ALSO BY THE EDITORS AT AMERICA'S TEST KITCHEN

The Science of Good Cooking
The Cook's Illustrated Cookbook
The America's Test Kitchen Menu Cookbook
The America's Test Kitchen Quick Family Cookbook
The America's Test Kitchen Healthy Family Cookbook
The America's Test Kitchen Family Baking Book
The America's Test Kitchen Family Cookbook

THE AMERICA'S TEST KITCHEN LIBRARY SERIES

The America's Test Kitchen DIY Cookbook
Pasta Revolution
Simple Weeknight Favorites
Slow Cooker Revolution
The Best Simple Recipes

THE COOK'S COUNTRY SERIES

From Our Grandmothers' Kitchens
Cook's Country Blue Ribbon Desserts
Cook's Country Best Potluck Recipes
Cook's Country Best Lost Suppers
Cook's Country Best Grilling Recipes
The Cook's Country Cookbook
America's Best Lost Recipes

THE TV COMPANION SERIES

The Complete Cook's Country TV Show Cookbook
The Complete America's Test Kitchen TV Show
Cookbook 2001–2013
America's Test Kitchen: The TV Companion Cookbook
(2002–2009, 2011, 2012, and 2013 Editions)

AMERICA'S TEST KITCHEN ANNUALS

The Best of America's Test Kitchen (2007–2013 Editions)
Cooking for Two (2010–2012 Editions)
Light & Healthy (2010–2012 Editions)

THE BEST RECIPE SERIES

The New Best Recipe
More Best Recipes
The Best One-Dish Suppers
Soups, Stews & Chilis
The Best Skillet Recipes
The Best Slow & Easy Recipes
The Best Chicken Recipes
The Best International Recipe
The Best Make-Ahead Recipe
The Best 30-Minute Recipe
The Best Light Recipe
The Cook's Illustrated Guide to Grilling and Barbecue
Best American Side Dishes
Cover & Bake
Steaks, Chops, Roasts & Ribs
Baking Illustrated
Italian Classics
American Classics

FOR A FULL LISTING OF ALL OUR BOOKS OR TO ORDER TITLES

http://www.cooksillustrated.com
http://www.americastestkitchen.com
or call 800-611-0759

THE BEST OF
America's
TEST KITCHEN

THE YEAR'S BEST RECIPES, EQUIPMENT REVIEWS, AND TASTINGS

2013

BY THE EDITORS AT
AMERICA'S TEST KITCHEN

PHOTOGRAPHY BY
CARL TREMBLAY, KELLER + KELLER, AND DANIEL J. VAN ACKERE

AMERICA'S TEST KITCHEN
17 Station Street, Brookline, MA 02445

THE BEST OF AMERICA'S TEST KITCHEN 2013
The Year's Best Recipes, Equipment Reviews, and Tastings

1st Edition

Hardcover: $35 US
ISBN-13: 978-1-936493-30-2 ISBN-10: 1-936493-30-6
ISSN: 1940-3925

Manufactured in the United States of America

10 9 8 7 6 5 4 3 2 1

Distributed by America's Test Kitchen
17 Station Street, Brookline, MA 02445

EDITORIAL DIRECTOR: Jack Bishop
EDITORIAL DIRECTOR, BOOKS: Elizabeth Carduff
EXECUTIVE EDITOR: Lori Galvin
ASSOCIATE EDITOR: Kate Hartke
ASSISTANT EDITOR: Alyssa King
DESIGN DIRECTOR: Amy Klee
ART DIRECTOR: Greg Galvan
ASSOCIATE ART DIRECTOR: Matthew Warnick
DESIGNERS: Tiffani Beckwith and Beverly Hsu
FRONT COVER PHOTOGRAPH: Carl Tremblay
STAFF PHOTOGRAPHER: Daniel J. van Ackere
ADDITIONAL PHOTOGRAPHY: Keller + Keller and Carl Tremblay
FOOD STYLING: Marie Piraino and Mary Jane Sawyer
PHOTOSHOOT KITCHEN TEAM:
    ASSOCIATE EDITOR: Chris O'Connor
    ASSISTANT TEST COOKS: Daniel Cellucci and Sara Mayer
ILLUSTRATOR: John Burgoyne
PRODUCTION DIRECTOR: Guy Rochford
SENIOR PRODUCTION MANAGER: Jessica Quirk
SENIOR PROJECT MANAGER: Alice Carpenter
PRODUCTION AND TRAFFIC COORDINATOR: Kate Hux
ASSET AND WORKFLOW MANAGER: Andrew Mannone
PRODUCTION AND IMAGING SPECIALISTS: Judy Blomquist, Heather Dube, and Lauren Pettapiece
COPYEDITOR: Barbara Wood
PROOFREADER: Elizabeth Emery
INDEXER: Elizabeth Parson

PICTURED ON THE FRONT COVER: Chocolate Espresso Daquoise (page 252)

CONTENTS

STARTERS & SALADS   2

SOUPS & STEWS   28

VEGETABLES & SIDE DISHES   50

BREAKFAST & BREADS   70

PASTA & PIZZA   106

MEAT   136

POULTRY   174

SEAFOOD   200

VEGETARIAN ENTRÉES   222

DESSERTS   238

TEST KITCHEN RESOURCES   276

INDEX   316

CHAPTER 1

STARTERS & SALADS

Stuffed Mushrooms with Boursin and Prosciutto   4

Baked Mini Falafel with Yogurt-Tahini Sauce   5

Broiled Shrimp Cocktail with Creamy Tarragon Sauce   8

Chinese Chicken Lettuce Wraps   9

Grilled Beef Satay   11
   Peanut Sauce

Grilled Thai Beef Salad   14

Classic Chicken Salad   18
   Curried Chicken Salad with Cashews
   Waldorf Chicken Salad
   Chicken Salad with Red Grapes and Smoked Almonds

Cucumber Salad with Olives, Oregano, and Almonds   20
   Cucumber Salad with Chile, Mint, and Basil
   Cucumber Salad with Ginger, Sesame, and Scallions
   Cucumber Salad with Jalapeño, Cilantro, and Pepitas

Fresh Corn Salad   23
   Arugula–Goat Cheese Fresh Corn Salad
   Chickpea-Avocado Fresh Corn Salad
   Tuscan Fresh Corn Salad
   Watermelon-Feta Fresh Corn Salad

Lentil Salad with Olives, Mint, and Feta   24
   Lentil Salad with Spinach, Walnuts, and Parmesan Cheese
   Lentil Salad with Hazelnuts and Goat Cheese
   Lentil Salad with Carrots and Cilantro

Sweet Potato Salad   26
   Asian-Style Sweet Potato Salad

STUFFED MUSHROOMS WITH BOURSIN AND PROSCIUTTO

THE IDEA OF BITE-SIZE STUFFED MUSHROOMS, served hot, with a good glass of wine, is always something I find appealing. That the reality typically falls far below my expectations is something that I relearn (and promptly seem to forget) every time I am offered stuffed mushrooms at a party. Without fail, I'm hit with instant regret when I encounter another bland, mushy filling. These disasters always involve a bread-based stuffing with multiple ingredients that are time-consuming to prepare and that invariably turn into a soggy, muddled mess. Tapas-style stuffed mushrooms, on the other hand, are a refreshingly simple affair—just a few well-chosen ingredients nestled inside each mushroom cap. Employing this "less is more" philosophy seemed key to an easy stuffed mushroom recipe that I'd want to both serve and eat.

First I selected the best mushrooms for the job. White button mushrooms are inexpensive and widely and consistently available—a reliable and approachable choice for entertaining. I found that size does matter, since mushrooms shrink considerably during cooking. Caps between 1½ and 2 inches in diameter proved best. Larger mushrooms were too big to eat in a single bite, and smaller mushrooms were difficult to stuff.

Next I was faced with a challenge all mushrooms pose: moisture. When filled and baked raw, the mushrooms release a significant amount of moisture, which can turn the whole hors d'oeuvre into a waterlogged sponge. This problem is particularly exacerbated by the aforementioned absorbent, bread-based stuffings, but after a few wet tests I quickly realized that no matter what the filling, I would have to rid the mushrooms of excess moisture first.

Preroasting was the most obvious way to achieve this, so I seasoned the mushrooms with oil, salt, and pepper before popping them (gill side down, so the released moisture could drain away) into a hot oven. After 30 minutes, these mushrooms were dry enough to stuff, but the edges verged on leathery, and I wondered if there was a quicker solution. Recently in the test kitchen, we've used the microwave to dehydrate eggplant before sautéing. I gave it a shot with the mushrooms and found that it worked, as long as I put a couple disposable coffee filters under the gills to keep the mushrooms from poaching in the leached-out liquid. After 10 minutes the mushrooms had released an amount of moisture comparable to that from 30 minutes of roasting, with no leathery exterior.

My mushrooms were finally ready to stuff. After considering various cheese options, I hit upon an unconventional but stellar choice. The soft, spoonable texture of Boursin made the otherwise tedious task of stuffing the caps significantly easier and less messy, and the cheese stayed buttery and supple long after the mushrooms came out of the oven. As an added bonus, Boursin comes conveniently preseasoned with potent herbs and garlic.

Looking for another heavy-hitter ingredient, I sprinkled the cheese with small strips of prosciutto before placing the mushrooms into a hot oven. Ten minutes at 450 degrees was enough to heat the Boursin and crisp the prosciutto. The salty, crunchy bites of pork played perfectly in both flavor and texture against the creamy, unctuous cheese. With such minimal prep, my knife looked abandoned, so I chopped up a little parsley to add some color and brightness.

—REBECCA MORRIS, *America's Test Kitchen Books*

Stuffed Mushrooms with Boursin and Prosciutto

SERVES 8

Be sure to buy mushrooms with caps that measure between 1½ and 2 inches in diameter; they will shrink substantially as they cook. Other flavors of Boursin will work fine here.

- 24 (1½- to 2-inch-wide) white mushroom caps, stems removed completely
- 2 tablespoons olive oil
  Salt and pepper
- 1 (5.2-ounce) package Boursin Garlic and Fine Herbs cheese, softened
- 1 ounce thinly sliced prosciutto, cut into ¼-inch strips
- 2 tablespoons minced fresh parsley or chives

1. Adjust oven rack to lower-middle position and heat oven to 450 degrees. Toss mushroom caps with oil and season with salt and pepper. Lay mushrooms gill side down on plate lined with 2 layers of coffee filters. Microwave mushrooms until they release their moisture and shrink in size, about 10 minutes.

2. Line rimmed baking sheet with aluminum foil. Transfer caps, gill side up, to prepared sheet. Spoon Boursin into mushroom caps and top with prosciutto. (Stuffed mushrooms can be covered and held at room temperature for up to 2 hours before baking.)

3. Bake mushrooms until cheese is hot and prosciutto begins to crisp, 10 to 12 minutes. Transfer to serving platter and sprinkle with parsley. Serve.

NOTES FROM THE TEST KITCHEN

EASIER STUFFED MUSHROOMS

1. Buy mushrooms that measure between 1½ and 2 inches in diameter. Be sure to remove stem completely before cooking.

2. Microwave mushrooms first to cut down on roasting time. Arrange mushrooms gill side down on coffee filter-lined plate before microwaving so that moisture will drain away.

3. Stuff with creamy, flavorful Boursin cheese to eliminate prep work. Top cheese with small strips of prosciutto to add even more flavor and nice crunch.

4. Bake 10 to 12 minutes in hot oven just before serving. Don't overbake mushrooms or they will turn out shriveled and chewy.

BAKED MINI FALAFEL WITH YOGURT-TAHINI SAUCE

WHEN I THINK OF CLASSIC HOT HORS D'OEUVRES, cocktail meatballs quickly come to mind. Easily skewered with a toothpick and eaten in one bite, they make great party food. Unfortunately, typical cocktail meatballs are bland and overly saucy. I wanted a bite-size savory appetizer with a fresh take.

Similar in size and shape to meatballs, falafel seemed like a good direction to take. Since they are meatless, falafel have a vegetarian-friendly edge as well. However, traditional falafel are deep-fried, which can be a bother. I wanted an easier approach that resulted in lighter, but still flavorful, falafel. Falafel are typically served with a rich, creamy tahini sauce. While it's tasty, I wondered if I could come up with a lighter sauce to match my lighter falafel. It was settled: My goal was to develop falafel with a moist, light interior, a well-browned, crisp crust, and a creamy but light sauce for dunking.

To come up with an alternative method to frying, I made a few batches of a basic falafel mixture and shaped it into 2-inch patties. First I tried cooking the patties in a skillet with a little oil. Unfortunately, the mixture quickly soaked up the oil, became soggy, and fell apart before cooking through. I also had to cook the falafel in so many batches that the first batch became cold before I was finished; this was not ideal for a party. Could I take a cue from a test kitchen recipe for big-batch meatballs and switch to the oven? I placed the patties on a lightly oiled baking sheet and cooked them at 375 degrees until they began to brown. When I reached in to flip them over, however, I discovered that they were completely fused to the pan. I gradually increased the amount of oil on the pan until the patties browned evenly and released cleanly.

Now that I had settled on baking the falafel, I got to work on the makeup of the patties themselves. I started by sorting through Middle Eastern and vegetarian cookbooks. I learned that Egyptian-style falafel are made entirely from dried split fava beans and Israeli-style are made with dried chickpeas, while others use some combination of the two. Unable to find dried split fava beans at my local markets, I chose Israeli-style falafel by process of elimination.

I started by testing several Israeli-style recipes that I had come across in my research. In initial tests, I decided to try canned chickpeas instead of dried for simplicity, but they were a disaster—they were simply too moist and made very mushy falafel. The key is that in none of the recipes I found were the dried chickpeas cooked, but rather they were soaked in water overnight, ground in the food processor with the other ingredients, then shaped and fried. No wonder the canned didn't work! I decided to follow the advice in the existing recipes and stick with dried beans.

Next I turned to the seasonings. While tasters welcomed the flavor of onion, it released moisture, which made the falafel mushy. And draining the minced onion seemed like too much of a bother. So instead, I turned to scallions, which tasters liked for their flavor and for the bright green color. Herbs added another hit of freshness; tasters preferred the complexity provided by a combination of cilantro and parsley over just a single herb. Garlic was a given, along with ground cumin, salt, and ground black pepper. Many recipes include ground cinnamon to season the falafel, and tasters liked the warm floral notes that it imparted.

In my initial tests, I realized that size matters when it comes to falafel. Larger falafel took longer to cook through, making them as dry as sawdust on the inside without enough of the contrasting outer crust. By contrast, smaller falafel (about 1 tablespoon each) had the perfect ratio of crispy crust to tender interior, and they were just the right size—two bites—for an appetizer. I formed some into balls and some into disks. Tasters unanimously preferred the disks, shaped ½ inch thick and 1 inch wide, which offered plenty of crisp exterior.

All that was left to do was whip up a sauce. Although falafel are traditionally served with a tahini-based sauce, I found tahini (a paste made from sesame seeds) too heavy for my light, fresh recipe. Instead, I created a creamy yogurt-based sauce with just enough tahini for a nice sesame flavor. I seasoned it simply with garlic, lemon juice, cilantro, salt, and pepper. My new sauce came together quickly and easily with a few flicks of a whisk. To transform the falafel from a street snack into a bite-size appetizer, I topped each patty with a slice of tomato for a touch of freshness and color, followed by a small dollop of sauce.

—JENNIFER LALIME, *America's Test Kitchen Books*

NOTES FROM THE TEST KITCHEN

THE BEST TAHINI

Tahini is a thick paste made from ground sesame seeds that's most often used to flavor Middle Eastern dishes. In our test of five supermarket brands, **Joyva Sesame Tahini** boasted the most tahini flavor. Tasters called it "very nutty," "buttery," and almost "peanut-butterish."

OUR FAVORITE GREEK YOGURT

The main difference between ordinary yogurt and Greek-style yogurt is that true Greek yogurt is strained to remove most of its liquid whey; the result is a yogurt that is thicker than the typical American stuff, higher in protein, and usually less acidic. It's good eaten plain or drizzled with honey, and we have found that it works well in creamy dips and a number of sauces. To find the best supermarket brand, we gathered 18 different nonfat, 2 percent low-fat, and full-fat plain Greek yogurts and called tasters to the table.

While some yogurts stood up in stiff peaks, others were loose and watery, and flavors ranged from bland to lightly tangy to strongly sour. A little digging revealed that some manufacturers are skipping the straining process and fortifying their yogurt with thickeners—tasters found these samples unpleasantly sour with unappealing textures.

The winner of both our nonfat and full-fat tastings was **Olympus Traditional Greek Yogurt**; the nonfat yogurt was described as "seriously creamy" and "pleasantly tangy," and the full-fat version (labeled "10% fat") was favored for its "satiny" texture and "buttery," "tangy" flavor. Interestingly, this was the only brand in our lineup imported from Greece. In the 2 percent category, tasters preferred **Fage Total 2%** for its "great dairy flavor."

Baked Mini Falafel with Yogurt-Tahini Sauce
SERVES 8 TO 10

Be sure to use Greek yogurt in the sauce, or the sauce will be too watery. To quick salt-soak the chickpeas, combine 2 quarts water, chickpeas, and 1½ tablespoons salt in a Dutch oven and bring to a boil over high heat. Remove the pot from the heat, cover, and let stand for 1 hour. Drain and rinse well.

SAUCE

- ½ cup 2 percent Greek yogurt
- 1 tablespoon tahini
- 2 teaspoons lemon juice
- 1½ teaspoons minced fresh cilantro or parsley
- ½ small garlic clove, minced
- Salt and pepper

BAKED MINI FALAFEL WITH YOGURT-TAHINI SAUCE

FALAFEL

        Salt
1   **cup dried chickpeas, picked over and rinsed**
6   **tablespoons olive oil**
5   **scallions, chopped coarse**
½   **cup fresh parsley leaves**
½   **cup fresh cilantro leaves**
3   **garlic cloves, minced**
¼   **teaspoon ground cumin**
⅛   **teaspoon ground cinnamon**
6   **ounces cherry tomatoes, sliced thin**

1. FOR THE SAUCE: Whisk yogurt, tahini, lemon juice, cilantro, garlic, ⅛ teaspoon salt, and pinch pepper together in bowl until smooth. Season with salt and pepper to taste. Cover and refrigerate until chilled, at least 1 hour or up to 1 day.

2. FOR THE FALAFEL: Dissolve 1½ tablespoons salt in 2 quarts cold water in large bowl. Add chickpeas and soak at room temperature for at least 8 hours or up to 24 hours. Drain and rinse well.

3. Adjust oven rack to middle position and heat oven to 375 degrees. Coat large baking sheet with ¼ cup oil.

4. Process remaining 2 tablespoons oil, drained chickpeas, scallions, parsley, cilantro, garlic, 1 teaspoon salt, ½ teaspoon pepper, cumin, and cinnamon together in food processor until smooth, about 1 minute. Working with 1 tablespoon chickpea mixture at a time, shape falafel into small patties, about 1 inch wide and ½ inch thick, and spread out on prepared sheet.

5. Bake until falafel are lightly browned on both sides, about 25 minutes, flipping falafel over halfway through baking. Transfer falafel to serving platter, top each with 1 slice tomato, and dollop each with 1 teaspoon yogurt-tahini sauce. Serve.

BROILED SHRIMP COCKTAIL

I DON'T THINK I CAN REMEMBER A HOLIDAY gathering growing up where there wasn't a platter of chilled shrimp cocktail on the table. Traditionally for this dish, shrimp are poached in a court-bouillon (water flavored with white wine, lemon juice, herbs, and spices), and then shocked in ice water to halt cooking and start their chill, so they could be served cold with tangy cocktail sauce. I don't want to rock the boat (well, maybe a little), but after years of the same shrimp cocktail, I craved a change. Having seen a few recipes for roasted shrimp cocktail, I was intrigued—and a little confused (after all, it's HOT shrimp cocktail). Basically this easier, modern interpretation uses the high heat of roasting to impart deep flavor rather than delicately infusing the shrimp with a bouquet of aromatics via poaching water. As long as the results are just as good, I was game for replacing a time-honored and somewhat tedious (i.e., French) technique with something less refined and more to the point.

After suiting up to step into the kitchen and give this method a try, I peeled a couple of pounds of shrimp before tossing them with oil, salt, and pepper and roasting them in a 400-degree oven. Ten minutes later the shrimp were done. Easy and quick, perhaps, but the results were not impressive. Anemic and flavorless, the shrimp had just steamed in their own juices. Even at higher oven temperatures, the interiors were rubbery and overcooked before any browning occurred.

I wasn't ready to give up on the oven, though. Roasting was a bust, but what about broiling? The intense direct heat of the broiler proved effective, finally producing shrimp with a moderate sear. But it still wasn't good enough, so I focused on improving the technique. Experimenting with adjusting the oven rack, I had the best results at close range, about 3 inches from the broiler element. Moisture was my enemy here, so I was careful to thoroughly pat the shrimp dry and place them in a single layer to minimize steaming. Switching from the large shrimp that I had been using to jumbo shrimp extended their cooking time, so they had time to develop a lightly browned exterior under the broiler without overcooking.

In addition to tossing the shrimp with salt and pepper before cooking, I included coriander and cayenne for more flavor. Tasters liked these subtle notes of bright citrus and heat, but the real game-changer was when I added a little sugar to the spice rub. The sugar caramelized quickly under the broiler, further boosting the browning and enhancing the fresh, sweet shrimp flavor.

Instead of traditional tomato-based cocktail sauce, we thought these shrimp paired better with a mayonnaise-based creamy sauce, aggressively brightened with lemon juice and plenty of fresh herbs. With my shrimp cocktail perfected, I look forward to my next holiday gathering so that I can stir up tradition with my new take on a beloved classic.

—ADELAIDE PARKER, *America's Test Kitchen Books*

Broiled Shrimp Cocktail with Creamy Tarragon Sauce
SERVES 8 TO 10

Other fresh herbs, such as dill, basil, cilantro, or mint, can be substituted for the tarragon. We prefer to use jumbo shrimp here, but extra-large shrimp (21 to 25 per pound) can be substituted; if using smaller shrimp, reduce the broiling time by about 2 minutes.

SAUCE

- ¾ cup mayonnaise
- 2 scallions, minced
- 3 tablespoons minced fresh tarragon
- 2 tablespoons lemon juice
- ½ teaspoon salt
- ¼ teaspoon pepper

SHRIMP

- ¾ teaspoon salt
- ¾ teaspoon ground coriander
- ½ teaspoon sugar
- ¼ teaspoon pepper
- ⅛ teaspoon cayenne pepper
- 2 pounds jumbo shrimp (16 to 20 per pound), peeled and deveined
- 2 tablespoons olive oil

NOTES FROM THE TEST KITCHEN

DEVEINING SHRIMP
Although the vein in shrimp doesn't affect flavor, it does affect appearance, so we prefer to remove it.

1. After removing shell, use paring knife to make shallow cut along back of shrimp to expose vein.

2. Use tip of knife to lift vein out of shrimp. Discard vein by wiping blade against paper towel.

---

1. FOR THE SAUCE: Stir all ingredients together in serving bowl, cover, and refrigerate until needed. (Sauce can be refrigerated for up to 1 day; season with additional lemon juice, salt, and pepper to taste before serving.)

2. FOR THE SHRIMP: Adjust oven rack 3 inches from broiler element and heat broiler. (If necessary, set upside-down rimmed baking sheet on oven rack to get closer to broiler element.) Combine salt, coriander, sugar, pepper, and cayenne in bowl. Pat shrimp dry with paper towels, then toss with oil and spice mixture in large bowl.

3. Spread shrimp in single layer on rimmed baking sheet. Broil shrimp until opaque and edges begin to brown, about 6 minutes. Transfer shrimp to serving platter and serve with sauce.

CHINESE CHICKEN LETTUCE WRAPS

THERE AREN'T MANY CHAIN RESTAURANT DISHES that are worth making at home, but Chinese chicken lettuce wraps are one exception. Originally part of Cantonese banquet spreads, this dish (known as *sung choy bao*) was popularized in this country by places like P. F. Chang's and the Cheesecake Factory. At its best, it offers tender morsels of chicken and crunchy vegetables stir-fried in a salty-sweet sauce and served in crisp lettuce cups—ideal either as an appetizer or as a light meal.

The recipes I found shared more or less the same technique: Stir-fry the chicken over high heat, add chopped vegetables, pour in the sauce and toss to coat, and spoon the mixture into Bibb lettuce leaves. I didn't bother trying recipes that called for ground chicken, since commercial ground meat is often processed so fine that it cooks up stringy and chalky. But even when I painstakingly diced the chicken breast by hand, the meat cooked up dry and bland; plus, all the sauces I tried needed a little punching up, too.

To introduce more flavor and juiciness, I tried briefly soaking the chopped chicken in soy sauce mixed with a little rice wine. When this step didn't do enough, I decided to switch to chicken thighs, which boast more intramuscular fat, making them less prone to drying out when stir-fried and giving them richer, meatier flavor.

I also wondered if instead of finely dicing the meat by hand, I could use the test kitchen's food processor method for grinding meat. This involved briefly freezing the thighs to firm them up and then pulsing them until coarsely chopped. The results? Not bad—and much faster than chopping by hand. But the machine introduced a new problem: Even after the meat had been frozen, a small amount of the chicken inevitably became overprocessed, releasing sticky meat proteins that glued the larger pieces together into chewy clumps during cooking. Tossing the chopped pieces with oil first helped but also turned the dish greasy.

The idea of coating the pieces wasn't a bad one, though, and it reminded me that a handful of the more traditional recipes I'd come across called for "velveting" the chicken. In this classic Chinese technique, the meat is dipped into a cornstarch slurry that forms a barrier against clumping and helps it retain moisture. I gave it a whirl, whisking a couple of teaspoons of cornstarch and a little sesame oil into the soy-wine mixture and tossing it with the chopped-up chicken before stir-frying. This was the breakthrough I'd been hoping for. My tasters raved about these tender, juicy, distinct bits of chicken.

The other major components—the vegetables and aromatics—were much simpler to nail down. Most recipes include either water chestnuts or celery for crunch, but tasters agreed that using both was even better. I also added a handful of sliced shiitake mushrooms for earthy depth and chew, along with garlic and scallions.

As for the sauce, I built complexity into the traditional oyster sauce, soy sauce, and rice wine mixture by adding a couple of teaspoons of toasted sesame oil, a little sugar, and dried chili pepper flakes. (Per tradition, I'd also be passing salty-sweet hoisin sauce with the lettuce wraps as a tableside condiment.) Spooned into the tender Bibb cups, this stir-fry was as bold and complex as it was light, and it came together in less than an hour.

—KEITH DRESSER, *Cook's Illustrated*

Chinese Chicken Lettuce Wraps

SERVES 6

To make it a meal, serve this dish with steamed white rice.

CHICKEN

- 1 **pound boneless, skinless chicken thighs, trimmed and cut into 1-inch pieces**
- 2 **teaspoons Chinese rice wine or dry sherry**
- 2 **teaspoons soy sauce**
- 2 **teaspoons toasted sesame oil**
- 2 **teaspoons cornstarch**

SAUCE

- 3 **tablespoons oyster sauce**
- 1 **tablespoon Chinese rice wine or dry sherry**
- 2 **teaspoons soy sauce**
- 2 **teaspoons toasted sesame oil**
- ½ **teaspoon sugar**
- ¼ **teaspoon red pepper flakes**

STIR-FRY

- 2 **tablespoons vegetable oil**
- 2 **celery ribs, cut into ¼-inch pieces**
- 6 **ounces shiitake mushrooms, stemmed and sliced thin**
- ½ **cup water chestnuts, cut into ¼-inch pieces**
- 2 **scallions, white parts minced, green parts thinly sliced**
- 2 **garlic cloves, minced**

- 1 **head Bibb lettuce, leaves separated and left whole**
  Hoisin sauce

1. FOR THE CHICKEN: Place chicken pieces on large plate in single layer. Freeze meat until firm and starting to harden around edges, about 20 minutes.

2. Whisk rice wine, soy sauce, oil, and cornstarch together in medium bowl. Pulse half of meat in food processor until coarsely chopped into ¼- to ⅛-inch pieces, about 10 pulses. Transfer meat to bowl with rice wine mixture and repeat with remaining chunks. Toss chicken to coat and refrigerate for 15 minutes.

3. FOR THE SAUCE: Whisk all ingredients together in bowl; set aside.

4. FOR THE STIR-FRY: Heat 1 tablespoon oil in 12-inch nonstick skillet over high heat until just smoking. Add chicken and cook, stirring constantly, until opaque, 3 to 4 minutes. Transfer to bowl and wipe out skillet.

5. Heat remaining 1 tablespoon oil in now-empty skillet over high heat until just smoking. Add celery and mushrooms; cook, stirring constantly, until mushrooms have reduced in size by half and celery is crisp-tender, 3 to 4 minutes. Add water chestnuts, scallion whites, and garlic; cook, stirring constantly, until fragrant, about 1 minute. Whisk sauce to recombine. Return chicken to skillet; add sauce and toss to combine. Spoon into lettuce leaves and sprinkle with scallion greens. Serve, passing hoisin sauce separately.

GRILLED BEEF SATAY

IN BANGKOK'S OUTDOOR MARKETS, THE PUNGENT fragrance of charring meat hovers in the air. It's grilled satay—Southeast Asia's most famous street fare, featuring tender swaths of assertively flavored pork, chicken, or beef that have been marinated for hours, threaded onto bamboo skewers, and then cooked over charcoal to achieve a lightly burnished crust.

But something funny happened on satay's journey from Thai food stall to stateside sit-down restaurant: The magic got lost. And the worst offender, hands down, is the beef version. Whether the meat is cut too thick and overcooked (making it chewy like leather) or "tenderized" by a lengthy marinade (giving it a mealy exterior), the texture is unappealing—to say nothing of the meat's lackluster flavor, which relies far too much on the chile-spiked peanut sauce served on the side. How hard could it be to bring beef satay back to its streetwise roots? I headed to the test kitchen to find out.

Figuring out the best cut of beef—and how to slice it—would go far toward improving the situation, so I started there. I ruled out luxury cuts from the outset and narrowed the field to less expensive flank, skirt, top round, and top sirloin steaks, all of which have good flavor and can be tender, too, if treated right.

I cut each of these steaks into pieces small enough to thread onto skewers, taking care to slice the flank and skirt against the grain (a tenderizing trick we use for heavily striated cuts of beef). I soaked the meat for 30 minutes in a simple coconut milk–based marinade before skewering it and throwing it onto the grill.

Top round was the loser, coming out tough with liver-y off-notes. Sirloin had great flavor but inconsistent texture. Skirt and flank ended up in a dead heat for first place, thanks to plenty of evenly distributed fat. I went with symmetrical flank, which would be far easier to prep than tapered skirt.

Experimenting with butchering methods, I found that halving the flank steak lengthwise first, and then slicing the two long, thin portions on a slight bias, about ¼ inch thick, yielded the optimal size and shape for skewering—and for consuming in a bite or two.

Small pieces of flank steak cook in a matter of minutes, and it's a race to get the exterior adequately crusted before the interior overcooks—a chronic problem in the satay recipes I'd tested. The solution seemed easy enough: Just make the fire hotter. Piling the coals on one side of the grill gave me the firepower I wanted but required seriously nimble work with tongs to keep every morsel on the 12-inch skewers directly over this more contained fire. Add basting, which I did right as I put the meat on the grill, again when I flipped the skewers, and once more right before I took them off, and the whole process became more trouble than it was worth.

Trolling the Internet for a better idea, I happened upon videos of satay vendors in action and was reminded of the unique style of grill they use for the job. Instead of a kettle with grates, the street vendors cook over a trough-shaped grill, about as wide as the skewers are long, which allows them to suspend the meat mere inches above the coals. To mimic this setup, I used a 13 by 9-inch disposable aluminum roasting pan as a makeshift "trough," poking several holes in the bottom of it (to allow for air circulation), positioning it atop the cooking grate of my kettle grill, and filling it with hot coals. I strategically threaded the steak onto only the middle 9 inches of each skewer—so the ends could rest on the edge of the pan—and positioned them just above the coals, Thai-style. I imagined street vendors in Bangkok giving me the thumbs-up for my ingenuity—until reality set in. The meat was now so close to the fire that I needed to flip it as constantly and frenetically as they did in the video, and doing so still didn't prevent me from overcooking it.

Maybe what I needed to do was mimic the setup but introduce a little more space between the coals and the meat. This time I positioned the pan inside the kettle, poured the hot coals inside, and replaced the cooking grate. I then lined up the skewers over the pan. This method worked like a charm. When I basted the satay, the coals smoldered just enough to impart a subtle smokiness, and with the coals corralled in the center of the grill, the heat was sufficiently powerful to yield a lovely burnished exterior—but not so hot that I had to flip the skewers more than once.

Finally, I turned my attention back to the marinade. The test kitchen has spent years determining what works and what doesn't, so it was with a touch of hubris that I picked off ingredients I knew would be problematic. Acids—gone. We've found that they do nothing but weaken the surface of the meat, giving it a mushy texture. Likewise, enzyme-rich juices like pineapple and papaya were sent packing. Though many recipes incorporate them to help "tenderize" tough cuts of meat, our tests have shown that all they do is break

GRILLED BEEF SATAY

down the exterior. Besides, my choice of cut and cooking method yielded ample tenderness; what I needed now was big flavor.

From the ingredients left standing, I assembled the marinade: oil, to facilitate the transfer of oil-soluble flavorings; salty fish sauce, for its brining and flavor-boosting qualities; brown sugar, for complexity and enhanced browning; plus coconut milk, a smattering of dried spices, and a generous amount of minced fresh lemon grass, shallots, and ginger.

Confidently, I tossed the sliced flank steak with the marinade, letting it chill in the refrigerator for an hour. (We've found that there is little benefit to longer marinating times.) I skewered the slices, grilled them, and dug in. As expected, the flavor was terrific. The problem was the texture: The exterior suffered from the mealiness I thought I'd taken every precaution to avoid. Cutting the marinating time in half, I tried again. The flavor was every bit as good, but the texture was just as mealy.

Puzzled, I went down the ingredient list, omitting each component of the marinade one by one in subsequent batches. It was only when I eliminated the ginger that I fingered the culprit—without this root, the meat wasn't mealy in the least. Additional research revealed that ginger contains zingibain, an enzyme that aggressively breaks down protein. And my recipe had called for 2 tablespoons of the stuff. I hated to remove such a key flavoring, but what could I do?

Then it occurred to me. What if I kept the marinade very simple and ramped up the basting sauce with ginger and most of the other flavorings instead? I cooked one more batch, this time marinating the steak in just fish sauce, oil, and sugar. During grilling, I basted the meat heavily with the coconut milk mixture, redolent with ginger, lemon grass, and spices. This was my breakthrough: The texture was flawless, and the flavors from the basting sauce really stuck to the meat, so no one missed them in the marinade.

Finally, I focused on the peanut sauce. Using chunky peanut butter as a base, I spiced things up with Thai red curry paste and garlic. Coconut milk contributed body, and chopped roasted peanuts offered additional texture. A final hit of lime juice, coupled with soy and fish sauces, lent brightness.

Served with the peanut sauce, this beef satay was as good as it gets. And who knows? Maybe one day a Thai street vendor will look to my method for tips.

—BRYAN ROOF, *Cook's Illustrated*

Grilled Beef Satay

SERVES 6

Bamboo skewers soaked in water for 30 minutes can be substituted for metal skewers. The aluminum pan used for charcoal grilling should be at least 2¾ inches deep; you will not need the pan for a gas grill. Kitchen shears work well for punching the holes in the pan. Unless you have a very high-powered gas grill, these skewers will not be as well seared as they would be with charcoal. Serve with Peanut Sauce (recipe follows). To make it a meal, serve this dish with steamed white rice.

BASTING SAUCE

- ¾   cup regular or light coconut milk
- 3   tablespoons packed dark brown sugar
- 3   tablespoons fish sauce
- 2   tablespoons vegetable oil
- 3   shallots, minced
- 2   lemon grass stalks, trimmed to bottom 6 inches and minced (see page 14)
- 2   tablespoons grated fresh ginger
- 1½ teaspoons ground coriander
- ¾   teaspoon red pepper flakes
- ½   teaspoon ground cumin
- ½   teaspoon salt

BEEF

- 2   tablespoons vegetable oil
- 2   tablespoons packed dark brown sugar
- 1   tablespoon fish sauce
- 1   (1½- to 1¾-pound) flank steak, halved lengthwise and sliced on slight angle against grain into ¼-inch-thick slices

  Disposable aluminum deep roasting pan

1. FOR THE BASTING SAUCE: Whisk all ingredients together in bowl. Reserve one-third of sauce in separate bowl.

2. FOR THE BEEF: Whisk oil, sugar, and fish sauce together in medium bowl. Toss beef with marinade and let stand at room temperature for 30 minutes. Weave beef onto 12-inch metal skewers, 2 to 4 pieces per skewer, leaving 1½ inches at top and bottom of skewer exposed. You should have 10 to 12 skewers.

3A. FOR A CHARCOAL GRILL: Punch twelve ½-inch holes in bottom of disposable roasting pan. Open bottom vent completely and place roasting pan in center of grill. Light large chimney starter mounded with charcoal briquettes (7 quarts). When top coals are partially covered with ash, pour into roasting pan. Set cooking grate over coals with grates parallel to long side of roasting pan, cover, and open lid vent completely. Heat grill until hot, about 5 minutes.

3B. FOR A GAS GRILL: Turn all burners to high, cover, and heat grill until hot, about 15 minutes. Leave all burners on high.

4. Clean and oil cooking grate. Place beef skewers on grill (directly over coals if using charcoal) perpendicular to grate. Brush meat with reserved one-third of basting sauce and cook (covered if using gas) until browned, about 3 minutes. Flip skewers, brush with half of remaining basting sauce, and cook until browned on second side, about 3 minutes. Brush meat with remaining basting sauce and cook 1 minute longer. Transfer to large platter and serve with Peanut Sauce.

NOTES FROM THE TEST KITCHEN

HOW TO PREP LEMON GRASS

When buying lemon grass, look for green (not brown) stalks that are firm and fragrant.

1. Trim dry leafy top (this part is usually green) and tough bottom of each stalk.

2. Peel and discard dry outer layer until moist, tender inner stalk is exposed.

3. Smash peeled stalk with bottom of heavy saucepan to release maximum flavor from fibrous stalk.

4. Cut smashed stalk into long, thin strips; cut crosswise to mince.

Peanut Sauce

MAKES ABOUT 1½ CUPS

- 1 **tablespoon vegetable oil**
- 1 **tablespoon Thai red curry paste**
- 1 **tablespoon packed dark brown sugar**
- 2 **garlic cloves, minced**
- 1 **cup regular or light coconut milk**
- ⅓ **cup chunky peanut butter**
- ¼ **cup dry-roasted unsalted peanuts, chopped**
- 1 **tablespoon lime juice**
- 1 **tablespoon fish sauce**
- 1 **teaspoon soy sauce**

Heat oil in small saucepan over medium heat until shimmering. Add curry paste, sugar, and garlic; cook, stirring constantly, until fragrant, about 1 minute. Add coconut milk and bring to simmer. Whisk in peanut butter until smooth. Remove from heat and stir in peanuts, lime juice, fish sauce, and soy sauce. Cool to room temperature.

GRILLED THAI BEEF SALAD

IN WINTER WHEN I CRAVE THAI FOOD, IT'S OFTEN a rich, coconut milk–based curry or a wok-charred noodle dish. But in the summer months, I'm more tempted by the country's famous salads, particularly the grilled beef rendition known as *nam tok*. Served warm or at room temperature, this preparation features slices of deeply charred steak tossed with thinly sliced shallots and handfuls of torn mint and cilantro in a bright, bracing dressing, traditionally served with steamed jasmine rice. In the best versions, the cuisine's five signature flavor elements—hot, sour, salty, sweet, and bitter—come into balance, making for a light but satisfying dish.

I paged through the test kitchen's stack of Thai cookbooks for some nam tok recipes to try and was pleased to find that both the shopping list and the cooking time—about half an hour from start to finish—were very manageable. The most unusual ingredient was toasted rice powder, which I knew would be easy enough to make at home. Still, the salads that I produced in the test kitchen, while not bad, fell short of the versions that I've eaten in good Thai restaurants. Either the dressing's flavors were unbalanced—too sweet, too salty, too sour—or the beef itself didn't boast enough char to give the salad its hallmark smoky, faintly bitter edge. Clearly, I had some tinkering to do.

The obvious place to start my testing was with the beef. Surprisingly, the recipes that I consulted were all over the map. Some specified lean cuts like tenderloin, others more marbled choices like skirt steak or New York strip steak. A few recipes called for marinating the meat before grilling; others suggested simply seasoning it with salt and white pepper (a staple ingredient in Thai cuisine). Most of them didn't even specify a grilling method. As a starting point, I built a standard single-level fire—a full chimney's worth of coals spread in an even layer over the kettle—and seared a variety of beef cuts—New York strip steak, boneless short ribs, tenderloin, and flank steak—sprinkled with salt and white pepper. Once each piece had developed a thick, dark crust, I pulled it off the fire, let it rest briefly (to allow the interior juices to be reabsorbed), cut thin slices, and tossed them in a standard dressing of equal parts fresh lime juice and fish sauce, a little sugar, and a thinly sliced Thai chile.

Just as I had expected, the more marbled pieces of beef fared better than the lean tenderloin, which started out woefully bland and ended up overcooked by the time it developed even the barest crust. Flavorwise, any of these fattier cuts would have been a fine choice, but two came with a caveat. Boneless short ribs vary in quality: Some are evenly marbled and ideally shaped, almost like small strip steaks, while others are misshapen and full of interior fat and connective tissue that require trimming. Meanwhile, New York strip steaks boast good flavor and pleasantly tender chew but don't come cheap. I settled on flank steak. The uniformly shaped, moderately priced slab was also beefy and juicy, and it sliced neatly.

Next decision: whether or not to marinate the meat in a mixture of the dressing ingredients. A quick side-by-side test made my decision easy. Since moisture thwarts browning, the crust on the marinated flank steak was markedly thin and pale compared with that on the non-marinated sample. And my goal with this recipe was nicely crusted beef. Besides, once the slices of grilled steak were tossed with the dressing, they were plenty flavorful.

With the cut of meat decided, I could now focus my attention on the grilling method. The single-level fire had produced decently charred results, but for this salad, the contrast of a crisp, smoky, faintly bitter crust and a juicy center was a must, and I knew I could do better. To get a true blaze going, I turned to the test kitchen's favorite high-heat grill method: a modified two-level fire, in which all the coals are concentrated in an even layer over half of the grill. This way, the meat's exterior would caramelize almost on contact and would cook faster, ensuring that the interior would stay medium-rare.

The recipes that I consulted may have been vague about the fire setup, but they did offer one grilling pointer: As the steak cooks, beads of moisture will appear on its surface—an indication that the meat is ready to be flipped. In fact, the dish is named for this visual cue; *nam tok* translates as "water falling." Grateful for the cue, I flipped the meat as soon as beads of moisture showed up, let it sear another five minutes on the second side, and pulled it off the grill. To my delight, this steak was not only perfectly charred on the exterior, but also spot-on medium-rare within.

With perfectly grilled and subtly, satisfyingly bitter meat in hand, I moved back indoors to address the other four flavor elements: hot, sour, salty, and sweet. Everyone agreed that my initial dressing needed some tweaking—a bit more sweetness, a more balanced (and less heady) salty-sour punch, and more complex heat. The first two requests were easy to fix: I quickly landed on a 2:3 ratio of fish sauce to lime juice, plus ½ teaspoon of sugar and 2 tablespoons of water to tone it all down a touch. But the chile situation required a bit more attention. A fresh chile was a given, and I'd been using a Thai chile; when sliced thin and tossed with the other vegetable components, it added a fruity, fiery blaze to each bite. So why did something still seem to be missing? I found the answer in a recipe from Thai cuisine guru David Thompson: His grilled beef salad calls for not only a fresh Thai chile, but also a powder made from the dried pods, called bird chiles.

Hoping that regular old cayenne powder toasted in a skillet would suffice, I compared its effect on the salad with that of a powder made with ground, toasted chiles following Thompson's instructions. The consensus was unanimous: The powder made from the dried bird chiles added a deeper, earthier complexity than the hotter, more one-dimensional cayenne. Just ½ teaspoon of cayenne, in fact, overpowered the meat's smoky char.

I was about to resign myself to the extra step of grinding my own powder when I spied a jar of sweet paprika in the spice cabinet. Could this give me the earthy, fruity red pepper flavor that was missing from the cayenne? As it turned out, a 50–50 mix of cayenne and paprika did the trick. I added just a dash of the toasted spice mixture to the dressing and put the rest aside as a seasoning for those who wanted to kick up the heat another notch.

NOTES FROM THE TEST KITCHEN

FIVE TASTES OF GRILLED THAI BEEF SALAD— AND ONE MORE

One of the keys to this salad is balancing the signature flavor elements of Thai cuisine. In addition to achieving this, we added one more complementary flavor: the earthiness of toasted cayenne and sweet paprika.

HOT
A fresh Thai chile creates bright, fruity heat in the dressing.

SOUR
A generous 3 tablespoons of fresh lime juice adds bracing acidity.

SALTY
Derived from salted, fermented fish, pungent fish sauce acts as a rich flavor enhancer.

SWEET
Half a teaspoon of sugar tames the dressing's salty-sour flavors without becoming cloying.

BITTER
Thoroughly charred steak adds both a pleasing textural contrast and a subtle bitter edge.

EARTHY
Though nontraditional, ground cayenne and sweet paprika add earthy flavor without too much heat.

The other condiment that I had to address was the *kao kua,* or toasted rice powder. These days most Thai recipes call for the commercially made product, but it can be hard to find. It was simple enough to make my own by toasting rice in a dry skillet and pulverizing it in a spice grinder. Tossing half of the powder with the salad components gave the dressing fuller body, and sprinkling on the rest at the table added faint but satisfying crunch.

As for the vegetable components, it was really a matter of personal taste. Some recipes called for incorporating only the requisite sliced shallots and torn mint leaves and cilantro, while others added green beans, cabbage, cucumbers, and lettuce. My tasters and I agreed that any accoutrements should complement—not compete with—the grilled beef. We settled on just one extra: a thinly sliced cucumber, which contributed a cool crispness to this nicely balanced, complexly flavored Thai classic.

—ANDREW JANJIGIAN, *Cook's Illustrated*

Grilled Thai Beef Salad

SERVES 4 TO 6

Serve with rice, if desired. If fresh Thai chiles are unavailable, substitute ½ serrano chile. Don't skip the toasted rice; it's integral to the texture and flavor of the dish. Any variety of white rice can be used. Toasted rice powder (kao kua) can also be found in many Asian markets; substitute 1 tablespoon rice powder for the white rice.

1 teaspoon paprika
1 teaspoon cayenne pepper
1 tablespoon white rice
3 tablespoons lime juice (2 limes)
2 tablespoons fish sauce
2 tablespoons water
½ teaspoon sugar
1 (1½-pound) flank steak, trimmed
  Salt and coarsely ground white pepper
1 seedless English cucumber, sliced ¼ inch thick on bias
4 shallots, sliced thin
1½ cups fresh mint leaves, torn
1½ cups fresh cilantro leaves
1 Thai chile, stemmed, seeded, and sliced thin into rounds

GRILLED THAI BEEF SALAD

1. Heat paprika and cayenne in 8-inch skillet over medium heat; cook, shaking pan, until fragrant, about 1 minute. Transfer to small bowl. Wipe skillet clean, then return to medium-high heat, add rice and toast, stirring constantly, until deep golden brown, about 5 minutes. Transfer to small bowl and let cool for 5 minutes. Grind rice with spice grinder, mini food processor, or mortar and pestle until it resembles fine meal, 10 to 30 seconds (you should have about 1 tablespoon rice powder).

2. Whisk lime juice, fish sauce, water, sugar, and ¼ teaspoon toasted paprika mixture together in large bowl and set aside.

3A. FOR A CHARCOAL GRILL: Open bottom vent completely. Light large chimney starter filled with charcoal briquettes (6 quarts). When top coals are partially covered with ash, pour in even layer over half of grill. Set cooking grate in place, cover, and open lid vent completely. Heat grill until hot, about 5 minutes.

3B. FOR A GAS GRILL: Turn all burners to high, cover, and heat grill until hot, about 15 minutes. Leave primary burner on high and turn off other burner(s).

4. Clean and oil cooking grate. Season steak with salt and pepper. Place steak on grate over hot part of grill and cook until beginning to char and beads of moisture appear on outer edges of meat, 5 to 6 minutes. Flip steak and continue to cook on second side until meat registers 120 to 125 degrees, about 5 minutes longer. Transfer to carving board, tent loosely with aluminum foil, and let rest for 10 minutes.

5. Line large platter with cucumber slices. Slice meat, against grain, on bias, into ¼-inch-thick slices. Transfer sliced steak to bowl with fish sauce mixture, add shallots, mint, cilantro, chile, and half of rice powder, and toss to combine. Arrange steak on cucumber-lined platter. Serve, passing remaining rice powder and toasted paprika mixture separately.

CLASSIC CHICKEN SALAD

CHICKEN SALAD CAN MEAN JUST ABOUT ANYTHING these days, from shredded meat dressed in vinaigrette to grilled strips tossed with leafy greens. But to me, there's no beating the classic version: tender chicken cubes lightly bound with creamy mayonnaise and freshened up with minced celery and herbs. It's ideal sandwiched between bread slices, scooped into crisp lettuce cups, or simply eaten by the forkful—provided, of course, that the chicken has been properly cooked. Over the years I've eaten enough disappointing versions to know that no amount of dressing or add-ins will camouflage dry, stringy meat. Chicken salad is only as good as the chicken itself.

I made it my goal to devise a method for making silky, juicy, delicately flavored chicken first and worry about finessing the accoutrements later. I paged through dozens of recipes, most of which specified the same cut of meat: bone-in, skin-on chicken breasts. (The bone, a poor conductor of heat, helps prevent the meat from overcooking.) For the cooking method, the majority of recipes called for poaching.

As with any chicken recipe, my target temperature for the white meat was 160 to 165 degrees, when it's safely cooked through but still juicy and tender. I stuck with a conventional poaching method, bringing a pot of water to a subsimmer of 180 degrees and adding four breasts. Then things got fussy: Because the water temperature plunged as soon as I added the meat, I had to continually adjust the heat to maintain the temperature. The results were succulent and tender, but having to constantly fiddle with the stove was a pain. Cranking the heat higher from the start wasn't the answer: The outside of the meat dried out before the inside was done. There had to be a simpler way to prevent the meat from overcooking.

That's when my thoughts turned to *sous vide*, a technique in which vacuum-sealed foods are submerged in a water bath that's been preset to the food's ideal cooked temperature. The beauty of this method is that it's impossible to overcook the food because the water temperature never exceeds the target doneness temperature. Temperature-controlled sous vide ovens cost a fortune, but if I could approximate this technique using ordinary kitchen equipment, I'd have a foolproof way to get perfectly cooked chicken.

Rather than heating the water before adding the chicken, I tried placing the breasts in a Dutch oven, covering them with cold water, and turning the burner to medium. When the water reached 165 degrees, I moved the pot off the heat and let it sit, covered, so that the chicken could continue climbing toward 165 degrees with no risk of overshooting the mark.

Unfortunately, this first sous vide attempt was too gentle; the water cooled before the chicken could fully cook through. I went through a dozen more tests, adjusting the cooking time, water temperature, and amount of water. It was a delicate balance: I needed enough water to fully submerge the chicken and hold the heat, but I didn't want to wait for several quarts of water heat up. At last, I hit on the ideal formula: four chicken breasts and 6 cups of water heated to 170 degrees then removed from the heat, covered, and left to stand for about 15 minutes until the meat was 165 degrees throughout. In fact, the method was so foolproof that I could swap bone-in meat for fuss-free boneless, skinless breasts and still get the same tender, juicy results. One final cooking trick: Adding 2 tablespoons of salt to the water seasoned the meat nicely. I popped the cooked meat onto a baking sheet to chill in the refrigerator while I finished the salad.

I knew that mayonnaise would be the dressing base, but I wanted to use as little of it as possible to keep the salad light and fresh-tasting. After some experimentation, I found that just ½ cup was sufficient to bind the meat together, and I brightened its rich flavor with lemon juice and Dijon mustard. Minced celery, shallot, tarragon, and parsley added freshness and a cool, contrasting crunch.

With the basic salad perfected, I updated a few other classic versions so that I'd have several options for picnic lunches: a curried salad punched up with fresh ginger and crunchy cashews; a Waldorf version with crisp apple and walnuts; and an iteration boasting juicy red grapes and smoked almonds.

—KEITH DRESSER, *Cook's Illustrated*

Classic Chicken Salad

SERVES 4 TO 6

To ensure that the chicken cooks through, don't use breasts that weigh more than 8 ounces or are thicker than 1 inch. Make sure to start with cold water in step 1. We like the combination of parsley and tarragon, but 2 tablespoons of one or the other is fine. This salad can be served in a sandwich or spooned over leafy greens.

  Salt and pepper
4 (6- to 8-ounce) boneless, skinless chicken breasts, no more than 1 inch thick, trimmed
½ cup mayonnaise
2 tablespoons lemon juice
1 teaspoon Dijon mustard
2 celery ribs, minced
1 shallot, minced
1 tablespoon minced fresh parsley
1 tablespoon minced fresh tarragon

1. Dissolve 2 tablespoons salt in 6 cups cold water in Dutch oven. Submerge chicken in water. Heat pot over medium heat until water registers 170 degrees. Remove from heat, cover pot, and let stand until chicken registers 165 degrees, 15 to 17 minutes.

2. Transfer chicken to paper towel–lined baking sheet. Refrigerate until chicken is cool, about 30 minutes. While chicken cools, whisk mayonnaise, lemon juice, mustard, and ¼ teaspoon pepper together in large bowl.

3. Pat chicken dry with paper towels and cut into ½-inch pieces. Transfer chicken to bowl with mayonnaise mixture. Add celery, shallot, parsley, and tarragon; toss to combine. Season with salt and pepper to taste. Serve. (Salad can be refrigerated for up to 2 days.)

VARIATIONS

Curried Chicken Salad with Cashews

Microwave 1 teaspoon vegetable oil, 1 teaspoon curry powder, and ⅛ teaspoon cayenne pepper together, uncovered, until oil is hot, about 30 seconds. Add curry oil to mayonnaise and substitute lime juice for lemon juice and 1 teaspoon grated fresh ginger for mustard in step 2. Substitute 2 tablespoons minced fresh cilantro for parsley and tarragon, and add ½ cup coarsely chopped toasted cashews and ⅓ cup golden raisins to salad with celery.

Waldorf Chicken Salad
Add ½ teaspoon ground fennel seeds to mayonnaise mixture in step 2. Substitute 1 teaspoon minced fresh thyme for parsley and add 1 peeled Granny Smith apple cut into ¼-inch pieces and ½ cup coarsely chopped toasted walnuts to salad with celery.

Chicken Salad with Red Grapes and Smoked Almonds
Add ¼ teaspoon grated lemon zest to mayonnaise mixture in step 2. Substitute 1 teaspoon minced fresh rosemary for tarragon, and add 1 cup quartered red grapes and ½ cup coarsely chopped smoked almonds to salad with celery.

CRISP CUCUMBER SALAD

A CRISP, COOL CUCUMBER SALAD WOULD BE THE ideal accompaniment to any hot-off-the-grill entrée if the typical recipe didn't result in soggy disks awash in an insipid dressing. The problem: Cucumbers are full of water. While all that moisture gives cucumber its fresh, clean bite, liquid begins to seep out as soon as the vegetable is cut, diluting the dressing almost as soon as the two come together.

Some recipes address this issue by salting the cucumbers and leaving them to drain before tossing them with dressing. The only dilemma? That process takes at least an hour and leaves the cucumbers slightly wilted. I found that I could get rid of some of the liquid with almost no added time by draining the slices on paper towels while I mixed the dressing, but this didn't entirely solve the problem. Could I do more?

I knew the variety of cucumber I chose would also affect the crispness of the salad. While seedless English cucumbers require less prep, we've found that common American cucumbers have more crunch than their English cousins. While all cucumbers contain a "softening" enzyme that's activated when the vegetable is cut, breaking down its cell walls, the cell structure of the English variety is naturally weaker and thus collapses more easily. I knew American cucumbers would fare better when peeled and tossed with dressing.

The cuke choice settled, I moved on to how I might compensate for the dressing's inevitable dilution. I tried doubling and even tripling the amount of dressing to lessen the impact of the cucumber water, but all that soupy liquid at the bottom of the bowl was unappealing. What if instead of trying to mask the excess liquid, I worked with it? For my next batch I tossed the cucumbers with an ultra-potent dressing made with 3 tablespoons of vinegar and just 2 teaspoons of oil. This latest batch was better, if a bit harsh. Could I do better?

I recalled a recipe that concentrated and smoothed out the flavor of the dressing by reducing the vinegar. I did the same: I boiled ½ cup of vinegar until it measured 3 tablespoons; let it cool for about 10 minutes; mixed it with oil, a little salt and sugar, and the cucumbers; and let the salad stand for a few minutes—just long enough for the cucumbers to shed some of their liquid into the dressing. But curiously, instead of tasting more concentrated, the flavor of the dressing had flattened out. It turns out that heating vinegar drives off some of the acetic acid that gives it its tartness, and boiling is the most detrimental way to heat it, driving off many of its other flavors. Our science editor suggested that gently simmering the vinegar might preserve more of its character while still mellowing its sharp bite. I gave it a whirl, this time reducing the ½ cup of vinegar over medium-low heat for about five minutes and then proceeding with my recipe. The results were remarkably improved. The dressing now had a concentrated depth that could hold up to an influx of water.

But all was still not perfect. I found I actually missed some of the brightness of the uncooked dressing. Adding back even a little raw vinegar would only result in the harshness I was trying to avoid, so I swapped in another, rounder-flavored source of acid: lemon juice. I cut the reduced vinegar to 2 tablespoons (⅓ cup before reducing) and added 1 tablespoon of fresh lemon juice, which punched up the flavors without oversharpening the acidity.

My tasters' only remaining complaint was that the ¼-inch-thick slices of cucumber were a bit chunky and didn't allow enough dressing to cling to them. They were happier when I sliced the cucumbers very thin (⅛ inch to 3/16 inch) so that each piece would be coated with plenty of vinaigrette.

All my salad needed now was some jazzing up. Clean-tasting cucumbers take well to bolder elements, so I added parsley and oregano, kalamata olives, and a handful of chopped almonds. And variations that embraced Thai, Chinese, and Mexican flavor profiles ensured that we could serve this salad with a variety of dishes.

—YVONNE RUPERTI, *Cook's Illustrated*

Cucumber Salad with Olives, Oregano, and Almonds

SERVES 4 TO 6

This salad is best served within 1 hour of being dressed.

    4 cucumbers, peeled, halved lengthwise, seeded,
       and sliced very thin
    ⅓ cup white wine vinegar
    1 tablespoon lemon juice
    2 teaspoons extra-virgin olive oil
 1½   teaspoons sugar
    1 teaspoon salt
    ⅛ teaspoon pepper
    ½ cup pitted kalamata olives, chopped coarse
    1 shallot, sliced very thin
    ½ cup chopped fresh parsley
    1 teaspoon minced fresh oregano
    3 tablespoons sliced almonds, toasted and
       chopped coarse

1. Spread cucumber slices evenly on paper towel–lined baking sheet. Refrigerate while preparing dressing.

2. Bring vinegar to simmer in small saucepan over medium-low heat; cook until reduced to 2 tablespoons, 4 to 6 minutes. Transfer vinegar to bowl and set aside to cool to room temperature, about 10 minutes. Whisk in lemon juice, oil, sugar, salt, and pepper.

3. When ready to serve, add cucumbers, olives, shallot, parsley, and oregano to dressing and toss to combine. Let stand for 5 minutes; retoss, sprinkle with almonds, and serve.

VARIATIONS

Cucumber Salad with Chile, Mint, and Basil

Substitute lime juice for lemon juice and vegetable oil for olive oil. Omit pepper and increase sugar to 2 teaspoons. Add 1 tablespoon fish sauce and 2 seeded and minced Thai chiles to dressing in step 2. Substitute ¼ cup chopped fresh mint and ¼ cup chopped fresh basil for parsley and ¼ cup coarsely chopped toasted peanuts for almonds. Omit olives, shallot, and oregano.

Cucumber Salad with Ginger, Sesame, and Scallions

Nori are thin sheets of seaweed commonly used for wrapping sushi. They can be found in most supermarkets in the international foods aisle.

Substitute lime juice for lemon juice and toasted sesame oil for olive oil. Omit pepper and increase sugar to 2 teaspoons. Add 2 teaspoons grated fresh ginger to dressing in step 2. Substitute 5 thinly sliced scallions for parsley, 1 toasted and crumbled sheet of nori for oregano, and 3 tablespoons toasted sesame seeds for almonds. Omit olives and shallot.

Cucumber Salad with Jalapeño, Cilantro, and Pepitas

Substitute lime juice for lemon juice. Omit pepper and add 1 seeded and minced jalapeño chile and 2 teaspoons grated lime zest to dressing in step 2. Substitute 1 cup chopped cilantro for parsley and toasted pepitas for almonds. Omit olives, shallot, and oregano.

NOTES FROM THE TEST KITCHEN

SEEDING A CUCUMBER

To seed a cucumber, peel it, then cut it in half lengthwise. Run small spoon inside each cucumber half to scoop out seeds and surrounding liquid.

WATERMELON–FETA FRESH CORN SALAD

FRESH CORN SALAD

IT'S NOT HARD TO FIND RECIPES FOR CORN SALAD, but, as I recently learned after making several of them, it's hard to find a good one. The standard method—stripping kernels off the cob, adding vegetables (usually tomatoes, onions, and/or peppers), and tossing with dressing—produced salads that were not up to snuff. Some were too sweet and meek. Others were so tart that I couldn't taste the corn through the pucker. And some were waterlogged, overwhelmed by the juices the vegetables released as they sat. I wanted a simple recipe that was nonetheless bold, balanced, and full of corn flavor.

My initial tests showed that raw corn is very sweet, yes, but its delicate taste can disappear in a salad. I hoped to heighten the flavor of the kernels by browning them lightly in a skillet for a few minutes. It worked, giving the corn—even inferior, out-of-season corn—a complex, nutty dimension. I learned the hard way, though, that using a nonstick pan was crucial. Otherwise, the corn's milky starch burned and stuck to the skillet.

When it came time to dress the salad, the sweetness of the corn still proved challenging. A standard vinaigrette (3 parts oil to 1 part vinegar) wasn't acidic enough to bring the salad into balance. Retooling the ratios, I found that it took equal parts oil and vinegar to create a dressing that offset the sugary corn. When we make potato salad in the test kitchen, we often sprinkle the hot cooked potatoes with vinegar, which seasons them deeply. I decided to borrow the technique to heighten the flavor of my corn salad further. As I'd hoped, the hot kernels absorbed the vinaigrette beautifully.

When incorporated into salads like these, tomatoes (and other juicy summer produce, like the watermelon and cucumber in our variations) weep water and make the salads soggy. Using another test kitchen technique, I tossed the tomatoes with ½ teaspoon of salt and let them sit in a colander for 30 minutes to draw out some of their liquid, which I then discarded. Unfortunately, as soon as I added the drained tomatoes to the warm corn, the tomatoes broke down and wept more water. To prevent a soupy salad, I waited until the corn had cooled in the dressing before stirring in the tomatoes

(or other juicy vegetables). At last, my corn salad was tasty and crunchy. But I found that letting it sit for at least 30 minutes before serving so that the flavors could meld greatly improved it.

This corn salad was so good that I developed four easy variations so you can enjoy different versions of the dish all summer long.

—KELLY PRICE, *Cook's Country*

Fresh Corn Salad
SERVES 4 TO 6

Don't add the tomatoes to the toasted corn until it is cool, as the heat from the corn will partially cook the tomatoes.

- 2   tomatoes, cored and cut into ½-inch pieces
     Salt and pepper
- 2   scallions, sliced thin
- 1½ tablespoons white wine vinegar
- 2½ tablespoons olive oil
- 5   ears corn, kernels cut from cobs
- ¼   cup minced fresh parsley

1. Toss tomatoes with ½ teaspoon salt in bowl. Transfer to colander set over bowl and let drain for 30 minutes. Combine scallions, vinegar, ¾ teaspoon salt, and ½ teaspoon pepper in large bowl. Slowly whisk in 1½ tablespoons oil

2. Meanwhile, heat remaining 1 tablespoon oil in 12-inch nonstick skillet over medium-high heat until shimmering. Add corn and cook, stirring occasionally, until spotty brown, 5 to 7 minutes. Transfer corn to bowl with vinaigrette, toss to coat, and let cool to room temperature, about 20 minutes. Stir in drained tomatoes and parsley. Let sit until flavors meld, about 30 minutes. Season with salt and pepper to taste and serve. (Salad can be refrigerated for up to 2 days.)

VARIATIONS
Arugula-Goat Cheese Fresh Corn Salad
Substitute 1½ tablespoons lemon juice for white wine vinegar. Stir in 2 ounces coarsely chopped baby arugula and 4 ounces crumbled goat cheese with tomatoes. Omit parsley.

Chickpea-Avocado Fresh Corn Salad

Substitute 1½ tablespoons red wine vinegar for white wine vinegar. Add ¾ teaspoon smoked paprika, 1 minced garlic clove, and ⅛ teaspoon cayenne pepper to skillet with corn for last 30 seconds of cooking. Toss 1 (15-ounce) can rinsed chickpeas with vinaigrette and hot corn. Stir in 1 avocado, pitted and cut into ½-inch pieces, with tomatoes.

Tuscan Fresh Corn Salad

Substitute 1½ tablespoons red wine vinegar for white wine vinegar. Toss 1 (15-ounce) can rinsed cannellini beans with vinaigrette and hot corn. Substitute 2 tablespoons chopped fresh basil for parsley.

Watermelon-Feta Fresh Corn Salad

Substitute 2 cups watermelon, cut into ½-inch pieces, and 2 cucumbers, peeled, quartered lengthwise, seeded, and cut into ½-inch pieces, for tomatoes. Stir 4 ounces crumbled feta cheese into cooked and cooled corn. Substitute ¼ cup minced fresh mint for parsley.

NOTES FROM THE TEST KITCHEN

EASY CORN OFF THE COB

Trying to cut kernels off wobbly, unsteady ears of corn is asking for trouble. To keep cob stable as you slice off kernels, cut each ear of corn in half crosswise, then turn each half on its cut side.

CORING TOMATOES

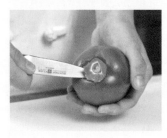

Using paring knife, cut out cone-shaped tomato core along with any hard flesh around core.

LENTIL SALAD

LENTILS MAY NOT GET POINTS FOR GLAMOUR, BUT when properly cooked and dressed up in a salad with bright vinaigrette and herbs, nuts, and cheeses, the legumes' earthy, almost meaty depth and firm-tender bite make a satisfying side dish for almost any meal.

The trouble is, perfectly cooked lentils are never a given. Too often, either their skins burst and their flesh disintegrates into unappealing starchy mush, or they don't cook through completely and retain chewy skins and hard, crunchy cores. Before I started adding accoutrements, I had to nail down a reliable way to produce tender, buttery lentils with soft, unbroken skins. And because the tiny, shape-retaining French green lentils we favor can be hard to come by, I was also determined to develop an approach that would yield perfect results with whatever lentil variety my supermarket had to offer.

Fortunately, the test kitchen's previous work with bean cookery gave me a good idea for how to keep the lentil skins intact. We've discovered that, odd as it may sound, brining beans overnight softens their outer shells and makes them less likely to burst. The explanation is twofold: As the beans soak, the sodium ions from the salt replace some of the calcium and magnesium ions in the skins. By replacing some of the mineral ions, the sodium ions weaken the pectin in the skins, allowing more water to penetrate and leading to a more pliable, forgiving texture. But with beans it took an overnight soak for the brining to be most effective. Fortunately, due to the lentils' smaller, flatter shape, I found that just a few hours of brining dramatically cuts down on blowouts. I also had one more idea for hastening the process: Since heat speeds up all chemical reactions, I managed to reduce the brining time to just an hour by using warm water in the salt solution.

To further reduce blowouts, I tried to cook the lentils as gently as possible. But I could see that even my stovetop's low setting still agitated the lentils too vigorously. I decided to try the oven, hoping that its indirect heat would get the job done more gently—and it did. And while the oven did increase the cooking time from less than 30 minutes to nearly an hour, the results were worth the wait: Virtually all of the lentil skins were tender yet intact.

Despite the lentils' soft, perfect skins, their insides tended to be mushy, not creamy. It occurred to me that I could try another simple trick with salt: adding it to the cooking water. Many bean recipes (including ours) shy away from adding salt during cooking because it produces firm, often gritty interiors. Here's why: While a brine's impact is mainly confined to the skin, heat (from cooking) affects the inside of the bean, causing sodium ions to move to the interior, where they slow the starches' ability to absorb water. But a firmed-up texture was exactly what my mushy lentils needed. Could a problem for beans prove to be the solution for lentils? Sure enough, when I added ½ teaspoon of salt to the cooking water, the lentils went from mushy to firm yet creamy.

I had just two remaining tasks to tackle: enriching the flavor of the lentils and creating a few salad variations. Swapping some of the cooking water for chicken broth solved the first problem, and tossing the lentils with tart vinaigrette and bold mix-ins feta, olives, and mint in one salad; spinach, walnuts, and Parmesan in another; hazelnuts and goat cheese in another; and carrots and cilantro in a final version—brightened and balanced their rich, earthy flavor.

—ANDREW JANJIGIAN, *Cook's Illustrated*

Lentil Salad with Olives, Mint, and Feta
SERVES 4 TO 6

French green lentils, or *lentilles du Puy*, are our preferred choice for this recipe, but it works with any type of lentil except red or yellow. Brining helps keep the lentils intact, but if you don't have time, they'll still taste good without it. The salad can be served warm or at room temperature.

 1 **cup lentils, picked over and rinsed**
    Salt and pepper
 6 **cups water**
 2 **cups low-sodium chicken broth**
 5 **garlic cloves, lightly crushed and peeled**
 1 **bay leaf**
 5 **tablespoons extra-virgin olive oil**
 3 **tablespoons white wine vinegar**
 ½ **cup pitted kalamata olives, chopped coarse**
 ½ **cup minced fresh mint**
 1 **large shallot, minced**
 1 **ounce feta cheese, crumbled (¼ cup)**

1. Place lentils and 1 teaspoon salt in bowl. Cover with 4 cups warm water (about 110 degrees) and soak for 1 hour. Drain well. (Drained lentils can be refrigerated for up to 2 days before cooking.)

NOTES FROM THE TEST KITCHEN

ALL ABOUT LENTILS

Lentils come in numerous varieties, each of which has a distinct appearance, flavor, and texture. We prepared different types using the slow-cooking method developed for our lentil salad recipes and asked our tasters to evaluate them.

TYPE	APPEARANCE	FLAVOR	TEXTURE	APPLICATION
French green	Small, dark green	Earthy, slightly starchy taste	Firm, resilient texture that won't fall apart even when long-cooked	Salads and side dishes
Black or "beluga"	Tiny, jet black	Robust, meaty taste	Firm, creamy texture that holds shape well	Salads and side dishes
Green, brown	Medium, pale green or brown	Vegetal, mineral taste	Relatively firm texture when cooked	Salads, soups, and side dishes
Red	Small, orange	Delicate taste with floral hints	Disintegrate completely when cooked	Soups, Indian dal
Yellow	Medium, pale golden	Bland, starchy taste	Disintegrate completely when cooked	Soups, Indian dal

2. Adjust oven rack to middle position and heat oven to 325 degrees. Combine drained lentils, remaining 2 cups water, broth, garlic, bay leaf, and ½ teaspoon salt in ovensafe medium saucepan. Cover and bake until lentils are tender but remain intact, 40 to 60 minutes. Meanwhile, whisk oil and vinegar together in large bowl.

3. Drain lentils well; remove garlic and bay leaf. Add drained lentils, olives, mint, and shallot to dressing and toss to combine. Season with salt and pepper to taste. Transfer to serving dish, sprinkle with feta, and serve.

VARIATIONS

Lentil Salad with Spinach, Walnuts, and Parmesan Cheese

Substitute sherry vinegar for white wine vinegar. Place 4 ounces baby spinach and 2 tablespoons water in bowl. Cover and microwave until spinach is wilted and volume is halved, 3 to 4 minutes. Remove bowl from microwave and keep covered for 1 minute. Transfer spinach to colander; gently press to release liquid. Transfer spinach to cutting board and roughly chop. Return to colander and press again. Substitute chopped spinach for olives and mint and 1½ ounces coarsely grated Parmesan cheese for feta. Sprinkle with ⅓ cup coarsely chopped toasted walnuts before serving.

Lentil Salad with Hazelnuts and Goat Cheese

Substitute red wine vinegar for white wine vinegar and add 2 teaspoons Dijon mustard to dressing in step 2. Omit olives and substitute ¼ cup chopped fresh parsley for mint. Substitute 2 ounces crumbled goat cheese for feta and sprinkle with ⅓ cup coarsely chopped toasted hazelnuts before serving.

Lentil Salad with Carrots and Cilantro

Substitute lemon juice for white wine vinegar. Toss 2 carrots, peeled and cut into 2-inch-long matchsticks, with 1 teaspoon ground cumin, ½ teaspoon ground cinnamon, and ⅛ teaspoon cayenne pepper in bowl. Cover and microwave until carrots are tender but still crisp, 2 to 4 minutes. Substitute carrots for olives and ¼ cup minced fresh cilantro for mint. Omit shallot and feta.

SWEET POTATO SALAD

I GREW UP EATING ORDINARY AMERICAN POTATO salad—the kind with mayonnaise, celery, and sometimes hard-cooked egg—at every family picnic and barbecue, but I've since fallen for the sweet potato version. Unlike classic potato salad, sweet potato salad is usually tossed with a light vinaigrette so the flavor of the potatoes really shines through. To perfect my own version of this sweet summer salad, I found a handful of recipes in our cookbook library and headed into the test kitchen with my trusty peeler to get to work.

All the recipes I prepared required boiling and then dressing sweet potato cubes. Terrible idea—the boiled sweet potatoes were mushy and waterlogged. I scrapped those recipes without ceremony and switched to steaming, which immediately produced fluffy, flavorful potatoes—until I stirred in a basic vinaigrette. Suddenly, the sweet potato salad turned oily. I was baffled until our science editor explained that steaming damages the cell walls of sweet potatoes, so they absorb oil more easily. I made a few additional batches, adjusting ratios of oil to vinegar, before deciding on a vinaigrette with the usual amount of oil reduced by one-third.

When we make ordinary potato salad in the test kitchen, we often toss the warm potatoes with a little vinegar—they drink it up and become deeply seasoned. I did the same with the sweet potatoes, but their edges broke down. The problem this time, our science editor explained, was that there's less pectin holding the cells together in sweet potatoes than in white potatoes. When the sweet potatoes are hot, the pectin begins to lose its grip. Cooling them lets the pectin rebond slightly. Could I get the same flavor impact without compromising texture by tossing cold potatoes with hot dressing? Happily, it worked.

Now that I had the technique down, I turned to flavor. The sweet potato salad cried out for a little heat, bite, and crunch. I added those with cayenne pepper, Dijon mustard, and chopped red bell pepper, respectively. A common refrain at *Cook's Country* is "Bacon makes it better," and it certainly did here; crisp, salty, meaty bacon was a welcome addition. We liked this sweet potato salad so well, I developed a variation that sent the dish on a trip to Asia.

—CAROLYNN PURPURA MACKAY, *Cook's Country*

Sweet Potato Salad

SERVES 4 TO 6

Be sure to rinse the sweet potatoes until they are completely cooled in step 1 or they will break down and become mushy when tossed with the dressing.

2 pounds sweet potatoes, peeled and cut into
¾-inch pieces

1 red bell pepper, stemmed, seeded, and
cut into ½-inch pieces

2 tablespoons cider vinegar

1 tablespoon Dijon mustard
Salt and pepper

⅛ teaspoon cayenne pepper

5 slices bacon, chopped

3 tablespoons vegetable oil

3 scallions, sliced thin

1. Add 1 inch water to Dutch oven and bring to boil. Place steamer basket in Dutch oven and add sweet potatoes. Reduce heat to medium-low and cook, covered, until potatoes are nearly tender, 16 to 20 minutes. Add bell pepper and cook, covered, until sweet potatoes and pepper are tender, 2 to 4 minutes. Drain vegetables and rinse with cold water until cool, about 2 minutes. Drain again briefly and transfer to large bowl.

2. Combine vinegar, mustard, ½ teaspoon salt, ¼ teaspoon pepper, and cayenne in bowl. Transfer half of vinegar mixture to small bowl and microwave until steaming, about 30 seconds. Drizzle hot vinegar mixture over vegetables and gently toss until evenly coated. Let sit at room temperature until flavors meld, about 15 minutes.

3. Meanwhile, cook bacon in 10-inch skillet over medium heat until crisp, 6 to 8 minutes. Using slotted spoon, transfer bacon to paper towel–lined plate. Slowly whisk oil into remaining vinegar mixture until thoroughly incorporated.

4. Pour dressing over vegetables and gently toss until evenly coated. Stir in bacon and scallions. Cover and refrigerate until chilled, about 30 minutes. Season with salt and pepper to taste and serve. (Salad can be refrigerated for up to 2 days.)

VARIATION

Asian-Style Sweet Potato Salad

Substitute 4 ounces snow peas, strings removed, sliced ½ inch thick on bias for bell pepper. In step 2, substitute 1 tablespoon lime juice and 1 tablespoon rice vinegar for the cider vinegar, 1 tablespoon grated fresh ginger for the mustard, and 1 tablespoon soy sauce for the salt. Replace 1 tablespoon vegetable oil with 1 tablespoon toasted sesame oil and substitute ⅓ cup chopped salted, dry-roasted peanuts for the bacon.

NOTES FROM THE TEST KITCHEN

PREPARING BELL PEPPERS

1. Slice ¼ inch from top and bottom of pepper. Remove stem from top lobe.

2. Pull core out of pepper. Make slit down one side of pepper and lay flat, skin side down, in one long strip.

3. Slide sharp knife along inside of pepper to remove ribs and seeds. Cut into strips, then cut strips into ½-inch pieces.

CHAPTER 2

SOUPS & STEWS

Corn Chowder   30

Farmhouse Vegetable and Barley Soup   31

Herbed Croutons

Lemon-Thyme Butter

Quinoa and Vegetable Stew   34

Italian Wedding Soup   37

Catalan-Style Beef Stew with Mushrooms   41

Green Bay Booyah   43

Easy Clam Chowder   46

Shrimp Bisque   48

CORN CHOWDER

I'M ALL FOR THE SIMPLICITY OF EATING SWEET summer corn straight from the cob, but sometimes I have a bumper crop of ears and need a good corn chowder recipe. I can't say I've ever made a really bad version, but I've never made a great one either. Usually, the results are excessively rich—and while I enjoy cream-based chowders as much as the next New Englander, too much dairy can muddle the bottom line: fresh corn flavor. My ideal version? A simple but substantial soup that lets the kernels' crisp sweetness stand out against a creamy (not stodgy) backdrop seasoned with bits of pork, aromatic vegetables, and fresh herbs.

The most promising recipe I tried was pretty traditional: The cobs were stripped of their kernels and "milked" with the back of a knife to extract all their pulp and juices; chopped onion was sautéed in rendered salt pork fat to build a flavor base, followed by a touch of flour for thickening. Liquid—a combination of chicken broth and milk—was added along with cubed red potatoes, herbs, and the corn pulp. Once the potatoes were tender, in went the kernels and a big glug of heavy cream just before serving. My tasters and I decided that, besides the almost undetectable pork, the key flavor elements were generally there, but given the weakness of the corn flavor, the proportions were clearly way off.

The pork problem was easily fixed. Salt pork may have been the go-to meat for early chowder recipes, but over time it has evolved from a meaty slab often cut from portions other than the belly to the muscle-streaked pieces of fat available today. Instead, I used bacon for its subtle sweet smokiness, adding it to the pot along with the onion and a pat of butter to keep it from browning and overwhelming the other elements.

As for the corn, I looked over the ingredient list and pinpointed the one component I knew was dulling its flavor: the dairy. I started dialing back on both the milk and the heavy cream until I had traded them for water and a mere cup of half-and-half, respectively. The results? Still plenty rich with much clearer corn flavor—but not fresh or sweet enough for a soup made with peak-season produce. Plus, without the cream, the broth lacked body. Adding more flour would have thickened things up a little, but not without undoing my flavor-boosting efforts.

As I thought more about the consistency problem, I realized that adding extra starch wasn't necessary.

I already had all the thickening power I needed right in the pot with the potatoes. The trick would be to treat this chowder like other hearty soups and puree a portion of it in a blender. Sure enough, this method worked beautifully; when I poured the pureed portion back into the pot and gave the contents a stir, I had exactly the fluid yet spoon-coating results I was hoping for. But the nutty, sweet corn flavor I was after was still a work in progress.

Looking for other opportunities to highlight the corn, I scanned my recipe again and stopped at the chicken broth. What if I swapped it for a homemade corn broth, as some recipes suggest? I tried—but with little success. Simmering the denuded cobs and husks in water didn't produce anything better than chowder made with plain water. There was only one outlier technique that looked intriguing: "juicing" the corn pulp and adding the flavorful liquid to a water base. I admit, I balked at the idea at first, but I couldn't ignore its potential.

So I stripped the kernels and milked the cobs as I had been doing, but instead of adding the pulp (2 cups or so) straight to the pot, I wrapped it in a clean kitchen towel, squeezed every last bit of liquid into a bowl, and discarded the solids. When I measured the output, I had about ⅔ cup of "jus," which I stirred into the chowder just before serving to preserve its fresh sweetness. That did it. When my tasters slurped up this batch and reached for seconds, I knew that shot of pure corn extract was worth the trouble. With one final flourish—a small handful of chopped basil sprinkled over the top—I had a chowder every bit as fresh and sweet as corn straight from the cob.

—DAVID PAZMIÑO, *Cook's Illustrated*

NOTES FROM THE TEST KITCHEN

STRIP IT OFF
To make chowder with fresh, sweet corn flavor, we first needed to remove the kernels from the cob. This can be done by running a sharp chef's knife down the length of the ear, but a good corn stripper can make the job easier and safer. Our favorite model, the **OXO Good Grips Corn Stripper**, $13.99, resembles a computer mouse and cleanly cuts several rows of kernels at a time as you run its oval body along the cob; even better, it deposits the kernels into an attached cup instead of all over your counter.

Corn Chowder

SERVES 6

Be careful to remove only the part of the kernel sticking out of the cob; cutting deeper will pull off fibrous material. Yukon Gold potatoes can be substituted for the red potatoes and minced chives for the basil. Depending on the sweetness of your corn, the finished chowder may need to be seasoned with sugar. For more information on cutting corn kernels from the cob, see page 24.

8	ears corn, husks and silk removed
3	tablespoons unsalted butter
1	onion, chopped fine
4	slices bacon, halved lengthwise, then cut crosswise into ¼-inch pieces
2	teaspoons minced fresh thyme
	Salt and pepper
¼	cup all-purpose flour
5	cups water
¾	pound red potatoes, cut into ½-inch pieces
1	cup half-and-half
	Sugar
3	tablespoons chopped fresh basil

1. Using chef's knife or corn stripper, cut kernels from corn; transfer to bowl and set aside (you should have 5 to 6 cups kernels). Holding cobs over second bowl, use back of butter knife to firmly scrape remaining pulp on cobs into bowl (you should have 2 to 2½ cups pulp). Transfer pulp to center of clean kitchen towel set in medium bowl. Wrap towel tightly around pulp and squeeze tightly until dry. Discard pulp in towel and set corn juice aside (you should have about ⅔ cup juice).

2. Melt butter in Dutch oven over medium heat; add onion, bacon, thyme, 2 teaspoons salt, and 1 teaspoon pepper; cook, stirring frequently, until onion is softened and edges are beginning to brown, 8 to 10 minutes. Stir in flour and cook, stirring constantly, for 2 minutes. Whisking constantly, gradually add water and bring to boil. Add corn kernels and potatoes. Bring to simmer; reduce heat to medium-low and cook until potatoes have softened, 15 to 18 minutes.

3. Process 2 cups chowder in blender until smooth, 1 to 2 minutes; return puree to chowder. Add half-and-half and return chowder to simmer. Remove pot from heat and stir in reserved corn juice. Season with salt, pepper, and up to 1 tablespoon sugar to taste. Sprinkle with basil and serve.

FARMHOUSE VEGETABLE AND BARLEY SOUP

WINTERTIME IS SOUP TIME, AND ALSO THE TIME OF year when our crisper drawers are overflowing with cold-weather vegetables like carrots, potatoes, leeks, cabbage, and turnips. That abundance of hearty produce would seem to have all the makings of a satisfying vegetable soup, but my attempts often turn out lackluster. The problem is time. The best soups—vegetable or otherwise—start with a rich, full-bodied broth, and I usually need the weekend to make a good one. Some recipes call for adding a little meat to the broth to beef up flavor, but it's hardly a shortcut. Many of the most flavorful cuts are also some of the toughest, and they take hours to turn tender. Cured meats such as bacon and pancetta impart distinctive smoky tastes that I sometimes don't want in a vegetable soup.

Rather than sideline rustic vegetable soup as a lazy Sunday afternoon project, I wanted to pack all the rich, earthy flavor and depth of a long-simmered stock into a recipe that took only about an hour's work. That narrowed my focus to a soup based on store-bought broth.

Curious to see how much mileage I could get out of simply doctoring commercial broth and tossing in vegetables, I threw together a test batch in which I sweated leeks, carrots, and celery in a few pats of butter; added staple aromatics like crushed garlic, a few sprigs of fresh thyme, and a bay leaf; and poured in 10 cups of vegetable broth. I simmered this base for 20 minutes, strained out the solids, then stirred in small chunks of potato and turnip and chopped green cabbage and let everything cook until the vegetables were just tender. My tasters had no complaints about the vegetables themselves; their flavors worked well together, and the crinkly cabbage leaves offered a nice crisp-tender crunch. Nor could I gripe about the time or labor involved, both of which were minimal. But there was no denying that the soup felt thin, in terms of both flavor and body.

The good news was that we'd been here before. A few years back the test kitchen developed a recipe for quick beef and vegetable soup and learned that the most effective way to get big flavor in a hurry is to bolster the prefab broth with ingredients rich in flavor-enhancing *umami*, the fifth taste that describes savory, "meaty" flavor. Among the ingredients at the top of the list were soy sauce and mushrooms, so I started my testing there, "seasoning" one pot with a few dashes of soy sauce and another with two large pieces of dried porcini (great for adding intense, earthy depth). The improvement to each batch was obvious but still insufficient. While both flavor boosters provided subtle depth, the commercial-broth taste still prevailed. I hesitantly added a little more of each ingredient to the pot in subsequent batches. But just as I'd feared, the soy and mushrooms began to overwhelm the broth.

Clearly soy sauce and mushrooms were imperfect solutions on their own, but I had yet to try them together. I worked up another batch of soup, this time limiting myself to 2 teaspoons of soy sauce and just a few of the dried mushroom slabs. To my delight, this broth was far better than I had expected. The soup took on a savory depth and complexity that had previously been missing. The only problem was that I couldn't reliably repeat the results. Sometimes the soup turned out a little less flavorful; other times it tasted a bit too mushroom-y.

It occurred to me that the issue was the dried mushroom pieces, which can vary a lot in size. I wondered if it would work better to grind the dried porcini to a powder and then measure out a set amount to add to the pot instead of rehydrating whole slices in the soup. This turned out to be a great solution: After experimenting with amounts, I found that 2 teaspoons of the porcini powder along with 2 teaspoons of soy sauce perfectly enhanced the broth's savory flavor.

The broth was now so good, I even found that I could substitute water for a good bit of the store-bought broth to eliminate any vestige of commercial flavor. The acidity of a little white wine (added along with the first batch of vegetables) further improved the soup, as did the last-minute addition of frozen peas, a splash of fresh lemon juice, and a fistful of minced parsley.

Flavorwise, I was in pretty good shape. The bigger hurdle was the soup's lack of body. The vegetables themselves were substantial, and roughly chopping (rather than dicing) them amped up their heartiness, but even the starchy potatoes didn't do much to thicken the broth. I thought about adding dairy but knew that the fat would dull the flavor of the broth that I'd just worked so hard to build. Recalling that a colleague had mentioned eating some stellar vegetable soups while in Ireland, I started flipping through some Irish cookbooks, and I stumbled on an interesting idea: adding oatmeal to the soup. I found this frugal trick for bulking up the broth charming in theory, but it didn't play out as I'd hoped. Tasters complained that even though the dish

took on a certain nuttiness, the chewy oats turned it into a vegetable-heavy gruel.

Nonetheless, I liked the idea of bulking up the soup with a grain and turned my attention to a more obvious choice: barley. I added half a cup of the pearl variety to the pot just as I poured in the liquids. The beads were partially plumped by the time I was ready to add the potatoes, turnip, and cabbage, and they were perfectly al dente about 20 minutes later, when the soup was ready to be served.

This was exactly the heft and substance that the soup needed—well, almost. A few of my tasters weren't keen on letting me wrap up testing before getting another dimension of flavor and richness into the pot. I had a holdout idea that I'd come across in one of the Irish cookbooks: finishing the soup with flavored butter. It would be an unusual addition for sure. Still, I held out hope that stirring in a dollop at the table would contribute not only a burst of fresh flavor (lemon and fresh thyme seemed like good soup-brightening additions) but also the plush body that only dairy can give without the cloying, flavor-dampening effect of milk or cream. When I caught my tasters sneaking an extra dollop into their bowls, I knew that I'd hit it right.

At last, I had a rustic, full-bodied vegetable soup thrown together in under an hour that didn't need even a speck of meat to taste hearty and satisfying.

—LAN LAM, *Cook's Illustrated*

Farmhouse Vegetable and Barley Soup

SERVES 6 TO 8

We prefer an acidic, unoaked white wine such as Sauvignon Blanc for this recipe. We love the richness added by the Lemon-Thyme Butter (recipe follows), and the soup can also be garnished with crisp bacon, crumbled cheddar cheese, or Herbed Croutons (recipe follows). You will need at least a 6-quart Dutch oven for this recipe.

⅛ ounce dried porcini mushrooms, rinsed

8 sprigs fresh parsley plus 3 tablespoons minced

4 sprigs fresh thyme

1 bay leaf

2 tablespoons unsalted butter

1½ pounds leeks, white and light green parts only, sliced ½ inch thick and washed thoroughly

2 carrots, peeled and cut into ½-inch pieces

- 2 celery ribs, cut into ¼-inch pieces
- ⅓ cup dry white wine
- 2 teaspoons soy sauce
  Salt and pepper
- 6 cups water
- 4 cups low-sodium chicken broth or vegetable broth
- ½ cup pearl barley
- 1 garlic clove, peeled and smashed
- 1½ pounds Yukon Gold potatoes, peeled and cut into ½-inch pieces
- 1 turnip, peeled and cut into ¾-inch pieces
- 1½ cups chopped green cabbage
- 1 cup frozen peas
- 1 teaspoon lemon juice

1. Grind porcini with spice grinder until they resemble fine meal, 10 to 30 seconds. Measure out 2 teaspoons porcini powder; reserve remainder for another use. Using kitchen twine, tie together parsley sprigs, thyme, and bay leaf.

2. Melt butter in Dutch oven over medium heat. Add leeks, carrots, celery, wine, soy sauce, and 2 teaspoons salt. Cook, stirring occasionally, until liquid has evaporated and celery is softened, about 10 minutes.

3. Add water, broth, barley, porcini powder, herb bundle, and garlic; increase heat to high and bring to boil. Reduce heat to medium-low and simmer, partially covered, for 25 minutes.

4. Add potatoes, turnip, and cabbage; return to simmer and cook until barley, potatoes, turnip, and cabbage are tender, 18 to 20 minutes.

5. Remove pot from heat and remove herb bundle. Stir in peas, lemon juice, and minced parsley; season with salt and pepper to taste. Serve, passing Lemon-Thyme Butter separately.

Herbed Croutons

MAKES ABOUT 2½ CUPS

Our favorite brand of sandwich bread is Arnold Country Classic White Bread.

- 1 tablespoon unsalted butter
- 1 teaspoon minced fresh parsley
- ½ teaspoon minced fresh thyme
- 4 slices hearty white sandwich bread, cut into ½-inch pieces
  Salt and pepper

BUILDING SAVORY FLAVOR ON THE DOUBLE

To ramp up savory flavor in our Farmhouse Vegetable and Barley Soup, we tried adding umami boosters like soy sauce and porcini mushrooms and made an interesting discovery. We found that using less of both ingredients—versus more of just one or the other—had a powerful impact on flavor. Here's why: Soy sauce contains high levels of naturally occurring, flavor-enhancing compounds called glutamates, while mushrooms are rich in flavor-amplifying compounds known as nucleotides. Used together, the two compounds can boost savory, umami-like flavors exponentially. Their effect is even more pronounced when the ratio of glutamates to nucleotides is very high. (Studies suggest that an effective ratio is 95:5.) Of course, we couldn't measure exactly how much of each compound was making it into the pot, so we tinkered with the amounts of soy and porcini we were adding until we hit it just right.

GLUTAMATES + NUCLEOTIDES = BIG SAVORY FLAVOR
Thanks to the synergistic effect of combining their different flavor-enhancing compounds, small amounts of both soy sauce and porcini mushrooms add up to a profound impact on flavor.

TESTING VEGETABLE CLEAVERS

Asian vegetable cleavers have a straight edge that, unlike curving Western-style knives, stays in contact with food as you cut, streamlining vegetable prep. Whereas meat cleavers have thick, heavy blades and a blunter edge for hacking through bone, these blades are thin and tapered. We found two types: Chinese-style, built like a slim meat cleaver, and shorter Japanese-style, which resembles a squared-off santoku.

We tested seven cleavers ($30 to $190), dicing onions, mincing parsley, slicing potatoes, and quartering butternut squash. Taller, heavier Chinese cleavers were easier to guide through large vegetables, as their heft did most of the work. But they were too unwieldy for some testers, who preferred the smaller, lighter Japanese blades. Spine width also proved important: Slimmer blades glided through food; thicker blades tore instead of sliced. Our favorite was the **MAC Japanese Series 6½-Inch Japanese Vegetable Cleaver**, $95. Weighing less than 5 ounces, with a 1.9-millimeter spine, it was light, sharp, and nimble. We don't consider this tool a replacement for an all-purpose Western-style chef's knife, but it's a pleasure to use if you chop a lot of vegetables.

Melt butter in 10-inch skillet over medium heat. Add parsley and thyme; cook, stirring constantly, for 20 seconds. Add bread and cook, stirring frequently, until light golden brown, 5 to 10 minutes. Season with salt and pepper to taste.

Lemon-Thyme Butter
MAKES 6 TABLESPOONS

6 **tablespoons unsalted butter, softened**
1 **tablespoon minced fresh thyme**
¾ **teaspoon finely grated lemon zest plus**
  ¼ teaspoon juice
  Pinch salt

Combine all ingredients in bowl.

QUINOA AND VEGETABLE STEW

QUINOA IS AN ANCIENT GRAIN THAT HAS GAINED a lot of popularity in the United States over the past several years because of its healthy profile: It has a high protein content, and it provides a good number of vitamins and minerals. In countries along the Andean highlands, this "super-food" plays a starring role in many dishes, among them a quinoa stew. It traditionally includes a good mix of vegetables, with potatoes and corn at the forefront, and while some recipes call for meat, many rely solely on the quinoa for protein; this version struck me as a great healthy vegetarian stew to add to our collection.

Most of the traditional recipes I found followed the same basic cooking method. First, a mix of cumin, coriander, and *annatto* powder (a flavoring common in Central and South America) was toasted in oil until fragrant. Next, onion, garlic, green pepper, and tomato were added and sautéed to form the background notes before broth, water, or a combination of the two was stirred into the pot along with native potatoes and giant kernels of Andean corn. When these were almost tender, quinoa was added and simmered until cooked through. Garnished with diced avocado, cilantro, and salty *queso fresco* (a fresh, crumbly cheese), the authentic stews were hearty, delicious, and filling. This method

seemed like the right place to start, but I needed to find a way to work around the obscure ingredients, like annatto powder and Peruvian varieties of potatoes and corn, to make a recipe with an accessible ingredient list .

I cooked a few batches of the stew to identify exactly what the annatto powder contributed. I found it to be slightly sweet and earthy, with just a hint of peppery bitterness. Although its flavor can be subtle, the color it lends to foods is anything but. Just a teaspoon or two was enough to turn a pot of my stew a rich shade of crimson. I realized that annatto powder has a flavor profile and color similar to those of sweet paprika, an easy switch for me to make. The cumin and coriander found in traditional recipes rounded out the flavor. To prevent the spices from burning (which happened in many of the recipes I tested), I added them to the pot only after I had sautéed the aromatics.

For the aromatics, the traditional combination of onion, green bell pepper, tomato, and garlic was OK, but tasters complained about the texture and flavor of the pepper, which turned army green and flavorless by the time the stew was done. Red bell pepper, on the other hand, remained sweet and fire-engine red. Tasters also felt the tomato flavor was spent by the end of cooking, so I waited to stir fresh tomatoes into the pot until the end, so that they could just warm through. With that tweak, they provided a welcome burst of freshness and clean tomato flavor. After adding a few cups of vegetable broth to the softened aromatics, I had to make a decision about the other vegetables that would give my stew its South American feel.

Without access to native Peruvian potatoes or Andean corn at local supermarkets, I had to find acceptable substitutes. After getting my hands on some Peruvian potatoes and comparing them with domestic varieties, I found the texture of red potatoes to be the closest option. As for the corn, nothing was similar to the dense, chewy, and nutty Andean corn, but tasters almost unanimously preferred the sweeter stew made with our own locally grown corn. Finally, to round out the vegetable selection and add some green to the pot, I stirred in some frozen peas. Happy with the hearty mix of vegetables, next I focused on the quinoa.

I've cooked a fair bit of quinoa in the test kitchen, so I knew it can go from crunchy to mushy almost instantly. Wary of overcooking, I added it to the pot only after the potatoes had softened (instead of when they were almost tender, as in the traditional recipes). After about

QUINOA AND VEGETABLE STEW

10 minutes, I was rewarded with firm yet cushy bites of quinoa. But tasters felt the broth still lacked body. One colleague suggested stretching the cooking time of the quinoa as far as I could in the hope that it would release additional starch into the stew without softening too much. After a few more minutes of gentle simmering, the quinoa still offered a slight chew and had given up sufficient starch to give the broth good body.

To finish, tasters liked citrusy cilantro and a garnish of creamy avocado. Some tasters also liked salty queso fresco, so I made it optional. This quinoa stew was the best of both worlds: a humble ode to its authentic roots and a streamlined yet flavorful offering ready for modern-day tastes.

—DAN SOUZA, *America's Test Kitchen Books*

Quinoa and Vegetable Stew

SERVES 6

This stew tends to thicken as it sits; add additional warm vegetable broth as needed before serving to loosen. Be sure to rinse the quinoa to remove its bitter coating (called saponin) before cooking. Garnish this stew with queso fresco, if desired.

- 1 onion, chopped fine
- 1 red bell pepper, stemmed, seeded, and cut into ½-inch pieces (see page 27)
- 2 teaspoons canola oil
   Salt and pepper
- 5 garlic cloves, minced
- 1 tablespoon paprika
- 2 teaspoons ground coriander
- 1½ teaspoons ground cumin
- 6 cups vegetable broth
- 1 pound red potatoes, cut into ½-inch pieces
- 1 cup quinoa, rinsed
- 1 large ear corn, kernels cut from cob (see page 24), or 1 cup frozen
- 2 tomatoes, cored and chopped coarse
- 1 cup frozen peas
- ½ cup minced fresh cilantro
- 1 avocado, halved, pitted, and cut into ½-inch pieces
- 8 ounces queso fresco, crumbled (2 cups) (optional)

1. Combine onion, bell pepper, oil, and ⅛ teaspoon salt in Dutch oven. Cover and cook over medium-low heat, stirring occasionally, until softened, 8 to 10 minutes.

Stir in garlic, paprika, coriander, and cumin and cook until fragrant, about 30 seconds. Stir in broth and potatoes and bring to boil. Reduce to gentle simmer and cook for 10 minutes.

2. Stir in quinoa and continue to simmer for 8 minutes. Stir in corn and continue to simmer until potatoes and quinoa are just tender, 5 to 7 minutes. Stir in tomatoes and peas and let heat through, about 2 minutes.

3. Off heat, stir in cilantro and season with salt and pepper to taste. Garnish individual bowls with avocado and queso fresco, if using, before serving.

NOTES FROM THE TEST KITCHEN

RINSING GRAINS AND RICE

Place grains or rice in fine-mesh strainer and rinse under cool water until water runs clear, occasionally stirring grains or rice around lightly with your hand. Let drain briefly.

PREPARING AVOCADOS

1. Slice avocado in half around pit, then lodge edge of knife blade into pit and twist to remove. Using large wooden spoon, pry pit safely off knife.

2. Use dish towel to hold avocado steady. Make ½-inch crosshatch incisions in flesh of each avocado half with knife, cutting down to but not through skin.

3. Separate diced flesh from skin with soupspoon inserted between skin and flesh. Gently scoop out avocado cubes.

ITALIAN WEDDING SOUP

I'VE NEVER BEEN TO A WEDDING BANQUET IN MILAN, Venice, or Palermo, but I'd hazard a guess that Italian wedding soup would not be on the menu. Its Italian name, *minestra maritata* ("married soup"), refers not to actual nuptials but to the marriage of hearty greens to a savory mixture of meats against the backdrop of a rich broth. The Italian-American rendition takes this pairing even further by transforming the meats into tender miniature meatballs and adding bits of wheaty pasta.

But over the years, Italian wedding soup has lost touch with its roots, sliding into the dodgy territory of convenience food. Most recipes seem to call for nothing more than simmering a few cans of broth, adding some ersatz "meatballs" in the form of dollops of Italian sausage, dumping in a bag of greens, and dusting it all with grated Parmesan. I didn't want a project that took an entire afternoon at the stove, but surely there was a middle ground that would bring back the deeper, more complex flavors of the old-fashioned version.

Traditionally, Italian wedding soup starts with a base of meaty *brodo*, broth brewed from cured meats and the bits, bobs, and bones of various animals, for a broth that doesn't taste strongly of any one particular kind of meat. Beyond gathering the requisite odd parts and specialty meats, cooks must spend hours simmering traditional brodo to fully develop its flavor—not to mention the constant skimming to remove foam and the tedious work of separating out the fat. Overall, this is more time and attention than most of us want to devote to a soup. I hoped that with the right collection of meats, aromatics, and flavorings I could render store-bought broth into something resembling a classic brodo in the 30-odd minutes it would take to prepare meatballs.

Since I wanted a base with a well-rounded, meaty taste, it made sense to use both chicken and beef broths. After a bit of experimentation, I found that a 2:1 ratio of chicken broth to beef broth, cut with a little water, tasted the most balanced. Some basic aromatics, like sautéed onion and a few smashed garlic cloves, nudged the broth in the right direction, especially when helped along by a sharpening splash of dry white wine. To further enrich the broth, I tried adding carrots and celery but found the sweetness of the former too cloying, and the metallic taste of the latter came on too strong. A fennel bulb turned out to be a better choice, lending a pleasant anise note and mild warmth.

With convenience in mind, I eschewed the odds and ends used in traditional brodo in favor of easy-to-find bone-in pieces. I tried out chicken wings, country-style pork ribs, and beef short ribs. They all contributed terrific flavor but made the broth too fatty, and my half-hour time frame was not enough to extract maximum flavor from the bones. Then it occurred to me: Since I would be using ground meat to make the meatballs, why not enlist some of it to lend flavor to the broth as well? After the meat had contributed its richness to the broth, I could strain out the hard bits—an easy enough step. I took a few ounces of the ground beef and pork that I'd bought to make the meatballs and lightly browned them along with the aromatics before adding the broth. The ground meats cooked quickly and the broth's meatiness was clearly amplified—another step in the right direction. But my soup base still tasted too thin, lacking the full-throated savor of a long-simmered stock.

Several traditional recipes that I'd consulted called for the leftover bone and scraps from a leg of prosciutto. Ever looked for a prosciutto bone? It's easier to find hens' teeth. A few thin slices of the salt-cured pork (which is packed with the glutamates that contribute savory richness to food) chopped and blended in with the ground meats did help matters. But I couldn't tolerate discarding $10 worth of top-shelf charcuterie when I strained the broth. I tried out a few other Italianate flavor enhancers: A Parmesan rind proved that it's easy to be too cheesy, sun-dried tomatoes tasted too sour and dyed the stock a ruddy color, and anchovies took the broth into overly salty territory.

Continuing my search for flavor-boosting ingredients, I borrowed an idea from our recipe for Farmhouse Vegetable and Barley Soup (page 32): combining dried porcini mushrooms and soy sauce. I loved the deep earthiness that the mushrooms provided, but soy sauce made the brodo too salty. I experimented with—and quickly ruled out—other umami boosters, including fish sauce and miso. They all added flavor but also muddied the primal meatiness that my brodo required. Then I remembered a condiment that tends to get pushed to the back of my pantry: Worcestershire sauce. This dark, old-fashioned liquid was bringing a jolt of savory flavor to meats and Bloody Marys long before umami became a household word. I added a dash of the stuff and noted that the broth's flavor was now somewhat deeper. A full tablespoon galvanized that flavor, highlighting the beef

ITALIAN WEDDING SOUP

and pork alike. With just 30 minutes and a well-edited handful of ingredients, I now had a full afternoon's worth of flavor in my pot.

Italian meatballs are often rolled from a blend of ground beef, pork, and veal and bound with a panade, a mixture of bread and dairy (and sometimes eggs) that moisturizes the meats and prevents their proteins from binding too tightly and growing tough. Why the blend of meats? Each brings something to the party: Beef packs big flavor; pork adds sweetness and richness; and veal's high concentration of gelatin gives the meatballs body while keeping them tender and light. Ground veal, though, can be hard to find. What happens if you simply skip it? My veal-less meatballs were a bit chewy and bland.

I wondered if I needed a substitute for veal, or if a cooking method could compensate for its missing attributes. Drawing on test kitchen experience, I ended up turning to both approaches. When we tackled Swedish meatballs (another meatball typically made from a beef-pork-veal blend), we found success using ground beef and pork alone by adding a secret ingredient: baking powder. Just 1 teaspoon ensured that the meatballs remained light once cooked. We'd also borrowed a technique from sausage making, whipping the ground pork in a stand mixer until it formed a smooth emulsion before adding the panade, seasonings, and ground beef. This step evenly distributes the pork's fat and moisture and traps them both within the meat's protein structure so that the meatballs remain juicy and pleasingly supple. (Pork has a lower proportion of muscle fibers to fat than beef and can be whipped without risk of toughening.) Both of these tricks brought the same great results to my mini meatballs.

Some Italian wedding soup recipes instruct you to pan-fry the meatballs before adding them to the brodo, but my tasters disliked the crisp exterior of browned meatballs in soup, plus the extra step was a hassle. But when I cooked the meatballs directly in the broth, the egg in the panade made the meatballs turn rubbery (the proteins in eggs and meat bind to form an elastic structure, which grows more resilient when cooked in liquid). Out went the egg—with no ill effect. I also learned that batches with a high ratio of panade to meat produced lighter, almost dumplinglike meatballs that paired well with the tender greens and pasta.

With the texture of the meatballs perfected, I just needed to fine-tune their flavor. Finely grated onion was a must, and a little Parmesan, blended into the panade, brought a subtle nuttiness. Dried herbs added little, but fresh oregano tied everything together and tempered the meatballs' richness.

All manner of greens find their way into this soup. I started my testing with spinach, a popular choice, but was disappointed by the way it quickly turned limp and slimy. Sturdier chard, cabbage, escarole, and kale were more successful, with kale's meaty texture and assertive flavor trumping the rest. Thinly sliced into a chiffonade, the kale strands wove themselves into an unwieldy clump; chopped bits worked better. The small pieces kept to themselves, fit tidily on a spoon, and softened in the time it took the pasta to cook.

And what about that pasta? Tiny bite-size shapes, like ditalini, worked best. To avoid mushy pasta, I added it at the last minute, testing it frequently. In just less than an hour in the kitchen, I had an elegant, satisfying soup tasting of far more work than I had invested—a successful compromise between tradition and convenience.

—MATTHEW CARD, *Cook's Illustrated*

Italian Wedding Soup

SERVES 6 TO 8

Use a rasp style grater to grate the onion and garlic for the meatballs. Tubettini or orzo can be used in place of the ditalini.

BROTH

- 1 onion, chopped
- 1 fennel bulb, stalks discarded, bulb halved, cored, and chopped
- 4 garlic cloves, peeled and smashed
- ¼ ounce dried porcini mushrooms, rinsed
- 4 ounces ground pork
- 4 ounces 85 percent lean ground beef
- 1 bay leaf
- ½ cup dry white wine
- 1 tablespoon Worcestershire sauce
- 4 cups low-sodium chicken broth
- 2 cups beef broth
- 2 cups water

FLAVORFUL SOUP STOCK ON THE FLY

Skipping the fuss of a typical brodo doesn't have to mean sacrificing flavor. By doctoring commercial chicken broth, we got comparably rich-tasting results in under an hour.

ATYPICAL AROMATIC

We rejected the standard carrots and celery for the anise notes of fennel. Onion and garlic, though, were musts.

TWO MEATS

No need to seek out meat scraps and bones for depth. A broth simmered with ground pork and beef is plenty savory.

TWO BROTHS

In addition to chicken broth, we use beef broth to mimic the flavor of traditional brodo.

UMAMI BOOSTERS

Umami-packed porcini mushrooms and Worcestershire sauce amp up the broth's meaty flavor.

MEATBALLS

- 1 slice hearty white sandwich bread, crusts removed, torn into 1-inch pieces
- 5 tablespoons heavy cream
- ¼ cup grated Parmesan cheese
- 4 teaspoons finely grated onion
- ½ teaspoon finely grated garlic
  Salt and pepper
- 6 ounces ground pork
- 1 teaspoon baking powder
- 6 ounces 85 percent lean ground beef
- 2 teaspoons minced fresh oregano

- 1 cup ditalini
- 12 ounces kale, stemmed and cut into ½-inch pieces (6 cups)

1. FOR THE BROTH: Heat onion, fennel, garlic, porcini, pork, beef, and bay leaf in Dutch oven over medium-high heat; cook, stirring frequently, until meats are no longer pink, about 5 minutes. Add wine and Worcestershire; cook for 1 minute. Add chicken broth, beef broth, and water; bring to simmer. Reduce heat to low, cover, and simmer for 30 minutes.

2. FOR THE MEATBALLS: While broth simmers, combine bread, cream, Parmesan, onion, garlic, and pepper to taste in bowl; using fork, mash mixture to uniform paste. Using stand mixer fitted with paddle, beat pork, baking powder, and ½ teaspoon salt on high speed until smooth and pale, 1 to 2 minutes, scraping down bowl as needed. Add bread mixture, beef, and oregano; mix on medium-low speed until just incorporated, 1 to 2 minutes, scraping down bowl as needed. Using moistened hands, form heaping teaspoons of meat mixture into smooth, round meatballs; you should have 30 to 35 meatballs. Cover and refrigerate until needed or up to 1 day.

3. Strain broth through fine-mesh strainer; discard solids. Wipe out Dutch oven and return broth to pot. (Broth can be refrigerated for up to 3 days. Skim off fat before reheating.)

4. Return broth to simmer over medium-high heat. Add pasta and kale; cook, stirring occasionally, for 5 minutes. Add meatballs; return to simmer and cook, stirring occasionally, until meatballs are cooked through and pasta is tender, 3 to 5 minutes. Season with salt and pepper to taste and serve.

CATALAN-STYLE BEEF STEW

FEW CUISINES CAN RIVAL THE COMPLEXITY OF Spanish food, with its influences from ancient Greece and Rome, North Africa, and even the Americas. This multilayering of flavors and textures is particularly apparent in the meat stews from the country's easternmost region of Catalonia. Almost all begin with a slow-cooked jam of onions and tomatoes known as *sofrito* and end with the stirring in of *picada,* a pestolike paste that includes fried bread, herbs, and ground nuts and gives the stew body and even more dimension. Cinnamon and smoked paprika are also common, along with a sherrylike fortified wine known as *vi ranci.* Though stews made from game, boar, or sausage are most typical in Catalonia, I was intent on investigating beef stew. When a search turned up only a handful of recipes, I consulted the renowned Spanish chef José Andrés, whose restaurants include Jaleo in Washington, D.C. Andrés explained the scarcity: Because Catalonia has little pastureland, beef stews are a special indulgence. I love beef, so there was no question that any Catalan-style stew I came up with would feature it. After jotting down a few pointers from Andrés, I set out to build my own recipe.

While most American beef stews are made with chuck roast, Spanish cooks employ a variety of cuts, including flank or skirt steak, blade steak, and short ribs. I tested all of these, comparing each one to chuck. The long, fibrous muscles of flank and skirt steak led to stringy results, and blade steak was flavorful but tended to dry out due to its lower fat content. I settled on boneless beef short ribs. Not only were these easier to butcher than a chuck roast, which is full of intramuscular fat and sinew, but they boasted outstanding beef flavor and became supremely tender and moist after a long, slow simmer. I seared chunks of short ribs in batches in a Dutch oven and then transferred them to a plate so I could prepare the foundation of my stew: the sofrito.

This flavor base is the cornerstone of not only Catalan cooking but also much of Spanish cuisine, lending remarkable depth to countless recipes. A traditional sofrito consists of finely chopped onions browned slowly over low heat and brightened with tomatoes (and sometimes herbs, spices, and aromatics). We've discovered that adding a small amount of salt and sugar to the onions helps draw out their moisture, both hastening and deepening the level of caramelization, so I sprinkled a bit of each onto two minced onions as they cooked over the traditional very low heat in olive oil. Once the onions were soft and dark brown (30 to 40 minutes later), I added tomatoes.

I experimented with canned and fresh tomatoes, preferring the latter for their greater acidity and brightness. I found, however, that fresh tomatoes had to be peeled or the skins made the stew stringy. Our standard method of blanching tomatoes before peeling seemed too fussy, particularly since I was using only two plum tomatoes. I decided to try a simpler method I'd seen in a Spanish cookbook: scraping the pulpy flesh of the tomatoes over the large holes of a box grater and then discarding the leathery skin. This worked beautifully. Along with the tomatoes, I stirred a bay leaf and a teaspoon of heady smoked paprika into the onions.

After 10 minutes more of cooking, the sweet and savory flavors of the sofrito had fully melded, and its texture was sticky and jamlike. But nearly 45 minutes had passed, and I couldn't help but wonder if I could cut back on some of the cooking time. When I sampled sofritos cooked for 15 and 30 minutes alongside a 45-minute flavor base, I had my answer: The long-cooked sample had a significantly richer, more developed taste; the shorter versions simply didn't have enough time to thoroughly caramelize. There would be no shortcuts taken here.

I nestled several batches of seared short-rib chunks atop the slow-cooked sofrito and poured in cooking liquids, experimenting with various combinations of chicken broth, beef broth, and water. Surprisingly, the broths actually detracted from the flavor of the beef and sofrito. Tasters preferred the cleanness of a stew made with water alone, which allowed more of the beef, onion, and tomato flavors to dominate.

As for the sherry that is typically added, the sofrito was already providing mild sweetness, and tasters thought that vi ranci (as well as American-made sherries) rendered the sauce too cloying. Instead, I turned to wine. I remembered a tip from Andrés that less assertive white wine is often preferred to red wine in stew as it complements, rather than overpowers, the flavor of the meat. I selected a dry Spanish white (Albariño), which my tasters agreed worked far better in the stew than red wine. In the end, I simmered the beef in just 1½ cups each of water and wine. To capture the warm spice flavor typical of Catalan stew, I also stirred a touch of cinnamon along with a sprig of fresh thyme into the pot.

My stew was coming along nicely, but after searing the short ribs and cooking the sofrito, I was an hour into my recipe, and I hadn't even started simmering the beef. I wondered whether searing the meat (a step that took about 15 minutes) was absolutely necessary. Spanish stews are usually simmered covered, but I had an idea.

In past test kitchen work for Hungarian beef stew, we were able to do away with searing since the meat was cooked on a bed of onions with no added liquid.

SHAKING UP STEW STANDARDS

To achieve the supremely beefy and complex flavor profile of Spanish beef stew, we learned a few new tricks—and gave up some long-held notions.

START WITH SOFRITO
A slow-cooked mixture of onions, tomatoes, spices, and herbs—known as *sofrito* in Spain—forms a flavor-packed base for the stew.

GO FOR WHITE WINE
We typically use red wine in beef stew. Here, we agreed with Spanish cooks that red wine competes with beefy flavor, so we reached for white instead.

SWAP THE ROAST FOR RIBS
Most stew recipes (including many of ours) call for chuck-eye roast. Boneless beef short ribs are even beefier-tasting and are easier to break down.

SKIP THE SEAR
When the stew is cooked in the oven and the pot is left uncovered, any part of the beef not submerged in liquid can brown, making searing unnecessary.

END WITH PICADA
A mixture of ground toasted bread, almonds, garlic, and parsley—the *picada*—stirred in before serving brightens the stew's flavor and thickens the broth.

Any portion of meat sitting above the liquid released by the onions was exposed to the heat of the oven and browned nearly as well as it would if it were seared, developing thousands of new flavor compounds. To see if I could eliminate searing in this recipe, I set the oven to a moderate 300 degrees and prepared a comparison of stews made with seared and unseared meat, leaving the unseared batch uncovered to fully expose it to the heat of the oven. When the stews emerged from the oven 2½ to 3 hours later, they tasted remarkably similar. I concluded that I could eliminate searing. An added benefit of this move was that the gentle, ambient heat of a low oven provided more reliable results than the stove, which runs the risk of scorching the meat on the bottom of the pot.

Now that I had achieved tender, intensely flavored beef, it was time for the critical final flourish: the picada. Some experts estimate that this bracing mixture of fried bread, nuts (most often almonds or hazelnuts), garlic, olive oil, and herbs (typically parsley) ground together has been used in Catalan cooking since the 13th and 14th centuries. In stews, the nuts and bread bulk up the braising liquid, and the garlic and parsley add flavor and freshness.

Opting for blanched almonds, which, unlike hazelnuts, require no fussy skinning, I sautéed ¼ cup of nuts with chunks of bread and a couple of cloves of minced garlic in olive oil before processing the whole lot with the parsley in a food processor. Stirred into the finished stew, the picada gave the dish a jolt of bright flavor, but I wondered if it would be even better if I left the garlic raw. Sure enough, a subsequent batch with raw garlic imparted a pungency to the stew that tasters loved. And although a food processor proved faster and more convenient than a mortar and pestle, its whizzing blade muddied the grassy flavor of the parsley, so I minced it with a knife before combining it with the ground ingredients.

So far, my stew contained no vegetables, and although I didn't plan on loading it up with carrots, peas, and potatoes like a typical American stew, some additional element seemed appropriate. It only made sense to feature a popular Catalan ingredient: oyster mushrooms. Rather than cook them directly in the stew, which spoiled their delicate flavor and texture, I sautéed them separately. The mushrooms went into the finished stew along with the picada and a shot of sherry vinegar. Here was a beef stew rich and fragrant with the flavors of Catalonia that employed classic Spanish techniques, plus a few of my own.

—BRYAN ROOF, *Cook's Illustrated*

Catalan-Style Beef Stew with Mushrooms

SERVES 4 TO 6

While we developed this recipe with Albariño, a dry Spanish white wine, you can also use a Sauvignon Blanc. Remove the woody base of the oyster mushroom stem before cooking. An equal amount of quartered button mushrooms may be substituted for the oyster mushrooms. Serve the stew with boiled or mashed potatoes or rice.

STEW

2	tablespoons olive oil
2	large onions, chopped fine
½	teaspoon sugar
	Kosher salt and pepper
2	plum tomatoes, halved lengthwise, pulp grated on large holes of box grater, and skins discarded
1	teaspoon smoked paprika
1	bay leaf
1½	cups dry white wine
1½	cups water
1	large sprig fresh thyme
¼	teaspoon ground cinnamon
2½	pounds boneless beef short ribs, trimmed and cut into 2-inch cubes

PICADA

¼	cup whole blanched almonds
2	tablespoons olive oil
1	slice hearty white sandwich bread, crusts removed, torn into 1-inch pieces
2	garlic cloves, peeled
3	tablespoons minced fresh parsley
½	pound oyster mushrooms, trimmed
1	teaspoon sherry vinegar

1. FOR THE STEW: Adjust oven rack to middle position and heat oven to 300 degrees. Heat oil in Dutch oven over medium-low heat until shimmering. Add onions, sugar, and ½ teaspoon salt; cook, stirring often, until onions are deeply caramelized, 30 to 40 minutes. Add tomatoes, smoked paprika, and bay leaf; cook, stirring often, until darkened and thick, 5 to 10 minutes.

2. Add wine, water, thyme, and cinnamon to pot, scraping up any browned bits. Season beef with 1½ teaspoons salt and ½ teaspoon pepper and add to pot. Increase heat to high and bring to simmer. Transfer to

oven and cook, uncovered. After 1 hour stir stew to redistribute meat, return to oven, and continue to cook, uncovered, until meat is tender, 1½ to 2 hours longer.

3. FOR THE PICADA: While stew is in oven, heat almonds and 1 tablespoon oil in 10-inch skillet over medium heat; cook, stirring often, until almonds are golden brown, 3 to 6 minutes. Using slotted spoon, transfer almonds to food processor. Return now-empty skillet to medium heat, add bread, and cook, stirring often, until toasted, 2 to 4 minutes; transfer to food processor with almonds. Add garlic and process until mixture is finely ground, about 20 seconds, scraping bowl as needed. Transfer mixture to bowl, stir in parsley, and set aside.

4. Return now-empty skillet to medium heat. Heat remaining 1 tablespoon oil until shimmering. Add mushrooms and ½ teaspoon salt; cook, stirring often, until tender, 5 to 7 minutes. Transfer to bowl and set aside.

5. Remove bay leaf. Stir picada, mushrooms, and vinegar into stew. Season with salt and pepper to taste and serve.

GREEN BAY BOOYAH

BOOYAH JUST MAY BE THE RICHEST, HEARTIEST chicken and beef soup you've never heard of—unless you happen to be from Green Bay, Wisconsin, that is. Little known even in the rest of the state, booyah is both a soup and an event in Green Bay, made in huge batches in outdoor kettles for fairs, fundraisers, and family gatherings. One cold, slushy morning at the Suamico United Methodist Church, just north of Green Bay, people were lining up for bowls of stick-to-your-ribs booyah at 7:30 a.m., never mind the 10:00 a.m. start time and the discouraging weather. Clearly, the soup is a celebration all by itself.

Later that same day, I attended my second booyah bash, this time sampling the handiwork of Suamico firefighters. When I got home, I tested several recipes I'd found in Wisconsin cookbooks. I was sure that this hearty soup could please crowds far beyond Green Bay, but first I'd have to bring it indoors, cutting back the 60-gallon batches to fit into a Dutch oven on a home stove. I'd also need to come up with a full-flavored

GREEN BAY BOOYAH

broth without the endless simmering called for by the booyah faithful. And I wanted to limit the ever-present fat (although Green Bay fans actually measure the success of booyah by the grease—a defense against bitter Wisconsin winters?). I'd also need to cook the vegetables to tenderness instead of mush and keep the chicken from overcooking.

Most recipes for booyah follow the same outline: Simmer whole chicken(s) in water to make broth. Turn that broth into the soup base, simmering beef and shredded cabbage in it until they practically disintegrate. At some point, add the other vegetables. Finally, discard the skin and bones from the chicken, dice the meat, and return it to the pot.

With an eye toward building a flavorful broth more quickly, I replaced the water with store-bought chicken broth. But I'd still need chicken meat for the booyah. Instead of waiting for a whole chicken to cook, I'd use parts. And to avoid stringy, overcooked white meat, I'd use dark meat thighs, which I knew would stand up better to simmering and contribute better flavor. (They did, on both counts.) As added insurance against overcooking, I learned to pull them out after 30 minutes, stirring in the boned, shredded meat at the end. Taking advantage of my considerably scaled-down batch, I made another break from booyah tradition: I browned the chicken before simmering it. This is standard test kitchen practice for building flavor in braises and stews, but I can see why booyah chefs in Wisconsin don't do it: Browning enough chicken for several hundred people would be highly impractical. Since my booyah would feed just 10, I could take advantage of the extra flavor that the technique supplies.

But while the flavor was good, the broth lacked the full-bodied, silken quality that comes from the gelatin released from bones that simmer for a long time (the thighs simmered for just 30 minutes). I enlisted the beef for help. Usually, booyah contains boneless beef chuck. I tried two bone-in cuts: short ribs and shin slices. Both "beefed up" the broth as I'd hoped. I opted for the short ribs, since they're easier to find. I handled them as I had the chicken, browning them to build flavor before simmering them in the broth. Unfortunately, the short ribs set me back on another score: The soup was greasier than ever. Eventually I forged a three-pronged approach to limit the grease. I trimmed (and discarded) the fat between the raw short-rib meat and bones, adding the two separately to the broth. I discarded the

fatty chicken skin (but only after browning, so I could capture its flavor). And I defatted the broth before adding the vegetables.

Booyah never met a vegetable it didn't like. In addition to the constants (onions, carrots, celery, tomatoes, cabbage, and potatoes), you find beans of every stripe (green, fresh, and dried), peas (frozen and split), corn (usually as a component of frozen mixed vegetables), turnips, and even rutabaga. Since I was making a comparatively small batch, I left the frozen mix in the freezer aisle and replaced it with fresh carrot coins and chunks of mellow rutabaga. I kept the frozen peas, as finding fresh ones is difficult in the fall and winter. Mushy vegetables may be unavoidable in 60-gallon batches, but all I had to do to prevent this in my scaled-down soup was add the vegetables in stages; the quickest-cooking went in at the end. I made an exception for the cabbage, which I added early so it would be very soft by serving time, just as I'd seen (and tasted) in Suamico. A final hit of lemon juice brightened the soup.

I sat down with a bowlful to assess. Warming, filling, and flavorful, this booyah could hold its own anywhere in the country, Green Bay included.

—ADAM RIED, *Cook's Country*

Green Bay Booyah

SERVES 8 TO 10

The bone side of a short rib is especially fatty and requires the most trimming.

2½ pounds beef short ribs (3 to 4 English-style ribs)
2½ pounds bone-in chicken thighs, trimmed
    Salt and pepper
1 tablespoon vegetable oil
2 onions, chopped fine
2 celery ribs, minced
8 cups low-sodium chicken broth
2 bay leaves
4 cups shredded green cabbage
1 (28-ounce) can diced tomatoes
½ pound rutabaga, peeled and cut into ½-inch pieces
1 pound russet potatoes, peeled and cut into ½-inch pieces
3 carrots, peeled and sliced ¼ inch thick
1 cup frozen peas
1 tablespoon lemon juice

1. Remove bones from short ribs; reserve. Trim fat from meat and bones. Pat beef and chicken dry with paper towels and season with salt and pepper. Heat oil in Dutch oven over medium-high heat until just smoking. Brown beef on all sides, about 10 minutes; transfer to plate. Cook chicken until browned all over, about 10 minutes; transfer to plate. When chicken is cool enough to handle, remove and discard skin.

2. Pour off all but 1½ teaspoons fat from pot. Add onions and celery and cook over medium heat until softened, about 5 minutes. Stir in broth and bay leaves, scraping up any browned bits. Add beef, beef bones, and chicken and bring to boil.

3. Reduce heat to low and simmer, covered, until chicken registers 175 degrees, about 30 minutes. Transfer chicken to bowl. When chicken is cool enough to handle, shred into bite-size pieces, discarding bones. Cover chicken and refrigerate. Continue to simmer stew until beef is tender, about 1¼ hours longer. Transfer beef to plate. When cool enough to handle, shred into bite-size pieces, discarding fat. Remove beef bones and bay leaves. Strain broth through fine-mesh strainer; discard solids. Allow liquid to settle, about 5 minutes, then skim off fat.

4. Add shredded beef, cabbage, tomatoes, rutabaga, 1¼ teaspoons salt, and 1 teaspoon pepper and bring to boil. Reduce heat to medium-low and simmer until rutabaga is translucent around edges, about 15 minutes. Stir in potatoes and carrots and cook until all vegetables are tender, about 20 minutes. Add chicken and peas and simmer until heated through, 2 to 3 minutes. Off heat, stir in lemon juice. Season with salt and pepper to taste. Serve.

NOTES FROM THE TEST KITCHEN

ADD BEEF BONES, NOT BEEF FAT
Normally, booyah features boneless beef chuck. We substituted bone-in short ribs so that we could take advantage of the gelatin that melts out of the bones to make a silken broth. To prevent the fatty short ribs from making the soup greasy, we separated meat from bone and trimmed the fat, adding both the flavorful bones and the meat to the broth to simmer and tossing out the fat.

SAVE THE BONES
Short-rib bones add body and richness.

EASY NEW ENGLAND CLAM CHOWDER

CLAM CHOWDER FROM SCRATCH IS FANTASTIC, BUT it's sure not quick: To serve six, you have to soak, scrub, steam, shuck, and mince some 7 pounds of clams, then collect and strain the seafood broth—all this before you so much as chop a single potato or onion. Also, if you don't hover over the (expensive) simmering clams, chances are good they'll turn to rubber. I wanted to develop a recipe that only tasted like I'd spent hours in the kitchen.

I collected and prepared a smattering of New England clam chowder recipes that claimed to accelerate the usual process. As a group, they sacrificed straight-from-the-sea flavor for speed and ease. Some were bland and milky. Others were very thin. A few called for canned clams—my tasters firmly vetoed those. Also, none nailed the delicate balance of cream, clam, and pork that defines good chowder. I cherry-picked features from among the test group to put together a basic working recipe: Sauté pork product for its fat; sauté onions in said fat; add milk, potato chunks, and seasonings; simmer until the potatoes are tender; then stir in clams.

New England clam chowders typically start with either salt pork or bacon. Each has its merits, so I let the clock determine the winner. I found I could chop, sauté, and extract flavor from diced bacon twice as fast as with salt pork (plus it gave me crispy bacon to sprinkle on at the end). Bacon it would be. Since I'd nixed fresh clams (too much work) and canned clams (nothing like the real deal), I went to the supermarket, returned with a tub of fresh chopped clams, and cooked a batch of soup. Fresh, preshucked and chopped clams, stirred in at the end to cook quickly, proved an excellent compromise between haste and taste.

But even with 2 pounds of clams, the soup tasted wan. It needed some supporting players. In a series of tests, I tried liquid bases of many sorts, alone and in combination: Milk, which I'd been using (milk or water is traditional in older recipes), made for pallid chowder, and an all-cream version was over-the-top rich. Plus, neither registered the sea. Some quicker chowder recipes call for bottled clam juice, so I pulled a bottle out of the pantry. In the end, a combination of bottled clam juice, heavy cream, and plain water

EASY CLAM CHOWDER

actually fooled a couple of tasters into thinking I'd gone to the trouble of making homemade clam stock. For seasonings, I stayed simple and classic, using fresh minced thyme and a single bay leaf.

My quicker chowder still had one serious drawback—it was as thin as skim milk. I tried thickening it with flour, as in many recipes, stirring it in with the sautéing onions. But the amount I needed to get the full-bodied texture I sought turned the chowder pasty. In search of ideas, I returned to the recipes I'd gathered, including some from the 19th century. These early recipes used crackers and potatoes as thickeners. The modern practice of floating a few crackers in chowder stems from these early thickeners. Curious, I made a new batch, this time adding roughly a sleeve of crushed saltines with the simmering potatoes. In 20 minutes, they disappeared into the soup, leaving behind body and a subtle, salty depth. It was a revelation. When the potatoes were tender, I fished out a few chunks and crushed them into the chowder for even more body.

Not even 40 minutes after I'd planted my cutting board in the kitchen, I ladled out a thick, fragrant bowl of chowder. Happily, I had managed to shortcut the work of clam chowder without shortchanging the flavor.

—DIANE UNGER, *Cook's Country*

Easy Clam Chowder

SERVES 6

If you buy frozen clams, thaw them before using.

- 4 slices bacon, chopped fine
- 1 onion, chopped fine
- 3 (8-ounce) bottles clam juice
- 2 cups water
- 1½ pounds russet potatoes, peeled and cut into ½-inch pieces
- 20 saltines, crushed
- 1 teaspoon minced fresh thyme
- 1 bay leaf
- 2 pounds chopped clams, rinsed, drained, and chopped fine
- 1 cup heavy cream
  Salt and pepper

1. Cook bacon in large saucepan over medium heat until crisp, 6 to 8 minutes. Using slotted spoon, transfer bacon to paper towel–lined plate. Pour off all but 1 tablespoon fat from saucepan. Add onion and cook over medium heat until softened, about 5 minutes. Stir in clam juice, water, potatoes, saltines, thyme, and bay leaf and bring to boil. Reduce heat to medium and simmer, stirring occasionally, until potatoes are tender, about 20 minutes.

2. Using slotted spoon, transfer ½ cup potatoes to bowl and mash with potato masher until smooth. Return mashed potatoes to pot. Reduce heat to low. Stir clams into pot and simmer until cooked through, 3 to 5 minutes. Off heat, stir in cream. Remove bay leaf. Season with salt and pepper to taste and sprinkle with bacon. Serve.

SHRIMP BISQUE

SHRIMP BISQUE IS ONE OF THOSE GREAT "FANCY" French soups. When done correctly, it's something to behold—luxuriously rich and creamy, mildly sweet and shrimpy, with a hint of sherry and a handsome pastel hue. But fancy often equals finicky and tedious. The recipes I tested were just that, ranging from antiquated and involved (making a shrimp stock in one pot, whisking a roux in another, sautéing aromatics in a third, and then straining the soup through a French chinois) to the downright strange (creating a compound butter from the boiled shells). And then there were those where the bisque was set on fire—literally. I wanted bisque that didn't chain me to the stove yet still delivered impressive shrimp flavor. I wanted "fancy" without the fuss.

From the initial recipes I tested, I could see two things right away: One, like most crustaceans, shrimp carry a lot of their flavor in their shells, and the trick is extracting it. Two, in an effort to extract that flavor, some recipes wasted as much as 1½ pounds of whole raw shrimp; whole, ground, or sautéed shrimp were used to make stock, then the spent crustaceans were discarded. I wanted the shrimp in my bisque, not in the trash.

Seeking to make easy, flavorful stock with no waste, I turned to bottled clam juice, a briny test kitchen staple for seafood soups. But far from highlighting the shrimp flavor, the clam juice screamed "Clam!" and overwhelmed the delicate shrimp. Next, I tried chicken stock, another go-to soup backbone in the test kitchen. Again, tasters vetoed it, gently reminding me that shrimp bisque should taste like, you know, shrimp.

I reconsidered making my own stock—but I'd use just the shells, and the process would have to be less complicated. I peeled the shrimp and separated the shells and meat. From there, I followed a streamlined seafood bisque method: I sautéed onions, carrots, and celery in butter and added flour (to thicken), white wine (for acidity), and tomato paste (a standard shrimp bisque ingredient for color and flavor). I poured in plain water and stirred in the reserved shrimp shells. I let everything simmer for about 30 minutes, and then I strained the pot and pitched the spent shells and vegetables. Finally, I returned my simple, homemade stock to the stove, added plenty of cream, and, in the last few minutes, stirred in the chopped shrimp meat.

This approach produced an acceptable bisque but not a great one. Simply boiling the shrimp shells had resulted in meek shrimp flavor. What could I do to amplify it? I knew that sautéing and browning any ingredient helps develop its flavor, and I remembered that in some of my initial test recipes this had been done with the shells. So I sautéed the shrimp shells in butter until they were golden brown, about five minutes, then added the vegetables and continued as before. Now my bisque had pronounced (and delicious) shrimp flavor.

Unfortunately, the shrimp themselves were like rubbery marbles, even though I was cooking them in the simmering broth for just three minutes. I tried adding the shrimp after I turned off the heat, covering the pot, and letting the bisque stand for five minutes. The gentle residual heat cooked the shrimp perfectly. Finished with the classic splash of sherry, my bisque looked and tasted as fancy and as fussy as the recipes I'd started with—but looks are deceiving.

—NICK IVERSON, *Cook's Country*

Shrimp Bisque
SERVES 6 TO 8

Be sure to buy shell-on shrimp for this recipe.

- 4 tablespoons unsalted butter
- 2 pounds medium-large (31 to 40 per pound) shrimp, peeled and shells reserved, shrimp deveined (see page 9) and chopped
- 2 onions, chopped
- 2 carrots, peeled and chopped
- 2 celery ribs, chopped
- ½ cup all-purpose flour
- 6 tablespoons tomato paste
- 2 garlic cloves, minced
- 2 cups dry white wine
- 6 cups water
- 2 sprigs fresh thyme
- 2 cups heavy cream
- 1 tablespoon dry sherry
  Salt and pepper

1. Melt butter in Dutch oven over medium heat. Cook shrimp shells until spotty brown, about 5 minutes. Add onions, carrots, and celery and cook until browned, 6 to 8 minutes. Stir in flour and cook, stirring constantly, until golden, about 2 minutes. Add tomato paste and garlic and cook until fragrant and paste begins to darken, about 2 minutes. Stir in wine and simmer, scraping up any browned bits, until thickened, 2 to 3 minutes. Add water and thyme and bring to boil. Reduce heat to medium-low and simmer until slightly thickened, about 30 minutes.

2. Strain broth through fine-mesh strainer; discard solids. Stir in cream and sherry and bring to simmer. Off heat, add chopped shrimp, cover pot and let sit until shrimp are cooked through, about 5 minutes. Season with salt and pepper to taste and serve.

NOTES FROM THE TEST KITCHEN

SHELL-ON SHRIMP
For a bisque with real shrimp flavor in record time, you need to use the shells, not just the meat. After peeling shrimp, sauté shells with vegetables and then simmer with water and wine to make a fast, flavorful shrimp stock.

CHAPTER 3

VEGETABLES & SIDE DISHES

Roasted Brussels Sprouts   52

   Roasted Brussels Sprouts with Garlic, Red Pepper Flakes, and Parmesan

   Roasted Brussels Sprouts with Bacon and Pecans

   Roasted Brussels Sprouts with Walnuts and Lemon

Parmesan-Crusted Asparagus   53

Fried Green Tomatoes   54

Shoestring Onions   57

Crispy Potato Tots   59

   Crispy Potato Tots for a Crowd

   Bacon-Ranch Potato Tots

   Parmesan-Rosemary Potato Tots

   Southwestern Potato Tots

Crisp Roasted Fingerling Potatoes   61

Salt-Baked Potatoes with Roasted Garlic and Rosemary Butter   62

Potato Casserole with Bacon and Caramelized Onion   64

Back-to-Basics Bread Stuffing   66

Cranberry Chutney with Apples and Crystallized Ginger   67

   Spicy Cranberry Chutney

   Cranberry Chutney with Fennel and Golden Raisins

   Cranberry-Orange Chutney

   Cranberry Chutney with Pear, Lemon, and Rosemary

ROASTED BRUSSELS SPROUTS

BRUSSELS SPROUTS ARE IN DIRE NEED OF A NEW publicist. The first order of business: to get the word out that this vegetable doesn't have to taste overly bitter or sulfurous. Like other members of the crucifer family (which also includes broccoli, cabbage, and mustard greens), Brussels sprouts are rich in flavor precursors that react with the vegetable's enzymes to produce pungent new compounds when the sprouts are cut, cooked, and even eaten. But when the sprouts are handled just right, this pungency takes on a nutty sweetness.

The problem is, achieving perfect results is usually a two-part process. To ensure that the interiors of this dense vegetable get sufficiently tender, the sprouts are first blanched or steamed, followed by roasting or pan-searing. The latter process lightly crisps the outer leaves and creates the nice browning that mellows the sprouts' bitter kick. But when Brussels sprouts are part of a holiday feast, this two-step approach is a little too fussy. Could I get the results I wanted using just one step?

I decided to skip the pan-searing, since one batch in a 12-inch skillet barely makes enough for four people, and I wanted my sprouts to feed a crowd. Roasting seemed like the best technique to play with.

I rounded up a little over 2 pounds of sprouts—enough for six to eight people—looking for same-size specimens about 1½ inches long. With parcooking ruled out, the obvious first step was to halve the sprouts, which would help ensure that they cooked through and would create a flat surface for browning. I then tossed them in a bowl with a bit of olive oil, salt, and pepper.

To maximize browning and to jump-start cooking, we often preheat the baking sheet before roasting vegetables. I did precisely this, placing the sprouts cut side down on the hot sheet, which I then put back in a 500-degree oven. But when I pulled the vegetables out 20 minutes later, they were dry, chewy, and even burnt in spots on the outside, while practically crunchy on the inside. Starting with a cool baking sheet didn't help matters, and turning down the heat merely meant that it took a little longer for the sprouts to reach the same unsatisfactory state.

To prevent the outer leaves from drying out too much before the center achieved the ideal tender-firm texture, it seemed clear that I needed to introduce moisture into the equation. I wondered if just covering the sprouts with aluminum foil as they roasted would trap enough steam to do the trick. Once again, I arranged the sprouts cut side down on the baking sheet, but this time I covered the pan tightly with foil before placing it in the oven. After 10 minutes, I removed the foil so that the slightly softened sprouts could brown and get just a little crisp. After 10 minutes more, the Brussels sprouts were perfectly browned on the outside. And undercooked on the inside. And a bit dry and chewy all around.

I reluctantly considered lowering the oven temperature—but that would almost certainly increase the cooking time, and I wanted a side dish that would be done when my turkey finished resting. The solution was as simple as tossing the sprouts with a tablespoon of water along with the oil and seasonings before I put them in the oven. Covered in foil, each halved sprout acted like its own little steam chamber, holding on to a tiny bit of water to finish cooking its interior even as its outside began to brown. The results were perfect: tender, sweet insides and caramelized exteriors.

Now that I'd made perfectly cooked Brussels sprouts in one easy step, I devised some quick variations. They could show off their image makeover not just during the holidays, but all year long.

—ANDREA GEARY, *Cook's Illustrated*

Roasted Brussels Sprouts
SERVES 6 TO 8

If you are buying loose Brussels sprouts, select those that are about 1½ inches long. Quarter Brussels sprouts longer than 2½ inches; don't cut sprouts shorter than 1 inch.

- 2¼ **pounds Brussels sprouts, trimmed and halved**
- 3 **tablespoons olive oil**
- 1 **tablespoon water**
- **Salt and pepper**

1. Adjust oven rack to upper-middle position and heat oven to 500 degrees. Toss Brussels sprouts, oil, water, ¾ teaspoon salt, and ¼ teaspoon pepper together in large bowl until sprouts are coated. Transfer sprouts to rimmed baking sheet and arrange cut sides down.

2. Cover sheet tightly with aluminum foil and roast for 10 minutes. Remove foil and continue to cook until

Brussels sprouts are well browned and tender, 10 to 12 minutes longer. Transfer to serving platter, season with salt and pepper to taste, and serve.

VARIATIONS

Roasted Brussels Sprouts with Garlic, Red Pepper Flakes, and Parmesan

While Brussels sprouts roast, heat 3 tablespoons olive oil in 8-inch skillet over medium heat until shimmering. Add 2 minced garlic cloves and ½ teaspoon red pepper flakes; cook until garlic is golden and fragrant, about 1 minute. Remove from heat. Toss roasted Brussels sprouts with garlic oil and season with salt and pepper to taste. Transfer to platter and sprinkle with ¼ cup grated Parmesan cheese before serving.

Roasted Brussels Sprouts with Bacon and Pecans

While Brussels sprouts roast, cook 4 slices bacon in 10-inch skillet over medium heat until crisp, 7 to 10 minutes. Using slotted spoon, transfer bacon to paper towel–lined plate and reserve 1 tablespoon bacon fat. Finely chop bacon. Toss roasted Brussels sprouts with 2 tablespoons olive oil, reserved bacon fat, chopped bacon, and ½ cup finely chopped toasted pecans. Season with salt and pepper to taste; transfer to platter and serve.

Roasted Brussels Sprouts with Walnuts and Lemon

Toss roasted Brussels sprouts with 3 tablespoons melted unsalted butter, 1 tablespoon lemon juice, and ⅓ cup finely chopped toasted walnuts. Season with salt and pepper to taste; transfer to platter and serve.

PARMESAN-CRUSTED ASPARAGUS

THE SWEET, INTENSELY CONCENTRATED FLAVOR OF simple roasted asparagus is irresistible, but I also love the richness of asparagus gratin with bread crumbs and Parmesan. I wanted a recipe that married the two for delicious roasted asparagus with a crispy, cheesy coating.

I thought it would be a simple matter of tossing raw spears with olive oil, seasonings, cheese, and bread crumbs. But when I tried this, I found that as the asparagus roasted, it released moisture. That's no problem when the spears roast on their own—the moisture

simply evaporates. But now that I'd coated them with crumbs and cheese, the moisture turned the topping soggy, and it fell off the spears in large, soggy clumps.

Clearly I had to get rid of some of the asparagus's moisture before adding the crumb topping. For my next test, I tried roasting the stalks in a 450-degree oven until the moisture evaporated, about 10 minutes, and then topping them with the bread-crumb mixture. I gave everything a few more minutes to crisp in the oven. The finished asparagus spears were dehydrated and leathery, and the coating didn't adhere. I tried parcooking the asparagus in the microwave, but it was limp by the time the moisture was gone.

What about salt? We often salt vegetables like tomatoes, eggplant, and cucumbers to draw out their moisture. I sprinkled ½ teaspoon of salt over the raw asparagus and let it sit on paper towels to drain. Thirty minutes later, the towels were sodden with exuded liquid. I tossed the asparagus with oil, sprinkled on the bread-crumb topping, and then let it roast for 20 minutes. This asparagus was markedly better. It improved further when I poked the spears with a fork before salting to facilitate the release of moisture.

But the topping still refused to stick. So I decided that, rather than tossing the crumbs on the spears, I'd "glue" them on. I moistened each spear in lightly beaten egg and pressed them in the bread-crumb mixture before roasting. This coating was too heavy for the delicate vegetable. To lighten it, I switched to using only the egg whites. To ensure that the cheese and bread crumbs would stay put, I mixed the whites with the stickiest (edible) thing I could think of: honey. Tasters liked its subtle sweetness, and I liked its adhesive properties.

For the coating, I pitted ordinary bread crumbs against extra-crunchy panko crumbs. We preferred the latter. With a few more tests, I determined that ¾ cup of crumbs to 1½ cups of Parmesan was the best ratio. I also found that if I set aside ½ cup of the cheese to sprinkle over the coated asparagus partway through roasting, I got the crispiest coating and the best cheese flavor. Yet tasters continued to ask for more crunch. I had one more idea—if I whipped the egg whites to soft peaks before coating the asparagus, the peaks and valleys would grip as much crunchy coating as possible. Each spear was now a perfect balance of crunchy, cheesy, salty, and roasted asparagus sweetness.

—NICK IVERSON, *Cook's Country*

Parmesan-Crusted Asparagus

SERVES 4 TO 6

This recipe works best with ½-inch-thick spears. Work quickly when tossing the asparagus with the egg whites, as the salt will rapidly begin to deflate the whites.

- 2 pounds thick asparagus, trimmed
  Salt and pepper
- 3 ounces Parmesan cheese, grated (1½ cups)
- ¾ cup panko bread crumbs
- 1 tablespoon unsalted butter, melted and cooled
  Pinch cayenne pepper
- 2 large egg whites
- 1 teaspoon honey

1. Adjust oven rack to middle position and heat oven to 450 degrees. Line rimmed baking sheet with aluminum foil and spray with vegetable oil spray. Using fork, poke holes up and down stalks of asparagus. Toss asparagus with ½ teaspoon salt and let stand for 30 minutes on paper towel–lined baking sheet.

2. Meanwhile, combine 1 cup Parmesan, panko, melted butter, ¼ teaspoon salt, ⅛ teaspoon pepper, and cayenne in bowl. Transfer half of bread-crumb mixture to shallow dish and reserve remaining mixture. Using stand mixer fitted with whisk, whip egg whites with honey on medium-low speed until foamy, about 1 minute. Increase speed to medium-high and whip until soft peaks form, 2 to 3 minutes. Scrape into 13 by 9-inch baking dish and toss asparagus with egg-white mixture. Working with 1 spear at a time, dredge half of asparagus in bread-crumb mixture and transfer to baking sheet. Refill shallow dish with reserved bread-crumb mixture and repeat with remaining half of asparagus.

3. Bake asparagus until just beginning to brown, 6 to 8 minutes. Sprinkle with remaining ½ cup Parmesan and continue to bake until cheese is melted and bread crumbs are golden brown, 6 to 8 minutes longer. Transfer to platter. Serve.

NOTES FROM THE TEST KITCHEN

MAKING THE COATING STICK

1. Perforate and salt asparagus to draw out excess moisture that could saturate crumbs.

2. Whip egg whites to help crumbs adhere. Add honey for flavor and extra sticking power.

3. Work with one spear at a time to keep bread crumbs from clumping.

FRIED GREEN TOMATOES

FRIED GREEN TOMATOES ARE JUST THAT—SLICES OF tart, unripe tomato coated in mellow, savory cornmeal (or flour, or both) and shallow-fried until crisp. But this prosaic description doesn't do them justice. If you've eaten them, you probably understand why novelists, movie directors, and many an ordinary Southerner wax lyrical (or at least nostalgic) about this homespun dish. Delicious as they are, though, fried green tomatoes still languish in relative obscurity north of the Mason-Dixon Line. I hoped to bring them into the (Northern) sun.

Unfortunately, the first crop of recipes I tested—despite their bona fide Southern-cookbook roots—was disappointing. One called for dipping slices of tomato in a mixture of flour and cornmeal; with no wet ingredients to cement the coating, it was soggy, thin, and patchy. Other recipes more sensibly required dipping the slices in milk or buttermilk mixed with egg before dredging, a method that yielded more substantial coatings, yes, but they were soggy or slid off—or both. These initial tests also revealed that green tomatoes dredged in flour alone were lackluster while those dredged in cornmeal alone were delicious but gritty. It became clear that a combination of the two would work best.

FRIED GREEN TOMATOES

But before turning to the coating, I took a hard look at the frying medium, pitting bacon fat, which some Southern cooks swear by, against peanut oil, the test kitchen's usual choice for frying. Some tasters complained that the porky, smoky bacon fat overwhelmed the green tomatoes. Since using peanut oil meant I could skip the step of cooking bacon, I stuck with it and turned to finding the right cornmeal-to-flour ratio.

Tasters liked the flavor of 2 parts cornmeal to 1 part flour; with any less cornmeal, the flavor lacked backbone. Unfortunately, even with finely ground cornmeal, this ratio made the coating gritty. No problem—I dumped the cornmeal into the blender and hit start. Eventually, I found that by grinding just half of the cornmeal, I achieved the right balance of full cornmeal flavor and subtle grit.

But my perfected coating continued to slip off the tomato slices somewhere between frying pan and mouth. To determine the function of each adhesion ingredient (buttermilk, milk, egg), I tested each separately, dipping and then dredging. The egg dip gave me a coating that stuck like white on rice. Too bad it was rubbery and tasted like overcooked eggs. The milk dip yielded a soggy coating that slipped off. The buttermilk didn't improve adhesion but made for a coating so crunchy tasters gobbled up the sloughed-off bits. (Our science editor explained that the acid in the buttermilk speeds the gelatinization—or absorption of moisture—of the starchy coating, making it especially brittle and crunchy when fried.) To get the coating to stick, I embarked on another series of ratio tests, eventually learning that one egg beaten with ⅔ cup of buttermilk produced a crunchy, not eggy, coating that stayed put. Almost.

Part of what makes fried green tomatoes a beloved Southern staple is the contrast between tart tomato and crunchy coating in every bite. "Almost" wouldn't cut it. The problem was that the green tomatoes released moisture while they fried. Despite my best efforts to make the coating stick, the moisture accumulated beneath the coating and loosened its grip. Just dry off the tomatoes, a practical colleague suggested. Good thinking. I pressed the slices between paper towels, dipped them in the egg-buttermilk mixture, and then dredged and fried them.

This time, the crunchy, sweet-tart tomatoes were so good, I actually found myself looking forward to the first frost with its bonanza of green tomatoes.

—SARAH GABRIEL, *Cook's Country*

Fried Green Tomatoes

SERVES 4

You'll need 4 to 5 green tomatoes. We recommend finely ground Quaker cornmeal for this recipe.

- 1½ **pounds green tomatoes, cored and sliced ¼ inch thick**
- ⅔ **cup cornmeal**
- ⅓ **cup all-purpose flour**
- 1½ **teaspoons salt**
- ½ **teaspoon pepper**
- ⅛ **teaspoon cayenne pepper**
- ⅔ **cup buttermilk**
- 1 **large egg**
- 2 **cups peanut or vegetable oil**

1. Place tomatoes on paper towel–lined rimmed baking sheet. Cover with more paper towels, let sit for 20 minutes, and pat dry. Meanwhile, process ⅓ cup cornmeal in blender until very finely ground, about 1 minute. Combine processed cornmeal, remaining ⅓ cup cornmeal, flour, salt, pepper, and cayenne in shallow dish. Whisk buttermilk and egg together in second shallow dish.

2. Working with 1 at a time, dip tomato slices in buttermilk mixture, then dredge in cornmeal mixture, pressing firmly to adhere; transfer to clean baking sheet.

3. Set wire rack in rimmed baking sheet. Heat oil in 12-inch skillet over medium-high heat to 350 degrees. Fry 4 tomato slices until golden brown on both sides, 4 to 6 minutes. Drain on prepared wire rack. Bring oil back to 350 degrees and repeat with remaining tomato slices. Serve.

NOTES FROM THE TEST KITCHEN

DRY BEFORE YOU FRY

To keep tomatoes from weeping as they fry (which will loosen coating), let them sit between paper towels for 20 minutes and then press dry.

SHOESTRING ONION RINGS

LET'S BE HONEST: THICK BEER-BATTERED RINGS are more about the puffy, crunchy coating than about the onions themselves. Shoestring onions, on the other hand, have a thinner, crisp coating that highlights the onions. At their best, shoestrings arrive at the table a salty, crunchy tangle of feathery fried onions that are hard to stop eating. At their worst, they're a greasy, soggy pile of breading.

My initial task was to determine which type of onion had the sweet yet robust flavor that would work best. I started with a simple recipe that called for tossing thinly sliced onions in flour seasoned with salt and pepper. I sliced red, white, yellow, and sweet onions, tossed each with the flour, fried them separately in peanut oil, and called over my tasters. Red onions browned faster than the flour coating did, while sweet onions were (duh) too sweet and didn't have much oniony oomph. White onions were a little flat and lacked sweet-savory balance, but yellow onions were identifiably "onion" without being offensively pungent. Now I had the best onion, but the seasoned flour coating was limp and greasy.

In search of something that would give these onions more crunch, I dug through dozens of recipes for fried foods. Baking soda and cornstarch were the most common dredge additives, so I gave them a try. Cornstarch did improve the crunch, but it made the coating a bit pasty. Baking soda sped up the browning too much, making for burnt coating and underdone onions. Shifting gears, I decided to look at wet ingredients. Some recipes call for soaking the sliced onions in milk or buttermilk for about 30 minutes before dredging in flour. I soaked one batch in milk and another in buttermilk and then dredged and fried them alongside a batch that hadn't been soaked. Only the buttermilk-soaked onions were really crisp, but they held on to so much flour that the onion flavor was diminished. Before I could solve this problem, I first had to figure out why the buttermilk improved crunch.

Buttermilk is made by adding live cultures (friendly bacteria of the sort used to produce yogurt or cheese) to milk; the cultures produce lactic acid, which gives buttermilk its signature tang. Our science editor explained that the acid in the buttermilk was helping the coating fry up crisper by speeding up the gelatinization of the starch and drawing more amylose out of the starch granules in the flour. I wondered if another acidic liquid would yield the same crunch yet release more of the flour. Soaking the onions in white vinegar did just that.

Unfortunately, while the vinegar made for a super-crunchy coating, the shoestring onions were now way too sour. Cider vinegar, while still too tart, improved matters, so I tried diluting it with water. That worked pretty well, but what worked even better was using apple juice. The juice contributed more acid (hence more crunch), plus it added sweetness to balance the vinegar. As a bonus, I discovered that the onions didn't need to soak for 30 minutes—a quick dip did the trick.

Having unlocked the secret to maximum crunch (acid), I wondered if I could take it one step further. The wet ingredients were working hard to create crunch, but what about the flour? Was there a dry acidic ingredient that I could add to the flour to promote even more crispness? Searching the test kitchen pantry, I came across cream of tartar, which is often used as an acidic activator in baked goods leavened with baking soda (the soda requires an acid to release its lift-giving bubbles). A few tests of cream of tartar in varying amounts determined that ¾ teaspoon added a crunchy boost without leaving a flavor trail.

You don't have to understand the science of why apple cider vinegar, apple juice, and cream of tartar make for the crispest, tastiest fried onions ever. All you have to do is try to stop eating them.

—SARAH GABRIEL, *Cook's Country*

Shoestring Onions

SERVES 4

You will need at least a 6-quart Dutch oven for this recipe. We prefer yellow onions here, but white onions will also work. Do not use red or sweet onions.

- 2 **quarts peanut or vegetable oil**
- 1½ **cups all-purpose flour**
  Salt and pepper
- ¾ **teaspoon cream of tartar**
- 1 **pound onions, sliced into ¼-inch-thick rings**
- ½ **cup apple juice**
- ¼ **cup cider vinegar**

1. Adjust oven rack to middle position and heat oven to 200 degrees. Heat oil in large Dutch oven over medium-high heat to 350 degrees. Set wire rack in rimmed baking sheet.

CRISPY POTATO TOTS

2. While the oil heats, combine flour, 1 teaspoon salt, cream of tartar, and ½ teaspoon pepper in large bowl. Toss onions with apple juice and vinegar to coat in another bowl. Drain onions and transfer to flour mixture, tossing to coat.

3. Fry half of onion rings, stirring occasionally and adjusting burner as necessary to maintain oil temperature between 325 and 350 degrees, until golden brown and crisp, 3 to 4 minutes. Drain onions on prepared wire rack and place in oven. Bring oil back to 350 degrees and repeat with remaining onions. Season with salt and pepper to taste and serve.

CRISPY POTATO TOTS

HAVING EATEN MY WEIGHT IN TATER TOTS® AS A child during the elder Bush's administration, I felt particularly qualified to develop a recipe for a homemade version. When my colleagues saw me researching recipes, many asked, "What's wrong with the frozen ones?" Good question. I prepared a big batch for the tasting table and was surprised to hear complaints about the powdery coating and raw-tasting, fishy-smelling interiors. Had tots always been this terrible? Even with a bad taste in my mouth, my childhood memory of super-crunchy, well-seasoned, fluffy potato pillows was unshaken. I wanted a recipe that lived up to those memories.

Bloodied but not unbowed after the store-bought frozen-tot tasting debacle, I gathered five promising recipes for homemade tots. (Yes, they're out there.) The standard method calls for chopping potatoes either by hand or in a food processor and then combining them (either raw or partly cooked) with egg, flour, salt, and pepper before shaping and deep-frying. I quickly learned two things: First, raw potatoes produced tots with decidedly undercooked interiors, so I'd need to start with partially cooked spuds. Second, the amount of flour that these recipes required (about ¼ cup per pound of potatoes) produced hard, rubbery tots, so I'd use less.

I started with five potatoes, peeled and roughly chopped. I pulsed them in the food processor, scraped them into a bowl, and microwaved them. After eight minutes, they were slightly cooked but still firm enough to hold their shape. Unfortunately, the spud pieces were brown in spots. Stirring a little salt into the raw potatoes corrected the color (frozen tots use a sodium-based preservative for the same reason). Now that I had bright white, partially cooked potatoes, I stirred in a beaten egg and just 1½ tablespoons of flour.

The good: The tots were unbelievably crunchy on the outside ("almost viciously crunchy," said one pleased taster). Our science editor explained that when I microwaved the potatoes, their starch granules expanded and absorbed water. When I fried the tots, the water evaporated and left behind the dry, brittle skeleton of the swollen starch molecules—the crunch. The bad: The mixture was very wet and hard to work with. I had to scoop it into the hot oil, tot by tot. And these tots fried up dense and gluey inside.

To reduce the glueyness, I'd have to reduce the amount of starch—but I had already taken most of the flour out. One recipe from the first round called for processing the potatoes with water, and I'd noticed that when I drained the spuds, the water was thick with potato starch. For my next test, I processed the potatoes with a cup of water (salted to prevent browning), drained them and discarded the starchy water, then microwaved them and stirred in the flour and beaten egg as before. With some of the potato starch removed, these tots were fluffy, not gluey. However, they were still wet inside. That proved an easy fix: I simply ousted the egg.

Now, for the shaping. As most of the recipes I'd found instructed, I had been scooping each tot individually into the hot oil. But without the egg, the mixture was drier and difficult to scoop. Was this a positive development? One recipe from my initial tests called for rolling the potato mixture into logs in plastic wrap, freezing the logs, then slicing them into individual tots. The rolling was messy, but slicing the chilled mixture was definitely easier than scooping each tot. I tried pressing my potato mixture into a foil-lined 8 by 8-inch baking dish and then freezing it. After an hour, it was easy to remove the foil and slice the mixture into tots.

To speed the cooling process, I spread the hot potato mixture on a large sheet of foil on the counter for 10 minutes before packing it into the pan and freezing it. Now the block was ready to slice neatly after just 30 minutes in the freezer. With six easy cuts in one direction and eight in the other, forming individual tots was as simple as slicing brownies. From there, all it took was a quick fry, and these tots were ready to roll. Watching tasters stuff their faces like 10-year-olds fresh from recess, I knew this recipe rated an A+.

—SARAH GABRIEL, *Cook's Country*

Crispy Potato Tots

MAKES 4 DOZEN TOTS

If your food processor has a capacity of less than 11 cups, you'll need to process the potatoes in two batches. If any large pieces of potato remain after processing, chop them coarsely by hand. To make handling the uncooked tots easier, use a wet knife blade and wet hands. Once the tots are added to the hot oil, they may stick together; resist the temptation to stir and break them apart until after they have browned and set. You will need at least a 6-quart Dutch oven for this recipe.

- 1 cup water
- 2¼ teaspoons salt
- 2½ pounds russet potatoes, peeled and cut into 1½-inch pieces
- 1½ tablespoons all-purpose flour
- ½ teaspoon pepper
- 4 cups peanut or vegetable oil

1. Whisk water and salt together in bowl until salt dissolves. Pulse potatoes and salt water together in food processor until potatoes are coarsely ground, 10 to 12 pulses, stirring occasionally. Drain mixture in fine-mesh strainer, pressing potatoes with rubber spatula until dry (liquid should measure about 1½ cups); discard liquid. Transfer potatoes to bowl and microwave, uncovered, until dry and sticky, 8 to 10 minutes, stirring halfway through cooking.

2. Stir flour and pepper into potatoes. Spread potato mixture into thin layer on large sheet of aluminum foil and let cool for 10 minutes. Push potatoes to center of foil and place foil and potatoes in 8-inch square baking pan. Push foil into corners and up sides of pan, smoothing foil flush to pan. Press potato mixture tightly and evenly into pan. Freeze, uncovered, until firm, about 30 minutes.

3. Meanwhile, adjust oven rack to middle position and heat oven to 200 degrees. Heat oil in large Dutch oven over medium-high heat to 375 degrees. Set wire rack in rimmed baking sheet. Using foil overhang, lift potatoes from pan and cut into 48 pieces (5 cuts in 1 direction and 7 in other). Fry half of potato tots until golden brown and crisp, 5 to 7 minutes, stirring only after they browned and set. Transfer to prepared baking sheet and place in oven. Return oil to 375 degrees and repeat with remaining potato tots. Serve.

VARIATIONS

Crispy Potato Tots for a Crowd

Double ingredients for Crispy Potato Tots. Process and drain potato mixture in 2 batches. Microwave entire potato mixture for 12 to 14 minutes, stirring halfway through cooking. Spread potato mixture on large

---

NOTES FROM THE TEST KITCHEN

KEYS TO MAKING TOTS AT HOME
Yes, ours are more work than commercial frozen tots—but they taste so much better.

1. After chopping, drain potatoes to remove starch that would otherwise make tots gluey and heavy.

2. Parcook potatoes, add flour, and press into baking pan to freeze briefly to make tots easy to cut.

3. Lift firmed mixture out of pan and cut potato into tots—it's as easy as slicing brownies.

KEYS TO DEEP-FRYING

THE IDEAL OIL TEMPERATURE
Most foods are fried at 350 to 375 degrees. But the oil temperature drops when food is added, so you have to adjust the burner to keep the oil at the right temperature.

THE RIGHT TOOLS
We like to fry in a Dutch oven because its relatively low sides allow good visibility and easy access. A metal slotted spoon or "spider" skimmer makes it easy to remove food from hot oil.

THE PROPER FINISH
Drain food on a wire rack set in a rimmed baking sheet and, if seasoning, season it hot out of the oil.

sheet of foil to cool and press into 13 by 9-inch baking pan. After freezing, cut potato rectangle in half crosswise before cutting into potato tots per recipe. Fry in 4 batches.

Bacon-Ranch Potato Tots

Stir 1 tablespoon cider vinegar into potatoes after microwaving. Add 4 slices finely chopped cooked bacon, 1 teaspoon onion powder, ½ teaspoon garlic powder, and ½ teaspoon dried dill to potatoes with flour in step 2.

Parmesan-Rosemary Potato Tots

Stir 2 minced garlic cloves into drained potatoes before microwaving. Add 1 cup grated Parmesan cheese and 2 tablespoons minced fresh rosemary to potatoes with flour in step 2.

Southwestern Potato Tots

Add ½ cup shredded smoked gouda cheese, 3 tablespoons minced fresh cilantro, and 2 tablespoons minced jarred jalapeños to potatoes with flour in step 2.

ROASTED FINGERLING POTATOES

COOKS PRIZE FINGERLING POTATOES FOR THEIR good flavor, ultra-thin skins, and creamy texture. They're usually cooked gently to showcase their delicate nature, but I had a tougher treatment in mind: I wanted roasted fingerling potatoes that were still fresh-tasting and creamy but had a crisp edge. The problem? It's the starch that facilitates crisp browning, and fingerlings have little of it.

My early tests proved that putting fingerlings (halved lengthwise to create a flat surface to brown) on an oiled sheet pan in a hot oven was a nonstarter; the potatoes were leathery by the time they picked up any color. I tried covering them with foil for half of the cooking time, but that didn't work either. I hit the back issues of *Cook's Country* and *Cook's Illustrated*. From previous recipes I learned that boiling potatoes in super-salty water helps season them throughout and maximizes a creamy interior. Also, with potato salad recipes we've added vinegar to the water to halt the release of starch; could I do the reverse here, making the water more alkaline (with baking soda) to encourage maximum starch release—and better browning?

Our science editor agreed, explaining that adding baking soda to boiling potatoes starts a chain reaction in which the pectin molecules that strengthen cell walls are unzipped, releasing the starch molecule amylose (a potato starch that facilitates browning) to the potatoes' surface. So I gave it a try, adding lots of salt and a little baking soda to the boiling water. Once the fingerlings were drained in the colander, I could see a thin layer of sticky starch on them. As I shook the potatoes dry in the colander, the starch became more abundant. I arranged the dried potatoes, cut side down, on a preheated, oiled baking sheet and roasted them at 500 degrees for 20 minutes.

These spuds came out of the oven tender and crisp—but became soggy as they cooled. They continued to release steam, even after a seared crust had formed. Clearly, I needed to cool the potatoes before roasting them, so I spread them out on a platter. After five minutes they'd stopped steaming. Now I placed them on a hot, oiled baking sheet and roasted them as before. These fingerlings were just as tender and creamy as boiled ones, but this time they had a crisp, flavorful crust.

—NICK IVERSON, *Cook's Country*

Crisp Roasted Fingerling Potatoes
SERVES 4

2 **pounds fingerling potatoes, halved lengthwise**
½ **cup salt**
½ **teaspoon baking soda**
2 **tablespoons olive oil**
¼ **teaspoon pepper**

1. Adjust oven rack to lowest position, place rimmed baking sheet on rack, and heat oven to 500 degrees. Bring 8 cups water to boil in large saucepan. Add potatoes, salt, and baking soda; bring to simmer; and cook until potatoes are tender but centers offer slight resistance when pierced with paring knife, 7 to 10 minutes. Drain potatoes in colander and shake vigorously to roughen edges. Transfer potatoes to large platter lined with kitchen towel and arrange cut side up. Let sit until no longer steaming and surface is tacky, about 5 minutes.

2. Transfer potatoes to large bowl and toss with 1 tablespoon oil and pepper. Working quickly, carefully remove baking sheet from oven and drizzle remaining 1 tablespoon oil over surface. Arrange potatoes on baking sheet, cut side down, in even layer. Bake until cut sides are crisp and skins are spotty brown, 20 to 25 minutes, rotating sheet halfway through roasting. Flip potatoes cut side up and let cool on sheet for 5 minutes. Serve.

SALT-BAKED POTATOES

I HAD ALWAYS ASSUMED THAT SALT-BAKED POTATOES were a novelty act akin to dishwasher-steamed salmon or manifold-roasted meatloaf. How could burying a potato beneath a mound of salt possibly improve on basic baking? Well, if you believe the press, all that salt intensifies the potato's flavor and makes its texture particularly moist and fluffy. After hearing yet another paean sung to the method, I decided it was time to separate fact from fiction.

I bought a sack of russets and rounded up some recipes. Most called for simply burying the potatoes in salt and popping them into the oven. Others instructed the cook to set the potatoes on a bed of salt in a baking dish and cover the whole thing with foil. I also found an approach that called for brushing the potatoes with an egg wash and then encrusting them in salt before baking. I tried all three methods—and to my great surprise, I was hooked. While each approach had drawbacks, they all significantly improved on plain baked potato.

Though their skins were as tough and desiccated as an old baseball mitt, the "buried" potatoes were remarkably light and flaky inside. The interiors of the salt-crusted potatoes were also wonderfully fluffy—plus their skins were less leathery—but painting on the egg wash was messy and chiseling off the crust at the table inelegant. And the potatoes cooked in the sealed dish? Really good—without a doubt some of the best baked potatoes I'd ever tasted. Their flesh was fluffy and moist, their flavor deep and well seasoned (though by no means salty). Even the skin was noticeably improved: Though the exposed portion was a tiny bit damp (a minor flaw I'd come back to), it was paper-thin and far more tender than the tough hide on a plain baked spud or the wet casing around one baked in foil.

After giving it some thought, I realized why baking potatoes on a bed of salt in a covered pan worked so much better than either of the conventional ways of baking potatoes: It allows for moisture exchange between the salt and the spud. The moisture that escapes from the potato is contained in the covered pan and absorbed by the salt crystals. Some of that moisture is then reabsorbed by the potato, helping to make its skin tender and its flesh light and fluffy.

Now that I had the mechanics behind the method straight, I began refining the details. After some experimentation, I settled on baking the potatoes in a spacious 13 by 9-inch baking dish (where the potatoes wouldn't touch one another) atop a thick 2½-cup layer of either kosher or table salt. Ninety minutes in a 450-degree oven also proved optimal.

But I wondered if I could perfect the skin by fixing the dampness of the exposed area. (I could live with the slight dryness where the skin touched the salt.) Figuring a bit of dry heat might help to burn off some moisture, I baked another batch, but this time I removed the foil once the potatoes were almost cooked through—about 75 minutes in. I then let them finish uncovered. This improved matters, but I was able to get rid of the dampness entirely (without any ill effects to the interior) by cranking the oven temperature to 500 degrees after I removed the foil. I also found that brushing the potatoes with olive oil after uncovering them boosted the skins' flavor and gave them an appealing glossy look.

The potatoes couldn't get much better, but I wondered if I could put this method to further use. As it turned out, a few rosemary sprigs laid over the salt scented the potatoes with their fresh, piney aroma.

SALT-BAKED POTATOES WITH ROASTED GARLIC AND ROSEMARY BUTTER

Even better, I threw a head of garlic alongside the spuds as they cooked and used their creamy, sweet flesh to whip up a quick roasted garlic–flavored butter.

I'm still not ready to steam fish in my dishwasher or cook meatloaf over my car engine, but in my household, salt-baked potatoes are here to stay.

—MATTHEW CARD, *Cook's Illustrated*

Salt-Baked Potatoes with Roasted Garlic and Rosemary Butter

SERVES 4

Kosher or table salt can be used in this recipe. The salt can be strained to remove solid bits and reused for this recipe. The potatoes can be prepared without the roasted garlic butter and topped with other garnishes such as sour cream, chives, crumbled bacon, and/or shredded cheese.

2½ cups plus ⅛ teaspoon kosher salt
4 russet potatoes, scrubbed and dried
2 sprigs fresh rosemary plus ¼ teaspoon minced
1 whole head garlic, outer papery skin removed and top quarter of head cut off and discarded
4 teaspoons olive oil
4 tablespoons unsalted butter, softened

1. Adjust oven rack to middle position and heat oven to 450 degrees. Spread 2½ cups salt in even layer in 13 by 9-inch baking dish. Gently nestle potatoes in salt, broad side down, leaving space between potatoes. Add rosemary sprigs and garlic, cut side up, to baking dish. Cover baking dish with aluminum foil and crimp edges tightly to seal. Bake for 1¼ hours; remove pan from oven. Increase oven temperature to 500 degrees.

2. Carefully remove foil from baking dish. Remove garlic and set aside to cool. Brush exposed portion of each potato with 1 teaspoon oil. Return uncovered baking dish to oven and bake until potatoes are tender when pierced with tip of paring knife and skins are glossy, 15 to 20 minutes.

3. Meanwhile, once garlic is cool enough to handle, squeeze root end until cloves slip out of their skins. Using fork, mash garlic, butter, ⅛ teaspoon kosher salt (or pinch table salt), and minced rosemary to smooth paste. Remove any clumped salt from potatoes (holding with kitchen towel if necessary), split lengthwise, top with portion of butter, and serve immediately.

FRENCH POTATO CASSEROLE

IN THE FRENCH DISH KNOWN AS *POMMES DE TERRE boulangère*, or "baker's potatoes," incredibly tender potatoes nestle in a rich, meaty sauce beneath a delicately browned crust. The name dates to a time when villagers used the residual heat of the baker's oven to cook dinner at the end of the day. Chicken, pork, or beef would roast on an upper oven shelf while this casserole of thinly sliced potatoes and onions bubbled away underneath, seasoned by the savory fat and juices dripping from above.

Today French chefs no longer cook pommes de terre boulangère beneath a blistering roast, but they impart the same unctuous flavor, deep brown color, and supreme tenderness using hearty meat stock and a well-calibrated oven. While I could spend hours making stock from scratch, it seemed like too much time and effort for a side dish. I wanted a potato casserole with deep flavor and a super-tender texture—after a reasonable amount of work.

Since I was seeking a creamy consistency, only one potato variety would do: the moderately starchy, buttery-tasting Yukon Gold. A mandoline was an ideal tool for slicing the peeled spuds since I wanted them to be wafer-thin (about ⅛ inch)—any thicker and the casserole would be too chunky, losing its refined nature. I added a thinly sliced onion to the Yukons, packed the mixture into a greased baking dish, poured in 3 cups of store-bought beef broth, and slid the casserole into a 350-degree oven. It was no surprise when this test batch revealed two big flaws. First, the sauce was bland and tasted . . . well, canned. And second, its consistency was soupy, lacking the requisite creaminess.

I tackled the flavor issue first. To temper the beef broth's undesirable qualities, I diluted it with an equal amount of commercial chicken broth. This mellowed the flavor of both, for a blend that didn't taste processed. But that doesn't mean it tasted meaty. Since potatoes boulangère were sometimes roasted beneath poultry, I experimented with scattering chicken wings atop the potatoes before baking, hoping that the wings would infuse the slices with rich flavor. But this was effective only if I first browned the chicken on both sides—an extra step that I wasn't willing to incorporate.

Next, I turned to flavor-packed pork options like ham hocks, pancetta, and bacon. I simmered a hock briefly in the broth, expecting it to impart smokiness, but the effect was negligible. (I could have cooked it longer but I wanted a quick fix.) For the pancetta and bacon, I simply rendered them until crisp and then tossed the pieces with the potatoes and onion. Both were much more effective at boosting meatiness than the ham hock was, but in the end, tasters preferred the smoky bacon.

Next up was the onion. I found inspiration from another French classic: onion soup, in which onions are deeply caramelized to concentrate their flavor. Cooking the sliced onion to a deep molasses-y brown made it too sweet for this dish, but sautéing it in some of the leftover bacon fat until golden brown was enough to bring out remarkable complexity.

With a scattering of fresh thyme, sprinkles of salt and pepper, and a few pats of butter, the flavor of my potatoes was in really good shape. But I still needed to improve the too-thin sauce and somehow make the overall texture silkier and more luscious.

My first attempt to remedy the consistency of the sauce was twofold: I decreased the amount of broth to 2½ cups and increased the oven temperature to 425 degrees so that more liquid would evaporate during baking. When I started to see improvement, I took things one step further by bringing the broth to a simmer in the pot used to cook the onion, giving it a jump start on reducing in the oven. As a bonus, this deglazing step captured all of the flavorful fond left behind by the bacon and caramelized onion.

The broth had now cooked down, but it was still neither thick nor creamy. Then it dawned on me. I had been submerging my sliced potatoes in water to keep them from discoloring while I prepped the remaining ingredients—a common practice, but one that also washes away most of the spuds' starch. Without that starch, my sauce couldn't thicken up. I tried again with unsoaked potatoes and witnessed a striking difference. The sauce now glazed the potatoes and onion in a velvety cloak. As a final measure, I made sure to allow the casserole to rest for a good 20 minutes before serving it. This went a long way toward developing a silky, creamy texture, since the starch granules in the potatoes continued to absorb moisture and swell as they cooled.

With a few modifications, I had been able to achieve a satisfying version of pommes de terre boulangère within a reasonable time frame, making this once-obscure dish now popular fare in my house.

—BRYAN ROOF, *Cook's Illustrated*

Potato Casserole with Bacon and Caramelized Onion

SERVES 6 TO 8

Do not rinse or soak the potatoes, as this will wash away their starch, which is essential to the dish. A mandoline makes slicing the potatoes much easier. For the proper texture, make sure to let the casserole stand for 20 minutes before serving.

3	slices thick-cut bacon, cut into ½-inch pieces
1	large onion, halved and sliced thin
1¼	teaspoons salt
2	teaspoons chopped fresh thyme
½	teaspoon pepper
1¼	cups low-sodium chicken broth
1¼	cups beef broth
3	pounds Yukon Gold potatoes, peeled
2	tablespoons unsalted butter, cut into 4 pieces

1. Adjust oven rack to lower-middle position and heat oven to 425 degrees. Grease 13 by 9-inch baking dish.

2. Cook bacon in medium saucepan over medium-low heat until crisp, 10 to 13 minutes. Using slotted spoon, transfer bacon to paper towel–lined plate. Pour off all but 1 tablespoon fat from pot. Return pot to medium heat and add onion and ¼ teaspoon salt; cook, stirring frequently, until onion is soft and golden brown, about 25 minutes, adjusting heat and adding water 1 tablespoon at a time if onion or bottom of pot becomes too dark. Transfer onion to large bowl; add bacon, thyme, remaining 1 teaspoon salt, and pepper. Add broths to now-empty saucepan and bring to simmer over medium-high heat, scraping up any browned bits.

3. Slice potatoes ⅛ inch thick. Transfer to bowl with onion mixture and toss to combine. Transfer to prepared baking dish. Firmly press down on mixture to compress into even layer. Carefully pour hot broth over top of potatoes. Dot surface evenly with butter.

4. Bake, uncovered, until potatoes are tender and golden brown on edges and most of liquid has been absorbed, 45 to 55 minutes. Transfer to wire rack and let stand for 20 minutes to fully absorb broth before cutting and serving.

BREAD STUFFING

IN RECENT YEARS, THERE'S BEEN A PROLIFERATION of bread stuffing recipes with delusions of grandeur. Sure, stuffing with a dozen or more ingredients (wild rice, dried cherries, Italian sausage, fennel seeds, pine nuts, eggs, cream…) can be delicious, but I wanted to revisit an older, simpler style of stuffing to counter both the excess of the Thanksgiving table and the stress of preparing it. I wanted purer flavors and no fussy custard that could curdle or break.

My nostalgia evaporated as soon as I started cooking. Most 19th- and early-20th-century recipes called for cooking the stuffing inside a bird to ensure moisture and meaty flavor, but the big batch I planned wouldn't fit inside the cavity. Plus, trading the rougher loaves of yore for today's supermarket sandwich bread rendered much of the century-old stuffing wisdom useless. Two popular older methods—soaking sliced bread in milk and using moistened bread crumbs—turned my more delicate modern bread into sludge.

But one batch had promise. The pared-down flavors and ingredient list were exactly what I had in mind— nothing but toasted bread, onions and celery sautéed in butter, poultry seasoning, and water. But this stuffing wasn't perfect. Despite the water, it was dry, and it lacked poultry flavor (no surprise, since the bird was gone).

This recipe called for toasting the bread and then dicing it, but others did the reverse or simply used up stale bread. In tests, toasting cubed bread yielded the maximum toasty-flavored surface area and proved most resistant to sogginess. Great—but the recipe I was using suffered from the opposite problem. With a mere 1½ cups of water for 2 pounds of bread, the stuffing was dry and crumbly.

To moisten it, I doubled the original amount of water. Not enough. Four cups? Still dry. At 5 cups, moist patches were interspersed with dry, cottony patches. I learned that if I let the mixture rest for 10 minutes (so the water could permeate) and gave the mix a stir halfway through, things evened out.

Without the turkey to flavor the stuffing as it cooked, I needed to trade the water for chicken broth. But that alone didn't give me deep roasted flavor. I tried doubling the usual amount of onions, and instead of merely sautéing them with the celery until translucent, I took them all the way to brown. For more pervasive herb flavor, I "bloomed" the poultry seasoning, cooking it briefly with the butter and vegetables. Now I reconsidered the broth: Could I get more out of it? I used some to deglaze the pan in which I'd cooked the vegetables and let it boil down. (To make up for the volume of liquid lost to evaporation, I added an extra cup of broth to the recipe.) As I'd hoped, scraping the flavorful browned bits from the pot and concentrating some of the broth deepened meatiness, but I still wasn't satisfied. If browned vegetables and toasty bread helped, what about browned butter? Cooking butter until the milk proteins began to brown finally gave the stuffing all the roasted, nutty flavor I was after.

"Now, how about a crunchy top?" tasters asked. Can do. Unlike many modern stuffings, mine contained no eggs. That meant I could go from the moderate 350 degrees I'd been using to 425 degrees, without any fear that I'd scramble a custard. While I was at it, I moved the stuffing to a higher rack, where it would brown better. I reserved 3 tablespoons of browned butter to drizzle over the top before baking, guaranteeing

that the top stayed moist. I had transformed this stuffing by browning the bread, vegetables, butter, and finished stuffing. It seemed that the key to successfully dusting off this classic wasn't more ingredients, but more cooking.

—SARAH GABRIEL, *Cook's Country*

Back-to-Basics Bread Stuffing

SERVES 10 TO 12

Use a hearty white sandwich bread for this recipe; our favorite brand is Arnold Country Classics White Bread.

- 2 **pounds hearty white sandwich bread, cut into ½-inch pieces**
- 16 **tablespoons unsalted butter, cut into 16 pieces**
- 4 **onions, chopped fine**
- 4 **celery ribs, chopped fine**
- 4 **teaspoons poultry seasoning**
- 1¾ **teaspoons salt**
- 1 **teaspoon pepper**
- 6 **cups low-sodium chicken broth**

1. Adjust oven racks to upper-middle and lower-middle positions and heat oven to 325 degrees. Divide bread between 2 rimmed baking sheets and bake until golden brown, 50 to 55 minutes, stirring bread and switching and rotating sheets halfway through baking. Cool completely on sheets, then transfer to large bowl.

2. Melt butter in 12-inch skillet over medium-low heat. Cook, stirring constantly, until butter is nutty brown, 5 to 7 minutes. Reserve 3 tablespoons browned butter in small bowl. Add onions and celery to skillet, increase heat to medium, and cook until browned, 12 to 15 minutes. Stir in poultry seasoning, salt, and pepper and cook until fragrant, about 30 seconds. Add vegetable mixture to bowl with toasted bread.

3. Increase oven temperature to 425 degrees. Add 2 cups broth to now-empty skillet and cook over high heat, scraping up any browned bits, until reduced to 1 cup, 6 to 8 minutes. Combine remaining 4 cups broth and reduced broth with vegetable-bread mixture and let sit for 10 minutes, stirring once. Transfer stuffing to 13 by 9-inch baking dish and press into even layer. Drizzle reserved browned butter evenly over top and bake on upper-middle rack until golden brown and crisp, 35 to 45 minutes. Let cool for 15 minutes. Serve.

HOLIDAY CRANBERRY CHUTNEY

THERE WILL ALWAYS BE A PLACE AT MY THANKSGIVING table for back-of-the-bag cranberry sauce made with just cranberries, water, and granulated sugar. With its sweet-tart flavor and soft jelled texture, this no-fuss condiment is a fine way to cut the richness of the roast turkey, mashed potatoes, and gravy. But when I want a sauce with more dimension and sharpness—whether as an accompaniment for turkey or for more robustly flavored, fattier cuts of pork, lamb, or game—I find the options for a dressed-up sauce disappointing. Usually these sauces incorporate just one more flavor note, and typically it's sweet—not what I had in mind.

As I cast about for ideas, I realized that I wanted something with the complexity of an Indian chutney, which, in addition to slow-cooked fruits, boasts vinegar, aromatics, and spices that give the jammy relish kick and savor. I began by thinking of an aromatic element that would add that subtle savory quality to the sauce. Garlic and red onion, both common additions in Indian chutneys, seemed too potent. I settled on milder shallot instead. For an assertive fruit to pair with cranberries, I chopped up tart Granny Smith apples. Fresh ginger was the perfect choice for incorporating spiciness. I mixed all of these ingredients in a pot with the cranberries, sugar, and a little salt. Because I didn't want an overly strong mixture, it seemed unwise to introduce the vinegar typically added to chutney to the two tart fruits. I opted instead for water as the only liquid, simmering the mixture until the cranberries and apples had completely broken down, about 20 minutes. The resulting chutney wasn't terrible, but overall, it lacked complexity. Also, the shallot and ginger were a little too prominent.

I wanted to keep my recipe relatively short, so developing depth via a bunch of additional ingredients was out. But what about my decision to omit vinegar? Indian cooks must have a good reason for its inclusion in chutney. Hoping that fruity cider vinegar would enliven the cranberry-apple mixture, I experimented with using it to replace some of the water, finally settling on swapping ⅓ cup of water for ¼ cup of cider vinegar. To my surprise, rather than making the sauce overly sour, the cider vinegar lent both brightness and depth, helping to pull the flavors back into balance. After consulting our science editor, I learned that the acetic acid in vinegar reacts with pectin in the cranberries

CRANBERRY CHUTNEY WITH APPLES AND CRYSTALLIZED GINGER

during cooking, reducing the vinegar's potency while preserving its lively taste.

For even more depth, I traded the granulated sugar for molasses-flavored brown sugar. Finally, I softened the shallot and ginger in oil along with some salt before adding the other ingredients, which drew out more of their flavor nuances while simultaneously toning down their harsh edges.

Now I was close to the chunky sauce that I had imagined, but I had inadvertently created a problem. While tasters appreciated the concentrated flavors of the sauce, many missed the fresh pop of the back-of-the-bag version, which cooks for just 10 minutes. I solved the problem by simmering half of the cranberries with the other ingredients for the full 20 minutes and reserving the other half until the last five minutes of cooking. This created a jamlike base dotted with soft but still intact berries that retained their zing. The textural contrast gave me the idea for one last tweak: I mixed ⅓ cup of minced crystallized ginger into the chutney along with the cranberries at the end of cooking, which added a slight, pleasing chewiness.

I used this concept to create four more versions. In addition to sweet-tart flavors, they all had a bit of punch, a bit of slow-cooked savor, a bit of fresh zing—and a whole lot of complexity.

—KEITH DRESSER, *Cook's Illustrated*

Cranberry Chutney with Apples and Crystallized Ginger

MAKES ABOUT 3 CUPS

If using frozen cranberries, thaw them before cooking.

- 1 teaspoon vegetable oil
- 1 shallot, minced
- 2 teaspoons finely grated fresh ginger
- ½ teaspoon salt
- ⅔ cup water
- ¼ cup cider vinegar
- 1 cup packed brown sugar
- 12 ounces (3 cups) fresh or frozen cranberries
- 2 Granny Smith apples, peeled, cored, and cut into ¼-inch pieces
- ⅓ cup minced crystallized ginger

1. Heat oil in medium saucepan over medium heat until shimmering. Add shallot, fresh ginger, and salt; cook, stirring occasionally, until shallot has softened, 1 to 2 minutes.

2. Add water, vinegar, and sugar. Increase heat to high and bring to simmer, stirring to dissolve sugar. Add 1½ cups cranberries and apples; return to simmer. Reduce heat to medium-low and simmer, stirring occasionally, until cranberries have almost completely broken down and mixture has thickened, about 15 minutes.

3. Add remaining 1½ cups cranberries and crystallized ginger; continue to simmer, stirring occasionally, until cranberries just begin to burst, 5 to 7 minutes. Transfer to serving bowl and cool for at least 1 hour before serving. (Sauce can be refrigerated for up to 3 days.)

VARIATIONS

Spicy Cranberry Chutney

Increase oil to 2 teaspoons and substitute 1 stemmed and seeded red bell pepper cut into ¼-inch pieces and 2 seeded and minced jalapeño chiles for fresh ginger in step 1. Increase cooking time in step 1 to 5 minutes. Increase water to ¾ cup and omit apples and crystallized ginger.

Cranberry Chutney with Fennel and Golden Raisins

Increase oil to 2 teaspoons and substitute 1 cored fennel bulb cut into ¼-inch pieces and ½ teaspoon fennel seeds for fresh ginger in step 1. Increase cooking time in step 1 to 5 minutes. Increase water to 1 cup, omit apples, and substitute ⅓ cup golden raisins for crystallized ginger.

Cranberry-Orange Chutney

Starting with 2 oranges, remove four 2-inch-wide strips zest from 1 orange, then peel both oranges and remove segments. Set aside zest and segments. Increase fresh ginger to 4 teaspoons and add 1 teaspoon yellow mustard seeds to oil together with fresh ginger in step 1. Increase water to ¾ cup and add orange zest and segments to pot with cranberries in step 2. Omit apples and crystallized ginger.

Cranberry Chutney with Pear, Lemon, and Rosemary

Remove two 2-inch-wide strips zest from 1 lemon, then peel and remove segments. Set aside zest and segments. Substitute 2 teaspoons chopped fresh rosemary for fresh ginger. Substitute 2 peeled Bosc pears cut into ¼-inch pieces for apples; omit crystallized ginger. Add lemon zest and segments to pot with cranberries in step 2.

CHAPTER 4

BREAKFAST & BREADS

Perfect Scrambled Eggs   72

    Perfect Scrambled Eggs for Two

    Perfect Scrambled Eggs for One

Light Quiche Lorraine   74

Almond Granola with Dried Fruit   77

    Hazelnut Granola with Dried Pear

    Pecan-Orange Granola with Dried Cranberries

    Spiced Walnut Granola with Dried Apple

    Tropical Granola with Dried Mango

Morning Glory Muffins   80

Cranberry-Pecan Muffins   83

Cinnamon Babka   85

Cinnamon Swirl Bread   88

Croissants   92

English Muffin Bread   98

Honey-Wheat Dinner Rolls   99

Dilly Casserole Bread   102

Indian Flatbread (Naan)   103

    Quicker Indian Flatbread

PERFECT SCRAMBLED EGGS

I TAKE PAINS WITH JUST ABOUT EVERYTHING I COOK, but not scrambled eggs. Usually my goal is just to get them on the table, fast. My method, such as it is, goes something like this: Whisk eggs, add a splash of milk, pour the mixture into a hot skillet, and stir over medium-high heat until the eggs puff up into large, moist curds. Trouble is, that's not what usually happens. All it takes is the merest distraction for my eggs to go from glossy, fluffy, and wobbly to tough, dry slabs. But even when I take my time and gently stir the eggs over lower heat, I still don't get the results I want. Instead, I end up with curds so pebbly and fine that the mixture looks like oatmeal. It was time to stop leaving everything to chance and nail down an approach to foolproof fluffy, tender scrambled eggs.

I did a little investigation into the science of cooking eggs, and the first thing I discovered was that to produce the ideal voluptuous curds, my slapdash approach over higher heat wasn't far off. Only relatively high heat will produce enough steam (from the dairy and the water in eggs) to puff up the scramble. As the proteins in the eggs continue to heat, they unfold and then bond together to form a latticed gel in a process known as coagulation. The texture of the eggs depends on exactly how much unfolding and bonding occur. To create moist curds, I needed the egg proteins to bond enough to transform from a liquid into a semisolid, but not so much that they seized up into a tough mass. Fortunately, I could fall back on some lessons learned in the test kitchen over the years to address this problem.

Lesson one: Adding salt to the raw eggs makes for more tender curds. In the same way that soaking a piece of pork in a brine solution tenderizes its protein network, salt dissolves egg proteins so that they are unable to bond as tightly when cooked. Lesson two: Don't overbeat the eggs or you'll have a tough scramble. This may seem counterintuitive (since physical agitation usually destroys structure), but the principle is easily

---

NOTES FROM THE TEST KITCHEN

TURN IT DOWN

Cooking temperature is key to perfect scrambled eggs. When your spatula just leaves a trail through eggs, that's your cue in our dual-heat method to turn dial from medium-high to low.

SCRAMBLED EGG EXTREMES

The best puffy scrambled eggs aren't hastily cooked over high heat. Nor are they gently cooked over low heat.

RUBBERY	WET
Blasting the eggs over high heat gets breakfast on the table in a hurry—but produces dried-out, rubbery curds.	Keeping the heat low might prevent the eggs from overcooking, but the result will be loose, tiny curds that look like lumpy custard.

THE BEST BREAKFAST SAUSAGE PATTIES

Dumping a box of fully cooked, frozen breakfast sausage patties into a skillet is easier and faster than shaping and cooking patties from tube-style rolls of raw sausage meat. But convenience aside, do these patties taste better, too? We pitted two brands of fully cooked breakfast sausage patties against four tubes of raw, "roll-style" breakfast sausage and one brand of raw patties to find out.

The most important factor to our tasters was texture. Brands with a fairly lean composition scored poorly, but brands with higher fat content didn't fare well, either; one was even labeled a "grease bomb" by a taster. Overall, we preferred sausage with a moderate amount of fat as this sausage was tender but not greasy. Flavor was also important; tasters preferred a harmonious blend of salty, sweet, and spicy and a noticeably "meaty" taste.

Our winner was **Jimmy Dean Fully Cooked Original Pork Sausage Patties**, which has a "tender yet substantial texture." It was fatty but not overly so, and it had an appealing blend of salt, sugar, and spices. (See page 290 for more information about our tasting results.)

illustrated by what happens when you whip egg whites into peaks. Vigorous whisking unfolds proteins in much the same way that heat does; once unfolded, the protein strands readily bond together to form a tighter structure. Since the last thing you want to do is accelerate the unfolding process before the eggs hit the heat, beat them until just combined with the gentler action of a fork rather than a whisk.

I kept those points in mind as I assumed the role of short-order cook, whipping up batch after batch of scrambled eggs to see how the other major component in the mix—dairy—affected the texture. Some of the recipes I consulted called for milk, others for half-and-half or heavy cream, but all three options contain two important tenderizers: water and fat. What I needed to know was how the water-to-fat ratio in each would affect coagulation and exactly how dairy-rich my tasters liked their eggs.

To feed four people, I beat eight eggs with both salt and pepper and varying proportions of each dairy option; poured the eggs into a butter-slicked 12-inch skillet over medium-high heat; and dragged a heatproof rubber spatula around the pan for about two minutes, until the eggs were clumpy but still shiny and wet. My tasters and I mulled over the pros and cons of each dairy ingredient. Milk produced slightly fluffier, cleaner-tasting curds, but they were particularly prone to weeping. Heavy cream, on the other hand, rendered the eggs very stable but dense, and some tasters found their flavor just too rich. One-quarter cup of half-and-half fared best. Though everyone agreed that these curds could stand to be fluffier, they were decently puffed and stable thanks to the tandem effects of the liquid's water and fat.

The benefits of the dairy are threefold. First, the water it contains (80 percent in half-and-half) interrupts the protein network and dilutes the molecules, thereby raising the temperature at which the eggs coagulate and providing a greater safety net against overcooking (and disproving the classic French theory that adding the dairy at the end of cooking is best). Second, as the water in the dairy vaporizes, it provides lift (just as in a loaf of baking bread), which causes the eggs to puff up. And third, the fat in the dairy also raises the coagulation temperature by coating and insulating part of the protein molecules so that they cannot stick together as tightly.

Half-and-half wasn't a perfect solution, however; some tasters still found the dairy flavor too prominent. Less dairy would only make the recipe less foolproof, so I researched ways to boost egg flavor. The best suggestion came from a colleague. She mentioned that when her grandmother makes fresh pasta, she adds an extra yolk or two to the dough to approximate the richer flavor of farm-fresh eggs. I followed suit, and sure enough, the more yolks I added to the mix, the richer the results. There was no need to overdo it, though: Two yolks per eight eggs balanced the flavor nicely. Even better, the high proportion of fat and emulsifiers in the yolks further raised the coagulation temperature, helping to stave off overcooking.

Before I moved on to fine-tune the cooking method, I tried a couple of unconventional stir-ins that promised either fluffier or more tender eggs: vinegar and baking powder. The acidity in the former tenderized the eggs in much the same way that salt did but far more drastically; just a drop rendered the curds mushy. A dash of baking powder was also too much of a good thing, puffing the eggs like a diner-style omelet as well as imparting a chemical aftertaste.

I also experimented with the advice of old-school French cookbooks to start with room-temperature eggs. While we've proved that egg temperature can influence the structure of some delicate cakes, I found that cold eggs and room-temperature eggs produced virtually identical scrambles. So much for "secret weapons." It was time to face the fire.

The bottom line was that no matter how perfectly I balanced the ratios of protein, fat, and water, the scrambled eggs would still fail if they overcooked. Low heat would curb overcooking, but I needed higher heat to produce nicely puffed curds. Suddenly it hit me: What if I used both high and low heat?

I mixed up another batch of eggs, tossed a piece of cold butter into the pan, and turned the heat to medium-high. Once the butter was melted but not brown (a cue that the pan is too hot), I added the eggs, constantly scraping the bottom and sides of the skillet to form large curds and prevent any spots from overcooking. As soon as my spatula could just leave a trail in the pan with minimal raw egg filling in the gap (about two minutes in), I dropped the heat to low and switched to a gentle folding motion to keep from breaking up the large curds. When the eggs looked cooked through but still glossy (about 45 seconds later), I slid them onto a plate to stop the cooking process. To my delight, the results were almost perfect—fluffy and tender, for sure—and the method was far more fail-safe than my high-heat-only attempts.

My tasters' only holdover request? Larger curds, please. I tried scraping a bit less frequently, but while the curds were certainly bigger, they were also overcooked in spots. Stymied, I looked over all the elements in my recipe and realized that there was one component I hadn't addressed: the size of the pan. In theory, my vessel choice mattered more here than in any other recipe, since a smaller skillet would keep the eggs in a thicker layer, thereby trapping more steam and producing heartier curds. Whisking together one more batch of eggs, I put aside my 12-inch skillet and grabbed a 10-inch pan instead, then proceeded with my recipe. About three minutes later, I had the best batch of scrambled eggs yet: big, billowy curds that were perfect with or without a last-minute sprinkle of fresh herbs.

I was finished with slapdash. A simple, foolproof version of my favorite breakfast was finally served.

—DAN SOUZA, *Cook's Illustrated*

Perfect Scrambled Eggs

SERVES 4

It's important to follow visual cues, as pan thickness will have an effect on cooking times. You can substitute 8 teaspoons whole milk and 4 teaspoons heavy cream for the half-and-half. Add 2 tablespoons minced fresh parsley, chives, basil, or cilantro or 1 tablespoon minced fresh dill or tarragon after reducing the heat to low, if desired.

- 8 **large eggs plus 2 large yolks**
- ¼ **cup half-and-half**
- **Salt and pepper**
- 1 **tablespoon unsalted butter, chilled**

1. Beat eggs, egg yolks, half-and-half, ¼ teaspoon salt, and ¼ teaspoon pepper together with fork until thoroughly combined and mixture is pure yellow; do not overbeat.

2. Melt butter in 10-inch nonstick skillet over medium-high heat (butter should not brown), swirling to coat pan. Add egg mixture and, using heatproof rubber spatula, constantly and firmly scrape along bottom and sides of skillet until eggs begin to clump and spatula leaves trail on bottom of pan, 1½ to 2½ minutes. Reduce heat to low and gently but constantly fold eggs until clumped and just slightly wet, 30 to 60 seconds. Immediately transfer eggs to warmed plates and season with salt to taste. Serve immediately.

VARIATIONS
Perfect Scrambled Eggs For Two
Reduce eggs to 4, egg yolks to 1, half-and-half to 2 tablespoons, salt and pepper to ⅛ teaspoon each, and butter to ½ tablespoon. Cook eggs in 8-inch skillet for 45 to 75 seconds over medium-high heat, then 30 to 60 seconds over low heat.

Perfect Scrambled Eggs for One
Reduce eggs to 2, egg yolks to 1, half-and-half to 1 tablespoon, salt and pepper to pinch each, and butter to ¼ tablespoon. Cook eggs in 8-inch skillet for 30 to 60 seconds over medium-high heat, then 30 to 60 seconds over low heat.

LIGHT QUICHE LORRAINE

IS REDUCED-FAT QUICHE LORRAINE EVEN WORTH attempting? After all, it's the heavy cream, bacon, and cheese that make this caloric French classic taste so good. The prospect of creating a low-fat version of the buttery crust was nerve-wracking. In my experience, tasty low-fat crust is an oxymoron. But the traditional quiche had a lot of room for improvement at 460 calories, 42 grams of fat, and 20 grams of saturated fat per slice, so I gathered a handful of recipes that promised healthier versions and headed to the kitchen, skepticism in tow.

These recipes replaced the heavy cream with everything from cottage cheese to evaporated milk to fat-free half-and-half. The results were predictably bland, gritty, and lean. The recipes swapped out the bacon, too, but I ask you: Is it even quiche Lorraine without bacon? In fairness, one recipe had some promise; tasters

LIGHT QUICHE LORRAINE

liked its silky buttermilk filling. True, the tang seemed out of place and the buttermilk refused to set up; when the edges of the quiche were done, the center was still too soft. But at least I had a place to start.

I grabbed some store-bought (for now) pie crusts and got to work on the filling. To begin, I gradually replaced a portion of the buttermilk with whole milk, stopping when the tang mellowed (at ⅓ cup of milk plus 1⅓ cups of buttermilk). Given the five eggs I was using, I couldn't understand why the filling wouldn't set up. Our science editor blamed the buttermilk, which has more water and less fat than heavy cream does (which is why I was using buttermilk in the first place). At his suggestion, I added cornstarch, which fixed the problem. In the spirit of giving everything a chance, I tested my quiche with turkey bacon, smoked ham, Canadian bacon, and even smoked tofu. I never extracted real bacon flavor from any of them. After checking the calorie and fat numbers thus far, I decided that I had some wiggle room and allowed myself four slices of bacon. I also retained the Gruyère cheese—a traditional choice in American versions of quiche Lorraine. But instead of the 1½ cups called for in some high-fat recipes, I used just ¼ cup.

Now came the real challenge—the crust. Nervously, I got out my rolling pin. Since I'm no fan of low-fat crusts, instead of tinkering around the edges, I decided to blow up the entire concept. To that end, I made a low-fat version from phyllo dough, brushing the phyllo sheets with egg whites instead of the usual melted butter. This "crust" tasted nothing like crust. A flour tortilla had the same problem, plus it was flimsy. Tasters vetoed a crust made from slices of bread, describing it as "hard, dry, stale toast."

Since my wacky ideas were going nowhere, I reconsidered standard low-fat crusts. Typically, recipes replace butter with fat-free dairy products or canola oil mixed with water. As I'd expected, these crusts looked and tasted like pale cardboard. While I knew I couldn't achieve the incredible flakiness of an all-butter French pastry crust, surely I could bake a low-fat crust that you'd actually want to eat. Ultimately, I managed it using olive oil plus a bit of bacon fat left over from the bacon I was frying for the filling (I'd already counted the fat in my calorie calculations), a good hit of pepper, and a dusting of Parmesan cheese. A spoonful of sugar helped the crust brown. Since lean dough can be hard to roll out, I simply patted it into the pie plate. With less fat, my crust had a tendency to tear. To fix that,

after it baked for 30 minutes, I sprinkled a bit more Parmesan onto its surface and returned the crust to the oven. As it melted, the Parmesan both repaired any tears and added flavor.

I checked the numbers one final time and was pleased to discover that one serving of my quiche weighed in at only 17 grams of fat and 290 calories—I had cut two-thirds of the fat and more than a third of the calories, proving that tasty low-fat quiche Lorraine is possible after all.

—CAROLYNN PURPURA MACKAY, *Cook's Country*

Light Quiche Lorraine

SERVES 8

The filling may look wet when you remove the quiche from the oven, but the water will disappear as the quiche cools.

CRUST

- **4** slices bacon, chopped
- **1¼** cups (6¼ ounces) all-purpose flour
- **¼** cup grated Parmesan cheese
- **1** tablespoon sugar
- **½** teaspoon salt
- **½** teaspoon pepper
- **3** tablespoons olive oil
- **4** tablespoons ice water

FILLING

- **1⅓** cups buttermilk
- **⅓** cup whole milk
- **5** large eggs
- **4** teaspoons cornstarch
- **½** teaspoon salt
- **¼** teaspoon pepper
- **1** ounce Gruyère cheese, shredded (¼ cup)

1. FOR THE CRUST: Spray 9-inch pie plate with vegetable oil spray. Cook bacon in 10-inch skillet over medium heat until crisp, 6 to 8 minutes. Using slotted spoon, transfer bacon to paper towel–lined plate. Reserve 1 tablespoon bacon fat; reserve bacon for filling.

2. Adjust oven rack to lowest position and heat oven to 350 degrees. Pulse flour, 1 tablespoon Parmesan, sugar, salt, and pepper together in food processor until combined, about 3 pulses. Add oil and reserved bacon fat and pulse until mixture resembles coarse meal, about

12 pulses. Add water and process until dough begins to clump into large pieces, about 10 seconds. Transfer dough to prepared pie plate and press into even layer on bottom and sides of plate. Cover with plastic wrap and freeze until firm, about 30 minutes.

3. Spray 12-inch square sheet of aluminum foil with oil spray and press sprayed side against dough. Fill with pie weights and bake until top edge starts to color, about 30 minutes. Remove crust from oven, remove foil and weights, and sprinkle remaining 3 tablespoons Parmesan evenly over bottom of crust. Return crust to oven and bake until cheese is melted, about 7 minutes. Set on wire rack to cool slightly, about 10 minutes.

4. FOR THE FILLING: Whisk buttermilk, milk, eggs, cornstarch, salt, and pepper together in bowl until smooth. Stir in bacon and Gruyère. Pour filling into crust. Bake until center of quiche is set, 40 to 45 minutes. Let quiche cool on wire rack for 15 minutes. Serve.

NOTES FROM THE TEST KITCHEN

EASIER THAN ROLLING

Our pat-in-pan crust is very easy—once dough comes together in food processor, scoop it out and pat it into even layer in pie plate.

MAKING FAT AND CALORIES COUNT
Here's how we maximized flavor while minimizing fat.

¼ CUP GRATED PARMESAN
Replaces some of the flour to add savory depth.

3 TABLESPOONS OLIVE OIL
Replaces some of the butter with unsaturated fat.

1 TABLESPOON BACON FAT
Replaces some of the butter while reinforcing the bacon flavor.

SUPER-CHUNKY GRANOLA

WHETHER PAIRED WITH MILK, FRESH FRUIT, OR yogurt—or eaten by the fistful as a snack—granola is a must-have in my kitchen. Too bad the commercially prepared kind is such a letdown. Whether dry and dusty, overly sweet, infuriatingly expensive ($10 for a 12-ounce bag?), or all of the above, it's so universally disappointing that I recently vowed never to purchase another bag. Of course, that meant that if I wanted to enjoy granola, I would have to make my own.

I expected a homemade version to dramatically improve matters, but it only partially helped. Sure, do-it-yourself granola afforded me the opportunity to choose exactly which nuts and dried fruits I wanted to include, as well as how much. But there was a downside: The slow baking and frequent stirring that most recipes recommend result in a loose, granular texture. I wanted something altogether different: substantial clumps of toasty oats and nuts. My ideal clusters would be markedly crisp yet tender enough to shatter easily when bitten—I definitely didn't want the density or tooth-chipping crunch of a hard granola bar. Starting from square one, I laid out my plan of attack: I would nail down particulars about the oats and nuts first and then set my sights on achieving substantial chunks.

I got down to business and set up my own little granola factory, baking test batches using instant, quick, steel-cut, and old-fashioned whole rolled oat varieties. It was no surprise that instant and quick oats baked up unsubstantial and powdery. Steel-cut oats suffered the opposite problem: Chewing them was like munching gravel. Whole rolled oats were essential for a hearty, crisp texture.

Nuts, on the other hand, offered much more flexibility. I chose almonds for my working recipe, but almost any type did just fine, contributing plenty of crunch and rich, toasty flavor that developed as the cereal roasted in the oven. While many recipes advocate adding them whole, I preferred chopping them first for more even distribution.

As for other potential additions, seeds (sunflower, flax, pumpkin, and so on) and more unusual grains (such as quinoa or amaranth) are terrific choices, but since I planned to make granola often, I wanted to keep things simple, with ingredients that I routinely stock in my pantry.

With two of the primary players settled, I mixed up a batch using 5 cups of rolled oats and 2 cups of chopped almonds coated with my placeholder liquids: honey and vegetable oil (plus a touch of salt). I used a rubber spatula to spread the sticky concoction on a baking sheet that I'd lined with parchment for easier cleanup. I deliberated over what oven temperature to choose, and I settled on a relatively moderate 375 degrees to ward off scorching and allow the ingredients to brown slowly and evenly. I stirred the mixture every 10 minutes or so until it was evenly golden, which took about 30 minutes. The granola boasted a fantastic toasty scent coming out of the oven, but just as I had feared, there were no hearty chunks.

Temporarily setting the textural issue aside, I considered the other ingredients, starting with the sweetener. Honey and maple syrup are the most common choices, but even in small amounts, the honey struck many tasters as too distinct. Maple syrup was preferred for its milder character, especially when I balanced it with the subtle molasses notes offered by light brown sugar. One-third cup of each for 7 cups of nuts and oats gave the granola just the right degree of sweetness.

The other major component in most granola recipes is fat. But because fat-free commercial versions are so popular and I didn't want to leave any stone unturned, I whipped up a batch in which I left the oil out of the recipe completely. No dice: The fat-free cereal was so dry and powdery that no amount of milk or yogurt could rescue it. I eventually determined that ½ cup was the right amount of oil for a super-crisp—but not greasy— texture. Our science editor explained that fat is essential for a substantial crisp texture versus a parched, delicate one: Fat and liquid sweeteners form a fluid emulsion that thoroughly coats ingredients, creating crunch as the granola bakes. Without any fat, the texture is bound to be dry and fragile. I did two final fat experiments, first swapping butter for the oil, only to find that it was prone to burning. In the second trial, extra-virgin olive oil gave the cereal a savory slant that divided tasters, so I stuck with my original choice: neutral-tasting vegetable oil.

My granola now possessed well-balanced flavor and perfectly crisp oats and nuts, but I still had to deal with the issue of how to create big clumps. As I paged through cookbooks looking for a magic bullet, I uncovered a lot of interesting suggestions, including adding dry milk powder, egg whites, and sweet, sticky liquids like apple juice or cider to the mix. Sadly, none produced the clusters of my dreams.

If an additional ingredient couldn't help create the substantial chunks I sought, how about adjusting my technique? I'd been reaching into the oven to repeatedly stir the granola as it baked, so I decided to try skipping this step. To make sure that the cereal wouldn't burn in the absence of stirring, I dropped the oven temperature to 325 degrees and extended the cooking time to 45 minutes. Sure enough, some olive-size pieces did form in a no-stir sample—but I wanted more (and larger) chunks. For my next try, I used a spatula to press the hot granola firmly into the pan as soon as it emerged from the oven so that the cooling syrup would bind the solids together as it hardened. This worked, but only to a point. Could I take this idea to the next level?

Since the raw granola mixture was so sticky with syrup and oil, I wondered if muscling it into a tight, compact layer in the pan before baking would yield larger nuggets. I gave it a try, happily finding that when I pulled the cereal from the oven, it remained in a single sheet as it cooled. Now the end product was more of a granola "bark," which was ideal, since I could break it into clumps of any size. Not only had I finally achieved hefty—yet still readily breakable—chunks, but as an added boon, this granola was now hands-off, aside from my having to rotate the pan halfway through baking.

All that my chunky granola needed now was sweet bits of dried fruit. I tested a variety of choices—raisins, apple, mango, pineapple, cranberries, and pear—finding that they all either burned or turned leathery when baked with the other ingredients. To rectify this, I tried plumping the fruit in water or coating it with oil to help prevent moisture loss. And yet time and time again, it emerged from the oven overcooked. It eventually became clear that the best way to incorporate the fruit was to keep it away from heat altogether, only stirring it in once the granola was cool.

My simple recipe was nearly complete, but I wanted to create a bit more depth. After some tinkering, I found that a healthy dose of vanilla extract (I used a whopping 4 teaspoons) was just the ticket, accenting the maple, nut, and fruit flavors without overwhelming them.

Finally, I developed a few twists on my basic formula by switching the fruit-and-nut pairings and accenting them with flavor boosters like coconut, citrus zest, and warm spices. Forget the store-bought stuff. Home is where you'll find the holy grail of granola: big, satisfying clusters and moist, chewy fruit.

—ADAM RIED, *Cook's Illustrated*

Almond Granola with Dried Fruit

MAKES ABOUT 9 CUPS

Chopping the almonds by hand is best for superior texture and crunch, but you can substitute an equal quantity of slivered or sliced almonds. Use a single type of your favorite dried fruit or a combination. Do not substitute quick oats.

- ⅓ cup maple syrup
- ⅓ cup packed (2⅓ ounces) light brown sugar
- 4 teaspoons vanilla extract
- ½ teaspoon salt
- ½ cup vegetable oil
- 5 cups old-fashioned rolled oats
- 2 cups (10 ounces) whole raw almonds, chopped coarse
- 2 cups (10 ounces) raisins or other dried fruit, chopped

1. Adjust oven rack to upper-middle position and heat oven to 325 degrees. Line rimmed baking sheet with parchment paper.

2. Whisk maple syrup, sugar, vanilla, and salt together in large bowl. Whisk in oil. Fold in oats and almonds until thoroughly coated.

3. Transfer oat mixture to prepared baking sheet and spread across sheet into thin, even layer (about ⅜ inch thick). Using stiff metal spatula, compress oat mixture until very compact. Bake until lightly browned, 40 to 45 minutes, rotating pan halfway through baking. Remove granola from oven and cool on wire rack to room temperature, about 1 hour. Break cooled granola into pieces of desired size. Stir in dried fruit. (Granola can be stored at room temperature for up to 2 weeks.)

VARIATIONS

Hazelnut Granola with Dried Pear

Substitute coarsely chopped, skinned hazelnuts for almonds. Use 2 cups chopped dried pear for dried fruit.

Pecan-Orange Granola with Dried Cranberries

Add 2 tablespoons finely grated orange zest and 2½ teaspoons ground cinnamon to maple syrup mixture in step 2. Substitute coarsely chopped pecans for almonds. Use 2 cups dried cranberries for dried fruit.

Spiced Walnut Granola with Dried Apple

Add 2 teaspoons ground cinnamon, 1½ teaspoons ground ginger, ¾ teaspoon ground allspice, ½ teaspoon ground nutmeg, and ½ teaspoon pepper to maple

NOTES FROM THE TEST KITCHEN

FOR BETTER GRANOLA, ADD FAT

When we tried leaving out the oil in a batch of granola, the resulting cereal was a real flop, the oats having taken on a crisp but overly dry consistency. It turns out that fat is essential for creating a likable crispness.

Here's why: When the water in a viscous liquid sweetener (like the maple syrup in our recipe) evaporates in the heat of the oven, the sugars left behind develop into a thin coating on the oats and nuts. But without any fat, the sugar coating becomes brittle and dry. Only oil can provide a pleasantly crisp coating with a sense of moistness.

KEYS TO CHUNKIER GRANOLA

1. Spread oat mixture on parchment-lined baking sheet. Press it firmly with spatula to create compact layer.

2. Bake granola at 325 degrees for 40 to 45 minutes. Rotate pan halfway through baking but don't stir.

3. Break cooled granola "bark" into pieces as large as you'd like.

GRANOLA GONE WRONG

Most store-bought granola is so bad (and so overpriced), we're surprised anyone ever buys it. Without oil to provide moisture, fat-free versions contain dry, dusty oats. Baked with the other ingredients, dried fruit turns tough and leathery. Loose oats, versus chunks, too readily absorb the milk or yogurt and turn soggy.

syrup mixture in step 2. Substitute coarsely chopped walnuts for almonds. Use 2 cups chopped dried apple for dried fruit.

Tropical Granola with Dried Mango

Reduce vanilla extract to 2 teaspoons and add 1½ teaspoons ground ginger and ¾ teaspoon ground nutmeg to maple syrup mixture in step 2. Substitute coarsely chopped macadamias for almonds and 1½ cups unsweetened shredded coconut for 1 cup oats. Use 2 cups chopped dried mango or pineapple for dried fruit.

MORNING GLORY MUFFINS

SOMETIMES COMPARED TO CARROT CAKE, MORNING glory muffins are the brainchild of 1970s wholesome hippie cooking. The various interpretations of these muffins have one thing in common: They are usually loaded to the brim with carrots, coconut, a multitude of nuts and seeds, fresh and dried fruits, and countless spices. Despite their appearance and wholesome billing, those first morning glory muffins were anything but healthy. In addition to an overabundance of nuts, they were loaded down with a cup or more of vegetable oil. Could I make this tasty treat healthy enough to live up to its original promise?

I started with a version of the original 1970s recipe. In addition to the usual muffin-batter ingredients (flour, sugar, eggs, oil, salt, and leavener), the recipe contained grated carrots and apples, canned crushed pineapple, coconut, walnuts, raisins, and cinnamon. It was a long list of ingredients, and I'd need to tackle them one by one to create a great foolproof, lightened recipe.

I started with the most obvious offender: the oil. Clearly, 1 cup of oil (and the 9 grams of fat per serving that came along with it) was far too much. Many muffin and quick-bread recipes include a significant amount of oil in order to maintain a moist crumb, but since all of the fruit in our muffins would contribute a great deal of moisture anyway, I figured I could cut the oil way back with no ill effects. I began my testing with 8 tablespoons and gradually reduced the amount, tablespoon by tablespoon, until there was a marked loss in texture. I was able to bring down the total amount of oil to a mere 4 tablespoons, but tasters pointed out that the oil wasn't doing much in terms of flavor. Replacing the

oil with melted butter made a huge difference in the right direction.

Yet even with half the fat, my muffins were gummy and wet. I evaluated the moist carrots, apples, and pineapple. I quickly learned that I couldn't cut back on the carrots without losing the carrot flavor entirely, so I decided to focus on the pineapple and apple. Instead of reducing the total amounts used (after all, I wanted as much healthy fruit as possible), I drained the fruits in a fine-mesh strainer, then pressed out and discarded the juice before mixing the fruit into the batter. As I had hoped, this method produced moist, but not soggy, muffins. But the missing fruit juice also meant missing fruit flavor.

When we make sauces and dressings in the test kitchen, we often boil down fruit juices to create a flavorful substitute for oil. This thickened liquid was exactly what the muffins needed. For my next test, after pressing the fruit, I boiled the cup of juices down to ¼ cup and added this syrup back to the batter. I also cut back on the sugar by ¼ cup to compensate for the added syrup, which helped to lighten the texture of the muffins and let the fruit flavors come to the forefront.

The moisture level in check, I broached the question of the coconut and walnuts. My working recipe contained ½ cup of nuts and almost a whole cup of coconut. I knew I'd need to cut back to bring the muffins into balance, but how far could I go before the character of the muffins suffered? I scaled the amounts down to ¼ cup of each and stirred the nuts and coconut into the batter. I could barely taste either ingredient, and they became unappealingly soggy in my moist muffins.

To increase their flavor and try to prevent sogginess, I toasted both the coconut and walnuts before adding them to the batter. This step indeed upped their flavor, but once they hit the batter they soaked up moisture and, once again, became soggy. Next I tried sprinkling the coconut and nuts on top of the muffins where they'd stand out and stay dry, but these muffins came out squat and flat-topped. It turned out that the nutty additions were contributing much-needed structure to the batter, and pulling them out made the muffins sink. Perhaps I could find a better way to incorporate them into the flour mixture. For my next batch, I ground the toasted coconut and walnuts finely in the food processor and mixed the meal into the dry ingredients. The result? Deep, nutty flavor and nicely domed muffins with no mealy bits.

MORNING GLORY MUFFINS

At this point, my muffins had great structure and flavor, but they were a bit small since reducing the nuts had removed a great deal of bulk. I decided to take a cue from the muffins' hodgepodge origins and add something new. Chopped dried pineapple did the trick, providing texture and sweetness without any extra moisture that might throw off the now-perfected balance. Finally, I had a moist, fruity, and nutty muffin that was as healthy as its origins claimed.

—KATE WILLIAMS, *America's Test Kitchen Books*

NOTES FROM THE TEST KITCHEN

THE BEST MUFFIN TIN

Six years ago, we tested muffin tins and decided on two must-have features: a nonstick coating and handles for easy gripping. Recently, we decided to revisit muffin tins and chose eight nonstick models that all had extended rims or silicone tabs for gripping. To find the winner, the test kitchen baked more than 300 muffins and cupcakes. While the nonstick coatings ensured easy release of baked goods, some coatings were more effective than others. To gauge durability, we smeared the tins with béchamel and let it harden overnight; the next day, testers scraped and scrubbed. We also shocked the pans by heating them empty to 500 degrees and then plunging them in ice water to see if any would warp. Our winner, the **Wilton Avanti Everglide Metal-Safe Non-Stick Muffin Pan**, gained praise for its wide, extended rims and raised lip, which made the pan easy to handle. Browning was acceptably even, though not stellar— but the price, $13.99, sure is right.

THE BEST GOLDEN RAISINS

When a recipe calls for golden raisins, your choices are surprisingly limited. Only a few brands are available, and they are processed the same way and from the same type of grapes, usually grown in California. A handful of specialty-food stores carry organic golden raisins; the first thing we noticed about the organic raisins was that they tended to be drier and less plump than the national brands. Sampled plain, we liked the organic raisins fine, but not as much as we liked the plump sugariness of conventional golden raisins. Tasters preferred their "malted" and "honeyed" flavors and tender texture. When we compared the raisins in recipes, all brands passed muster, but we preferred **Sun-Maid California Golden Raisins**, which had a pleasing sweet flavor "with just enough tang," and "moist, substantial" texture in the muffins.

Morning Glory Muffins

MAKES 12 MUFFINS

We prefer golden raisins for their color, but you can substitute brown if desired.

- ¼ cup (¾ ounce) sweetened shredded coconut, toasted
- ¼ cup walnuts, toasted
- 2¼ cups (11¼ ounces) all-purpose flour
- ¾ cup (5¼ ounces) sugar
- 1½ teaspoons baking soda
- ½ teaspoon baking powder
- 1 teaspoon ground cinnamon
- ¾ teaspoon salt
- 1 (8-ounce) can crushed pineapple in juice
- 1 Granny Smith apple, peeled, cored, and shredded
- 3 large eggs
- 4 tablespoons unsalted butter, melted and cooled
- 1 teaspoon vanilla extract
- 1½ cups shredded carrots (3 carrots)
- 1 cup golden raisins
- ¾ cup finely chopped dried pineapple

1. Adjust oven rack to middle position and heat oven to 350 degrees. Lightly coat 12-cup muffin tin with vegetable oil spray. Process coconut and walnuts together in food processor until finely ground, about 15 seconds. Add flour, sugar, baking soda, baking powder, cinnamon, and salt and pulse until combined, about 3 pulses. Transfer mixture to large bowl.

2. Pour crushed pineapple into fine-mesh strainer set over liquid measuring cup, then add shredded apple to strainer. Press fruit dry (juice should measure about 1 cup). Transfer juice to small saucepan and bring to boil over medium-high heat. Reduce heat to medium and simmer briskly until juice has reduced to ¼ cup, about 10 minutes. Let cool slightly.

3. Transfer juice to medium bowl and whisk in eggs, melted butter, and vanilla until smooth. Gently fold egg mixture into flour mixture until just combined. Gently fold in pineapple and apple mixture, carrots, raisins, and dried pineapple.

4. Divide batter evenly among muffin cups. Bake until toothpick inserted in center of muffin comes out clean, 24 to 28 minutes, rotating muffin tin halfway through baking. Let muffins cool in tin on wire rack for 10 minutes. Remove muffins from tin and let cool for at least 10 minutes before serving.

CRANBERRY-NUT MUFFINS

MOST RECIPES FOR CRANBERRY-NUT MUFFINS follow the same course as those for any fruit-studded muffin: Just toss a few handfuls of fresh berries and coarsely chopped nuts into the batter and bake. It's an approach that works well enough when using ripe, sweet blueberries or raspberries, but the method is never as successful with cranberries. I find that cranberries' ultra-sour burst can completely overwhelm the delicate flavor of the muffin. As for the nuts, they steam in the moist batter, and their rich, toasty flavor washes away. And then there's the usual problem of uneven distribution. Depending on where you bite, you might get a mouthful of sour berries, a cluster of nuts, or plain old cake. Hankering for a not-so-sweet breakfast pastry, I decided to reinvent the concept. My muffin would feature a moist crumb with plenty of its own flavor, punctuated by zingy but not harsh cranberries and rich-tasting, crunchy nuts.

First things first: creating a muffin that could stand up to the heft of two mix-ins. As with all cake recipes, I could choose either the creaming method or the hand-mixed "quick-bread" method. In this case, only the latter's coarser, sturdier crumb would do. I whisked sugar, eggs, melted butter, and milk in one bowl and flour, baking powder, and salt in another. Then I gently combined the two components with a generous 2 cups of whole cranberries and 1¼ cups of toasted chopped pecans (my preference over more-common walnuts for their richer, sweeter, more buttery flavor) before filling and loading the pan into a 425-degree oven. About 18 minutes later, I had a good-looking batch of muffins—nicely domed and sturdy enough to accommodate the fruit and nuts. But that's all this batch had going for it, as the nuts offered nothing but a little crunch, and the cake's ho-hum flavor was no match for the sour berries.

Brainstorming ways to enliven the muffin base, I gave my spice pantry a quick glance—and then thought better of it. Hits of cinnamon, cloves, or allspice would not add the kind of complexity I had in mind. My next idea was to trade some of the all-purpose flour for a heartier grain like cornmeal, oat flour, or whole wheat flour, but those batches baked up respectively gritty, gummy, and dense.

However, cutting the all-purpose flour with a heftier, more flavorful flour wasn't a bad idea. It then dawned on me that just the right kind of ingredient had been sitting under my nose the whole time: nuts. Nut flours are often used in conjunction with regular flour in nut cakes. Why not muffins? Almond flour might remedy both the blandness of the muffin and the washed-out flavor of the steamed chopped nuts. I knew the trade would mean losing some of the flour's gluten-forming proteins and, in turn, some of the muffins' tall, sturdy structure, but I decided to worry about that later. I processed the toasted pecans into a coarse, sandlike meal, which I then substituted for the regular flour in varying amounts—from just ¼ cup all the way up to 1¼ cups.

The results bore out my suspicion: These batches of muffin batter looked looser than those made with regular flour, and rather than baking up tall and self-contained, they spread out—particularly those with more nut flour. But once my tasters took a bite, I knew the trade-off hadn't been for naught. Despite their now-disappointing structure, these nut-based muffins boasted a richer-tasting, heartier crumb that helped counter the cranberries' acidity. As for how much nut flour to put in the batter, tasters were definitive: the more, the better.

To compensate for the nut flour's inability to form gluten, I committed baker's treason: I overmixed the batter. Though doing so is a surefire way to overdevelop the gluten strands and toughen up the final product, I thought it might be exactly what this batter needed. I even went for a second count by mixing up another batch and trading the remaining all-purpose flour for bread flour, hoping that the latter's protein boost would build up some structure. But instead of the domed tops that I wanted, I got squat, chewy muffins with stunted peaks—two classic signs of overworking. Apparently, I'd been wrong; more gluten was not the answer.

But if a lack of gluten wasn't the problem, what was? I was pondering this question while throwing together another batch of batter when I was called across the kitchen to a colleague's tasting. When I returned 30 minutes later, a curious thing had happened: The batter had thickened up considerably. Intrigued, I baked the muffins and was rewarded with the best batch yet. The batter hadn't spread across the pan, and the muffins were symmetrical, with gently rounded tops. When I described the outcome to our science editor, he explained that, while the rest undoubtedly allowed a little more gluten to form, its main effect was to hydrate the batter. Because this batter contained relatively little flour, there were very few starch granules to absorb the liquid and thicken the batter. Letting the batter rest allowed what starch granules were available to more fully absorb the free water, which, in turn, resulted in batter with more body.

The mystery of the spreading batter solved, it was time to temper the berries' sour punch. Sugar was the obvious go-to, but further sweetening the batter

NOTES FROM THE TEST KITCHEN

RAMPING UP NUTTINESS, TONING DOWN TANG

1. Incorporate homemade toasted pecan "flour," instead of chopped nuts, into batter for muffins with richer, heartier flavor.

2. Process berries with confectioners' sugar to sweeten them and add a dash of salt to mask their bitter edge.

3. Sprinkle classic nut streusel over top of muffins to add rich, buttery crunch and just a hint of sweetness.

THICKENING THIN BATTER

We thought a lack of gluten was making our nut flour–based muffin batter too thin. But when we accidentally let the batter rest when we walked away for 30 minutes, the batter thickened and the muffins baked up nice and tall. After a chat with our science editor, we understood why: As batter rests, a small amount of gluten develops, providing structure. But the main effect is that water more fully hydrates the starches, causing them to swell. This swelling thickens the batter and helps prevent it from spreading during baking.

| JUST MIXED | AFTER 30 MINUTES |

wouldn't help once the whole berries burst and released their sharp juice. The more effective solution was chopping the berries to expose some of their inner flesh—a fix that also helped distribute the fruit more evenly throughout the batter—and tossing them with sugar. I saved myself some knife work and pulsed the berries in the food processor with a spoonful of confectioners' sugar (which dissolves more quickly than granulated sugar). Sugar took the edge off, but tasters complained that the rough-chopped berries were still too tart—even bitter. That latter description triggered an idea: In the past, we've used salt to tame bitterness in eggplant and coffee. Sure enough, adding ¼ teaspoon to the processor bowl along with the berries and sugar did the trick.

These muffins were in good shape, but my tasters requested still more nut flavor. They also wanted to get back the crunchy element that had been eliminated when I switched from chopped to ground pecans. To meet the first request, instead of grinding the nuts by themselves, I processed them with the granulated sugar. The sugar's abrasiveness helped the nuts break down further, releasing more of their flavorful oils and preventing clumping. Recovering some of the crunchy texture was as simple as creating a topping. A sweet streusel mixture of flour, sugar, butter, and chopped pecans worked perfectly. The nuts browned nicely during baking and lent a toasty, buttery touch along with satisfying crunch.

With its crunchy topping and the pop of tart berries against the nutty-tasting crumb, here, finally, was a cranberry muffin I could go nuts for.

—YVONNE RUPERTI, *Cook's Illustrated*

Cranberry-Pecan Muffins

MAKES 12 MUFFINS

If fresh cranberries aren't available, substitute frozen cranberries and microwave until they are partially thawed, 30 to 45 seconds.

STREUSEL TOPPING
- ¼ cup (1¼ ounces) all-purpose flour
- 2 tablespoons packed light brown sugar
- 2 tablespoons granulated sugar
- 2 tablespoons unsalted butter, cut into ½-inch pieces and softened
- ½ cup pecans

MUFFINS

1⅓ cups (6⅔ ounces) all-purpose flour

2 teaspoons baking powder

Salt

1¼ cups (5 ounces) pecans, toasted and cooled

1 cup (7 ounces) plus 1 tablespoon granulated sugar

2 large eggs

6 tablespoons unsalted butter, melted and cooled

½ cup whole milk

8 ounces (2 cups) fresh cranberries

1 tablespoon confectioners' sugar

1. Adjust oven rack to upper-middle position and heat oven to 425 degrees. Spray 12-cup muffin tin with vegetable oil spray.

2. FOR THE STREUSEL TOPPING: Pulse flour, brown sugar, granulated sugar, and butter together in food processor until mixture resembles coarse sand, 4 to 5 pulses. Add pecans and pulse until mixture forms small clumps, 4 to 5 pulses. Transfer to small bowl; set aside.

3. FOR THE MUFFINS: Whisk flour, baking powder, and ¾ teaspoon salt together in bowl; set aside.

4. Process toasted pecans and granulated sugar together until mixture resembles coarse sand, 10 to 15 seconds. Transfer to large bowl and whisk in eggs, melted butter, and milk until combined. Whisk flour mixture into egg mixture until just moistened and no streaks of flour remain. Set batter aside for 30 minutes to thicken.

5. Pulse cranberries, confectioners' sugar, and ¼ teaspoon salt together in food processor until very coarsely chopped, 4 to 5 pulses. Using rubber spatula, fold cranberries into batter. Divide batter equally among prepared muffin cups (batter should completely fill cups and mound slightly). Evenly sprinkle streusel topping over muffins, gently pressing into batter to adhere.

6. Bake until muffin tops are golden and just firm, 17 to 18 minutes, rotating muffin tin halfway through baking. Let muffins cool in tin on wire rack for 10 minutes. Remove muffins from tin and let cool for at least 10 minutes before serving.

CINNAMON BABKA

THE ROOTS OF THE TRADITIONAL JEWISH BREAD known as babka (a diminutive of *baba*, the Polish word for grandmother) are planted firmly in Eastern Europe. Over there, it was a round yeast bread reserved for holidays. But after immigrants brought the bread to America—specifically the New York City area—it gradually morphed into a loaf-shaped coffee cake served year-round. Popular in both Jewish and other bakeries, babka also came to accommodate different fillings, such as chocolate or jam. But across time and geography, the defining characteristics of the classic version have remained constant: a moist, rich yeasted bread layered with sweet, gooey cinnamon-sugar filling.

Unfortunately, if you don't live within striking distance of New York City, it's hard to get your hands on really great babka. With no Jewish grandmother to bake me treats, I was tired of mail-ordering babka from New York bakeries, so I decided to devise a foolproof recipe to use in my own kitchen.

I started by baking four of the most promising of the wildly varying recipes I'd found. The babkas I wound up with ran the gamut from lean and bready (like cinnamon bread) to too rich and inundated with oozing filling (like too-indulgent cinnamon buns). But at least I had zeroed in on what I was looking for: a bread that was moist, rich, and tender but also sturdy enough to support lots of layers of filling. The filling should be sweet and gooey but not so abundant that it oozed out of the bread. And most important of all, the filling should swirl in layer after layer throughout the bread.

I started by searching for the right dough. From those initial tests, I had selected brioche-style dough (a yeasted dough made with butter, eggs, sugar, and milk) as the best model. But once I introduced the standard filling (a generous amount of brown sugar, cinnamon, and melted butter), the bottom layers of dough got weighed down, and the loaf emerged from the oven with a huge gap at the bottom. I backed off on the butter by a couple of tablespoons, but if I removed more than that, the dough seemed too lean to qualify as babka. To increase its richness without adding too much liquid, I substituted two egg yolks for the whole egg and injected just a splash more milk. This mimicked the tenderness of the lost butter without compromising the structure of the dough.

Next, I needed to plug the leak. The filling was pooling in the bottom of the pan, causing the dough to steam

CINNAMON BABKA

instead of bake and leaving me with huge pockets of filling interspersed with chunks of plain bread. The simple jelly roll–style shaping method didn't integrate the filling very well. After a long phone call to the very helpful folks at Green's, a Brooklyn bakery famous for its babka, I decided to try what they described as the traditional babka approach; though more labor-intensive than the jelly roll technique, it'd be worth it if it worked. The key concept is to roll out the dough super-thin. Next, the rectangle gets rolled up, creating a much longer and skinnier jelly roll, which is then folded in half lengthwise, given a couple of twists, and deposited in the loaf pan.

This traditional shaping technique was a challenge with a tender dough and slippery filling. I struggled with it until I realized that I could make my work a lot easier by chilling the dough before handling it. This made the new technique well worth the extra time and effort, since it almost quadrupled the number of layers in my babka, ensuring cinnamony goodness in every bite. A perfectionist, I went so far as to reserve a small amount of filling for the fold in the roll (where dough meets dough) to ensure cinnamon in the center of the babka.

But despite all the folds and undulations, the filling still sank some in the oven, leaving the top layers thin and wimpy and tasters fighting over the delicious gooey bottom. I'd need to thicken the filling to get it to stay put during baking. To do so, some recipes suggest introducing ground nuts or dried fruit like raisins or currants, but since I didn't want to alter the pure cinnamon-sugar filling, I chose additional flour as the best course of action. The extra starch bound the filling nicely but also left an unpleasantly pasty aftertaste. I could get away with ¼ cup of flour without my tasters noticing, but that alone wasn't enough to do the job of thickening.

A few chocolate babka recipes call for a layer of whipped egg whites in the filling. My first attempt to borrow this technique for my cinnamon babka resulted in some sadly deflated egg whites once I'd plopped on the heavy, flour-thickened streusel filling. However, the filling did stay put, so I knew I was on the right track. The second time, I didn't bother with whipping the egg white to peaks; instead, I just mixed it in with the other filling ingredients. Easy to spread, this filling stayed evenly distributed throughout the babka.

The loaf was beautiful. The aroma in the kitchen was heavenly, and the babka tasted so good, we practically inhaled it. My mail-order days were behind me.

—ERIKA BRUCE, *Cook's Country*

Cinnamon Babka
SERVES 8

Once you've added the butter in step 3, if the dough still sticks to the sides of the bowl after five minutes of mixing, add 2 to 4 tablespoons extra flour. The test kitchen's favorite loaf pan measures 8½ by 4½ inches; if you use a standard 9 by 5-inch loaf pan, start checking the babka for doneness after 40 minutes.

FILLING
- 1 cup packed (7 ounces) light brown sugar
- ¼ cup (1¼ ounces) all-purpose flour
- 2 tablespoons unsalted butter, melted and cooled
- 1 large egg white
- 2 teaspoons ground cinnamon
- ⅛ teaspoon salt

DOUGH
- ½ cup whole milk, heated to 110 degrees
- 1 large egg plus 2 large yolks
- 1 teaspoon vanilla extract
- 2 cups (10 ounces) all-purpose flour
- ¼ cup (1¾ ounces) sugar
- 1½ teaspoons instant or rapid-rise yeast
- ½ teaspoon salt
- 8 tablespoons unsalted butter, cut into 8 pieces and softened

1. FOR THE FILLING: Combine all ingredients in medium bowl. Set aside 1 tablespoon filling.

2. FOR THE DOUGH: Grease large bowl. Whisk milk, egg yolks, and vanilla together in 1-cup liquid measuring cup.

3. Using stand mixer fitted with dough hook, mix flour, sugar, yeast, and salt on low speed until combined. Slowly add milk mixture and mix until dough comes together, about 3 minutes. Increase speed to medium-low and add butter, 1 piece at a time, until incorporated, about 1 minute. Continue to mix until dough is smooth and comes away from sides of bowl, 10 to 12 minutes. Transfer dough to prepared bowl, cover with plastic wrap, and let rise at room temperature until risen slightly, about 1 hour. Place bowl in refrigerator until dough is firm and has doubled in size, at least 1 hour.

4. Line 8½ by 4½-inch loaf pan with parchment paper, allowing excess to hang over edges. Punch down dough on lightly floured counter. Roll out dough to 20 by 14-inch rectangle. Spread all but 1 tablespoon reserved filling over dough, leaving ½-inch border

SHAPING CINNAMON BABKA

1. Roll out chilled dough into 20 by 14-inch rectangle and spread all but 1 tablespoon filling over dough, leaving ½-inch border around edges.

2. Starting at short edge, roll filled dough into tight cylinder and pinch to seal seam. Stretch log to 18 inches by gently rolling it back and forth with seam side up.

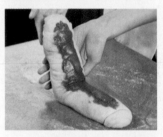

3. Spread remaining 1 tablespoon filling over top of cylinder and fold cylinder on top of itself, pinching ends together to seal.

4. Gently twist folded dough twice to form double figure eight and place seam side down in parchment-lined loaf pan.

THE BABKA GAP

By its very definition, babka is a rich, tender dough. But make it too tender and the dough will collapse under the weight of the cinnamon-sugar filling, leaving large holes in the bread. To add richness yet preserve the loaf's structural integrity, we cut back on the butter and swapped 2 egg yolks for a whole egg.

BAD BABKA
If it's too rich, babka will resemble Swiss cheese.

around edges. Working from short side, roll dough into cylinder and pinch along seam to seal. Position cylinder seam side up and roll back and forth until stretched to 18-inch length. Spread reserved filling over top of cylinder. Fold cylinder on top of itself and pinch ends to seal. Gently twist double cylinder twice to form double figure eight. Place shaped dough seam side down in prepared pan, cover loosely with plastic, and let rise at room temperature until doubled in size, about 1 hour.

5. Adjust oven rack to middle position and heat oven to 350 degrees. Lightly beat whole egg in bowl. Discard plastic and brush loaf with beaten egg. Bake until deep golden brown and loaf registers 190 degrees, about 45 minutes. Let cool in pan on wire rack for 20 minutes. Remove loaf from pan and cool completely, about 2 hours. Serve.

CINNAMON SWIRL BREAD

CINNAMON SWIRL BREAD ALWAYS SOUNDS APPEALING in theory, but I've been disappointed every time I've tried it. My ideal is a fluffy, delicate crumb studded with plump raisins and laced with a substantial swirl of gooey cinnamon sugar. But most versions are either austere white sandwich loaves rolled up with a bare sprinkle of cinnamon and sugar or overly sweet breads ruined by gobs of filling oozing from the cracks.

When I finally stumbled upon the solution, it was in the unlikeliest of places: Tokyo's Narita airport. I took a bite of a lightly toasted slice of swirl bread from a bakery kiosk and realized I'd found it. Beneath the lightly crisp exterior, the crumb was so springy, moist, and feathery it could be pulled into cotton candy–like strands. I vowed to replicate this style of wispy, milky-sweet Japanese white sandwich bread, called *shokupan*, at home.

I decided to focus first on the bread, but when English recipes for shokupan proved hard to come by, I sought out an expert: Takeo Sakan, head baker at Boston's acclaimed Japonaise Bakery & Café. To help me better understand how shokupan is made, we compared it with American sandwich bread. The two styles share a number of the same ingredients: flour, yeast, salt, water, milk, sugar, and butter. Shokupan, however, boasts considerably more fat (roughly twice as much butter, plus an egg) and more sugar, which accounts for its particularly tender crumb. Shokupan also contains more gluten—the network of proteins that builds structure and allows bread to rise high and retain its springy crumb. To develop that gluten, Sakan uses a combination of thorough kneading and specialty high-gluten flour, which contains even more protein than the bread flour used in most American sandwich breads. It's that marriage of particularly strong gluten and tenderizers like fat and sugar that produces shokupan's airy yet sturdy crumb.

I returned to the test kitchen to mix up a batch, with one change: Since the high-gluten flour he used requires mail-ordering, I'd have to stick with bread flour and worry about making up for the lack of gluten later. Otherwise, I followed his lead: I mixed the flour with yeast, sugar, and nonfat dry milk powder; added water plus an egg and 8 tablespoons of softened butter for richness; and kneaded the mixture in a stand mixer until it formed a cohesive mass. After letting the dough rest for about 20 minutes, I kneaded it for a longer stretch—about 10 minutes—until it was smoother and more workable. I mixed in a generous handful of golden raisins and let the dough proof in a turned-off oven. Because warm, humid air stimulates yeast activity and speeds rising time, I placed a pan of boiling water on the oven floor. Forty-five minutes later, I patted the dough into a rectangle, sprinkled a simple cinnamon-sugar filling over the surface, rolled it into a spiral, fitted it into a loaf pan, and let it proof for another 45 minutes, until the dough had doubled in size. I brushed the dough with an egg wash for shine and baked it until the crust was dark brown.

But while the color of the bread was handsome, the crumb itself was far from ideal. Among other problems, it didn't have the hallmark lift and airy texture. The reason, no doubt, had a lot to do with the lower-protein bread flour. I had one solution in mind to strengthen the dough: Work in more air. Not only does oxygen provide lift to baked goods, but it also drives gluten development. To add oxygen, I tried introducing two sets of "folds" into the process. By deflating the dough and folding it back onto itself several times, I incorporated more air into it, encouraging the bread to expand and rise more. I also increased the kneading time to about 15 minutes, rendering it even more elastic and better able to trap gas for a taller rise. This bread baked up noticeably higher, but still not as tall as the shokupan loaves I'd tasted.

I scanned my ingredient list for other ways to boost the bread's height. When I got to the butter, I paused.

MAKING A STICKY FILLING THAT STICKS

The cinnamon-sugar swirl isn't just for flavor; it needs to function as an adhesive between the pieces of dough. Here's how we altered the typical formula.

POWDERED SUGAR
Confectioners' sugar contains cornstarch that thickens the filling.

LOTS OF CINNAMON
Cinnamon contains starches that thicken the filling and help it form a sticky paste.

SPRITZ OF WATER
Lightly misting the dough before and after adding the filling creates extra adhesiveness.

I knew that incorporating it into the dough at the outset was coating the flour proteins with fat, preventing them from bonding and inhibiting gluten formation. A better method, I reasoned, would be to knead the dough almost completely to develop gluten and then work in some softened butter during the final minutes of kneading. But the soft butter pieces smeared into the dough rather than incorporating evenly. My quick fix: Tossing the pieces with a tablespoon of flour before letting them soften helped the dough grip the butter. The resulting loaf was gorgeously lofty—by far the best bread yet. It would serve as the perfect counterpoint for my next challenge: a gooey cinnamon-sugar swirl.

I thought perfecting a thick cinnamon swirl would be the easy part of making this bread—until my first attempt. Halfway through baking, the bread sprang a leak and spewed molten cinnamon sugar from its crevices. When I sliced it open, I found a mangled mix of dense bread, huge gaps, and puddles of cinnamon filling.

Our science editor explained: All of these issues boil down to the fact that the sugary filling and the bread don't easily bind. During proofing, the gas produced by the yeast leaks from the dough into the spiral, and because it has no place to go, the gas pushes apart the layers of dough. During baking, steam also fills the gaps. All that pressure compresses the dough, allowing the cinnamon-sugar filling to flow to the bottom of the bread and leak through its seam. What I needed was a way to encourage binding between the swirl and the dough. I added a slew of different ingredients to the filling to see if any would help it adhere: flour, eggs, pectin, corn syrup, pureed raisins, cooked caramel, crushed cinnamon cereal, and ground-up nuts. But the loaves still baked up with comically large gaps.

That's when I realized that adding extra ingredients to the swirl might not be as effective as examining the ingredients that were already in it: ½ cup of granulated sugar and 1 tablespoon of ground cinnamon per loaf. I baked more loaves, this time trading the granulated stuff for confectioners' sugar as well as tripling the cinnamon. The loaves showed significant improvement. The powdery confectioners' sugar absorbed water from the dough, dissolving and forming a sticky paste, which was thickened by the cornstarch in the confectioners' sugar and the carbohydrates in the cinnamon. The thickened paste didn't pool at the bottom of the bread and was sticky enough to help hold the layers together as the bread expanded during proofing.

This was by far the best loaf I had made to date, but unfortunately, I still got the occasional spewing leak or gaping hole. Having already fiddled with the filling ingredients, I got to thinking about the swirl itself. A spiral was attractive but impractical, and it made me wonder if there wasn't a better way to shape the dough. I tested a multitude of different shaping techniques that created crevices in the dough that would allow the problematic gas to escape, including those for monkey bread and braids. The easiest was an attractive weave called a Russian braid, which cut down on gapping and leaking considerably. To make it, I sprinkled the filling over the dough, rolled it into a cylinder, and then halved it lengthwise to reveal the striations of dough and filling. I then stretched these two halves slightly and twisted them together to form a tight loaf. This way, any gas that would have been trapped between the layers was able to escape, and the bread baked up tightly seamed and beautifully marbled. One last tweak: To prevent any risk of burning the raisins or

the bread's sugary surface, I pushed the exposed pieces of fruit into the braid and tented the loaves with aluminum foil halfway through baking.

Finally I'd come up with the bread I'd envisioned: a burnished crust encasing airy, slightly sweet bread streaked with thick lines of gooey cinnamon filling.

—DAN SOUZA, *Cook's Illustrated*

Cinnamon Swirl Bread

MAKES 2 LOAVES

To achieve the proper dough consistency, make sure to weigh your ingredients. The dough will appear very wet and sticky until the final few minutes of kneading; do not be tempted to add supplemental flour.

DOUGH

- 8 tablespoons unsalted butter
- 3¾ cups (20⅔ ounces) bread flour
- ¾ cup (2¾ ounces) nonfat dry milk powder
- ⅓ cup (2⅓ ounces) granulated sugar
- 1 tablespoon instant or rapid-rise yeast
- 1½ cups (12 ounces) water, heated to 110 degrees
- 1 large egg, lightly beaten
- 1½ teaspoons salt
- 1½ cups (7½ ounces) golden raisins

FILLING

- 1 cup (4 ounces) confectioners' sugar
- 3 tablespoons ground cinnamon
- 1 teaspoon vanilla extract
- ½ teaspoon salt

- 1 large egg, lightly beaten with pinch salt

1. FOR THE DOUGH: Cut butter into 32 pieces and toss with 1 tablespoon flour; set aside to soften while mixing dough. Whisk remaining flour, milk powder, sugar, and yeast together in bowl of stand mixer fitted with dough hook. Add water and egg and mix on medium-low speed until cohesive mass forms, about 2 minutes, scraping down bowl if necessary. Cover mixing bowl with plastic wrap and let stand for 20 minutes.

2. Adjust oven rack to middle position and place loaf or cake pan on bottom of oven. Grease large bowl. Remove plastic from mixer bowl, add salt, and mix on medium-low speed until dough is smooth and elastic and clears sides of bowl, 7 to 15 minutes. With mixer running, add butter a few pieces at a time, and continue to knead until butter is fully incorporated and dough is smooth and elastic and clears sides of bowl, 3 to 5 minutes longer. Add raisins and mix until incorporated, 30 to 60 seconds. Transfer dough to prepared bowl and, using bowl scraper or rubber spatula, fold dough over itself by gently lifting and folding edge of dough toward middle. Turn bowl 90 degrees; fold again. Turn bowl and fold dough 6 more times (total of 8 folds). Cover tightly with plastic and transfer to middle rack of oven. Pour 3 cups boiling water into loaf pan in oven, close oven door, and allow dough to rise for 45 minutes.

3. Remove bowl from oven and gently press down on center of dough to deflate. Repeat folding (making total of 8 folds), re-cover, and return to oven until doubled in volume, about 45 minutes.

4. FOR THE FILLING: Whisk all ingredients together in bowl until well combined; set aside.

5. Grease two 8½ by 4½-inch loaf pans. Transfer dough to lightly floured counter and divide into 2 pieces. Working with 1 piece of dough, pat into rough 6 by 11-inch rectangle. With short side facing you, fold long sides in like a business letter to form 3 by 11-inch rectangle. Roll dough away from you into ball. Dust ball with flour and flatten with rolling pin into 7 by 18-inch rectangle with even ¼-inch thickness. Using spray bottle, spray dough lightly with water. Sprinkle half of filling mixture evenly over dough, leaving ¼-inch border on sides and ¾-inch border on top and bottom; spray filling lightly with water. (Filling should be speckled with water over entire surface.) With short side facing you, roll dough away from you into firm cylinder. Turn loaf seam side up and pinch closed; pinch ends closed. Dust loaf lightly on all sides with flour and let rest for 10 minutes. Repeat with second ball of dough and remaining filling.

6. Working with 1 loaf at a time, use bench scraper to cut loaf in half lengthwise; turn halves so cut sides are facing up. Gently stretch each half into 14-inch length. Line up pieces of dough and pinch 2 ends of strips together. Take piece on left and lay over piece on right. Repeat, keeping cut side up, until pieces of dough are tightly twisted. Pinch ends together. Transfer loaf, cut side up, to prepared loaf pan; push any exposed raisins into seams of braid. Repeat with second loaf. Cover loaves loosely with plastic, return to oven, and allow to rise for 45 minutes. Remove loaves and water pan from oven; heat oven to 350 degrees. Allow loaves to rise at room temperature until almost doubled in size, about

45 minutes (tops of loaves should rise about 1 inch over lip of pans).

7. Brush loaves with egg mixture. Bake until crust is well browned, about 25 minutes. Reduce oven temperature to 325 degrees, tent loaves with aluminum foil, and continue to bake until internal temperature registers 200 degrees, 15 to 25 minutes longer.

8. Transfer pans to wire rack and let cool for 5 minutes. Remove loaves from pans, return to rack, and cool to room temperature before slicing, about 2 hours.

NOTES FROM THE TEST KITCHEN

WEAVING CINNAMON SWIRL BREAD, RUSSIAN-STYLE

The benefit of a Russian braid—other than good looks—is that it solves the gapping that plagues swirl breads. The twisted shape tightly seals the pieces of dough together while providing plenty of escape routes for the excess air that would otherwise compress the dough and create tunnels in the loaf.

1. Using bench scraper or sharp chef's knife, cut filled dough in half lengthwise. Turn halves so cut sides are facing up.

2. With cut sides up, stretch each half into 14-inch length.

3. Pinch 2 ends of strips together. To braid, take left strip of dough and lay it over right strip of dough.

4. Repeat braiding, keeping cut sides face up, until pieces are tightly twisted. Pinch ends together.

CROISSANTS

I CAN THINK OF TWO REASONS WHY ALMOST nobody makes croissants. First, most folks buy them from a bakery, or even a coffee shop or supermarket. Second, the process is long and daunting. It pairs the challenge of preparing a laminated pastry (one composed of many layers of fat and dough) with the potential unpredictability of yeast. Even if you follow a recipe to the letter, the results aren't always what they should be: a deep golden brown, shatteringly crisp surface that gives way to delicate layers of buttery and rich yet light pastry within.

I can also think of two reasons why making your own croissants is absolutely worth the effort. For starters, most commercial croissants are squat, dense, or just plain bland. Plus, there's nothing quite as satisfying as pulling off this feat yourself—from folding and shaping the dough, to filling your kitchen with the scent of warm pastry, to watching your brunch guests swoon.

That said, achieving consistent results is difficult. Sometimes the croissants collapse during baking and turn dense, losing their signature layers; other times the butter leaks out onto the baking sheet, yielding thick-crusted specimens that have essentially fried in their own fat. And then there's the sheer force required to muscle the gluten-heavy dough into submission. It would be a challenge, but I decided to get into the kitchen and learn where I was veering off course.

Before homing in on specific problems, I reviewed the basics of laminated pastry. Flour, milk, yeast, a bit of melted butter, sugar, and salt are mixed together, rested briefly, rolled into a rectangle, and refrigerated. The dough is then rolled into a larger rectangle and wrapped around a large block of cold butter, and the dough-butter package (known as a plaque) is rolled into a long rectangle. This is where the trademark layering happens: The plaque is folded into thirds, yielding layers of dough separated by layers of butter. This rolling and folding process (called a "turn") is repeated up to five times, tripling the number of layers with each turn. Finally, the plaque is rolled out again, cut into triangles, shaped into crescents, left to rise, brushed with egg wash, and baked.

To get started, I rounded up several recipes and found that the techniques—specifically the number of turns—varied widely: anywhere from two (which makes nine layers of dough) to a biceps-punishing five (which would theoretically produce 243 layers). Figuring out the ideal number of turns would be an important first step, as the turning process has a twofold effect: It not only creates layers in the dough but also develops gluten (the elastic protein that is formed when the flour is moistened), which causes the dough to stubbornly bounce back and resist rolling. Strong dough is no problem for bake shops, which use machines called sheeters (similar to huge pasta machines) to roll out the plaque. But for my at-home recipe, I'd need a dough that I could manage with just my hands.

To my great relief, too many turns ended up being detrimental. As the layers of fat became thinner, they were more easily absorbed into the dough, eventually yielding a pastry more akin to brioche—rich and tender, but with a homogeneous, bready crumb. Three turns seemed to be the magic number for producing the most distinct layers.

But rolling and folding the dough three times was still hard. Knowing that the protein content of the flour was directly affecting the gluten development, I made three new batches with different types (and brands) of flour: one with moderate-protein (10.5 percent) Gold Medal all-purpose flour, another with higher-protein (11.7 percent) all-purpose flour from King Arthur, and a final sample with high-protein (14 percent) bread flour. As I expected, the higher the protein, the more gluten developed, and the more difficult the plaque was to roll out. Still, the test was informative. The bread-flour croissants were the best I'd ever made: tall, crisp, and filled with airy spirals of buttery pastry.

It turns out that gluten doesn't just make a dough more elastic; it also makes it more resistant to tearing during rolling, rising, and baking (when it expands), and strong enough to maintain the thin sheets necessary for distinct layering. But since my hands were blistered from rolling out this sturdy bread-flour dough, I decided to compromise with the higher-protein all-purpose flour, hoping that I could find another way to make the dough more compliant.

That left me with the butter. From the start I'd defaulted to Land O'Lakes (about 81 percent butterfat), but some recipes called for European-style butter, the butterfat content of which typically starts at around 83 percent and goes up as high as 86 percent. Another point I noted: Recipes using standard butter called for kneading it with a bit of flour before shaping it into a block, while in those that specified European-style

CROISSANTS

butter no flour was added to the block. Not sure what effect the flour or the extra fat might have, I made three batches of croissants using European-style butter, standard butter mixed with flour, and unadulterated standard butter, respectively.

The differences were remarkable. When I tried shaping the unfloured standard butter, it broke into pieces, and the resulting dough baked up heavy. Flouring the standard butter helped, and the croissants were nicely layered—but didn't compare with those made with European-style butter. The higher-fat dough not only proved easier to work with but also boasted superior layering and ultra-rich flavor.

I did some homework and learned two reasons why more butterfat made such a difference. First, butter with less fat contains more water. Butter with 81 percent fat, for example, contains about 15 percent water, while butter with 83 percent fat has about 13 percent. This variance may sound small, but in fact the lower-fat butter has roughly 15 percent more water than the higher-fat butter—a difference significant enough that the extra water in the regular-butter dough was gluing the layers together, leading to a dense crumb. It also explained the purpose of adding flour to the standard butter: It soaked up the extra moisture.

Second, higher-fat butter remains solid over a wider temperature range, meaning that it's more pliable when cold and also holds its shape better as it warms up. This is advantageous since the butter for laminated dough must be firm to function as a barrier between distinct layers of dough and, therefore, must remain solid as the dough is handled.

I'd made great progress but had one more problem to iron out. For consistently tall, flaky results, I needed the butter and dough to be at exactly the same degree of malleability during rolling. I had been refrigerating the plaque between turns, but this resulted in butter that was firmer than the dough and therefore prone to breaking (and sticking where the butter was absent). Conversely, if I left the plaque at room temperature, the butter became softer than the dough and leaked out during rolling. The secret would be ensuring that these two markedly different components had the same puttylike texture. But how?

It wasn't until I contacted a local baker, Christy Timon of Clear Flour Bread, in Brookline, Massachusetts, that I came upon the solution: freezing the dough. As Timon demonstrated, super-chilling the butter-dough square

for 30 minutes before rolling firms the dough to the consistency of the butter without appreciably altering the texture of the butter. Together with the higher-protein all-purpose flour and the European-style butter, this freezer technique added up to a hat trick of discoveries that led to layering so distinct that it was visible even in the raw dough.

Confident that I had finally mastered croissants, I prepared a final batch. When I removed the bronzed beauties from the oven, the layers that had been subtly suggested in the raw dough had bloomed into crisp, delicate tiers. My colleagues declared them a triumph, regretting only that the testing had come to an end.

—ANDREA GEARY, *Cook's Illustrated*

Croissants

MAKES 22

Twelve croissants are baked first; the remaining 10 can be frozen. These croissants take at least 10 hours to make from start to finish, but the process can be spread over 2 days. European-style cultured butters have a higher butterfat content, which makes it easier to fold them into the dough. Any brand of all-purpose flour will produce acceptable croissants, but we recommend using King Arthur All-Purpose Flour, which has a slightly higher protein content. Do not attempt to make these croissants in a room that is warmer than 80 degrees. If at any time during rolling the dough retracts, fold it loosely, wrap it, and return it to the freezer to rest for 10 to 15 minutes.

3	tablespoons unsalted butter plus 24 tablespoons (3 sticks) unsalted European-style butter, very cold
1¾	cups whole milk
4	teaspoons instant or rapid-rise yeast
4¼	cups (21¼ ounces) all-purpose flour
¼	cup (1¾ ounces) sugar
	Salt
1	large egg
1	teaspoon cold water

1. Melt 3 tablespoons butter in medium saucepan over low heat. Remove from heat and immediately stir in milk (temperature should be lower than 90 degrees). Whisk in yeast; transfer milk mixture to bowl of stand mixer. Add flour, sugar, and 2 teaspoons salt. Using dough hook, knead on low speed until cohesive dough

MAKING THE BUTTER BLOCK

1. Fold 24-inch length of parchment in half to create 12-inch rectangle. Fold over 3 open sides of rectangle to form 8-inch enclosed square. Crease folds firmly.

2. Using rolling pin, beat butter until it is just pliable, then fold butter in on itself using bench scraper. Beat butter into rough 6-inch square.

3. Unfold envelope and, using bench scraper, transfer butter to parchment, refolding at creases to enclose.

4. Turn packet over; gently roll butter to fill parchment square, taking care to achieve even thickness.

LAMINATING THE DOUGH

1. Roll dough into 17 by 8-inch rectangle. Unwrap butter and place in center of dough so that edges of butter and dough are flush at top and bottom.

2. Fold two sides of dough over butter so they meet in center of butter square. Press seam together with fingertips.

3. Using rolling pin, press firmly on each open end of packet. Roll dough out lengthwise until it is 24 inches long and 8 inches wide.

4. Starting at bottom of dough, fold it into thirds. Turn dough 90 degrees; roll and fold again. Place it on baking sheet, wrap with plastic wrap, and return to freezer for 30 minutes. Roll and fold into thirds one more time.

THE BEST BUTTERS

At one time, cultured butter (also known as European butter) was hard to come by. Not anymore—many supermarket shelves now hold more brands of this pricier condiment than the sweet-cream stuff. We wanted to know if we should be spending more on our butter and sampled 10 butters, seven cultured and three sweet cream, spread on crackers and baked into French butter cookies.

While sweet-cream butters are quickly and cheaply mass-produced by churning cream that has undergone little or no storage, cultured butters are made more slowly, with cream that's allowed to ripen for a few days to develop flavor and then inoculated with bacterial cultures before churning. Given the time and effort that go into their production, we weren't surprised when cultured butters took three of the top four spots. But we were surprised that the second-place butter was of the sweet-cream variety.

Our favorite butter, **Plugrá European-Style Unsalted Butter**, offered everything we look for in a good butter: flavor that's sweet and creamy and overlaid with a complex, slightly sour tang. But at $10 a pound, it's a pricey topping for toast. For a Best Buy, we liked **Land O'Lakes Unsalted Sweet Butter**, which cost about half the price and was praised for its "fresh-cream," "clean dairy flavor." As a sweet-cream butter, how did it manage to do so well? Land O'Lakes butter comes wrapped in parchment paper that's been treated with a patented coating called FlavorProtect, which helps lock in the butter's clean flavor and keep intruding odors out. (See page 294 for more information about our testing results.)

SHAPING THE CROISSANTS

1. Transfer dough from freezer to lightly floured counter and roll it into 18 by 16-inch rectangle. (If it begins to retract, fold it into thirds, wrap it, and return it to freezer for 10 to 15 minutes.) Fold upper half of dough over lower half.

6. Grasp triangle by 2 corners on either side of slit and stretch gently, then grasp point and stretch.

2. Using ruler, mark dough at 3-inch intervals along bottom edge. Move ruler to top of dough, measure in 1½ inches from left, then use this mark to measure out 3-inch intervals.

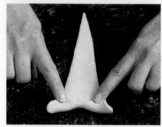

7. Place triangle on counter so point is facing toward you. Fold both sides of slit down.

3. Using sharp pizza wheel or knife, cut dough into triangles from mark to mark; discard any scraps.

8. Positioning your palms on folds, roll partway toward point.

4. You should have 12 single triangles and 5 double triangles. Unfold double triangles and cut in half to form 10 single triangles (making 22 triangles in all).

9. Gently grasp point with one hand and stretch again. Resume rolling, tucking point underneath.

5. Cut ½-inch slit in center of short end of triangle. If dough begins to soften, return it to freezer for 10 minutes.

10. Curve ends gently toward one another to form crescent shape. Repeat with remaining triangles.

forms, 2 to 3 minutes. Increase speed to medium-low and knead for 1 minute. Remove bowl from mixer and cover bowl with plastic wrap. Let dough rest at room temperature for 30 minutes.

2. Transfer dough to parchment paper–lined rimmed baking sheet and shape into 10 by 7-inch rectangle about 1 inch thick. Wrap tightly with plastic and refrigerate for 2 hours.

3. FOR THE BUTTER BLOCK: While dough chills, fold 24-inch length of parchment in half to create 12-inch rectangle. Fold over 3 open sides of rectangle to form 8-inch square with enclosed sides. Crease folds firmly. Place 24 tablespoons cold butter directly on counter and beat with rolling pin for about 60 seconds until butter is just pliable, but not warm, folding butter in on itself using bench scraper. Beat into rough 6-inch square. Unfold parchment envelope. Using bench scraper, transfer butter to center of parchment square, refolding at creases to enclose. Turn packet over so that flaps are underneath and gently roll butter packet until butter fills parchment square, taking care to achieve even thickness. Refrigerate for at least 45 minutes.

4. TO LAMINATE THE DOUGH: Transfer dough to freezer. After 30 minutes, transfer dough to lightly floured counter and roll into 17 by 8-inch rectangle with long side of rectangle parallel to edge of counter. Unwrap butter and place in center of dough so that butter and dough are flush at top and bottom. Fold 2 sides of dough over butter square so they meet in center. Press seam together with fingertips. With rolling pin, press firmly on each open end of packet. Roll out dough, perpendicular to edge of counter, to rectangle 24 inches long and 8 inches wide. Bring bottom third of dough up, then fold upper third over it, folding like business letter into 8-inch square. Turn dough 90 degrees counterclockwise. Roll out dough again, perpendicular to edge of counter, into 24 by 8-inch rectangle and fold into thirds. Place dough on baking sheet, wrap tightly with plastic, and return to freezer for 30 minutes.

5. Transfer dough to lightly floured counter so that top flap of dough is facing right. Roll once more, perpendicular to edge of counter, into 24 by 8-inch rectangle and fold into thirds. Place dough on baking sheet, wrap tightly with plastic, and refrigerate for 2 hours.

6. TO SHAPE THE CROISSANTS: Transfer dough to freezer. After 30 minutes, transfer to lightly floured counter and roll into 18 by 16-inch rectangle with long side of rectangle parallel to edge of counter. Fold upper half of dough over lower half. Using ruler, mark dough at 3-inch intervals along bottom edge with bench scraper (you should have 5 marks). Move ruler to top of dough, measure in 1½ inches from left, then use this mark to measure out 3-inch intervals (you should have 6 marks). Starting at lower left corner, use pizza wheel or knife to cut dough into triangles from mark to mark. You will have 12 single triangles and 5 double triangles; discard scraps. Unfold double triangles and cut into 10 single triangles (making 22 equal-size triangles in total). If dough begins to soften, return to freezer for 10 minutes.

7. Position 1 triangle on counter. (Keep remaining triangles covered with plastic while shaping.) Cut ½-inch slit in center of short end of triangle. Grasp triangle by 2 corners on either side of slit and stretch gently, then grasp bottom point and stretch. Place triangle on counter so point is facing toward you. Fold both sides of slit down. Positioning palms on folds, roll partway toward point. Gently grasp point again and stretch. To finish, continue to roll, tucking point underneath. Curve ends gently toward one another to create crescent shape. Repeat with remaining triangles.

8. Place 12 croissants on 2 parchment-lined rimmed baking sheets, leaving at least 2½ inches between croissants, 6 croissants per sheet. Loosely wrap baking sheets with plastic, leaving room for croissants to expand. Let stand at room temperature until nearly doubled in size, 2½ to 3 hours. (Shaped croissants can be refrigerated on trays for up to 18 hours. Remove from refrigerator to rise and add at least 30 minutes to rising time.)

9. After croissants have been rising for 2 hours, adjust oven racks to upper-middle and lower-middle positions and heat oven to 425 degrees. In small bowl, whisk together egg, water, and pinch salt. Brush croissants with egg wash using pastry brush. Place croissants in oven and reduce temperature to 400 degrees. Bake for 12 minutes, then switch and rotate baking sheets. Continue to bake until deep golden brown, 8 to 12 minutes longer. Transfer croissants to wire rack and allow to cool until just warm, about 15 minutes. Serve warm or at room temperature.

ENGLISH MUFFIN BREAD

WITH THEIR CHEWY INTERIOR, CRUNCHY CRUST, and craggy, dimpled texture that sops up butter and jam, English muffins are the perfect companion to that first cup of coffee. I wanted a no-fuss recipe that would give me everything good about English muffins without any of the hassles—specifically, the kneading, rolling, cutting, and griddling.

Fortunately, someone had thought of this before me—ergo, English muffin bread. The bread, a type known as "yeasted batter bread," is easy by definition: You scrape the wet, sticky batter directly into a loaf pan (or pans) and let it rise. No kneading or shaping required. To my surprise, I discovered recipes for these loaves that dated all the way back to the turn of the 19th century. Old or new, most were made from flour, milk, salt, sugar, and yeast. In one of the older recipes the flour was heated before it was added. Weird. Another included baking soda. Odd enough, but even stranger was how the soda was incorporated (more on that later). Beyond that, some recipes used milk and others dry milk powder; some called for all-purpose flour and others for bread flour. I'd test every detail in my quest for the easiest, chewiest, most satisfying English muffin bread ever.

I started by baking eight test loaves, following an assortment of recipes. The bread that used baking soda was swirled with nasty-tasting streaks of brown. The others were tasty enough but noticeably short on nooks and crannies; they seemed more like ordinary white bread than like an English muffin. I picked one as my starting point, combining all-purpose flour with yeast, salt, and sugar (to help the bread brown and give the yeast a kick start); pouring in hot milk (110 degrees, the test kitchen standard to activate the yeast); stirring for less than a minute; and leaving the batter to rise. Once it had doubled in size, I scraped it into the loaf pans for a second rise and then baked the loaves. The results were mixed: While the crumb was nice and moist, when I slathered the bread with butter, it lacked the proper porous quality and the characteristic chew.

Fixing the latter was easy: High-gluten bread flour turned the texture satisfyingly chewy. While I was making simple swaps, I wondered which made for a more perfect loaf: milk or dry milk powder. I couldn't tell the difference, so I opted for milk, which is always in my kitchen. Since I wanted larger holes, and more of them, I took a second look at baking soda. Before, following

instructions, I'd mixed it with liquid and added it to the thick batter just before the second rise. It had been impossible to stir in effectively. After more research, I found recipes where the soda was mixed in with the other dry ingredients. That technique yielded loaves that were appropriately coarse and honeycombed.

Earlier, I'd dismissed as bizarre the directions in an old recipe for warming flour. On reflection, might warm flour speed the rise? To see, I heated the flour in the oven. It did shorten the proofing, and I was considering adding the step to my recipe when I realized it'd be simpler to adjust the temperature of the hot milk. Since I mixed the yeast with the other dry ingredients before adding the milk, those combined ingredients would dilute the heat, preventing dangerously hot milk from killing the yeast. I slowly increased the temperature and watched the proofing time melt away. Ultimately, using milk 10 degrees hotter than usual let me cut the first rise in half.

I baked two final loaves, counted the minutes until they cooled, and then toasted a slice. It turned an attractive speckled brown, walked the line between crunch and chew, and soaked up butter like nobody's business. It tasted like the store-bought English muffins we know and love. Only better. Much better.

—SARAH WILSON WITH CHRIS DUDLEY,
Cook's Country

English Muffin Bread
MAKES 2 LOAVES

We prefer bread flour in this recipe for its stronger gluten proteins; do not substitute all-purpose flour.

	Cornmeal
5	cups (27½ ounces) bread flour
4½	teaspoons instant or rapid-rise yeast
1	tablespoon sugar
2	teaspoons salt
1	teaspoon baking soda
2½	cups whole milk, heated to 120 degrees

1. Grease two 8½ by 4½-inch loaf pans and dust with cornmeal. Combine flour, yeast, sugar, salt, and baking soda in large bowl. Stir in hot milk until combined and dough pulls away from sides of bowl, about 1 minute. Cover dough with greased plastic wrap and let rise in warm place for 30 minutes, or until dough is bubbly and has doubled in size.

2. Stir dough and divide between prepared loaf pans, pushing into corners with greased rubber spatula. (Pans should be about two-thirds full.) Cover pans with greased plastic and let dough rise at room temperature until it reaches edge of pans, about 30 minutes. Adjust oven rack to middle position and heat oven to 375 degrees.

3. Discard plastic and transfer pans to oven. Bake until bread is well browned and registers 200 degrees, about 30 minutes, rotating and switching pans halfway through baking. Turn bread out onto wire rack and let cool completely, about 1 hour. Slice, toast, and serve.

HONEY-WHEAT DINNER ROLLS

IN MY EXPERIENCE, THERE ARE TWO TYPES OF honey–whole-wheat dinner rolls, and neither hits the mark: Commercially produced versions are light and fluffy, but they're usually too sweet and taste only faintly of wheat. Commercial bakeries rely on chemical dough softeners to lighten their rolls and use more artificial sweeteners than honey. Homemade honey-wheat rolls present a different set of problems. The ones I tried tasted wheaty and nutty all right, but they were as dense as wet sand. In either case, these rolls are often "honey" in name only. I wanted tender, fluffy honey-wheat rolls that actually tasted like their namesake ingredients.

Since I love the texture of the test kitchen's favorite white dinner roll, I decided to start with that recipe and reverse-engineer it into a whole-wheat roll. Our recipe calls for all-purpose flour, yeast, milk, butter, honey, and salt. As a starting point, I exchanged all the white flour for an equal amount of whole-wheat flour. Our resident test kitchen bread-baking expert warned me that I'd need more liquid than usual, so I dutifully added an extra ¼ cup of milk. Then I kneaded the dough, let it rise, shaped it into rolls, let it rise again, and baked. A few hours later, I stared unhappily at the tray of tough, dense honey-wheat rolls I'd produced. Along with an unpleasant texture, using all whole-wheat flour had made the rolls almost bitter.

I thought that adding more butter (I was working with 4 tablespoons) would yield softer, more tender rolls.

Instead, it made them greasy and even denser than before. Some recipes for rolls include eggs; the protein in the egg whites traps air bubbles in the dough, helping the bread to rise, while the fat in the yolks tenderizes the dough. Adding an egg did help to lighten the dough a bit, so I tried adding a second. I'd gone too far. Now the crumb was crumbly instead of soft.

Several more tests showed that no matter what I added, the rolls were heavy, coarse, and bitter. I finally admitted to myself that a 100-percent-wheat dinner roll wasn't going to work. Wheat flour and white flour function differently. The bran in whole-wheat flour inhibits gluten development, which is why wheat rolls don't rise as well as white flour rolls. To get a light, fluffy roll, I'd have to put some all-purpose white flour back into the dough to allow more gluten to develop. I gradually removed wheat flour and replaced it with all-purpose, at the same time cutting back on the extra milk I'd added. I could take it only so far before the nuttiness that defines whole grains disappeared. After a few tests, I figured out that a 2:3 ratio of white to wheat flour was where I had to stop. At this point, while the texture of the rolls had improved, they still didn't wow me. I needed another idea.

On a particularly rainy day, as I poured the liquid ingredients into the dry, I noticed that the dough was much wetter than usual. I attributed it to the weather: The dough seemed to be absorbing extra moisture from the humid air. I figured my test was ruined, but, not wanting to have wasted time, I went ahead and shaped the loose dough rounds into rolls anyway. Because the dough was so floppy and wet, in the oven the rolls spread out, not up. But it wasn't all bad news. The interiors were decidedly lighter and fluffier than in my other tests thus far. Why?

Our science editor explained that whole-wheat flour has a lot more bran than white flour. I knew that, but what I didn't know was that bran is sharp, so sharp that it can slice right through the gluten strands that give height and structure to bread (and cakes, for that matter). To stop the bran from doing so, I needed to soften it. How? By letting it absorb a lot of water. (Alternatively, I could let the bran soak for a long time, but I was unwilling to wait around any longer than necessary for these rolls.) By sheer good luck (and bad weather), I'd found the key to fluffy wheat rolls— a super-wet (or "super-hydrated") dough.

HONEY-WHEAT DINNER ROLLS

With this in mind, I once again increased the amount of liquid called for in my recipe (I couldn't rely on rain) to make an especially sticky dough. To force the loose dough to rise up, not spread out, I snuggled the shaped rolls against one another in a baking dish. Placing them close together also translated into less crust and more fluffy interior. Indeed, these rolls were the best yet: tall and soft yet still unequivocally wheaty.

I still wanted to bump up the honey flavor, though. Most recipes used just 2 tablespoons of honey, basically replacing the sugar that's usual in yeast dough. I needed to increase the honey to 6 tablespoons before we could actually taste it. For a second hit of honey flavor, I mixed another teaspoon with some melted butter and brushed the honey butter on the rolls after they came out of the oven.

After several weeks of testing, my rolls were simultaneously fluffy and wheaty, and the taste of honey came through loud and clear.

—LYNN CLARK, *Cook's Country*

Honey-Wheat Dinner Rolls

MAKES 16 ROLLS

This dough will be sticky; do not be tempted to add flour.

- 1¾ cups whole milk, heated to 110 degrees, plus 1 tablespoon
- 6 tablespoons plus 1 teaspoon honey
- 5 tablespoons unsalted butter, melted and cooled
- 1 large egg
- 2½ cups (13¾ ounces) whole-wheat flour
- 1¾ cups (8¾ ounces) all-purpose flour
- 1 tablespoon instant or rapid-rise yeast
- 2¼ teaspoons salt

1. Grease large bowl and 13 by 9-inch baking dish. Combine 1¾ cups milk, 6 tablespoons honey, 4 tablespoons melted butter, and egg in 4-cup liquid measuring cup.

2. Using stand mixer fitted with dough hook, mix together whole-wheat flour, all-purpose flour, yeast, and salt on low speed until combined. Slowly add milk mixture and mix until dough comes together, about 1 minute. Increase speed to medium and mix until dough is smooth and almost clears sides of bowl yet still sticks to bottom, 6 to 8 minutes.

NOTES FROM THE TEST KITCHEN

SHAPING HONEY-WHEAT ROLLS

1. To get evenly sized rolls, cut dough into quarters and then quarters again.

2. Shape each piece of dough into ball by pulling edges under and pinching to seal.

3. Working on clean counter, cup dough with your palm and roll it into taut ball.

4. Nestle balls closely in dish for maximum rise: 6 down center and 5 on either side.

WET? YOU BET
Whole-wheat flour contains a lot of healthy bran, but bran is so sharp that it actually cuts the strands of gluten that give bread its height and structure. To soften the bran, we learned to make an especially hydrated (wet) honey-wheat dough.

JUST COMBINED
The dough looks very wet. Relax and trust us. It will come together.

AFTER KNEADING
The dough still looks relatively wet, with a sticky ring around the bowl. That's good.

3. Transfer dough, scraping sides of bowl, to prepared bowl. Cover with plastic wrap and let rise at room temperature until doubled in size, about 45 minutes.

4. Punch down dough on lightly floured counter. Divide dough into quarters and cut each quarter into 4 equal pieces. Form each piece into rough ball by pinching and pulling dough edges under so that top is smooth. On clean counter, cup each ball with your palm and roll into smooth, tight ball. Arrange in prepared baking dish and cover loosely with plastic. Let rolls rise at room temperature until doubled in size, about 20 minutes. Discard plastic.

5. Adjust oven rack to lower-middle position and heat oven to 400 degrees. Combine remaining 1 tablespoon melted butter and remaining 1 teaspoon honey in bowl. Brush rolls with remaining 1 tablespoon milk. Bake rolls until golden brown and register 200 degrees, about 20 minutes, rotating dish halfway through baking. Brush with honey butter and let cool in dish on wire rack for 10 minutes. Remove rolls from dish. Serve.

DILLY CASSEROLE BREAD

FOR LEONA SCHNUELLE OF CRAB ORCHARD, Nebraska, the ninth time was the charm. After years of trying, she took home the $25,000 grand prize in the 1960 Pillsbury Bake-Off for her Dilly Casserole Bread, an easy yeast bread that requires no kneading. The ingredients, including onion and dill seeds, are quickly mixed, and the dough rises twice before being baked in a round casserole dish. The loaf emerges large-crumbed, distinctly chewy, and amazingly moist. The very first loaf I baked rose to form a perfect golden brown dome, and the fragrance of dill and onion filled the test kitchen—a winner. But as we nibbled on wedges a while later, we could barely taste the dill and onion, and a strange hole the size of a golf ball lurked in the middle of the loaf. I couldn't understand. This was a famous, prize-winning recipe. What had gone wrong?

I quickly homed in on the baking soda and cottage cheese, the two oddball ingredients in Dilly Bread. The baking soda, in tandem with the yeast, produces gas bubbles that create the bread's signature network of uneven holes. The cottage cheese keeps the bread moist and adds chew. Were they to blame? Since the bread already uses yeast to rise, was the baking soda overleavening it? I tried using less baking soda, none at all, and baking powder in its place. I experimented with yeast every which way. Some loaves came out dense. Others lost their mesh of small holes. The giant central hole mostly stayed put.

I turned to the other atypical ingredient. At the time the recipe for Dilly Bread was created, manufacturers made cottage cheese by allowing milk to sour and slowly thicken from naturally occurring bacteria. Today, they speed the process by adding acid to milk. Our science editor told me that the large, very strong curds this shortcut creates don't break down as easily as those smaller, weaker curds of yore did. So as the Dilly Bread dough heats, the large curds create channels that the gas bubbles can move through. Gases naturally migrate to the coolest spot, he said, in this case the center of the dough, where they were meeting and forming a large hole. For my next loaf, I used small-curd cottage cheese. Smaller curds equals smaller hole, right? Wrong. Next, I tried mashing the curds with a potato masher before adding the cheese to the dough. Later that afternoon, I nervously cracked open the cooled loaf. To my relief, the hole was gone.

It was time to freshen up the spices. True to its mid-century roots, the original recipe called for shelf-stable dried dill seeds and dehydrated minced onion. I replaced them with minced fresh dill and grated onion, but the onion tasted harsh. Heating the onion in the microwave along with the cottage cheese softened its flavor. For a finishing touch, I mixed more fresh dill with butter, which I brushed on the loaf after it baked. This easy, homey loaf was back in the winner's circle.

—LYNN CLARK, *Cook's Country*

NOTES FROM THE TEST KITCHEN

MASH THE CHEESE
Because of changes over the years in the manufacturing process of cottage cheese, the classic recipe for Dilly Bread repeatedly produced a loaf with a large hole in the center. Happily, the fix was simple: Mash the cheese before mixing it into the dough.

Dilly Casserole Bread

SERVES 8

You can use either small- or large-curd cottage cheese in this recipe. If you don't own a 1½-quart soufflé dish, use a loaf pan.

8 ounces (1 cup) cottage cheese
¼ cup water
2 tablespoons sugar
1 tablespoon plus 1 teaspoon unsalted butter, softened
1 tablespoon grated onion
1 large egg, room temperature
2¼ cups (11¼ ounces) all-purpose flour
2¼ teaspoons instant or rapid-rise yeast
2½ tablespoons minced fresh dill
1 teaspoon salt
¼ teaspoon baking soda

1. Grease large bowl and 1½-quart soufflé dish. Using potato masher, mash cottage cheese until no large lumps remain. Combine cottage cheese, water, sugar, 1 tablespoon butter, and onion in 2-cup liquid measuring cup. Microwave until mixture registers 110 degrees, about 30 seconds. Whisk in egg until combined.

2. Using stand mixer fitted with paddle, mix 1¼ cups flour, yeast, 2 tablespoons dill, salt, and baking soda on low speed until combined. Slowly add cottage cheese mixture and mix until dough just comes together, about 1 minute. Using rubber spatula, stir in remaining 1 cup flour until just combined.

3. Transfer dough to prepared bowl. Cover with plastic wrap and let rise at room temperature until dough has doubled in size, about 45 minutes. Stir dough to remove air bubbles and transfer to prepared soufflé dish. Cover loosely with plastic and let rise at room temperature until doubled in size, about 20 minutes. Discard plastic.

4. Combine remaining ½ tablespoon dill and remaining 1 teaspoon butter in bowl. Adjust oven rack to lower-middle position and heat oven to 350 degrees. Bake loaf until deep golden brown, about 25 minutes, rotating dish halfway through baking. Brush bread with dill butter and let cool in dish on wire rack for 20 minutes. Remove bread from dish and let cool completely, about 2 hours. Serve.

NAAN

I'VE RE-CREATED PLENTY OF INDIAN CURRIES, biryanis, and chutneys in my home kitchen, but naan, the cuisine's famous leavened flatbread, is something I had yet to tackle. That might be because it's considered "restaurant" bread, even in India. To create the ideal version featuring a light, airy interior and a pliant, chewy crust, the dough is baked in the traditional barrel-shaped, charcoal- or wood-fired clay oven known as a tandoor. These vessels weigh upwards of 600 pounds and often top 1,000 degrees, which explains how the crust gets so beautifully blistered—and also why few home cooks own tandoors. At the same time, I've often wondered if I really have to venture out for something as simple as flatbread. I decided it was time to give home-baked naan a shot.

I scoured the test kitchen's collection of Indian cookbooks and came away feeling optimistic. The ingredient list would be no problem. Most of the recipes I found called for some combination of flour, yeast, water, salt, yogurt, and sugar. And though I'd worried that getting good char on the bread without a tandoor would be tricky, most sources seemed to suggest that it could be done in a conventional oven on a preheated baking stone.

Aiming for a dough that was wet enough to stay moist during cooking but not so hydrated that it was too sticky or soupy to handle, I mixed a few cups of all-purpose flour with a pinch of yeast, about ⅓ cup of low-fat yogurt, a little sugar, and some salt, along with enough water to make the dough pliable. I let the dough rise for a few hours, divided it into four balls, rolled them into thin disks, and slid them onto a baking stone that I'd preheated as hot as my oven would go (500 degrees).

Trouble started early, when I was rolling out the dough rounds and they snapped back like rubber bands. When I finally managed to get them flat, the loaves baked up dry and tough before they'd even had a chance to properly brown on the bottom, let alone develop any of those dark patchy blisters that, in my opinion, are the best part of naan. They also continued to rapidly lose more moisture as they cooled—a problem since, unlike in a restaurant, I couldn't exactly make each piece to order. Although I was still unsure whether the oven was the best stand-in for a tandoor, I decided the first

FINDING THE RIGHT HEAT TO REPLICATE A TANDOOR
We initially thought that a grill or preheated pizza stone would best approximate the intense heat of a tandoor, which cooks naan mainly by heat conducted through its walls. We were wrong. The best alternative? A trusty cast-iron skillet.

GRILL? NO
A grill's searing heat gets close to that of a tandoor. The problem: It only chars the bottom of the bread, while the top remains barely cooked. (Flipping only dries out the bread.)

PIZZA STONE IN OVEN? NO
Baked on a pizza stone in the oven, the bread encounters the conductive heat of the stone, which we wanted, and the drying heat of the oven's air currents, which we didn't.

COVERED SKILLET? YES
A covered skillet delivers heat to the bottom and top of the bread, producing loaves that are nicely charred but still moist. To ensure a tender interior, we mist the dough with water.

order of business was to create a dough that was softer but still pleasantly chewy.

One change I made right off the bat: switching from low-fat yogurt to the whole-milk kind. The extra fat would coat the flour proteins, weakening gluten formation by preventing them from binding to each other too tightly, as well as hold in more moisture for a more tender bread. With this change, my next batch of dough was easier to roll out, but it baked up too soft; the inside was like sandwich bread. I wondered if the higher protein (as much as 14 percent) in bread flour might be a better bet. But bread flour created so much chew that the resulting bread was leathery. High-protein all-purpose flour, such as King Arthur brand, was a better choice, producing naan that boasted a near-ideal texture. As I pulled apart an oven-fresh piece, I couldn't help but admire its tender chew. But then the inevitable happened: The thin rounds cooled almost instantly and were tough by the time I pulled the next batch off the baking stone a few minutes later. To buy each piece some time, I needed to figure out a way to keep the dough from drying out.

The solution wasn't more water; that would just make the dough loose and sticky. More fat was a better idea, since besides impeding gluten formation it limits water evaporation from the starches during baking, minimizing moisture loss. To that end, I tried adding vegetable oil to the dough, 1 teaspoon at a time, discovering that the more I added, the more tender the breads became and the more moisture they retained. The dough maxed out at 5 teaspoons per cup of flour; any more and the bread was greasy. But I had one more fat source in mind to boost moisture retention: an egg yolk. While unusual in naan recipes, egg yolks often turn up in other types of bread for just this reason. (I stayed away from whole eggs, knowing that the white's structure-enhancing proteins would toughen the dough.)

The last tweak I made before moving on to the cooking method was refrigerating the dough for several hours to keep it from snapping back during stretching. I learned this trick while developing a thin-crust pizza recipe: Cold fermentation encourages the relaxation of gluten strands so that the dough is more flexible. As an added bonus, preparing the dough the day before freed up time the next day for cooking the rest of the meal.

With the dough formula nailed down, I moved on to face the real challenge of making naan at home: getting good color and char without a tandoor. Since the oven wasn't browning the bread fast enough, I figured my best alternative was the hottest, most powerful heat source I had: a grill. I fired up some charcoal, expecting to come away with beautifully grill-marked breads. To say my first attempt was a disaster would be an understatement. Like a poorly cooked piece of meat, the bottom blackened while the top remained practically raw. I thought the fire was just too hot so I downsized it on my next test, but even a smaller fire produced the same charred result. Flipping the dough midway through cooking also wasn't the answer—it merely dried out the bread.

I took a step back to consider what really happens when naan cooks in a tandoor. The shaped dough is slapped directly onto the tandoor's inside wall, where it sticks and cooks in minutes, without ever being flipped. While heat radiating from the coals at the bottom of the oven helps cook the bread's exposed side, more important is the heat conducted through its walls, which also trap moisture to keep the bread soft. I could see now that a grill wasn't the best substitute for a tandoor. But neither was a pizza stone in the oven, since that method also exposed the bread to drying air currents. My choice became clear: a skillet on the stovetop.

So for my next test, I slipped my stretched and shaped dough onto a preheated cast-iron skillet. It puffed up quickly, and after a few minutes the bottom had browned a bit; I flipped it to finish cooking the top side. The result was a dramatic improvement on anything I'd made so far—lightly browned and bubbled in spots and tender inside. It wasn't perfect, though. The bread ballooned as it baked, which made it cook unevenly when I flipped it; the crust was a bit floury; and the loaves still dried out too quickly as they sat.

None of these issues were hard to fix. I poked the dough with a fork before putting it in the pan to let steam escape and prevent puffing. Improving the crust and prolonging the optimal tender texture of the bread required a two-tiered approach. First, I misted the dough with water before cooking it to moisten the flour that coated it. I also covered the pan to trap steam around the bread as it baked.

My simple approach created naan as good as any from a restaurant. Brushed with a little melted butter after cooking, it makes for a delicious edible utensil, perfect for tearing into bite-size pieces to dip into curries, chutneys, or even stew.

—ANDREW JANJIGIAN, *Cook's Illustrated*

Indian Flatbread (Naan)

MAKES 4 BREADS

This recipe works best with a high-protein all-purpose flour such as King Arthur brand. Do not use nonfat yogurt in this recipe. A 12-inch nonstick skillet may be used in place of the cast-iron skillet. For efficiency, stretch the next ball of dough while each naan is cooking.

½ cup ice water
⅓ cup plain whole-milk yogurt
3 tablespoons plus 1 teaspoon vegetable oil
1 large egg yolk
2 cups (10 ounces) all-purpose flour
1¼ teaspoons sugar
½ teaspoon instant or rapid-rise yeast
1¼ teaspoons salt
1½ tablespoons unsalted butter, melted

1. In measuring cup or small bowl, combine water, yogurt, 3 tablespoons oil, and egg yolk. Process flour, sugar, and yeast together in food processor until combined, about 2 seconds. With processor running, slowly add water mixture; process until dough is just combined and no dry flour remains, about 10 seconds. Let dough stand for 10 minutes.

2. Add salt to dough and process until dough forms satiny, sticky ball that clears sides of workbowl, 30 to 60 seconds. Transfer dough to lightly floured counter and knead until smooth, about 1 minute. Shape dough into tight ball and place in large, lightly oiled bowl. Cover tightly with plastic wrap and refrigerate for 16 to 24 hours.

3. Adjust oven rack to middle position and heat oven to 200 degrees. Place ovensafe plate on rack. Transfer dough to lightly floured counter and divide into 4 equal pieces. Shape each piece into smooth, tight ball. Place dough balls on lightly oiled baking sheet, at least 2 inches apart; cover loosely with plastic coated with vegetable oil spray. Let stand for 15 to 20 minutes.

4. Transfer 1 ball to lightly floured counter and sprinkle with flour. Using hands and rolling pin, press and roll piece of dough into 9-inch round of even thickness, sprinkling dough and counter with flour as needed to prevent sticking. Using fork, poke entire surface of round 20 to 25 times. Heat remaining 1 teaspoon oil in 12-inch cast-iron skillet over medium heat until shimmering. Wipe oil out of skillet completely with paper towels. Mist top of dough lightly with water. Place dough in pan, moistened side down; mist top surface of dough with water; and cover. Cook until bottom is browned in spots across surface, 2 to 4 minutes. Flip naan, cover, and continue to cook on second side until lightly browned, 2 to 3 minutes longer. (If naan puffs up, gently poke with fork to deflate.) Flip naan, brush top with about 1 teaspoon melted butter, transfer to plate in oven, and cover plate tightly with aluminum foil. Repeat rolling and cooking remaining 3 dough balls. Once last naan is baked, serve immediately.

VARIATION

Quicker Indian Flatbread

This variation, which can be prepared in about 2 hours, forgoes the overnight rest, but the dough may be a little harder to roll out.

After shaping dough in step 2, let dough rise at room temperature for 30 minutes. After 30 minutes, fold partially risen dough over itself 8 times by gently lifting and folding edge of dough toward middle, turning bowl 90 degrees after each fold. Cover with plastic wrap and let rise for 30 minutes. Repeat folding, turning, and rising one more time, for total of three 30-minute rises. After last rise, proceed with recipe from step 3.

CHAPTER 5

PASTA & PIZZA

Fresh Pasta without a Machine   108

    Olive Oil Sauce with Anchovies and Parsley

    Tomato and Browned Butter Sauce

    Walnut Cream Sauce

Campanelle with Roasted Garlic, Chicken Sausage, and Arugula   113

    Orecchiette with Roasted Garlic, Chicken, and Broccoli Rabe

    Campanelle with Roasted Garlic, Shrimp, and Feta

Pasta with Broccoli Rabe and Sausage   115

Spaghetti with Turkey-Pesto Meatballs   118

Ragu alla Bolognese   119

Rigatoni with Genovese Ragu   122

Reduced-Fat Chicken Tetrazzini   124

Vegetable Lasagna   125

Potato Gnocchi with Browned Butter and Sage   130

Grandma Pizza   133

FRESH PASTA

ONE CHALLENGE I'VE ALWAYS WANTED TO SET FOR myself is figuring out how to make pasta with nothing more than dough, a rolling pin, and some elbow grease. While mechanical pasta rollers aren't all that expensive, many home cooks don't own them. But as anyone who has ever attempted to roll out a block of hard pasta dough by hand knows, it's no easy task. The dough has a tendency to spring back, and if it isn't rolled out gossamer thin, the pasta will never achieve the right al dente texture when cooked. So how do Italian cooks manage to pull off this feat? One answer: years of perseverance.

In her *Essentials of Classic Italian Cooking* (1992), Marcella Hazan devotes no fewer than six pages to the classic hand-rolling technique perfected in the Emilia-Romagna region of Italy. Employing extra-thin, super-long rolling pins measuring 1½ inches in diameter and 32 inches in length, Italians in this part of the country have developed a series of stretching movements that can transform a lump of firm dough into a thin, delicate sheet. Besides the obvious drawback of needing a generous work surface to accommodate the pin, Hazan is the first to admit that this traditional technique must be exhaustively practiced "until the motions are performed through intuition rather than deliberation."

While I'm typically game for a hard-won lesson in authenticity, even I have limits. I wanted a dough that any cook could roll out with ease on the first try and that would cook up to that incomparably tender yet slightly chewy texture that makes fresh pasta so worth making.

In addition to centuries of experience, Italians have another hand-rolling advantage—the best kind of flour for the job: *doppio zero*, or 00. The name denotes the fine talcumlike grind that gives pasta an almost creamy texture. Also important is its protein content (around 9 percent). To see what I was missing, I mail-ordered some and mixed up a typical batch of dough. Sure enough, the 00 flour produced a malleable dough that was far easier to work with than dough made from all-purpose flour.

To achieve similarly soft dough without the specialty flour, my first inclination was to dilute the protein content of all-purpose flour (which boasts 10 to 12 percent protein) by cutting it with cake flour (which has 6 to 8 percent protein). I substituted increasing amounts of cake flour for all-purpose and saw a dramatic impact.

With just 25 percent cake flour in the mix, my dough was much softer, less elastic, and easier to roll out. Unfortunately, the cooked strands, which released a lot of starch into the cooking water, emerged with a pitted, pebbly surface. Our science editor explained why: For noodles to remain intact and leach only a little starch into the cooking water, the starch granules in the flour need to be fully surrounded by a strong network of proteins. But the bleach in cake flour weakens the proteins and makes the starch more absorbent and prone to bursting—a good thing when you want a tender cake but not when you're making pasta. Clearly, I needed a different strategy, so I turned my attention to the amount of liquid in the recipe.

Traditional pasta dough is about 30 percent water (compared with around 55 percent hydration for a basic sandwich loaf), all of which comes from the eggs. I figured that simply upping the hydration level would create a softer dough that would be easier to roll out, so I experimented with adding plain water to one batch of dough and an extra egg white to another. Just as I'd hoped, these more hydrated doughs were softer, but the wetter surface of the dough caused considerable sticking, which required more flour during rolling and led to cooked pasta with a starchy, gummy surface. Still, I felt I was on to something by increasing the liquid in my recipe. Olive oil is a common addition to many fresh pasta recipes. What if I used it instead of water?

I mixed up a few more batches of dough, adding increasing amounts of olive oil. As the oil amount increased, the dough became more supple and easier to roll out. But because fat coats the proteins, inhibiting gluten formation, too much oil once again weakened the dough's structure, leading to excess starch loss in the water and a compromised texture. I found my upper limit at 2 tablespoons of oil. I was finally getting somewhere, but this dough was still far from user-friendly.

In many pasta doughs yolks are substituted for some of the whole eggs, and for good reason. While yolks still contain about 50 percent water, they are also loaded with fat and emulsifiers, both of which limit gluten development. However, unlike doughs made with cake flour or excessive amounts of oil, dough made with extra yolks still has plenty of structure thanks to the coagulation of the egg proteins. I tried adding more yolks until I had a truly soft, easy-to-work dough that also boiled up nice and tender. The magic number proved to be six extra yolks. This dough took on a

FRESH PASTA WITH OLIVE OIL SAUCE WITH ANCHOVIES AND PARSLEY

beautiful yellow hue, yielded to gentle pressure with a rolling pin, and cooked up into delicate ribbons with a springy bite.

I had cleared some big hurdles, but I wasn't finished. I turned my attention to finding the best way to rest, roll, and cut the pasta. After being mixed, pasta dough is often rested for 20 to 30 minutes to allow the flour to fully hydrate and the newly formed gluten to cross-link into a network and then relax. Given that 30 minutes makes for friendlier dough, would longer be even better? To find out, I made a batch and let the dough sit at room temperature for an extended period of time, cutting and rolling out pieces every 30 minutes. As I suspected, after an hour, my dough was significantly more malleable—and it continued to soften over the next three hours (I found four hours of resting time to be ideal, though not critical for success). All I had to do now was divide the dough into manageable pieces and grab a heavy rolling pin—right?

Well, almost. This dough was worlds away from the dense blocks I'd struggled with in the past, but it still required a bit of technique. I knew I needed to avoid using too much bench flour; a little stickiness is a good thing, as it prevents the dough from springing back too easily. Plus, as I'd already learned, the excess flour turns the surface of the pasta coarse and gummy once cooked.

With that in mind, I first cut the dough into six manageable pieces. Working with one at a time, I dusted each piece lightly with flour and used my fingers to flatten it into a 3-inch square. From there I switched to a rolling pin and doubled it to a 6-inch square. After another light dusting of flour, I began working the dough. I started with the pin in the middle of the dough and first rolled away, returned to the middle, and then rolled toward me. When the dough reached 6 by 12 inches, I gave it another dusting of flour and then repeated the rolling process until the dough measured roughly 6 by 20 inches.

From here, the possibilities were limitless. For ribbon-style pasta, I let the sheets dry on kitchen towels until firm around the edges (a step that enabled me to avoid dusting with more flour) before folding them up at 2-inch intervals and slicing crosswise to the desired thickness.

With an easy-to-roll-out dough that cooks up into wonderfully springy, delicate noodles, I'd wager that even cooks with pasta machines might be tempted to leave them in the cabinet.

—DAN SOUZA, *Cook's Illustrated*

Fresh Pasta without a Machine
MAKES 1 POUND; SERVES 4 TO 6

If using a high-protein all-purpose flour like King Arthur brand, increase the number of egg yolks to 7. The longer the dough rests in step 2, the easier it will be to roll out. When rolling out the dough, avoid adding too much flour, which may result in excessive snapback.

- 2 **cups (10 ounces) all-purpose flour**
- 2 **large eggs plus 6 large yolks**
- 2 **tablespoons olive oil**
- 1 **tablespoon salt**
- 1 **recipe sauce (recipes follow)**

1. Process flour, eggs and yolks, and oil together in food processor until mixture forms cohesive dough that feels soft and is barely tacky to touch, about 45 seconds. (If dough sticks to fingers, add up to ¼ cup flour, 1 tablespoon at a time, until barely tacky. If dough doesn't become cohesive, add up to 1 tablespoon water, 1 teaspoon at a time, until it just comes together; process 30 seconds longer.)

2. Turn dough ball out onto dry counter and knead until smooth, 1 to 2 minutes. Shape dough into 6-inch-long cylinder. Wrap with plastic wrap and set aside at room temperature to rest for at least 1 hour or up to 4 hours.

3. Cut cylinder crosswise into 6 equal pieces. Working with 1 piece of dough (rewrap remaining dough), dust both sides with flour, place cut side down on clean counter, and press into 3-inch square. Using heavy rolling pin, roll into 6-inch square. Dust both sides of dough lightly with flour. Starting at center of square, roll dough away from you in 1 motion. Return rolling pin to center of dough and roll toward you in 1 motion. Repeat steps of rolling until dough sticks to counter and measures roughly 12 inches long. Lightly dust both sides of dough with flour and continue rolling dough until it measures roughly 20 inches long and 6 inches wide, frequently lifting dough to release it from counter. (You should be able to easily see outline of your fingers through dough.) If dough firmly sticks to counter and wrinkles when rolled out, dust dough lightly with flour.

4. Transfer pasta sheet to kitchen towel and let stand, uncovered, until firm around edges, about 15 minutes; meanwhile, roll out remaining dough. Starting with short end of 1 pasta sheet, gently fold sheet at 2-inch intervals until sheet has been folded into flat, rectangular roll.

ROLLING AND CUTTING PASTA DOUGH BY HAND

What's the trick to turning a lump of pasta dough into long, silky strands—without a pasta roller? Starting with a soft, malleable dough is half the battle. The other half: dividing the dough into small, manageable pieces and working with them one at a time.

1. Shape dough into 6-inch cylinder; wrap in plastic wrap and let rest for at least 1 hour. Divide into 6 equal pieces. Reserve 1 piece; rewrap remaining 5.

2. Working with reserved piece, dust both sides with flour, then press cut side down into 3-inch square. With rolling pin, roll into 6-inch square, then dust both sides again with flour.

3. Roll dough to 12 by 6 inches, rolling from center of dough 1 way at a time, then dust with flour. Continue rolling to 20 by 6 inches, lifting frequently to release from counter. Transfer dough to kitchen towel and air-dry for about 15 minutes.

4. Starting with short end, gently fold dried sheet at 2-inch intervals to create flat, rectangular roll.

5. With sharp knife, cut into ³⁄₁₆-inch-wide noodles.

6. Use fingers to unfurl pasta; transfer to baking sheet.

TROUBLESHOOTING FRESH PASTA

This dough is designed to be tacky enough to stick lightly to the counter, giving it traction to be stretched ultra-thin, but not so sticky that it wrinkles when rolled out. Variables such as flour brand, measuring technique, and size of the eggs may lead to slight differences in consistency. Here are tips on how to address texture-related problems and other issues that may arise.

PROBLEM: Dough doesn't come together in food processor.
SOLUTION: Add up to 1 tablespoon water, 1 teaspoon at a time, until dough forms cohesive mass that's barely tacky to touch.

PROBLEM: Dough is too sticky.
SOLUTION: Add up to ¼ cup flour, 1 tablespoon at a time, until dough is barely tacky to touch.

PROBLEM: Dough wrinkles when rolled out.
SOLUTION: Lift dough from counter; dust both sides lightly with flour.

PROBLEM: Dough has too much extra flour, doesn't stick to counter, and snaps back when rolled.
SOLUTION: Use pastry brush to dust off excess flour from dough.

PROBLEM: Dough sheet is too dry and cracks when folded.
SOLUTION: Mist sheet lightly with water; let sit for few minutes to allow dough to absorb water before folding again.

PROBLEM: Dough pieces aren't same size.
SOLUTION: When rolling out, pay more attention to visual cue provided—dough should be rolled thin enough that outline of fingers is visible through it—than final dimensions.

With sharp chef's knife, slice crosswise into 3/16-inch-wide noodles. Use fingers to unfurl pasta and transfer to baking sheet. Repeat folding and cutting remaining sheets of dough. Cook noodles within 1 hour.

5. Bring 4 quarts water to boil in large pot. Add pasta and salt and cook, stirring often, until al dente, about 3 minutes. Reserve 1 cup pasta cooking water, then drain pasta. Toss with sauce; serve immediately.

TO MAKE AHEAD: Follow recipe through step 4, transfer baking sheet of pasta to freezer, and freeze until pasta is firm. Transfer to zipper-lock bag and store for up to 2 weeks. Cook frozen pasta straight from freezer as directed in step 5.

Olive Oil Sauce with Anchovies and Parsley

MAKES 1 CUP; ENOUGH FOR 1 POUND PASTA

Mincing the anchovies ensures that their flavor gets evenly distributed. Use a high-quality extra-virgin olive oil in this recipe; our preferred brand is Columela.

⅓ cup extra-virgin olive oil

2 garlic cloves, minced

2 anchovy fillets, rinsed, patted dry, and minced

Salt and pepper

4 teaspoons lemon juice

2 tablespoons minced fresh parsley

1. Heat oil in 12-inch skillet over medium-low heat until shimmering. Add garlic, anchovies, ⅛ teaspoon salt, and ½ teaspoon pepper; cook until fragrant, about 30 seconds. Remove pan from heat and cover to keep warm.

2. To serve, return pan to medium heat. Add pasta, ½ cup reserved cooking water, lemon juice, and parsley; toss to combine. Season with salt and pepper to taste and add remaining cooking water as needed to adjust consistency. Serve immediately.

Tomato and Browned Butter Sauce

MAKES 3 CUPS; ENOUGH FOR 1 POUND PASTA

1 (28-ounce) can whole peeled tomatoes

4 tablespoons unsalted butter, cut into 4 pieces

2 garlic cloves, minced

½ teaspoon sugar

Salt and pepper

2 teaspoons sherry vinegar

3 tablespoons chopped fresh basil

Grated Parmesan cheese

1. Process tomatoes and their juice in food processor until smooth, about 30 seconds. Melt 3 tablespoons butter in 12-inch skillet over medium-high heat, swirling occasionally, until butter is dark brown and releases nutty aroma, about 1½ minutes. Stir in garlic and cook for 10 seconds. Stir in processed tomatoes, sugar, and ½ teaspoon salt and simmer until sauce is slightly reduced, about 8 minutes. Remove pan from heat; whisk in remaining 1 tablespoon butter and vinegar. Season with salt and pepper to taste; cover to keep warm.

2. To serve, return pan to medium heat. Add pasta, ¼ cup reserved cooking water, and basil; toss to combine. Season with salt and pepper to taste and add remaining cooking water as needed to adjust consistency. Serve immediately, passing Parmesan separately.

Walnut Cream Sauce

MAKES 2 CUPS; ENOUGH FOR 1 POUND PASTA

1½ cups (6 ounces) walnuts, toasted

¾ cup dry white wine

½ cup heavy cream

1 ounce Parmesan cheese, grated (½ cup)

Salt and pepper

¼ cup minced fresh chives

1. Process 1 cup walnuts in food processor until finely ground, about 10 seconds. Transfer to small bowl. Pulse remaining ½ cup walnuts in food processor until coarsely chopped, 3 to 5 pulses. Bring wine to simmer in 12-inch skillet over medium-high heat; cook until reduced to ¼ cup, about 3 minutes. Whisk in cream, walnuts, Parmesan, ¼ teaspoon salt, and ½ teaspoon pepper. Remove pan from heat and cover to keep warm.

2. To serve, return pan to medium heat. Add pasta, ½ cup reserved cooking water, and chives; toss to combine. Season with salt and pepper to taste and add remaining cooking water as needed to adjust consistency. Serve immediately.

WEEKNIGHT PASTA WITH ROASTED GARLIC

PASTA WITH GARLIC IS THE ULTIMATE IN QUICK weeknight dining. Bring a pot of water to a boil for your noodles, whip up a simple garlic-and-oil sauce, marry the two, and you're done. But all too often, this formula results in a disappointing dinner. Sure, it's got speed on its side, but the flavor leaves a lot to be desired. Whether they're overly greasy, rife with burnt garlic bits, or simply one-dimensional in their flavor, these easy entrées aren't worth the little time it takes to make them. I vowed to remedy this situation with a recipe that would deliver an ultra-satisfying dinner of tender pasta, intense, sweet garlicky flavor, and a lightly clingy sauce—all in about half an hour.

I started with the sauce, which I hoped to infuse with sweet, nutty, garlicky flavor. Though sautéing garlic takes no time at all, there's a fine line between perfectly softened, mellowed garlic and garlic that's burnt and bitter—just a few extra seconds can push it over the edge. Roasting, on the other hand, doesn't run the same risk, as the gentle, ambient heat of the oven allows the cloves to soften slowly and become nicely caramelized. But getting to this point can take up to an hour; I needed a way to speed up the process.

Standard test kitchen protocol calls for roasting the garlic head whole with the top quarter sliced off; the head is drizzled with olive oil, wrapped in aluminum foil, and roasted on a baking sheet in a 350-degree oven. To cut the hour-long roasting time in half, I made a few changes to our established roasting procedure. My first move was to separate the cloves, which I hoped would allow them to cook through more quickly than when bunched together in a compact head. I also cranked up the oven to 475 degrees. Finally, I swapped the baking sheet for a small baking dish, which would keep the cloves, plus a generous pour of olive oil, in close quarters and ideally prevent burning.

After half an hour, I checked the oven and was met by tough, dark brown garlic cloves that were worlds away from the tender, richly caramelized garlic I'd hoped for. Thinking back to the traditional roasting method, I realized that the separated cloves of garlic still needed some protection from the direct heat of the oven. For my next test, I covered the baking dish with aluminum foil and lowered the oven temperature to 425 degrees.

In just 20 minutes, the garlic had become nicely caramelized and taken on a rich, sweet flavor. But although the flavor and texture of the garlic were spot-on, dealing with the scorching hot, papery skins was a hassle; removing them prior to roasting solved the problem. Now I could mash the tender cloves right in the baking dish into a simple garlic-and-oil paste that would ensure that the rich garlicky flavor was evenly distributed throughout the dish. With a bit of salt and pepper, I had a flavorful start to my sauce. Now I just needed to select a few additional ingredients to turn this effortless dish into a satisfying, well-balanced supper.

Looking for something to add more richness, I decided to include some cheese and tested a number of varieties. In the end, tasters preferred crumbles of creamy goat cheese. Stirring it into the still-hot pasta along with the garlic-and-oil mixture gave my pasta a thick, velvety coating. To give it plenty of sauciness and some body, I also stirred in a good amount of the starchy, flavorful pasta cooking water, which I reserved before draining the pasta.

The dish still needed heartiness, and tasters clamored for something meaty. Crumbled Italian sausage resulted in a greasy, heavy dish. Swapping the raw sausage for precooked chicken sausage worked much better, providing substance and meaty flavor without making the dish greasy. It sped up the process, too—the thin sausage slices needed less than 5 minutes of browning time. For a slightly bitter note that would punch up the complexity of the dish, I stirred in a few handfuls of baby arugula.

Now that I had my perfect pantry pasta dinner, I wanted a couple of easy variations. For one, I swapped out the chicken sausage and arugula for shredded chicken and subtly spicy broccoli rabe. For a pasta supper with a definitively Greek flavor, I traded the sausage and goat cheese for shrimp and feta.

After just a few forkfuls of this easy, creamy pasta dish, I had to pause to pat myself on the back. I had successfully cut the time it takes to roast garlic in half—but I'd kept all the sweet, roasted garlic flavor intact. I'd call that a win-win.

—ASHLEY MOORE, *America's Test Kitchen Books*

Campanelle with Roasted Garlic, Chicken Sausage, and Arugula

SERVES 4 TO 6

Chicken sausage is available in a wide variety of flavors; feel free to choose any flavor that will work well in this dish.

⅓ cup plus 1 tablespoon olive oil

16 garlic cloves, peeled

Salt and pepper

12 ounces cooked chicken sausage, sliced ½ inch thick on bias

1 pound campanelle

5 ounces (5 cups) baby arugula

4 ounces goat cheese, crumbled (1 cup)

1. Adjust oven rack to upper-middle position and heat oven to 425 degrees. Combine ⅓ cup oil, garlic, ½ teaspoon salt, and ½ teaspoon pepper in 8-inch square baking dish and cover with aluminum foil. Bake, stirring occasionally, until garlic is caramelized and soft, about 20 minutes. Let cool slightly, then mash garlic and oil into paste with fork.

2. Heat remaining 1 tablespoon oil in 12-inch skillet over medium-high heat until shimmering. Add sausage and cook until lightly browned, about 4 minutes. Off heat, stir in garlic mixture.

3. Meanwhile, bring 4 quarts water to boil in large pot. Add pasta and 1 tablespoon salt and cook, stirring often, until al dente. Reserve 1½ cups cooking water, then drain pasta and return it to pot. Add sausage-garlic mixture, arugula, cheese, and ½ cup reserved cooking water and toss to combine. Season with salt and pepper to taste and add remaining cooking water as needed to adjust consistency. Serve.

NOTES FROM THE TEST KITCHEN

PREPEELED VERSUS FRESH GARLIC

Many supermarkets carry jars or deli containers of prepeeled garlic cloves, but how do they compare to fresh garlic bought by the head? We tasted both kinds, both raw and cooked in various recipes, and the results were mixed. However, we did find that a whole head of garlic stored in a cool, dry place will last for at least a few weeks, while prepeeled garlic in a jar lasts for only about two weeks before turning yellowish and overly pungent. But if you go through a lot of garlic, prepeeled cloves can be a fine alternative. Just make sure they look firm and white and have a matte finish when you purchase them.

VARIATIONS

Orecchiette with Roasted Garlic, Chicken, and Broccoli Rabe

SERVES 4 TO 6

To make this dish even faster, you can substitute leftover cooked chicken or store-bought rotisserie chicken for the chicken breasts in step 2.

⅓ cup plus 1 tablespoon olive oil

16 garlic cloves, peeled

Salt and pepper

12 ounces boneless, skinless chicken breasts, trimmed

1 pound broccoli rabe, trimmed and cut into 1½-inch pieces

1 pound orecchiette

2 ounces Parmesan cheese, grated (1 cup), plus extra for serving

1. Adjust oven rack to upper-middle position and heat oven to 425 degrees. Combine ⅓ cup oil, garlic, ½ teaspoon salt, and ½ teaspoon pepper in 8-inch square baking dish and cover with aluminum foil. Bake, stirring occasionally, until garlic is caramelized and soft, about 20 minutes. Let cool slightly, then mash garlic and oil into paste with fork.

2. Meanwhile, pat chicken breasts dry with paper towels and season with salt and pepper. Heat remaining 1 tablespoon olive oil in 12-inch skillet over medium-high heat until just smoking. Carefully lay chicken in skillet and cook until well browned on first side, 6 to 8 minutes. Flip chicken, add ½ cup water, and cover. Reduce heat to medium-low and continue to cook until chicken registers 160 degrees, 5 to 7 minutes longer. Transfer chicken to carving board, let cool slightly, then shred into bite-size pieces. Return to skillet, stir in garlic mixture, and cover until needed.

3. Bring 4 quarts water to boil in large pot. Add broccoli rabe and 1 tablespoon salt and cook until crisp-tender, 1 to 3 minutes; transfer to paper towel–lined plate.

4. Return pot of water to boil, add pasta, and cook, stirring often, until al dente. Reserve ½ cup cooking water, then drain pasta and return it to pot. Add chicken-garlic mixture, broccoli rabe, and Parmesan and toss to combine. Season with salt and pepper to taste and add reserved cooking water as needed to adjust consistency. Serve, passing extra Parmesan separately.

Campanelle with Roasted Garlic, Shrimp, and Feta
SERVES 4 TO 6

If your shrimp are larger or smaller, alter the cooking time in step 1 accordingly.

⅓ cup olive oil

16 garlic cloves, peeled

Salt and pepper

1 pound medium-large shrimp (31 to 40 per pound), peeled, deveined, and tails removed

1 pound campanelle

4 ounces feta cheese, crumbled (1 cup)

1 cup chopped fresh basil

1. Adjust oven rack to upper-middle position and heat oven to 425 degrees. Combine oil, garlic, ½ teaspoon salt, and ½ teaspoon pepper in 8-inch square baking dish and cover with aluminum foil. Bake, stirring occasionally, until garlic is caramelized and soft, about 20 minutes. Let cool slightly, then mash garlic and oil into paste with fork. Stir in shrimp and continue to bake until shrimp are cooked through, about 10 minutes.

2. Meanwhile, bring 4 quarts water to boil in large pot. Add pasta and 1 tablespoon salt and cook, stirring often, until al dente. Reserve ½ cup cooking water, then drain pasta and return it to pot. Add shrimp mixture, feta, and basil; toss to combine. Season with salt and pepper to taste and add reserved cooking water as needed to adjust consistency. Serve.

PASTA WITH BROCCOLI RABE AND SAUSAGE

IF EACH REGION IN ITALY CAN BE SAID TO HAVE A signature dish, then orecchiette with broccoli rabe is the one most often associated with the southeastern region of Puglia. Italian-American versions frequently include sausage to create a satisfying study in contrasts: the richness of the meat taming the peppery rabe. Pulled together with a generous helping of garlic, a dash of hot pepper flakes, and a shower of grated Pecorino, it's one of those quick, satisfying, one-pot meals that are invaluable as part of a winter weeknight repertoire.

But, as in any marriage of dissimilar personalities, the relationship takes finesse to work properly—and it's the broccoli rabe that requires the most attention. Most recipes agree that rabe requires pretreatment to tame its bitter edge, but they differ in their solution: Sautéing, blanching, and boiling are all common.

I gave each method a go, finishing the rough-chopped stalks in the skillet with the rendered sausage fat and aromatics before mixing them with the meat and tossing the two components with lightly sauced pasta. The rabe pretreatments produced remarkably different results, and tasters overwhelmingly preferred the crisp-tender bite of the greens that had been simply sautéed. Their intensely bitter flavor, however, needed some work.

I started by doing some rabe research to understand why the water-based treatments had softened the vegetable's sharp edge. It turns out that broccoli rabe is rich in flavor precursors that release pungent, bitter compounds called isothiocyanates when the vegetable is cut. Exposing the rabe to boiling water inactivates these acrid compounds. I wondered, though: Since we preferred the firmer texture of the sautéed rabe, was a full pot of boiling water necessary, or could I get by with adding just a splash of water to the skillet?

I had my answer after one test, as the boiled and lightly pan-steamed greens tasted virtually identical. I'd not only eliminated the wait time for the broccoli water to boil but also saved myself the trouble of washing another pot. In fact, I didn't even need to add water to the skillet; I just needed to forgo drying the greens. The water left clinging to the rabe after washing was enough to render it crisp-tender without the bitter edge.

As I turned to fine-tuning the dish itself, I considered one of my tasters' milder criticisms: that the large (1- to 3-inch) rabe pieces were clumping together in the pasta. No problem; I simply chopped the stalks into small (¼-inch) pieces. But while this remedied the clumping, it reintroduced the rabe's bitterness. I shouldn't have been surprised—the more the vegetable was broken down, the more of its bitter compounds were released.

Taking a step back, I tried balancing the bitterness by tweaking the other ingredients. The obvious test—ramping up the sausage, garlic, and pepper flakes—didn't so much round out the flavors as add heft and heat. I had more luck adjusting the sauce. Along with the ladle full of pasta cooking water I'd been adding to the pan (the starchy liquid lends body to the sauce and helps it cling to the pasta), I poured in 1 cup of chicken broth, then reduced the liquid to about 1 cup. This gave the

PASTA WITH BROCCOLI RABE AND SAUSAGE

sauce more depth. I further enriched it with a pat of butter and some grated Pecorino. Definitely better—but still not quite there.

Then I remembered that in my research I'd seen many recipes for broccoli rabe sautéed with anchovies mashed to a paste, a step intended to lend subtle depth. I followed suit, mashing a couple of fillets with some olive oil and a drop of fresh lemon juice and whisking the mixture into the reduced sauce before tossing it with the reserved pasta, sausage, rabe, and cheese (with salty anchovies in the mix, I swapped the super-salty Pecorino for milder Parmesan). That did it: Each bite was bold but balanced, with an addictively bitter—but not overwhelming—edge. Best of all, after cooking more than 40 pounds of rabe, I'd taken a standard weeknight pasta recipe and made it even easier to prepare.

—RAQUEL PELZEL, *Cook's Illustrated*

Pasta with Broccoli Rabe and Sausage

SERVES 4 TO 6

It's important that some water still cling to the rabe after washing to help it steam during cooking. We prefer orecchiette in this dish, but fusilli and campanelle also work well.

- 2 anchovy fillets, rinsed
- 4 tablespoons extra-virgin olive oil
- 1 tablespoon lemon juice
- 4 garlic cloves, minced
- 1 pound orecchiette
  Salt
- 8 ounces hot Italian sausage, casings removed, cut into ¼-inch pieces
- ½ teaspoon red pepper flakes
- 1 pound broccoli rabe, trimmed and cut into ¼-inch pieces
- 1 cup low-sodium chicken broth
- 1½ tablespoons unsalted butter
- 1 ounce Parmesan cheese, grated (½ cup), plus extra for serving

1. Using fork, smear anchovies on cutting board into uniform paste (you should have about 1 teaspoon). Combine anchovy paste, 1 tablespoon oil, lemon juice, and 1 teaspoon garlic in bowl; set aside.

2. Bring 4 quarts water to boil in large pot. Add pasta and 1 tablespoon salt and cook, stirring often, until al dente. Reserve 1 cup cooking water, then drain pasta and return it to pot.

3. While pasta cooks, heat 1 tablespoon oil in 12-inch nonstick skillet over medium-high heat until shimmering. Add sausage and cook, stirring often, until browned and cooked through, 2 to 4 minutes. Using slotted spoon, transfer sausage to paper towel–lined plate. Do not wipe out skillet.

4. Return skillet to medium heat, add remaining 2 tablespoons oil, remaining garlic, and pepper flakes; cook, stirring often, until fragrant, 1 to 2 minutes. Increase heat to high and add half of broccoli rabe; cook, stirring often, until just wilted, about 1 minute. Add remaining broccoli rabe and ½ teaspoon salt; cook, stirring often, until crisp-tender, 2 to 3 minutes. Transfer broccoli rabe to colander set in bowl. Do not wipe out skillet.

5. Bring broth and ¾ cup pasta water to boil in now-empty skillet over high heat. Reduce heat to medium and simmer until reduced to about 1 cup, 4 to 6 minutes. Remove skillet from heat and whisk in reserved anchovy mixture and butter. Add sauce, broccoli rabe, sausage, and ½ cup Parmesan to pasta and toss to combine. Add remaining cooking water as needed to adjust consistency. Serve immediately, passing extra Parmesan separately.

NOTES FROM THE TEST KITCHEN

PREPPING BROCCOLI RABE

1. To trim broccoli rabe, cut off and discard tough stalk ends.

2. Cut remaining stems and florets into ¼-inch pieces.

SPAGHETTI WITH TURKEY-PESTO MEATBALLS

TO KEEP DINNERTIME INTERESTING, SOMETIMES I like to stray from the predictable culinary course. Take spaghetti and meatballs. I love the classic version, but preparing it can be an all-day affair. I wanted a simpler spaghetti-and-meatballs recipe—and at the same time, I wanted meatballs with a fresh, modern spin.

I started with the meatballs. In addition to a combination of ground beef and ground pork, classic recipes rely on the usual suspects for seasoning (garlic, parsley, and Parmesan), a panade (made with bread crumbs and milk) to keep the meatballs tender, plus an egg yolk to bind it all together. After roaming the aisles of the supermarket looking for something that would simplify the shopping list and bump up the flavor, I landed on prepared pesto. It was perfect; in one fell swoop, I could replace the garlic, Parmesan, and even the egg yolk, thanks to the olive oil in the pesto. Best of all, the basil would pack a much bigger hit of flavor than the parsley. But as soon as I got to work, I quickly realized these meatballs were far too moist; the olive oil was making a bigger difference than I had expected. Luckily, simply cutting out the milk from the panade brought the moisture back into balance.

To keep the cooking technique simple and straightforward, I decided to begin by browning the meatballs in a skillet to give them a good crust and deeper flavor. Recipes sometimes call for up to a cup of oil for this step, but I found that 1 tablespoon was all that was required. At first my tender meatballs were falling apart in the skillet, so I chilled them in the refrigerator for an hour before browning to help them firm up. Once the meatballs were nicely browned, I added some pasta sauce (just a basic working recipe for now) to the skillet and finished cooking them through by simmering them right in the sauce. This gave the meatballs a chance to soak up more flavor and ensured that they stayed tender—and it gave the sauce some meaty flavor as well. The meatballs were perfectly cooked through in just 10 minutes. They were tender and had decent flavor, but I was disappointed to find that the pesto flavor wasn't at the fore. Swapping out the duo of ground beef and pork for milder ground turkey did the trick; now the pesto flavor could really come through.

With the revamped meatballs perfected, I turned my attention to the sauce. I certainly wasn't going to stoop to jarred sauce, but I also didn't want to spend hours tending a simmering sauce. To keep the shopping list short, I picked up just three cans of diced tomatoes, an onion, and some garlic. I pulsed two cans of tomatoes in the food processor until the tomatoes were mostly smooth. The third I left as is so that the end result would be a mostly smooth sauce with a few bigger bites of tomato. After browning the meatballs, I set them aside momentarily and started the sauce in the same skillet. I first browned the onion, then added the garlic and some red pepper flakes. Next I added all of the tomatoes and simmered them for 10 minutes to thicken the sauce and allow the aromatics to infuse the sauce with their flavors. Then it was time to nestle the meatballs into the sauce and let them simmer until cooked through. Meanwhile, I boiled and drained my noodles so they were ready to go when the sauce and meatballs were done.

This recipe was packed with flavor and came together like clockwork. And while it didn't completely buck tradition, I was confident it would be just unconventional enough to liven up my next spaghetti-and-meatballs supper.

—ADELAIDE PARKER, *America's Test Kitchen Books*

NOTES FROM THE TEST KITCHEN

MAKING SMALL-BATCH PESTO
Process 2 cups packed fresh basil leaves, 6 tablespoons extra-virgin olive oil, 2 tablespoons toasted pine nuts, and 1 small minced garlic clove together in food processor until smooth, scraping down bowl as needed. Transfer pesto to bowl, stir in ¼ cup grated Parmesan cheese, and season with salt and pepper to taste. Makes about ⅔ cup.

THE BEST SPAGHETTI
Spaghetti makes a versatile partner for just about any type of sauce. Plus, it promises a cheap dinner—or at least it used to. When we recently checked out brands at the supermarket, we saw a few boxes priced around a dollar, while others cost four times that. We sampled eight brands of spaghetti to find out if we had to spend more money for great pasta. After cooking and tasting six Italian imports and two domestic brands dressed simply with olive oil and tossed with a tomato sauce, we found our winner. Our favorite spaghetti—and also one of the two cheapest brands we tasted (less than $2 a pound)—was an Italian import. Tasters preferred **DeCecco Spaghetti no. 12** for its "clean wheat flavor" and "firm" strands with "good chew." (See page 298 for more information about our testing results.)

Spaghetti with Turkey-Pesto Meatballs
SERVES 4 TO 6

You can make your own pesto (see page 118) or use store-bought pesto from the refrigerated section of the supermarket—it has a fresher flavor than the jarred pesto sold in the grocery aisles. Do not use ground turkey breast meat (sometimes also labeled as 99 percent fat-free); it will make meatballs that are dry and grainy. You can substitute ground chicken, pork, or 90 percent lean beef for the ground turkey if desired. You will need a 12-inch skillet with at least 2-inch sides to accommodate both the meatballs and the sauce; the skillet will be quite full.

1½ pounds 93 percent lean ground turkey
1 (7-ounce) container basil pesto (⅔ cup)
⅔ cup panko bread crumbs
    Salt and pepper
3 (14.5-ounce) cans diced tomatoes
1 tablespoon olive oil
1 onion, chopped fine
4 garlic cloves, minced
    Pinch red pepper flakes
1 pound spaghetti
3 tablespoons chopped fresh basil

1. Gently mix turkey, pesto, panko, ½ teaspoon salt, and ¼ teaspoon pepper together in bowl using hands until uniform. Roll mixture into eighteen 1½-inch meatballs. Lay meatballs on large plate, cover, and refrigerate until firm, about 1 hour.

2. Pulse 2 cans diced tomatoes and their juice in food processor until mostly smooth, about 12 pulses; set aside. Heat oil in 12-inch nonstick skillet over medium heat until just smoking. Brown meatballs well on all sides, about 10 minutes; transfer to paper towel–lined plate.

3. Add onion and ⅛ teaspoon salt to fat left in skillet and cook over medium heat until softened, 5 to 7 minutes. Stir in garlic and pepper flakes and cook for 30 seconds. Stir in processed tomatoes and remaining 1 can diced tomatoes and their juice. Bring to simmer and cook for 10 minutes. Return meatballs to skillet, cover, and simmer gently until meatballs are cooked through, about 10 minutes.

4. Meanwhile, bring 4 quarts water to boil in large pot. Add pasta and 1 tablespoon salt and cook, stirring often, until al dente. Reserve 1 cup cooking water, then drain pasta and return it to pot. Add several large spoonfuls of tomato sauce (without meatballs) to pasta and toss to combine. Season with salt and pepper to taste and add reserved cooking water as needed to adjust consistency. Divide pasta among individual bowls. Top each bowl with remaining sauce and meatballs and sprinkle with basil. Serve.

RAGU ALLA BOLOGNESE

RAGU ALLA BOLOGNESE, THE HEARTY MEAT SAUCE native to the northern Italian city for which it is named, has always been a simple concept—but with a lot of complications to hamper its simplicity. Despite its undisputed Bolognese pedigree, there are countless "authentic" interpretations on record. While ground beef is the common starting point, many versions include ground pork and often veal as well. In others the ground meat is supplemented with finely chopped *salumi*, usually pancetta or prosciutto. Some recipes call for brightening the ragu with crushed tomatoes; others lean toward the drier, more concentrated depth of tomato paste. One version may call for white wine, another for red; some call for no wine at all. Cooking times range from 90 minutes to three hours.

But the most controversial point of all? Dairy. Depending on which source you consult, milk and/or cream either is an essential component, lending further richness and tenderizing the long-cooked meat, or it has no place in the sauce whatsoever. In other words, what constitutes "real" ragu Bolognese is largely a matter of interpretation. The only thing that all Italian cooks seem to agree on is this: The end product should be hearty and rich but not cloying, with a velvety texture that lightly clings to the noodles—and tomatoes should be a bit player in this show. The true star is the meat.

I'd never felt strongly about the dairy issue myself until recently, when I sampled a Bolognese sauce made by Dante de Magistris, an Italian chef in Boston with a big following. His version was by far the meatiest, most complex version I'd ever had. I was so taken with it that I asked him for a breakdown of the recipe. Two points stood out. First, he used a whopping six meats: ground beef, pork, veal, pancetta, mortadella (bologna-like Italian deli meat), and, to my surprise, chicken livers. Second, de Magistris stood squarely in the no-dairy camp, saying that when he learned to make the dish in

Bologna, milk and cream were definitely not included.

Those clues—plus the test kitchen's library of Italian cookbooks—were enough to get me started on my own dairy-free Bolognese. I was determined to make my version home cook–friendly and yet satisfying to even the most discriminating Italian palate.

I started with a test batch that I cobbled together based on de Magistris's version, loading up the pot with the components of the flavor base, or *soffritto* (chopped carrot, celery, and onion), followed by five different meats. (I wasn't sure I really needed the chicken livers, so I left them out for the time being.) I then stirred in crushed tomatoes. I let it all simmer, covered, for a

NOTES FROM THE TEST KITCHEN

BUILDING A MEATY, SATINY-TEXTURED BOLOGNESE

1. Cook ground meats, then add depth by sautéing chopped mortadella, pancetta, and sage in rendered fat.

2. Add soffritto and sweat it until softened, then add concentrated tomato flavor with tomato paste.

3. Deglaze pot with wine; stir in broth plus bloomed gelatin to develop luxurious silky texture.

4. Stir in pureed chicken livers for subtle but rich taste.

couple of hours. The result was acceptably rich and flavorful, but it still needed a good bit of tweaking, to both the ingredient list and the technique.

I made several more batches, adding a fistful of minced sage to the meat—considered an essential component by some sources—and trying various proportions of all five meats until I landed on equal amounts of the ground beef, pork, and veal and 4 ounces each of pancetta and mortadella. Some of the other classic Bolognese recipes I'd consulted specified that the ground meat should be cooked only until it loses its pink color, lest the browning lead to toughness. But I found the textural compromise in the finished sauce to be far subtler than the flavor benefit of a good sear. I also decided to ignore tradition and add the meat to the pot before the soffritto. Without the interference of moisture from the vegetables, I could get a much better sear on the meat, and sautéing the veggies in the rendered fat built up even richer flavor.

What gave me pause was a more minor complaint: finely chopping the pancetta and mortadella. It was tedious work, so I called on my food processor to take over. The job was literally done with the push of a button. In fact, the appliance worked so efficiently that I also pulsed the soffritto components before sautéing them.

I moved on to the next major decision: the best kind of tomato product to use. The recipes I'd read didn't help narrow things down—I'd seen everything from the crushed tomatoes I had been using to tomato sauce to paste. One source I consulted even suggested that tomatoes were not originally part of the sauce. That reminded me that I had liked the unobtrusive texture of tomato paste in de Magistris's version, so I added a healthy dollop to the pot. Once the fond had taken on a deep rust tone, I poured in a few big glugs of red wine, deglazed the pan by scraping up the browned bits with a wooden spoon, and let the sauce simmer gently for the better part of two hours. When the sauce was nearly done, I boiled some pasta, then tossed the noodles with the ragu.

Flavor-wise, the sauce was in good shape: rich and complex and, thanks to the wine and tomato paste, balanced with just enough acidity. But as my tasters noted, this ragu had a textural flaw: Its consistency was pebbly, dry, and not particularly saucelike.

There was one element of de Magistris's recipe that I had overlooked in my earlier attempts: Just before the long simmering step, he ladled some homemade *brodo* (or broth) into the ragu, repeating the step twice more during cooking to moisten the reduced sauce. I suspected that the brodo—and the technique of adding the brodo in stages—had an important effect on the texture of the Bolognese. Besides boosting the meaty flavor, the bones used to make the broth give up lots of gelatin as they simmer, which renders the liquid glossy and viscous. The more the broth reduced in the Bolognese, the more savory and satiny it became. But homemade broth was out of the question for me. Simmering bones for hours on top of making the ragu was just too much fuss; I'd have to make do with commercial broth.

No surprise here: The ragus I made with store-bought broth didn't measure up to Bolognese made with homemade broth—especially in regard to texture. I started brainstorming other ways to mimic the velvetiness contributed by the gelatin in real brodo—and realized that the answer was simple: powdered gelatin. It's a trick we've used to lend suppleness to all-beef meatloaf and viscosity to beef stew—two qualities that I was looking for in my ragu. I prepped multiple batches of the sauce, blooming varying amounts of gelatin—from 1 teaspoon all the way up to a whopping 8—in a combination of store-bought beef and chicken broths before proceeding with the recipe. Every batch was an improvement over the gelatin-free version, but the effect was relatively subtle until I got up into the higher amounts of gelatin, which rendered the sauce ultra-silky. That settled it: Eight teaspoons it was.

I had one more thought about the store-bought broth: Since the flavor and body of the store-bought stuff hardly equaled that of a real brodo, I wondered if the reduction step was really doing that much for the sauce. One side-by-side test gave me my answer: The batch to which I'd added all the broth at once boasted just as much meatiness and body as the one with the staggered additions. It also finished cooking in about 90 minutes.

And yet while store-bought broth plus gelatin nicely solved the texture problem, the sauce still lacked a certain depth and roundness of flavor. Fortunately, I still had one card left to play: chicken livers. They'd seemed superfluous to me at first, but I wondered if finely chopping them and tossing them in at the end might get at the complexity I was after. That they did—but according to my tasters, their effect was a bit too strong. Pureeing them in the food processor worked much better; this way, their rich, gamy flavor incorporated seamlessly into the sauce.

Though my sauce could hardly get any more perfect, I just couldn't push away the thought that kept sneaking into my head: What would happen if the sauce included a little dairy? I made one last batch, adding 1 cup of milk along with the broth. But when my tasters sampled this latest version, the consensus was unanimous: Dairy muted its meaty flavor, and they liked it better without.

Without dairy, I knew that some Italian cooks out there would not consider my recipe authentic. But no matter: The sauce was undeniably complex, rich-tasting, and lusciously silky. And besides, how could any version be Bolognese without a little controversy?

—BRYAN ROOF, *Cook's Illustrated*

Ragu alla Bolognese
MAKES ABOUT 6 CUPS

This recipe makes enough sauce for 2 pounds of pasta. Eight teaspoons of gelatin is equivalent to one (1-ounce) box of gelatin. If you can't find ground veal, use an additional ¾ pound of ground beef.

- 1 cup low-sodium chicken broth
- 1 cup beef broth
- 8 teaspoons unflavored gelatin
- 1 onion, chopped coarse
- 1 large carrot, peeled and chopped coarse
- 1 celery rib, chopped coarse
- 4 ounces pancetta, chopped
- 4 ounces mortadella, chopped
- 6 ounces chicken livers, trimmed
- 3 tablespoons extra-virgin olive oil
- ¾ pound 85 percent lean ground beef
- ¾ pound ground veal
- ¾ pound ground pork
- 3 tablespoons minced fresh sage
- 1 (6-ounce) can tomato paste
- 2 cups dry red wine
- Salt and pepper
- 1 pound pappardelle or tagliatelle
- Grated Parmesan cheese

1. Combine chicken broth and beef broth in bowl; sprinkle gelatin over top and set aside. Pulse onion, carrot, and celery together in food processor until finely chopped, about 10 pulses, scraping down bowl as needed; transfer to separate bowl. Pulse pancetta and mortadella together in now-empty food processor until

finely chopped, about 25 pulses, scraping down bowl as needed; transfer to second bowl. Process chicken livers in now-empty food processor until pureed, about 5 seconds; transfer to third bowl.

2. Heat oil in Dutch oven over medium-high heat until shimmering. Add beef, veal, and pork; cook, breaking up pieces with wooden spoon, until all liquid has evaporated and meat begins to sizzle, 10 to 15 minutes. Add pancetta mixture and sage; cook, stirring frequently, until pancetta is translucent, 5 to 7 minutes, adjusting heat as needed to keep fond from burning. Add chopped vegetables and cook, stirring frequently, until softened, 5 to 7 minutes. Add tomato paste and cook, stirring constantly, until rust-colored and fragrant, about 3 minutes.

3. Stir in wine, scraping up any browned bits. Simmer until sauce has thickened, about 5 minutes. Stir in broth mixture and return to simmer. Reduce heat to low and cook at bare simmer until thickened (wooden spoon should leave trail when dragged through sauce), about 1½ hours.

4. Stir in pureed chicken livers, bring to boil, and remove from heat. Season with salt and pepper to taste; cover and keep warm.

5. Bring 4 quarts water to boil in large pot. Add pasta and 1 tablespoon salt and cook, stirring often, until al dente. Reserve ¾ cup cooking water, then drain pasta and return it to pot. Add half of sauce and cooking water to pasta and toss to combine. Transfer to serving bowl and serve, passing Parmesan separately. (Leftover sauce may be refrigerated for up to 3 days or frozen for up to 1 month.)

RIGATONI WITH GENOVESE RAGU

HEARTY, RICH BOLOGNESE MIGHT BE THE MOST famous of the Italian ragus, but there are others that are equally delicious but for one reason or another have been paid far less attention. One such sauce is la Genovese, a hearty beef and onion sauce that has been around for centuries but still isn't all that familiar outside its place of origin, Naples. That's right—despite its name, la Genovese sauce doesn't even come from Genoa; in fact, it's hardly known there. But whatever its origin, when I recently discovered a recipe for it, I quickly decided this one-of-a-kind sauce had to be added to my hearty wintertime cooking repertoire. While most Neapolitan pasta sauces feature tomatoes—tomatoes grow well in this southern region of Italy—la Genovese is tomato-free. Instead, this hearty ragu features beef braised slowly with white wine and an abundance of onions until the meat is fall-apart tender and the onions and wine cook down into a rich, almost creamy sauce. I wanted to find out if this little-known regional dish had as much satisfying, flavorful potential as I suspected.

I couldn't find more than a handful of recipes worth testing, but the cooking method across these few was relatively similar. In each a large beef roast, such as a chuck or top round, was browned, then gently braised with onions (anywhere from 2 to 4 pounds) as well as a smattering of carrot, celery, and sometimes herbs. The braising liquid was always white wine, but as with the onions, the amounts I came across varied from recipe to recipe. The meat and vegetables were braised in the wine until the beef became incredibly tender and the onions turned sweet, rich, and velvety. The sauce was then served over a sturdy short pasta that would catch the meat and onions.

My first move was to swap out the large roast for short ribs. Most recipes called for a 2-pound beef roast, a slightly unusual size, and it would require more prep than the ribs. Plus, I knew the bones from the ribs would add great meaty flavor and a richness to the sauce that I wouldn't get from a boneless roast.

Most recipes also included some other meaty addition, such as a few ounces of salami, prosciutto, and/or pancetta. The salami seemed like an odd fit, and the pieces of prosciutto dried out and became unappealingly tough after the long cooking time. However, the more tender pancetta was a winner, melting into the sauce and adding a nice boost of meaty flavor.

I began by browning the ribs, then set them aside so I could add vegetables and pancetta to the pot. I stuck with the standard carrot and celery, which I sautéed until just softened before adding the onions. Some recipes used just 2 pounds of onions, but once cooked down, this seemed like far too little for a starring ingredient, so I doubled the amount to 4 pounds. In most of the recipes I found the onions were added and the meat was returned to the pot for the long braise all at once, but having sampled the results from this method, I knew the onions would benefit from building up a little more flavor in the pot on their own first. After adding them to the sautéed carrot and celery, I cooked the onions covered for 10 minutes until they released their moisture, then I turned down the heat and cooked them uncovered just until they started to turn golden brown. This extra step dramatically deepened their flavor.

At this point, I added the wine, returned the meat to the pot, and let it gently simmer. Once the meat was tender and falling off the bone, which took about two hours, I removed the ribs and shredded the meat, throwing out the bones and excess fat. The sauce at this point was still a little loose, so I let it continue to simmer until it was thick and creamy before stirring the shredded meat back into the pot. A few tests proved that the 3 cups of wine some recipes called for was way too much; it resulted in a sauce that was out of balance and too loose. Just 1 cup of wine allowed the meat to properly cook through while staying moist, and it cooked down with the vegetables to just the right consistency.

NOTES FROM THE TEST KITCHEN

THE BEST INEXPENSIVE STOCKPOT

Stockpots come in handy when preparing big batches of soup or making pasta for a crowd. But given that it's not a daily-use pot, we didn't want to shell out the big bucks. We gathered seven 12-quart stockpots, each costing less than $40, and used them to boil a double batch of spaghetti and a dozen ears of corn and simmer big batches of chili.

With more surface area in contact with the heat, a wide bottom heats water faster. Wider pots accommodated the corn more comfortably, and pots with lower, shorter sides let us see the contents and stir without burning our knuckles. Our top-ranking pots were both under 9 inches tall, with bottoms more than 10 inches wide. The handles were more important: Big, sturdy, protruding handles gave us a good grip, even with oven mitts. We also demanded that pots have lids, which confine the steam and expedite boiling. When it came to the chili, we confirmed our suspicion that a thick, heavy Dutch oven would work much better; there was at least some scorching in every stockpot, although the higher-ranked pots performed slightly better.

We found our winner in the **Alpha Heavy Gauge 12-Quart Stainless Steel Stock Pot with Glass Lid**, which cost just $26. With a low, wide profile, easy-to-grasp handles, generous capacity, sturdy construction, and affordable price, it's our top pick for a big pot devoted to boiling. (See page 305 for more information about our testing results.)

As for seasonings, recipes ran the gamut in terms of herbs. One used none at all while another included a veritable herb garden of parsley, basil, sage, bay leaves, and rosemary. I wanted to keep things simple but flavorful; a tablespoon of thyme or marjoram did the trick. I also found that while this is traditionally a tomato-free recipe, a couple of tablespoons of tomato paste lent great depth without adding a distinctly tomato flavor.

It required a little work at the outset, but for several hours my recipe was hands-off. And by the end, I had a meaty, hearty, and just slightly sweet ragu that was unlike any I'd had before. Served over rigatoni with a dusting of grated Pecorino Romano, I knew my take on la Genovese would be a welcome change of pace for any ragu fan.

—ADELAIDE PARKER, *America's Test Kitchen Books*

Rigatoni with Genovese Ragu
SERVES 8 TO 10

To prevent the sauce from becoming greasy, trim as much fat as possible from the ribs. You will need at least a 6-quart Dutch oven and a 12-quart stockpot for this recipe.

4	pounds beef short ribs, trimmed
	Salt and pepper
1	tablespoon vegetable oil
4	ounces pancetta, cut into ¼-inch pieces
2	carrots, peeled and cut into ¼-inch pieces
2	celery ribs, cut into ¼-inch pieces
4	pounds onions, halved and sliced thin
2	tablespoons tomato paste
1	tablespoon minced fresh marjoram or thyme
1	cup dry white wine
2	pounds rigatoni
	Grated Pecorino Romano cheese

1. Pat ribs dry with paper towels and season with salt and pepper. Heat oil in large Dutch oven over medium-high heat until just smoking. Brown half of ribs well on all sides, 8 to 10 minutes; transfer to plate. Repeat with remaining ribs using fat left in pot; transfer to plate.

2. Pour off all but 1 tablespoon fat left in pot, add pancetta, and cook over medium heat until pancetta is lightly browned, about 6 minutes. Stir in carrots and celery and cook until just softened, 5 to 7 minutes.

3. Stir in onions and ¼ teaspoon salt. Increase heat to

high, cover, and cook, stirring occasionally, until onions are wilted and release their moisture, about 10 minutes. Uncover, reduce heat to medium-high, and continue to cook, stirring often, until onions are golden brown, 8 to 10 minutes longer.

4. Stir in tomato paste and marjoram and cook until fragrant, about 1 minute. Add wine and simmer for 2 minutes. Nestle beef with any accumulated juices into pot and bring to gentle simmer. Reduce heat to low, cover, and simmer gently, turning ribs occasionally, until meat is very tender and falling off bones, about 2 hours.

5. Transfer ribs to plate, let cool slightly, then shred meat into bite-size pieces, discarding fat and bones. Meanwhile, return sauce to simmer and cook, stirring often, until slightly thickened and creamy, 12 to 15 minutes. Stir in shredded meat and season with salt and pepper to taste.

6. Meanwhile, bring 8 quarts water to boil in 12-quart pot. Add pasta and 2 tablespoons salt and cook, stirring often, until al dente. Reserve 1½ cups cooking water, then drain pasta and return it to pot. Add sauce and ½ cup cooking water; toss to combine. Season with salt and pepper to taste and add remaining reserved cooking water as needed to adjust consistency. Serve with Pecorino.

CHICKEN TETRAZZINI

TETRAZZINI IS THE ULTIMATE COMFORT FOOD— noodles, poultry, and vegetables baked in cream sauce, with a crumb topping and loads of cheese and butter. Although I could swear my grandmother invented it, it was actually created in the early 1900s, long before the age of calorie counting and concern about fat. No surprise, then, that just a single serving contains almost 450 calories and as much as 25 grams of fat. (It's even named after a famously full-figured opera star.)

And no surprise, either, that many low-fat recipes exist. I gathered a handful and got to work. For the sauce, these recipes variously combined egg whites, cornstarch, canned evaporated milk, and margarine or vegetable oil—which were fine if you like bland, tinny flavors and punishingly lean, pasty sauces.

I switched to a high-fat recipe, opting to whittle it down myself. I sautéed mushrooms and onions in butter, made a white sauce (melting more butter, whisking in flour for a roux, and pouring in heavy cream),

and stirred in sherry—a classic Tetrazzini flavor—and Parmesan cheese. I combined the sauce, vegetables, boiled noodles, and cubed leftover chicken (turkey is traditional, but I'm less likely to have it on hand), dumped everything into a casserole dish, and baked.

Before I cut a single calorie or gram of fat, I noticed that the chicken was chalky. Chicken tends toward dryness under the best of circumstances. Cooked twice, it didn't stand a chance. A few tests showed I could use diced raw chicken (boneless, skinless breasts for ease) if I let it begin cooking in the sauce on the stovetop. A quick marinade in soy sauce both added flavor and helped keep the chicken juicy (a soak in salty soy sauce mimics a saltwater brine). Then I turned to my main concern—fat and calories.

The cream would have to go. Borrowing an idea from a low-fat recipe I'd seen, I replaced it with low-fat milk and low-fat mozzarella. As the mild cheese melted, it gave the sauce body (good) and made it stringy (bad). Searching for a mild, low-fat cheese that could perform the same function more smoothly, I tried neufchatel (cream cheese with one-third less fat). It yielded a full-bodied, less caloric sauce. To cut down further, I replaced part of the milk with some of the starchy water in which the noodles had boiled; this helped thicken the sauce. Come to think of it, was that roux absolutely necessary? I skipped the butter and whisked the flour right into the pasta water—with excellent results.

The consistency of the sauce was on target, but it tasted bland. We test cooks put our heads together, and someone suggested I toast the flour. I wasn't convinced it would help, but in fact, toasting added a pleasant, nutty dimension. Next, since the neufchatel provided creaminess to spare, I replaced the remaining milk with more flavorful chicken broth. The sauce went from blah to bright.

Finally, I reconsidered the vegetables. In recipes for full-fat Tetrazzini, the mushrooms and the chopped onion are sautéed in as much as a stick of butter. I cut back tablespoon by tablespoon, and surprisingly I found that just a single tablespoon offered enough buttery presence.

Altogether, I had reduced the recipe by 160 calories and 18 grams of fat per serving. The numbers were so good that I was able to leave the crunchy (and, all things considered, only moderately caloric and fatty) bread-crumb topping alone. This reduced-fat Tetrazzini is so satisfying that it is destined to become a weeknight staple.

—CAROLYNN PURPURA MACKAY, *Cook's Country*

Reduced-Fat Chicken Tetrazzini

SERVES 6

You can substitute 2 cups chopped cooked turkey for the chicken, omitting the marinade and the simmer in step 4.

- 12 ounces boneless, skinless chicken breasts, trimmed and cut into ¾-inch pieces
- 2 tablespoons soy sauce
- 1 slice hearty white sandwich bread, torn into quarters
- 7 tablespoons grated Parmesan cheese Salt and pepper
- 5 ounces spaghetti, broken in half
- 2 tablespoons all-purpose flour
- 1 tablespoon unsalted butter
- 8 ounces white or cremini mushrooms, trimmed and sliced thin
- 1 onion, chopped fine
- 1 cup frozen peas
- 1 cup low-sodium chicken broth
- 2 tablespoons dry sherry
- 3 ounces neufchatel cream cheese

1. Combine chicken and soy sauce in zipper-lock bag and refrigerate for 30 minutes to 1 hour. Pulse bread, 2 tablespoons Parmesan, ¼ teaspoon salt, and ¼ teaspoon pepper in food processor until finely ground, 8 to 10 pulses.

2. Meanwhile, adjust oven rack to upper-middle position and heat oven to 400 degrees. Bring 2 quarts water to boil in large saucepan. Add pasta and 1½ teaspoons salt and cook, stirring often, until just al dente. Reserve ½ cup cooking water, then drain pasta and return it to saucepan. Toast flour in 12-inch skillet over medium heat, stirring constantly, until just beginning to brown, about 5 minutes. Whisk flour into reserved cooking water; set aside.

3. Melt butter in now-empty skillet over medium-high heat. Add mushrooms, onion, ½ teaspoon salt, and ½ teaspoon pepper and cook until browned, 6 to 8 minutes. Stir in peas and add mixture to saucepan with pasta.

4. Add broth and sherry to now-empty skillet, scraping up any browned bits. Stir in reserved flour mixture, cream cheese, and remaining 5 tablespoons Parmesan and bring to boil, whisking until smooth. Add chicken and simmer until exterior of chicken is opaque, about 1 minute. Add chicken mixture to pasta mixture and toss until combined. Scrape into 8-inch square baking dish and top with bread-crumb mixture. Bake until golden brown, 12 to 14 minutes. Let cool on wire rack for 10 minutes. Serve.

VEGETABLE LASAGNA

VEGETABLE LASAGNA MADE WITH THE CLASSIC TRIO of eggplant, zucchini, and summer squash sounds like a perfect hearty summer supper, especially when the produce is in season and locally grown. But I've rarely cooked one that I've been moved to make again. Some look tempting enough with a topcoat of bubbly cheese and thick tomato gravy, but they invariably reveal trouble at the core. Often placed between the pasta sheets raw, the zucchini and squash turn out steamed and limp, flooding the dish with their juices—or, in some instances, undercooked and crunchy. Then there's the eggplant, which is typically not only soggy but greasy from prefrying. Add to that the usual patches of dry, grainy ricotta, and it's a wonder this dish ever became an Italian-American standard. So what would it take to make a full-flavored lasagna with vegetables that could stand up to—not wash out—the cheese and sauce? Ridding the produce of some of its moisture and boosting its flavor before adding it to the dish would be steps in the right direction.

I first focused my efforts on the most challenging element: the eggplant. Besides being full of water, eggplant is extremely porous and readily soaks up any available liquid (including oil). It therefore requires some sort of pretreatment that not only rids the fruit of water but also breaks down its absorbent air pockets. Fortunately, the test kitchen had already devised an effective—and novel—approach to both problems in

another recipe: salting the eggplant and then heating it in the microwave. Salt pulls water out of the fruit through osmosis, and the microwave causes it to steam. Microwaving also collapses the eggplant's air pockets, leaving the fruit shrunken, wrinkled, and less prone to absorbing oil or liquid. Following this method, I cut the eggplant into ½-inch cubes, sprinkled them with 1 teaspoon of salt, and placed the pieces on a double layer of coffee filters. (The filters absorb moisture so that liquid doesn't pool on the plate.) I then microwaved the eggplant for 10 minutes. When I sautéed the pretreated eggplant to give it more flavor and color, it hardly picked up any oil at all.

I considered salting the zucchini and yellow squash to remove their excess water, but I was fairly certain that a turn in the skillet would burn off enough fluid, and it would also deepen their flavor. I cut the squashes (1 pound of each) into ½-inch cubes and, to save myself an extra step, combined them in a bowl with the microwaved eggplant. I then sautéed the mixture in two batches with minced garlic and healthy dashes of salt and pepper. About seven minutes later, the vegetables had developed good color and picked up some garlicky flavor, but I wondered if I could do better. I minced a few more cloves of garlic, this time letting the bits soak in a tablespoon of olive oil along with some minced fresh thyme. Added to the skillet as each batch of vegetables finished cooking, this super-garlicky, herb-infused mixture gave the eggplant and squash so much flavor that they were good enough to eat straight from the pan.

Now it was time to see how the vegetables would fare in the lasagna. I made a placeholder tomato sauce by briefly simmering crushed tomatoes with garlic, olive oil, basil, and a dash of pepper flakes. I then layered a dozen no-boil noodles (our favorite speedy alternative to fresh pasta) with the sauce, the sautéed eggplant and vegetables, and generous helpings of ricotta, mozzarella, and nutty Parmesan cheese. I baked the casserole in a 375-degree oven until golden and bubbly.

The good news was that starting with precooked vegetables allowed me to cut the baking time from the usual hour-plus down to about 35 minutes. But improvements were still needed here and there. Instead of acting as a creamy binder, the ricotta had cooked up into grainy slicks, and some tasters wanted the dairy

element to be even richer. Plus, we all agreed that the tomato sauce tasted a bit flat.

I had one quick idea about the ricotta, thanks to the efforts of another colleague who'd encountered similar graininess when he tried incorporating the tiny, pebbly curds into baked ziti. To solve the problem, he substituted cottage cheese, which boasts a creamier consistency (not to mention slightly tangier flavor), for the ricotta. When I made the switch in my next batch, everyone agreed that things were looking up, but that the cheese was still a bit dry and lean-tasting. In fact, this round of testing convinced me that what we all really wanted was the richness and creaminess of a béchamel sauce, the classic roux-thickened milk mixture found in countless meat and vegetable lasagna recipes. My only hesitation was that it involved extra work. I didn't want to add more fuss to the dish by cooking a third element, so I tried a lazy man's approach and whipped up a no-cook white sauce by whisking together 1 cup each of milk and cottage cheese with a generous 2 cups of Parmesan and a couple of minced garlic cloves.

I wasn't expecting much from this experiment, but the results were surprisingly good. All that cheese produced a "sauce" that was considerably richer, if still a bit thin and curdled. The first problem I easily fixed by swapping the milk for an equal amount of heavy cream. The second took a bit more experimentation, but a glossy, silky-smooth sauce finally came together after I whisked 1 teaspoon of cornstarch with the dairy ingredients. (When the starch granules in cornstarch absorb water and swell, they get in the way of the dairy proteins and prevent them from clumping together in curds.)

As for the tomato sauce, I couldn't help but wonder if a similar no-cook approach might liven up its dull flavor—and save a few extra minutes at the stove. I prepared another batch, this time simply stirring together the ingredients and adding the sauce to the casserole without simmering it first. The results were better than ever. Even after baking and cooling, the sauce still tasted bright, punching up the filling with just enough acidity.

And yet balancing the complexity of the dairy-rich "béchamel" sauce with the fruity tomato sauce didn't quite perk up tasters' interest in the filling. I needed

VEGETABLE LASAGNA

KEYS TO HEARTY VEGETABLE LASAGNA

1. Use cottage cheese for a tangier flavor and creamier consistency than drier, more pebbly ricotta.

2. For a quick version of traditional cooked béchamel, whisk together heavy cream, Parmesan, cottage cheese, and garlic, then add directly to casserole.

3. Stir together crushed tomatoes, basil, garlic, and olive oil for a sauce with bright flavor that saves time at the stove.

4. Salt, then microwave cubes of eggplant for 10 minutes to eliminate moisture that would flood lasagna and to collapse air pockets so eggplant soaks up less oil.

5. Toss microwaved eggplant into hot skillet with squashes to rid them of water and develop flavorful browning.

6. Stir in garlic-thyme oil with sautéed eggplant, summer squash, and zucchini near the end of cooking for added depth.

THE BEST GRATER

To grate piles of mozzarella for pizza or pasta, we've always reached for a four-sided box grater. But given that we tend to use only the one side with large holes—rarely do we grate on the panel with medium-size holes, and we never use the slicing blade or pinhole-style grating holes (mandolines and rasp graters work much better)—we got to thinking: Does it really make sense to buy a tool with three out of four functions that you never even use? So we gathered nine graters, including two flat paddles, a few two- or three-sided models, and a few standard four-sided brands to find a sturdy tool that could easily produce perfect shreds of everything from cheeses to carrots and potatoes.

In the mozzarella test, we found that a generous-size grating plane and large holes mattered more than the sharpness of the grater's teeth. We also preferred simpler designs with uncomplicated features: comfortable handles that eased the repetitive motion of grating and wide, rubber-lined feet that kept the grater securely anchored to the counter. When grating carrots and potatoes, hole design was the most critical feature. We preferred graters with stamped designs over etched graters; stamped designs sported thicker, more rigid grating surfaces that didn't budge when we pressed firmly against them, while etched graters, made by corroding thin, flexible steel, have super-sharp teeth that indent just enough to snag foods—and fingers.

In the end, we found the best grater in a paddle-style model. With its sharp, extra-large holes and spacious, inflexible stamped grating surface, the **Rösle Coarse Grater**, $35, whizzed through cheese, potatoes, and carrots faster than any other model, and its rubber-bottomed feet ensured that it stayed put. Its bent legs hooked around the lip of large bowls, and without the enclosed tower design, we never had to worry about unloading shreds. Another big plus: Its flat design makes for easy storage. (See page 309 for more information about our testing results.)

SHRINKING EGGPLANT DOWN TO SIZE

Eggplant is full of water that will wash out the flavors of lasagna as it bakes in the oven. It's also riddled with air pockets that act as a magnet for oil. Salting the cubed fruit and then microwaving it solves both problems: Microwaving not only speeds up salt's ability to pull moisture out of the eggplant but also collapses the eggplant's air pockets. (We set the eggplant on a double layer of coffee filters to absorb the excess moisture as it is released.) The result: low-moisture, meaty-tasting eggplant that doesn't soak up too much oil when sautéed.

RAW   SALTED + MICROWAVED

something bolder and fresher to complement the eggplant, zucchini, and squash. Rummaging through the refrigerator for ideas, I spotted a jar of kalamata olives. A handful of chopped olives added meaty texture and a briny, salty jolt of flavor. For freshness, I added a bag of baby spinach, which took no time to sauté in a touch of olive oil until wilted and then drain before layering it into the filling. My final touch was a generous amount of chopped fresh basil leaves sprinkled on the casserole right before serving. Each of these additions was small, but together they made a big difference in the flavor of the dish.

At last, this lasagna more than had it all with its rich flavors, creamy cheese, and substantial texture—along with a summery brightness that set it apart from the meat versions. I had to restrain a smile when I saw that even the most dedicated meat lovers among my tasters couldn't help but come back for more.

—BRYAN ROOF, *Cook's Illustrated*

Vegetable Lasagna

SERVES 8 TO 10

We prefer the lasagna made with our favorite whole-milk, block-style mozzarella from Sorrento, but Kraft part-skim preshredded mozzarella will also work. (See page 291 for more information about our testing results.) Our preferred brands of crushed tomatoes are Tuttorosso and Muir Glen.

TOMATO SAUCE

- 1 (28-ounce) can crushed tomatoes
- ¼ cup chopped fresh basil
- 2 tablespoons extra-virgin olive oil
- 2 garlic cloves, minced
- 1 teaspoon kosher salt
- ¼ teaspoon red pepper flakes

CREAM SAUCE

- 4 ounces Parmesan cheese, grated (2 cups)
- 1 cup whole-milk cottage cheese
- 1 cup heavy cream
- 4 garlic cloves, minced
- 1 teaspoon cornstarch
- ½ teaspoon kosher salt
- ½ teaspoon pepper

FILLING

- 1½ pounds eggplant, peeled and cut into ½-inch cubes (7 cups)
  Kosher salt and pepper
- 1 pound zucchini, cut into ½-inch pieces (4 cups)
- 1 pound yellow squash, cut into ½-inch pieces (4 cups)
- 5 tablespoons plus 1 teaspoon extra-virgin olive oil
- 4 garlic cloves, minced
- 1 tablespoon minced fresh thyme
- 12 ounces (12 cups) baby spinach
- 12 no-boil lasagna noodles
- ½ cup pitted kalamata olives, minced
- 12 ounces low-moisture whole-milk mozzarella cheese, shredded (3 cups)
- 2 tablespoons chopped fresh basil

1. FOR THE TOMATO SAUCE: Whisk all ingredients together in bowl; set aside.

2. FOR THE CREAM SAUCE: Whisk all ingredients together in bowl; set aside.

3. FOR THE FILLING: Adjust oven rack to middle position and heat oven to 375 degrees. Toss eggplant with 1 teaspoon salt in large bowl. Line surface of large plate with double layer of coffee filters and lightly spray with vegetable oil spray. Spread eggplant in even layer on filters. Wipe out and reserve now-empty bowl. Microwave eggplant, uncovered, until dry to touch and slightly shriveled, about 10 minutes, tossing once halfway through cooking to ensure that eggplant cooks evenly. Let cool slightly. Return eggplant to bowl and toss with zucchini and squash.

4. Combine 1 tablespoon oil, garlic, and thyme in small bowl. Heat 2 tablespoons oil in 12-inch non-stick skillet over medium-high heat until shimmering. Add half of eggplant mixture, ¼ teaspoon salt, and ¼ teaspoon pepper; cook, stirring occasionally, until vegetables are lightly browned, about 7 minutes. Push vegetables to sides of skillet; add half of garlic mixture to center of skillet and cook, mashing with spatula, until fragrant, about 30 seconds. Stir to combine garlic mixture with vegetables and transfer to medium bowl. Repeat with remaining eggplant mixture, 2 tablespoons oil, and remaining garlic mixture.

5. Return skillet to medium-high heat, add remaining 1 teaspoon oil, and heat until shimmering. Add spinach and cook, stirring frequently, until wilted, about

3 minutes. Transfer spinach to paper towel–lined plate and drain for 2 minutes. Stir into eggplant mixture.

6. TO ASSEMBLE: Spray 13 by 9-inch baking dish with oil spray. Spread 1 cup tomato sauce in bottom of baking dish; shingle 4 noodles on top of sauce. Spread half of vegetable mixture over noodles, followed by half of olives, half of cream sauce, and 1 cup mozzarella. Repeat layering with 4 noodles, 1 cup tomato sauce, remaining vegetables, remaining olives, remaining cream sauce, and 1 cup mozzarella. Place remaining 4 noodles on top layer of cheese. Spread remaining 1 cup tomato sauce over noodles and sprinkle with remaining 1 cup mozzarella. Lightly spray large sheet of aluminum foil with oil spray and cover lasagna. Bake until bubbling, about 35 minutes. Cool on wire rack for 25 minutes. Cut into pieces, sprinkle with basil, and serve.

GNOCCHI

IN ITALY, GNOCCHI CAN MEAN ANY NUMBER OF different styles of dumpling, from ricotta to semolina. In this country, gnocchi usually means the potato-based type. At their best, these thimble-size dumplings boast a pillowy texture and an earthy flavor, needing nothing more than a gloss of browned butter sauce to be fit for the table. Making them always looks straightforward enough: Just mash cooked potatoes, bind them with flour and knead into dough, shape into dumplings, and boil. And yet the surplus of mediocre versions is astonishing. Most of the time, these dumplings turn out dense, gluey, or rubbery—and sometimes all of the above.

The fact is that even in a seemingly simple recipe such as this, there's plenty of room for error. First, the moisture in the potatoes will affect how much flour the dough absorbs—and, in turn, will impact the density of the gnocchi. Second, mashing the potatoes presents a catch-22. While obviously necessary, the action of mashing bursts starch cells in the potatoes, and the more they burst, the gluier the gnocchi. Third, developing a modest amount of gluten is what lends these dumplings their pleasantly faint chew, but mix in too much flour or overknead the dough, and you'll end up with

leaden sinkers. Add to this the fact that sometimes even the most perfectly textured gnocchi can lack distinct potato flavor, and the challenge looms even larger.

Surely there was some way to make this simple recipe foolproof so that light, delicate, and potato-y gnocchi were not a happy accident, but a guarantee.

I wasn't shocked to find that the majority of gnocchi recipes I surveyed called for russet potatoes, since their low-moisture flesh absorbs less flour than other spuds. The trouble is, they're also comparatively bland. I tried out two other types of potato, but the resulting dumplings were as dense as rubber balls. Clearly, russets were the way to go.

No need to give up on potato flavor just yet, however. The precooking step was my opportunity to enhance the spuds' earthiness, and I quickly set up a side-by-side test of baked and boiled samples. Not surprisingly, the oven deepened the potatoes' flavor, while the hot water bath washed them out. Even better, the former's dry heat evaporated some of the spuds' moisture, yielding fluffier results. I pulled out an old test kitchen trick to hasten the process. I zapped the potatoes in the microwave for 10 minutes before moving them into a hot 450-degree oven, where they needed just 20 minutes to finish cooking. (Cooking them entirely in the microwave gave me unevenly cooked, bland potatoes.) I then pulled the spuds from the oven and grabbed an oven mitt and paring knife to remove the skins. Since the drier the potatoes the better, working quickly was essential to ensuring that the spuds would give off as much steam as possible.

It was time to mash, and for the gentlest method possible, I chose a ricer. We've found that this tool ruptures fewer starch cells than hand mashing, since it compresses the potatoes only once. I then followed the lead of many recipes and spread the riced strands on a baking sheet, where they continued to release steam.

Once the potatoes had cooled slightly, the flour could be incorporated—but exactly how much was not clear. The existing recipes I'd tried didn't specify an amount of flour but offered a range that varied by as much as 1 cup in some cases. The idea is to form the dough with the lesser amount of flour and boil a few test dumplings to see if it's enough. If the gnocchi fall apart, gradually work more flour into the dough.

But therein lies the problem: Because you're starting on the low end of the scale, the dough invariably requires more flour, which means extra kneading—and more gluten development—as you work it in. To limit the dough manipulation, the trick would be to weigh out an exact amount of cooked potato and then determine the precise amount of flour needed to develop structure. Not only would I avoid guesswork during mixing, but the dough would turn out the same way every time.

To determine the minimum amount of flour required to bind 16 ounces of potato together, I made several batches of dough, using a fork to gently stir different amounts into each and kneading them for just a minute. The magic number turned out to be 5 ounces; any less and the gnocchi feathered apart in the water. But although these gnocchi cooked up relatively light and airy, they still weren't the delicate puffs I had envisioned.

Reasoning that I could do no more than I already had with just the potatoes and flour, I pulled out what I thought might be a ringer from my pantry: baking powder. This batch definitely puffed up but, unfortunately, also absorbed some cooking water and turned mushy. The same was true for baking soda. With so little gluten, the dough couldn't hold the gases created by leavening, and it blew apart, allowing water to seep in.

I was running low on ideas when a colleague asked why I hadn't tried incorporating an egg, a relatively common addition. I'd avoided recipes calling for egg because I thought its proteins would coagulate during cooking and bind the dough together too firmly. But at this point, I had nothing to lose.

I whipped up another batch of dough, this time stirring in a beaten egg before adding the 5 ounces of flour. Predictably, the dough was a little wetter than usual. Because I resisted compensating with flour, I was skeptical about the gnocchi holding together when they hit the boiling water. I needn't have feared. These gnocchi not only held their shape but also emerged from the water puffed and tender. The egg turned out to be exactly what the dough needed after all: a more tender building block than gluten-rich flour, with the proteins creating just the right amount of structure.

KEYS TO AIRY, EARTHY-TASTING POTATO GNOCCHI

1. Jump-start potatoes in microwave then finish cooking in oven to avoid dull flavor of boiling.

2. Peel hot potatoes to release steam and ensure drier spuds that hold together with less flour.

3. Press cooked potatoes through ricer then allow more steam to escape by spreading potatoes on sheet pan.

4. Start with exact amount of cooked potato and flour so you knead only once. Knead dough until it just holds together to avoid overdeveloping gluten.

MAKE THE RIGHT IMPRESSION

Ridges help gnocchi hold on to sauce. To make them, hold fork with tines facing down. Press dough piece (cut side down) against tines with thumb to make indentation. Roll dumpling down tines to create ridges on sides.

I wondered if I could press this advantage even further. I made another batch, dropping the flour to a mere 4 ounces. After 90 seconds of simmering, the gnocchi had the impossibly light texture and rich potato flavor I'd been aiming for.

As for shaping, I kept my method traditional: Cut the dough into eight pieces, roll each into a ½-inch-thick rope, and cut ¾-inch lengths. From there, I simply pressed each dumpling against the back of a fork to create an indentation and then rolled it down the tines to create ridges. This classic technique serves two purposes: The ridges trap sauce, and the indentation helps each gnocchi cook more evenly.

These potato-y puffs were good enough to eat straight from the pot, drizzled with a little extra-virgin olive oil, but I also wanted to whip up a simple sauce. The traditional nutty browned butter with shallot and fresh sage fit the bill perfectly—and took just three minutes to make.

In the end, it turns out that you don't need to be Italian or an accomplished cook to make perfect gnocchi. All it takes is a little precision—and an egg.

—DAN SOUZA, *Cook's Illustrated*

Potato Gnocchi with Browned Butter and Sage

SERVES 2 TO 3

For the most accurate measurements, weigh the potatoes and flour. After processing, you may have slightly more than the 3 cups (16 ounces) of potatoes required for this recipe. Discard any extra or set it aside for another use.

GNOCCHI

2 pounds russet potatoes
1 large egg, lightly beaten
¾ cup plus 1 tablespoon (4 ounces) all-purpose flour
1 teaspoon plus 1 tablespoon salt

SAUCE

4 tablespoons unsalted butter, cut into 4 pieces
1 small shallot, minced
1 teaspoon minced fresh sage
1½ teaspoons lemon juice
¼ teaspoon salt

1. FOR THE GNOCCHI: Adjust oven rack to middle position and heat oven to 450 degrees. Poke each potato 8 times with paring knife over entire surface. Microwave potatoes until slightly softened at ends, about 10 minutes, flipping potatoes halfway through cooking. Transfer potatoes directly to oven rack and bake until skewer glides easily through flesh and potatoes yield to gentle pressure, 18 to 20 minutes.

2. Holding each potato with potholder or kitchen towel, peel with paring knife. Process potatoes through ricer or food mill onto rimmed baking sheet. Gently spread potatoes into even layer and let cool for 5 minutes.

3. Transfer 3 cups (16 ounces) warm potatoes to bowl. Using fork, gently stir in egg until just combined. Sprinkle flour and 1 teaspoon salt over potato mixture. Using fork, gently combine until no pockets of dry flour remain. Press mixture into rough ball, transfer to lightly floured counter, and gently knead until smooth but slightly sticky, about 1 minute, lightly dusting counter with flour as needed to prevent sticking.

4. Line 2 rimmed baking sheets with parchment paper and dust liberally with flour. Cut dough into 8 pieces. Lightly dust counter with flour. Gently roll piece of dough into ½-inch-thick rope, dusting with flour to prevent sticking. Cut rope into ¾-inch lengths. Holding fork with tines facing down in 1 hand, press each dough piece, cut side down, against tines with thumb of other hand to create indentation. Roll dough down tines to form ridges on sides. If dough sticks, dust thumb or fork with flour. Transfer formed gnocchi to prepared sheets and repeat with remaining dough.

5. FOR THE SAUCE: Melt butter in 12-inch skillet over medium-high heat, swirling occasionally, until butter is browned and releases nutty aroma, about 1½ minutes. Off heat, add shallot and sage, stirring until shallot is fragrant, about 1 minute. Stir in lemon juice and salt; cover to keep warm.

6. Bring 4 quarts water to boil in large pot. Add remaining 1 tablespoon salt. Using parchment paper as sling, gently lower gnocchi from 1 sheet into water and cook until firm and just cooked through, about 90 seconds (gnocchi should float to surface after about 1 minute). Using slotted spoon, transfer cooked gnocchi to skillet with sauce. Repeat with remaining gnocchi. Gently toss gnocchi with sauce and serve.

GRANDMA PIZZA

PIZZA IS IN NEW YORK CITY'S BLOOD. TOURISTS know they can get a slice on every block, and locals hotly debate the merits of old-school coal-oven pizzerias like Patsy's and Lombardi's versus relative newcomers like Motorino and Forcella. The pizza that rarely gets talked about, however, lives on Long Island. Grandma pizza is a thin-crust, rectangular pan pizza topped in reverse order: first with a modest amount of cheese and then with chunks of tomato. It traces its origins to Umberto's Pizzeria in New Hyde Park. The story goes that in the early 1970s proprietor Umberto Corteo would ask his pizza man to create a simple pizza like the one his mother used to make in Italy. Soon, other Long Island pizzerias were offering the pie, and a phenomenon was born. But in order to fully understand this pizza, I'd have to take an eating tour of Long Island pizzerias.

What did I find out on my whirlwind, gut-busting trip? That this is good pizza. Of the dozen or so samples I tried, there was no single version that stood out from the rest, but there were elements of each that I wanted to pull into my recipe. The crusts I liked best were thin and crunchy, like the one I'd sampled at the iconic pizzeria King Umberto. Smaller, more uniformly distributed chunks of tomato were preferable to larger, sporadically placed hunks. And fresh basil was a great complement.

The dough for grandma pizza is stretched and baked on an oiled sheet pan. Starting with a test kitchen recipe for a sheet pan pizza, I mixed all-purpose flour, yeast, salt, sugar, water, and oil in the stand mixer, let it rise in a bowl, stretched it on an oiled pan, and topped it with mozzarella and a can of drained diced tomatoes. My plan was to taste this admittedly crude interpretation and then adjust it to bring it into line with the best of the pizzas I'd eaten on Long Island.

The dough was tender and easy to stretch, but when baked, it puffed up much thicker and denser than quintessential grandma slices, and it didn't have the crisp-bottomed, chewy crust I was after. Cutting the dough recipe in half still made for a crust that was too thick, but cutting it by two-thirds yielded just enough dough for a properly thin crust. Baking it for 15 minutes at 500 degrees on the lowest rack nicely browned the crust, and sliding the pizza onto a wire rack when it came out of the oven kept the bottom from getting soggy in the pan. But the crust was still too dense and tender. To add chew, I switched from all-purpose to higher-protein bread flour and increased the kneading time. Ten minutes in the stand mixer gave me the elastic, gluten-rich dough I wanted. But this time, when I stretched the taut dough, it snapped back, refusing to stay in the corners of the pan.

I knew that adding water would make the dough less dense, and I hoped it would also make stretching a bit easier. An extra quarter-cup of water fixed the dense and bready texture. But while it did make stretching the dough a tad easier, I still had to stretch it little by little, letting it rest periodically to allow the dough to slacken. I noticed that just moving it from the rising bowl to the oiled sheet pan was building elasticity. What if I didn't have to move it?

I mixed a batch of dough, this time letting it rise directly on the oiled sheet pan. Not hemmed in by the sides of a bowl, the dough stretched a little itself while rising. When it had proofed, stretching it to the corners was much easier, though it still required a 10-minute rest before the last bit of fitting. In the end, I found that pressing the dough to a 10 by 6-inch rectangle before letting it rise gave me just the head start I needed for easy stretching.

Now I could work on the toppings. Tasters found the plain mozzarella lackluster. In a few of the pizzas I'd sampled it was augmented with nutty, salty Parmesan cheese. Adding ¼ cup of Parmesan to my 2 cups of mozzarella rounded out the flavor. The diced tomatoes alone tasted bright but unbalanced. Adding ¼ teaspoon of salt, a tablespoon of olive oil, minced garlic, and dried oregano introduced the necessary aromatic depth.

I mixed up one more batch of dough, let it rise on the pan, stretched it out, let it rise a second time, and then topped it with cheese and the seasoned diced tomatoes. I baked it, sprinkled on some basil, slid it onto the wire rack, and called my tasters. Before I could ask what they thought, the pizza was gone.

—SARAH GABRIEL, *Cook's Country*

GRANDMA PIZZA

Grandma Pizza

SERVES 4

If the dough snaps back when pressing it into the baking sheet, cover it, let it rest for 10 minutes, and try again.

DOUGH

- 3 tablespoons olive oil
- ¾ cup water
- 1½ cups (8¼ ounces) bread flour
- 2¼ teaspoons instant or rapid-rise yeast
- 1 teaspoon sugar
- ¾ teaspoon salt

TOPPING

- 1 (28-ounce) can diced tomatoes
- 1 tablespoon olive oil
- 2 garlic cloves, minced
- 1 teaspoon dried oregano
- ¼ teaspoon salt
- 8 ounces mozzarella cheese, shredded (2 cups)
- ¼ cup grated Parmesan cheese
- 2 tablespoons chopped fresh basil

1. FOR THE DOUGH: Coat rimmed baking sheet with 2 tablespoons oil. Combine water and remaining 1 tablespoon oil in 1-cup liquid measuring cup. Using stand mixer fitted with dough hook, mix flour, yeast, sugar, and salt together on low speed until combined. With mixer running, slowly add water mixture and mix until dough comes together, about 1 minute. Increase speed to medium-low and mix until dough is smooth and comes away from sides of bowl, about 10 minutes.

2. Transfer dough to prepared baking sheet and turn to coat. Stretch dough to 10 by 6-inch rectangle. Cover with plastic wrap and let rise at room temperature until doubled in size, 1 to 1½ hours. Stretch dough to corners of pan, cover loosely with plastic, and let rise at room temperature until slightly puffed, about 45 minutes. Meanwhile, adjust oven rack to lowest position and heat oven to 500 degrees.

3. FOR THE TOPPING: Place tomatoes in colander and drain well. Combine drained tomatoes, oil, garlic, oregano, and salt in bowl. Combine mozzarella and Parmesan in second bowl. Sprinkle cheese mixture over dough, leaving ½-inch border around edges. Top with tomato mixture and bake until well browned and bubbling, about 15 minutes. Slide pizza onto wire rack, sprinkle with basil, and let cool for 5 minutes. Serve.

NOTES FROM THE TEST KITCHEN

EASY RISE

Our method lets the dough proof right on the sheet. Spread the dough on an oiled baking sheet and then set it aside to rise.

THE BEST LOW-MOISTURE MOZZARELLAS

Mozzarella is the most popular cheese in the United States, overtaking cheddar in per-capita consumption in 2006. Most supermarkets stock two main varieties: fresh (usually packed in brine) and low-moisture (available either as a block or preshredded). We prefer the sweet richness and tender bite of fresh mozzarella for snacking, sandwiches, and caprese salad but avoid using it in cooked applications; its delicate flavor and texture don't stand up well to heat. For cooking, we use the low-moisture kind. It offers mellow flavor that blends seamlessly with bolder ingredients and melts nicely in everything from lasagna to pizza. But even amongst low-moisture varieties, there are seemingly endless options in the supermarket cheese case. So which one should you reach for? We recently sampled nine brands of low-moisture supermarket mozzarella, both block-style and preshredded, made with whole or part-skim milk. After tasting the brands plain, we tried them on pizzas, looking for one that offered creamy flavor with a bit of soft (not rubbery) chew, plenty of gooey stretch, and a touch of flavorful browning.

In the end, our winner was the block-style **Sorrento Whole Milk Mozzarella**. Its gooey creaminess and clean dairy flavor were exactly what we wanted on pizza. Tasters raved that its flavor was "clean," "mellow," and "buttery"—which makes sense considering this brand uses only fresh milk as its milk product, whereas some other brands rely on processed milk products, such as condensed skim milk or nonfat dry milk. When it came to the shredded mozzarella samples, tasters disliked most of them, with the exception of one: **Kraft Low-Moisture Part-Skim Mozzarella**. Unlike the other shredded brands, this one had a little more fat and melted nicely on pizza, giving way to a "smooth" texture with "nice chewiness" and "good brown spots." (See page 291 for more information about our testing results.)

CHAPTER 6

MEAT

Grilled Steak with New Mexican Chile Rub   138

Grilled Steak with Ancho Chile–Coffee Rub

Grilled Steak with Spicy Chipotle Chile Rub

Grilled Steak Burgers   140

Best Prime Rib   143

French-Style Pot-Roasted Pork Loin   145

French-Style Pot-Roasted Pork Loin with Port and Figs

Grilled Stuffed Pork Tenderloin   149

Olive and Sun-Dried Tomato Stuffing

Piquillo Pepper and Manchego Stuffing

Porcini and Artichoke Stuffing

Slow-Cooker Holiday Glazed Ham   151

Crown Roast of Pork   152

Country-Fried Pork with Gravy   154

Hawaiian-Style Smoked Pork (Kalua Pork)   157

Spicy Pork Tacos (al Pastor)   160

Red Wine–Braised Pork Chops   162

Barbecued Country-Style Ribs   166

Smoky Indoor Ribs   167

Sichuan Stir-Fried Pork in Garlic Sauce   170

SPICE-RUBBED STEAK ON THE GRILL

AS A DEDICATED PRACTITIONER OF THE SILK-PURSE-out-of-a-sow's-ear approach to cooking, I enjoy the challenge of transforming inexpensive ingredients into a memorable meal. But I've always conceded that when it comes to grilled steaks, you get what you pay for.

With their tender texture and big-time beef flavor, pricey cuts from the middle of the steer (like rib eyes and T-bones) need little more than salt, pepper, and a few minutes over a hot fire. Try that technique on cheaper steaks from farther down the animal (like the sirloin and the round) and you get meat that's chewy and dry, with flavors that veer toward liver-y and gamy. It's probably these flavor and texture challenges that inspire cooks to take a page from the barbecue manual and apply spice rubs to less expensive steaks. Unfortunately, in my experience that approach doesn't really work. Because cheap steaks exude little fat to bond with the spices, the rub tends to fall off in chunks. If by some stroke of luck the rub remains intact, it usually tastes dry and dusty, plus nuances of flavor can vaporize over the fire.

Still, my skinflint tendencies aren't easily subdued. Surely there was a way to create a recipe for inexpensive grilled steak that was also tender and juicy, with a flavorful, crunchy crust that stayed in place.

First I had to find a steak that provided the best taste and texture for the money, so I looked to the sirloin and the round, settling on what we here in New England call the shell sirloin steak. Tasters described the shell steak as having a relatively beefy taste, unlike cuts from the round, which were liver-y.

Salting the shell steaks before cooking was a given. Salt sprinkled liberally on the surface of the meat draws moisture from inside, which over time is then reabsorbed as the meat sits, seasoning it and changing the structure of the muscle fibers so that they hold on to more juices. But I'd have to do more than that to close the gap between a $6 steak and a $12 steak. Some recipes suggest that allowing a spice rub to sit on the meat for a period of time enables its flavors to be absorbed for more complex-tasting results. Science, however, refutes this: Most flavor compounds in spices are fat-soluble rather than water-soluble, so they can't penetrate below the surface of the steak. Furthermore, in tests of marinades, we've found that, other than salt, the only water-soluble flavor compounds that can travel deep into the meat are glutamates.

So, what about glutamates? Scanning my pantry, I singled out two of the most potent sources of these compounds: tomato paste and—odd as it may sound—fish sauce, a condiment that we've called upon in other unlikely applications to amp up savory taste. I applied a rub made with kosher salt and a couple of teaspoons each of these two ingredients (to compensate for their extra sodium I cut back a little on the salt) and applied it to a set of steaks an hour before grilling. The difference in these steaks was remarkable: They boasted a much deeper flavor without any trace of my secret enhancements. Spurred by this success, I decided to add ½ teaspoon each of garlic powder and onion powder to the rub. Though neither substance contains significant levels of glutamates, their water-soluble flavors are potent enough (especially in concentrated powdered form) that even if they penetrated only ¼ inch into the meat, they might make a difference in the overall flavor. Tasters confirmed that my hunch was correct: The steaks treated with the powdered alliums along with salt, tomato paste, and fish sauce had noticeably richer flavor. On to the spice rub.

My plan was to treat the steak with the salt-and-glutamate-packed paste first, wait an hour, and then apply a second, more conventional dry rub right before grilling. I tried a variety of rubs, but I found that those made mostly with dried herbs lost their flavor, while those based on spices fared better. It turns out that the flavors in herbs like rosemary, sage, and thyme fade in the intense heat of the grill, but the compounds in spices do much better, particularly those containing capsaicin—namely, peppers, chiles, and paprika. Thus, rubs made predominantly from chile or pepper were clearly the way to go.

First I tried rubs made with preground spices, but these formed a coating that was more pasty than crunchy. Since I had some time to spare between applying the salty glutamate rub and firing up the grill, I tried toasting some whole spices (cumin, coriander, red pepper flakes, and black peppercorns) in a skillet along with some earthy-tasting dried New Mexican chiles, and then I ground them coarsely in a coffee grinder. To round out the flavors, I also incorporated sugar, paprika, and ground cloves before pressing the rub onto the surface of the steaks.

Tasters pronounced these steaks juicy, tender, and flavorful, and they greatly preferred the more robust texture of this home-ground rub. Still, there were two problems to be solved. First, despite the toasting step, the spices retained a slightly raw taste, the result of being cooked with very little fat, so the flavors couldn't "bloom." Second, tasters requested a more substantial crust. I sheepishly informed them that there had been more rub when I started grilling, but half of it had been left on the cooking grate. Clearly, I needed to find a way to help the spices stick to the steak and not to the grate.

I remembered when a coworker who was developing a recipe for pan-fried pork chops had difficulty persuading the breading to adhere to the meat. He eventually came up with the clever solution of making shallow cuts into the meat to give the breading more purchase. Doing the same with my steaks before adding the first rub seemed likely to be doubly advantageous:

It would increase the surface area, which could give that first rub more opportunity to really get into the meat, plus it could help the spice rub stick to the meat.

As I liberally greased the cooking grate in preparation for grilling my newly crosshatched steaks, I wished that there were some way to put a layer of oil on the steaks themselves without disturbing their spice crust (which—I was pleased to see—was sticking quite nicely). The easy solution: A light spritz of vegetable oil spray or oil from a mister helped the steaks keep their rub intact throughout the grilling process.

These steaks were crusty and crunchy on the outside, with just enough heat and spice to complement the meat's rich flavor, and that little bit of added fat imparted by the oil spray gave the spices the fully developed "bloomed" flavor that tasters were after. The tender and juicy meat belied its $5.99-per-pound price tag. My inner cheapskate quietly rejoiced.

—ANDREA GEARY, *Cook's Illustrated*

NOTES FROM THE TEST KITCHEN

TURNING CHEAPER STEAK INTO "CHOICE"

1. Cut shallow slits into steak to help salt paste and spice rub adhere to meat and penetrate more deeply.

2. Tenderize meat and boost beefy flavor with paste of onion and garlic powders, salt, tomato paste, and fish sauce.

3. Toast, then grind dried chiles and spices for substantial crust with complex flavor.

4. Lightly mist spice rub with oil to bloom spices on grill and help rub cling to meat.

Grilled Steak with New Mexican Chile Rub
SERVES 6 TO 8

Shell sirloin steak is also known as top butt, butt steak, top sirloin butt, top sirloin steak, and center-cut roast. Spraying the rubbed steaks with oil helps the spices bloom, preventing a raw flavor.

STEAK

- 2 teaspoons tomato paste
- 2 teaspoons fish sauce
- 1½ teaspoons kosher salt
- ½ teaspoon onion powder
- ½ teaspoon garlic powder
- 2 (1½- to 1¾-pound) boneless shell sirloin steaks, 1 to 1¼ inches thick, trimmed

SPICE RUB

- 2 dried New Mexican chiles, stemmed and seeded, flesh torn into ½-inch pieces
- 4 teaspoons cumin seeds
- 4 teaspoons coriander seeds
- ½ teaspoon red pepper flakes
- ½ teaspoon black peppercorns
- 1 tablespoon sugar
- 1 tablespoon paprika
- ¼ teaspoon ground cloves
  Vegetable oil spray

1. FOR THE STEAK: Combine tomato paste, fish sauce, salt, onion powder, and garlic powder in bowl. Pat steaks dry with paper towels. With sharp knife, cut 1/16-inch-deep slits on both sides of steaks, spaced 1/2 inch apart, in crosshatch pattern. Rub salt mixture evenly on both sides of steaks. Place steaks on wire rack set in rimmed baking sheet; let stand at room temperature for at least 1 hour. After 30 minutes, prepare grill.

2. FOR THE SPICE RUB: Toast chiles, cumin seeds, coriander seeds, pepper flakes, and peppercorns in 10-inch skillet over medium-low heat, stirring frequently, until just beginning to smoke, 3 to 4 minutes. Transfer to plate to cool, about 5 minutes. Grind spices in spice grinder or in mortar with pestle until coarsely ground. Transfer spices to bowl and stir in sugar, paprika, and cloves.

3A. FOR A CHARCOAL GRILL: Open bottom vent completely. Light large chimney starter mounded with charcoal briquettes (7 quarts). When top coals are partially covered with ash, pour two-thirds evenly over grill, then pour remaining coals over half of grill. Set cooking grate in place, cover, and open lid vent completely. Heat grill until hot, about 5 minutes.

3B. FOR A GAS GRILL: Turn all burners to high, cover, and heat grill until hot, about 15 minutes. Leave primary burner on high and turn other burner(s) to medium.

4. Clean and oil cooking grate. Sprinkle half of spice rub evenly over 1 side of steaks and press to adhere until spice rub is fully moistened. Lightly spray rubbed side of steak with vegetable oil spray, about 3 seconds. Flip steaks and repeat process of sprinkling with spice rub and spraying with oil spray on second side.

5. Place steaks over hotter side of grill and cook until browned and charred on both sides and center registers 120 to 125 degrees (for medium-rare) or 130 to 135 degrees (for medium), 6 to 8 minutes. If steaks have not reached desired temperature, move to cooler side of grill and continue to cook. Transfer steaks to clean wire rack set in rimmed baking sheet, tent loosely with aluminum foil, and let rest for 10 minutes. Slice meat thin against grain and serve.

VARIATIONS

Grilled Steak with Ancho Chile–Coffee Rub

Substitute 1 dried ancho chile for New Mexican chiles, 2 teaspoons ground coffee for paprika, and 1 teaspoon cocoa powder for ground cloves.

Grilled Steak with Spicy Chipotle Chile Rub

Substitute 2 dried chipotle chiles for New Mexican chiles, 1 teaspoon dried oregano for paprika, and 1/2 teaspoon ground cinnamon for ground cloves.

GRILLED STEAK BURGERS

MOST STEAKHOUSES FEATURE A BURGER ON THEIR menus. The meat is usually ground from intensely beefy steak trimmings, cooked on a ripping-hot grill (or under the broiler) to crusty perfection, and served with steak sauce—in essence, the steak experience on a bun. I wanted the same results from my backyard grill.

Fancy burger recipes call for grinding various cuts of beef at home. For an easier route to similarly big flavor, I started by grilling burgers made with ground beef readily available in markets (chuck, round, and sirloin), seasoned with salt and pepper, and grilled over high heat to medium-rare. Round was fine, chuck was better, but neither tasted as "steak-y" as the robust sirloin (from which steaks are cut). But sirloin is about 90 percent lean, so these burgers were a little dry. I decided to add butter to the meat. Melted butter blended easily and took on a texture similar to that of beef fat. Perfect.

But I still wanted more flavor. In the test kitchen, we often add soy sauce to beef recipes because it contains a lot of savory, meaty-tasting glutamates. Two teaspoons increased meatiness without tasting like soy. Onions and garlic are always great for adding flavor, so I sautéed some in the butter before mixing it into the meat. But the moisture from the chopped onions made the burgers mushy. I kept the minced garlic but switched to onion powder for depth without dampness.

I moved on to the sauce. A taste test showed that all commercial steak sauces (yes, even A.1.) tasted harsh—I'd have to make my own. Following the lead of most recipes, I sautéed garlic and onion in butter, then added tomato paste, water, raisins, vinegar, Worcestershire, and mustard. This sauce was good, but it got even better when I added a few tablespoons of soy sauce and traded white vinegar for balsamic and water for beef broth. I let it simmer for a few minutes, then buzzed the sauce in the blender and was good to go.

But my burgers still had one problem: They lacked serious steakhouse char. I was grilling them over high heat, but if I left them on long enough to develop good

GRILLED STEAK BURGERS

char, they overcooked. I looked for something sweet to brush on the raw patties to encourage browning. With tomato paste, raisins, and balsamic, my homemade sauce already fit the bill, so I tried that. These burgers came off the grill still a perfect medium-rare but now with a perfectly charred crust.

As a final flourish, I brushed steak sauce mixed with butter onto rolls and toasted them on the grill. I was almost done, but before I put this recipe to bed, I realized I could streamline it by starting with a big batch of garlic and onion powder sautéed in melted butter, then dividing it for triple use in the burgers, sauce, and buns. These burgers require nothing but a big appetite—and plenty of napkins.

—SARAH GABRIEL, *Cook's Country*

Grilled Steak Burgers

SERVES 4

Use Kaiser rolls or other hearty buns for these burgers.

BURGERS

8	tablespoons unsalted butter
2	garlic cloves, minced
2	teaspoons onion powder
1	teaspoon pepper
½	teaspoon salt
2	teaspoons soy sauce
1½	pounds 90 percent lean ground sirloin
4	hamburger buns

STEAK SAUCE

2	tablespoons tomato paste
⅔	cup beef broth
⅓	cup raisins
2	tablespoons soy sauce
2	tablespoons Dijon mustard
2	tablespoons balsamic vinegar
1	tablespoon Worcestershire sauce

1. FOR THE BURGERS: Melt butter in 8-inch skillet over medium-low heat. Add garlic, onion powder, pepper, and salt and cook until fragrant, about 1 minute. Pour all but 1 tablespoon butter mixture into bowl and let cool slightly, about 5 minutes.

2. FOR THE STEAK SAUCE: Meanwhile, add tomato paste to skillet and cook over medium heat until paste begins to darken, 1 to 2 minutes. Stir in broth, raisins,

soy sauce, mustard, vinegar, and Worcestershire and simmer until raisins are plump, about 5 minutes. Process sauce in blender until smooth, about 30 seconds; transfer to bowl.

3. Add 5 tablespoons cooled butter mixture and soy sauce to ground beef and gently knead until well combined. Shape into four ¾-inch-thick patties and press shallow divot in center of each. Brush each patty all over with 1 tablespoon steak sauce. Combine remaining

NOTES FROM THE TEST KITCHEN

BUTTER MAKES IT BETTER

Why are our steakhouse burgers so good? Yep, butter. Ground sirloin has great flavor, but it's a little dry; butter helps keep the burgers moist. Butter also gives richness and body to our homemade steak sauce, and we slather butter on the buns before toasting them on the grill.

FLAVORED BUTTER
For the meat, sauce, and buns

FIGHTING THE BATTLE OF THE BULGE

The collagen, or connective tissue, in ground meat shrinks when heated. This causes the bottom and sides of the patty to tighten like a belt, which forces the surface of the burger to expand. To prevent a bubble burger, press a ¼-inch divot in the center of each patty. The collagen will still tighten, but the indented meat won't bulge.

FLAT PATTY = BULGING BURGER

DIVOTED PATTY = FLAT BURGER

2 tablespoons cooled butter mixture with 2 tablespoons steak sauce; set aside.

4A. FOR A CHARCOAL GRILL: Open bottom vent completely. Light large chimney starter filled with charcoal briquettes (6 quarts). When top coals are partially covered with ash, pour evenly over grill. Set cooking grate in place, cover, and open lid vent completely. Heat grill until hot, about 5 minutes.

4B. FOR A GAS GRILL: Turn all burners to high, cover, and heat grill until hot, about 15 minutes. Leave all burners on high.

5. Clean and oil cooking grate. Cook burgers (covered if using gas) until meat registers 120 to 125 degrees (for medium-rare), 6 to 8 minutes, or 130 to 135 degrees (for medium), 8 to 10 minutes, flipping burgers halfway through cooking. Transfer burgers to plate, tent loosely with aluminum foil, and let rest for 5 to 10 minutes. Brush cut sides of buns with butter–steak sauce mixture. Cook buns, cut side down, until golden, 2 to 3 minutes. Place burgers on buns. Serve with remaining steak sauce.

THE BEST PRIME RIB

A CHEF FRIEND OF MINE RECENTLY SERVED ME A slice of prime rib as close to beef perfection as anything I've ever tasted. It featured a crisp, salty crust encasing a large eye of juicy, rose-hued meat interspersed with soft pockets of richly flavored fat. The meat had the buttery texture of tenderloin but the beefiness of a chuck roast—and the usual gray band of overcooked meat under the surface of the crust was practically nonexistent. I found myself reassessing my expectations for this primo cut and asked my friend for his recipe. While he wouldn't divulge all the details, he did direct me to the formula on which he based his own: famed British chef Heston Blumenthal's recipe for "Steak" (translation: a two-rib roast from which he cuts steaks), published in his book *In Search of Perfection*.

To say that Blumenthal goes to extremes for his prime rib would be an understatement. The recipe breaks down as follows: Sear the exterior of the roast with a blowtorch; place the meat in a preheated 120-degree oven until the internal temperature hits 120 degrees—and then hold it there for 18 hours. (You read that right: 18 hours.) Finally, pull the meat out of the oven, let it rest, slice it into steaks, and pan-sear the slabs until crisp.

This exact approach was out of the question. For one thing, even if a cook were willing to keep the meat in the oven all night and most of a day, no home oven can reliably go below 200 degrees. But it did give me some ideas—and an ideal to strive for.

I had one major decision—the meat selection—made before I even got started. In the test kitchen, our preferences for the exact grade and cut of beef are definitive: a prime first-cut roast for its supreme marbling and large rib-eye muscle. As I would with any other roast, I patted the meat dry and seasoned it with a handful of coarse salt. Then came the first hurdle: how best to replicate the effects of a blowtorch. Blumenthal blast-sears meat with this instrument because its intense heat output (over 3,000 degrees) immediately starts to render fat and brown the exterior while leaving the meat beneath the surface virtually untouched (hence the remarkably thin gray band). My options were a hot oven or a skillet—and neither was ideal. Oven searing at 500 degrees was easy but far too slow; by the time the roast got some decent color, a good half-inch of meat below the surface had turned ashen. Unacceptable. Meanwhile, a blazing-hot skillet seared the meat faster, but evenly browning a three-bone roast in a 12-inch pan was cumbersome to say the least.

I came up with a quick fix for the unwieldiness problem: I cut the bones off the roast before searing to make it easier to maneuver the meat in the skillet, then tied them back on before roasting so that they could still provide insulation, helping the roast cook more evenly. I even discovered two extra benefits to the method: The exposed meat on the bone side could now be thoroughly seasoned, and carving the finished roast required nothing more than snipping the twine before slicing. But getting a deep sear on the roast (even when I skipped browning the bone side) still took 10 minutes—not because the pan wasn't hot (it clocked 450 degrees), but because even after I had carefully blotted it dry, the meat straight out of the package was still damp. That meant that the surface directly underneath my roast couldn't rise above 212 degrees (the boiling point of water) until the moisture had evaporated. I didn't need a hotter pan. I needed drier meat.

Fortunately, this was familiar territory. We routinely air-dry poultry to allow its moisture to evaporate so that we can get the skin extra-crisp. I took the same tack here, prepping and seasoning another roast before moving it into the fridge for a 24-hour rest. When I seared this roast, the exterior did indeed brown better (and faster) than it had in my previous attempts. But that wasn't the only perk. The meat below the surface was beefier and much more tender, and I had the combination of salt and time to thank for it. Given a chance to penetrate deep into the meat, salt enhanced the beefy flavor while dissolving some of the proteins, yielding a buttery-tender roast. In fact, I found that the longer I let the roast sit—up to four days—the beefier, juicier, and more tender the results. (If I let it sit any longer than four days, however, I risked desiccating the exterior.) I also scored the larger swaths of fat on the exterior, which gave the salt a head start on the meat and encouraged rendering.

Things were progressing nicely—but I still had a home oven to reckon with. There was good reason for Blumenthal's incredibly long cooking time and incredibly low temperature. By gently raising the temperature of the meat and then holding it at 120 degrees for all those hours, he was cleverly manipulating two active enzymes in the meat: calpains and cathepsins. When the meat is held around the 120-degree mark, these enzymes work at a rapid pace to break down connective tissues and tenderize the meat. (This tenderizing effect is equivalent to aging the beef for almost a month.) Since it was impossible to use the same method with my conventional home oven, I focused my efforts on finding another way to keep my beef close to 120 degrees for as long as I could.

The lowest my oven would go was 200 degrees, so I set the dial there and popped in another salted, seared roast. When the meat hit 125 degrees (medium-rare) almost four hours later, the crust was decent and the interior well seasoned and rosy from center to edge. But the texture wasn't ideal: more like run-of-the-mill strip steak than prime-grade rib eye. I wasn't sure what to do next. Then it occurred to me that I actually did have a way to lower the temperature of my oven: I could turn it off. I ran a series of tests, shutting off the oven when the roasts hit various degrees of doneness. The magic number turned out to be 110 degrees, my trusty probe thermometer indicating exactly when the roast had hit the target temperature. This was a breakthrough technique. In the shut-off oven, the beef stayed in the enzyme sweet spot far longer, about an hour more to reach 120 for rare. I then took it out of the oven to let it rest and to allow the exuded juices to be drawn back into the meat. Thanks to the roast's hefty size, the meat stayed at an ideal serving temperature for more than an hour, giving me plenty of time to cook or reheat side dishes.

Only one imperfection remained: The crust had lost some of its crispness as it rested under a tent of foil. A quick stint under the broiler before serving was all it took to restore it—well, almost all of it. To ensure that the fatty portion at the top of the ribs got enough exposure to the heat, I rolled up the piece of foil I'd used to tent the roast into a ball and sandwiched it under the ribs to elevate the fat.

All that was left was to snip the twine, lift the meat from the bones, and slice it into hefty ¾-inch-thick slabs. This prime rib was truly the king of all roasts—a deep-colored, substantial crust encasing a rosy-pink center. And making it took nothing more than a humble skillet and regular oven.

—DAN SOUZA, *Cook's Illustrated*

Best Prime Rib

SERVES 6 TO 8

Look for a roast with an untrimmed fat cap (ideally ½ inch thick). We prefer the flavor and texture of prime-grade beef, but choice grade will work as well. Monitoring the roast with a meat-probe thermometer is best. If you use an instant-read thermometer, open the oven door as little as possible and remove the roast from the oven while taking its temperature. If the roast has not reached the correct temperature in the time range specified in step 3, heat the oven to 200 degrees, wait for 5 minutes, then shut it off, and continue to cook the roast until it reaches the desired temperature.

1　(7-pound) first-cut beef standing rib roast (3 bones), meat removed from bones, bones reserved
　　Kosher salt and pepper
2　teaspoons vegetable oil

1. Using sharp knife, cut slits in surface layer of fat, spaced 1 inch apart, in crosshatch pattern, being careful to cut down to, but not into, meat. Rub 2 tablespoons salt over entire roast and into slits. Place meat back on bones (to save space in refrigerator), transfer to large plate, and refrigerate, uncovered, for at least 24 hours or up to 4 days.

2. Adjust oven rack to middle position and heat oven to 200 degrees. Heat oil in 12-inch skillet over high heat until just smoking. Sear sides and top of roast (reserving bones) until browned, 6 to 8 minutes total (do not sear side where roast was cut from bones). Place meat back on ribs so bones fit where they were cut and let cool for 10 minutes; tie meat to bones with 2 lengths of twine between ribs. Transfer roast, fat side up, to wire rack set in rimmed baking sheet and season with pepper. Roast until meat registers 110 degrees, 3 to 4 hours.

3. Turn off oven; leave roast in oven, opening door as little as possible, until meat registers about 120 degrees for rare or about 125 degrees for medium-rare, 30 minutes to 1¼ hours longer.

4. Remove roast from oven (leave roast on baking sheet), tent loosely with aluminum foil, and let rest for at least 30 minutes or up to 1¼ hours.

5. Adjust oven rack to about 8 inches from broiler element and heat broiler. Remove foil from roast, form into 3-inch ball, and place under ribs to elevate fat cap. Broil until top of roast is well browned and crisp, 2 to 8 minutes.

6. Transfer roast to carving board; cut twine and remove ribs from roast. Slice meat into ¾-inch-thick slices. Season with coarse salt to taste and serve.

NOTES FROM THE TEST KITCHEN

PREPARING PRIME RIB

1. Removing the ribs makes it easier to sear the prime rib in a skillet. Run sharp knife down length of bones, following contours as closely as possible to remove ribs.

2. Score fat cap in 1-inch crosshatch pattern to allow salt to contact meat directly and to improve fat rendering and crisping.

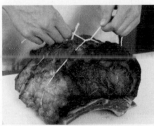

3. After searing meat, place meat back on ribs so bones fit where they were cut and let cool for 10 minutes; tie meat to bones with 2 lengths of twine between ribs.

FRENCH-STYLE POT-ROASTED PORK LOIN

FRENCH CUISINE IS WELL KNOWN FOR ITS MANY dishes featuring a lackluster cut of meat turned sumptuous and flavorful by surprisingly simple methods, but the one that impresses me most is *enchaud Périgourdin*. A specialty in the southwest Périgord region of France, it consists of a seared pork loin—one of the least promising cuts for slow-cooking—thrown into a covered casserole with garlic and a trotter (or pig's foot) to bake for several hours. You'd expect that a roast with so little fat or collagen to protect it would emerge from the pot dried out and tasteless. Instead, the finished meat is astonishingly moist and flavorful, with plenty of rich-tasting, viscous jus to drizzle on top.

Unfortunately, my attempts to make this dish at home have always turned out exactly as I had expected: bland and stringy meat sitting in a flavorless pool of juice. I'm never sure what gets lost in translation, but the promise of a dish that eked out juicy, tender, savory results from this bland roast was motivation enough for me to find a successful approach of my own. I had just one stipulation: The trotter had to go. Though it imparts body and flavor to the sauce, hunting one down would complicate this genuinely simple dish.

I gave a few recipes a try, and when not one of the roasts—cooked at both high heat and more moderate temperatures—turned out like the juicy, rich-tasting pot-roasted loins I've enjoyed in Périgord, I realized I had a very fundamental problem to deal with: the pork itself. While French pigs are bred to have plenty of fat, American pork contains far less marbling, with the center-cut roast that I was using perhaps being the leanest cut of all.

I wondered if I could improve the results by dropping the oven temperature (the lowest I'd tried so far was 325 degrees) and pulling out the roast when it hit the medium mark (140 degrees). Sure enough, this test proved that the lower the oven temperature, the more succulent the roast. My tasters clearly favored the pork cooked in the 225-degree oven for about 70 minutes. In this very low oven, the outer layers of the loin absorbed less heat (and consequently squeezed out less moisture) during the time it took the center to climb to 140 degrees. And not only was it far juicier than any of my previous attempts, but a small pool of concentrated jus had accumulated at the bottom of the pot.

There was just one texture-related setback: The bottom of the roast, which was in direct contact with the pot, cooked more quickly than the top. I solved this problem by searing just the top and sides of the roast while leaving the bottom raw.

But I still had work to do. Engineering juicier meat hadn't improved its bland flavor. Plus, without the trotter, the sauce lacked body. Salting and brining are our go-to methods when we want to draw seasoning into large cuts of pork and help the meat retain moisture during cooking. Brining wouldn't be helpful here, because soaking in a salt solution adds extra water to the meat, which would simply leach out and dilute the jus. Salting was the better option. The downside was that it took at least six hours (with superior results after 24 hours) for the salt to penetrate deep into the thick roast. I wondered if I could find a faster way.

It seemed that splitting the loin lengthwise into two smaller pieces and liberally sprinkling each one with salt might hasten the seasoning process, but when I gave it a shot, tasters complained that the interior of each mini loin was still bland. Slicing a pocket into the top of the loin and sprinkling the interior with salt was strike two. Though the center of the roast was well seasoned, we were just as likely to get an unseasoned bite.

NOTES FROM THE TEST KITCHEN

"DOUBLE-BUTTERFLYING" A ROAST

1. Holding chef's knife parallel to cutting board, insert knife one-third of way up from bottom of roast and cut horizontally, stopping ½ inch before edge. Open up flap.

2. Make another horizontal cut into thicker portion of roast about ½ inch from bottom, stopping about ½ inch before edge. Open up this flap, smoothing out rectangle of meat.

After some further experimentation I landed on an effective technique: "double-butterflying." By making two sweeping cuts—the first one-third of the way up the loin and the second into the thicker portion that I created with the first cut—I was able to open up the loin like a trifold book and expose a vast amount of surface area. Then I rubbed each side with 1½ teaspoons of kosher salt, folded the loin back up, and secured it with twine. While this method required a bit more knife work, it produced perfectly seasoned meat. Even better, this technique made it possible to add fat and flavor directly to the meat, bringing me closer to the French original.

For "fattening up" the roast, bacon fat, rendered salt pork fat, and butter all seemed like viable options. Though each produced richly flavorful, supremely juicy roasts, tasters particularly enjoyed the subtly sweet flavor imparted by butter. In fact, I pushed that sweetness one step further and added 1 teaspoon of sugar to the salt rub. To round out the roast's savory depth, I then sliced a few garlic cloves and caramelized them in the butter before using the mixture to coat the meat. Finally, I sprinkled the rolled roast with herbes de Provence, a heady combination that includes dried basil, fennel, lavender, marjoram, rosemary, sage, and thyme.

That left just the flavorful but thin jus to attend to. I knew one way to bulk up the jus would be to put bones in the pot. Not only do the bones themselves contain gelatin, but the connective tissue surrounding them also turns into gelatin over the course of long cooking. I wanted to see what would happen if I started with a bone-in loin, removed the bones, and then used them to make a quick stock to add to the pork as it roasted. This worked beautifully. When I opened the pot about an hour later, the jus was as glossy and thickened as the trotter-enhanced liquid. The only problem was that making the stock tacked 30 minutes onto an already lengthy cooking time. I wondered if adding powdered gelatin, which we've used in the past to mimic slow-cooked stocks, would do the trick here; I found that 1 tablespoon bloomed in ¼ cup of chicken broth lent just the right viscosity.

But bones also contribute flavor, and I still had to make up for that loss. Reducing ⅓ cup of white wine (after sautéing some onions) and whisking in 1 tablespoon of butter along with the gelatin rendered the sauce rich and balanced but not remarkable. It was only my final inspiration—a diced apple cooked along with the onions—that really brought the sauce together. Enchaud is traditionally served with pickles as a counterpoint to its rich flavors, and tasters raved that the softened bits of sweet-tart fruit worked in the same way. A variation with port and figs was equally satisfying.

The French method had inspired me, but it was kitchen testing that made slow-cooking this super-lean cut something truly great.

—DAN SOUZA, *Cook's Illustrated*

French-Style Pot-Roasted Pork Loin

SERVES 4 TO 6

We strongly prefer the flavor of natural pork in this recipe, but if enhanced pork (injected with a salt solution) is used, reduce the salt to 2 teaspoons (1 teaspoon per side) in step 2.

    2 tablespoons unsalted butter, cut into 2 pieces
    6 garlic cloves, sliced thin
    1 (2½-pound) boneless center-cut pork loin roast, trimmed
       Kosher salt and pepper
    1 teaspoon sugar
    2 teaspoons herbes de Provence
    2 tablespoons vegetable oil
    1 Granny Smith apple, peeled, cored, and cut into ¼-inch pieces
    1 onion, chopped fine
    ⅓ cup dry white wine
    2 sprigs fresh thyme
    1 bay leaf
 ¼–¾ cup low-sodium chicken broth
    1 tablespoon unflavored gelatin
    1 tablespoon minced fresh parsley

1. Adjust oven rack to lower-middle position and heat oven to 225 degrees. Melt 1 tablespoon butter in 8-inch skillet over medium-low heat. Add half of garlic and cook, stirring frequently, until golden, 5 to 7 minutes. Transfer mixture to bowl and refrigerate.

2. Position roast fat side up. Insert knife one-third of way up from bottom of roast along 1 long side and cut horizontally, stopping ½ inch before edge. Open up flap. Keeping knife parallel to cutting board, cut through

thicker portion of roast about ½ inch from bottom of roast, keeping knife level with first cut and stopping about ½ inch before edge. Open up this flap. If uneven, cover with plastic wrap and use meat pounder to even out. Sprinkle 1 tablespoon salt over both sides of loin (½ tablespoon per side) and rub into pork until slightly tacky. Sprinkle sugar over inside of loin, then spread with cooled toasted garlic mixture. Starting from short side, fold roast back together like business letter (keeping fat on outside) and tie with twine at 1-inch intervals. Sprinkle tied roast evenly with herbes de Provence and season with pepper.

3. Heat 1 tablespoon oil in Dutch oven over medium heat until just smoking. Add roast, fat side down, and brown on fat side and sides (do not brown bottom of roast), 5 to 8 minutes. Transfer to large plate. Add remaining 1 tablespoon oil, apple, and onion to pot; cook, stirring frequently, until onion is softened and browned, 5 to 7 minutes. Stir in remaining sliced garlic and cook until fragrant, about 30 seconds. Stir in wine, thyme, and bay leaf; cook for 30 seconds. Return roast, fat side up, to pot; place large sheet of aluminum foil over pot and cover tightly with lid. Transfer pot to oven and cook until pork registers 140 degrees, 50 minutes to 1½ hours (short, thick roasts will take longer than long, thin ones).

4. Transfer roast to carving board, tent loosely with foil, and let rest for 20 minutes. While pork rests, sprinkle gelatin over ¼ cup chicken broth and let sit until gelatin softens, about 5 minutes. Remove thyme sprigs and bay leaf from jus. Pour jus into 2-cup measuring cup and, if necessary, add chicken broth to measure 1¼ cups. Return jus to pot and bring to simmer over medium heat. Whisk softened gelatin mixture, remaining 1 tablespoon butter, and parsley into jus and season with salt and pepper to taste; remove from heat and cover to keep warm. Slice pork into ½-inch-thick slices, adding any accumulated juices to sauce. Serve pork, passing sauce separately.

VARIATION

French-Style Pot-Roasted Pork Loin with Port and Figs

Substitute ¾ cup chopped dried figs for apple and port for white wine. Add 1 tablespoon balsamic vinegar to sauce with butter in step 4.

GRILLED STUFFED PORK TENDERLOIN

GRILLED STUFFED PORK TENDERLOIN

WHEN I HAVE PLENTY OF TIME ON MY HANDS, MY go-to summer pork roast is a well-marbled, bone-in cut that I can throw on the grill for as long as it takes for the meat to become tender and juicy while picking up plenty of smoky flavor from the fire. But when a laid-back meal isn't possible, a fast-cooking alternative like pork tenderloin can come in handy. This readily available cut has the added advantages of being supremely tender and uniformly shaped for even cooking and slicing. But what it offers in convenience, this lean, mild-mannered roast—basically the pork equivalent of boneless, skinless chicken breast—sorely lacks in flavor and juiciness. Throw the unpredictable heat of the grill into the equation, and you're well on your way to producing a dry, bland log.

Most recipes tackle these issues by using relishes or sauces to dress the cooked roast, but those solutions are only skin deep. For a flavor boost that would literally get at the interior of the tenderloin—arguably the blandest part—I wanted to try stuffing the roast with a rich-tasting filling.

I decided to work with two tenderloins, which would make enough to feed four to six people. The average pork tenderloin is only 2 inches in diameter, so I had to think carefully about the most effective way to butterfly it for stuffing. One option was a simple hinge method, in which the meat is bisected lengthwise about half an inch shy of its back edge, opened up like a book and stuffed, and then closed and secured with twine. The other approach took this method further, calling for pounding the butterflied meat until it was wide and thin, so that once stuffed, it could be rolled up. The first technique seemed less fussy, but I found that it allowed too much stuffing to ooze from the seams. Though it took a little more effort, pounding and rolling turned out to have two benefits: Pounding the meat created more surface area for the filling, and rolling the pork around the stuffing helped prevent leakage during cooking and carving.

But even with this wider plane to work with, I had to keep the filling's bulk to a minimum. That meant forgoing a traditional bread stuffing. What I needed was some sort of intense-tasting paste, of which a little would go a long way. I perused the test kitchen's pantry for flavor-packed ingredients that wouldn't require extensive prep or precooking. It didn't take me long to come up

with three robustly flavored combinations that required nothing more than a whirl in the food processor. One featured briny kalamata olives, sweet sun-dried tomatoes, and a few flavor-enhancing anchovies. Another balanced spicy roasted piquillo peppers with buttery Manchego cheese and smoked paprika. The third brought together porcini with artichoke hearts and Parmesan. Layering raw baby spinach leaves over the fillings freshened their rich flavors and added bright color.

Now for the grilling method. Lean pork tenderloin needs a forgiving heat source that won't parch the meat's exterior before the interior has a chance to cook through. I opted for a modified two-level fire, where all the coals are spread evenly over one side of the grill, leaving the other side cooler. But when I grilled the roasts across from the coals for 25 minutes, I found that the indirect heat produced mixed results. While the roasts were quite tender with perfectly warmed-through fillings, they looked utterly pale.

Fortunately, this was a problem the test kitchen had tackled before. When we want to boost browning on lean meat, we coat the exterior with a little sugar. Sure enough, when I mixed about 4 teaspoons of sugar with the salt and pepper I was rubbing on the roasts just before grilling, they came off the fire nicely browned with deeper flavor. The effect was even more pronounced when I traded granulated sugar for dark brown sugar.

When I have the time, I still like to take it slow with a fatty bone-in cut. But my tender, faintly smoky tenderloins with their robustly flavored fillings were on the table in less than an hour. Who could argue with that?

—BRYAN ROOF, *Cook's Illustrated*

Grilled Stuffed Pork Tenderloin
SERVES 4 TO 6

When trimming the tenderloins, be sure to remove the silver skin, the thin swatch of connective tissue underneath the fat. To do so, simply slip a knife under the silver skin, angle it slightly upward, and use a gentle back-and-forth motion to release it from the meat.

- 4 teaspoons packed dark brown sugar
  Kosher salt and pepper
- 2 (1¼- to 1½-pound) pork tenderloins, trimmed
- 1 recipe stuffing (recipes follow)
- 1 cup baby spinach
- 2 tablespoons olive oil

1. Combine sugar, 2 teaspoons salt, and 1 teaspoon pepper in bowl. Cut each tenderloin in half horizontally, stopping ½ inch from edge so halves remain attached. Open up tenderloins, cover with plastic wrap, and pound to ¼-inch thickness. Trim any ragged edges to make rough rectangle about 10 inches by 6 inches. Sprinkle interior of each tenderloin with ⅛ teaspoon salt and ⅛ teaspoon pepper.

2. With long side of pork facing you, spread half of stuffing mixture over bottom half of 1 tenderloin followed by ½ cup spinach. Roll away from you into tight cylinder, taking care not to squeeze stuffing out ends. Position tenderloin seam side down, evenly space 5 pieces of twine underneath, and tie. Repeat with remaining tenderloin, stuffing, and spinach.

3A. FOR A CHARCOAL GRILL: Open bottom vent completely. Light large chimney starter filled with charcoal briquettes (6 quarts). When top coals are partially covered with ash, pour evenly over half of grill. Set cooking grate in place, cover, and open lid vent completely. Heat grill until hot, about 5 minutes.

3B. FOR A GAS GRILL: Turn all burners to high, cover, and heat grill until hot, about 15 minutes. Leave primary burner on high and turn off other burner(s).

4. Clean and oil cooking grate. Coat pork with oil, then rub entire surface with sugar mixture. Place pork on cooler side of grill, cover, and cook until center of stuffing registers 140 degrees, 25 to 30 minutes, rotating pork once halfway through cooking.

5. Transfer pork to carving board, tent loosely with aluminum foil, and let rest for 5 to 10 minutes. Remove twine, slice pork into ½-inch-thick slices, and serve.

Olive and Sun-Dried Tomato Stuffing
MAKES ABOUT 1 CUP; ENOUGH FOR 2 TENDERLOINS

- ½ **cup pitted kalamata olives**
- ½ **cup oil-packed sun-dried tomatoes, rinsed and chopped coarse**
- 4 **anchovy fillets**
- 2 **garlic cloves, minced**
- 1 **teaspoon minced fresh thyme**
- 1 **teaspoon finely grated lemon zest**
  Salt and pepper

Pulse all ingredients except salt and pepper in food processor until coarsely chopped, 5 to 10 pulses; season with salt and pepper to taste.

Piquillo Pepper and Manchego Stuffing
MAKES ABOUT 1 CUP; ENOUGH FOR 2 TENDERLOINS

Roasted red peppers may be substituted for the piquillo peppers.

- 1 **slice hearty white sandwich bread, torn into ½-inch pieces**
- ¾ **cup jarred piquillo peppers, rinsed and patted dry**
- 2 **ounces Manchego cheese, shredded (½ cup)**
- ¼ **cup pine nuts, toasted**
- 2 **garlic cloves, minced**
- 1 **teaspoon minced fresh thyme**
- ½ **teaspoon smoked paprika**
  Salt and pepper

Pulse all ingredients except salt and pepper in food processor until coarsely chopped, 5 to 10 pulses; season with salt and pepper to taste.

Porcini and Artichoke Stuffing
MAKES ABOUT 1 CUP; ENOUGH FOR 2 TENDERLOINS

½ ounce dried porcini mushrooms, rinsed
3 ounces frozen artichoke hearts, thawed and
   patted dry (¾ cup)
1 ounce Parmesan cheese, grated (½ cup)
¼ cup oil-packed sun-dried tomatoes, rinsed and
   chopped coarse
¼ cup fresh parsley leaves
2 tablespoons pine nuts, toasted
2 garlic cloves, minced
1 teaspoon finely grated lemon zest plus
   2 teaspoons juice
   Salt and pepper

Microwave ½ cup water and porcini together in covered bowl until steaming, about 1 minute. Let stand until softened, about 5 minutes. Lift mushrooms from bowl with fork and pat dry with paper towels. Discard soaking liquid. Pulse porcini with remaining ingredients except salt and pepper in food processor until coarsely chopped, 5 to 10 pulses; season with salt and pepper to taste.

SLOW-COOKER GLAZED HAM

COOKING A BIG HAM DINNER PRESENTS A SERIOUS real estate problem: My oven is pushed to its limits as I try to juggle the ham with all the pies, sides, and biscuits that also need baking. Putting my slow cooker to use seemed like the perfect solution. And sure enough, recipes abound for slow-cooker ham. These recipes called for a variety of hams: spiral and uncut, boneless and bone-in, and even ham steaks, dressed up with spice rubs, jelly glazes, sugar smears, and juice braises.

After making seven recipes that represented all the various cuts and techniques, I was dispirited by the array of dry, pale, sorry-looking hams they produced. If I wanted moist ham with a dark, burnished glaze, I'd have to figure out the method myself.

Anyone who has ever cooked a ham knows the two main challenges: keeping the ham from drying out and getting a flavorful, caramelized glaze. In the test kitchen, we usually solve the first problem by cooking the ham in the steamy confines of an oven bag. The small, enclosed space of the slow cooker inherently replicates the moisture-retaining capability of an oven bag—to a degree. My early tests taught me a few keys to creating really moist slow-cooker ham. First, use a good-size (at least 6 pounds) bone-in, uncut ham to minimize moisture loss (smaller cuts and boneless and spiral-sliced hams were more apt to dry out). Second, when placing the ham in the cooker, add about a cup of liquid to the cooker insert to ensure moist meat (recipes without this liquid emerged much drier).

Since I knew I had to add liquid, I hoped I could add flavor at the same time. I tried cooking hams with plain apple and pineapple juices, and with juice seasoned with vegetables and spices, but the meat picked up scant flavor. Water it would be.

As for getting the glaze right, I had already learned that rubs and glazes melted right off the ham after many hours in the slow cooker—even when I cross-hatched the ham's exterior for more traction—so I knew I'd need a different approach. I tried making a simple thick and clingy glaze on the stovetop and then brushing it on the pale cooked ham. I started with brown sugar cooked down in a saucepan with a little water and butter. But once I brushed it on the cooked ham and let it set up, it became crystalline and gritty. One taster described it as "ham praline." Not exactly what I was aiming for.

Thinking that honey would be both smoother and stickier, I replaced some of the brown sugar with honey and again reduced the mixture slightly before brushing it on the cooked ham. But if the first glaze was praline, this one was caramel: It stuck to the pot, the stove, and even our teeth, and it sheared off the ham in one large sheet. I tried swapping the honey for another common glaze ingredient, apple jelly. Now I was getting somewhere, as tasters appreciated the sweet, fruity dimension of this glaze. But although the glaze seemed to be the right consistency in the saucepan, it was too loose to completely adhere to the ham. A tablespoon of cornstarch fixed that, making the glaze thick enough to cling. The addition of Dijon mustard and black pepper rounded out the glaze's flavor. Now this ham would both look and taste great as the centerpiece of any holiday dinner.

—CAROLYNN PURPURA MACKAY, *Cook's Country*

Slow-Cooker Holiday Glazed Ham

SERVES 16 TO 20

Do not substitute spiral-cut ham, as it will be dry. Let the glaze cool for 5 minutes before applying (it should be just warm). For a hint of spiciness, add ¼ teaspoon cayenne to the sugar mixture at the beginning of step 2.

- 1 (6- to 7½-pound) cured bone-in ham
- ½ cup packed dark brown sugar
- ½ cup apple jelly
- 2 tablespoons Dijon mustard
- 1 tablespoon cornstarch
- 1 teaspoon pepper

1. Remove skin from exterior of ham and trim fat to ¼-inch thickness. Score remaining fat at 1-inch intervals in crosshatch pattern. Place ham, cut side down, in slow cooker. Add 1 cup water, cover, and cook on low until fat is rendered and meat registers 100 degrees, 5 to 6 hours. Transfer to carving board and let rest for 15 to 20 minutes.

2. Bring sugar, jelly, mustard, cornstarch, and pepper to boil in small saucepan over medium-high heat. Cook, whisking until smooth, until glaze begins to darken and is slightly thickened, 2 to 3 minutes. Off heat, let glaze cool for 5 minutes in saucepan. Brush ham evenly with glaze and let sit for 5 minutes. Carve and serve.

NOTES FROM THE TEST KITCHEN

HAM PREP

Spiral-sliced hams dry out in the slow cooker. Bone-in, uncut hams turn out moist and succulent but require some prep work.

1. Use chef's knife to remove tough skin or rind. Then carefully trim fat to about ¼-inch thickness.

2. Slice grid pattern into ham's exterior fat to help glaze adhere to ham.

CROWN ROAST OF PORK

FOR AN IMPRESSIVE PRESENTATION AROUND THE holidays, butchers take two bone-in pork loin roasts, strip the meat off the bone ends (a technique called frenching), and tie the roasts together in a crown shape. But the striking appearance hides a culinary challenge: The odd shape—think big spiky doughnut—makes it difficult to cook a crown roast evenly.

Most recipes treat a crown roast like any other big roast: Season, brush with oil or butter, set in a roasting pan, and cook in a moderate oven. But the ring of meat and bone insulates the pork on the inside; because the oven's heat can't efficiently travel into the hole, that section takes much longer to cook. This leads to a dry, overcooked perimeter by the time the interior meat is done. Additionally, simply salting and peppering the exterior amounts to seasoning that's only superficial. Staring at 40 pounds of nearly inedible pork and a pile of problems on the heels of my initial tests, my goal crystallized: an evenly cooked, richly seasoned, and well-browned roast.

To get the hot oven air to circulate through the hole in the center of the meat, I tried elevating the roast on a V-rack. Lifting the meat off the pan this way only marginally improved the doneness discrepancy and did nothing to even out the browning. As I was staring dejectedly at yet another unevenly cooked roast, a colleague asked me if I had tried roasting the crown upside down. It sounded a little crazy, but the usual techniques weren't getting me any-where. I flipped a roast, rubbed it with salt and pepper, brushed on 4 tablespoons of melted butter, and put it in a 300-degree oven. Because the large mass of meat on the bottom was now exposed to more heat, this roast emerged much more evenly cooked, although the browning still needed work.

It took a battery of tests to find a cooking technique that resulted in both evenly cooked and well-browned meat, but eventually I got there. To blast the thick, meaty bottom of the ring with heat and start the browning, I cooked the roast upside down for about an hour (until it registered 110 degrees) at 475 degrees. Then I turned down the oven to 300 degrees and flipped the roast right side up to gently finish cooking for about 40 more minutes (until the roast hit 140 degrees).

The meat was perfectly cooked, but I still hadn't solved the problem of superficial seasoning. A crown roast is too unwieldy to easily brine (one of the test kitchen's favorite techniques to deeply season meat), but I knew that salting the roast and letting it sit overnight should have the same effect. Sure enough, a roast handled this way was seasoned throughout. For even more flavor, I added thyme, rosemary, and garlic to the mix. I did a few more tests to see if I could cut back on the salting time and determined that six hours of salting was enough to get the job done. The added seasoning also made the savory pan drippings (of which I had about half a cup) even more flavorful.

Crown roasts are often presented with stuffing or a side dish filling the hole in the middle. Stuffing seemed a little heavy with so much meat, so I concentrated on roasting some potatoes and shallots along with the pork. Because I was cooking the crown roast on a rack and flipping it, cooking the vegetables inside the hole was

obviously out (although I could certainly serve them there). But roasting them in the pan, under the rack, imbued them even more completely with the meaty drippings.

One taster suggested that I add apples, a classic pork accompaniment. Apple pieces that I cooked with the vegetables were too mushy to serve but added a pleasantly sweet-tangy dimension to the drippings. Instead of discarding them, I pureed the softened apples with the pan drippings. This mixture, bolstered with a little chicken broth, made a delicious sauce. Adding ½ cup of apple cider to the roasting pan midway through cooking reinforced the apple flavor, making the sauce even better.

Juicy and perfectly cooked, with simple roasted vegetables in the center and a sweet and tangy sauce on the side, this roast was just the crown I needed for the head of my Christmas table.

—SARAH GABRIEL, *Cook's Country*

NOTES FROM THE TEST KITCHEN

CROWN ROAST OF PORK
When roasted directly on a roasting pan, the perimeter of a crown roast overcooks by the time the interior ring is done. Here's how we solved that problem and produced evenly cooked pork.

1. Using kitchen twine, make 2 loops around widest part of roast and tie securely to help crown hold its shape when flipped.

2. Place pork bone side down on V-rack and adjust bones to steady roast. Roast about 1 hour, until meat registers 110 degrees.

3. Using paper towels to protect your hands, flip hot roast bone side up and set it back on V-rack to finish cooking in 300-degree oven.

Crown Roast of Pork
SERVES 10 TO 12

Buy a pork loin roast with rib bones that have been trimmed clean, or "frenched." Check with the butcher that the chine bone has been cut from the crown roast; leaving this bone attached hinders even cooking. You want to buy the roast tied, but we tie it an extra time for more support during flipping. Use potatoes that measure 1 to 2 inches in diameter.

    Kosher salt and pepper
3   tablespoons minced fresh thyme
2   tablespoons minced fresh rosemary
5   garlic cloves, minced
1   (8- to 10-pound) bone-in pork loin crown roast
    (chine bone removed)
2   pounds small red potatoes
10 ounces shallots, peeled and halved
2   Golden Delicious apples, peeled, cored, and halved
8   tablespoons unsalted butter, melted
½   cup apple cider
1   cup low-sodium chicken broth

1. Combine 3 tablespoons salt, 1 tablespoon pepper, thyme, rosemary, and garlic in bowl; reserve 2 teaspoons for vegetables. Pat pork dry with paper towels and rub with remaining salt mixture. Wrap kitchen twine twice around widest part of roast and tie tightly. Refrigerate roast, covered, for 6 to 24 hours.

2. Adjust oven rack to lower-middle position and heat oven to 475 degrees. Place V-rack inside large roasting pan. Toss potatoes, shallots, apples, 4 tablespoons melted butter, and reserved herb salt together in large bowl and transfer to pan. Arrange roast bone side down in V-rack and brush with remaining 4 tablespoons melted butter. Roast until meat is well browned and registers 110 degrees, about 1 hour.

3. Remove roast from oven and reduce oven temperature to 300 degrees. Using 2 bunches of paper towels, flip roast bone side up. Add apple cider to pan and return to oven, rotating pan. Roast until meat registers 140 degrees, 30 to 50 minutes. Place meat on carving board, tent loosely with aluminum foil, and let rest for 15 to 20 minutes.

4. Transfer apple halves to blender and potatoes and shallots to bowl. Pour pan juices into fat separator, let liquid settle, then pour into blender. Process apples with pan juices until smooth, about 1 minute. Strain sauce through fine-mesh strainer into medium saucepan. Add broth and bring to simmer. Season with salt and pepper to taste. Remove twine and slice meat between bones. Serve with vegetables and sauce.

COUNTRY-FRIED PORK

COUNTRY FRIED IS A CONTROVERSIAL TERM THAT means different things in different parts of the country. Call me stubborn, but no matter where I'm hanging my hat, country fried means tender, juicy meat that's shallow fried and firmly encased in a crunchy flour coating. The meat that's most often country fried is beef (as in chicken-fried steak). But I'd seen recipes for country-fried pork, and I wanted to give that a try. I had in mind moist, tender pork with a crisp, bumpy coating with lots of nooks and crannies to capture the flavorful, creamy gravy.

Country-fried meats are always boneless, so I started with boneless pork loin, slicing and pounding it into thin cutlets before dredging and frying. But tasters found the pounded loin a little chewy. Why not use a cut of pork that is supremely tender to begin with: the tenderloin?

A single 1-pound tenderloin is easy to cut into four pieces. Instead of flipping the tenderloin pieces onto their cut sides to pound them out (as in other recipes), I found I got more even pieces if I pounded them without flipping. What's more, pounding them to ¼ inch thick this way resulted in oblong cutlets that easily fit two at a time in the skillet.

Now that I had the right cut of pork, I got to work on the coating. I took a cue from our recipe for chicken-fried steak and scored the pork to help the coating adhere, then lightly coated it with seasoned flour before pounding it. But this was not your standard seasoned flour. In addition to the usual seasonings, I added baking powder (for lightness) and cornstarch (to dry the surface and create a super-crisp crust). I also found that sticking the dredged pork in the refrigerator for 15 minutes helped the coating set. (Later tests showed that it could hold up to four hours at this stage.) When fried, this crust was light and nicely browned, but it still felt a little bit thin. To get the craggy coating I was looking for, I moistened part of the flour mixture with milk and rubbed until it resembled coarse meal. Then I tested the pork in bubbling oil. Happily, this method gave me a perfectly fried coating.

Now I had the crisp coating, but there was still the matter of flavor. To compensate for the tenderloin's blandness, I'd create a super-charged gravy. Most recipes called for making the gravy after frying, but since I didn't want my country-fried pork sitting around getting soggy while awaiting its mate, I'd need to reverse the order. The drawback, though, was that I wouldn't have those browned bits that stick to the bottom of the pot after cooking the pork, which give the gravy much of its flavor. So I turned to other flavor enhancers. I replaced some of the milk in traditional cream gravy with chicken broth; then added chopped onion along with garlic, lots of dried sage, and paprika; and simmered everything for about 10 minutes to thicken. To finish, I stirred in a generous amount of Worcestershire sauce and took the "more is better" approach with the pepper mill.

The bold gravy lent the lean pork big flavor that one taster described as "the opposite of bland." And that's just what you want out of country-fried pork, no matter where you hang your hat.

—DIANE UNGER, *Cook's Country*

COUNTRY-FRIED PORK WITH GRAVY

Country-Fried Pork with Gravy

SERVES 4

Make the gravy first so the crisp pork doesn't turn soggy waiting for it.

GRAVY

  3 tablespoons unsalted butter
  ¼ cup finely chopped onion
  3 tablespoons all-purpose flour
  1 garlic clove, minced
  1 teaspoon dried sage
  ½ teaspoon paprika
  2 cups low-sodium chicken broth
  1 cup whole milk
  4 teaspoons Worcestershire sauce
     Salt and pepper

PORK

  2 cups all-purpose flour
  ½ cup cornstarch
  2 teaspoons garlic powder
  2 teaspoons onion powder
     Salt and pepper
  1½ teaspoons baking powder
  ¼ teaspoon cayenne pepper
  ½ cup whole milk
  2 large eggs
  1 (1-pound) pork tenderloin, trimmed,
     cut crosswise into 4 pieces
  1 cup peanut or vegetable oil

1. FOR THE GRAVY: Melt butter in medium saucepan over medium heat. Add onion and cook until softened, about 5 minutes. Stir in flour, garlic, sage, and paprika and cook, whisking constantly, until golden and fragrant, about 1 minute. Slowly whisk in broth and milk and bring to boil. Reduce heat to medium-low and simmer until thickened, about 10 minutes. Off heat, stir in Worcestershire and season with salt and pepper to taste. Cover and set aside. (Gravy can be refrigerated for up to 2 days.)

2. FOR THE PORK: Meanwhile, combine flour, cornstarch, garlic powder, onion powder, 2 teaspoons pepper, 1 teaspoon salt, baking powder, and cayenne in bowl. Transfer 1 cup seasoned flour to shallow dish. Whisk 6 tablespoons milk and eggs together in second shallow dish. Stir remaining 2 tablespoons milk into remaining seasoned flour, rub with fingers until

mixture resembles coarse meal, and transfer to third shallow dish.

3. Pat pork dry with paper towels and season with salt and pepper. Lightly score both uncut sides of pork pieces in ¼-inch crosshatch pattern. Working with 1 piece at a time, coat pork lightly with seasoned flour. Place pork between 2 sheets of plastic wrap and pound to ¼-inch thickness; remove plastic. Coat pork again with seasoned flour, dip into egg mixture, and dredge in milk and flour mixture, pressing firmly to adhere. Arrange pork on wire rack set in rimmed baking sheet and refrigerate for 15 minutes or up to 4 hours.

4. Adjust oven rack to middle position and heat oven to 200 degrees. Warm gravy over medium-low heat, stirring occasionally. Heat oil in 12-inch skillet over medium heat until shimmering. Fry 2 pieces pork until deep golden brown and crisp, 2 to 3 minutes per side. Drain on clean wire rack set in rimmed baking sheet and place in oven. Fry remaining pork. Serve with gravy.

NOTES FROM THE TEST KITCHEN

KEYS TO BETTER BREADING
For a craggy, crisp coating that sticks to the pork, follow these steps.

1. Use chef's knife to mark meat in crosshatch pattern on both sides. This helps flour adhere.

2. Dredge scored tenderloin pieces in seasoned flour, wrap in plastic wrap, and pound to ¼ inch.

3. Dredge pounded pork in flour again, dip it in egg mixture, and coat it in moistened, seasoned flour.

KALUA PORK

I FIRST ENCOUNTERED KALUA PORK—A SUCCULENT, smoked suckling pig that's the centerpiece of Hawaiian luaus—on a trip to Oahu. It was fantastic, but it was clear why I'd never run into it before. The word *kalua* refers to the traditional Hawaiian pit-cooking method using an *imu*, a deep hole in the ground with a native kiawe wood fire and a lining of hot rocks and banana leaves. The leaves flavor the meat and help keep it moist. Seasoned with only local pink sea salt, the pork roasts at low heat in the pit for hours, emerging tender, juicy, and smoky and bearing the unique flavor stamp of the leaves. How could I ever make that happen at home—minus the whole pig, the banana leaves, and (sigh) the Hawaiian beaches?

Understandably, recipes in most modern Hawaiian cookbooks skip the imu, too. They use the oven, rely on bottled liquid smoke for the essential smoky flavor, and bypass the vegetation altogether. Imu aside, in terms of cooking method, true kalua pork resembles any barbecued pork in that it cooks "low and slow"—at a low temperature for a long time. The test kitchen has plenty of experience using a grill to barbecue pork, so I was confident that we could employ that technique here, too. Mimicking the elusive, herbaceous flavor of the banana leaves, however, would be another matter entirely.

To start, in place of the traditional but obviously impractical whole pig, I opted for boneless pork shoulder roast, often labeled "pork butt" or "Boston butt" in supermarkets. Comprising several well-exercised muscles with plenty of fat and connective tissue that melts during cooking to keep the meat moist, the rich, flavorful shoulder roast stands up well to long, slow cooking (it's the cut usually used for pulled pork).

Unlike most pulled pork and other types of barbecue, though, kalua pork is not sauced, so it wasn't a surprise that some tasters found my first attempt a bit dry and bland. I decided to capture the flavorful juices that were dripping into the fire by placing the pork in a disposable aluminum pan on top of the grill grate. This allowed me to moisten the finished pork by adding back some of the collected, defatted juices, which, of course, are rich in pork flavor. A few tests showed me that it was also necessary to loosely cover the pan with foil in order to replicate the steamy environment of the imu. I poked holes in the foil to let the smoke through.

The test kitchen's first choice for building smoky flavor is a charcoal fire topped with a packet of wood chips.

While choosing the type of wood, I learned that mesquite is related to Hawaiian kiawe wood, so it was the natural choice for this recipe (both types of wood produce smoke that is more assertive than hickory or oak). Refueling the fire to keep it burning (and smoking) for an extended cooking time is inconvenient to say the least (you have to remove the roast, then the hot grill grate to add more charcoal, then replace the grate and meat), which is why we've developed a terrific hybrid method: Start by smoking the meat with gentle indirect heat and then, when after two hours the coals and chips have burned out, move the meat to a 325-degree oven to cook (covered or wrapped in foil) until it's fork-tender, another two to three hours.

To get a better idea of the flavor imparted by the banana leaves, I ordered some online, wrapped a pork butt in the leaves, and slow-smoked it. The herbal, mineral-y flavor played off the smoke perfectly and really was unusual. Thinking about how to re-create that flavor, I paced the produce department for inspiration, picking up various large, leafy greens to try wrapping around the pork.

I wrapped each of seven pork butts with a different type of leaf: collard greens, kale, Swiss chard, green cabbage, napa cabbage, savoy cabbage, and corn husks. It was an interesting experiment but not a successful one. The corn husks burned, and the rest of these vegetables infused the smoked pork with cabbage-y, sulfuric flavors. Yuck. I rubbed more pork butts with pastes made from parsley, watercress, and spinach. These flavors weren't unpleasant; they were just plain wrong for kalua pork.

Back to the supermarket produce aisle. This time I focused on the tropical nature of the banana leaves and chose bananas and pineapple. It took some doing (and fellow test cooks looked at me as if I'd lost my mind), but I used kitchen twine to lash pork roasts with fancy patchworks of banana peels and pineapple rind. I got—no surprise—pork that tasted like bananas and pineapples. Not what I was going for, either. I was running out of steam.

I had one last banana leaf in the freezer, so I tried it again to jog my memory and further analyze the flavor: aromatic, earthy, and mildly grassy, with a tea-like quality. Ding, ding, ding! I hit the tea aisle at the market, bringing home smoky Lapsang Souchong, a few herbal tea blends, and green tea, each of which I made into seasoning rubs. Several more tests later, I was delighted to find that a rub made from 3 tablespoons of crumbled green tea and 4 teaspoons of kosher salt

HAWAIIAN-STYLE SMOKED PORK (KALUA PORK)

hit very close to the mark, and rubbing it on was far easier than tying leaves or peels around a large pork roast. A little brown sugar helped the rub caramelize and made the meat's crust a more attractive (and delicious) shade of deep brown.

Luau or not, now I can enjoy kalua pork wherever I want.

—ADAM RIED, *Cook's Country*

Hawaiian-Style Smoked Pork (Kalua Pork)

SERVES 8

You'll need 10 to 15 tea bags. Boneless pork butt is often labeled Boston butt in the supermarket. If your pork butt comes with an elastic netting, remove it before you rub the pork with the tea. When using a charcoal grill, we prefer wood chunks to wood chips whenever possible; substitute 6 medium wood chunks, soaked in water for one hour, for the wood chip packets. To eat kalua pork as the Hawaiians do, serve it with steamed rice, macaroni salad, and cabbage salad.

- 3 tablespoons green tea leaves
- 4 teaspoons kosher salt
- 1 tablespoon packed brown sugar
- 2 teaspoons pepper
- 1 (4- to 5-pound) boneless pork butt roast, trimmed
- 1 (13 by 9-inch) disposable aluminum roasting pan
- 6 cups mesquite wood chips

1. Combine tea, salt, sugar, and pepper in bowl. Pat pork dry with paper towels and rub with tea mixture. Wrap meat tightly with plastic wrap and refrigerate for 6 to 24 hours. Just before grilling, soak wood chips in water for 15 minutes, then drain. Place pork in pan and cover pan loosely with aluminum foil. Poke about twenty ¼-inch holes in foil. Using large piece of heavy-duty foil, wrap 2 cups soaked chips in foil packet and cut several vent holes in top. Make 2 more packets with additional foil and remaining 4 cups chips.

2A. FOR A CHARCOAL GRILL: Open bottom vent halfway. Light large chimney starter three-quarters full with charcoal briquettes (4½ quarts). When top coals are partially covered with ash, pour into steeply banked pile against side of grill. Place wood chip packets on coals. Set cooking grate in place, cover, and open lid

vent halfway. Heat grill until hot and wood chips are smoking, about 5 minutes.

2B. FOR A GAS GRILL: Place wood chip packets over primary burner. Turn all burners to high, cover, and heat grill until hot and wood chips are smoking, about 15 minutes. Turn primary burner to medium-high and turn off other burner(s). (Adjust primary burner as needed to maintain grill temperature around 300 degrees.)

3. Place pan on cool side of grill. Cover (positioning lid vent over meat if using charcoal) and cook for 2 hours. During last 20 minutes of grilling, adjust oven rack to lower-middle position and heat oven to 325 degrees.

4. Remove pan from grill. Cover pan tightly with new sheet of foil, transfer to oven, and bake until tender and fork inserted into meat meets no resistance, 2 to 3 hours. Let pork rest, covered, for 30 minutes. Unwrap and, when meat is cool enough to handle, shred into bite-size pieces, discarding fat. Strain contents of pan through fine-mesh strainer into fat separator. Let liquid settle, then return ¼ cup defatted pan juices to pork. Serve. (Pork can be refrigerated for up to 3 days.)

NOTES FROM THE TEST KITCHEN

TASTING SUPERMARKET GREEN TEA

The Japanese and Chinese have sipped green tea for more than a millennium. And now Westerners are drinking it, too, as well as using it to give astringent, slightly bitter flavor to custard, ice cream, and even pork roast. (It's made from the same plants as black tea but is unfermented, which accounts for its distinctive flavor.) Connoisseurs have their pick among high-end selections, but cooking with $14-an-ounce tea makes about as much sense as cooking with a $100 bottle of wine. We wanted a tea we could both sip and cook with on occasion. Supermarket green teas are affordable, but would any suit our two needs? We set the teakettles a-boiling and gathered 21 tasters to sample five nationally available supermarket brands of bagged green tea, tasting each on its own (following manufacturers' brewing instructions) and in green-tea-infused custard. None dazzled us, but we did identify a few that were both drinkable and imparted nice flavor to recipes. We liked the mild grassiness and clean flavor of **Celestial Seasonings Authentic Green Tea** best, sipped, infused, and rubbed on Kalua Pork.

TACOS AL PASTOR

TACOS AL PASTOR, OR "SHEPHERD-STYLE" TACOS, are a Mexican taqueria classic made from thin slices of chile-marinated pork that's been tightly packed onto a vertical spit with layers of pork fat and then roasted. The cone-shaped stack is often topped with a whole pineapple whose tangy, sweet juices trickle down, encouraging the meat to caramelize as it turns. When the exterior is browned and crisp, thin shavings of the roasted pork and pineapple are carved off directly onto a warm tortilla and then topped with garnishes that contrast with the rich meat: minced raw onion, cilantro, and a squeeze of fresh lime.

It's an adaptation of the lamb shawarmas (themselves inspired by Turkish doner kebabs) introduced to Mexico by Arab immigrants in the late 19th century, and it's my favorite kind of taco filling. I've often given thought to a homemade version to satisfy my frequent al pastor cravings but have always been deterred by the fact that my home kitchen lacks what you'd think would be an essential piece of equipment: a vertical spit. This time, however, my appetite got the better of me. I decided to see what it would take to make this super-flavorful meat at home.

I pored over the test kitchen's library of Mexican cookbooks and came away with a half-dozen recipes. All but one called for pork shoulder, which made sense; it's what the taquerias use because it's a flavorful, well-marbled cut.

Most of the marinade formulas I found looked relatively similar, too: Some assortment of whole dried guajillo, pasilla, and/or chipotle chiles (all readily available at most supermarkets) is toasted in a skillet and then combined with tomatoes or tomatillos, cumin, garlic, citrus juices, herbs and spices, and water. The mixture is simmered until the chiles are soft and is then pureed, strained, and married with the thin-cut strips of meat. But what sounded like recipes for flavor-packed results turned out to be bland disappointments across the board. It wasn't that the marinades themselves weren't bold—the one I liked best (with fruity guajillos, tomatoes, lots of garlic, bay leaves, cumin, and cloves) was full-bodied and concentrated—but that no marinade travels more than a few millimeters beyond the surface of the meat.

That meant it was crucial that the pork be sliced as thin as possible to allow the heady chile mixture to permeate every bite—a point, I soon realized, that would be one of the biggest challenges of pulling off tacos al pastor at home. Many taquerias have the benefit of a meat slicer to shave the roast paper-thin before coating it with the marinade. I'd have to make do with a sharp chef's knife. But since raw pork is squishy and hard to control with a knife, the thinnest uniform slices I could manage still measured a good half-inch—too thick for the marinade to come through in each bite. Partially freezing the roast did make the meat firm enough to slice but also tacked an extra hour onto the process, and I didn't want to wait that long. Stymied, I decided to turn my attention to the cooking method in hopes of finding an alternative solution.

With the exception of one that opted for a skillet, all of the recipes I tried employed the broiler or a grill. The logic here seemed sound enough: Mimic the deep browning and crispy edges of authentic al pastor by exposing the marinated meat to the hottest possible heat source. According to tasters, there was no contest between the two methods; the grilled pork strips (for now, I was using my ½-inch slabs) boasted better charring and crispier edges. The downside was that neither method produced the tender, juicy results you get at a taqueria, and the problem again boiled down to a matter of equipment. When spit-roasted, the pork turns out extra-succulent because it's continually basted by the layers of melting fat. But how could I get this result without a rotisserie?

It was time to seek professional help, and I turned to my favorite local source for tacos al pastor, Taqueria el Amigo in Waltham, Massachusetts. When I stepped into owner Jorge Calderón's kitchen, I made a surprising discovery: He doesn't own a vertical spit either. Instead, he makes tacos al pastor the way his grandmother did at her roadside stand in Mexico. First, he braises finely cubed pork butt in a tomato-based chile sauce until it's supremely tender and deeply infused with flavor, and then he scoops portions of the meat onto a griddle, where it sizzles to a browned patina.

His unusual approach sounded promising: Braising the pork in the chile sauce would simultaneously tenderize it and infuse it with flavor, putting to bed the problems associated with slicing the roast by hand. I hurried back to the test kitchen to try replicating his results. After whipping up a batch of my chile-tomato sauce, I nestled the ½-inch slabs of pork (for now, I was hoping to avoid painstakingly cubing the meat) into the liquid; let it all simmer for a good two hours, by which time the meat was fall-apart tender; and then moved the pork slabs into a hot skillet to crisp.

It seemed my battle was half won. The braised meat was incredibly tender, juicy, and infused with the complex chile sauce, which confirmed that there was no need to cube the pork butt. But tasters missed the charred crispness of the grilled versions. Easy fix, I figured; I'd simply brown the braised strips on the grill rather than in a skillet. Indeed, searing the meat for about five minutes per side over a single-level fire seemed to work well until I went to flip the pieces, which fell apart and slipped through the grill grate in shreds. Tender meat was one thing, but it had to be grillable, too, so I dialed back the braising time by 30 minutes. The result: meat that was plenty tender but still held its shape. It was also a snap to grill some pineapple rounds right next to the pork; I coarsely chopped them and transferred them to a bowl for garnishing each taco.

To replicate the appearance and texture of meat shaved from a spit, I sliced the crisped slabs crosswise into short ⅛-inch-thick strips. Now the meat was getting really good—full-flavored, crisp at the edges, and fork-tender—but I wished it were as succulent as the spit-roasted versions I'd had. That's when it dawned on me that a crucial part of the classic setup was missing: the melted fat that drips down, basting the meat as it cooks. I wasn't about to start grilling pieces of pork fat, but I did have a potful of braising liquid that was loaded with rendered drippings. I brushed the unctuous liquid over both sides of each pork slab before grilling and then, just before serving, tossed a little more of it, spiked with a bit of lime juice for brightness, with the grilled slices.

Now my tacos al pastor, imbued with all of the complexity and rich flavor of the spit-roasted originals, brought the taste of a taqueria into my own kitchen.

—DAN SOUZA, *Cook's Illustrated*

Spicy Pork Tacos (al Pastor)
SERVES 6 TO 8

Boneless pork butt is often labeled Boston butt in the supermarket. If you can't find guajillo chiles, New Mexican chiles may be substituted, although the dish may be spicier. To warm tortillas, place them on a plate, cover with a damp kitchen towel, and microwave for 60 to 90 seconds. Keep tortillas covered and serve immediately.

10   large dried guajillo chiles, wiped clean
1½   cups water
1¼   pounds plum tomatoes, cored and quartered
8   garlic cloves, peeled
4   bay leaves
     Salt and pepper
¾   teaspoon sugar
½   teaspoon ground cumin
⅛   teaspoon ground cloves
1   (3-pound) boneless pork butt roast
1   lime, cut into 8 wedges
½   pineapple, peeled, cored, and cut into
     ½-inch-thick rings
     Vegetable oil
18   (6-inch) corn tortillas, warmed
1   small onion, chopped fine
½   cup coarsely chopped fresh cilantro

1. Toast guajillos in large Dutch oven over medium-high heat until softened and fragrant, 2 to 4 minutes. Transfer to large plate and, when cool enough to handle, remove stems.

2. Return toasted guajillos to now-empty Dutch oven, add water, tomatoes, garlic, bay leaves, 2 teaspoons salt, ½ teaspoon pepper, sugar, cumin, and cloves, and bring to simmer over medium-high heat. Cover, reduce heat, and simmer, stirring occasionally, until guajillos are softened and tomatoes mash easily, about 20 minutes.

3. While sauce simmers, trim excess fat from exterior of pork, leaving ¼-inch-thick fat cap. Slice pork against grain into ½-inch-thick slabs.

4. Transfer guajillo-tomato mixture to blender and process until smooth, about 1 minute. Strain puree through fine-mesh strainer, pressing on solids to extract as much liquid as possible. Return puree to pot, submerge pork slices in liquid, and bring to simmer over medium heat. Partially cover, reduce heat, and gently simmer until pork is tender but still holds together, 1½ to 1¾ hours, flipping and rearranging pork halfway through cooking. (Pork can be left in sauce, cooled to room temperature, and refrigerated for up to 2 days.)

5. Transfer pork to large plate, season both sides with salt, and cover tightly with aluminum foil. Whisk sauce to combine. Transfer ½ cup sauce to bowl for grilling; pour off all but ½ cup remaining sauce from pot and reserve for another use. Squeeze 2 lime wedges into sauce in pot and add spent wedges; season with salt to taste.

RE-CREATING TACOS AL PASTOR

Our at-home approach achieves juicy meat with crisp edges—without specialized equipment.

1. Gently simmer pork roast (cut into ½-inch slabs) in chile sauce to tenderize meat and infuse it with rich flavor.

2. Sear braised pork on grill to crisp edges; brush it with fatty braising liquid to lend succulence.

3. Toss grilled pork (cut into ⅛-inch slices) with lime juice and braising liquid for brightness and richness.

SMOKY SPICE

This mild, fruity dried chile is easy to find in supermarkets and brings smoky flavor to the pork.

GUAJILLO CHILE

THE BEST PINEAPPLE CUTTERS

To simplify the messy, time-consuming job of prepping fresh pineapples, we test-drove six tools, from $7.99 to $30, that promised faster results. Our favorite, the **Rösle Pineapple Cutter**, made effortless, 30-second work of the job, but at $30, it's only for hard-core pineapple lovers. Our Best Buy, the **MIU France Pineapple Corer/Slicer**, $12.33, performed nearly as well at less than half the price.

6A. FOR A CHARCOAL GRILL: Open bottom vent halfway. Light large chimney starter filled with charcoal briquettes (6 quarts). When top coals are partially covered with ash, pour evenly over grill. Set cooking grate in place, cover, and open lid vent halfway. Heat grill until hot, about 5 minutes.

6B. FOR A GAS GRILL: Turn all burners to high, cover, and heat grill until hot, about 15 minutes. Turn all burners to medium.

7. Clean and oil cooking grate. Brush 1 side of pork with ¼ cup reserved sauce. Place pork on 1 side of grill, sauce side down, and cook until well browned and crisp, 5 to 7 minutes. Brush pork with remaining ¼ cup reserved sauce, flip, and continue to cook until second side is well browned and crisp, 5 to 7 minutes longer. Transfer to carving board. Meanwhile, brush both sides of pineapple rings with vegetable oil and season with salt to taste. Place on other half of grill and cook until pineapple is softened and caramelized, 10 to 14 minutes; transfer pineapple to carving board.

8. Coarsely chop grilled pineapple and transfer to serving bowl. Using tongs or carving fork to steady hot pork, slice each piece crosswise into ⅛-inch pieces. Bring remaining ½ cup sauce in pot to simmer, add sliced pork, remove pot from heat, and toss to coat pork well. Season with salt to taste.

9. Spoon small amount of pork into each warm tortilla and serve, passing chopped pineapple, remaining 6 lime wedges, onion, and cilantro separately.

BRAISED PORK CHOPS

WHEN I THINK OF PORK CHOPS, I THINK OF A SIMPLE, no-frills cut that I can just slap into a hot skillet and have on the table in minutes. But lately I've been hearing people talk about braised pork chops. The more I considered this option, the better it seemed. Not only did the slow, gentle approach of braising promise flavorful, tender chops, but it also meant that I'd end up with a rich, glossy sauce. This, I thought, would take pork chops to a whole new level. I was also attracted to the idea of braising smaller cuts like chops in place of the more typical roast—I wouldn't have to trim intramuscular fat or tough silver skin from the roast and retie it with twine before it went into the pan, nor would there be any carving to do after cooking. Sounded good to me.

But when I went into the test kitchen to try out a few recipes, none lived up to their promise. The meat was dry and bland, swimming in liquid that lacked both complexity and the silky body of a long, gently simmered sauce. Clearly I had some work to do.

Before I started fiddling with the cooking method, I had an important decision to make at the supermarket: exactly which chops to buy. Butchers cut four different chops: blade, rib, center cut, and sirloin. I knew that the muscle and fat makeup of the four chops varies considerably and that the only way to find the best cut for the job would be to test them all. I brined each set of chops (to season the chops and ensure juiciness), patted them dry, and seared them in a Dutch oven just long enough to develop some flavorful browning on the meat and the fond on the bottom of the pot—a crucial step for creating a richly flavored sauce. Then I browned the aromatics and deglazed the pot with red wine, which I hoped would temper the meaty richness of the chops. Finally, I poured in some chicken broth, covered the pot, and pushed it into a low (275-degree) oven to simmer gently for about 90 minutes.

When I sliced the meat and called my tasters, the results were unanimous: All but one of the chops had cooked up stringy and bland, officially disqualifying the center-cut, rib, and sirloin contenders from the running. But the blade chops were promising; they contained a good bit of marbling and connective tissue, both of which were breaking down during cooking, lending the meat flavor and also helping to preserve its juiciness. The drawback was that the chops buckled considerably during searing and, as a result, didn't take on much browning or supply much fond to the bottom of the pot. Without that foundation of flavor, the sauce was lackluster and thin, and the wine's contribution one-dimensional and a bit harsh. Blade chops were also a little harder to find in the store, but I decided they were worth seeking out. All in all, this was a good start.

I seared another batch to get a closer look at the buckling problem and watched as the chops' dense rim of connective tissues immediately began to contract like a rubber band. The chops' contortions were keeping them from browning evenly, and the lack of fond on the bottom of the vessel also explained why the sauce tasted so anemic. For the sake of both aesthetics and flavor, I had to figure out a way to keep the chops flat. What would happen if I trimmed away the offending portion of connective tissue before searing?

I placed a new batch of trimmed chops in the hot Dutch oven, where they stayed flat and took on an even layer of color. Everything looked great until I took a peek at the bottom of the pot. Where I expected to find a thick, crusty layer of fond I found a few faint patches of browning—hardly the makings of a flavorful sauce. Where had all the fond gone? I realized that the real ingredient for fond was the pile of fatty scraps I was about to pitch into the trash.

That gave me an idea: Rather than toss the fatty trimmings, I chopped them into 1-inch pieces and seared them to generate fond. In less than 10 minutes, I had the most substantial layer of browning yet, thanks to the increased surface area of the smaller pieces. In fact, the fond was so impressive that I wondered if I needed to sear the chops themselves. One side-by-side test gave me my answer: The braise made with unseared chops was every bit as meaty as that made with the seared batch. To take full advantage of their flavor, I left the chunks in the pot during braising, knowing that their rich fat would only add to the porky flavor and unctuousness of the sauce.

As an added bonus, the chopped-up scraps served a structural function as well. When I nestled the chops on top of the fatty chunks, they rested well above the liquid line. When I pulled this batch out of the oven roughly 90 minutes later, not only was the sauce richer and more flavorful, but the chops were noticeably juicier than they had been when they'd cooked more thoroughly submerged in the liquid.

Our science editor had an explanation: The secret to braising is ensuring that the temperature of the meat hovers for as long as possible between 160 and 180 degrees. In that range, the meat's collagen converts into gelatin, which holds on to the meat's juices. Too little heat and the meat won't produce enough gelatin; too much and its muscle fibers will wring out moisture before the gelatin can soak it up. In this case, the combination of air and liquid was holding the less-submerged chops at a temperature that allowed them to produce a good bit of gelatin and retain their moisture. And to ensure that they held on to every bit of their flavorful juices, I rested the braised chops for 30 minutes before slicing into them, which gave the juices ample time to redistribute throughout the meat.

Thanks to the trimmings and staple aromatics like garlic, thyme, and bay leaves, the braising liquid now had decent flavor, but a few tasters remarked that it lacked

KEYS TO BETTER BRAISED PORK CHOPS

1. Sear trimmed scraps from blade chops to build flavorful browning without searing chops themselves.

2. Sauté onions in rendered pork fat until golden brown with garlic, thyme, bay leaves, ginger, and allspice for complex flavor.

3. Deglaze pot with combination of red wine, ruby port, and red wine vinegar to add acidity, sweetness, and complexity to braising liquid.

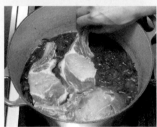

4. Lay chops on top of trimmings to raise them well above liquid, where they will cook more gently and retain their flavorful juices.

TRIM YOUR CHOPS

The band of fatty connective tissue and shoulder meat along the outer edge of blade chops contributes body and flavor to the braise—but it also causes the chops to buckle. To cut out the structural issues without sacrificing flavor, we trim away the band, chop it up, and save the pieces for searing.

ON THE CHOPPING BLOCK

Trim off swath of fatty meat and any cartilage running along edge of chop. Cut scraps into 1-inch pieces.

body, depth, and even some brightness. Fixing the first problem was easy; I simply strained and defatted the liquid and reduced it for about five minutes. A pat of butter whisked in off the heat added silkiness and a bit more viscosity.

As for the latter critiques, I tried finishing the pot with a splash of wine, but everyone agreed that only furthered the harshness we'd detected early on. To take the edge off, I went in search of something sweeter in the pantry and came across a bottle of ruby port. Replacing some of the red wine with the fortified stuff went a long way but also flattened the flavor a bit. I wasn't crazy about upping the booziness, so instead I added a touch of red wine vinegar along with the wines, the bright acidity of which brought the sweet-tart balance into equilibrium. I also tossed in a knob of crushed fresh ginger and a dash of allspice, both of which lent this latest batch a rich, spicy aroma.

Just before serving, I added a final splash of vinegar and a handful of chopped parsley, spooned the liquid over the tender, juicy chops, and knew I had finally done right by this classic technique.

—LAN LAM, *Cook's Illustrated*

Red Wine–Braised Pork Chops

SERVES 4

Look for chops with a small eye and a large amount of marbling, as these are the best suited to braising. The pork scraps can be removed when straining the sauce in step 4 and served alongside the chops. (They taste great.)

> Salt and pepper
> 4 (10- to 12-ounce) bone-in pork blade chops, 1 inch thick
> 2 teaspoons vegetable oil
> 2 onions, halved and sliced thin
> 5 sprigs fresh thyme plus ¼ teaspoon minced
> 2 garlic cloves, peeled
> 2 bay leaves
> 1 (½-inch) piece ginger, peeled and crushed
> ⅛ teaspoon ground allspice
> ½ cup red wine
> ¼ cup ruby port
> 2 tablespoons plus ½ teaspoon red wine vinegar
> 1 cup low-sodium chicken broth
> 2 tablespoons unsalted butter
> 1 tablespoon minced fresh parsley

RED WINE–BRAISED PORK CHOPS

1. Dissolve 3 tablespoons salt in 1½ quarts cold water in large container. Submerge chops in brine, cover, and refrigerate for 30 minutes or up to 1 hour.

2. Adjust oven rack to lower-middle position and heat oven to 275 degrees. Remove chops from brine and pat dry with paper towels. Trim off meat cap and any fat and cartilage opposite rib bones. Cut trimmings into 1-inch pieces. Heat oil in Dutch oven over medium-high heat until shimmering. Add trimmings and brown on all sides, 6 to 9 minutes.

3. Reduce heat to medium and add onions, thyme sprigs, garlic, bay leaves, ginger, and allspice. Cook, stirring occasionally, until onions are golden brown, 5 to 10 minutes. Stir in wine, port, and 2 tablespoons vinegar and cook until reduced to thin syrup, 5 to 7 minutes. Add broth, spread onions and pork scraps into even layer, and bring to simmer. Arrange pork chops on top of pork scraps and onions.

4. Cover, transfer to oven, and cook until meat is tender, 1¼ to 1½ hours. Remove from oven and let chops rest in pot, covered, for 30 minutes. Transfer chops to serving platter and tent with aluminum foil. Strain braising liquid through fine-mesh strainer; discard solids. Transfer braising liquid to fat separator and let stand for 5 minutes.

5. Wipe out now-empty pot with wad of paper towels. Return defatted braising liquid to pot and cook over medium-high heat until reduced to 1 cup, 3 to 7 minutes. Off heat, whisk in butter, minced thyme, and remaining ½ teaspoon vinegar. Season with salt and pepper to taste. Pour sauce over chops, sprinkle with parsley, and serve.

BARBECUED COUNTRY-STYLE RIBS

"COUNTRY-STYLE PORK RIBS" IS A MISNOMER: They aren't actually ribs. A more accurate (but probably less marketable) name would be hybrid loin/shoulder pork chops. This affordable cut contains both tender loin (light) and flavorful shoulder (dark) meat, meaning that each "rib" represents the best of both worlds. These ribs sound grand for the grill, I thought. I set out to infuse country-style ribs with smoky, tangy barbecue flavor.

Recipes for barbecued country-style ribs don't agree on much. For starters, some call for boneless ribs; some call for bone-in. Bone-in ribs were harder to find, and when I did find them, often many in the package were actually boneless. To keep things consistent, I went with boneless ribs. Next, grilling methods ranged from searing them over a hot fire for eight minutes, to smoking them with indirect heat for two hours, to everything in between—and I tried them all. I quickly realized that country-style ribs are finicky. Long cooking times were great for the dark meat, but they made the light meat dry and chalky. Short cooking times meant tender light meat but left the dark meat chewy. My big challenge, then, would be to somehow manipulate the ribs so that both white and dark meat were done at the same time.

Since I was after smoky barbecue flavor, I decided to start with a low-and-slow method (which was, again, great for the dark meat) and figure out how to fix the white meat. My first thought was to try to simultaneously insulate the white meat and add smoky flavor by wrapping each rib with bacon. Fabulous idea, right? But although the flavor was good and the light meat was slightly less dry than before, it was still a long way from moist. For once, bacon wasn't the solution. Brining the ribs (soaking them in a saltwater solution) helped them stay somewhat juicier but still not sufficiently so. After attempting dozens of batches of ribs, I came to the conclusion that I couldn't keep the white meat moist through long cooking. I'd have to do the opposite: find a way to get the dark meat to become tender on the white meat's timetable.

Obviously, thinner cuts cook more quickly than thicker cuts do, so I tried pounding the boneless ribs into ¼-inch-thick cutlets before brining. When the ribs were out of the brine, I dried them off; seasoned them with a simple barbecue dry rub of brown sugar, chili powder, paprika, onion powder, dry mustard, and pepper; and then grilled the ribs (using smoke and indirect heat) until cooked but still tender, about 15 minutes. The brining and the shorter cooking time meant that the white meat was juicy; the pounding meant that the dark meat finally cooked to tenderness at the same rate as the white meat. Disappointingly, the finished product looked more like cutlets than ribs. But pounding a little less, to about ¾ inch, fixed that.

From here, the recipe came together easily. To get a nice saucy, caramelized lacquer on the meat, I mixed half of the dry rub spices with ketchup and vinegar for an easy barbecue sauce that I could sear onto the ribs (over high heat) at the end of cooking. I had been using 1 cup

SHOPPING FOR COUNTRY-STYLE RIBS
Country-style ribs aren't ribs at all. They're well-marbled pork chops cut from the blade end of the loin. We bought dozens of these chops while testing this recipe and found that they were inconsistently shaped and sized. What's more, these "ribs" had widely varying proportions of light and dark meat. To help level the culinary playing field and ensure even cooking, we pounded each piece into an even ¾-inch thickness.

of soaked wood chips to impart smoke flavor, but my tasters complained through every test that the ribs tasted too smoky (even with the short cooking time). I reduced the chips to ½ cup—still too smoky. One-quarter cup of wood chips was plenty for this quick smoke.

Country-style ribs may be inaccurately named, and my method may not technically be "barbecue," but who's quibbling? This recipe is a terrific weeknight alternative to slow-smoked ribs.

—CAROLYNN PURPURA MACKAY, *Cook's Country*

Barbecued Country-Style Ribs

SERVES 4 TO 6

For easier pounding, cut any ribs that are longer than 5 inches in half crosswise. Wood chunks are not recommended for this recipe.

- 1 tablespoon salt
- 2 pounds boneless country-style pork ribs, trimmed
- ¾ cup packed dark brown sugar
- 2 tablespoons chili powder
- 2 tablespoons paprika
- 1 tablespoon dry mustard
- 1 tablespoon onion powder
- ¾ teaspoon pepper
- ¼ teaspoon cayenne pepper
- 6 tablespoons ketchup
- 1 tablespoon cider vinegar
- ¼ cup wood chips, soaked in water for 15 minutes and drained

1. Dissolve salt in 2 cups cold water in large container. Place ribs, cut side down, between 2 sheets of plastic wrap

and pound to ¾-inch thickness. Submerge pork in brine, cover, and refrigerate for 30 minutes or up to 1 hour.

2. Combine sugar, chili powder, paprika, dry mustard, onion powder, pepper, and cayenne in shallow dish. Transfer half of mixture to bowl and stir in ketchup and vinegar; set aside.

3. Remove pork from brine and pat dry with paper towels. Dredge pork in remaining spice mixture and transfer to plate. Using large piece of heavy-duty aluminum foil, wrap soaked chips in foil packet and cut several vent holes in top.

4A. FOR A CHARCOAL GRILL: Open bottom vent halfway. Light large chimney starter filled with charcoal briquettes (6 quarts). When top coals are partially covered with ash, pour evenly over half of grill. Place wood chip packet on coals. Set cooking grate in place, cover, and open lid vent halfway. Heat grill until hot and wood chips are smoking, about 5 minutes.

4B. FOR A GAS GRILL: Place wood chip packet over primary burner. Turn all burners to high, cover, and heat grill until hot and wood chips are smoking, about 15 minutes. Leave primary burner on high and turn off other burner(s).

5. Clean and oil cooking grate. Place pork on cool side of grill, cover (positioning lid vent over meat if using charcoal), and cook until meat registers 125 degrees, 3 to 5 minutes. Brush pork with ketchup mixture and grill, brushed side down, over hot side of grill until lightly charred, 2 to 3 minutes. Brush second side of pork with sauce and grill until lightly charred and meat registers 145 degrees, 2 to 3 minutes. Transfer pork to platter, tent loosely with foil, and let rest for 5 to 10 minutes. Serve.

SMOKY INDOOR RIBS

"SMOKE IS NO JOKE" IS THE BARBECUE MANTRA IN my native North Carolina. What this means is that you can't have real barbecue without smoke. I was in full agreement until I moved to Boston, where barbecuing through the long winter is impractical. But living without the smoky, tangy, slightly spicy barbecue ribs I was raised on was not an option.

So I gathered a representative sampling of recipes for indoor "smoked" ribs and got cooking. The recipes used three approaches to try to introduce smoke flavor: placing wood chips on the oven floor, rubbing the raw ribs with smoked paprika, and broiling a liquid smoke–enhanced barbecue sauce onto cooked ribs. Fail, fail, and fail. The chips never smoked, the rubs didn't add much, and the smoky sauce didn't get inside the meat. If I wanted deeply smoky, tender ribs with a sticky, saucy crust, I'd have to start from scratch.

I knew to start with St. Louis–cut spareribs, which are meatier than baby backs but more manageable than

regular spareribs (the latter have extra meat, bone, and bulk on one end). Next, I focused on getting smoky flavor into the meat. Traditional barbecue relies on long exposure to wood smoke (generated by soaked wood chips in backyard recipes). Could I get wood chips to work in the oven? Even at the highest temperature, even on ripping-hot baking sheets and pizza stones, the chips never smoked. Time to give up on the chips.

I'd already discovered that brushing a smoky sauce onto cooked ribs added only superficial smokiness. But what if I braised the ribs in a smoky liquid? I tested every smoky ingredient I could think of: chipotle powder, smoked paprika, liquid smoke, espresso powder, and Lapsang Souchong tea, all mixed with water. After the ribs had braised for about 1½ hours—enough time to start tenderizing and, I hoped, drink up some braising liquid—I baked them "dry" for another 1½ hours to get a crusty exterior that approximated real barbecue "bark." Except for a faint whiff of smoke in the liquid smoke batch, tasters detected no smoke. I upped the liquid smoke from 1 teaspoon to 2 tablespoons, and now I was on to something. I added espresso powder; it hadn't done much on its own, but the two worked nicely together to deepen the smoke flavor.

To create a sticky coating, I slathered the test kitchen's basic barbecue sauce on the ribs twice while they were baking. That was good, and it got even better when I added some of the liquid smoke and espresso powder. Replacing the paprika with smoked paprika contributed yet more smoky depth. These ribs were good, but I knew the true test was with the test kitchen's Southern contingent. "Tastes like home," said one tester. "Smoke is no joke," said another. Little did they know.

—KELLY PRICE, *Cook's Country*

NOTES FROM THE TEST KITCHEN

BRINGING THE SMOKER INSIDE

Braise ribs in mixture of water, espresso powder, and liquid smoke. After 1½ hours, slowly roast ribs with sauce for caramelized "bark."

THE BEST KETCHUPS

For most people, a burger isn't complete until it's topped with a liberal dose of ketchup. But with so many options lining the condiment shelves these days, which one should you pick? We sampled eight brands plain and with fries to find the best one.

It was clear that our panel wanted ketchup that tasted the way they remembered it from childhood: boldly seasoned, with all the flavor elements—salt, sweet, tang, and tomato—assertive yet harmonious. Many brands are now sweetened with high-fructose corn syrup, not sugar, because it's cheap and easy to mix with other ingredients, but our tasters were not in favor of this trend, preferring instead those brands that relied on sugar. High-fructose corn syrup can exhibit off-flavors because of the manufacturing process, while sugar is perceived as having a cleaner, purer sweetness. Tasters also liked ketchups that had enough acid and a good amount of salt to balance the sugar.

In the end, two brands (both of which use white sugar, not high-fructose corn syrup) were virtually tied for first place. Tasters slightly preferred **Heinz Organic Tomato Ketchup** for its "bright, fresh flavor," calling it "tangy, salty, smooth," and "full bodied." **Hunt's Tomato Ketchup** came in a close second and was praised for its "classic" flavor; at nearly a third the price of Heinz, we recommend it as our Best Buy. (See page 296 for more information about our testing results.)

Smoky Indoor Ribs

SERVES 4 TO 6

Use liquid smoke that contains no salt or additional flavorings. Our favorite brand of liquid smoke is Wright's All Natural Hickory Seasoning Liquid Smoke.

RIBS

2 **tablespoons instant espresso powder**

2 **tablespoons liquid smoke**

1 **tablespoon salt**

2 **(2½- to 3-pound) racks pork spareribs, preferably St. Louis cut, trimmed and membrane removed**

SMOKY INDOOR RIBS

BARBECUE SAUCE

- 1 tablespoon vegetable oil
- 1 onion, chopped fine
    Salt and pepper
- 1 tablespoon smoked paprika
- 1½ cups low-sodium chicken broth
- ¾ cup cider vinegar
- ¾ cup dark corn syrup
- ¾ cup ketchup
- ½ cup molasses
- 2 tablespoons brown mustard
- 1 tablespoon hot sauce
- 1 tablespoon instant espresso powder
- ½ teaspoon liquid smoke

1. FOR THE RIBS: Adjust oven rack to middle position and heat oven to 300 degrees. Bring 3 cups water, espresso powder, liquid smoke, and salt to boil in small saucepan. Pour mixture into large roasting pan. Place ribs, meat side down, in liquid. Cover pan tightly with aluminum foil and bake for 1½ hours. Line rimmed baking sheet with foil and set wire rack inside.

2. FOR THE BARBECUE SAUCE: Meanwhile, heat oil in large saucepan over medium heat until shimmering. Add onion and ¼ teaspoon salt and cook until softened, about 5 minutes. Stir in paprika and cook until fragrant, about 30 seconds. Add broth, vinegar, corn syrup, ketchup, molasses, mustard, hot sauce, and espresso powder and simmer, stirring occasionally, until thickened and reduced to 2 cups, 50 to 60 minutes. Stir in liquid smoke and season with salt and pepper to taste. Let cool for 20 minutes. (Sauce can be refrigerated for up to 1 week.)

3. Reserve ½ cup sauce for serving. Remove ribs from roasting pan and transfer, meat side up, to prepared wire rack; discard braising liquid. Brush both sides of ribs with sauce. Bake until tender and fork inserted into meat meets no resistance, about 1½ hours, brushing meat side with sauce after 30 and 60 minutes of cooking. Tent ribs loosely with foil and let rest for 30 minutes. Slice meat between bones and serve with reserved sauce.

SICHUAN STIR-FRIED PORK IN GARLIC SAUCE

I REMEMBER STIR-FRIED PORK IN GARLIC SAUCE, but not fondly. When I was growing up, this was the dish of wormy pork strips swimming in a generic "brown sauce" that my parents ordered as kid-friendly (read: not spicy) fare to follow up the egg rolls. I liked it well enough then, but my appreciation for this Cantonese-American mainstay nose-dived sharply over the years, and with it went any expectation I had that a pork dish featuring garlic sauce would be something other than gloppy, greasy, and boring.

Fast-forward decades later to my introduction to *yu xiang* pork. With thin-cut strips of pork, a soy-based sauce, and plenty of garlic, this Sichuan staple looks similar to the Cantonese version, but its punched-up flavors make it seem anything but related. Yu xiang translates literally as "fish-fragrant," but the sauce isn't the least bit fishy. (The name refers to its origins as a condiment for seafood.) Rather, it's a mix of salty, sweet, hot, and—thanks to a healthy splash of Chinese black vinegar—sour flavors that, when prepared well, balance out into a bold-tasting, silky sauce that coats the super-tender meat and accompanying vegetables. These usually feature a crunchy element like celery, bamboo shoots, or water chestnuts, plus dark, wrinkly wood ear mushrooms.

That's what it tastes like in a restaurant, anyway. But since I'd found plenty of recipes for yu xiang pork in Chinese cookbooks, I figured I'd make it myself. The method looked easy enough: Gently parcook the meat in oil, drain it, and set it aside; turn up the heat and add aromatics and Asian broad-bean chili paste, followed by the vegetables; return the meat to the pan along with the sauce ingredients and simmer until thickened.

But my attempts were all disappointments. None achieved the requisite balance of yu xiang; one tasted cloyingly sweet, and another overdid it on the vinegar and left tasters puckering. Some were thin and watery, others slick and greasy. The biggest problem of all, however, was the pork itself. In most cases, its texture was dry, chewy, and stringy, and the sauce wasn't sufficiently camouflaging those flaws.

Figuring I'd tackle the meat itself first, I spread my test recipes out in front of me and discovered the common problem: Almost all of them called for pork loin, a lean, notoriously unforgiving cut that tends to cook up dry and fibrous. Switching to another cut was an obvious move, so I surveyed the butcher case and came back with two fattier cuts that promised more flavor and tenderness—pork shoulder and country-style ribs. Both cuts tasted markedly richer and juicier, but shoulder meat came with its own set of challenges. Not only was it hard to find in quantities small enough for stir-fry purposes (I needed only about 12 ounces), but it required quite a bit of knife work to trim out the excess fat and pare it down to matchstick-size pieces. Country-style ribs, cut from the shoulder end of the loin, were a lot easier to butcher, so I went with them.

Now that I was using a fattier cut, I wondered if the low-temperature fat bath was actually necessary. It seemed to me that the only purpose of that step was to ensure that the lean tenderloin emerged moist and silky. But when I tried to eliminate the step, even this more marbled cut didn't cook up as supple as the best yu xiang pork I've eaten in restaurants. If I wanted supremely tender, juicy pork without the mess of all that oil, I'd have to look for another way.

Fortunately, there's a far simpler technique from Chinese cookery that tackles the problem of meat drying out in a stir-fry: velveting. This approach involves coating the meat in a cornstarch slurry to provide an insulating barrier that shields the meat from the pan's high temperatures. I gave it a whirl, mixing 2 teaspoons of cornstarch with an equal amount of rice wine and tossing it with the pork before proceeding with the recipe. Though this was a definite improvement, the leaner pieces of meat were still less tender and juicy than I wanted. For the results that I was after, I needed a technique that offered more than just a starch over-coat; it would have to actually tenderize the meat, too.

As it happens, we learned an interesting fact about meat texture during a recent tasting: Tenderness, especially in pork, is highly dependent on the pH of the meat; the higher the pH, the more tender it will be. If I could find a way to artificially boost the pH of the meat, it might just soften up a bit. And I had just the ingredient in mind to help: alkaline baking soda.

My plan was to soak the pork in a solution of baking soda (1 tablespoon) and water (½ cup) for an hour or so and then proceed with velveting. And the results were promising; even the leaner strips of meat were considerably more tender. Too tender, in fact, and also soapy-tasting. I'd overcompensated a bit, so in the next batch I cut back to 1 teaspoon of baking soda and soaked the meat for just 15 minutes. I also rinsed the pork afterward, to remove any residual soda. This time the pork was perfect: marvelously juicy and supple. Even better, I needed only a few tablespoons of oil to cook the meat.

Meanwhile, the other half of the equation—the sauce—needed adjusting to achieve just the right balance of salty, sour, sweet, and spicy flavors. Starting with a base of equal parts soy sauce and rice wine, plus 4 teaspoons of tangy Chinese black vinegar and a tablespoon of sesame oil, I diluted the mixture with enough chicken broth to amply coat the meat and vegetables and stirred in 2 teaspoons of cornstarch for thickening. Then I fried up some minced garlic and scallion whites and a few teaspoons of broad-bean chili paste in a nonstick skillet, poured in the sauce mixture, and simmered it until it turned glossy. Not bad, tasters said, but they wanted more—particularly more sweetness and more savory depth.

The first request was easy to fulfill with a couple of tablespoons of sugar. It was boosting the savoriness of the dish that was more challenging. I spent more than 30 subsequent tests tinkering with the ratios of sesame oil, vinegar, garlic, and bean paste, but each batch still lacked a certain full-bodied depth that I remembered in the restaurant versions I'd tried. Two likely reasons: Many restaurants build the sauce from a base of home-made stock (instead of store-bought chicken broth), and some also add monosodium glutamate to punch up the savoriness. Neither of those ingredients would be in my recipe, so I started rooting through my pantry for ingredients that I thought might do the trick and came away with two successful (albeit untraditional) additions: fish sauce and ketchup, both of which are naturally packed with flavor-enhancing glutamates. Just 2 teaspoons of each rounded out the savory flavor we were looking for. As an added bonus, the ketchup also contributed to the smooth viscosity of the sauce.

SICHUAN STIR-FRIED PORK IN GARLIC SAUCE

A few last substitutions were necessary. Instead of hard-to-find wood ear mushrooms, I went with shiitakes. I also settled on readily available celery over water chestnuts for a contrasting crunch. Though Chinese black vinegar and Asian broad-bean chili paste are popping up in more and more supermarkets, I found that equal parts balsamic and rice vinegars provided a fine alternative to the former, and either Asian chili-garlic paste or Sriracha sauce made a good sub for the latter (but in smaller amounts).

At last, I had a version of yu xiang pork as good as anything I'd find in a Sichuan restaurant.

—ANDREW JANJIGIAN, *Cook's Illustrated*

Sichuan Stir-Fried Pork in Garlic Sauce

SERVES 4 TO 6

If Chinese black vinegar is unavailable, substitute 2 teaspoons balsamic vinegar and 2 teaspoons rice vinegar. If Asian broad-bean chili paste is unavailable, substitute 2 teaspoons Asian chili-garlic paste or Sriracha sauce. Serve with steamed white rice.

SAUCE

- ½ **cup low-sodium chicken broth**
- 2 **tablespoons sugar**
- 2 **tablespoons soy sauce**
- 4 **teaspoons Chinese black vinegar**
- 1 **tablespoon toasted sesame oil**
- 1 **tablespoon Chinese rice wine or dry sherry**
- 2 **teaspoons ketchup**
- 2 **teaspoons fish sauce**
- 2 **teaspoons cornstarch**

PORK

- 12 **ounces boneless country-style pork ribs, trimmed**
- 1 **teaspoon baking soda**
- ½ **cup cold water**
- 2 **teaspoons Chinese rice wine or dry sherry**
- 2 **teaspoons cornstarch**

STIR-FRY

- 1 **garlic cloves, minced**
- 2 **scallions, white parts minced, green parts sliced thin**
- 2 **tablespoons Asian broad-bean chili paste**
- 4 **tablespoons vegetable oil**
- 6 **ounces shiitake mushrooms, stemmed and sliced thin**
- 2 **celery ribs, cut on bias into ¼-inch slices**

1. FOR THE SAUCE: Whisk all ingredients together in bowl; set aside.

2. FOR THE PORK: Cut pork into 2-inch lengths, then cut each length into ¼-inch matchsticks. Combine pork with baking soda and water in bowl. Let sit at room temperature for 15 minutes.

3. Rinse pork in cold water. Drain well and pat dry with paper towels. Whisk rice wine and cornstarch together in bowl. Add pork and toss to coat.

4. FOR THE STIR-FRY: Combine garlic, scallion whites, and chili paste in bowl.

5. Heat 1 tablespoon oil in 12-inch nonstick skillet over high heat until just smoking. Add mushrooms and cook, stirring frequently, until tender, 2 to 4 minutes. Add celery and continue to cook until celery is crisp-tender, 2 to 4 minutes. Transfer vegetables to separate bowl.

6. Add remaining 3 tablespoons oil to now-empty skillet and place over medium-low heat. Add garlic-scallion mixture and cook, stirring frequently, until fragrant, about 30 seconds. Transfer 1 tablespoon garlic-scallion oil to small bowl and set aside. Add pork to skillet and cook, stirring frequently, until no longer pink, 3 to 5 minutes. Whisk sauce mixture to recombine and add to skillet. Increase heat to high and cook, stirring constantly, until sauce is thickened and pork is cooked through, 1 to 2 minutes. Return vegetables to skillet and toss to combine. Transfer to serving platter, sprinkle with scallion greens and reserved garlic-scallion oil, and serve.

NOTES FROM THE TEST KITCHEN

THE OTHER MEAT TENDERIZER

Meat soaked in a solution of baking soda and water? We admit it sounds pretty unappetizing, but there's a good reason we worked this step into our recipe for Sichuan Stir-Fried Pork in Garlic Sauce. Simply put, alkaline baking soda makes the meat more tender by raising its pH. As this happens, enzymes in the meat called calpains become more active and cut the meat's muscle fibers. The tenderizing effect is twofold. First, as the meat's fibers break down, its texture softens. Second, since the meat's looser consistency retains water better, it's less likely to contract and expel moisture when heated, ensuring that the meat stays juicy throughout. The succulent results are well worth it. And don't worry; the baking soda solution gets washed off before cooking.

CHAPTER 7

POULTRY

Weeknight Roast Chicken   176

Tarragon-Lemon Pan Sauce

Citrus-and-Spice Grilled Chicken   178

Grilled Chicken Wings   180

BBQ Grilled Chicken Wings

Creole Grilled Chicken Wings

Tandoori Grilled Chicken Wings

Crispy Chicken Nuggets   182

Sweet and Sour Sauce

Honey-Mustard Sauce

Baked Chicken Imperial   185

Chicken Marbella   188

Filipino Chicken Adobo   190

Moravian Chicken Pie   194

Braised Turkey with Gravy   196

WEEKNIGHT ROAST CHICKEN

IF THERE'S ONE THING WE'VE LEARNED FROM OUR years of experience in the test kitchen, it's that the best way to guarantee a juicy, well-seasoned roast chicken is to brine or salt the bird (at least 30 minutes for brining and up to 24 hours for salting) before it hits the oven. We've found that such pretreatment reliably solves the classic roast-poultry predicament: how to keep the lean, delicate breast meat from overcooking in the time it takes for the fattier leg quarters to come up to temperature. The salt buffers the meat against overcooking by restructuring its proteins, enabling it to retain more of its natural juices. But on a weeknight, many cooks just don't have time to salt or brine. We got to thinking: Wouldn't it be great if we could come up with a foolproof way to roast chicken that didn't call for any preroasting treatment?

The best approach, it seemed to me, was to modify our standard method for roasting chicken, which calls for submerging the bird in a salt-sugar brine (sugar encourages good browning) for an hour, brushing it with melted butter, and roasting it on a V-rack in a 375-degree oven. I would skip the brine and then put every other step in that recipe under the microscope—from the roasting pan, to the V-rack, to the oven temperature.

I started with the V-rack. This piece of equipment elevates the bird so that the oven's heat can circulate evenly around it. The V-rack also prevents the skin from sitting in juices that would keep it from crisping up. I definitely wanted crisp skin, but I also knew that I could use the pan's surface to my advantage. If I preheated the pan and then placed the chicken in it breast side up, the thighs would get a jump start on cooking, much as they would if I seared them first in a skillet. I compared a pan-seared bird to one roasted in the traditional rack setup and found the results surprisingly decent. The skin was poorly browned, but tasters agreed that the breast meat was better now that the thigh meat had a head start in the pan, and I could shave a few minutes off the cooking time. The V-rack was out; preheating the roasting pan was in.

Now what about oven temperature? The 375-degree oven wasn't really doing the breast meat any favors, so I reasoned my next move should be lowering the heat to cook that delicate meat more gently. I experimented with dropping the temperature to 300 degrees, but the results were disappointing. Though the white meat became marginally juicier, there was an obvious—and unacceptable—trade-off: The skin had gone from patchily browned to pale.

Without any clear idea of how to proceed, I decided to roast a chicken according to a recipe developed by celebrated French chef Joël Robuchon that is widely regarded as one of the best. He places the bird in a buttered baking dish and rubs it with softened butter—and then does something totally unexpected: He puts it in a cold oven and promptly cranks the heat to 410 degrees. I found that while the hotter temperature did color the skin a deeper shade of bronze, it didn't produce meat any juicier than on chickens I'd roasted in preheated ovens.

But could there be something to the idea of a dramatic shift in oven temperature? What if I reversed Robuchon's method by starting the chicken at a relatively hot temperature to brown the skin, but then turned off the oven midway through cooking? I decided to give this radical approach a shot. I set the dial to Robuchon's recommended 410 degrees, brushed the chicken with melted butter, seasoned it aggressively with salt and pepper, and lowered it into the hot pan. After about 30 minutes, I shut off the heat, let the bird idle in the oven until the breast and thigh meat hit their target temperatures about 30 minutes later, then let it sit on the counter for its requisite 20-minute rest, during which juices would be released and then drawn back into the meat.

This latest bird was a huge success. Beneath the layer of nicely tanned skin was white meat so tender and moist that even the dark meat loyalists among us were reaching for second helpings. A quick conversation with our science editor helped me understand why the approach was so effective: In meat with a lot of surface area like chicken, most of the moisture loss that occurs during cooking is through surface evaporation. Shutting off the oven cools the chicken's exterior relatively rapidly, in turn slowing the evaporation of juices. In the meantime, heat that's already inside the chicken continues to be conducted deeper into the interior, eventually bringing it to the desired safe temperature (the same carryover cooking that occurs when meat is resting). The net result is a juicier chicken with virtually no chance of overcooking.

I was very happy with the progress I'd made with the meat, but I wondered if I could darken the skin on the breast even more by increasing the oven's heat. I tested temperatures all the way up to 500 degrees, but the finest of the flock emerged from a 450-degree oven with beautifully dark amber skin encasing tender, juicy meat.

Still, all was not well. The higher heat forced more of the juices to evaporate, leaving me with less for a pan sauce. I reasoned that if I replaced the roasting pan with a skillet, the juices would pool in the smaller space and not evaporate as quickly. Plus, its long handle and less cumbersome shape would make shuffling the chicken in and out of the oven easier. The only minor downside was that the skin on the back of the chicken sat in the juices, which turned it soggy. But since this skin is rarely eaten anyway—and the rest of the skin was so gorgeous—I wasn't too bothered.

I made two other small adjustments: I swapped the melted butter for olive oil, which gave me equally good results with even less work. I also decided to truss the legs. We usually avoid this technique because it can slow down the cooking of the inner thigh, but now that I was relying on carryover cooking, trussing would help keep the heat in.

The only item left on my checklist? Making good use of the pan drippings. I spooned out and discarded all but 1 tablespoon of the fat, making sure to leave the flavorful browned bits in the pan, and whipped up a simple sauce with mustard, tarragon, and lemon juice.

I checked my watch. I had started cooking only an hour beforehand, but thanks to my new foolproof, dead-simple technique, I was already sitting down to the best roast chicken I'd ever made without brining or salting. This was definitely going to be my standard method for weeknight roast chicken.

—BRYAN ROOF, *Cook's Illustrated*

Weeknight Roast Chicken

SERVES 4

We prefer to use a 3½- to 4-pound chicken for this recipe. If roasting a larger bird, increase the time that the oven is on in step 2 to 35 to 40 minutes. Cooking the chicken in a preheated skillet will ensure that the breast and thigh meat finish cooking at the same time.

- 1 tablespoon kosher salt
- ½ teaspoon pepper
- 1 (3½- to 4-pound) whole chicken, giblets discarded
- 1 tablespoon olive oil
- 1 recipe Tarragon-Lemon Pan Sauce (optional; recipe follows)

1. Adjust oven rack to middle position, place 12-inch ovensafe skillet on rack, and heat oven to 450 degrees. Combine salt and pepper in bowl. Pat chicken dry with paper towels. Rub entire surface with oil. Sprinkle evenly all over with salt mixture and rub in mixture with hands to coat evenly. Tie legs together with twine and tuck wingtips behind back.

2. Transfer chicken, breast side up, to preheated skillet in oven. Roast chicken until breast registers 120 degrees and thighs register 135 degrees, 25 to 35 minutes. Turn off oven and leave chicken in oven until breast registers 160 degrees and thighs register 175 degrees, 25 to 35 minutes.

3. Transfer chicken to carving board and let rest, uncovered, for 20 minutes. While chicken rests, prepare pan sauce, if using. Carve chicken and serve.

Tarragon-Lemon Pan Sauce

MAKES ABOUT ¾ CUP

- 1 shallot, minced
- 1 cup low-sodium chicken broth
- 2 teaspoons Dijon mustard
- 2 tablespoons unsalted butter
- 2 teaspoons minced fresh tarragon
- 2 teaspoons lemon juice
- Pepper

While chicken rests, remove all but 1 tablespoon fat from now-empty skillet (handle will be very hot) using large spoon, leaving any browned bits and jus in skillet. Place skillet over medium-high heat, add shallot, and cook until softened, about 2 minutes. Stir in broth and mustard, scraping up any browned bits. Simmer until reduced to ¾ cup, about 3 minutes. Off heat, whisk in butter, tarragon, and lemon juice. Season with pepper to taste; cover and keep warm. Serve with chicken.

CITRUS-AND-SPICE GRILLED CHICKEN

I'D WAGER THAT ALMOST EVERY MEXICAN TAQUERIA in America serves grilled citrus- and spice-marinated chicken. For a standard dish, the range in quality is dramatic. Sometimes you luck out with chicken that is juicy and full of flavor from a marinade of citrus juices, onions, garlic, oregano, and spices like cinnamon, cumin, and cloves. More often, though, the chicken is as dry, leathery, and bland as it is at the taco joint around the corner from my house (where it's served with a side of earsplitting Mexican karaoke). To give my ears some relief and my tastebuds something to celebrate, I decided to come up with a great version to grill at home.

Recipes often call for marinating chicken halves in a combination of orange and lime juices (to substitute for the juice of sour oranges, the fruit that's authentic to the dish but hard to come by), along with the aromatics, spices, and herbs. Using chicken parts, which are easier to find than halves, I tried these recipes, but none delivered bold flavors, even after I tinkered with the seasonings, the amounts of juices, and the marinating times and tried toasting the garlic or charring the onion.

Since the juices did little on their own, I offered them a helping hand: grated zest. The zest is, after all, home to the oils that give citrus fruits much of their fragrance and flavor. A teaspoon of grated lime zest with a tablespoon of orange zest worked so well that I did away with the orange juice entirely. Into the food processor went the onion, garlic, orange and lime zest, and lime juice, along with the spices. I added just enough olive oil to make a paste that could cling to the chicken. Grilled after an hour's rest in the pungent paste, this chicken had the best flavor yet.

But I still needed a grilling technique that would fix the chewy, leathery texture. With a gas grill, cooking the pieces over medium-low heat was just the ticket. But a medium-low charcoal fire was dicey: If the fire was a little too hot, flare-ups burned the chicken. If the fire was a little too cool, the fat didn't render properly by the time the meat was cooked. The solution for cooking over charcoal was using indirect heat—that is, positioning the meat away from (and not directly over) the fire. The most foolproof way to set this up is to place a disposable aluminum pan in the center of the bottom grill grate, then pour half of the lit charcoal on either side. Grilling the pieces with indirect heat with the skin

CITRUS-AND-SPICE GRILLED CHICKEN

side up allowed the paste to cook gently until the end, when I flipped the chicken and moved it over the fire for a few minutes of direct heat, crisping the skin and giving the paste a substantial char (on a gas grill, just turn up the heat to sear the pieces at the end of cooking).

Finally, no more flare-ups, and I got the succulent meat, crisp skin, and nicely caramelized seasonings I'd been aiming for. Now I can have citrus chicken whenever I want—and I get to choose the soundtrack.

—ADAM RIED, *Cook's Country*

Citrus-and-Spice Grilled Chicken

SERVES 4 TO 6

If using a charcoal grill, you will need a 13 by 9-inch disposable aluminum roasting pan for this recipe.

- 1 onion, chopped coarse
- 1 teaspoon grated lime zest plus ¼ cup juice (2 limes)
- 6 garlic cloves
- 2 tablespoons olive oil
- 1 tablespoon grated orange zest
- 2 teaspoons dried oregano
- 1½ teaspoons salt
- ½ teaspoon pepper
- ½ teaspoon ground cinnamon
- ½ teaspoon ground cumin
- ⅛ teaspoon ground cloves
- 3 pounds bone-in chicken pieces, trimmed and breasts halved crosswise

1. Process onion, lime zest and juice, garlic, oil, orange zest, oregano, salt, pepper, cinnamon, cumin, and cloves together in food processor until smooth, about 30 seconds; transfer to zipper-lock bag. Pat chicken dry with paper towels and add to bag, turning to coat. Refrigerate for 1 hour or up to 24 hours, turning occasionally.

2A. FOR A CHARCOAL GRILL: Open bottom vent completely and place roasting pan in center of grill. Light large chimney starter filled with charcoal briquettes (6 quarts). When top coals are partially covered with ash, pour into 2 even piles on either side of pan. Set cooking grate in place, cover, and open lid vent completely. Heat grill until hot, about 5 minutes.

2B. FOR A GAS GRILL: Turn all burners to high, cover, and heat grill until hot, about 15 minutes. Turn all burners to medium-low. (Adjust burners as needed to maintain grill temperature around 350 degrees.)

SOUR ORANGE SUBSTITUTE

THE ORIGINAL
Bright, tart sour oranges can be hard to find.

THE FACSIMILE
Orange zest, lime zest, and lime juice mimic the sour orange flavor.

3. Clean and oil cooking grate. Place chicken skin side up on grill (in center of grill if using charcoal). Cover and cook until bottom is browned and chicken registers 155 degrees, about 25 minutes.

4. Flip chicken skin side down. If using charcoal, slide chicken to hot side of grill. If using gas, turn all burners to high. Cook until well browned and breasts register 160 degrees and thighs/drumsticks register 175 degrees, 5 to 10 minutes. Transfer chicken to platter, tent loosely with aluminum foil, and let rest for 5 to 10 minutes. Serve.

GRILLED CHICKEN WINGS

CHICKEN WINGS ARE MY THING, BUT DEEP-FRYING them in the summertime is most definitely not. So I decided to try grilling them. I found plenty of recipes for grilled wings, each selling the idea that the fat and connective tissue render and drip away through the grill grate, leaving the skin crisp and lightly charred, the meat succulent and smoky.

But I've grilled enough skin-on chicken to foresee the problem with grilling wings: The fat drips away over a fire—and fat mixed with fire means flare-ups. The recipes I rounded up used three basic strategies to get around this problem, and I gave all three a go. The "firefighter" approach: Grill over high heat and hose down the flare-ups with a spray bottle of water. Well, the flare-ups were impossible to control and I ended up with burnt, sooty wings. The "parcook" approach: Start the wings in the oven to render the fat and then finish them on a hot grill to crisp the skin. Although successful, this technique was a bother. And finally, the "low-and-slow" approach: Grill the wings using indirect heat and wait for them to cook to about 170 degrees. With this method, the fat easily rendered with no flare-ups. But the skin was more leathery than crisp, plus the wings took almost two hours to cook.

Determined to come up with a better strategy, I started with a riff on the low-and-slow approach. Instead of using indirect heat, I placed the wings directly over the low fire to accelerate the cooking. There were no flare-ups and the fat did render. So far, so good. But the fire was so weak that the chicken never developed any char, and the skin stuck to the grill grate like bubblegum to hot asphalt. I tested varying heat levels, ultimately finding that a medium-low fire was just hot enough to prevent sticking yet cool enough to avoid a conflagration as the fat rendered.

But the wings still lacked proper char. Turning up the heat was a nonstarter—even a medium-hot fire brought back the flare-ups. Could I just leave the wings on the grill longer? A little extra time on the grill meant a marked improvement for the char, but it also left the wings overcooked—about 180 to 185 degrees, well above the 170 degrees most recipes suggest. Still, I was intent on getting feedback, so I brought the "over-cooked" wings to the tasting table.

As I guessed, tasters complained that the wings were dry, but that wasn't the end of the story. They also thought the meat was significantly more tender than previous batches cooked to 170 degrees. I was confused by these seemingly contradictory contentions—until I spoke with our science editor. Apparently, the tasters were experiencing two separate phenomena. First, as the internal temperature of a piece of meat rises, protein fibers within the meat constrict and force out juices. The higher the internal temperature, the more juices are expelled. The result, as noted by my tasters, was that the 180-degree wings were drier than those cooked to 170 degrees.

But chicken wings also contain a large amount of collagen. Collagen is naturally chewy until it starts breaking down into gelatin, which happens most efficiently at temperatures above 170 degrees. So if wings are grilled to only 170 degrees, the collagen barely has any time to break down, and the result is chewy wings. At 180-plus degrees, much of the collagen turns to gelatin. The result is more tender wings. How could I fix the dry meat yet keep the tenderness?

From past experience, I knew that brining (soaking meat in a saltwater solution) helps meat retain moisture even if it is overcooked. But most recipes call for brining for an hour, and I didn't want to wait that long. Cutting the wings into sections (called drumettes and flats in restaurants; some wings are sold already sectioned) and piercing the pieces all over with a fork allowed the brine to soak down to the bone in just 30 minutes. Now the wings cooked to 180 degrees were tender and juicy.

This approach had one downside, though: The moisture from the brine made the wings steam and stick to the grill again. A colleague suggested tossing the wings with a little cornstarch before grilling to discourage sticking. The thin layer of cornstarch worked like a charm—no more sticking. Whether tossed with salt and pepper or rubbed with a sophisticated spice blend, these grilled wings were good enough to make me forget the fryer forever—at least until winter rolls around.

—JEREMY SAUER, *Cook's Country*

NOTES FROM THE TEST KITCHEN

PREPPING CHICKEN WINGS FOR GRILLING

1. Using a fork, puncture each wing all over to allow brine to easily penetrate and give rendered fat an escape route.

2. Brine wings to season them and keep them juicy, even when cooked to 180 degrees.

3. Dust wings with mixture of cornstarch (to prevent sticking) and black pepper right before grilling.

Grilled Chicken Wings

MAKES 2 DOZEN WINGS

If you buy whole wings, cut them into 2 pieces before brining. Don't brine the wings for more than 30 minutes or they'll be too salty.

½ cup salt
2 pounds chicken wings, wingtips removed
1½ teaspoons cornstarch
1 teaspoon pepper

1. Dissolve salt in 2 quarts cold water in large container. Prick chicken wings all over with fork. Submerge chicken in brine, cover, and refrigerate for 30 minutes.

2. Combine cornstarch and pepper in bowl. Remove chicken from brine and pat dry with paper towels. Rinse and dry container. Transfer wings to now-empty container and sprinkle with cornstarch mixture, tossing until evenly coated.

3A. FOR A CHARCOAL GRILL: Open bottom vent completely. Light large chimney starter half filled with charcoal briquettes (3 quarts). When top coals are partially covered with ash, pour evenly over grill. Set cooking grate in place, cover, and open lid vent completely. Heat grill until hot, about 5 minutes.

3B. FOR A GAS GRILL: Turn all burners to high, cover, and heat grill until hot, about 15 minutes. Turn all burners to medium-low.

4. Clean and oil cooking grate. Cook wings (covered if using gas), thicker skin side up, until browned on bottom, 12 to 15 minutes. Flip chicken and cook until skin is crisp and lightly charred and meat registers 180 degrees, about 10 minutes. Transfer chicken to platter, tent loosely with aluminum foil, and let rest for 5 to 10 minutes. Serve.

VARIATIONS

BBQ Grilled Chicken Wings
Reduce pepper to ½ teaspoon. Add 1 teaspoon chili powder, 1 teaspoon paprika, ½ teaspoon garlic powder, ½ teaspoon dried oregano, and ½ teaspoon sugar to cornstarch mixture in step 2.

Creole Grilled Chicken Wings
Add ¾ teaspoon dried oregano, ½ teaspoon garlic powder, ½ teaspoon onion powder, ½ teaspoon white pepper, and ¼ teaspoon cayenne pepper to cornstarch mixture in step 2.

Tandoori Grilled Chicken Wings
Reduce pepper to ½ teaspoon. Add 1 teaspoon garam masala, ½ teaspoon ground cumin, ¼ teaspoon garlic powder, ¼ teaspoon ground ginger, and ⅛ teaspoon cayenne pepper to cornstarch mixture in step 2.

CRISPY CHICKEN NUGGETS

WE'VE ALL EATEN CHICKEN NUGGETS, WHETHER they were from the drive-through or surreptitiously plucked from a child's plate (consider me guilty on both counts). But let's be honest. The typical fast-food and frozen nuggets features gristly ground meat in a bland, greasy coating. It's time to take a stand. Homemade chicken nuggets made from tender, juicy chicken and sporting a substantial crunch—something you needn't feel bad about your children eating—shouldn't be too much to ask.

The biggest problem with chicken nuggets is the chicken itself. Most nugget manufacturers start with the least desirable parts of the bird and feed these "off cuts" through a grinder: Like laws and sausages, it's best not to see them being made. While I did try a recipe that used ground breast meat, the pasty texture of those nuggets persuaded me to instead cut nuggets from the breast (nuggets are usually white meat). But while tender, the meat from boneless, skinless breasts was bland and, if even slightly overcooked, dry. Happily, I discovered that a simple saltwater brine helped season the meat and protected it from drying out during cooking. After some quick tests I determined that I could cut my brining time from 1 hour to 30 minutes if I cut the meat into nuggets first. Adding some pungent, salty Worcestershire sauce to the brine ensured that the nuggets had plenty of flavor.

The second problem with most nuggets is their greasy, soft exterior. I wanted a craggy, crunchy crust to contrast with the tender meat. As with every fried food, there are three ways to coat: batter, bread crumbs, or a simple flour dredge. After I tried recipes representing each category, it was easy to pick a winner. Batters were light and doughnut-y (chicken cruller, anyone?). Homemade bread crumbs weren't quite crunchy or craggy enough, while panko, the light Japanese crumbs, were crisp to a fault; the thin shards coated the nuggets like a porcupine's quills. A flour dredge, which gave the nuggets a proper

CRISPY CHICKEN NUGGETS

fried-chicken crunch, proved best (especially when I seasoned the flour with onion and garlic powders). Still, my tasters wanted the coating to have a little more texture. Would a mixture of flour and panko work? Still spiky. What if I crumbled the panko a bit? Success! The coating was now plenty crisp and pleasantly craggy. A pinch of baking soda encouraged the crust to take on color during its quick dip (just 3 minutes) in the oil.

Most recipes dip each nugget in beaten egg to get the coating to adhere. This works for larger pieces of chicken, but the ratio was off for a nugget: The egg coating was thick and tasted, well, eggy. To lighten the crust, I tried using beaten egg whites instead of whole eggs. That solved one problem, but the coating was now sheeting off the chicken. To keep the breading in place, some recipes suggest resting the breaded nuggets, sometimes for up to an hour, before frying. I found that as little as 10 minutes' rest solved the sheeting problem—and gave me another idea. After resting, the

exterior of the dredged nuggets looked slightly tacky. I tossed the nuggets back into the flour-crumb mixture right before frying. The slightly moist exterior picked up another light coating. The result? An ultra-crunchy coating that had tasters downing these nuggets with the zeal of 10-year-olds at the drive-through.

Dipped in simple homemade sauces, my crunchy chicken nuggets were a whole new—and comparatively wholesome—take on a fast-food favorite.

—JEREMY SAUER, *Cook's Country*

Crispy Chicken Nuggets
SERVES 4 TO 6

Do not brine the chicken longer than 30 minutes or it will be too salty. To crush the panko, place it inside a zipper-lock bag and lightly beat it with a rolling pin. You will need at least a 6-quart Dutch oven for this recipe. This recipe doubles easily and freezes well.

- 4 **(6-ounce) boneless, skinless chicken breasts, trimmed**
- 2 **cups water**
- 2 **tablespoons Worcestershire sauce**
  Salt and pepper
- 1 **cup all-purpose flour**
- 1 **cup panko bread crumbs, crushed**
- 2 **teaspoons onion powder**
- ½ **teaspoon garlic powder**
- ½ **teaspoon baking soda**
- 3 **large egg whites**
- 1 **quart peanut or vegetable oil**
- 1 **recipe dipping sauce (recipes follow)**

1. Cut each chicken breast diagonally into thirds, then cut each third diagonally into ½-inch-thick pieces. Whisk water, Worcestershire, and 1 tablespoon salt in large bowl until salt dissolves. Add chicken pieces and refrigerate, covered, for 30 minutes.

2. Remove chicken from brine and pat dry with paper towels. Combine flour, panko, onion powder, 1 teaspoon salt, ¾ teaspoon pepper, garlic powder, and baking soda in shallow dish. Whisk egg whites in second shallow dish until foamy. Coat half of chicken with egg whites and dredge in flour mixture, pressing gently to adhere. Transfer to plate and repeat with remaining chicken (do not discard flour mixture). Let sit for 10 minutes.

NOTES FROM THE TEST KITCHEN

CUTTING CHICKEN BREASTS FOR NUGGETS

1. Cut each chicken breast diagonally into three pieces.

2. Slice largest piece crosswise into ½-inch-thick pieces.

3. Slice two smaller pieces crosswise on bias into ½-inch-thick pieces.

3. Adjust oven rack to middle position and heat oven to 200 degrees. Set wire rack in rimmed baking sheet. Add oil to large Dutch oven until it measures about ¾ inch deep and heat over medium-high heat to 350 degrees. Return chicken to flour dish and turn to coat, pressing flour mixture gently to adhere. Fry half of chicken until deep golden brown, about 3 minutes, turning halfway through cooking. Transfer chicken to prepared wire rack and place in oven. Return oil to 350 degrees and repeat with remaining chicken. Serve with dipping sauce.

TO MAKE AHEAD: Let fried nuggets cool, transfer to zipper-lock bag, and freeze for up to 1 month. To serve, adjust oven rack to middle position and heat oven to 350 degrees. Place nuggets on rimmed baking sheet and bake, flipping once, until heated through, about 15 minutes.

Sweet and Sour Sauce
MAKES ¾ CUP; ENOUGH FOR 1 RECIPE CRISPY CHICKEN NUGGETS

- ¾ cup apple, apricot, or hot pepper jelly
- 1 tablespoon white vinegar
- ½ teaspoon soy sauce
- ⅛ teaspoon garlic powder
- Pinch ground ginger
- Pinch cayenne pepper
- Salt and pepper

Whisk jelly, vinegar, soy sauce, garlic powder, ginger, and cayenne in bowl until smooth. Season with salt and pepper to taste.

Honey-Mustard Sauce
MAKES ¾ CUP; ENOUGH FOR 1 RECIPE CRISPY CHICKEN NUGGETS

- ½ cup yellow mustard
- ⅓ cup honey
- Salt and pepper

Whisk mustard and honey in medium bowl until smooth. Season with salt and pepper to taste.

CHICKEN IMPERIAL

"CHICKEN IMPERIAL" MAY SOUND FANCY, BUT IT'S actually an easy weeknight dish of chicken baked under a thick blanket of buttery, seasoned bread crumbs. When it's done well, you're rewarded with tender chicken and crisp bread crumbs in every bite. If things go like my first kitchen tests did, however, the crumbs end up bland, greasy, and heaped in the pan instead of on the chicken where they belong. There was plenty to do to make this dish worth eating.

Selecting the cut of chicken to use was straightforward. Some recipes call for chicken parts and others specify boneless, skinless breasts. Tasters strongly favored the latter. The mild flavor of the white meat was a better partner for the buttery crumbs, and the meat proved to be a stronger anchor for the crumbs than the skin. That mild flavor can also be a problem, though. White meat can verge on bland, so the test kitchen often treats it to deep seasoning with salting or a liquid brine.

This time I skipped the liquid (it's more useful when the heat source will be intense, as with direct grilling, and I knew I'd be baking this dish) and stuck with salting. When chicken is salted, the salt on the surface of the chicken draws moisture from the meat, which mixes with the salt and then moves back into the chicken, taking the salt with it for deep seasoning. I gave the salted chicken 30 to 60 minutes to do its thing while I prepared the bread crumbs and sauce mixture.

Now on to those problematic bread crumbs. Store-bought dry bread crumbs tasted as old and dusty as they looked in the container, and Japanese panko crumbs were not quite supple enough for this job. Fresh bread crumbs are a test kitchen favorite (and a breeze to make: Just grind fresh bread in the food processor for a few seconds), and tasters wanted that flavor here, too. Usually we use white sandwich bread, but in this case it got too dark while the chicken cooked because of sweeteners in the bread. Instead, I reached for more savory French or Italian bread. Seasoning the crumbs was easy: Fresh parsley and thyme, minced garlic, and freshly grated Parmesan (don't even think about reaching for the green can) went right into the processor along with the bread.

Emperors must have a taste for butter because many recipes used up to an entire stick for just four pieces of chicken. I'm all for butter, but in deference to

BAKED CHICKEN IMPERIAL

democracy and modern times I dramatically reduced the amount. Processing 3 tablespoons of softened butter into the bread crumbs provided plenty of richness without greasiness and gave the crumb mixture just enough moisture to stay put on the chicken without a messy, laborious bound breading (flour, then egg, then crumbs). Brushing a little melted butter onto the chicken before packing on the crumbs also helped them adhere.

The chicken was great at this point, but many recipes for this dish call for serving it with either Cumberland sauce (a potent mix of jelly, citrus, and spices) or a cream sauce. Tasters voted in favor of a cream sauce to complement the butter, cheese, and herbs in the crumbs. Chicken broth gave the sauce a savory underpinning, and white wine, Dijon mustard, and shallot gave it complexity.

I wanted the sauce to benefit from the flavorful juices the chicken exuded while cooking, so I combined the two in the baking pan. The problem was that the sauce didn't reduce enough in the oven; it required a stint on the stovetop while the chicken rested. For simplicity's sake (and to save on dishes), I switched from a baking dish to a 12-inch ovensafe skillet that could go from the oven right onto the stovetop for that final reduction. The large skillet was big enough to keep the crumb coating dry and crisp while the chicken and sauce mingled in the oven.

Juicy, tender chicken with a generous coat of golden, buttery, cheesy, garlicky bread crumbs and a rich, velvety sauce—that sounds imperial for sure, but with this recipe you can get it done in a single skillet in about an hour. It doesn't get much more down-to-earth than that.

—ADAM RIED, *Cook's Country*

Baked Chicken Imperial

SERVES 4

Do not salt the chicken for longer than the recommended hour or it will become too salty. Don't worry if some of the crumb topping falls into the skillet in step 3. It will disappear into the sauce.

- 4 **(6- to 8-ounce) boneless, skinless chicken breasts, trimmed**
  Salt and pepper
- 4 **ounces French baguette, cut or torn into 1-inch pieces (4 cups)**

- ⅓ **cup grated Parmesan cheese**
- 3 **tablespoons unsalted butter, softened, plus 2 tablespoons melted and cooled**
- 3 **tablespoons minced fresh parsley**
- 2 **garlic cloves, minced**
- 2 **teaspoons minced fresh thyme**
- 1 **cup heavy cream**
- ¾ **cup low-sodium chicken broth**
- ⅓ **cup dry white wine**
- 1 **shallot, minced**
- 2 **teaspoons Dijon mustard**

1. Sprinkle chicken all over with 1½ teaspoons salt, cover with plastic wrap, and refrigerate for 30 minutes or up to 1 hour. Adjust oven rack to middle position and heat oven to 425 degrees.

2. Meanwhile, process bread in food processor until coarsely ground, about 20 seconds. Add Parmesan, softened butter, 2 tablespoons parsley, garlic, thyme, and ½ teaspoon pepper and process to combine, about 15 seconds, scraping down bowl as needed.

3. Pat chicken dry with paper towels and season with pepper. Arrange chicken, skinned side up, in 12-inch

---

NOTES FROM THE TEST KITCHEN

ODD—BUT EFFECTIVE—SETUP

Cooking the chicken right in the sauce allows for maximum flavor transfer between the two. We use a skillet instead of a baking dish so that we can reduce the sauce to the proper consistency after the chicken has baked.

1. Arrange uncoated chicken breasts with narrow ends meeting in center of skillet. Pack one-quarter of crumb mixture on top of each piece.

2. Carefully pour 1½ cups cream mixture around chicken. Move skillet to 425-degree oven and bake.

ovensafe skillet with narrow ends pointing toward center of skillet. Brush chicken with melted butter. Top each breast with equal amount (generous ½ cup) of crumb mixture, pressing firmly to adhere.

4. Whisk cream, broth, wine, shallot, and mustard together in 4-cup liquid measuring cup. Carefully pour 1½ cups around chicken breasts, taking care not to wet crumbs on top of chicken. Transfer skillet to oven and bake until crumbs are deep golden brown and chicken registers 160 degrees, 30 to 35 minutes.

5. Using spatula, carefully transfer chicken to platter and tent loosely with aluminum foil. Pour remaining ½ cup sauce mixture into skillet and bring to boil over medium-high heat. Cook until thickened and reduced to 1 cup, about 5 minutes. Stir in remaining 1 tablespoon parsley. Season with salt and pepper to taste. Serve, passing sauce with chicken.

CHICKEN MARBELLA

IN 1977, A GOURMET SHOP CALLED THE SILVER Palate opened in Manhattan's Upper West Side and introduced New Yorkers to their first bite of chicken Marbella. Inspired by the Moroccan tagines and Spanish braises that owners Julee Rosso and Sheila Lukins had sampled while traveling abroad in the 1960s, the shop's signature dish offered Americans a taste of then-exotic flavors: briny capers and bold Spanish olives baked with chicken and tender prunes in a sweet and tangy sauce. The shop closed in 1993, but the dish lives on in kitchens throughout America.

The original recipe starts with four whole chickens that are quartered into split breasts and legs and marinated overnight in olive oil, red wine vinegar, garlic, olives, prunes, capers, oregano, bay leaves, and plenty of salt and pepper. Everything is then transferred to shallow baking dishes, moistened with white wine, topped with a cup of brown sugar, and baked (with frequent basting) in a 350-degree oven for about an hour.

When I made this modern classic in the test kitchen, it was easy to see why its unique balance of flavors has made it such an enduring hit. But there were also a

number of problems. While the chicken was juicy, its flavor was very subtle despite the overnight soak. The skin remained pale and flabby, and the sauce, though well seasoned, was quite sweet, lacking the pungency that its ingredient list would suggest. In the enterprising spirit of Rosso and Lukins, I set out to create an updated version of this classic dinner-party favorite.

To make the dish more feasible as a weeknight supper, I first scaled it down to four to six servings (the original recipe serves 16 to 24). I also saved myself the trouble of butchering by switching from whole chickens to split breasts and leg quarters.

Next to go: the overnight marinade. Years of testing have taught us that marinades aren't miracle cure-alls for bland, dry meat. We've found that regardless of how long a marinade remains in contact with meat, its flavor never penetrates more than a few millimeters into the meat. And forget about crisp skin: The lengthy soak waterlogs poultry skin, which in turn inhibits rendering and browning. There is one element of a marinade that does live up to the hype, however: salt. Salt in a marinade acts like a brine, penetrating the muscle fibers, seasoning the meat, and helping it hold on to its juices. When I ran a side-by-side test pitting chicken pieces treated with the original marinade against a batch that was simply salted (both sat overnight in the fridge), both samples emerged equally succulent. In fact, tasters preferred the salted chicken, noting that the vinegar had turned the marinated chicken mealy.

Unfortunately, salting worked well, but it took at least six hours to have an impact (with better results after 24 hours). Brining was faster but—just like the marinade—left me with limp, waterlogged chicken skin that resisted browning and diluted the sauce during baking. Reluctantly, I scratched these pretreatments off of my list and turned my attention to the cooking method, hoping to find an alternative path to moist, flavorful meat.

I decided to sear the chicken to jump-start browning and build a sauce from the fond. I seasoned two split breasts and two leg quarters with salt and pepper and placed them, skin side down, in a smoking-hot 12-inch skillet. Once the skin turned golden, I flipped the parts over and transferred them to a shallow baking dish.

Then I set about building the sauce. I stirred in the oil, vinegar, olives, capers, and other ingredients and cooked them for a minute. I deglazed the skillet with white wine, poured the sauce around the chicken, and transferred everything to a 400-degree oven (leaving the skin exposed to the direct heat of the oven). To allow the skin to continue rendering, I scrapped the brown sugar coating (relying on the prunes for sweetness) and skipped the basting, since moist skin doesn't render or brown much.

The good news was that the sauce was more flavorful, albeit still a little thin. But despite my efforts, the skin hadn't rendered or colored much more than it had after the initial browning—the straight sides of the baking dish were trapping moisture. I'd already dirtied a skillet; could I take advantage of its shallow walls and cook the chicken through in the same pan? I gave it a shot, returning the seared chicken to the skillet after building my sauce and then placing the skillet in the oven to finish cooking. Sure enough, the skillet allowed more steam to escape, resulting in well-browned skin and a more concentrated sauce. Finally, I was getting somewhere.

But there was still more work to do. Tasters complained that the dish didn't seem cohesive, and none of the sauce's flavor had transferred to the chicken. Perhaps a more concentrated sauce was the answer. I ramped up the amounts of olives, capers, prunes, and garlic, and to boost meatiness and complexity, I tried adding onions, anchovies, and red pepper flakes. Onions didn't impress tasters, but minced anchovies (which added a rich depth without tasting fishy) and a pinch of pepper flakes earned rave reviews. The sauce finally came together with the addition of ¾ cup of chicken broth. The chicken, however, was still bland.

Desperate for a fix, I went back to basting, but the technique proved both inconvenient and ineffective. Even with frequent basting, the sauce merely dripped back into the pan, and I ran into the same old problem of soggy, unrendered skin. While mulling over how I could get the flavor to "stick" to the chicken, I hit on the solution: I'd make a paste that would literally adhere to the skin.

I prepped another batch, pureeing some of the prunes, olives, and capers with garlic, anchovies, oregano, pepper flakes, and olive oil. After searing the chicken, I spread an even layer of paste on each piece before transferring the skillet to the oven. Things looked promising during the first half of cooking, as the paste started to develop a rich, dark patina. But it continued to darken, and by the time the meat was cooked through, the surface was charred. For the next test, I waited until the chicken was about half cooked and the skin well rendered and browned before adding the paste. After another 10 minutes in the oven, the paste had caramelized and the flavors had bloomed, making this the best-tasting chicken yet.

Wondering if I could use the paste to deepen the flavor of the sauce as well, I caramelized some of the paste in the skillet after browning the chicken. Just as I had hoped, the sauce was deeply flavorful and possessed a velvety texture thanks to the pureed prunes. A last-minute knob of butter, a teaspoon of red wine vinegar, and a sprinkle of fresh parsley pulled everything into balance.

With these changes, my colleagues agreed I'd made a good dish even better—and a version that might live on for another 25 years.

—DAN SOUZA, *Cook's Illustrated*

NOTES FROM THE TEST KITCHEN

MAKING OVER MARBELLA
The original chicken Marbella featured chicken parts marinated overnight and then baked.

PROBLEM: Pale, flabby skin
SOLUTIONS: Ditch the marinade since it turns skin soggy (and never permeates the flesh anyway). Sear the chicken to crisp the skin before adding liquid.

PROBLEM: Bland meat
SOLUTION: Smear a potent paste of capers, garlic, anchovies, olives, prunes, oregano, and red pepper flakes onto the chicken during the last 10 minutes of cooking.

PROBLEM: Overly sweet, lackluster sauce
SOLUTIONS: Eliminate brown sugar and use the flavorful fond from searing the chicken (plus more caper-prune-olive paste) to form the base of the sauce. Balance the flavors with butter, vinegar, and parsley.

Chicken Marbella

SERVES 4 TO 6

Any combination of split breasts and leg quarters can be used in this recipe.

PASTE

⅓ cup pitted green olives, rinsed

⅓ cup pitted prunes

3 tablespoons extra-virgin olive oil

4 garlic cloves, peeled

2 tablespoons capers, rinsed

3 anchovy fillets, rinsed

½ teaspoon dried oregano

½ teaspoon pepper

¼ teaspoon kosher salt

Pinch red pepper flakes

CHICKEN

2½–3 pounds bone-in split chicken breasts and/or leg quarters, trimmed

Kosher salt and pepper

2 teaspoons olive oil

¾ cup low-sodium chicken broth

⅓ cup white wine

⅓ cup pitted green olives, rinsed and halved

1 tablespoon capers, rinsed

2 bay leaves

⅓ cup pitted prunes, chopped coarse

1 tablespoon unsalted butter

1 teaspoon red wine vinegar

2 tablespoons minced fresh parsley

1. FOR THE PASTE: Adjust oven rack to middle position and heat oven to 400 degrees. Pulse all ingredients together in food processor until finely chopped, about 10 pulses. Scrape down bowl and continue to process until mostly smooth, 1 to 2 minutes. Transfer to bowl. (Paste can be refrigerated for up to 24 hours.)

2. FOR THE CHICKEN: Pat chicken dry with paper towels. Sprinkle chicken pieces with 1½ teaspoons salt and season with pepper.

3. Heat oil in 12-inch ovensafe skillet over medium-high heat until just smoking. Add chicken, skin side down, and cook without moving until well browned, 5 to 8 minutes. Transfer chicken to large plate. Drain off all but 1 teaspoon fat from skillet and return to medium-low heat.

4. Add ⅓ cup paste to skillet and cook, stirring constantly, until fragrant and fond forms on bottom of pan, 1 to 2 minutes. Stir in broth, wine, olives, capers, and bay leaves, scraping up any browned bits. Return chicken, skin side up, to pan (skin should be above surface of liquid) and transfer to oven. Cook, uncovered, for 15 minutes.

5. Remove skillet from oven and use back of spoon to spread remaining paste over chicken pieces; sprinkle prunes around chicken. Continue to roast until paste begins to brown, breasts register 160 degrees, and leg quarters register 175 degrees, 7 to 12 minutes longer.

6. Transfer chicken to serving platter and tent loosely with aluminum foil. Remove bay leaves from sauce and whisk in butter, vinegar, and 1 tablespoon parsley; season with salt and pepper to taste. Pour sauce around chicken, sprinkle with remaining 1 tablespoon parsley, and serve.

FILIPINO CHICKEN ADOBO

ADOBO MAY BE CONSIDERED THE NATIONAL DISH of the Philippines, but thanks to the country's melting-pot ancestry, the formula for making it is remarkably varied. The core concept is meat marinated and braised in vinegar and soy sauce, with lots of garlic, bay leaves, and black pepper. Everything from that point on, however, is open to interpretation. Chicken is the usual choice, but pork is also used. In the Philippines, coconut-sap vinegar is preferred, but when that isn't available, rice vinegar is a popular substitute. Plenty of recipes also call for cider or plain old distilled vinegar. Some versions go heavy on the soy sauce, rendering the dish a distant relative of Japanese teriyaki, while others use the soy more sparingly with rich coconut milk stirred in for a result that is more currylike.

What most Filipino recipes do seem to agree on: This dish is simple and easy to prepare, the ingredients are few and mostly pantry staples, and the finished product—tender meat napped with a reduction of the tangy braising liquid—boasts bold, well-developed flavors.

I armed myself with Filipino cookbooks and tried a bunch of recipes based on chicken, my protein of choice. The recipes all started with combining all the ingredients in a large bowl. Marinating times, however,

FILIPINO CHICKEN ADOBO

were anywhere from 30 minutes to as long as 24 hours. The results were predictably varied, but unfortunately all were problematic, with aggressively tart and salty flavors and sauce that was too thin to cling to the meat. Most troubling of all was the meat, which more often than not sported a tough, mealy outer layer. With the goal of bringing more balance and body to the dish and producing meat that was juicy and tender, I started to work up my own take on adobo.

Using the best elements of my research recipes, I built a working formula using bone-in, skin-on chicken thighs. With more fat and collagen than breasts and more meat on the bone than drumsticks, thighs are rich, flavorful, and particularly well suited to braising. And the meat's skin would give the sauce something to cling to.

I tested marinating times from one end of the spectrum to the other, using cider vinegar for its round, fruity flavor. Each test resulted in the same tough, mealy texture. If anything, I expected that the chicken would be mushy, as we've always found that to be the effect of acidic marinades on meat. Puzzled, I relayed the result to our science editor, who offered an explanation: While soaking meat in moderately acidic marinades causes its surface to become mushy, strongly acidic mixtures like this one can cause surface proteins to bind and squeeze out moisture, drying out and toughening the meat's exterior. And it doesn't take long; tasters reported that even the 30-minute samples showed the effects.

I tried skipping the marinade altogether, but that knee-jerk reaction was too drastic. While I'd done away with the meat's tough chew, I'd also inadvertently wiped out its flavor, and tasters complained that the chicken and sauce now tasted like separate entities. I reviewed our previous research on marinades and came up with my next idea: marinating in only soy sauce. Salt is one of the few marinade ingredients that actually makes its way beyond the surface of the meat; in fact, it's the most important one, as it both seasons and tenderizes the meat. Sure enough, when I repeated the marinade test using only soy sauce, the flavor and tenderness of the meat improved radically after only 30 minutes. But I was far from finished. The tartness of the sauce was still way off base, and even after reducing, it lacked enough body to cling to the meat.

As I found myself at an impasse, a colleague suggested that I stop into Filipino chef Romy Dorotan's acclaimed

Purple Yam restaurant in Brooklyn to try his adobo. His version was terrific, and when I inquired about the recipe, Dorotan revealed that he adds coconut milk to the braising liquid, which is customary in adobos native to southern Luzon, the largest of the Philippine islands. I'd shied away from the super-rich milk in my earlier tests, fearing that it would muddy the flavor of the braise. But his version convinced me otherwise, as it perfectly tempered the salt and acidity while still allowing for plenty of tanginess.

I returned to the test kitchen and whisked a can of coconut milk into the braising liquid of my next batch. Tasters praised the balanced flavors and declared this my best adobo yet, save for one objection: The double dose of fat from the chicken skin and the coconut milk had rendered the sauce a little greasy. I also had a related demand of my own: This being a braise, I wasn't banking on crackly crisp skin, but thus far it had been downright soggy. Discarding the skin altogether might have been one option, but I was counting on its craggy exterior to grip the sauce.

The problem was that my one-step cooking method wasn't exposing the chicken to any high, dry heat, so there was no opportunity to render any of the skin's gummy fat layer and crisp its surface. Easy fix, right? Just throw the thighs skin side down into a ripping-hot skillet for a few minutes before moving them into the braising liquid. Wrong. Sure, the skin looked crisp and nicely browned, but slicing below the surface revealed that the thick fat pad was still there. Leaving the thighs in the hot pan for several more minutes to render the fat wasn't any better; by the time the skin had shed most of its fat, it was also literally burned to a crisp.

The problem reminded me of cooking duck breasts. When I worked in French bistros, I learned a standard method for melting down the dense white layer in duck: Place the meat skin side down in a "cold" (read: room-temperature) pan and then turn up the heat. As the pan gradually gets hotter, the fat under the skin has enough time to melt away before the exterior burns. Hoping the technique would translate to chicken, I placed the marinated thighs skin side down in a 12-inch nonstick skillet and then turned the heat to medium-high. Sure enough, after about 10 minutes the skin was not only sheer but also gorgeously browned. Even better, when I emptied the pan, I dumped out nearly ⅓ cup of fat.

Greasiness problem solved. And although I knew that the skin wouldn't stay super-crisp, I did employ one last trick to keep as much of its crackly texture as possible. When I braised the chicken thighs, I started them skin side down and then flipped them halfway through so that they finished skin side up, allowing the skin to dry out a little before serving.

I'd been at the stove for less than an hour when I removed the chicken from the pan and briefly reduced the cooking liquid. I poured the tangy, coconut milk–enriched sauce over the tender pieces of chicken, sprinkled on a handful of sliced scallion for color and freshness, and dug in, admiring how perfectly these bold flavors had melded together.

—BRYAN ROOF, *Cook's Illustrated*

Filipino Chicken Adobo

SERVES 4

Light coconut milk can be substituted for regular coconut milk. Serve this dish over rice.

    8   (5- to 7-ounce) bone-in chicken thighs, trimmed
    ⅓   cup soy sauce
    1   (13.5-ounce) can coconut milk
    ¾   cup cider vinegar
    8   garlic cloves, peeled
    4   bay leaves
    2   teaspoons pepper
    1   scallion, sliced thin

1. Toss chicken with soy sauce in large bowl. Refrigerate for at least 30 minutes or up to 1 hour.

2. Remove chicken from soy sauce, allowing excess to drip back into bowl. Transfer chicken, skin side down, to 12-inch nonstick skillet; set aside soy sauce.

3. Place skillet over medium–high heat and cook until chicken skin is browned, 7 to 10 minutes. While chicken is browning, whisk coconut milk, vinegar, garlic, bay leaves, and pepper into soy sauce.

4. Transfer chicken to plate and discard fat in skillet. Return chicken to skillet skin side down, add coconut milk mixture, and bring to boil. Reduce heat to medium-low and simmer, uncovered, for 20 minutes. Flip chicken skin side up and continue to cook, uncovered, until chicken registers 175 degrees, about

15 minutes. Transfer chicken to platter and tent loosely with aluminum foil.

5. Remove bay leaves and skim any fat off surface of sauce. Return skillet to medium-high heat and cook until sauce is thickened, 5 to 7 minutes. Pour sauce over chicken, sprinkle with scallion, and serve.

NOTES FROM THE TEST KITCHEN

BALANCING ACT

The two core components of Filipino adobo—vinegar and soy sauce—add up to a predictably sharp, salty braising liquid. To even out the acidity and salt, we took a cue from a regional variation and added a can of coconut milk. The thick, rich milk mellows those harsher flavors while still allowing for plenty of tanginess. It also adds welcome body to the sauce.

SALTY AND SOUR
Soy sauce and vinegar are staples in Filipino adobo.

THICK AND CREAMY
We add coconut milk for body and richness.

MICROWAVE RICE COOKERS

Cooking rice is never as easy as it seems. The grains blow out or don't soften, and the pot often boils over or burns the bottom layer. So we were hopeful about microwave rice cookers' claims to produce perfect rice with easier cleanup. We tested five of these plastic containers (all BPA-free) with vented lids. Since microwave oven wattage varies, included instructions were presented as "guidelines," and getting good results from any of the cookers involved a lot of trial and error. We finally hit on a formula that worked for all models: five minutes on full power, 15 minutes on 50 percent power, and then a five-minute rest. Our favorite model, **The Progressive International Microwave Rice Cooker Set**, $8.99, is intuitive, easy to clean, and much cheaper than a traditional rice cooker. That said, it's no better than our homegrown microwave method (cover a glass bowl with a plate and use the same low-and-slow timing), but it's a fine product—once you've fine-tuned the technique.

MORAVIAN CHICKEN PIE

FOR MORE THAN 40 YEARS, MY GRANDMOTHER and the ladies of Fairview Moravian Church in Winston-Salem, North Carolina have gathered on the second Tuesday of every month, a flurry of chicken and chatter, to make The Pies. They simmer the chicken, whisk the gravy, fill the crust, and exchange updates on everything from gardening to grandchildren. To raise money for their churches, a lot of other local ladies are making the very same homespun pies: tender chicken in a rich, golden-brown crust and a good dousing of gravy. But as with many old dishes, recipes are vague at best, merely instructing the cook to "boil the chicken until cooked" and "bake until ready."

Almost a thousand miles from home, I was frustrated that there were only a few times a year that I could enjoy Moravian chicken pie. I needed to develop my own reliable recipe. I looked up some online, in the test kitchen cookbook library, and in my own Moravian cookbooks. I found, among others, one from the Old Salem Tavern, a 200-year-old tavern in the Moravian village of Old Salem that's renowned for its pie. In most cookbooks, the writers plainly assumed that the cook already had plenty of chicken pie expertise. If you couldn't fill in the missing information yourself, you could expect pies that were either dry or so soupy that they couldn't be sliced, as well as soggy, tricky-to-make crusts. Plus, these recipes required the cooks to spend many hours in the kitchen.

Most older Moravian chicken pie recipes start by simmering a whole chicken in water until tender, then shredding the meat and concentrating the broth into rich chicken stock. Doubtless it was a fine method back when flavorful yard-roaming hens were the norm, but made with supermarket chickens today, the filling was bland. To develop old-fashioned chicken flavor, I borrowed a test kitchen technique we use for chicken soup: I browned bone-in, skin-on breasts and thighs to develop fond and flavor, discarded the skin, and simmered the chicken pieces in store-bought broth. Now I had both juicy chicken and a quick broth with amplified chicken flavor to use for my gravy.

To build the gravy, I made a roux by stirring flour and a little butter into the chicken fat from browning the chicken. I whisked in the fortified broth and some half-and-half, simmered the mixture for 10 minutes, and ended up with a thick, full-bodied gravy. As most recipes suggest, I intended to use some of the gravy to moisten the filling—1 cup produced a juicy yet sliceable pie—and to serve the remainder with the pie. But while my gravy was perfect for the filling, it was too thick to serve with the pie. To get pourable gravy, I thinned out a portion of the thick stuff with additional fortified broth.

With the filling and double-duty gravy settled, I turned to the crust. Among the recipes I'd tested, the Old Salem Tavern pie crust stood out. Typically, pie crust doughs are made from flour, butter, shortening, and water. The tavern's crust had no shortening, but it did include two less common ingredients: sour cream and egg. Surprising, these unusual additions made an especially flaky, tender pie crust that was unusually easy to roll out.

Our science editor explained that acidic sour cream inhibits gluten development. Gluten, the protein that's formed when water bonds with flour, is necessary to hold a crust together, but too much can toughen it. The egg was providing emulsifiers to help disperse the fat evenly throughout the dough, resulting (again) in less gluten development, hence more tenderness.

But the crust wasn't quite perfect. As with most pie dough recipes, my working recipe required a variable amount of water to make the dough come together, depending on the humidity in the air, the age of the flour, and other factors. Frustrating. To eliminate the guesswork, I tried using more sour cream, which has water in it. I discovered that if I used exactly ½ cup, I could skip the water entirely. My crust was flaky and tender. The dough was a dream to work with. Best of all, the recipe was precise and turned out perfect every single time.

Well, almost perfect: The bottom crust was soggy. Fortunately, the test kitchen knows how to handle that. I simply turned up the heat, baking the pie on the bottom rack in a 450-degree oven to let the bottom crust crisp. After 20 minutes, I turned down the oven to keep the pie from overbrowning before cooking through.

I pulled my fragrant chicken pie out of the oven. A labor of love and an antidote to homesickness, this golden pie didn't make my grandmother, the church ladies, or Fairview Moravian Church materialize. But on every other count, it delivered.

—KELLY PRICE, *Cook's Country*

Moravian Chicken Pie

SERVES 8

If you have less than 2 tablespoons fat after browning the chicken in step 4, supplement it with butter. The pie may seem loose when it comes out of the oven; it will set up as it cools.

CRUST

- ½ cup sour cream, chilled
- 1 large egg, lightly beaten
- 2½ cups (12½ ounces) all-purpose flour
- 1½ teaspoons salt
- 12 tablespoons unsalted butter, cut into ½-inch pieces and chilled

PIE

- 2 (10- to 12-ounce) bone-in split chicken breasts, trimmed and halved crosswise
- 3 (5- to 7-ounce) bone-in chicken thighs, trimmed
  Salt and pepper
- 1 tablespoon vegetable oil
- 3 cups low-sodium chicken broth
- 1 bay leaf
- 2 tablespoons unsalted butter
- ¼ cup all-purpose flour
- ¼ cup half-and-half
- 1 large egg, lightly beaten

1. FOR THE CRUST: Combine sour cream and egg in bowl. Process flour and salt in food processor until combined, about 3 seconds. Add butter and pulse until only pea-size pieces remain, about 10 pulses. Add half of sour cream mixture and pulse until combined, 5 pulses. Add remaining sour cream mixture and pulse until dough begins to form, about 10 pulses.

2. Transfer mixture to lightly floured counter and knead briefly until dough comes together. Divide dough in half and form each half into 4-inch disk. Wrap each disk in plastic wrap and refrigerate for at least 1 hour or up to 2 days. (Dough can be wrapped tightly in plastic and foil and frozen for up to 2 months. Thaw completely at room temperature before using.)

3. Line rimmed baking sheet with parchment paper. Remove 1 dough disk from refrigerator and let sit for 10 minutes. Working on lightly floured counter, roll into 12-inch round and transfer to 9-inch pie plate, leaving ½-inch overhang all around. Repeat with second dough disk and transfer to prepared baking sheet.

Cover both dough rounds with plastic and refrigerate for 30 minutes.

4. FOR THE PIE: Pat chicken dry with paper towels and season with salt and pepper. Heat oil in large Dutch oven over medium-high heat until just smoking. Cook chicken until browned, about 10 minutes, transfer to plate. Pour fat (you should have 2 tablespoons) into bowl; reserve. When chicken is cool enough to handle, remove and discard skin. Add broth, chicken, and bay leaf to now-empty pot and bring to boil. Reduce heat to low and simmer, covered, until breasts register 160 degrees and thighs register 175 degrees, 14 to 18 minutes. Transfer chicken to bowl. When chicken is cool enough to handle, shred into bite-size pieces, discarding bones. Strain broth through fine-mesh strainer into separate bowl and reserve (you should have about 2¾ cups); remove bay leaf.

5. Adjust oven rack to lowest position and heat oven to 450 degrees. Heat butter and reserved fat in now-empty pot over medium heat until shimmering. Add flour and cook, whisking constantly, until golden, 1 to 2 minutes. Slowly whisk in 2 cups reserved broth and half-and-half and bring to boil. Reduce heat to medium-low and simmer gravy until thickened and reduced to 1¾ cups, 6 to 8 minutes. Season with salt and pepper to taste. Combine 1 cup gravy with shredded chicken; reserve remaining gravy for serving.

6. Transfer chicken mixture to dough-lined pie plate and spread into even layer. Top with second dough round, leaving at least ½-inch overhang all around. Fold dough under so that edge of fold is flush with rim

---

NOTES FROM THE TEST KITCHEN

REALLY EASY PIE CRUST

Most recipes for pie crust call for a variable amount of ice water to bind the dough, depending on the humidity, the flour, and the phases of the moon. OK, we made up that last part, but still, making crust is nerve-racking enough without having to guess how much water to add. Fall short and the dough won't ever come together. Overdo it and you'll get a tough crust. The magic of our recipe is that by including exactly one egg and precisely ½ cup of sour cream, we produce an especially tender crust and we eliminate the water and the guesswork.

of pie plate. Flute edges using thumb and forefinger or press with tines of fork to seal. Cut four 1-inch slits in top. Brush pie with egg and bake until top is light golden brown, 18 to 20 minutes. Reduce oven temperature to 375 degrees and continue to bake until crust is deep golden brown, 10 to 15 minutes. Let pie cool on wire rack for at least 45 minutes.

7. When ready to serve, bring remaining ¾ cup reserved gravy and remaining ¾ cup reserved broth to boil in medium saucepan. Simmer over medium-low heat until slightly thickened, 5 to 7 minutes. Season with salt and pepper to taste. Serve pie with gravy.

BRAISED TURKEY WITH GRAVY

ROAST TURKEY HAS BECOME SYNONYMOUS WITH Thanksgiving, but many early American cookbook authors actually advocated a very different method: cooking the whole bird (or its parts) in liquid in a covered pot set over an open fire. Braising would have been uniquely suited to the tough wild fowl put on the table in those days, as hours of simmering would have broken down the dark meat's chewy connective tissue and turned it meltingly tender.

But it's also a terrific way to cook today's mass-produced domestic turkey. Since the temperature in the pot can never rise above the boiling point of water (212 degrees), the method is inherently gentle, minimizing the risk of drying out the breast. On top of that, simmering the pieces in broth creates a flavor exchange between the meat and the liquid, giving the turkey a flavor boost and producing a rich, ready-made gravy. (The only trade-off I could think of might be less-than-crisp skin, but it was a compromise I was willing to make for supremely tender, juicy meat.) Braising parts instead of a whole bird makes the method even more advantageous as the white and the dark meat cook at a more even rate.

But I knew that a successful recipe would require more than just sticking some turkey parts in broth and placing the whole thing in the oven. Contrary to what you might expect, simmering meat in liquid is no guarantee of juiciness. In fact, if cooked too long or at the wrong temperature, braised meat can dry out just as readily as roasted meat. The trick would be to find the optimal cooking time and oven temperature and just the right ingredients to add deeper complexity to the meat.

Turkey parts are readily available at the supermarket, so I wouldn't have to bother with any butchering myself. I started with about 10 pounds of bone-in, skin-on breasts, drumsticks, and thighs—enough to feed a crowd of 10 to 12. I wanted to start by getting the basics of the cooking method down. To that end, I arranged the parts skin side up in a roasting pan, which was big enough to fit them all in one layer. I added about 5 cups of chicken broth—just enough to come about three-quarters of the way up the sides of the thighs. Then I covered the pan tightly with aluminum foil.

The oven temperature was a more complicated matter. The curious thing about braising is that despite the fact that the meat is sitting in liquid, it never actually absorbs moisture. On the contrary, once its muscle fibers reach around 140 degrees, they begin to contract and wring out juices. But when the meat in the pot has a lot of collagen, this contraction is mitigated by a second reaction: Between 160 and 180 degrees, the collagen rapidly dissolves into gelatin, which then holds on to some of the juices squeezed from the muscle fibers. The challenge in braising turkey, however, is that the dark meat has a good bit of collagen while the breast meat has almost none. I'd need to keep the thighs above the minimum temperature for dissolving collagen long enough for most of it to turn into gelatin—but not so long that the breast dried out.

Playing it safe, I dialed the oven temperature to a very gentle 275 degrees and put the turkey parts in. Without the insulating effect of the backbone and the breast, the thighs and drumsticks came up to their ideal temperature of 175 degrees at the same time that the breast reached its ideal 160 degrees: about four hours later. Both types of meat were very tender and juicy. Even the outermost layers of the breast were moist and succulent—an almost impossible feat when roasting. Still, as good as the turkey tasted, monopolizing the oven for four hours during the holidays was something I wanted to avoid.

BRAISED TURKEY WITH GRAVY

Wondering what would happen if I took the opposite tack and cranked the heat a lot higher, I prepped a new batch of turkey parts and braised them in a 400-degree oven. That got things moving for sure—it took barely more than an hour for the meat to come up to temperature—but the results were markedly inferior. Though the center of the breast was still juicy, the outer layers were dried out and the thighs, while moist, were tough. The higher heat was obviously to blame. Because the liquid was at a rapid boil, the cooking time sped up and, as a result, the collagen in the thighs didn't have a chance to sufficiently break down.

The compromise solution was 325 degrees. At this temperature, braising took a reasonable two hours, but the collagen still had a chance to break down into gelatin, while the breast meat remained relatively moist. Still, I couldn't get the super-juiciness of the low-and-slow-cooked batch out of my head. What if I introduced brining into the equation? I'd been avoiding the extra step until now, but brining both seasons meat and helps it hold on to its moisture. I also amped up the flavor of the solution by stirring in some sugar. Finally, both the breast and the dark meat were super juicy and tender.

Now that the meat was perfect, it was time to address the turkey's sallow skin. I knew that truly crisp skin wasn't in the cards, but some browning was a must. Not only would it improve the look of the skin, but it would also add flavor that would make its way into the braising liquid. Searing the pieces in the oven before adding the liquid would be the most efficient method, so I cranked the heat to 500 degrees, brushed another batch of turkey parts with melted butter, and roasted them until they were lightly tanned. After 20 minutes, I poured the chicken broth into the pan and returned the meat to a 325-degree oven. Some of the color washed away during the long braise, but the rich, roasted flavor that it added to the broth made for a worthy compromise.

I wasn't finished yet: The braising liquid still needed some tweaking. I started by swapping out 1 cup of the chicken broth for white wine to add bright sweetness. To further round out the flavor, I tossed chopped onions, celery, carrots, and garlic with melted butter and arranged them in the pan before placing the parts on top, browning the whole lot at once. The flavor was much improved, but I did even better by adding pepper, bay leaves, thyme, parsley, and a handful of ultra-savory dried porcini mushrooms. Best of all, as the flavors of the braising liquid improved, so did the flavor of the turkey itself.

All that remained was to turn this rich braising liquid into gravy. Once the turkey was cooked, I let the parts rest while I skimmed the liquid and used some of the flavorful fat to produce a golden roux. Then I whisked in a few cups of the liquid and let the mixture simmer until it thickened into glossy gravy.

With its juicy, rich meat and sumptuous gravy, braised turkey is worth celebrating. An approach so good—and so tailor-made for turkey—should be as much the stuff of legend as the roasted bird.

—ANDREW JANJIGIAN, *Cook's Illustrated*

Braised Turkey with Gravy

SERVES 10 TO 12

Instead of drumsticks and thighs, you can use 2 whole leg quarters, 1½ to 2 pounds each. The recipe will also work with turkey breast alone; in step 1, reduce the salt and sugar to ½ cup each and the water to 4 quarts. If you are braising kosher or self-basting turkey parts, skip the brining step and instead season the turkey parts with 1½ teaspoons salt.

TURKEY

Salt and pepper
1 cup sugar
1 (5- to 7-pound) whole bone-in turkey breast, trimmed
4 pounds turkey drumsticks and thighs, trimmed
3 onions, chopped
3 celery ribs, chopped
2 carrots, peeled and chopped
6 garlic cloves, peeled and crushed
2 bay leaves
6 sprigs fresh thyme
6 sprigs fresh parsley
½ ounce dried porcini mushrooms, rinsed
4 tablespoons unsalted butter, melted
4 cups low-sodium chicken broth
1 cup dry white wine

GRAVY

3 tablespoons all-purpose flour

Salt and pepper

1. FOR THE TURKEY: Dissolve 1 cup salt and sugar in 2 gallons cold water in large container. Submerge turkey pieces in brine, cover, and refrigerate for 3 hours or up to 6 hours.

2. Adjust oven rack to lower-middle position and heat oven to 500 degrees. Remove turkey from brine and pat dry with paper towels. Toss onions, celery, carrots, garlic, bay leaves, thyme, parsley, porcini, and 2 tablespoons butter together in large roasting pan; arrange in even layer. Brush turkey pieces with remaining 2 tablespoons butter and season with pepper. Place turkey pieces, skin side up, on vegetables, leaving at least ¼ inch between pieces. Roast until skin is lightly browned, about 20 minutes.

3. Remove pan from oven and reduce temperature to 325 degrees. Pour broth and wine around turkey pieces (it should come about three-quarters of way up legs and thighs). Place 12 by 16-inch piece of parchment paper over turkey pieces. Cover roasting pan tightly with aluminum foil. Return covered roasting pan to oven and cook until breast registers 160 degrees and thighs register 175 degrees, 1¾ to 2¼ hours. Transfer turkey to carving board, tent loosely with foil, and let rest for 20 minutes.

4. FOR THE GRAVY: Strain vegetables and liquid from roasting pan through fine-mesh strainer set in large bowl; discard solids. Transfer liquid to fat separator; allow to settle, about 5 minutes. Reserve 3 tablespoons fat and 3 cups braising liquid (reserve any remaining broth for another use).

5. Heat reserved fat in medium saucepan over medium-high heat. Add flour and cook, stirring constantly, until flour is dark golden brown and fragrant, about 5 minutes. Whisk in reserved braising liquid and bring to boil. Reduce heat to medium-low and simmer, stirring occasionally, until gravy is thick and reduced to 2 cups, 15 to 20 minutes. Remove gravy from heat and season with salt and pepper to taste.

6. Carve turkey and serve, passing gravy separately.

HOW BRAISING CREATES JUICY, FLAVORFUL TURKEY—PLUS RICH GRAVY

Contrary to what you might expect, it's possible for braised meat to turn out dry. To guarantee moist, juicy meat, we brine the turkey and cook it in a low oven.

1. Brine turkey parts in water, salt, and sugar to not only ensure that outer layers of breast don't dry out during cooking but also to season meat thoroughly.

2. Briefly brown turkey parts in 500-degree oven along with aromatics and flavorings to boost complexity and lend roasted flavor.

3. Pour 1 cup wine and 4 cups broth into pan—just enough to partially submerge meat—to ensure concentrated braising liquid.

4. Cover pan with parchment paper and aluminum foil and braise gently in 325-degree oven until white and dark meat are cooked through, about 2 hours.

5. To make gravy from rich-flavored braising liquid, strain liquid, use some of its fat to make roux, add back liquid, and simmer until thickened.

CHAPTER 8

SEAFOOD

Best Crab Cakes   202

Easy Salmon Cakes   204

    Easy Salmon Cakes with Smoked Salmon, Capers, and Dill

Baked Fish with Crispy Bread Crumbs   207

Grilled Cumin-Crusted Bluefish with Corn Relish   209

Poached Fish Fillets with Crispy Artichokes and Sherry-Tomato Vinaigrette   210

    Poached Fish Fillets with Crispy Scallions and Miso-Ginger Vinaigrette

    Poached Fish Fillets with Crispy Jalapeños and Spicy Vinaigrette

Thai-Style Fish and Creamy Coconut Rice Packets   214

Pan-Seared Shrimp with Tomato and Avocado   217

Light Seafood Risotto   218

Clams with Israeli Couscous, Leeks, and Tomatoes   220

    Clams with Israeli Couscous, Chorizo, and Tomatoes

BEST CRAB CAKES

IT'S A GIVEN THAT THE BEST CRAB CAKES ARE MADE with meat that's just been picked from the shell. But since fresh crabmeat is usually impossible to come by, I almost never make the cakes at home. That's a shame, because crab cakes are relatively quick and easy to throw together. Most recipes call for simply mixing the shucked meat with aromatics, herbs, spices, and a binder like mayo or beaten egg; forming cakes and dredging them in bread crumbs; then quickly pan-frying them until they're golden brown and crisp.

But is fresh-shucked meat really the only acceptable option? We did some tasting and discovered that a couple of brands of pasteurized crabmeat (available either canned or in the refrigerated section of most supermarkets) are surprisingly good alternatives to the fresh stuff. I decided to make it my goal to come up with the best possible crab cakes—sweet, plump meat delicately seasoned and seamlessly held together with a binder that didn't detract from the seafood flavor—regardless of whether I was starting with fresh crabmeat or not.

The obvious first step: figuring out what type of packaged crabmeat to use. Species aside, all crabmeat is graded both by size and by the part of the crab from which it's taken. Most crab cake recipes call for plump (pricey) jumbo lump or lump, while some suggest finer, flakier backfin crabmeat.

I was pretty sure my colleagues would prefer the meatier texture of jumbo lump or lump, but I made crab cakes with all three grades to be sure. I put together a bare-bones recipe, mixing 1 pound of meat with mayonnaise and eggs, forming the mixture into eight cakes, rolling them in panko (super-crisp Japanese bread crumbs), and pan-frying them. No contest: Tasters overwhelmingly preferred the cakes made with jumbo lump or lump crabmeat. Flavor was another matter. Not only were the binders dulling the sweet crabmeat flavor, but all three batches tasted and smelled inescapably fishy. When I mentioned the results to our science editor, he suggested soaking the meat in milk to rid it of its unpleasant fishiness. It was a great quick trick. When I submerged the crabmeat in 1 cup of milk, the fishiness washed away after just a 20-minute soak.

Figuring I'd solved the toughest problem, I moved on to consider more conventional crab cake decisions like flavors and binders. Celery and onion (both briefly sautéed before joining the crabmeat) plus Old Bay seasoning were classic additions that nicely rounded out the rich flavor of the crabmeat. But the flavor-muting binders were a trickier issue. Reducing or leaving out the mayonnaise or egg allowed the clean crabmeat flavor to come through. However, the unfortunate (if predictable) consequence was that the binder-free batches fell apart during cooking.

Putting aside the mayo and eggs for the moment, I tried the first two out-of-the-box ideas that came to mind: a béchamel and a panade. Unfortunately, both tests flopped. The former, a combination of milk, flour, and butter, rendered the crab mixture mushy. The latter, a thick paste made from milk and bread that's often used in meatballs, was sticky and difficult to incorporate without breaking apart the crabmeat. Even worse, the starches and dairy in both binders deadened the crab flavor just as much as the mayonnaise and eggs had.

I was feeling short on ideas when I remembered a product I had used when I worked in high-end restaurants. "Meat glue," as it's commonly called, is a powdered protein that some chefs use to help bind foods together. Buying this stuff was out of the question here, but what about coming up with my own version? I couldn't turn protein into powder, but I could puree it. More specifically, I could call on another idea from my restaurant days: a mousseline. This delicate, savory mousse is composed mainly of pureed meat or fish and just a little cream. To enhance the briny sweetness and plump bite of the crabmeat, I figured I'd use shrimp. I wouldn't need much of it, and since the shrimp would be pureed, I could use whatever size was cheapest.

To that end, I pureed 6 ounces of shrimp in the food processor with 6 tablespoons of cream, plus the Old Bay, a little Dijon mustard, hot sauce, and fresh lemon juice for punchy flavor. As I'd hoped, the resulting mousse was a great stand-in; in fact, our science editor noted that this was a true meat glue. Pureeing the shrimp released fragments of sticky muscle proteins that delicately held the clumpy pieces of crabmeat together through the breading and cooking process. When tasters raved about the clean crab flavor that I had achieved, I knew this idea was a keeper. Their only quibble: The inside texture of the cakes was a bit too springy and bouncy, and a few stray clumps of crabmeat were falling off during cooking. Scaling back the mousse mixture by a third took care of the bounce, but pieces were still breaking off as I flipped the cakes.

I had one other, more subtle idea in mind to help make the crab cakes a bit sturdier: Briefly chilling them before cooking allowed them to firm up, resulting in less fragile cakes. I ran a side-by-side test, refrigerating one batch for a half-hour before pan-frying, while immediately cooking the other. The chill paid off; these cakes not only felt noticeably sturdier than the unrested batch but also held up considerably better during cooking.

My tasters' one lingering request concerned the breading. The panko was definitely crisper than traditional bread crumbs, but the flakes soaked up moisture from the cakes, losing some of their crunch and falling off the sides. Color was also a problem, as the only surfaces that browned nicely were those that came in contact with the pan. My two quick fixes: crushing half of the panko to make smaller pieces that would adhere better to the cakes, and toasting all of the crumbs before coating to deepen and even out their color and beef up their crunch.

With just a few easy tricks to clean up the crab's flavor and keep the meat neatly bound, I'd created a recipe for classic crab cakes that were delicious whether made with the freshest crab or with readily available pasteurized crabmeat.

—LAN LAM, *Cook's Illustrated*

Best Crab Cakes

SERVES 4

Either fresh or pasteurized crabmeat can be used in this recipe. With packaged crab, if the meat smells clean and fresh when you first open the package, skip steps 1 and 4 and simply blot away any excess liquid. Serve the crab cakes with lemon wedges.

- 1 pound lump crabmeat, picked over for shells
- 1 cup milk
- 1½ cups panko bread crumbs
    Salt and pepper
- 2 celery ribs, chopped
- ½ cup chopped onion
- 1 garlic clove, peeled and smashed
- 1 tablespoon unsalted butter
- 4 ounces shrimp, peeled, deveined (see page 9), and tails removed
- ¼ cup heavy cream
- 2 teaspoons Dijon mustard
- ½ teaspoon hot sauce
- 1 teaspoon lemon juice
- ½ teaspoon Old Bay seasoning
- 4 tablespoons vegetable oil

1. Place crabmeat and milk in bowl, making sure crab is totally submerged. Cover and refrigerate for 20 minutes.

2. Meanwhile, place ¾ cup panko in small zipper-lock bag and finely crush with rolling pin. Transfer crushed panko to 10-inch nonstick skillet and add remaining ¾ cup panko. Toast over medium-high heat, stirring constantly, until golden brown, about 5 minutes. Transfer panko to shallow dish and stir in ¼ teaspoon salt and pepper to taste. Wipe out skillet.

3. Pulse celery, onion, and garlic together in food processor until finely chopped, 5 to 8 pulses, scraping down bowl as needed. Transfer vegetables to large bowl. Rinse processor bowl and blade and reserve. Melt butter in now-empty skillet over medium heat. Add chopped vegetables, ½ teaspoon salt, and ⅛ teaspoon pepper; cook, stirring frequently, until vegetables are softened and all moisture has evaporated, 4 to 6 minutes. Return vegetables to large bowl and let cool to room temperature. Rinse out pan and wipe clean.

4. Strain crabmeat through fine-mesh strainer, pressing firmly to remove milk but being careful not to break up lumps of crabmeat.

5. Line rimmed baking sheet with parchment paper. Pulse shrimp in now-empty food processor until finely ground, 12 to 15 pulses, scraping down bowl as needed. Add cream and pulse to combine, 2 to 4 pulses, scraping down bowl as needed. Transfer shrimp puree to bowl with cooled vegetables. Add mustard, hot sauce, lemon juice, and Old Bay; stir until well combined. Add crabmeat and fold gently with rubber spatula, being careful not to overmix and break up lumps of crabmeat. Divide mixture into 8 balls and firmly press into ½-inch-thick patties. Place cakes on prepared baking sheet, cover tightly with plastic wrap, and refrigerate for 30 minutes.

6. Coat each cake with panko, firmly pressing to adhere crumbs to exterior. Heat 1 tablespoon oil in now-empty skillet over medium heat until shimmering. Place 4 cakes in skillet and cook without moving them until golden brown, 3 to 4 minutes. Using 2 spatulas, carefully flip cakes. Add 1 tablespoon oil, reduce heat to medium-low, and continue to cook until second side is golden brown, 4 to 6 minutes. Transfer cakes to platter. Wipe out skillet and repeat with remaining 4 cakes and remaining 2 tablespoons oil. Serve immediately.

SALMON CAKES

AS A CHILD, I WAS CONVINCED THAT ALL FISH WERE perfectly cylindrical—sort of like dachshunds with fins—because when my family ate fish, it was in the form of puck-shaped cakes. While I have a soft spot for those starch-heavy cod and haddock cakes of my youth, I sometimes crave a more refined version, in which the fish itself isn't camouflaged by gluey binders (usually potatoes) and heavy-handed seasoning. Enter salmon cakes. When done well, these pan-fried patties are tender and moist on the inside, crisp and golden brown on the outside. The seasoning complements—rather than overpowers—the flavor of the fish, and there is just enough binder to hold the cakes together. Unfortunately, most salmon cakes I've tried stray far from this ideal. Their interiors are mushy and their flavor overly fishy. And then there's the fussy breading process.

With a lifetime of fish cake–eating experience, I knew I could do better. My goal: salmon cakes that tasted first and foremost of salmon, with a moist, delicate texture. I'd dump the potatoes in favor of a less stodgy binder and keep it to a minimum. And although I'd make them from scratch, these cakes would be quick and simple to prepare.

Fish cakes have long been a mainstay of New England cuisine, designed for using up leftover fish and potatoes. But today, most of us buy and cook only as much fish as we plan to eat in one sitting. Which led me to my first question: Should I use cooked or raw fish? I was pretty sure raw would be the way to go if I wanted a moist cake. But to be sure, I tried both approaches. I chopped both raw and cooked salmon fillets by hand into small pieces, then stirred in two typical binders (bread crumbs and mayonnaise), shaped the mixture into cakes, and (per standard breading procedure found in other salmon cake recipes) coated them with all-purpose flour, egg, and bread crumbs. I fried the cakes on both sides in vegetable oil until they were crisp and golden brown.

Just as I'd expected, the cakes made with cooked salmon lacked moisture. Plus, they tasted noticeably "fishier" than the raw-fish batch. But making raw salmon cakes was no joy either. Chopping slippery raw fish by hand into ¼-inch pieces was messy, sticky, and tedious. Larger chunks weren't an option—with

EASY SALMON CAKES

bigger salmon bits the cakes fell apart, even with strong binders. That said, my colleagues deemed the cakes made from raw salmon "pretty darn good." They were tender and moist inside and boasted pleasantly rich, almost creamy flavor with none of the "fishiness" of the twice-cooked samples. They just needed a bit of flavor enhancement and, for the sake of weeknight cooking, an easier method.

To that end, I took out my food processor. I cut the fillet into 2-inch pieces, chucked them in, and let the processor whirl. This resulted in big chunks of salmon bound by finely ground fish paste. Processing the salmon in two batches yielded smaller pieces, but the mixture was still too pasty; when I formed it into rounds and fried them, the finished cakes had a ground-meat consistency that was dense rather than delicate.

But that ground-meat analogy gave me an idea. When we make burgers, we grind the meat ourselves using an easy three-step process: We cut the meat into 1-inch pieces, briefly freeze them to firm them up, and then batch-grind them into smaller chunks in the food processor. The method ensures small, discrete pieces rather than mush. I didn't have time for the freezer, but smaller pieces and smaller batches were both doable. I cut the salmon into 1-inch chunks and gently pulsed them in three batches. This approach—pulsing, rather than letting the processor run continuously—allowed for more even chopping. Some of the pieces were still a bit bigger than the ideal ¼-inch morsels and some were smaller, but they produced cakes very similar to those I'd made with tediously hand-minced fish.

Having succeeded in making the chopping easier, I now could address an issue that had been annoying me from the start: The raw cakes were so wet and sticky that dipping them in egg made them as slippery and awkward to handle as mud pies. Adding more bread crumbs made the patties less goopy but masked the delicate sweetness of the fish. I had a radical thought: Was the three-step breading process really necessary for salmon cakes? In the test kitchen's recipe for Best Crab Cakes (page 203), we coat the cakes in bread crumbs alone. What if I followed suit here—ditching the egg and flour and simply coating the salmon cakes in bread crumbs before frying? This approach made the patties easier to handle, and the bread crumbs clung surprisingly well

to the fish on their own, but the results weren't stellar. Without a little bit of flour to act as a buffer from the moisture in the cakes, the fresh bread crumbs came out too pale and soft. But when I traded the fresh crumbs for ultra-crisp Japanese panko (just as we used in our crab cakes), the salmon cakes emerged from the pan crisp and golden brown. For convenience, I decided to use panko for a binder as well.

Though this simple solution was a happy state of affairs that both cut down on mess and resulted in a simpler process, I was curious why the traditional breading procedure proved superfluous in this case. Our science editor explained that a typical breading process works because the egg contains sticky soluble proteins called ovalbumin that (along with the flour) help the mixture hold together. But it turns out that salmon also contains tacky soluble proteins, called myosin, that migrate to the surface with the moisture in the fish and help the

---

NOTES FROM THE TEST KITCHEN

THREE EASY STEPS TO PERFECT SALMON CAKES

1. Hand-chop fish into 1-inch pieces before adding them to food processor. Any bigger, and you'll end up with some large chunks and some finely ground paste.

2. To ensure that pieces grind evenly, pulse chopped fish in 3 batches into ¼-inch bits. (Be careful not to overprocess.) Mix with bread-crumb binder and flavorings.

3. Gently coat shaped cakes with coarse panko bread crumbs. Salmon's high concentration of tacky water-soluble proteins glues crumbs to patties without need for egg or flour.

bread crumbs stick. Salmon has more of these water-soluble proteins than many other kinds of fish, as well as chicken and shrimp, making it the perfect candidate for a nontraditional breading.

Now that I had settled on a technique, it was time to jazz up the plain cakes in a way that would enhance the fish flavor rather than disguise it. I added some finely chopped shallot for depth and both scallion and parsley for freshness. Lemon juice brightened the flavor and cut the richness of the salmon, and a teaspoon of mustard and a pinch of cayenne added punch.

Served with tartar sauce or simply with a wedge of lemon, these moist yet crisp salmon cakes managed to be both elegant fare and comfort food. What's more, I could easily whip them up for a weeknight dinner.

—ANDREA GEARY, *Cook's Illustrated*

Easy Salmon Cakes

SERVES 4

If buying a skin-on salmon fillet, purchase 1⅓ pounds fish. This will yield 1¼ pounds fish after skinning. When processing the salmon, it is OK to have some pieces that are larger than ¼ inch. It is important to avoid overprocessing the fish. Serve the salmon cakes with lemon wedges and/or tartar sauce.

- 3 tablespoons plus ¾ cup panko bread crumbs
- 2 tablespoons minced fresh parsley
- 2 tablespoons mayonnaise
- 4 teaspoons lemon juice
- 1 scallion, sliced thin
- 1 small shallot, minced
- 1 teaspoon Dijon mustard
- ¾ teaspoon salt
- ¼ teaspoon pepper
  Pinch cayenne pepper
- 1 (1¼-pound) skinless salmon fillet, cut into 1-inch pieces
- ½ cup vegetable oil

1. Combine 3 tablespoons panko, parsley, mayonnaise, lemon juice, scallion, shallot, mustard, salt, pepper, and cayenne in bowl. Working in 3 batches, pulse salmon in food processor until coarsely chopped into ¼-inch pieces, about 2 pulses, transferring each batch to bowl with panko mixture. Gently mix until uniformly combined.

2. Place remaining ¾ cup panko in pie plate. Using ⅓-cup measure, scoop level amount of salmon mixture and transfer to baking sheet; repeat to make 8 cakes. Carefully coat each cake with panko, gently patting into disk measuring 2¾ inches in diameter and 1 inch high. Return coated cakes to baking sheet.

3. Heat oil in 12-inch skillet over medium-high heat until shimmering. Place salmon cakes in skillet and cook without moving until bottoms are golden brown, about 2 minutes. Carefully flip cakes and cook until second side is golden brown, 2 to 3 minutes. Transfer cakes to paper towel–lined plate to drain for 1 minute. Serve.

VARIATION

Easy Salmon Cakes with Smoked Salmon, Capers, and Dill
Reduce fresh salmon to 1 pound and salt to ½ teaspoon. Substitute 1 tablespoon minced fresh dill for parsley. Add 4 ounces finely chopped smoked salmon and 1 tablespoon chopped capers to bowl with salmon mixture.

BETTER BAKED FISH

BAKED FISH HAS MANY VIRTUES: IT'S MILD-FLAVORED, healthy, and quick-cooking. Add a crunchy, flavorful crumb topping and there's a lot to like. In the real world, though, baked fish is often dry and overcooked yet sitting in a pool of liquid. I've also eaten more than my share of wet, boring crumb toppings—assuming they haven't fallen off the fillet. Surely moist, flavorful fish with a crisp crown of crumbs was an achievable goal.

I know that as fish cooks, its proteins denature and its moisture is squeezed out, which explains why overcooked fish is dry yet sits in a puddle of its own juices. Most recipes use a relatively hot oven (375 to 450 degrees), but when the window for perfect doneness is small, as it is for fish fillets, isn't this asking for trouble? My strategy was to slow down the cooking so I could get the fish out of the oven before it overcooked. As extra insurance, I'd use fillets at least 1 inch thick, which are less likely to overcook. Also, I wanted a recipe that would work with a variety of white fish. Putting the bread crumbs aside for now, I jumped in.

I put my naked fish fillets in a baking dish, set them in a 300-degree oven, and waited, thermometer at the ready. I checked the temperature of the fillets at five-minute intervals until they reached the optimum temperature (135 degrees). The fish wasn't bad, but it was slightly tough and soggy on the underside. A fellow test cook suggested elevating the fish on a wire rack, which would allow gentle heat to circulate all around it and also lift it out of its juices. So I switched from a baking dish to a rack (greased so the fish wouldn't stick) set in a rimmed baking sheet. After 35 minutes, the fish was perfectly cooked.

On to the crumbs. Fresh bread crumbs are prone to sogginess, so I went with a proven test kitchen favorite: super-crunchy Japanese panko crumbs. To get them to stick, I smeared the tops of the fillets with mayonnaise before pressing on the crumbs. Though the crumbs were anchored, let's face it: White fish is lean and the flavor is subtle. After several tests, I found that adding an egg yolk to the mayonnaise enriched the fish nicely, and pepper and lemon zest rounded out the flavors.

My tasters loved the crunch that panko provided, but the crumbs were pale and bland. The oven temperature was simply too low to brown them in the 35 minutes it took to cook the fish. Obviously, I'd have to brown the panko before baking the fish. For my next test, I sautéed the panko in melted butter (fortified with garlic, thyme, salt, and shallot) until they were deep golden. I let the crumbs cool, then "glued" them onto the fillets with the mayonnaise. Now the crumbs not only stayed put but also tasted delicious. Flavorful, satisfying, and simple? This baked fish just earned a place in my weekly repertoire.

—REBECCAH MARSTERS, *Cook's Country*

Baked Fish with Crispy Bread Crumbs

SERVES 4

Haddock or halibut fillets are good alternatives to cod.

- 3 **tablespoons unsalted butter**
- 1 **large shallot, minced**
  Salt and pepper
- 1 **garlic clove, minced**
- 1 **teaspoon minced fresh thyme**
- ¾ **cup panko bread crumbs**
- 2 **tablespoons minced fresh parsley**
- 2 **tablespoons mayonnaise**
- 1 **large egg yolk**
- ½ **teaspoon grated lemon zest**
- 4 **(6- to 8-ounce) skinless cod fillets, 1 to 1½ inches thick**

1. Adjust oven rack to middle position and heat oven to 300 degrees. Set wire rack in rimmed baking sheet and spray with vegetable oil spray. Melt butter in 12-inch skillet over medium heat. Add shallot and ½ teaspoon salt and cook until softened, about 3 minutes. Add garlic and thyme and cook until fragrant, about 30 seconds. Add panko and ¼ teaspoon pepper and cook, stirring constantly, until evenly browned, 5 to 7 minutes. Remove from heat and stir in parsley. Transfer panko mixture to shallow dish and let cool for 10 minutes.

2. Whisk mayonnaise, egg yolk, lemon zest, and ¼ teaspoon pepper together in bowl. Pat fish dry with paper towels and season with salt and pepper. Coat tops of fillets evenly with mayonnaise mixture. Working with 1 fillet at a time, dredge coated side in panko mixture, pressing gently to adhere, and place fish crumb side up on prepared wire rack. Bake until centers are just opaque and fish registers 135 degrees, 30 to 40 minutes, rotating pan halfway through baking. Serve.

CUMIN-CRUSTED BLUEFISH WITH CORN RELISH

IF GRILLED FISH IS WHAT YOU ARE AFTER, CHANCES are that salmon, tuna, and trout are at the top of your list—they certainly are for me. But I was up for trying something new. Bluefish, a favorite for the grill on the northeast coast, came to mind as something I had been passing over. While bluefish is an oily fish, I knew that, just like salmon, it could also be a healthy choice when properly prepared. Given its bold flavor, I thought it was an ideal candidate for pairing with a spice rub.

First, I had to settle on the best way to grill bluefish. I chose skin-on fillets to give the flesh added protection, then coated them with a basic working rub: a mixture of cumin, chili powder, cayenne, salt, and pepper. For these quick-cooking fillets, I felt that intense heat would be necessary in order to sear the exterior without overcooking the interior. I started with a half-grill fire on a charcoal grill, where the coals are concentrated on one side of the grill to produce a very hot fire. For the gas grill I found that leaving all the burners on high was the best way to achieve the same intense level of heat. However, the fish fused to the cooking grate, and because the skin shrank as the fish cooked, the fillets were curling midway through, leading to burnt edges and arched, barely seared centers. Even worse was the raw flavor of the spices. Addressing the curling problem turned out to be a quick fix. Scoring the skin ensured that the fillets stayed flat and seared nicely. Next, I needed to address the pesky sticking problem.

Giving the grill plenty of time to heat up and incinerate anything left on the grate from previous grilling helped somewhat, but not enough. In previous grilling recipes where sticking was a particular problem, I learned that I needed to first give the grate a good brushing to remove any charred remnants, then take extra care to oil the grate several times until the surface was well lubricated and glossy. Using this method better ensured that the bluefish would not stick and allowed me to finally grill with confidence.

The final problem to address was the harsh, raw flavor of the spice rub. "Blooming" is usually a sure bet for fixing raw-tasting spices. To bloom spices, we typically sauté them in a few tablespoons of butter or oil until they intensify in flavor and emit a fragrant aroma.

Blooming the spices before applying them to the fish worked great, but after one test I knew it required too much oil for an already naturally oily fish. I wondered if I could get similar results by lightly coating the fillets with oil before adding the spice rub. In doing so, the oil would heat up while the fish cooked and bloom the spices, streamlining and lightening the method in one fell swoop. One test proved that my idea was right on the money. By the time the fillets were fully cooked, the spice rub had acquired the depth and richness I was after, without any raw flavor.

Now that I had perfectly cooked bluefish fillets, I wanted something to complement them. A sweet corn relish sounded like a perfect match. I was curious if more convenient canned or frozen corn could work as well as fresh, so I had tasters sample relishes made with each. Fresh corn was the clear winner; its superior taste and texture made it worth the small amount of additional preparation. Red bell pepper, some scallion, and a little cilantro contributed to the base of the relish, and a vibrant lime, chipotle, and honey dressing completed the picture. This recipe was a sure way to spice up my weeknight summer grilling routine.

—DAN ZUCCARELLO, *America's Test Kitchen Books*

Grilled Cumin-Crusted Bluefish with Corn Relish

SERVES 4

Fresh corn is essential to the relish; don't be tempted to substitute frozen or canned corn here. If your fish fillets are thicker or thinner, adjust the cooking time accordingly. You can substitute snapper for the bluefish if desired.

RELISH

- 1 ear corn, kernels cut from cob (see page 24)
- ½ red bell pepper, chopped fine
- 2 scallions, sliced thin
- 3 tablespoons minced fresh cilantro
- 2 tablespoons lime juice
- ½ teaspoon minced canned chipotle chile in adobo sauce
- ½ teaspoon honey
- ½ teaspoon salt
- ½ teaspoon pepper

4 teaspoons ground cumin

1 teaspoon chili powder

¼ teaspoon cayenne pepper

¼ teaspoon salt

¼ teaspoon pepper

4 (6-ounce) skin-on bluefish fillets, ¾ inch thick

2 teaspoons canola oil

1. FOR THE RELISH: Mix all ingredients together in bowl until well combined. Cover and refrigerate until ready to serve.

2. FOR THE FISH: Combine cumin, chili powder, cayenne, salt, and pepper in bowl. Pat fish dry with paper towels. Using sharp knife, make shallow diagonal slashes every inch along skin side of fish, being careful not to cut into flesh. Rub both sides of fillets with oil, then rub evenly with spice mixture.

3A. FOR A CHARCOAL GRILL: Open bottom vent completely. Light large chimney starter three-quarters filled with charcoal briquettes (4½ quarts). When top coals are partially covered with ash, pour evenly over half of grill. Set cooking grate in place, cover, and open lid vent completely. Heat grill until hot, about 5 minutes.

3B. FOR A GAS GRILL: Turn all burners to high, cover, and heat grill until hot, about 15 minutes. Leave all burners on high.

4. Clean cooking grate, then repeatedly brush grate with well-oiled paper towels until grate is black and glossy, 5 to 10 times. Place fish skin side down on grill (on hot side if using charcoal) with fillets diagonal to grate. Cook until skin is dark brown and crisp, 3 to 5 minutes. Carefully flip fish and continue to cook until fish flakes apart when gently prodded with paring knife and registers 140 degrees, about 5 minutes longer. Serve, passing corn relish separately.

POACHED FISH FILLETS WITH SHERRY-TOMATO VINAIGRETTE

IF YOUR EXPERIENCE WITH POACHED FISH IS LIMITED to the lean, bland preparations you might be served at a wedding or a weight-loss spa, a poaching technique popular at high-end restaurants will permanently change your perception. The key perk: Submerging fish in liquid and gently cooking it at below-simmer temperatures—anywhere from 130 to 180 degrees—renders the delicate flesh silky and supple. But in this case there is one amendment to the technique that elevates it above any poached fish I'd ever tasted: Rather than the usual lean bath of water, wine, or broth, the poaching liquid is olive oil.

I had to admit that on paper, cooking delicate fish fillets in a pot of fat sounded like a recipe for greasy disaster, but the results were stunning—lighter, moister, and more fragrant than any traditionally poached fish—and they explained why this technique has become so popular in top restaurants. Another plus: The flavor-infused poaching oil can be whirled into a rich, glossy emulsion and drizzled over the fish as a sauce. The dish would make elegant fare, provided I could get around one obvious challenge: the cost—and mess—of heating up a large amount of olive oil for just one meal. I would have to figure out how to scale the oil way back.

Since the oil would never get hot enough to crisp the skin, I went with skinless fillets. I settled on cod for its firm, meaty flesh and clean flavor. As for the amount of oil, I reasoned that the smaller the surface area of the cooking vessel, the deeper the liquid would pool, so I swapped my trusty 12-inch nonstick skillet for its 10-inch sibling. Unfortunately, this setup still demanded about 1½ cups of oil to cover the four 6-ounce fillets. My only other idea was to displace some of the oil by placing half an onion in the skillet and arranging the fillets around it—a trick that helped but got me down only another ¼ cup. Clearly, I needed a more drastic solution.

That's when I started to wonder if completely immersing the fillets in oil was necessary. The alternative—pouring enough oil into the pan to come roughly halfway up the sides of the fish (about ¾ cup)—would mean flipping the fish partway through poaching to ensure that it cooked through. But that seemed a small price to pay for significantly reducing the amount of expensive oil. I gave it a shot, basting the exposed half of each fillet with a few spoonfuls of oil (to prevent evaporation), popping a lid on the pan, and placing the skillet over the lowest burner setting. The good news was that the method worked; the fillets were supremely moist and tender and not at all oily.

The bad news was that it was fussy. With relatively little oil in the pan, the temperature spiked quickly and required that I constantly fiddle with the burner knob to keep the oil in my target range (140 to 150 degrees), which would slowly bring my fish to an

POACHED FISH FILLETS WITH CRISPY ARTICHOKES AND SHERRY-TOMATO VINAIGRETTE

ideal internal temperature of 130 degrees with little risk of overcooking. What I needed was a steadier, less direct heat source—and for that I turned to the oven.

I figured that I could simply bring the oil to 140 degrees on the stovetop, add the fish, then transfer the skillet into a low oven. But the oil temperature immediately plummeted when I added the still-cold fillets, and the temperature recovery time in the oven was slow. I had an idea: I'd heat the oil on the stovetop to well above my target temperature then rely on the oven's even heat to keep it in the poaching sweet spot.

After a slew of tests, I hit upon a winning combination: Heat the oil to 180 degrees, nestle in the fillets (each sprinkled with kosher salt), and set the pan in a 250-degree oven. The oil temperature recovered within 15 minutes, by which point the lower half of the fish was cooked. I flipped the fillets, replaced the lid, and returned the pan to the oven. This batch emerged incredibly moist and velvety, and thanks to my oven method, the process was now largely hands-off. What I had was good—but I wanted to make it even better.

We often salt meat and allow it to rest before cooking, both to enhance juiciness and to bring seasoning deep into the interior. Why not try this with fish? For my next round of testing, I salted the fillets about 20 minutes before cooking. This technique worked beautifully: Moisture beaded on the surface of the fish, where it dissolved the salt and created a concentrated brine that was eventually absorbed back into the flesh to bolster flavor.

I also wanted something that could serve as a textural contrast to the silky fish. Restaurants often garnish their oil-poached fillets with lightly fried vegetables and fresh herbs, and I reasoned that I could approximate that by crisping something in the oil before cooking the fish. Fried artichoke hearts have always been a favorite of mine, so I defrosted a bag of artichokes, patted them dry, and halved them lengthwise before tossing them with cornstarch (for extra crunch) and dropping them into the shimmering oil with some minced garlic.

Tasters loved the crisp garnish, but after cranking up the heat to fry, I then had to wait more than 10 minutes for the oil to cool to my target of 180 degrees before the pan went into the oven. The solution proved easy: Rather than dump in all the oil at once, I'd fry the garnishes in ½ cup of oil, strain it, and add the remaining ¼ cup of room-temperature oil to the pan to speed the cooling. The tweak made all the difference; about five minutes after frying, the oil was cool enough for poaching.

Frying up a garnish had also left me with an added bonus: flavor-infused oil to use for a sauce. I poured ½ cup into the blender and whirled it with whole cherry tomatoes (for bright sweetness), half a shallot, sherry vinegar, and salt and pepper. After a quick spin on high speed and a pass through a fine-mesh strainer, I had a silky-smooth vinaigrette.

Dressed up with the sauce, crispy artichoke garnish, a few slices of fresh cherry tomato, and a fistful of minced parsley, my elegant plate was complete—not to mention simple enough to pull off at home.

—DAN SOUZA, *Cook's Illustrated*

Poached Fish Fillets with Crispy Artichokes and Sherry-Tomato Vinaigrette
SERVES 4

Fillets of meaty white fish like cod, halibut, sea bass, or snapper work best in this recipe. Make sure the fillets are at least 1 inch thick. A neutral oil such as canola can be substituted for the pure olive oil. A 4-ounce porcelain ramekin can be used in place of the onion half in step 3. Serve with couscous or steamed white rice.

FISH
- 4 (6-ounce) skinless white fish fillets, 1 inch thick
  Kosher salt
- 4 ounces frozen artichoke hearts, thawed, patted dry, and sliced in half lengthwise
- 1 tablespoon cornstarch
- ¾ cup olive oil
- 3 garlic cloves, minced
- ½ onion, peeled

VINAIGRETTE
- 4 ounces cherry tomatoes
- ½ small shallot, peeled
- 4 teaspoons sherry vinegar
  Kosher salt and pepper

- 1 tablespoon minced fresh parsley
- 2 ounces cherry tomatoes, cut into ⅛-inch-thick rounds

1. FOR THE FISH: Adjust oven racks to middle and lower-middle positions and heat oven to 250 degrees. Pat fish dry with paper towels and season each fillet with ¼ teaspoon salt. Let sit at room temperature for 20 minutes.

2. Meanwhile, toss artichokes with cornstarch in bowl to coat. Heat ½ cup oil in 10-inch nonstick ovensafe skillet over medium heat until shimmering. Shake excess cornstarch from artichokes and add to skillet; cook, stirring occasionally, until crisp and golden, 2 to 4 minutes. Add garlic and continue to cook until garlic is golden, 30 to 60 seconds. Strain oil through fine-mesh strainer into bowl. Transfer artichokes and garlic to ovensafe paper towel–lined plate and season with salt. Do not wash strainer.

3. Return strained oil to skillet and add remaining ¼ cup oil. Place onion half in center of pan. Let oil cool until it registers about 180 degrees, 5 to 8 minutes. Arrange fish fillets, skinned side up, around onion (oil should come roughly halfway up fillets). Spoon a little oil over each fillet, cover skillet, transfer to middle oven rack, and cook for 15 minutes.

4. Remove skillet from oven. Using 2 spatulas, carefully flip fillets. Cover skillet, return to middle rack, and place plate with artichokes and garlic on lower-middle rack. Continue to cook fish until it registers 130 to 135 degrees, 9 to 14 minutes longer. Gently transfer fish to serving platter, reserving ½ cup oil, and tent fish loosely with aluminum foil. Turn off oven, leaving plate of artichokes in oven.

5. FOR THE VINAIGRETTE: Process cherry tomatoes, shallot, vinegar, ¾ teaspoon salt, and ½ teaspoon pepper with reserved ½ cup fish cooking oil in blender until smooth, 1 to 2 minutes. Add any accumulated fish juices from platter, season with salt to taste, and blend for 10 seconds. Strain sauce through fine-mesh strainer; discard solids.

6. To serve, pour vinaigrette around fish. Garnish each fillet with warmed crisped artichokes and garlic, parsley, and tomato rounds. Serve immediately.

VARIATIONS

Poached Fish Fillets with Crispy Scallions and Miso-Ginger Vinaigrette

For fish, substitute 8 scallion whites, sliced ¼ inch thick, for artichoke hearts; omit garlic; and reduce cornstarch to 2 teaspoons. For vinaigrette, process 6 scallion greens, 8 teaspoons lime juice, 2 tablespoons mirin, 4 teaspoons white miso paste, 2 teaspoons minced ginger, and ½ teaspoon sugar with ½ cup reserved fish cooking oil as directed in step 5. Garnish fish with 2 thinly sliced scallion greens and 2 halved and thinly sliced radishes.

NOTES FROM THE TEST KITCHEN

POACHING FISH OUT OF WATER

Oil poaching is not only a foolproof technique for cooking delicate fish but also a seamless way to create a crispy garnish and elegant sauce from the same oil.

1. Fry artichoke hearts and garlic in oil for crisp garnish that provides nice contrast to fish.

2. Pour ¼ cup fresh oil into strained frying oil to help cool it to gentle poaching temperature. Add onion half to displace oil, so it comes up higher in pan—and so less oil is needed.

3. Poach in low oven (rather than on stovetop) for more even cooking.

4. Use flavorful poaching oil to create simple vinaigrette that adds brightness.

WHY POACH IN OIL?

Poaching in oil allows fish to retain more of its juices than poaching in wine or broth, leading to remarkably moist, velvety results. This is because cooking in oil is inherently gentler than cooking in water. And while you might expect that fish poached in fat would be greasy, it actually absorbs very little oil. Why? In order for oil to penetrate the fish, moisture must exit first. But because oil and water repel each other, it's very difficult for moisture inside the fish to readily enter the oil. Hence, more of the juices stay in the fish. In fact, in our tests, oil-poached fish lost just 14 percent of its weight during cooking, while water-poached fillets lost 24 percent.

Poached Fish Fillets with Crispy Jalapeños and Spicy Vinaigrette

To make this dish spicier, add some of the reserved chile seeds to the vinaigrette in step 4. Serve with steamed white rice.

For fish, substitute 2 jalapeño chiles, stemmed, seeded, and cut into ⅛-inch-thick rings, for artichoke hearts and reduce cornstarch to 2 teaspoons. For vinaigrette, process 4 jalapeños, stemmed, halved, and seeded (seeds reserved); ½ small shallot, peeled; 6 sprigs fresh cilantro; 8 teaspoons lime juice; and ½ teaspoon kosher salt with ½ cup reserved fish cooking oil as directed in step 5. Garnish fish with 2 tablespoons fresh cilantro leaves and ½ avocado, pitted and cut into ¼-inch pieces.

THAI-STYLE FISH WITH COCONUT RICE PACKETS

COOKING EN PAPILLOTE—BAKING FOOD IN A tightly sealed, artfully folded parchment package that is slit open just before serving for dramatic presentation—may seem outdated or showy, not to mention unnecessarily laborious. But there's a practical reason the technique has held up through countless culinary fads and fashions. It does an excellent job of enhancing delicately flavored foods, particularly fish, since the food is allowed to steam in its own juices. The fish cooks quickly in the moist environment, and because there's no water added to dilute flavors, it's a more flavorful method than ordinary poaching. It's also appealingly tidy. I set out to simplify the pouch-making process (i.e., forgo the exercise in origami) and include a complementary side (one that required minimal prep) for a quick and flavorful "one-pouch" meal.

I would have to keep in mind that fish en papillote is not trouble-free in terms of technique. Without the right blend of flavorings, the fish can taste so lean and bland you might as well be dining on third-rate diet food. And while there are recipes that include vegetables in the pouch—since steaming vegetables is pretty foolproof—I was after something a little more satisfying. Could I possibly figure out a way to make a starchy side cook properly in the pouch along with the fish?

Classic en papillote recipes call for cutting parchment paper into attractive shapes such as teardrops, hearts, and butterflies. The fish is placed between two of these identical shapes, which are then crimped together. The result makes for a dramatic visual—the paper balloons and browns in the oven, to be slit open just before serving. An easier way, albeit less dramatic, is to simply use aluminum foil. I cut one piece of foil per serving, each a bit over a foot long. Then I arranged the food in the center of the packet and simply folded the foil over and crimped the edges to seal it tightly, ensuring that no steam would escape. I was happy to leave the theatrics to the restaurant chefs; this much simpler method got the job done just as well.

My next step was to figure out what type of fish worked best. After trying a variety of fillets, I decided to use a flaky, mild white fish, like halibut or cod. More assertively flavored fish like salmon also worked well, but white fish usually offers broader appeal, and its more neutral flavor would give me more room to play with the flavor profile of the sauce.

Determining when the fish was done proved somewhat challenging. The old rule of thumb for fish—10 minutes of cooking time per inch of thickness—failed in this case, as the fish was barely opaque within that period. After experimenting with oven temperatures, I found that ¾- to 1-inch-thick fillets cooked best at 400 degrees for 16 to 19 minutes. While this seemed like a long time at such high heat, the fish was insulated within the sealed packets and came out flaky and moist.

Next I moved on to choosing the right starchy side. Potatoes seemed like a good idea at first, but I ruled them out after one test; they took far too long to cook through. What about rice? Raw, uncooked rice would never be ready in the brief amount of cooking time, but what about precooked? Whether it was my own leftover rice or the variety available precooked from the supermarket, it seemed like a good option. With the starch chosen, I turned my attention to coming up with a sauce that would bring this duo together.

With its combination of sweet, sour, salty, and spicy flavors, Thai cuisine seemed like the perfect inspiration for my sauce. Using fish sauce, rice vinegar, and coconut milk as the base seemed like the right starting place.

A little sugar would lend a light sweetness, red pepper flakes, ginger, and garlic a touch of heat, and cilantro a fresh finish. I heated the sugar, vinegar, and pepper flakes together just long enough to dissolve the sugar, then stirred in the other ingredients. Now all I had to do was assemble my packets. I mounded some rice on each sheet of foil, laid a piece of fish on top, poured over the sauce, then crimped the packets closed and moved them to the oven. Putting the packets on a single baking sheet made it easier to move them in and out of the oven.

When I pulled the sheet of packets from the oven and took a taste, the results were even better than I had expected. The rice and fish were not only perfectly cooked, but the sauce had transformed the rice into a rich, creamy side dish, and both the fish and the rice were infused with flavor. It took a little more tweaking to get the proportions of the sauce ingredients into perfect balance and to make sure the amount of liquid was just right (this was the trickiest part, since the fish releases moisture and the rice soaks some up). Once all these little details were fine tuned, I had a flavor-packed entrée and side dish that could be on the table in less than 45 minutes and required less than a dozen ingredients. With that, fish en papillote went from fussy to fast and foolproof.

—SARAH WILSON, *America's Test Kitchen Books*

Thai-Style Fish and Creamy Coconut Rice Packets

SERVES 4

Any white fish will work here, but we prefer the thickness and meaty texture of halibut or cod. Serve with lime wedges.

- ⅓ **cup rice vinegar**
- 1½ **tablespoons sugar**
- ⅛ **teaspoon red pepper flakes**
- ½ **cup minced fresh cilantro**
- ½ **cup coconut milk**
- 2 **tablespoons fish sauce**
- 1 **tablespoon grated fresh ginger**
- 3 **garlic cloves, minced**
- 4 **(6 to 8 ounce) skinless halibut fillets, ¾ to 1 inch thick**
  Salt and pepper
- 4 **cups cooked rice**

1. Adjust oven rack to middle position and heat oven to 400 degrees. Combine vinegar, sugar, and pepper flakes in small saucepan and cook over medium-high heat until sugar dissolves, about 1 minute. Off heat, stir in ¼ cup cilantro, coconut milk, fish sauce, ginger, and garlic.

2. Season halibut with salt and pepper. Lay four 14-inch lengths of aluminum foil flat on counter. Pile rice in center of foil pieces, then lay fish on top and spoon sauce over fish. Fold foil over fish and rice into packets and crimp edges to seal.

3. Place packets in rimmed baking sheet and bake until fish flakes apart when gently prodded with paring knife, 16 to 19 minutes. To serve, open packets and sprinkle with remaining ¼ cup cilantro.

NOTES FROM THE TEST KITCHEN

PREPARING FISH AND RICE POUCHES

1. Lay four 14-inch lengths of aluminum foil flat on counter. Pile rice on one side of each piece.

2. Lay fish on top of rice and spoon sauce over top.

3. Fold foil over fish and rice to make packets, then crimp edges to seal.

PAN-SEARED SHRIMP WITH TOMATO AND AVOCADO

PAN-SEARED SHRIMP WITH TOMATO AND AVOCADO

SHRIMP ALWAYS COME TO MIND WHEN I WANT A meal that can be on the table in minimal time and with minimal fuss. They're convenient—I can stock them in my freezer and simply pull them out as needed. After a quick thaw, they cook through in just a few minutes. Their light, briny flavor means they pair well with simple, fresh flavors, which translates to minimal shopping and minimal cooking. That said, making a good meal with shrimp can be tricky. Given a short cooking time and only a handful of ingredients, every step and every ingredient in a shrimp recipe has to count toward maximizing flavor.

In my search for inspiration, I landed on a coastal Mexican dish known as *camarones a la plancha*. Fresh shrimp are seared on a hot griddle (the plancha) and topped with a fresh salsa–like mixture of tomatoes, chiles, cilantro, and lime juice. I wondered if I could capture the flavors of the authentic version here in the test kitchen.

Quickly searing shrimp on a hot griddle produces a well-caramelized exterior while maintaining a moist, tender interior. In the absence of a plancha, my next-best option was a 12-inch skillet; its large surface area would keep the shrimp from crowding in the pan and steaming, which is a surefire way to prevent caramelization. As for the shrimp themselves, for this simple recipe, 1½ pounds of extra-large shrimp seemed just right for serving four people.

In addition to a really hot skillet, heating a little oil in the pan first helped ensure a perfect sear. And to further increase the shrimp's caramelization, I seasoned them with sugar in addition to the usual salt and pepper before placing them in the skillet, a trick we often use in the test kitchen when cooking seafood or meat. Just ⅛ teaspoon of sugar promoted browning and accentuated the shrimp's natural sweetness.

Even in a 12-inch skillet, I found I needed to cook the shrimp in two batches, or they couldn't be arranged in a single layer, and they steamed instead of searing. Furthermore, a few tests proved that searing the shrimp on both sides took too long; the result was rubbery shrimp every time. So I seared the shrimp on the first side, which took about a minute, then took the pan off

the heat, flipped the shrimp over, and let them sit for another 30 seconds in the hot pan before setting them aside. When my sauce was finished, I could add the shrimp back to the skillet with the sauce and let them gently finish cooking to perfection while the flavors of the shrimp and sauce married.

With the shrimp figured out, I moved onto the salsa-like sauce. I began with the classic camarones a la plancha components: chopped fresh tomatoes, onions, garlic, jalapeño, lime juice, and cilantro. I knew the sauce would need to come together quickly to ensure that the shrimp didn't turn cold. With that in mind, the easiest tactic was an all-in approach. I added all the sauce ingredients to the now-empty skillet and cooked the sauce until the tomatoes broke down slightly, which allowed just enough time for the flavors to meld. Unfortunately, I ended up with a sauce that was too loose, and tasters complained of undercooked onions. They also agreed that the dish overall needed a little more pizzazz.

For an easy fix of the onion issue, I switched to soft-textured scallions. The scallion whites could replace the onion in the sauce, and their green tops could serve as a colorful garnish that also lent a fresh hint of onion flavor at the end. To give the sauce the smokiness that typifies foods prepared on a hot plancha, I replaced the fresh jalapeño with a teaspoon of canned chipotle chiles in adobo sauce. This gave the final dish a deeper, richer flavor as well as a hint of spiciness. My tasters approved.

Finally, I needed to fix the thin texture of my sauce. To reduce the amount of liquid, I tried seeding the tomatoes as well as seeding and draining them in a colander. Tasters vastly preferred the sauce with tomatoes that were only seeded; the sauce made with seeded and drained tomatoes was just too dry (and I didn't mind that they preferred the faster option). I also adjusted the length of time that I cooked the sauce. Instead of cooking the mixture long enough for the tomatoes to release their liquid, I simply warmed the ingredients through in the hot skillet for about a minute. Then all I had to do was stir in the shrimp and transfer it all to a platter to serve. For a touch of richness, I garnished the dish with diced avocado along with the scallion greens before serving. These shrimp were terrific on their own with a quick squeeze of lime juice and even better served over steamed rice to catch the flavorful juices.

—BRYAN ROOF, *America's Test Kitchen Books*

Pan-Seared Shrimp with Tomato and Avocado

SERVES 4

If your shrimp are larger or smaller, be sure to alter the cooking time in step 2 accordingly. This dish is fairly spicy; to make it milder, use less chipotle chile. Serve with lime wedges.

    3 tomatoes, cored, seeded, and cut into ½-inch pieces
    6 scallions, white and green parts separated and
       sliced thin
    ¼ cup minced fresh cilantro
    3 garlic cloves, minced
    1 tablespoon lime juice
    1 teaspoon minced canned chipotle chile in adobo sauce
       Salt and pepper
    2 tablespoons vegetable oil
 1½ pounds extra-large shrimp (21 to 25 per pound),
       peeled, deveined (see page 9), and tails removed
    ⅛ teaspoon sugar
    1 avocado, halved, pitted, and cut into ½-inch pieces
       (see page 36)

1. Combine tomatoes, scallion whites, cilantro, garlic, lime juice, chipotle, and ¼ teaspoon salt in bowl.

2. Heat 1 tablespoon oil in 12-inch nonstick skillet over high heat until just smoking. Pat shrimp dry with paper towels and season with sugar, salt, and pepper. Add half of shrimp to skillet in single layer and cook, without moving, until spotty brown and edges turn pink, about 1 minute. Remove skillet from heat, flip shrimp, and let sit until opaque in center, about 30 seconds; transfer to bowl. Repeat with remaining 1 tablespoon oil and remaining shrimp.

NOTES FROM THE TEST KITCHEN

SEEDING TOMATOES

To seed tomato, first cut in half through equator, then use finger to pull out seeds and surrounding gel.

---

3. Return now-empty skillet to high heat, add tomato mixture, and cook until tomatoes soften slightly, about 1 minute. Off heat, stir in shrimp, cover, and let sit until shrimp are cooked through, 1 to 2 minutes. Season with salt and pepper to taste, transfer to platter, and sprinkle with scallion greens and avocado. Serve.

SEAFOOD RISOTTO

SEAFOOD RISOTTO BEGINS WITH NATURALLY low-fat shellfish paired with Arborio rice and either broth or fumet (a concentrated fish stock). So why does this potentially healthy, minimalist dish get such a bad rap? First of all, it tends to entail a lot of work, traditionally demanding 30 minutes of constant stirring to produce evenly cooked, ultra-creamy rice. Hot broth is ladled into the pot in small amounts while the cook stirs almost constantly until the rice is tender but still maintains a slight bite. Time-consuming, yes, but unhealthy? Unfortunately, in many seafood risotto recipes the "creaminess" of the rice's naturally occurring starch is also buoyed with heavy cream and high-fat cheeses. My goal was to create a rich-tasting weeknight seafood risotto without breaking the scale or the bank. I also wanted to keep dirty dishes to a minimum and develop a more hands-off approach.

I started with streamlining the method. Medium-grain Arborio rice is the best choice for risotto since it is higher than both short- and long-grain rice in an important starch called amylopectin, which gives risotto its creamy consistency. Stirring hot broth into the rice releases the surface starches, which dissolve into and thicken the broth. Since stirring is essential to this technique, I knew that eliminating it entirely wasn't an option, but I was hopeful I could reduce the amount of hands-on time required. I tried testing some almost-no-stir methods, but their specific liquid requirements made it impossible to add raw seafood directly to the pot, and I knew I wanted an easy one-pot meal. To see how infrequently I could add broth and stir and still get the creamy results I desired, I made dozens of batches of risotto, tweaking both factors.

Surprisingly, batches stirred roughly half of the time were hard to distinguish from those stirred constantly.

In the end, I settled on a technique of adding almost half of the liquid at the beginning and stirring infrequently for the first 13 to 17 minutes. Then I added the remaining broth in 1-cup increments and stirred the rice frequently (but not constantly) for the final 13 to 17 minutes. This gave me flawlessly creamy risotto with significantly less tedious pot watching.

Next I needed to tackle the broth. For my simple dish, homemade seafood broth was out of the question. While some seafood risotto recipes opt for plain water, tasters found the resulting risotto thin and bland. Substituting bottled clam juice for a portion of the water was more promising, offering a welcome briny hit, but the broth still lacked depth. Stepping away from the sea for a moment, I tried substituting store-bought low-sodium chicken broth for some of the water. This was certainly my richest batch yet, but tasters were missing a certain seafood essence.

At this point, a fellow test cook pointed out that since I knew I wanted my risotto to include shrimp, I could use their shells to add the missing seafood flavor to the broth. I tried simmering the broth with the shells from ½ pound of shrimp, along with onion, bay leaves, and peppercorns (a few classic broth additions). Simmering the shells for just 15 minutes infused the broth with a light but distinct seafood flavor that, along with the clam juice, gave the risotto briny depth. Final touches of saffron and drained diced tomatoes added color and acidity to the broth.

Before I started cooking the rice, I built up some flavor by sautéing an onion and some garlic and thyme in a little butter. A single minced anchovy added with the aromatics lent some body and a savory richness. I added the rice to the skillet and toasted it for a few minutes to give the risotto a delicious nutty flavor before adding some dry white wine and the broth.

Next I focused on which seafood I wanted to use. In addition to the shrimp, I decided to include squid, which tasters liked for its mild flavor and gentle bite. I cut the bodies into rings but left the tentacles whole to showcase their unique texture and visual appeal. In the end, I excluded clams and mussels (their steaming would require another pot and I wanted to keep the risotto simple), but scallops lent their trademark gentle brininess and richness and were easy to prepare. I chose small bay scallops over large sea scallops because they

NOTES FROM THE TEST KITCHEN

PREPARING SCALLOPS

The small, crescent-shaped muscle that is sometimes attached to scallops will be incredibly tough when cooked. Use your fingers to peel it away from side of each scallop before cooking.

cooked quickly and fit nicely on a fork with a bite of rice. Now I just needed to determine when to add the seafood to the pot.

I tested a number of recipes that called for adding the seafood to the rice as it stood off the heat for a few minutes. Unfortunately, I found that this method often produced undercooked shrimp and squid. Instead, heating the seafood in the pot for about three minutes while stirring frequently produced the best results, allowing every bite of seafood to cook through evenly. Then I just let the pot sit off the heat for five minutes until the risotto was slightly thickened and the seafood was perfectly cooked. As a final touch, I stirred in a tablespoon of butter for richness as well as parsley and lemon juice for brightness.

With just a few labor- and pot-saving techniques, I now had a deceptively light, easy-to-prepare seafood risotto.

—CHRISTIE MORRISON, *America's Test Kitchen Books*

Light Seafood Risotto

SERVES 6

Do not buy peeled shrimp; you will need the shrimp shells in order to make the broth. You can substitute ½ pound sea scallops, quartered, for the bay scallops. We recommend buying "dry" scallops, which don't have chemical additives and taste better than "wet." Dry scallops will look ivory or pinkish; "wet" scallops are bright white. If using wet scallops, soak them in a solution of 1 quart water, ¼ cup lemon juice, and 2 tablespoons salt for 30 minutes, then rinse and pat dry before step 5.

BROTH

- 3 (8-ounce) bottles clam juice
- 3 cups water
- 2 cups low-sodium chicken broth
- 1 (14.5-ounce) can diced tomatoes, drained
- Shells from ½ pound shrimp (see risotto ingredients)
- 1 onion, chopped coarse
- 10 black peppercorns
- 2 bay leaves
- ⅛ teaspoon saffron threads, crumbled
- Hot water

RISOTTO

- 2 tablespoons unsalted butter
- 1 onion, chopped fine
- Salt and pepper
- 5 garlic cloves, minced
- 1 teaspoon minced fresh thyme or ¼ teaspoon dried
- 1 anchovy fillet, rinsed and minced
- 2 cups Arborio rice
- 1 cup dry white wine
- ½ pound medium-large shrimp (31 to 40 per pound), peeled and deveined (see page 9) (shells reserved)
- ½ pound small bay scallops, tendons removed
- ½ pound squid, bodies cut crosswise into ½-inch rings, tentacles left whole
- 1 tablespoon lemon juice
- 2 tablespoons minced fresh parsley

1. FOR THE BROTH: Combine all ingredients except water in large saucepan over medium-high heat and bring to boil. Reduce heat to medium-low and simmer for 15 minutes. Strain broth through fine-mesh strainer into large measuring cup; discard solids. (You should have 8 cups broth; if not, add hot water as needed.) Wipe out saucepan and transfer stock to clean saucepan; return saucepan to lowest possible heat to keep broth warm.

2. FOR THE RISOTTO: Melt 1 tablespoon butter in Dutch oven over medium-low heat. Add onion and ¼ teaspoon salt, cover, and cook, stirring occasionally, until softened, 8 to 10 minutes. Stir in garlic, thyme, and anchovy and cook until fragrant, about 30 seconds. Increase heat to medium, stir in rice, and cook, stirring frequently, until grains are translucent around edges, about 3 minutes.

3. Stir in wine and cook, stirring frequently, until fully absorbed, 2 to 3 minutes. Stir in 3½ cups warm broth. Bring to simmer and cook, stirring about every 3 minutes, until broth is absorbed and bottom of pot is dry, 13 to 17 minutes.

4. Continue to cook rice, stirring frequently and adding more hot broth, 1 cup at a time, every few minutes as pan bottom turns dry, until rice is cooked through but still somewhat firm in center, 13 to 17 minutes.

5. Stir in shrimp, scallops, and squid and continue to cook, stirring frequently, until seafood is just cooked through, about 3 minutes longer. Remove pot from heat, cover, and let stand for 5 minutes until risotto is slightly thickened.

6. Stir in remaining 1 tablespoon butter, lemon juice, and parsley and season with salt and pepper to taste. If desired, add remaining broth, ¼ cup at a time, to loosen consistency of risotto before serving.

CLAMS WITH ISRAELI COUSCOUS, LEEKS, AND TOMATOES

WHENEVER I EAT CLAMS AT A RESTAURANT, I wonder why I don't cook them at home more often. Flavorful, economical, and easy to cook, clams infuse any dish they grace with their sweet, slightly salty, fresh-from-the-sea flavor. I wanted to turn all the juicy brininess of a bowl of steamed clams into a complete weeknight meal, but I needed to find the perfect starch to round out the meal.

Bored by the old standby of linguine with clams and thinking that the brothy base I envisioned would be too sloppy to twirl, I looked around the test kitchen pantry for a more suitable (and perhaps more interesting) starch. Rice and couscous were closer to the size and shape I wanted, but they still didn't seem quite substantial enough. Then I spied a bag of Israeli couscous. Also known as pearl couscous, Israeli couscous is larger than traditional couscous (with grains about the size of a caper) and is not precooked like its bread-crumb-size brethren. Excited about my find, I tested Israeli couscous using both the rice pilaf method (toasting the grains in fat, then simmering in liquid for 15 minutes) and the pasta method (boiling the couscous in 2 quarts of salted water until tender). While both tests were successful, I preferred the pasta method because it produced well-separated grains with mostly hands-off cooking. Best of all, the couscous was fully cooked in just 8 minutes.

Satisfied with my Israeli couscous, I focused on the rest of the dish. Most recipes for clams begin with an aromatic base and just enough liquid to provide steam. Tasters liked small clams that were easy to eat in one bite, so I went with littleneck clams, the smallest variety. The clams, which remain closed while they're alive, open their shells as they cook and release their plentiful liquid into the pot to mingle with the other flavors.

While it seemed that the world was my oyster (or clam) when it came to seasonings, I wanted to avoid flavors that would overpower the mild flavor of the clams. I started by sautéing onions, garlic, and thyme in melted butter, then added white wine as my liquid. In went the clams, and after about eight minutes in the covered pot, the clams opened. I stirred in the drained, cooked couscous and was … underwhelmed. While the texture of the couscous was satisfying, it was the flavor that disappointed.

The onion flavor was overwhelming, the wine was barely discernible, and the clams added little more than a briny background note. Switching to milder (and more colorful) leeks solved the onion problem, and I substituted dry vermouth for the white wine, hoping its more herbaceous, concentrated flavor would stand up to the aromatics and complement the fresh thyme and the brininess of the clams. Tasters were amazed at the difference in flavor, but the dish still needed a splash of acidity to balance the saltiness. Chopped fresh tomatoes were the answer, adding a hat trick of color, fresh flavor, and bright acidity to the mix. Plus, the juices released by the tomatoes during cooking provided additional flavor and steam for the clams.

A sprinkling of parsley added freshness to the finished dish, which came together in well under an hour. Not quite a stew, but brothy enough to warrant a bowl, my clams and couscous dish was just the kind of comfort food I could turn to again and again.

—REBECCAH MARSTERS, *America's Test Kitchen Books*

Clams with Israeli Couscous, Leeks, and Tomatoes
SERVES 4

Small quahogs or cherrystones are good alternatives to the littleneck clams. We like the punch that dry vermouth adds to this dish, but dry white wine will also work well. Be sure to use Israeli couscous in this dish; regular (or fine-grain) couscous won't work here.

    2   cups Israeli couscous
        Salt and pepper
    2   tablespoons unsalted butter
    1½ pounds leeks, white and light green parts only, halved lengthwise, sliced thin, and washed thoroughly
    3   garlic cloves, minced
    1   tablespoon minced fresh thyme
    1   cup dry vermouth or dry white wine
    3   tomatoes, cored, seeded, and chopped
    4   pounds littleneck clams, scrubbed
    ½   cup minced fresh parsley

1. Bring 2 quarts water to boil in medium saucepan. Stir in couscous and 2 teaspoons salt and cook until al dente, about 8 minutes; drain.

2. Meanwhile, melt butter in Dutch oven over medium-high heat. Add leeks and cook until tender, about 4 minutes. Stir in garlic and thyme and cook until fragrant, about 30 seconds. Stir in vermouth and cook until slightly reduced, about 1 minute. Stir in tomatoes and clams and cook, covered, until clams open, 8 to 10 minutes.

3. Use slotted spoon to transfer clams to large serving bowl, discarding any that do not open. Stir drained couscous and parsley into pot with tomatoes and leeks and season with salt and pepper to taste. Portion couscous into bowls, top with clams, and serve.

VARIATION

Clams with Israeli Couscous, Chorizo, and Tomatoes

Add 6 ounces chorizo sausage, halved lengthwise and sliced thin, to pot with leeks.

CHAPTER 9

VEGETARIAN ENTRÉES

Wild Mushroom Ragu with Farro   224

Mushroom and Leek Galette with Gorgonzola   225

  Potato and Shallot Galette with Goat Cheese

  Butternut Squash Galette with Gruyère

Cheesy Polenta with Eggplant and Tomato Ragu   230

Easier Spinach Strudel   231

  Spinach Strudel with Olives and Goat Cheese

Lighter Cuban-Style Black Beans and Rice (Moros y Cristianos)   234

Thai Vegetable Green Curry with Jasmine Rice Cakes   236

WILD MUSHROOM RAGU WITH FARRO

TYPICALLY, A RAGU IS MADE WITH MEAT OR POULTRY; mushroom ragu, however, is a rich, well-seasoned stew made with a variety of mushrooms. Mushroom ragu is luxurious in texture with a hearty, deep brown color. Although this dish is wonderful when prepared with an assortment of exotic wild mushrooms, I wanted my recipe to include only commonly available varieties. I also wanted my version to be vegetarian, so I would need to find a way to amplify the mushrooms' rich, meaty flavor to make it hearty and satisfying.

I began my tests with the mushrooms. My goal was to include mushrooms that offered variety in flavor, texture, and appearance. To start, I focused on portobello, cremini, white, shiitake, and oyster mushrooms, all of which are typically found fresh in most supermarkets. Cremini are baby portobellos, and testing revealed that their flavors were similar enough that including both was unnecessary. I opted for portobellos since they are meatier in texture and can be cut into thick, hearty slices. I found that white, shiitake, and oyster mushrooms all worked well in the ragu, but an assortment of all three was best for complex flavor.

Sautéing the mushrooms until their liquid had evaporated and they were browned and tender developed lots of flavor, but it took nearly 20 extra minutes at the stovetop. I wondered if I could simplify and speed up the process by using the microwave. After just eight hands-off minutes in the microwave, the mushrooms were tender and had released their excess liquid, which intensified their flavor. And I could get started on the rest of the ragu while they cooked, saving me even more time. I simply drained the mushrooms—reserving their potent liquid to add back to the ragu later on—and sautéed them for a few minutes until they were dry and lightly browned for richly flavorful mushrooms in half the time.

Porcini mushrooms are rarely found fresh in this country, but they are available dried. They are treasured throughout Italy and France for their smoky, pungent, and earthy flavor. Tasters loved the intense flavor they added to the ragu. Because they are so potent, I needed just ½ ounce. Sautéing the porcini until lightly browned brought out their complex flavor even further.

With my mushrooms chosen, I turned my attention to the aromatics. I tried carrot, celery, and onion, but the carrot and celery looked out of place in this stew, and their flavors and textures took away from the mushrooms rather than enhancing them. I shifted my focus to alliums, testing onions, shallots, garlic, and leeks. The leeks were too delicate in flavor and texture, and shallots turned out to be too subtle as well. Onions, however, stood up nicely to the assortment of assertive mushroom flavors. Garlic added a pungent note and some depth.

My ragu thus far was pretty good, but it needed some wine to cut through the richness. I found that white wine didn't have enough muscle to brighten the flavors, and red wine was too strong and sharp. Next I tried dry Madeira and dry sherry. These fortified wines are often found in mushroom ragus, and testing revealed why: They are stronger in flavor than white wine but not as overpowering as red wine, adding just the right amount of bright flavor to balance the stew.

Many mushroom ragu recipes also include tomatoes for brightness and acidity. I tried both canned diced tomatoes and tomato paste. The tomato paste dulled both the flavor and color of the stew, so I stuck with the canned tomatoes, which added some color and sweetness and just the right amount of liquid.

After lightly browning the onion and mushrooms and cooking the garlic until just fragrant, I deglazed the pot with the Madeira and the reserved mushroom juices, then added the tomatoes and simmered the stew until it thickened, which took just eight minutes. As for herbs, the clean, grassy flavor of parsley gave the stew a hit of freshness, and woodsy thyme paired perfectly with the mushrooms. The thyme went into the pot along with the garlic, and I garnished the stew with the parsley just before serving

---

NOTES FROM THE TEST KITCHEN

OUR FAVORITE BALSAMIC VINEGAR
Traditional balsamic vinegar takes a minimum of 12 years to make and costs an astonishing $60 per ounce. We were happy to discover that you don't need to book a flight to Italy or spend a fortune for this ingredient; we found a great balsamic at our local supermarket. Tasters thought **Lucini Gran Riserva Balsamico** had a "sweet, nuanced flavor" and most closely resembled traditional balsamic vinegar with its balance of sweet and tart and its viscosity.

But while my ragu was delicious on its own, tasters wanted a grain to accompany it to make it a complete meal. After scanning the pantry shelves, I landed on farro. Farro is a whole-grain form of wheat popular in Italy and traditionally cooked in the same manner as Arborio rice. It has a slightly sweet, nutty flavor and chewy texture perfect for pairing with a ragu. Although it can be cooked in water, tasters preferred vegetable broth; its sweetness balanced the earthiness of the mushrooms. All I had to do was simmer the farro and broth gently for about 20 minutes while I made the ragu.

The nutty farro grains topped with my savory, rich mushroom ragu made for a seriously satisfying meal in well under an hour—and I didn't have to go foraging to put it on the table.

—SUZANNAH MCFERRAN,
America's Test Kitchen Books

Wild Mushroom Ragu with Farro

SERVES 4

For the best flavor, we prefer to use a combination of white, shiitake, and oyster mushrooms; however, you can choose just one or two varieties if you like. The woody stems of shiitakes are unpleasant to eat, so be sure to remove them. Consider drizzling individual portions with good balsamic vinegar before serving.

FARRO

1½   cups farro
3½   cups vegetable broth
       Salt and pepper

RAGU

1   pound portobello mushroom caps, halved and
       sliced ½ inch thick
18   ounces assorted mushrooms, trimmed and halved
       if small or quartered if large
1   onion, chopped fine
2   tablespoons extra-virgin olive oil
½   ounce dried porcini mushrooms, rinsed and minced
3   garlic cloves, minced
1   teaspoon minced fresh thyme or ¼ teaspoon dried
¼   cup dry Madeira
1   (14.5-ounce) can diced tomatoes, drained and chopped
2   tablespoons minced fresh parsley
       Salt and pepper

1. FOR THE FARRO: Simmer farro and broth together in large saucepan over medium heat until farro is tender and creamy, 20 to 25 minutes. Season with salt and pepper to taste; cover to keep warm.

2. FOR THE RAGU: Meanwhile, microwave portobello and assorted mushrooms in covered bowl until tender, 6 to 8 minutes. Drain, reserving mushroom juices.

3. Cook onion, oil, and porcini together in Dutch oven over medium-high heat until softened and lightly browned, 5 to 7 minutes. Stir in drained mushrooms and cook, stirring often, until mushrooms are dry and lightly browned, 4 to 6 minutes.

4. Stir in garlic and thyme and cook until fragrant, about 30 seconds. Stir in Madeira and reserved mushroom juices, scraping up any browned bits. Stir in tomatoes and simmer gently until sauce is slightly thickened, about 8 minutes. Off heat, stir in parsley and season with salt and pepper to taste. Top individual portions of farro with mushroom ragu and serve.

MUSHROOM AND LEEK GALETTE WITH GORGONZOLA

COMPARED WITH MORE FORMAL TARTS BAKED IN fluted pans, a free-form tart's beauty lies in its rustic simplicity. You roll out the dough, add the filling, and then draw in the edges of the dough to form a pleated crust. This method requires far less effort than precisely fitting pastry into a molded pan, and it looks just as attractive.

But when it comes to savory applications, free-form tarts can have their flaws. Many recipes simply borrow a standard pastry dough intended for fruit and swap in vegetables. After trying a few such versions, I realized that for vegetables, this wouldn't work. Vegetables have far less of the pectin that holds on to moisture and binds a fruit filling together, so they are particularly prone to leaking liquid into the crust or falling apart when the tart is sliced. What's more, vegetables don't pack the concentrated, bright flavors of fruit. To make up for these deficiencies, I needed a crust that was extra-sturdy and boasted a complex flavor of its own. I also wanted a robust-tasting filling with enough sticking power to hold together when cut.

I started by putting together a basic all-butter pie dough, trading half of the white flour for whole wheat.

The earthy flavor of whole-wheat flour, I hoped, would complement the savory filling, and its coarser consistency would turn out a pleasantly hearty crumb. I pulsed the dry ingredients and butter in the food processor a few times, then dumped the mixture into a bowl, added a little water, and stirred it until thoroughly combined. To ensure that the butter stayed firm enough to leave air pockets as it melted in the oven, creating flakiness, I chilled the dough for about an hour before rolling it out.

The good news: The butter and all of that whole-wheat flour added up to a great-tasting crust. The bad news: It had none of the flaky yet sturdy texture that I'd been looking for. Instead, it was crumbly and dense. And I was pretty sure I knew why. All doughs, pastry or otherwise, get their structure from gluten, the network of proteins that forms when flour is mixed with water. The challenge when working with whole-wheat flour is that it contains the fibrous outer layers of the wheat berry, the bran and germ (which are stripped away in white flour, leaving only the inner core, or endosperm). Since the bran and germ contain none of the gluten-forming proteins found in the endosperm, the more whole-wheat flour there is in a dough, the heavier and more prone to falling apart it will be.

To strengthen the dough, I'd need to cut back on the whole-wheat flour, but 25 percent was as low as I could go before I lost too much of the whole wheat's nice nutty taste. And there was another problem: As the proportion of white flour, and therefore gluten, increased, the dough became tough. I didn't think I was overworking the dough (a typical cause). Then it occurred to me that the problem might be water. Because the bran and germ need more water than the endosperm to become fully hydrated, I'd added a little extra to the dough. I realized that the extra liquid was being absorbed by the white flour's gluten-forming proteins, thus creating more gluten and making the dough more susceptible to overworking. To reduce toughness, then, I'd need to either cut back on the water or find an even gentler way to handle the dough.

I knew that acids can weaken the bonds that form between gluten strands, so I decided to try adding vinegar. I found that a teaspoon—the most I could add before the dough tasted too vinegary—did tenderize it a little, but not enough. What if I took a hands-off approach to mixing and let the flour absorb the water on its own? I hoped that partially mixing the dough so that not all of the flour was mixed in and then letting it rest before rolling it out might allow the water to migrate to drier parts and produce pastry that was workable—but not overworked.

I gave it a shot, just barely mixing the dry and wet ingredients together and then chilling the dough briefly. When I pulled the dough out an hour or so later, it was clear that I was on to something: Without any effort on my part, most of the dry flour had disappeared; even better, the dough was remarkably supple but not floppy. I gently nudged it together and then rolled it out and baked it at 375 degrees. The result: a tender, moist, and decently flaky crust without the least bit of toughness.

But the perfectionist in me wouldn't settle for decently flaky. I wanted a crust with the long, striated layers in puff pastry, which would also make the crust more resistant to splitting when sliced. But the hundreds of layers in puff pastry are created through a painstaking process of rolling and folding the dough, chilling it in between. Curious to see what would happen if I mimicked this approach in a more modest way, I dumped the rested dough onto the counter, rolled it into a rectangle, and folded it into thirds, like a business letter. I repeated the process just twice more. The results were even better than I'd hoped: The increase in layers rendered the crust wonderfully flaky and less apt to shatter when cut.

Working with a sturdy crust, however, didn't mean that I could just throw in the vegetables raw. The shiitake mushrooms and leeks I'd chosen for a hearty yet fresh and springy filling still leached far too much moisture, rendering the crust soggy. Fortunately, sautéing the leeks took only a few minutes and helped concentrate their flavor as well as reduce their liquid. For the mushrooms, I hastened the evaporation process by heating them in the microwave. To introduce rich, complex flavor and not too much moisture, I worked in a hefty dollop of crème fraîche and some Dijon mustard and layered a few handfuls of crumbled Gorgonzola between the vegetables just before baking.

With its hearty filling bound by a buttery crust, this rustic tart amounted to a perfect cold-weather meal— one so good I'd be tempted to make it year-round.

—ANDREW JANJIGIAN, *Cook's Illustrated*

MUSHROOM AND LEEK GALETTE WITH GORGONZOLA

Mushroom and Leek Galette with Gorgonzola

SERVES 6

Cutting a few small holes in the dough prevents it from lifting off the pan as it bakes. A pizza stone helps to crisp the crust but is not essential. An overturned baking sheet can be used in place of the pizza stone.

DOUGH

- 1¼ cups (6¼ ounces) all-purpose flour
- ½ cup (2¾ ounces) whole-wheat flour
- 1 tablespoon sugar
- ¾ teaspoon salt
- 10 tablespoons unsalted butter, cut into ½-inch pieces and chilled
- 7 tablespoons ice water
- 1 teaspoon white vinegar

FILLING

- 1¼ pounds shiitake mushrooms, stemmed and sliced thin
- 5 teaspoons olive oil
- 1 pound leeks, white and light green parts only, sliced ½ inch thick and washed thoroughly (3 cups)
- 1 teaspoon minced fresh thyme
- 2 tablespoons crème fraîche
- 1 tablespoon Dijon mustard
  Salt and pepper
- 3 ounces Gorgonzola cheese, crumbled (¾ cup)

- 1 large egg, lightly beaten
  Kosher salt
- 2 tablespoons minced fresh parsley

1. FOR THE DOUGH: Pulse flours, sugar, and salt together in food processor until combined, 2 to 3 pulses. Add butter and pulse until it forms pea-size pieces, about 10 pulses. Transfer mixture to medium bowl.

2. Sprinkle water and vinegar over mixture. With rubber spatula, use folding motion to mix until loose, shaggy mass forms with some dry flour remaining (do not overwork). Transfer mixture to center of large sheet of plastic wrap, press gently into rough 4-inch square, and wrap tightly. Refrigerate for at least 45 minutes.

3. Transfer dough to lightly floured counter. Roll into 11 by 8-inch rectangle with short side of rectangle parallel to edge of counter. Using bench scraper, bring bottom third of dough up, then fold upper third over it, folding like business letter into 8 by 4-inch rectangle. Turn dough 90 degrees counterclockwise. Roll out dough again into 11 by 8-inch rectangle and fold into thirds again. Turn dough 90 degrees counterclockwise and repeat rolling and folding into thirds. After last fold, fold dough in half to create 4-inch square. Press top of dough gently to seal. Wrap in plastic and refrigerate for at least 45 minutes or up to 2 days.

4. FOR THE FILLING: Microwave mushrooms in covered bowl until just tender, 3 to 5 minutes. Transfer to colander to drain; return to bowl. Meanwhile, heat 1 tablespoon oil in 12-inch skillet over medium heat until shimmering. Add leeks and thyme, cover, and cook, stirring occasionally, until leeks are tender and beginning to brown, 5 to 7 minutes. Transfer to bowl with mushrooms. Stir in crème fraîche and mustard. Season with salt and pepper to taste. Set aside.

5. Adjust oven rack to lower-middle position, place pizza stone on rack, and heat oven to 400 degrees. Line rimmed baking sheet with parchment paper. Remove dough from refrigerator and let stand at room temperature for 15 to 20 minutes. Roll out on generously floured (up to ¼ cup) counter to 14-inch circle about ⅛ inch thick. (Trim edges as needed to form rough circle.) Transfer dough to prepared baking sheet. With tip of paring knife, cut five ¼-inch circles in dough (one at center and four evenly spaced halfway from center to edge of dough). Brush top of dough with 1 teaspoon oil.

6. Spread half of filling evenly over dough, leaving 2-inch border around edge. Sprinkle with half of Gorgonzola, cover with remaining filling, and top with remaining Gorgonzola. Drizzle remaining 1 teaspoon oil over filling. Grasp 1 edge of dough and fold up outer 2 inches over filling. Repeat around circumference of tart, overlapping dough every 2 to 3 inches; gently pinch pleated dough to secure but do not press dough into filling. Brush dough with egg and sprinkle evenly with kosher salt.

7. Lower oven temperature to 375 degrees. Bake until crust is deep golden brown and filling is beginning to brown, 35 to 45 minutes. Cool tart on baking sheet on wire rack for 10 minutes. Using offset or wide metal spatula, loosen tart from parchment and carefully slide tart off parchment onto cutting board. Sprinkle with parsley, cut into wedges, and serve.

THE BEST OVEN MITTS

The obvious purpose of a good oven mitt is to protect your hands from hot surfaces. But besides being heat-resistant, it should also be comfortable, durable, and allow the cook to easily maneuver piping-hot items around the kitchen. Looking for one that would fit the bill, we tested eight mitts by moving hot sheet trays loaded with baking cookies, scorching-hot oven racks, and full casserole dishes that had just come out of a 450-degree oven.

Our favorite mitt was the **Kool-Tek 15-Inch Oven Mitt** (left) by KatchAll, $44.95. Made with layers of Nomex (a fireproof fabric) and Kevlar (which is found in bullet-resistant body armor) for heat protection, this mitt won fans for heat resistance and all-around dependability. Plus, it came out of the washing machine looking as good as new. Testers also liked the **OrkaPlus Silicone Oven Mitt with Cotton Lining** (right), which performed almost on a par with our winner. Its removable cotton-terry lining kept our hands at a comfortable temperature, and it laundered perfectly. At $14.95, it's our Best Buy. (See page 310 for more information about our testing results.)

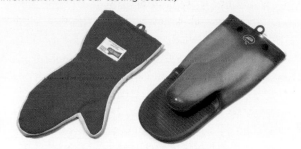

PLEATING A FREE-FORM TART

It's surprisingly simple to create pleated edges around free-form tarts.

Gently grasp 1 edge of dough and make 2-inch-wide fold over filling. Lift and fold another segment of dough over first fold to form pleat. Repeat every 2 to 3 inches.

DON'T DOUBT YOUR DOUGH

Barely mixing the dough and then resting it in the refrigerator hydrates the flour while minimizing gluten development, for a more tender crust. Don't worry if the dough looks loose and shaggy—it's supposed to.

SHAGGY DOUGH

VARIATIONS

Potato and Shallot Galette with Goat Cheese

Substitute 1 pound Yukon Gold potatoes, sliced ¼ inch thick, for mushrooms and increase microwave cooking time to 4 to 8 minutes. Substitute ¼ pound thinly sliced shallots for leeks and rosemary for thyme. Increase amount of crème fraîche to ¼ cup and substitute ¼ cup chopped pitted kalamata olives and 1 teaspoon finely grated lemon zest for Dijon mustard. Substitute goat cheese for Gorgonzola.

Butternut Squash Galette with Gruyère

1. Microwave 6 ounces baby spinach and ¼ cup water in bowl until spinach is wilted and decreased in volume by half, 3 to 4 minutes. Using potholders, remove bowl from microwave and keep covered for 1 minute. Carefully remove plate and transfer spinach to colander. Gently press spinach with rubber spatula to release excess liquid. Transfer spinach to cutting board and roughly chop. Return spinach to colander and press again with rubber spatula; set aside.

2. Substitute 1¼ pounds butternut squash, peeled and cut into ½-inch cubes, for mushrooms and increase microwave cooking time to about 8 minutes. Substitute 1 thinly sliced red onion for leeks and ½ teaspoon minced fresh oregano for thyme. Substitute 1 teaspoon sherry vinegar for Dijon mustard and stir reserved spinach and 3 ounces shredded Gruyère cheese into filling along with crème fraîche and vinegar in step 4. Omit Gorgonzola.

THE BEST CANNED WHOLE TOMATOES

San Marzano tomatoes are often praised as being the best canned tomatoes—bright, sweet, and tangy, with meat that's plush and soft but doesn't dissolve in long-simmered sauce—so we held a taste-off: San Marzanos versus everything else. We sampled 10 brands—three labeled San Marzano and the remaining seven a mix of Italian, Canadian, and American products—plain, in a quick-cooked tomato sauce, and in a slow-simmered version.

Overall, tasters liked tomatoes that had higher levels of sugar balanced by a lot of acidity. Surprisingly, the San Marzano tomatoes were either not sweet enough or too sweet and lacking the acidity necessary to counter the sweetness. When it came to texture, we liked tomatoes with a firm yet tender bite, even after a lengthy simmer. Tomatoes that were rubbery or broke down completely and became mushy scored poorly. Again, the San Marzano tomatoes fell behind, with domestic brands performing better and retaining a firmer texture due to being treated with calcium chloride; the imported brands did not use this additive.

In the end, our favorite brand was domestic. **Muir Glen Organic Whole Peeled Tomatoes** won tasters over with their bold acidity, appealing sweetness, and firm bite. These tomatoes were "sweet in a natural way," "vibrant," and had a "nice firm texture" that held up even after hours of simmering. (See page 299 for more information about our testing results.)

SHOPPING FOR INSTANT POLENTA

Whether topped with a vegetable ragu or a meaty braise, polenta is a delicious way to round out a meal. But cooking traditional polenta from scratch takes at least 30 minutes and requires constant attention, so when we're looking for an easier option, we swap in quick-cooking instant polenta, which takes just a few minutes to whip together. Just be aware that shopping for instant polenta can be confusing— it looks just like traditional polenta and is often identifiable only by the word "instant" in its title, which in our experience can be somewhat hidden.

CHEESY POLENTA WITH EGGPLANT AND TOMATO RAGU

IT'S TRUE THAT POLENTA IS NOTHING MORE THAN dried, ground corn cooked with a little water or broth, but it's hard to beat that simple, homey appeal and nutty flavor. I'm a big fan of traditional soft, porridgelike polenta embellished with a little butter or cheese for richness and flavor. And it's even better topped with a stew or hearty ragu to create a satisfying, wintry meal. That is exactly what I was envisioning for this recipe— with a few stipulations. I wanted this polenta and ragu meal to come together fast, and I wanted it to be vegetarian. I set out to see what I could do.

I started with the polenta; made the traditional way, it can be fussy and time-consuming: Coarse cornmeal is slowly added to boiling salted water and stirred constantly (to prevent scorching) for 30 to 40 minutes. After ten minutes, you'll feel like you've been arm wrestling Arnold Schwarzenegger. For an easy weeknight meal, I wanted to prepare both polenta and topping in less than 30 minutes.

I always raise an eyebrow when I hear the word *instant*, but I thought if I was going to find a way to make a quick polenta and ragu dinner, instant polenta was worth a shot. Instant polenta, like quick-cooking grits and instant rice, has been partially cooked, then dried. So all I needed to do was reconstitute it with boiling water. I gave it a try, and I was pleasantly surprised. While the instant didn't taste quite the same as traditional polenta, it had good flavor and took only five minutes to cook over medium heat. I had to whisk constantly, but given the short cooking time, I didn't mind. Once the pan was off the heat, I stirred in some Parmesan (a full ¾ cup to ensure good cheesy flavor), salt, and pepper. It couldn't have been easier.

With the polenta sorted out, I moved on to the topping. I knew I wanted a hearty vegetarian ragu, but from there the options were endless. I was particularly drawn to the idea of using eggplant. Its nutty flavor is a classic pairing with polenta, and it's a vegetable that adds heft and meatiness to vegetarian dishes. After cooking a few batches of the vegetable, which I cut into manageable ¾-inch chunks, I found that the key to achieving good eggplant flavor and texture was to brown the pieces well in a generous amount of oil (with very little stirring so it wouldn't fall apart) and cook until just tender. I started it over medium-high heat and didn't touch the eggplant until it had been in the skillet for at least five minutes and was just beginning to brown on the first side. Only then did I reduce the heat and stir occasionally, cooking it for another five minutes until it was tender and browned all over. I then added a couple of cloves of garlic for depth and bite and a can of whole tomatoes I crushed myself (which tasters preferred over looser canned crushed tomatoes) for an acidic, bright component that would round out the sauce. I let this mixture simmer for a bit, seasoned it, and gave it a try.

Tasters were pleased but thought that the ragu could use even more garlicky oomph, so I upped the garlic to three cloves for an easy fix. My ragu was now hearty and filling, with bright, balanced flavor and just enough bite. Since polenta will stiffen as it sits, I found it was best to make the topping first, cover it to keep warm and set it aside, then make the polenta. To serve, I simply topped bowls of polenta with a generous helping of eggplant and tomato ragu. Garnished with a bit of fresh basil and some extra Parmesan, not only was this polenta dish rich and flavorful, but I could get it on the table in just 30 minutes.

—CHRISTIE MORRISON, *America's Test Kitchen Books*

Cheesy Polenta with Eggplant and Tomato Ragu

SERVES 4

Be sure to use instant polenta here; traditional polenta requires a different cooking method. Leaving the skin on the eggplant helps keep the pieces intact during cooking.

RAGU

- 1 **pound eggplant, cut into ¾-inch chunks**
- ¼ **cup olive oil**
   Salt and pepper
- 1 **(28-ounce) can whole peeled tomatoes**
- 3 **garlic cloves, minced**

POLENTA

- 4 **cups water**
- 1 **cup instant polenta**
   Salt and pepper
- 1½ **ounces Parmesan cheese, grated (¾ cup), plus extra for serving**
- ⅓ **cup chopped fresh basil**

1. FOR THE RAGU: Cook eggplant, oil, and ¼ teaspoon salt in 12-inch nonstick skillet over medium-high heat until eggplant begins to brown, 5 to 7 minutes. Reduce heat to medium and cook, stirring occasionally, until eggplant is tender and lightly browned, about 5 minutes.

2. Meanwhile, pour tomatoes into bowl and crush with hands into 1-inch pieces.

3. Add garlic to skillet and cook until fragrant, about 30 seconds. Stir in tomatoes and simmer until slightly thickened, about 3 minutes. Season with salt and pepper to taste; cover and keep warm.

4. FOR THE POLENTA: Meanwhile, bring water to boil in large saucepan. Gradually whisk in polenta and ½ teaspoon salt. Cook over medium heat, whisking constantly, until very thick, about 5 minutes. Off heat, stir in Parmesan and season with salt and pepper to taste. Portion polenta into 4 individual serving bowls, top with eggplant mixture, and sprinkle with basil. Serve with extra Parmesan.

SPINACH STRUDEL

SPANAKOPITA, A TRADITIONAL GREEK DISH, IS A savory baked pie made of an aromatic mixture of spinach, onion, and feta cheese layered between sheets of buttered phyllo dough. The problem is, when you consider the time needed to assemble the filling, layer the delicate pastry, and bake it, you have quite a project on your hands—certainly not easy weeknight fare. Spinach pie, I thought, was definitely in need of an easier, quicker adaptation. Rather than layering the sheets of phyllo dough in a baking dish, I wondered if I could simply roll them up around the spinach mixture to form a crisp, flaky strudel that could easily be sliced and served. My savory strudel would have to be as good as the real thing and perfect for a weeknight dinner.

I decided to focus on perfecting the spinach filling before handling the phyllo dough, which is notoriously difficult to work with. Wilted fresh spinach and frozen spinach both worked well once chopped, so I went with frozen spinach, the more convenient option of the two. The only preparation required was thawing it and squeezing it dry in a kitchen towel before chopping. Feta cheese was a given for any version of spanakopita;

EASIER SPINACH STRUDEL

I crumbled it into small pieces before mixing it with the spinach so that it would be evenly distributed throughout the filling. I found that about ¾ cup added just enough tangy flavor without overwhelming the spinach.

For the aromatics, tasters liked the combination of scallions, garlic, and oregano the best. Grated nutmeg is commonly used in spinach pie, so I added a pinch to my strudel. Some toasted pine nuts provided a nice textural contrast to the soft filling, as did a handful of raisins, and fresh lemon juice added brightness and a clean flavor. However, at this point, some tasters were finding the filling a little dry and lacking richness. Although it's not traditional, I took the suggestion of a fellow test cook and folded in some ricotta cheese. Tasters agreed that the ricotta rounded out the flavors and gave the filling a moist, creamy texture.

Now ready to roll up my strudel, I prepared myself for working with the phyllo. Phyllo is notorious for drying out and cracking when left sitting out even briefly; to prevent this from happening, I kept the layers of phyllo covered with damp towels while I worked. Coating each sheet of phyllo with olive oil spray, rather than brushing on melted butter, sped up the layering process and still provided the additional moisture needed to help the sheets adhere to each other and promote a crispy texture once baked. I also tried to keep the number of layers to a minimum and found that 10 layers of phyllo formed an ample crust—any less and the strudel had a weak structure.

Traditional strudels are formed by mounding the filling in a log on the pastry, folding in the two sides, then rolling the whole thing up into a tight package. Working with my delicate dough of just a few layers of phyllo was challenging enough, and folding in the sides seemed like an extra step I could do without. I found that the easiest method worked best: I left the sides of the phyllo open as I rolled up the strudel and left a ½-inch margin at the ends to guard against leaking filling. As for baking, most recipes recommended about 40 minutes in a moderate oven—too long for my quick recipe. Instead, I tried baking the strudel at a higher temperature—400 degrees—for just 20 minutes. This crust was perfect: toothsome yet slightly yielding, with a golden exterior. Cut into attractive slices, this savory strudel is perfect when you're in the mood for something fast, fresh, and flavorful.

—SUZANNAH MCFERRAN,
America's Test Kitchen Books

NOTES FROM THE TEST KITCHEN

MAKING SPINACH STRUDEL

1. On clean counter, layer phyllo sheets on top of one another, coating each sheet thoroughly with olive oil spray (about 3 seconds per sheet).

2. Mound spinach mixture into narrow log along bottom edge of phyllo, leaving 2-inch border at bottom and ½-inch border on sides.

3. Fold bottom edge of dough over filling, then continue to roll dough around filling into tight log, leaving ends open.

4. Gently transfer strudel, seam side down, to prepared baking sheet. Lightly spray strudel with oil spray and cut four 1½-inch vents at diagonal across top.

THE BEST FETA CHEESE

Within the European Union, only cheese made in Greece from a mixture of sheep's and goat's milk can legally be called feta, but most of the feta in American supermarkets is made from pasteurized cow's milk that has been curdled, shaped into blocks, sliced (*feta* is Greek for slice), and steeped in brine. Feta can range from soft to semihard and has a tangy, salty flavor. It dries out quickly when removed from its brine, so always store it in the brine it's packed in (we do not recommend buying precrumbled feta, which is more expensive and lacking in flavor and texture). Our favorite brand is **Mt. Vikos Traditional Feta**, which tasters found to be flavorful yet mild and to have a pleasing "creamy, crumbly" texture.

Easier Spinach Strudel

SERVES 4

Make sure to squeeze the spinach thoroughly until it's dry, or else the filling will be wet and may leak. Be sure to use phyllo that is fully thawed or it will crack and flake apart when handled. To thaw frozen phyllo, let it sit either in the refrigerator overnight or on the counter for several hours.

10   ounces frozen spinach, thawed, squeezed dry, and chopped coarse

6   ounces (¾ cup) whole-milk ricotta cheese

3   ounces feta cheese, crumbled (¾ cup)

6   scallions, sliced thin

½   cup golden raisins

2   tablespoons pine nuts, toasted

2   tablespoons lemon juice

2   garlic cloves, minced

1   tablespoon minced fresh oregano

½   teaspoon ground nutmeg

     Salt and pepper

10   (14 by 9-inch) sheets phyllo, thawed

     Olive oil spray

1. Adjust oven rack to middle position and heat oven to 400 degrees. Mix spinach, ricotta, feta, scallions, raisins, pine nuts, lemon juice, garlic, oregano, and nutmeg together in bowl and season with salt and pepper to taste.

2. Line baking sheet with parchment paper. On clean counter, layer phyllo sheets on top of one another, coating each sheet thoroughly with oil spray. Mound spinach mixture into narrow log along bottom edge of phyllo, leaving 2-inch border at bottom and ½-inch border on sides. Fold bottom edge of dough over filling, then continue to roll dough around filling into tight log, leaving ends open.

3. Gently transfer strudel, seam side down, to prepared baking sheet. Lightly spray with oil spray and cut four 1½-inch vents at diagonal across top of strudel.

4. Bake strudel until golden, about 20 minutes, rotating sheet halfway through baking. Let cool on sheet for 5 minutes, then slice and serve.

VARIATION

Spinach Strudel with Olives and Goat Cheese
Substitute ½ cup chopped pitted kalamata olives for raisins and 3 ounces crumbled goat cheese for feta.

CUBAN-STYLE BLACK BEANS AND RICE

RICE AND BEANS IS A CLASSIC COMBINATION, BUT honestly, most incarnations are a bit mundane. And sadly, superior versions often contain so much fat that the dish loses its healthy appeal. But Cuban-style rice and beans, traditionally called *moros y cristianos*, has such an intensely appealing blend of aromatic vegetables and spices that I was loath to relegate it to guilty-pleasure food. Could I slim down this fantastic dish without losing its character?

I knew that part of the allure of moros y cristianos is the flavor and texture of the beans. Not exactly a last-minute recipe, the dish begins with dried black beans that soak overnight in a brine. Using dried beans is key to the success of the dish; canned beans lack the firm texture needed to withstand an extended cooking time. This dish is also unique in that the rice is cooked in the inky concentrated liquid left over from cooking the beans, which renders the grains just as flavorful. Clearly, any shortcut taken with the beans would prove detrimental to the flavor of the rice, so I decided to stay true to the traditional method in that regard.

Even before tinkering with the beans and rice, I needed to address the *sofrito*. This mixture of aromatic vegetables, spices, and herbs is a cornerstone of Latin cooking and the starting point for this dish. The specific elements in the mix differ from one Latin cuisine to another, but a Cuban sofrito usually consists of a trio of onion, green pepper, and garlic, typically flavored with cumin and oregano. Recipes also often include some sautéed pork (usually salt pork or bacon); the sofrito is cooked in the rendered fat. I understood the concept: Cooking the sofrito in the oil and rendered fat from the salt pork imparts a smoky, meaty flavor to the vegetables, and the browned pieces of pork add textural interest to the dish. But all that fat seemed unnecessary for an otherwise healthy recipe, and since the pork was the only ingredient preventing this dish from being vegetarian, I decided it had to go.

I needed to find an acceptable substitute for the pork, but I didn't want to lose the meaty flavor it provided altogether. So I turned to one of the test kitchen's favorite tricks for adding savory flavor: tomato paste. Just a tablespoon provided enough moisture and intense flavor to replace the pork entirely. And by sautéing the sofrito covered, I avoided the need to add any oil. Now I had a base with deep flavor but a fraction of the fat.

To build even more flavor, I tried amping up the intensity of the sofrito by increasing the spices and doubling the amount of vegetables, but these tests yielded problematic results. More spices gave the sofrito an intense but dusty flavor, and more sofrito weighed down the rice and beans in a kind of sofrito sludge. But I hit the bull's-eye when I cooked some of the sofrito vegetables (half an onion, half a green pepper, a garlic head, and bay leaves) with the beans, as they infused the beans with flavor, increasing the overall flavor of the dish.

A splash of red wine vinegar perked up the dish with bright acidity, and a sprinkling of thinly sliced scallions and a squeeze of lime brought it to life. While I had cut the meat and the fat from traditional moros y cristianos, I hadn't sacrificed the complex flavor. Even rabid fans of the classic version were clamoring for more, excited to enjoy its rich flavor without a trace of guilt.

—YVONNE RUPERTI, *America's Test Kitchen Books*

Lighter Cuban-Style Black Beans and Rice (Moros y Cristianos)
SERVES 6 TO 8

The success of the dish relies upon the texture and flavor of the black beans. Do not substitute canned beans for dried beans in this recipe. To quick salt-soak the beans, combine 2 quarts water, beans, and 1½ tablespoons salt in a Dutch oven and bring to a boil over high heat. Remove the pot from the heat, cover, and let stand for 1 hour. Drain and rinse well.

  Salt
1 cup dried black beans, picked over and rinsed
4 cups water
2 large green bell peppers, halved and seeded
1 large onion, halved at equator and peeled, root end left intact
1 head garlic, 5 cloves removed and minced, remainder of head halved at equator with skin left intact
2 bay leaves
1 tablespoon tomato paste

4 teaspoons ground cumin
1 tablespoon minced fresh oregano
1½ cups long-grain white rice, rinsed
2 tablespoons red wine vinegar
2 scallions, sliced thin
  Lime wedges

1. Dissolve 1½ tablespoons salt in 2 quarts cold water in large bowl or container. Add beans and soak at room temperature for at least 8 hours or up to 24 hours. Drain and rinse well.

2. In Dutch oven with tight-fitting lid, stir together drained beans, water, 1 pepper half, 1 onion half (with root end), halved garlic head, bay leaves, and ½ teaspoon salt. Bring to simmer over medium-high heat. Cover, reduce heat to low, and cook until beans are just soft, 30 to 40 minutes. Using tongs, remove pepper, onion, garlic, and bay leaves. Drain beans in colander set over large bowl, reserving 3 cups bean cooking liquid. (If you don't have enough bean cooking liquid, add water to equal 3 cups.) Do not wash Dutch oven.

3. Adjust oven rack to middle position and heat oven to 350 degrees. Cut remaining peppers and onion into 2-inch pieces and pulse in food processor until broken into rough ¼-inch pieces, about 8 pulses, scraping down sides of bowl as needed; set vegetables aside.

4. Cook chopped peppers and onion, tomato paste, cumin, and oregano, covered, in now-empty Dutch oven over medium-low heat until vegetables are softened, 6 to 8 minutes. Uncover, increase heat to medium, and continue to cook until water has evaporated and vegetables are beginning to brown, about 5 minutes

NOTES FROM THE TEST KITCHEN

OUR TOP PICK FOR DRIED BLACK BEANS
Canned beans may be convenient, but their flavor and texture never measure up to those of dried. We tested three brands of dried black beans by sampling them cooked plain and in Cuban-Style Black Beans and Rice. Surprisingly, the mail-order heirloom variety became blown out and mushy, but the beans from the two national supermarket brands emerged from the pot perfectly intact and creamy. Our favorite was **Goya Dried Black Beans,** which offered "nutty," "buttery" bean flavor and a reliably uniform texture.

longer. Add minced garlic and cook, stirring constantly, until fragrant, about 30 seconds. Add rice and stir to coat, about 30 seconds.

5. Stir in beans, reserved bean cooking liquid, vinegar, and ¼ teaspoon salt. Increase heat to medium-high and bring to simmer. Cover and transfer to oven. Bake until liquid is absorbed and rice is tender, about 30 minutes. Fluff with fork and let sit, uncovered, for 5 minutes. Serve, passing scallions and lime wedges separately.

THAI VEGETABLE GREEN CURRY WITH JASMINE RICE CAKES

MAKING A DEEPLY FLAVORED AND SATISFYING curry is hard. Making a curry that is flavorful, quick, and vegetarian is incredibly hard. But the appeal of the hearty, aromatic stew with long, slow-simmered flavor on a weeknight was undeniable; I had to find a way to make it work.

Thai curries blend a variety of tastes, textures, temperatures, and colors to work their magic. They almost always contain coconut milk, which not only blends with and carries the flavors but also forms the base of the sauce. The balance is tilted toward aromatics, which are added in the form of a paste usually consisting of garlic, ginger, shallots, lemon grass, kaffir lime leaves, shrimp paste, and chiles. These curry pastes can be quite involved and may require an hour of preparation. Fortunately, the curries themselves come together rather quickly and gently simmer for a short amount of time.

Since my goal was a weeknight meal, when time is of the essence, I would have to eschew the long preparation of making my own curry paste. Instead, I would try a store-bought paste and balance the flavors with additional ingredients as needed. Thai chile pastes are available in green curry or red curry; green curry paste is made with fresh green chiles, and red curry paste is made with dried red chiles. I opted for green curry paste, thinking that its fresher, brighter flavor would be better suited to my vegetarian dish. I started by sautéing the curry paste in hot oil to bloom and intensify its flavor, then whisked in the coconut milk. The thick gravy was delightfully unctuous (the word *curry* comes from the Tamil word *kari*, which means "sauce" or

"gravy"), but the richness of the coconut milk muted the flavors of the jarred curry paste. The spicy flavors of garlic, ginger, and chiles came through, but the more delicate flavor of kaffir lime was lacking.

Since making a trip to the Asian market wasn't an option, I tried to mimic the flavor with fresh lime juice, adding it at the end of cooking to keep the flavor bright. Tasters were almost satisfied, but something was still missing. Then it hit me: sweetness. I recalled that many Thai recipes use palm sugar to balance the flavors. Since its rich, caramel-like sweetness is similar to that of brown sugar, I added a tablespoon to the curry. Finally, the flavors came into line.

Next, I focused on the vegetables. I wanted this vegetarian dish to make no apologies; it needed to be rich and hearty. My goal was to pack as many different textures and colors into the dish as possible. Looking for

NOTES FROM THE TEST KITCHEN

CURRY PASTE AND COCONUT MILK

Curry paste, which can be either green or red, is a handy ingredient for adding deep, well-rounded flavor to Thai curries. It is made from a mix of lemon grass, kaffir lime leaves, shrimp paste, ginger, garlic, chiles, and other spices. It is the type of chile that gives a curry paste its color. Fresh green Thai chiles are used to make green curry paste, while dried red Thai chiles are used to make red curry paste. It's not surprising that making curry paste at home can be quite a chore. We have found that the store-bought variety does a fine job and saves significant shopping and prep time. It is usually sold in small jars next to other Thai ingredients at the supermarket. Be aware that these pastes can vary in spiciness depending on the brand, so use more or less as desired.

Coconut milk is another common ingredient in Thai cuisine. Coconut milk is not the thin liquid found inside the coconut itself; that is called coconut water. Coconut milk is a product made by steeping equal parts shredded coconut meat and either warm milk or water. The meat is pressed or mashed to release as much liquid as possible, then the mixture is strained. Coconut milk imparts a rich creamy element that blends well with the spicy, sweet, and sour flavors of Thai dishes.

a hearty vegetable to anchor the dish, I considered eggplant and cauliflower, two substantial, almost meaty vegetables that would maintain their texture in the thick curry. Eggplant proved disappointing, however. Without a lengthy sear to brown and dry out the flesh, it became spongy and unappealing. The cauliflower, on the other hand, cooked perfectly, retaining its integrity and texture in the curry. Since it required the longest cooking time, I added the cauliflower to the skillet with the curry paste, giving it an extra hit of flavor and a sear in the hot oil before adding the coconut milk. I settled on a trio of zucchini, red bell pepper, and snap peas to add near the end of cooking to preserve their more delicate textures. They added heft, sweetness, and crunch respectively, as well as giving the curry a burst of color.

Since the stewlike consistency of the curry begged for some rice to sop up the sauce, I considered my options. Fragrant jasmine or basmati rice seemed a perfect fit for the flavors of the dish, but I was loath to simply heap my curry on a pile of rice. Just because it was a weeknight meal didn't mean it needed to be boring, after all. Plus, I really wanted to add a little more texture to the dish; with all that creaminess, it needed a little crunch. What if I fashioned my cooked jasmine rice into a cake that I could sauté to develop a browned, crispy crust?

While the rice was still warm, I mixed in a beaten egg and a couple of tablespoons of flour and formed it into patties. Then I added them to a hot skillet to sauté them on both sides until they were brown. But when I went to flip the cakes, they broke into craggy pieces. Clearly, I needed to work on the binder. Adding another egg made them too wet, and adding more flour was equally unsuccessful. Then I thought of our recipe for black bean burgers, where we pulse a portion of the beans to serve as a gluey binder to hold the burgers together. Would that work with my rice cakes? I took half of the warm rice and pulsed it in the food processor until it was coarsely ground, then I added it to the unprocessed rice, egg, and flour.

The starchy, sticky rice bits were just what my rice cakes needed. The next batch came out of the skillet browned and crisp on the outside, soft and tender on the inside. Served with a heaping ladle of my Thai vegetable green curry, they made an easy, elegant entrée for any night of the week.

—EVA KATZ AND CHRISTIE MORRISON,
America's Test Kitchen Books

Thai Vegetable Green Curry with Jasmine Rice Cakes

SERVES 4

Though we like the flavor of jasmine rice here, regular long-grain rice can be substituted. Consider garnishing the curry with a handful of chopped fresh herbs such as basil, mint, and/or cilantro.

- ¼ cup vegetable oil
- 12 ounces cauliflower florets, cut into 1-inch pieces
- 3 tablespoons Thai green curry paste
- 1 (14-ounce) can coconut milk
- 2 tablespoons fish sauce
- 1 tablespoon packed brown sugar
- 2 zucchini, cut into ¾-inch pieces
- 1 red bell pepper, stemmed, seeded, and cut into matchsticks
- 8 ounces snap peas, strings removed
- 2 tablespoons lime juice
  Salt and pepper
- 4 cups cooked jasmine rice
- 1 large egg
- 2 tablespoons all-purpose flour

1. Heat 2 tablespoons oil in Dutch oven over medium-high heat until shimmering. Add cauliflower and curry paste and cook until cauliflower begins to soften, about 5 minutes. Stir in coconut milk, fish sauce, and sugar and bring to simmer. Stir in zucchini, bell pepper, and snap peas, cover, and cook, stirring occasionally, until vegetables are just tender, about 4 minutes. Uncover and cook until sauce is slightly thickened, about 2 minutes. Off heat, stir in lime juice and season with salt and pepper to taste.

2. Meanwhile, pulse half of rice in food processor until coarsely ground, about 12 pulses; return to bowl with unprocessed rice. Stir in egg, flour, ¾ teaspoon salt, and ½ teaspoon pepper. Using hands, pack rice mixture into 4 patties.

3. Heat remaining 2 tablespoons oil in 12-inch nonstick skillet over medium-high heat until shimmering. Add rice patties and cook until crisp and browned on both sides, about 3 minutes per side. Serve rice cakes with vegetable curry.

CHAPTER 10

DESSERTS

Black and White Cookies   240

Gingersnaps   241

Peanut Butter Sandwich Cookies   245

Peanut Butter Sandwich Cookies with Honey-Cinnamon Filling

Peanut Butter Sandwich Cookies with Milk Chocolate Filling

Cream Cheese Pound Cake   247

Chocolate Pound Cake   248

Italian Cream Cake   250

Carrot Layer Cake   252

Texas-Style Blueberry Cobbler   256

Paris-Brest   257

Danish Puff Pastry   262

Chocolate Espresso Dacquoise   266

Vanilla Ice Cream   270

Creamy Chocolate Pudding   273

Creamy Mexican Chocolate Pudding

Creamy Mocha Pudding

BLACK AND WHITE COOKIES

YOU WOULD BE HARD-PRESSED TO FIND A DELI OR bakery in New York City that doesn't sell black and white cookies. If you're not from the Big Apple, here's what you need to know: They're gigantic, tender iced cookies with an ardent following. The base is flavored with vanilla or lemon. The icing is half chocolate and half vanilla or lemon. "Cookie" may be a misnomer, as what you get when you mix the ingredients together is closer to cake batter than to cookie dough, and the cookie itself is definitely cakey.

But bakery black and white cookies rarely live up to their billing. Former *New York Times* food writer Molly O'Neill should know, and here's what she wrote in 2001: "The black-and-white cookie, that frumpy and oversize mainstay of New York City bakeries and delis, has not endured by dint of its taste. Unlike other edible icons, like New York cheesecake or bagels, there is no such thing as a delicious black-and-white cookie. They are either edible or inedible." I took what O'Neill wrote as a personal challenge. I grabbed recipes from every New York City cookbook I could track down and headed into the test kitchen.

These recipes mainly produced cookies about the size of coasters, yet the range of textures was wider than I had expected. Some were like sugar cookies, others resembled sponge cake, and a third group was nearest to tender yellow cake. None were bad (it's a cookie, folks), but none were perfect, either. As a group, they were bland, and even the one we liked best and considered truest to form was too crunchy and coarse, plus it was pocked with air bubbles. Still, it was clear that I wouldn't have to reinvent the wheel here; I would focus on fine-tuning. Before buckling down to work, I made an executive decision and abandoned the lemon. Lemon and chocolate? Whatever some New Yorkers say, the combination is as wrong as cheering for the Yankees at Fenway Park. I'd stick with vanilla.

The recipe I used as my jumping-off point read like a yellow cake recipe: Cream butter with sugar, beat in the egg, then add the dry ingredients (all-purpose flour with leavener) alternately with milk. The batter that it produced was thicker than cake batter, though, so the raw cookies would hold their shape. But the cookies baked up too coarse. As an experienced baker, I knew that cake flour equals tender crumb and soft interior, so I tried it. It was tender all right—so tender that the cookies fell apart. I went back to all-purpose flour. Next I substituted sour cream for the milk. Sour cream typically makes for tender baked goods, and it did so here. But the one-for-one swap made the cookies so moist that they stuck to the baking sheet. I dialed back on the amount of sour cream until the cookies came off the sheet cleanly. Getting rid of the air bubbles in the cookies was as easy as using less baking soda and powder. Finally, I doubled the vanilla extract and sat back as the complaints about blandness disappeared. When I started seeing tasting sheets with comments like "Killer!" "So right!" I knew it was time to move on to the icing.

The most heated debate during my early tests had been over which side of the cookies to frost: flat or domed. After a couple of trial runs, I settled on the flat side—it was simpler to frost, and there was less risk of the glaze running down the edges. With that settled, we debated the texture. Should the frosting be creamy or "snap" when a cookie was broken in half? To please everybody, I set myself the goal of making a creamy icing that set up to a hard sheen.

NOTES FROM THE TEST KITCHEN

GLAZING BLACK AND WHITE COOKIES

Using butter knife or mini offset spatula, glaze half of bottom of each cookie with vanilla glaze. Chill cookies for 15 minutes. Glaze other half of each cookie with chocolate glaze and let sit until glaze sets, about 1 hour.

THE BEST COCOA POWDER

Cocoa powder is a chocolate powerhouse, packing in more flavor ounce for ounce than any other type of chocolate. We reach for it often in the test kitchen for cookies, cake, pudding, hot chocolate and more. We selected eight widely available supermarket brands, baked them into chocolate butter cookies and chocolate cake, and stirred them into our recipe for hot chocolate. We asked tasters to rate them on the intensity and complexity of chocolate flavor and overall appeal. **Hershey's Cocoa, Natural Unsweetened** had full, strong chocolate flavor with notes of deeper complexity that tasters singled out again and again, in cake, cookies and hot chocolate.

Some recipes for black and white frosting are actually fondant: water and sugar boiled to what candy makers call the "soft-ball stage." I had no intention of making such a fuss and opted for a streamlined approach. I'd combine confectioners' sugar with water, milk, or heavy cream, whisking together a base glaze and adding chocolate to half. The water made the glaze look dull and taste chalky. The cream kept it too soft. Milk proved perfect but for one thing: As the soft cookies sat, the icing soaked in. To prevent that, I peered into my pastry chef's bag of tricks and pulled out corn syrup. I replaced a portion of the milk with syrup for a thicker, stickier, and shinier glaze. For the chocolate glaze, I tested chocolate in every form before settling on cocoa powder as the simplest. No need to melt; just open the tin.

As I was wrapping up my testing, a New York friend announced that she was coming to town. I requested a box of black and white cookies. When she (and they) arrived, I pitted them against my homemade version. My tender, flavorful cakey cookies were the hands-down winner. New York, here I come.

—CAROLYNN PURPURA MACKAY, *Cook's Country*

Black and White Cookies

MAKES 12 COOKIES

You'll get neater cookies if you spread on the vanilla glaze first. This recipe provides a little extra glaze, just in case.

COOKIES

1¾   cups (8¾ ounces) all-purpose flour

½   teaspoon baking powder

¼   teaspoon baking soda

⅛   teaspoon salt

10   tablespoons unsalted butter, softened

1   cup (7 ounces) granulated sugar

1   large egg

2   teaspoons vanilla extract

⅓   cup sour cream

GLAZE

5   cups (20 ounces) confectioners' sugar, sifted

7   tablespoons whole milk

2   tablespoons corn syrup

1   teaspoon vanilla extract

½   teaspoon salt

3   tablespoons cocoa, sifted

1. FOR THE COOKIES: Adjust oven racks to upper-middle and lower-middle positions and heat oven to 350 degrees. Line 2 baking sheets with parchment paper. Combine flour, baking powder, baking soda, and salt in bowl.

2. Using stand mixer fitted with paddle, beat butter and sugar together on medium-high speed until pale and fluffy, about 2 minutes. Add egg and vanilla and beat until combined. Reduce speed to low and add flour mixture in 3 additions, alternating with 2 additions of sour cream, scraping down bowl as needed. Give dough final stir by hand.

3. Using greased ¼-cup measure, drop portions of cookie dough 3 inches apart on prepared baking sheets. Bake until edges are lightly browned, 15 to 18 minutes, switching and rotating sheets halfway through baking. Let cookies cool on sheets for 5 minutes, then transfer to wire rack to cool completely, about 1 hour.

4. FOR THE GLAZE: Whisk sugar, 6 tablespoons milk, corn syrup, vanilla, and salt together in bowl until smooth. Transfer 1 cup glaze to small bowl; reserve. Whisk cocoa and remaining 1 tablespoon milk into remaining glaze until combined.

5. Working with 1 cookie at a time, spread 1 tablespoon vanilla glaze over half of underside of cookies. Refrigerate until glaze is set, about 15 minutes. Cover other half of each cookie with 1 tablespoon chocolate glaze and let cookies sit at room temperature until glaze is firm, at least 1 hour. Serve. (Cookies can be stored at room temperature for up to 2 days.)

GINGERSNAPS

SWEETENED DOUGH SPICED WITH GINGER HAS BEEN around since medieval times, but the term *gingersnap* wasn't coined until the 19th century. In my mind, this nomenclature should have settled once and for all the question of whether a ginger cookie should be crisp or chewy. I've never doubted that "snap" speaks to a cookie that breaks cleanly in half and crunches with every bite.

But most gingersnap recipes that I've tried don't live up to the name. Once you get past their brittle edges, the cookies turn soft and chewy. In fact, the only gingersnaps I've had that actually snap come from a box. But these cookies always fall short on flavor. I wanted freshly baked gingersnaps with a crackly top and a

GINGERSNAPS

texture to rival the store-bought kind, but with all-natural ginger flavor and lingering heat.

I started with the best of all of the flawed recipes I'd tried—one that at least yielded a cookie that boasted crisp edges. Like most gingersnap recipes, it called for creaming butter and brown sugar (preferred to white sugar for its caramel-like undertone) in a stand mixer, then whipping in eggs, molasses, and vanilla and incorporating the dry ingredients (flour, baking soda, salt, and ground ginger). You then chill the dough until firm, form it into balls, and bake.

I wondered if transforming this cookie from mainly chewy to crunchy could be as straightforward as cutting down on moisture. I opted not to tinker with the molasses since the cookies wouldn't be true gingersnaps without its pleasantly bitter, smoky edge. And with just a single egg and a yolk in the recipe, the idea of adjusting the egg amount didn't seem promising either. That left me with just two potential moisture sources to work with: the brown sugar and the butter.

I turned to the sugar first. I knew that brown sugar is a double-edged sword. It contributes rich, molasses-y flavor—but it also creates chewiness in cookies, attracting moisture during baking. Switching to granulated sugar did produce a crisper, less chewy cookie, but the loss of flavor wasn't worth it. My only choice was to cut back on the sweetener. I found that slashing the brown sugar almost in half—from 2 to 1¼ cups—resulted in cookies that were noticeably drier and crunchier. Reducing the sugar also allowed the ginger flavor to move to the fore.

On to the butter, which is about 16 percent water. Using less butter dehydrated the cookies a bit, but new problems emerged. Without ample fat, the leaner, stiffer dough refused to spread as it baked. More importantly, these cookies didn't taste as good. Then it occurred to me that if I browned the butter, I'd eliminate some of its water while keeping its fat (and creating richer, nutty flavor). I was pleased to find that this lower-moisture dough yielded considerably firmer cookies, and the subtle nutty taste of the browned butter turned out to be an ideal backdrop for the ginger. Stirring in the melted butter rather than creaming seemed to help matters, too: Since I was no longer whipping air into the dough, the cookie crumb was more densely packed and firmly textured. But all was not perfect: The center of the cookie was still a little too moist and didn't have the crackly top I wanted.

Previous experiments in the test kitchen gave me an idea for creating crackles: increasing the leavening. In the next series of tests, I gradually upped the baking soda. The intentional overdose caused the cookies to rise dramatically but then collapse, leaving attractive fissures on their surfaces. After experimenting with varying amounts of baking soda, I settled on a full 2 teaspoons, which created nice deep cracks without imparting any soapy flavor. I found that the overdose had several other positive effects: better browning and crisper cookies, since the cracks in the dough were allowing more moisture to escape.

Though these cookies were getting close, they still didn't have quite the clean, definitive snap of the box kind, so I moved on to consider the other major variable: the oven. By reducing the temperature from 350 to 300 degrees, I nearly doubled the overall baking time, which allowed the gingersnaps to gradually (and fully) dry out without burning. I also transferred the cookies to a wire rack immediately after baking, which allowed air to circulate and steam to escape from their undersides. At last, my cookies turned out crackly crisp to the core.

There was just one glitch. When I baked two sheets at once, only the cookies on the upper rack developed a uniformly crackled top. Rotating the sheets halfway through baking didn't improve the situation, suggesting that the cracks were produced right at the beginning of baking, when the heat radiating down from the top of the oven caused the cookies to rise and fall rapidly. The sheet on the lower rack was partially shielded from the oven's heat by the sheet above, causing its cookies to expand more gradually, which resulted in smoother tops. The solution proved as simple as staggering the baking: I popped one tray onto the upper rack for 15 minutes until fissures formed, moved it to the lower rack to finish baking, then placed the second sheet of cookies on the upper rack.

With the texture and appearance of my gingersnaps right where I wanted them, all that remained was to punch up their rather mild flavor. Doubling the amount of dried ginger was an obvious starting point, as was incorporating freshly grated ginger. Warm spices seemed appropriate here, and I followed the lead of many other recipes by incorporating cinnamon and cloves. But I wanted yet another layer of heat. I perused the spice cabinet once more, landing on cayenne and black pepper. The combination lent the cookies a judicious but lingering heat. Finally, to make the spices really sing, I bloomed them in the browned butter, the hot fat helping to fully release the spices' pungent aromatic compounds.

As a finishing touch, I rolled the balls of dough in granulated sugar before baking to provide a sweet exterior foil to the spicy interiors. At last, I'd found the gingersnap that I'd been craving: snappy-textured, snappy-flavored, and a snap to make.

—ANDREW JANJIGIAN, *Cook's Illustrated*

Gingersnaps

MAKES 80 1½-INCH COOKIES

For the best results, use fresh spices. For efficiency, form the second batch of cookies while the first batch bakes. The 2 teaspoons of baking soda are essential to getting the right texture.

2½	cups (12½ ounces) all-purpose flour
2	teaspoons baking soda
½	teaspoon salt
12	tablespoons unsalted butter
2	tablespoons ground ginger
1	teaspoon ground cinnamon
¼	teaspoon ground cloves
¼	teaspoon pepper
	Pinch cayenne pepper
1¼	cups packed (8¾ ounces) dark brown sugar
¼	cup molasses
2	tablespoons finely grated fresh ginger
1	large egg plus 1 large yolk
½	cup (3½ ounces) granulated sugar

1. Whisk flour, baking soda, and salt together in bowl. Heat butter in 10-inch skillet over medium heat until melted. Lower heat to medium-low and continue to cook, swirling pan frequently, until foaming subsides and butter is just beginning to brown, 2 to 4 minutes. Transfer butter to large bowl and whisk in ground ginger, cinnamon, cloves, pepper, and cayenne. Cool slightly, about 2 minutes. Add brown sugar, molasses, and fresh ginger to butter mixture and whisk to combine. Add egg and yolk and whisk to combine. Add flour mixture and stir until just combined. Cover dough tightly with plastic wrap and refrigerate until firm, about 1 hour.

2. Adjust oven racks to upper-middle and lower-middle positions and heat oven to 300 degrees. Line 2 baking sheets with parchment paper. Place granulated sugar in shallow baking dish or pie plate. Divide dough into heaping teaspoon portions; roll dough into 1-inch balls. Working in batches of 10, roll balls in sugar to coat. Evenly space dough balls on prepared baking sheets, 20 dough balls per sheet.

3. Place 1 sheet on upper rack and bake for 15 minutes. Transfer partially baked top sheet to lower rack, rotating 180 degrees, and place second sheet of dough balls on upper rack. Continue to bake until cookies on lower tray just begin to darken around edges, 10 to 12 minutes longer. Remove lower sheet of cookies and

NOTES FROM THE TEST KITCHEN

PUTTING THE SNAP IN GINGERSNAPS
The hallmark of gingersnap cookie texture—big crunch—came down to one key factor: drying out the dough.

1. Butter is 16 percent water. Brown it before whisking it with sugar, eggs, and flour to eliminate moisture.

2. Brown sugar holds on to water, even after baking. Use just 1¼ cups for crisper cookies.

3. Bake cookies in low (300-degree) oven to give dough ample time to gradually—but thoroughly—dry out.

4. Stagger baking by baking each tray on top rack before moving it to cooler bottom rack to create fissures that allow moisture to escape.

transfer upper sheet to lower rack, rotating 180 degrees, and continue to bake until cookies begin to darken around edges, 15 to 17 minutes longer. Slide baked cookies, still on parchment, to wire rack and cool completely before serving. Cool sheets slightly and line with parchment again. Repeat step 3 with remaining dough balls. (Cooled cookies can be stored at room temperature for up to 2 weeks.)

TO MAKE AHEAD: Dough can be refrigerated for up to 2 days or frozen for up to 1 month. Let frozen dough thaw overnight before proceeding with recipe. Let dough stand at room temperature for 30 minutes before shaping.

PEANUT BUTTER SANDWICH COOKIES

TO A PEANUT BUTTER OBSESSIVE LIKE ME, THAT distinguishing crosshatch on top of a traditional peanut butter cookie feels like a cheat. A cookie shouldn't have to rely on a homey hieroglyph to proclaim its identity; great flavor speaks for itself. Their looks aside, I've always had another issue with peanut butter cookies: The raw dough tastes better than the baked treats. This is because in the presence of heat, the starch granules in flour soak up peanut flavor molecules like a sponge, reducing their aroma and limiting their ability to interact with our taste buds. The upshot is that a traditional peanut butter cookie becomes flavor challenged as soon as it hits the oven.

It occurred to me that a sandwich cookie—two peanut butter cookies enclosing a filling made primarily with uncooked (read: full-flavored) peanut butter—might be the solution. The cookies themselves would have to be quite thin and flat (so you could comfortably eat two of them sandwiched with filling) as well as crunchy, to contrast with the creamy center. I also wanted my cookies to have the simplicity of a drop cookie: no chilling of the dough, no slicing, no rolling, and no cutting.

Because a good sandwich cookie is all about balanced flavors and textures, I knew that the filling would influence my cookie and vice versa. I chose to start with the simpler filling. Most recipes call for blending peanut butter and confectioners' sugar (granulated sugar remains too gritty and doesn't provide much thickening power) with a creamy element, such as butter,

cream cheese, or marshmallow crème. I settled on butter, which gave me the silkiest consistency and the purest peanut butter flavor. I softened 3 tablespoons of butter with ¾ cup of creamy peanut butter in the microwave and, to keep the peanut flavor in the forefront, stirred in a modest ½ cup of confectioners' sugar. This low-sugar filling tasted great, but it was far too soft, squirting out from my placeholder cookies as soon as I pressed them together. To thicken things up, I ultimately had to double the sugar amount. I would have to balance the filling with a significantly less sweet cookie.

Setting the filling aside, I put together a dough with 3 tablespoons of butter, ½ cup of peanut butter, 2 eggs, 1 cup of sugar, 2 cups of flour, and ½ teaspoon each of baking soda and salt. After portioning the dough and baking it at 350 degrees for about 12 minutes, I had cookies that weren't bad for a first try, offering just the right degree of sweetness to complement the sugary filling. But they were too thick and soft. I wanted more spread, more crunch, and—if I could pack it in—more peanut flavor.

My first change was to scrap one of the eggs (they contribute protein that traps air and makes baked goods cakey), replacing it with 3 tablespoons of milk. I knew that moisture level influences how much cookie dough will spread in the oven, so I tried to increase the moisture level by cutting back on flour. Since my goal was also a super-nutty-tasting cookie, I decided to replace a full cup of flour with finely chopped peanuts, which would absorb far less moisture as well as add welcome crunch and peanut flavor. These changes helped, but the cookies still weren't spreading enough.

What would happen if I actually took out all of the flour? Flourless peanut butter cookie recipes abound on the Internet, and I'd always been curious about them. I eliminated the flour and, to my surprise, found that the resulting cookies were not that much thinner or flatter—but they tasted great. However, they were also far too crumbly. I added flour back incrementally, finding that a ratio of ¾ cup of flour to the ½ cup of peanut butter created relatively thin, nutty-tasting cookies that were still sturdy enough to serve as a shell for the filling. Finally, to get them thinner, I relied on brute force: After portioning the dough on the baking sheet, I used my wet hand to squash the dough into even 2-inch rounds.

I was almost there, but I had one final trick up my sleeve: tinkering with the baking soda. In other cookie recipes, we have found that adding extra soda causes the bubbles within dough to inflate so rapidly that they burst before the cookies set, flattening them. A mere ¼ teaspoon of baking soda would be sufficient to leaven the ¾ cup of flour in my recipe; when I quadrupled that amount to a full teaspoon, the cookies quickly puffed up in the oven and then deflated. Voilà: greater spread, just as I had hoped. In addition, these cookies boasted a coarser, more open crumb, which provided extra routes through which moisture could escape. This left the cookies even drier and crunchier—a better foil for the creamy filling.

With my creamy, peanut-y filling and ultra-crunchy cookies ready to go, it was time to put the two components together. But on my first few maddening attempts, the cookies shattered into pieces as I tried to spread the too-firm filling. Then I realized that it was a matter of timing: If I prepared the filling right before assembly, it could be easily scooped and squished between the cookies while it was still warm from the microwave—no painstaking spreading necessary—after which it would cool and set to an ideal firm texture.

At last, I had a cookie with a simple, understated appearance that delivered the powerful peanut wallop promised by those pretenders sporting the traditional fork marks. These cookies are unmistakably of the peanut butter variety, no crisscrosses required.

—ANDREA GEARY, *Cook's Illustrated*

NOTES FROM THE TEST KITCHEN

FILLING COOKIES EVENLY

1. Using #60 scoop or tablespoon measure, portion warm filling onto bottom cookies (turned upside down).

2. Rather than spreading filling with knife or offset spatula, top bottom cookie with second cookie and press gently until filling spreads to edges.

Peanut Butter Sandwich Cookies

MAKES 24 COOKIES

Do not use unsalted peanut butter for this recipe.

COOKIES
1¼ cups (6¼ ounces) raw peanuts, toasted and cooled
¾ cup (3¾ ounces) all-purpose flour
1 teaspoon baking soda
½ teaspoon salt
3 tablespoons unsalted butter, melted
½ cup creamy peanut butter
½ cup (3½ ounces) granulated sugar
½ cup packed (3½ ounces) light brown sugar
3 tablespoons whole milk
1 large egg

FILLING
¾ cup creamy peanut butter
3 tablespoons unsalted butter
1 cup (4 ounces) confectioners' sugar

1. FOR THE COOKIES: Adjust oven racks to upper-middle and lower-middle positions and heat oven to 350 degrees. Line 2 baking sheets with parchment paper. Pulse peanuts in food processor until finely chopped, about 8 pulses. Whisk flour, baking soda, and salt together in bowl. Whisk melted butter, peanut butter, granulated sugar, brown sugar, milk, and egg together in second bowl. Stir flour mixture into peanut butter mixture with rubber spatula until combined. Stir in peanuts until evenly distributed.

2. Using #60 scoop or tablespoon measure, place 12 mounds, evenly spaced, on each prepared baking sheet. Using damp hand, flatten mounds until 2 inches in diameter.

3. Bake until deep golden brown and firm to touch, 15 to 18 minutes, switching and rotating sheets halfway through baking. Let cookies cool on sheets for 5 minutes. Transfer cookies to wire rack and let cool completely, about 30 minutes. Repeat portioning and baking remaining dough.

4. FOR THE FILLING: Microwave peanut butter and butter together until butter is melted and warm, about 40 seconds. Using rubber spatula, stir in confectioners' sugar until combined.

5. TO ASSEMBLE: Place 24 cookies upside down on counter. Place 1 level tablespoon (or #60 scoop) warm filling in center of each cookie. Place second cookie on top of filling, right side up, pressing gently until filling spreads to edges. Allow filling to set for 1 hour before serving. Assembled cookies can be stored at room temperature for up to 3 days.

VARIATIONS

Peanut Butter Sandwich Cookies with Honey-Cinnamon Filling

Omit butter from filling. Stir 5 tablespoons honey and ½ teaspoon ground cinnamon into warm peanut butter before adding confectioners' sugar.

Peanut Butter Sandwich Cookies with Milk Chocolate Filling

Reduce peanut butter to ½ cup and omit butter from filling. Stir 6 ounces finely chopped milk chocolate into warm peanut butter until melted, microwaving for 10 seconds at a time if necessary, before adding confectioners' sugar.

CREAM CHEESE POUND CAKE

ONCE UPON A TIME, BAKERS MADE POUND CAKES by combining a pound each of butter, sugar, flour, and eggs. Such a simple formula is an irresistible blank canvas for bakers, so over the years they've tinkered with the cake, adding items as wide-ranging as peanut butter, 7UP, and poppy seeds. One variation that caught my interest was cream cheese pound cake. Fans claim that cream cheese adds tang, plus it makes a thicker batter, which can hold more air, thereby creating an especially velvety texture. I was dubious: With protein, moisture, and fat, wouldn't the cream cheese throw off pound cake's delicate balance? I gathered a few recipes and set out to discover if the claims were true.

I baked and ate my way through a half-dozen sample recipes. I had plenty of help in the eating department, but the reviews were mixed. Overall, we agreed that while the cream cheese added a pleasant tang, most of the cakes were either dense and gummy or coarse and marred by tunnels. A coarse, open crumb suits white layer cake, but pound cake should be fine-crumbed, lusciously tender, and rich. As for flavor, tasters voted for simplicity. Classic pound cake, we felt, is defined by pure flavors: butter, vanilla, and, in this case, cream cheese. We also preferred the cakes that weren't cloyingly sweet.

Informed by those tests and armed with the test kitchen's recipe for plain pound cake, I cobbled together a new recipe as a place to begin my testing. I beat three sticks of butter (this is pound cake, after all) with 3 cups of sugar and 1 package (8 ounces) of cream cheese. I added six eggs and several spoonfuls of vanilla extract, followed by 3 cups of all-purpose flour mixed with baking powder and salt. I scraped the batter into a Bundt pan and baked the cake. A few hours later, we tasted. The verdict: too cakey. On top of that, I spied the occasional tunnel worming its way through the cake.

Tunnels can be caused by overleavening. For my next test, I cut the baking powder in half (to ¼ teaspoon), which alleviated but didn't eliminate the holes. Maybe baking powder wasn't necessary in the first place. I knew that old recipes for pound cakes don't call for leaveners. When cakes are made, air is beaten into the batter during "creaming" (beating the butter and sugar together until fluffy). This forms small holes that eventually make the cake's crumb. The job of the leavener is to enlarge those holes. So if I wanted a tighter crumb, eliminating the baking powder might get me there. Indeed it did: When I cut out all the baking powder, the tunnels disappeared.

But I still hadn't achieved my ideal "velvet" texture. Cake flour was the obvious next thing to try: It's a little more acidic than all-purpose flour. Our science editor explained that acidity lowers the temperature at which proteins coagulate and starches gelatinize, making for a tighter crumb. Experience had taught me that cake flour absorbs more moisture than all-purpose flour does. To account for that, I replaced 2 ounces of the cream cheese that I had been using with ¼ cup of neutral-tasting milk. These changes in place, I baked another pound cake.

I was definitely on the right track: This latest version was more tender, fine-crumbed, and velvety than any other I'd baked thus far. Encouraged, I moved down the ingredient list, looking for more ways to improve the cake; I spied eggs. Egg yolks tenderize, but the whites actually have a drying effect. Here's why: Whites are 90 percent water, but during baking, that water evaporates. Yolks are just 56 percent water, but all the emulsifiers in the yolks help them hold on to that water; that, in turn, keeps cake moist. If I cut back on whites, maybe I could make a cake that was the most moist and tender yet. Several cakes later, I concluded that four whole eggs and two yolks gave me the fine crumb that I'd been after.

My cream cheese pound cake was getting better and better—so much so that my tastings were drawing a crowd. But a layer of gumminess on top stood between me and perfect pound cake. A gummy top is a telltale sign of an underbaked cake. But if I baked my cake any longer, the sides of the cake burned—unless I decreased the oven temperature. I inched the dial down to 300 degrees (from 350). Ninety minutes later I was in business. This cake was moist, tender, golden brown, and very velvety. It had even more richness and all the pure buttery flavor of classic pound cake, but with a delicate tang. Breaking with tradition, it seems, can be downright delicious.

—REBECCAH MARSTERS, *Cook's Country*

Cream Cheese Pound Cake

SERVES 12 TO 14

We prefer whole milk in this recipe, but any percentage fat will work.

3	cups (12 ounces) cake flour
1	teaspoon salt
4	large eggs plus 2 large yolks, room temperature
¼	cup milk
2	teaspoons vanilla extract
3	cups (21 ounces) sugar
24	tablespoons (3 sticks) unsalted butter, softened
6	ounces cream cheese, softened

1. Adjust oven rack to middle position and heat oven to 300 degrees. Grease and flour 12-cup nonstick Bundt pan. Combine flour and salt in bowl. Whisk eggs and yolks, milk, and vanilla together in 2-cup liquid measuring cup.

2. Using stand mixer fitted with paddle, beat sugar, butter, and cream cheese together on medium-high speed until pale and fluffy, about 3 minutes. Reduce speed to low and very slowly add egg mixture until incorporated (batter may look slightly curdled). Add flour mixture in 3 additions, scraping down bowl as needed. Give batter final stir by hand.

3. Scrape batter into prepared pan and gently tap pan on counter to release air bubbles. Bake until toothpick inserted in center comes out clean, 80 to 90 minutes, rotating pan halfway through baking. Cool cake in pan on wire rack for 15 minutes. Remove cake from pan and cool completely, about 2 hours. Serve. (Cake can be wrapped tightly in plastic wrap and stored at room temperature for up to 3 days.)

CHOCOLATE POUND CAKE

I LOVE POUND CAKE AND I LOVE CHOCOLATE CAKE. So why don't I love chocolate pound cake? Because most versions fail to capture the best of either: the buttery, mild, dense, and velvety nature of pound cake or the deep, rich chocolate of chocolate cake. You would think it would be simple: Just add chocolate to a proven recipe for plain pound cake and voilà: chocolate pound cake.

Instead, the chocolate pound cakes that I tested missed the mark. Some were so timid that I barely pegged them as chocolate. Others went to the other extreme: Chocolate (and sometimes sugar) overload annihilated all traces of pound cake. Textures ranged from coarse to crumbly to fudgy; none evinced the tight, compact crumb that should characterize pound cake. I was determined to develop a recipe that walked the line between pound and chocolate cake.

I decided to start with a classic recipe for plain pound cake: Cream 1 cup of sugar with two sticks of butter. Add ½ teaspoon of vanilla extract and five eggs, beating after adding each egg to help the cake rise in the oven (most pound cakes have no chemical leaveners). To finish, stir in 1 cup of flour and bake.

CHOCOLATE POUND CAKE

To this basic cake I added cocoa, figuring that it was the simplest way to add chocolate flavor. After testing varying amounts, I settled on ¾ cup. However, by introducing this additional dry ingredient into the batter, I turned my formerly moist pound cake dry as well. I looked into adding milk or buttermilk but came up with a better idea: I'd "bloom" the cocoa. The test kitchen uses this technique—stirring cocoa into hot water (in this case ⅓ cup of water)—because it frees the cocoa's flavor particles, amping up chocolate taste. In one stroke, I hoped to get a cake that was both more moist and more flavorful. And I did.

But the chocolate flavor remained a little bit harsh. To fix that, I pitted the natural cocoa I'd been using against Dutch-processed cocoa; there was no question that the mellow, rounded flavor of the latter suited pound cake better. At this point, a fellow test cook asked why I was limiting myself to cocoa. Wouldn't chopped bar chocolate further soften and deepen the cake's flavor? Good question. Many pound cakes later, I determined that 2 ounces was the right amount and milk chocolate the right type. One final change assured both optimal chocolate flavor and moist texture: I added ¼ cup of brown sugar to the batter. Brown sugar is more moist than granulated sugar, and its complex, caramel nuance underlined the taste of the chocolate.

Despite all the work I'd done, tasters continued to insist that the cake tasted "flat." Fortunately, that complaint disappeared when I quadrupled the vanilla (it seems counterintuitive, but vanilla actually enhances chocolate flavor) and doubled the salt. Finally, my cake was moist, buttery, and mildly sweet, with a tight crumb and deep, rounded chocolate flavor. A hybrid of pound cake and chocolate cake, this version did both proud.

—SHANNON FRIEDMANN HATCH AND
LYNN CLARK, *Cook's Country*

Chocolate Pound Cake

SERVES 8

The test kitchen's favorite loaf pan measures 8½ by 4½ inches; if you're using a standard 9 by 5-inch pan, start checking the cake for doneness after 55 minutes.

- 1 **cup (5 ounces) all-purpose flour**
- 1 **teaspoon salt**
- ⅓ **cup boiling water**
- ¾ **cup (2¼ ounces) Dutch-processed cocoa**
- 2 **ounces milk chocolate, chopped fine**
- 16 **tablespoons unsalted butter, softened**
- 1 **cup (7 ounces) granulated sugar**
- ¼ **cup packed (1¾ ounces) light brown sugar**
- 2 **teaspoons vanilla extract**
- 5 **large eggs, room temperature**

1. Adjust oven rack to lower-middle position and heat oven to 325 degrees. Grease and flour 8½ by 4½-inch loaf pan. Combine flour and salt in bowl. Pour water over cocoa and chocolate in second bowl and stir until chocolate is melted and no dry streaks of cocoa remain. Let mixture cool for 5 minutes.

2. Using stand mixer fitted with paddle, beat butter, cocoa-chocolate mixture, granulated sugar, brown sugar, and vanilla together on medium-high speed until fluffy, 2 to 3 minutes. Add eggs, 1 at a time, beating after each addition until combined. Reduce speed to low and add flour mixture in 3 additions, scraping down bowl as needed, mixing until just combined. Give batter final stir by hand (it may look curdled).

3. Scrape batter into prepared pan and gently tap pan on counter to release air bubbles. Bake until toothpick inserted in center comes out clean, 60 to 70 minutes. Cool cake in pan on wire rack for 10 minutes. Remove cake from pan and cool for 2 hours. Serve.

ITALIAN CREAM CAKE

OTHER THAN ITS NAME, THERE ISN'T ANYTHING remotely Italian about Italian cream cake (and for the record, it doesn't contain cream, either). Its name be damned, for more than 40 years this moist coconut-pecan layer cake swathed in cream cheese frosting has been a favorite in the American South—a region that knows a thing or two about gorgeously showy layer cakes. You may find it sitting on bakery shelves, big and tempting, easily holding its own right next to the red velvet and caramel cakes. I had to learn how to make a cake this enticing.

There was scant disagreement among recipes: 1 cup of fat (usually half butter and half shortening) beaten with 2 cups of sugar; five eggs (separated); 2 cups of all-purpose flour mixed with 1 teaspoon of baking soda; 1 cup of buttermilk; and, finally, shredded coconut and chopped pecans. The frosting called for cream cheese, butter, and a lot of confectioners' sugar.

The results were disappointing. While plenty sweet, the cake was bland; if I hadn't stirred in the coconut and pecans myself, I wouldn't have known they were there, and what nuts I could detect were soggy. Although I had taken the trouble to whip and fold in the egg whites, the cake was heavy and gummy and sank slightly. To top it off, the frosting was too sweet. I got to work simplifying, balancing, and boosting the flavors.

Because I am firmly pro-butter, I immediately ditched the shortening. But due to all the nuts and coconut, my all-butter cake was even denser than before. Shortening, I learned, has small fat crystals that trap air bubbles and make a higher and less dense cake. Butter's larger fat crystals, in contrast, tend to rise in the batter and escape. Eventually, I found that a ratio of 3 parts butter to 1 part shortening balanced buttery flavor with lightness. At the same time, I switched from all-purpose to cake flour to return the cake to its original tenderness, adding a little extra flour for structural support. I made a few more flavor adjustments—adding salt, upping the vanilla extract, and cutting back on the sugar—before turning my attention to a recurring problem: gummy cake.

The recipe called for baking soda, which produces gas bubbles upon contact with the buttermilk, but no baking powder, a leavener that reacts to heat for a longer, more gradual rise. Cakes that rely solely on baking soda are unusual. Was that the source of the trouble? The cake was collapsing before the structure could set and the whipped whites weren't picking up the slack. I skipped the steps of separating the eggs and whipping the whites (saving me trouble and dirty dishes) and supplemented the baking soda with baking powder. Now the cake had an even, airy crumb.

To bring out the flavors of the coconut and pecans, I increased the amounts of each and I toasted them before adding them to the batter. The nuts now had lots of presence. But while the toasted coconut gave the cake a fabulous, macaroon-like flavor, it was dry and fibrous. I tried pulverizing the toasted strands, but even the crumbs made the cake dry. To remoisten them, I soaked them briefly in the buttermilk while I readied the other ingredients. To my relief, this fixed the problem. The cake was ready for its cream cheese cap.

After doubling the amount of cream cheese called for in most recipes and cutting back on the confectioners' sugar, I had a rich, tangy frosting. To make it a vehicle

for extra coconut flavor, I added some flavorful canned cream of coconut. After pressing a cup of chopped pecans onto the sides of the cake, I was ready to dish out some genuine Southern hospitality.

—ERIKA BRUCE, *Cook's Country*

Italian Cream Cake

SERVES 8 TO 10

Toast the coconut and nuts in a 350-degree oven until golden brown, 10 to 12 minutes. Watch carefully and stir occasionally to prevent burning.

CAKE

- 1½ cups sweetened shredded coconut, toasted
- 1 cup buttermilk, room temperature
- 2 teaspoons vanilla extract
- 2½ cups (10 ounces) cake flour
- 2 teaspoons baking powder
- ½ teaspoon baking soda
- ¾ teaspoon salt
- 12 tablespoons unsalted butter, cut into 12 pieces and softened
- 4 tablespoons vegetable shortening, cut into 4 pieces
- 1¾ cups (12¼ ounces) granulated sugar
- 5 large eggs, room temperature
- 2 cups (8 ounces) pecans, toasted and chopped

FROSTING

- 12 tablespoons unsalted butter, softened
- 2¼ cups (9 ounces) confectioners' sugar
- ½ cup cream of coconut
- ½ teaspoon vanilla extract
  Pinch salt
- 16 ounces cream cheese, cut into 8 pieces and softened

1. FOR THE CAKE: Adjust oven rack to middle position and heat oven to 350 degrees. Grease two 9-inch round cake pans, line with parchment paper, grease parchment, then flour pans. Process coconut in food processor until finely ground, about 1 minute. Combine coconut, buttermilk, and vanilla in 2-cup liquid measuring cup and let sit until coconut is slightly softened, about 10 minutes; reserve.

2. Combine flour, baking powder, baking soda, and salt in bowl. Using stand mixer fitted with paddle, beat butter, shortening, and sugar together on medium-high speed until pale and fluffy, about 3 minutes. Add eggs,

1 at a time, and beat until combined. Reduce speed to low and add flour mixture in 3 additions, alternating with 2 additions of reserved coconut-buttermilk mixture, scraping down bowl as needed. Add ¾ cup pecans and give batter final stir by hand.

3. Divide batter evenly between prepared pans and bake until toothpick inserted in center comes out clean, 28 to 32 minutes. Cool cakes in pans on wire rack for 10 minutes. Remove cakes from pans, discard parchment, and let cool completely, about 2 hours. (Cooled cakes can be wrapped tightly in plastic wrap and stored at room temperature for up to 2 days.)

4. FOR THE FROSTING: Using stand mixer fitted with paddle, mix butter and sugar together on low speed until combined, about 30 seconds. Increase speed to medium-high and beat until pale and fluffy, about 2 minutes. Add cream of coconut, vanilla, and salt and beat until smooth, about 30 seconds. Add cream cheese, 1 piece at a time, and beat until incorporated, about 1 minute. Refrigerate until ready to use.

NOTES FROM THE TEST KITCHEN

COCONUT: TOAST, GRIND, SOAK

To bring out the flavor of the shredded coconut, we toast it in a 350-degree oven until it is golden brown. To help the coconut flavor permeate the cake, we grind it to meal in the food processor. But toasted, ground coconut is hard and dry, a real problem in such a deliciously soft, moist cake. To moisten and soften the coconut meal, we soak it in buttermilk before adding it to the cake batter.

RATING MANUAL NUT CHOPPERS

Could a simple manual nut chopper work faster and better than a chef's knife or food processor? We pitted five choppers, from $7 crank-style jars to mills costing almost $30, against our favorite food processor (the KitchenAid 750) and timed ourselves chopping pecans, hazelnuts, almonds, and walnuts. The highest-priced chopper fared the worst, processing nuts into gritty, mushy bits, but only one did much better: The **Progressive International Heavy Duty Nut Chopper**, $8.89, chopped a cup of pecans into mostly even-size pieces with minimal dust. Its sharp stainless steel tines pushed the nuts through slats that gave us a coarse texture as we turned the handle in one direction, a slightly finer texture in the other. It is the only manual nut chopper worth buying. Not only that, but chopping with our chef's knife actually took twice as long for worse results, plus we had to corral scooting nuts.

5. When cakes are cooled, cover edges of cake platter with strips of parchment paper. Place 1 cake layer on platter. Spread 1½ cups frosting evenly over top, right to edge of cake. Top with second cake layer, press lightly to adhere, then spread remaining frosting evenly over top and sides of cake. Press remaining 1¼ cups pecans onto sides of cake. Carefully remove parchment strips before serving. (Cake can be refrigerated for up to 2 days. Bring to room temperature before serving.)

BEST CARROT LAYER CAKE

AS SHOWSTOPPER DESSERTS GO, CARROT CAKE IS often overlooked, and that's a shame. Carrot cake is a relatively easy option since the typical "dump and stir" method means there's no need to haul out the stand mixer. And between its moist, fragrantly spiced crumb chock-full of plump raisins and crunchy nuts and its luxurious cream cheese frosting, it brings more to the table than many desserts. But traditional carrot cake is a rather homely confection, a snack cake typically baked in a serviceable 13 by 9-inch pan and topped with frumpy-looking frosting. That's fine for an informal family dinner but not as the finale for a fancier occasion.

Building a layer cake would be the obvious way to dress it up, but stacking delicately slim slabs into a lofty tower presents plenty of obstacles. For starters, the carrots make the cake sticky and prone to breaking—and a real nightmare to slice horizontally. Additionally, a stack of moist, heavy cake comes with a risk of toppling. I've seen bakeries pull off tall, stately carrot cakes but not without compromising the frosting. To make it thick enough to keep the cake structurally sound, they load it up with powdered sugar, dulling the characteristic tang of the cream cheese. For layers that were both slender and sturdy, I'd have to lighten the crumb without sacrificing moisture and rework the frosting to support a taller profile, but I was determined to avoid a sickly sweet concoction.

Putting aside the frosting for the moment, I made a first attempt at the cake: I whisked flour, baking powder, salt, cinnamon, cloves, and nutmeg together in one bowl, and eggs, brown sugar, vanilla extract, and vegetable oil (oil, not butter, is almost always used) in another. I folded shredded carrots, raisins, and chopped pecans into the wet ingredients; added the dry; divided the batter between two 9-inch round cake pans; and pushed them into a 350-degree oven to bake for 45 minutes. (Because the vegetable adds moisture to the batter, carrot cakes bake longer than other types.) Once the cakes were cool, I tried to neatly trim and halve them. It was a disaster. The tacky crumbs stuck to my knife as I tried to shave off the domed top of each layer, and the blade seemed to snag every nut as I sliced the cakes horizontally. Moving the sliced layers without breaking them also proved nearly impossible.

I was starting to reconsider the layers when, on a visit to a wholesale club, I spotted a rectangular layer cake that stood four tiers high. The layers had been baked in shallow jelly roll pans, then stacked with frosting in between. The slender, uniform layers were intriguing. Could I bake my cake in a rimmed baking sheet, slice it into four equal pieces, and stack them into a tall, rectangular cake?

As it turned out, this concept had a lot going for it: In a standard 18 by 13-inch rimmed baking sheet, the cake baked in a mere 16 minutes and took only 30 minutes to cool. And because the middle set almost as quickly as the edges, the cake didn't dome, rendering the trimming step unnecessary. Feeling smug, I summoned tasters—but it took only one bite of my four-tier confection for them to identify a major flaw that brought me down to earth: The carrots were crunchy. Thanks to the drastically reduced baking time, the coarse shreds hadn't had a chance to soften.

I tried cooking and pureeing the carrots before incorporating them into the batter, but their texture was completely lost. I didn't want crunch, but I did want the star of the dessert to be identifiable. Then a light bulb went on: What if I added baking soda—an alkali—to the batter to raise its pH and help the carrots break down? I added a teaspoon of baking soda to another batch and crossed my fingers. Thanks to the baking soda's pH-boosting effect, the carrots were visible but tender, and the crumb was incredibly light yet moist, with no off-flavors. I had just two more changes to make before moving on to the frosting: Since the nuts that caught on my knife during slicing caused the cake to tear, I eliminated them for now. And because the raisins looked clunky in these slim, lighter-than-ever layers, I swapped in daintier currants.

The next step: a tangy frosting. Most recipes are basic mixtures of butter, cream cheese, and confectioners' sugar, but the ratios vary. Go heavy on the cream cheese

and you get a rich, bright frosting, but one that is perilously soft and likely to trickle down the sides of the cake or—even worse—cause the layers to slip and slide. Adding sugar solves the structural issues but masks the cream cheese flavor. The standard recipe I tried fell victim to both of these faults: It was too soft and too sweet. Adding acidic lemon juice, sour cream, and yogurt punched up the tang but also introduced more liquid, necessitating more sugar for thickening—a vicious circle.

It wasn't until I started rummaging through the test kitchen pantry for ideas that I came across a potential fix: buttermilk powder. I wondered if its pleasant tang would do the trick in my frosting. I added 2 tablespoons to my frosting and was delighted to find that the mixture was not only flavorful but also markedly tangy. In fact, adding ⅓ cup of powder made the frosting so potent that I could increase the sugar by 1 cup, for a consistency that was structurally sound but still not overly sweet.

I was getting close, but my cake was not yet special-occasion ready. The cut surfaces released crumbs as I assembled the layers, so while the frosting on top of the cake looked pristine, the sides were a wreck. So I brought the nuts back into the equation. To camouflage the imperfections—and satisfy tasters who missed the crunch of the pecans in the cake—I pressed toasted nuts onto the crumb-speckled sides.

With nothing but a sheet pan and the surprise help of a few pantry ingredients, I'd managed to reengineer humble carrot cake as a four-tier, nut-crusted confection that could claim its place among the most glamorous desserts.

—ANDREA GEARY, *Cook's Illustrated*

Carrot Layer Cake

SERVES 10 TO 12

Shred the carrots on the large holes of a box grater or in a food processor fitted with the shredding disk. Do not substitute liquid buttermilk for the buttermilk powder. To ensure the proper spreading consistency for the frosting, use cold cream cheese. If your baked cake is of an uneven thickness, adjust the orientation of the layers as they are stacked to produce a level cake. Assembling this cake on a cardboard cake round trimmed to a 6 by 8-inch rectangle makes it easy to press the pecans onto the sides of the frosted cake.

CARROT LAYER CAKE

CAKE

1¾ cups (8¾ ounces) all-purpose flour

2 teaspoons baking powder

1 teaspoon baking soda

1½ teaspoons ground cinnamon

¾ teaspoon ground nutmeg

½ teaspoon salt

¼ teaspoon ground cloves

1¼ cups packed (8¾ ounces) light brown sugar

¾ cup vegetable oil

3 large eggs

1 teaspoon vanilla extract

2⅔ cups shredded carrots (4 carrots)

⅔ cup dried currants

FROSTING

3 cups (12 ounces) confectioners' sugar

16 tablespoons unsalted butter, softened

⅓ cup buttermilk powder

2 teaspoons vanilla extract

¼ teaspoon salt

12 ounces cream cheese, chilled and cut into
12 equal pieces

2 cups (8 ounces) pecans, toasted and chopped coarse

1. FOR THE CAKE: Adjust oven rack to middle position and heat oven to 350 degrees. Grease 18 by 13-inch rimmed baking sheet, line with parchment paper, and grease parchment. Whisk flour, baking powder, baking soda, cinnamon, nutmeg, salt, and cloves together in large bowl.

2. Whisk sugar, oil, eggs, and vanilla together in second bowl until mixture is smooth. Stir in carrots and currants. Add flour mixture and fold with rubber spatula until mixture is just combined.

3. Transfer batter to prepared sheet and smooth surface with offset spatula. Bake until center of cake is firm to touch, 15 to 18 minutes. Cool in pan on wire rack for 5 minutes. Invert cake onto wire rack (do not remove parchment), then reinvert onto second wire rack. Cool cake completely, about 30 minutes.

4. FOR THE FROSTING: Using stand mixer fitted with paddle, beat sugar, butter, buttermilk powder, vanilla, and salt together on low speed until smooth, about 2 minutes, scraping down bowl as needed. Increase speed to medium-low; add cream cheese, 1 piece at a time; and mix until smooth, about 2 minutes.

5. Transfer cooled cake to cutting board, parchment side down. Using sharp chef's knife, cut cake and parchment in half crosswise, then lengthwise, to make 4 equal rectangles, about 6 by 8 inches each.

6. Place 6 by 8-inch cardboard rectangle on cake platter. Place 1 cake layer, parchment side up, on cardboard and carefully remove parchment. Using offset spatula, spread ⅔ cup frosting evenly over top, right to edge of cake. Repeat with 2 more layers of cake, pressing lightly to adhere and frosting each layer with ⅔ cup frosting. Top with last cake layer and spread 1 cup frosting evenly over top. Spread remaining frosting evenly over sides of cake. (It's fine if some crumbs show through frosting on sides, but if you go back to smooth top of cake, be sure that spatula is free of crumbs.)

7. Hold cake with 1 hand and gently press chopped pecans onto sides with other hand. Chill for at least 1 hour before serving. (The frosted cake can be refrigerated for up to 24 hours before serving.)

TEXAS-STYLE BLUEBERRY COBBLER

IN MOST OF AMERICA, COBBLER MEANS LOTS OF sweet, jammy fruit under a biscuit topping. But at many a barbecue joint in the Hill Country region of central Texas, the same word applies to a very different dessert, one with a moist, tender interior and a crisp, craggy top. As the cobbler bakes, the fruit (which starts out on top) sinks and forms juicy pockets throughout. Whatever you call it, it tastes delicious.

Working my way through a stack of Texas community cookbooks, I found a version of the homey recipe in almost every one. They went under several different names, but the techniques and ingredients were nearly identical. "Don't Stir Cobbler" seemed particularly apt, since you melt lots of butter in a baking dish; pour a simple batter of milk, flour, baking powder, and sugar over it; scatter on fruit; and simply bake. In Texas, peaches are standard cobbler fare, but summer in New England means blueberries, so I made a handful of the recipes that I'd found, substituting berries for the sliced peaches. It was very easy, but I did uncover a few problems: The cobblers were thin and a little bland, and the tops were underbaked. I rolled up my sleeves and got to work.

All the versions that I'd tested were skimpy, barely reaching halfway up the sides of 13 by 9-inch baking dishes. So my first alteration was to increase all the ingredients by 50 percent for a more ample amount. The adjustment meant that I was melting 12 tablespoons of butter in the baking dish, so it was no surprise when tasters complained that the bottom was greasy. I found I could cut the grease if I divided the butter between the pan and the batter. I settled on half a stick of butter melted in the dish and twice that amount stirred into the batter. As an added bonus, the cobbler's crisp brown edges were now so good that my tasters fought over them.

To turn the berries into a more cohesive filling, I realized that I needed to get their juices flowing before the fruit went into the oven. I grabbed a potato masher and went to work. Adding a little sugar helped further break down the berries, and for a bright note, I stirred in grated lemon zest. But in the baked cobbler, the zest was barely discernible. Processing the lemon zest with the sugar in the food processor helped release the zest's flavorful oils, amping up the flavor.

Now I just had to fix the problem of the underbaked top. To get a crisp, nicely browned top, I sprinkled the cobbler with sugar to help it caramelize. This technique worked perfectly, giving me a nicely browned top with little extra sweetness. It also occurred to me that I had another chance to reinforce the lemon flavor. Before I mashed the lemon-sugar mixture with the berries, I set some aside to sprinkle over the unbaked cobbler.

A couple of hands-off hours later, I was contentedly eating a cobbler that was nothing like the sort I'd grown up with. But with its crisp, buttery crust and moist, tender interior studded with sweet, juicy blueberries, I'm not complaining.

—REBECCAH MARSTERS, *Cook's Country*

Texas-Style Blueberry Cobbler
SERVES 8 TO 10

Keep a close eye on the butter as it melts in the oven so that it doesn't scorch. Place the hot baking dish with butter on a wire rack after removing it from the oven. Avoid untreated aluminum pans here. If using frozen blueberries, thaw them first.

- 4 tablespoons unsalted butter, cut into 4 pieces, plus 8 tablespoons melted and cooled
- 1½ cups (10½ ounces) sugar
- 1½ teaspoons grated lemon zest
- 15 ounces (3 cups) blueberries
- 1½ cups (7½ ounces) all-purpose flour
- 2½ teaspoons baking powder
- ¾ teaspoon salt
- 1½ cups milk

1. Adjust oven rack to upper-middle position and heat oven to 350 degrees. Place 4 tablespoons cut-up butter in 13 by 9-inch baking dish and transfer to oven. Heat until butter is melted, 8 to 10 minutes.

2. Meanwhile, pulse ¼ cup sugar and lemon zest together in food processor until combined, about 5 pulses; set aside. Using potato masher, mash blueberries and 1 tablespoon lemon sugar together in bowl until berries are coarsely mashed.

3. Combine flour, remaining 1¼ cups sugar, baking powder, and salt in large bowl. Whisk in milk and 8 tablespoons melted, cooled butter until smooth. Remove baking dish from oven, transfer to wire rack, and pour batter into prepared pan.

4. Dollop mashed blueberry mixture evenly over batter, sprinkle with remaining lemon sugar, and bake until golden brown and edges are crisp, 45 to 50 minutes, rotating pan halfway through baking. Let cobbler cool on wire rack for 30 minutes. Serve warm.

NOTES FROM THE TEST KITCHEN

A DIFFERENT KIND OF COBBLER

Many of us know cobbler as a jammy fruit base with a baked biscuit topping. In the Lone Star State, they start with the batter on the bottom and the fruit on top. In the oven, the batter rises over the berries.

1. First, melt butter right in baking pan to give finished cobbler rich, crisp edges.

2. Next, pour batter into baking pan over melted butter.

3. Finally, scatter on mashed berries.

BUYING BLUEBERRIES

In the peak of summer, locally grown blueberries are sweet and flavorful, making them the only choice in the test kitchen. But the "fresh" berries sold in our supermarkets the rest of the year are expensive and either bland or sour. From fall through early summer, we rely on frozen wild blueberries, which have more flavor than their cultivated cousins. We particularly like **Wyman's** brand from Maine.

PARIS-BREST

PARIS-BREST IS A SHOWSTOPPER DESSERT WITH A rather curious history. To make it, a large ring of pâte à choux—the same pastry used to make éclairs and cream puffs—is filled with hazelnut praline pastry cream, then sprinkled with chopped almonds and powdered sugar. Its quirky name dates back to 1910, when an enterprising baker whose shop was located along the route of the Paris-Brest-Paris bicycle race—a 1,200-kilometer journey from Paris to the city of Brest, in Brittany, and back again—invented the dessert to honor the cyclists. His creation was in the shape of a bicycle tire, complete with a pastry "inner tube"—a recent invention at the time. Despite the irony of associating a calorie-laden, decadent confection with grueling feats of athleticism, Paris-Brest cake was an instant hit in France.

Although it looks as though it would take a professional pastry chef to create it, the dessert is actually assembled from relatively easy-to-prepare elements, each of which can be made hours or days in advance. That said, I knew that coming up with a foolproof recipe was going to require a bit of athleticism of my own. The recipes I rounded up in my research—from such culinary luminaries as Julia Child, Alain Ducasse, and Pierre Hermé—yielded "wheels" of all shapes and sizes. Often the pastry ring was crusty and tough; other rings were so tender that they collapsed upon cooling. The praline cream presented challenges as well: I didn't want it to be overly rich, yet I needed it to be sturdy enough to stay put in the pastry. The praline paste—a puree of toasted hazelnuts and caramelized sugar—was straightforward enough, but I'd need to make it foolproof.

I started my tests with the pastry dough. Creating pâte à choux is a particularly rewarding process because it's so easy and the results are so dramatic. To make it, you simmer milk, water, granulated sugar, and butter, stir in all-purpose flour to make a paste, then cook it briefly before whipping eggs into the hot mixture. The dough is piped out through a pastry bag and baked. Leavened by steam alone, the dough puffs up, creating a crisp, hollow shell surrounding a tender, ethereal lining of soft dough. For a pastry this large, it would take some work to achieve just the right balance between a too-crisp shell and one so tender that it would slump once removed from the oven.

To start, I compared the ratios of each ingredient in the various recipes I'd tested. The differences were clear.

PARIS-BREST

The recipes that yielded the crispest, most rigid pastries called for the addition of extra egg whites and only small amounts of milk. Egg whites give the pastry structure, and both milk and egg yolks contain tenderizing fat and proteins. After testing several ratios of my own, I eventually landed on a dough made with ⅔ cup of whole eggs (an exact amount was essential) and half that amount of both water and milk. These measurements yielded the balance of tenderness and strength that I was looking for. To add crunch to the tender pastry, I sprinkled it with chopped hazelnuts before baking it.

With a reliable dough in hand, I began to sort out the best way to bake my tire and inner tube. Choux pastry is typically baked in three stages. Starting the dough in a high-temperature oven quickly generates steam that inflates the pastry. The oven temperature is then lowered and the pastry is cooked until the exterior is well browned and fully set. Finally, it is removed from the oven, sliced open in spots to help release moisture trapped in its interior, then returned until dry to a turned-off but still-warm oven with its door propped open.

But when baking two sets of rings, one thick and one narrow, the standard method was unworkable: The larger tire never completely set, and the narrow inner tube tended to burn by the end of the baking time. I first tried opening the oven door to remove the narrow ring as soon as it was crisp, but that let so much heat escape that the larger ring collapsed. After a long series of tests, I came up with a two-part solution.

First, I discovered that when the narrow ring was placed on the lower rack, it was partially shielded from the oven's heat by the tray above, which helped prevent burning. Second, I lowered the temperature of the initial bake from the standard 450 to 400 degrees and held it there for 25 minutes—more than double the standard duration. This longer, gentler early cooking period ensured that by the time the narrow ring was browned, the thick ring would be fully set, so I could remove the narrow ring without the larger ring collapsing. (Because the narrow ring was so thin, it did not need to dry out in the turned-off oven.)

Next, I got down to the business of creating that light yet sturdy cream filling. Praline cream is made by combining pastry cream with praline paste—a pulverized mixture of hardened caramel and nuts—and lightening it with whipped butter or cream or a meringue. The praline paste was the sticking point, since caramel making can be tricky business. But when I got to the stove, I was pleasantly surprised to find the paste considerably less finicky than standard caramel. The key is that praline calls for adding nuts to the sugar syrup as soon as it turns golden. Standard caramel requires careful monitoring to avoid scorching. Adding nuts, however, immediately arrests the cooking, making praline practically foolproof. I was also able to improve on the basic recipe by adding a touch of lemon juice to the sugar and water mixture. The acidity of the juice speeds up the breakdown of the sugars and catalyzes browning. Once the nuts are in, the mixture is transferred to a baking sheet to harden. To turn the praline into a smooth paste, I broke it into small pieces and ground it fine in a food processor along with salt and a little oil.

For the pastry cream, I used the test kitchen's standard recipe, which uses flour to thicken the dairy rather than the usual cornstarch, as the latter is less stable and can break down if overheated or overwhisked. As for lightening up the pastry cream, there were a number of options to try, including whipped butter, softened butter, Italian meringue, and whipped cream. Not surprisingly, butter—even when whipped—added too much richness, and the meringue fussily required the use of a candy thermometer. In the end, my tasters were happiest with the texture and flavor of whipped cream, since it added little to the filling besides much-needed air.

Ensuring that the filling had enough structure was more complicated. More flour thickened it up somewhat, but it also added an unpleasant pastiness. A few teaspoons of gelatin (added after the pastry cream had finished cooking) worked far better, providing the necessary amount of body without rendering the filling firm or bouncy. To fully set, the cream needed to sit in the refrigerator for three to 24 hours, well in advance of dinner.

With each component in place, all that remained was the assembly. After halving the larger cooled ring horizontally with a serrated knife, I used a ½-inch star tip to pipe a ribbon of praline cream onto the bottom half of the ring in a zigzag pattern. Working my way up, I pressed the narrow inner tube into the bed of cream to secure it in place, piped the remaining praline cream over the inner tube in a wider zigzag pattern, and gently placed the top half of the large ring on top of it. With a last-minute dusting of confectioners' sugar, this dazzling cake was ready for its grand debut on my holiday table.

—ANDREW JANJIGIAN, *Cook's Illustrated*

Paris-Brest

SERVES 8 TO 10

An equal amount of slivered almonds can be substituted for the hazelnuts. To skin the hazelnuts, simply place them in a clean kitchen towel after toasting, while they are still warm, and rub gently. Use a serrated knife to cut the dessert.

PRALINE

- ½ cup (3½ ounces) granulated sugar
- ¼ cup water
- 1 teaspoon lemon juice
- 1 cup (4 ounces) hazelnuts, toasted and skinned
- ½ teaspoon salt
- 1 tablespoon vegetable oil

PASTRY DOUGH

- 3 large eggs
- 6 tablespoons unsalted butter, cut into 12 pieces
- ⅓ cup whole milk
- ⅓ cup water
- 2 teaspoons granulated sugar
- ½ teaspoon salt
- ¾ cup (3¾ ounces) all-purpose flour
- 2 tablespoons toasted, skinned, and chopped hazelnuts

CREAM FILLING

- 2 teaspoons unflavored gelatin
- ¼ cup water
- 1½ cups half-and-half
- 5 large egg yolks
- ⅓ cup (2⅓ ounces) granulated sugar
- 3 tablespoons all-purpose flour
- 3 tablespoons unsalted butter, cut into 3 pieces and chilled
- 1½ teaspoons vanilla extract
- 1 cup heavy cream, chilled

  Confectioners' sugar

1. FOR THE PRALINE: Line rimmed baking sheet with parchment paper; spray parchment with vegetable oil spray and set aside. Bring sugar, water, and lemon juice to boil in medium saucepan over medium heat, stirring once or twice to dissolve sugar. Cook without stirring until syrup is golden brown, 10 to 15 minutes. Remove saucepan from heat, stir in nuts, and immediately pour mixture onto prepared baking sheet. Place baking sheet on wire rack and allow caramel to harden, about 30 minutes.

2. Break hardened caramel into 1- to 2-inch pieces; process pieces in food processor until finely ground, about 30 seconds. Add salt and vegetable oil and continue to process until uniform paste is formed, 1 to 2 minutes longer. Transfer mixture to bowl, cover with plastic wrap, and set aside.

3. FOR THE PASTRY DOUGH: Adjust oven racks to upper-middle and lower-middle positions and heat oven to 400 degrees. Draw or trace 8-inch circle in center of two 18 by 12-inch sheets of parchment paper; flip parchment over. Spray 2 baking sheets with oil spray and line with parchment (keeping guide rings on underside).

4. Beat eggs in measuring cup or small bowl; you should have ⅔ cup (discard excess). Heat butter, milk, water, sugar, and salt in medium saucepan over medium heat, stirring occasionally. When mixture reaches full boil (butter should be fully melted), immediately remove saucepan from heat and stir in flour with heatproof spatula or wooden spoon until combined and no mixture remains on sides of pan. Return saucepan to low heat and cook, stirring constantly, using smearing motion, until mixture is slightly shiny and tiny beads of fat appear on bottom of saucepan, about 3 minutes.

5. Immediately transfer mixture to food processor and process with feed tube open for 30 seconds to cool slightly. With machine running, gradually add eggs in steady stream. When all eggs have been added, scrape down sides of bowl, then process for 30 seconds until smooth, thick, sticky paste forms.

6. Transfer ¾ cup dough to pastry bag fitted with ⅜-inch round tip. To make narrow inner ring, pipe single ½-inch-wide circle of dough directly on traced guide ring on 1 baking sheet. For large outer ring, squeeze out any excess dough in pastry bag and change pastry bag tip to ½-inch star tip. Put all remaining dough into pastry bag. Pipe ½-inch-wide circle of dough around inside of traced guide ring on remaining baking sheet. Pipe second ½-inch circle of dough around first so they overlap slightly. Pipe third ½-inch circle on top of other 2 circles directly over seam. Sprinkle chopped nuts evenly over surface of ring.

7. Place sheet with larger outer ring on upper rack and sheet with narrow inner ring on lower rack and bake until narrow ring is golden brown and firm, 22 to

PUTTING TOGETHER PARIS-BREST

Although this showstopper dessert seems daunting, it's actually assembled from relatively easy-to-prepare elements, each of which can be made hours or days in advance. The praline can be made up to 1 week in advance and refrigerated. Bring the praline to room temperature before using. The pastry dough can be covered and stored at room temperature for up to 2 hours. The cooled pastry rings can be wrapped tightly and stored at room temperature for up to 24 hours or frozen for up to 1 month. Before using, recrisp rings in 300-degree oven for 5 to 10 minutes. The dessert can be assembled and refrigerated up to 3 hours in advance.

1. ADD NUTS TO CARAMEL: As soon as caramel turns golden brown, stir in toasted hazelnuts and pour mixture onto parchment paper–lined baking sheet to set.

2. MAKE PRALINE PASTE: Process broken caramel pieces in food processor until finely ground, about 30 seconds. Add salt and vegetable oil and process again until uniform paste forms, 2 to 3 minutes longer.

3. PIPE INNER RING: Using bag fitted with ⅜-inch round tip, pipe narrow circle of pastry dough directly on top of guide ring traced on parchment. Set aside.

4. PIPE 2 CIRCLES FOR LARGE OUTER RING: Use ½-inch star tip to pipe circle of dough around inside of remaining guide ring. Then pipe second circle around first so they overlap slightly.

5. PIPE THIRD CIRCLE FOR OUTER RING: Finish outer ring by piping third circle on top of other 2 circles, directly over seam. Sprinkle with nuts and bake.

6. HALVE BAKED OUTER RING: After cooling outer ring, halve horizontally using serrated knife.

7. PIPE PRALINE CREAM: Using pastry bag fitted with ½-inch star tip, pipe narrow zigzag of praline cream onto bottom half of outer ring.

8. TOP WITH INNER RING: Place inner ring on top of praline cream and press down gently.

9. PIPE PRALINE CREAM: Pipe remaining praline cream over inner ring in zigzag pattern to cover.

10. TOP AND DUST: Gently place top half of outer ring over filling and dust with confectioners' sugar.

26 minutes. Remove narrow ring and transfer to wire rack. Reduce oven temperature to 350 degrees and continue to bake larger ring for another 10 minutes. Remove baking sheet from oven and turn oven off. Using paring knife, cut 4 equally spaced ¾-inch-wide slits around edges of larger ring to release steam. Return larger ring to oven and prop oven door open with handle of wooden spoon. Let ring stand in oven until exterior is crisp, about 45 minutes. Transfer ring to wire rack to cool, about 15 minutes.

8. FOR THE CREAM FILLING: Sprinkle gelatin over water in small bowl and let sit until gelatin softens, about 5 minutes. Heat half-and-half in medium saucepan over medium heat until just simmering. Meanwhile, whisk yolks and sugar together in medium bowl until smooth. Add flour to yolk mixture and whisk until incorporated. Remove half-and-half from heat and, whisking constantly, slowly add ½ cup to yolk mixture to temper. Whisking constantly, add tempered yolk mixture to half-and-half in saucepan.

9. Return saucepan to medium heat and cook, whisking constantly, until mixture thickens slightly, 1 to 2 minutes. Reduce heat to medium-low and continue to cook, whisking constantly, 8 minutes longer.

10. Increase heat to medium and cook, whisking vigorously, until bubbles burst on surface, 1 to 2 minutes. Remove saucepan from heat; whisk in butter, vanilla, and softened gelatin until butter is melted and incorporated. Strain pastry cream through fine-mesh strainer set over large bowl. Press lightly greased parchment paper directly on surface and refrigerate until chilled but not set, about 45 minutes.

11. Using stand mixer fitted with whisk, whip cream on medium-low speed until foamy, about 1 minute. Increase speed to high and whip until soft peaks form, 1 to 3 minutes. Whisk praline paste and half of whipped cream into pastry cream until combined. Gently fold in remaining whipped cream until incorporated. Cover and refrigerate until set, at least 3 hours or up to 24 hours.

12. TO ASSEMBLE: Using serrated knife, slice larger outer ring in half horizontally; place bottom on large serving plate. Fill pastry bag fitted with ½-inch star tip with cream filling. Pipe ½-inch-wide strip of cream filling in narrow zigzag pattern around center of bottom half of ring. Press narrow inner ring gently into cream filling. Pipe cream filling over narrow ring in zigzag pattern to cover. Place top half of larger ring over cream filling, dust with confectioners' sugar, and serve.

TO MAKE AHEAD: Cooled pastry rings can be wrapped tightly and stored at room temperature for up to 24 hours or frozen for up to 1 month. Before using, recrisp rings in 300-degree oven for 5 to 10 minutes. Praline can be made up to 1 week in advance and refrigerated. Bring praline to room temperature before using. Pastry dough can be transferred to bowl, with surface covered with sheet of lightly greased parchment, and stored at room temperature for up to 2 hours. Dessert can be assembled and refrigerated up to 3 hours in advance.

DANISH PUFF PASTRY

DANISH PUFF PASTRY IS NEITHER DANISH NOR PUFF pastry. It is, however, buttery, almond-y, and incredibly delicious. Inspired by the many-leaved traditional Danish pastry known as kringle, the Betty Crocker kitchens developed Danish puff pastry in 1961, seemingly to capture some of kringle's fancy, layered pastry appeal without the complex, time-consuming process of laminating (that's how pastry chefs say "layer dough with butter"). Even 50 years later, this was a goal I could definitely get behind.

When I collected recipes for Danish puff pastry, I made two surprising discoveries. First, Danish puff pastry is simply ordinary pie crust with flavored pâte à choux, or cream puff dough, spread on top of it. And second, all recipes for it are virtually identical. These recipes start with instructions to make basic pie dough. In place of a rolling pin, they call for shaping the dough into two long ropes, then simply patting them flat to form two rectangles. The "topping" is made from typical cream puff dough: Boil a cup of water with half a cup of butter, stir in a cup of flour to make a paste, then turn off the heat and mix in three eggs. Unlike classic choux paste, Danish puff gets an injection of almond extract. This choux paste is spread over the long, narrow pie dough rectangles, baked in a 350-degree oven for about an hour, cooled, and topped with an almond or vanilla glaze and sliced, toasted almonds.

A pastry made from two completely different doughs seemed bizarre to me, but my colleague Becky practically drooled as she recalled her mother making Danish puffs for special occasions during Becky's childhood. Based on her description, I had visions of a sky-high Danish puff, with a crisp, flaky pie crust supporting a buttery, creamy interior, its labyrinthine network of dough walls and air channels resembling the many layers of a traditional laminated dough. A sweet and easy glaze (basically confectioners' sugar and milk) united the two parts. Unfortunately, my test puffs weren't like that at all. Instead, the choux top was stunted and the pie crust bland and dry.

I quickly remedied the bland flavor by adding salt and sugar to both crust and puff dough. Getting the top to puff up was more complicated. A comparison of the Danish puff topping recipes with cream puff and éclair recipes suggested that more egg would help elevate my puff. One extra egg helped a bit, so I tried two. That knocked the flavor out of balance, making the puff too eggy. My next idea—bake the puff for a short time in a very hot oven, then decrease the temperature to finish baking—did give the puff a jump start, as I'd intended, but it still didn't achieve the heights I had in mind.

I was getting a cramp in my forearm from stirring my umpteenth batch of choux paste when I got to wondering if the dough was too stiff: A stiff, dry dough is harder to inflate than a loose, wet dough. To make it looser, I added more water. At the same time, I tried out two standard choux paste techniques that are aimed at drying the interior of baked puffs to prevent collapse. Using a paring knife, I slit the baked choux topping to let the steam escape, and I cooled the puffs in a partially open oven. To my relief, these three adjustments combined to make my puffs tall and airy.

But alas, the pie crust was burnt, and every change of oven rack location and oven temperature that fixed the pie crust bottom ruined the choux paste top. What I needed, I realized, was insulation for the bottom. For my next test, I baked the puffs on two stacked baking sheets and produced a well-browned, not scorched, crust.

All along, I'd been thinking about pie dough and choux dough as two completely different things, but as I was measuring out the ingredients for another test, it suddenly occurred to me how similar the two dough recipes actually were. Could I save time and effort by making just one dough? After some trial and error, I was able to consolidate the two parts of the recipe into one. I created a dough of flour, butter, sugar, salt, and water and used half of it to make the two 12 by 3-inch pie dough rectangles. To the remaining dough I added boiling water and eggs. Voilà—choux paste! The results were indistinguishable from a puff made with the two doughs mixed independently. The process, however, was much more efficient—definitely a boon for a sweet intended to mimic a fancy pastry in every way except the amount of effort required to make it.

The final step, the sweet glaze and nut topping, was a snap: I stirred together confectioners' sugar, milk, salt, almond extract, and melted butter; drizzled the mixture on the puffs; and sprinkled them with toasted, sliced almonds. The original Danish puff didn't quite live up to promises of an easy yet elegant mile-high pastry. With better seasoning, an extra egg, and a couple of tricks, this updated Danish puff delivers. It may not be Danish and it may not be puff pastry, but in the end, tasters were too busy eating to argue the point.

—SARAH GABRIEL, *Cook's Country*

Danish Puff Pastry

SERVES 10 TO 12

Baking the pastry on 2 stacked baking sheets prevents it from burning on the bottom. Be sure to cool the pastries completely before glazing. If the glaze is too thick to spread smoothly, whisk in an additional tablespoon of milk.

PASTRY

- 2 cups (10 ounces) all-purpose flour
- 2 tablespoons granulated sugar
- 1¾ teaspoons salt
- 16 tablespoons unsalted butter, cut into ½-inch pieces and chilled
- 1½ cups cold water
- 4 large eggs
- ¾ teaspoon almond extract

GLAZE

- 1½ cups (6 ounces) confectioners' sugar, sifted
- 3 tablespoons milk
- ¼ teaspoon salt
- ⅛ teaspoon almond extract
- 3 tablespoons unsalted butter, melted and cooled
- ⅓ cup sliced almonds, toasted

HOW TWO DOUGHS BECOME ONE PASTRY

1. After making pie dough, set half of it aside to be used to start choux pastry. Roll other half into two equal ropes.

2. Press ropes into 12 by 3-inch rectangles. Chill rectangles in refrigerator while you make choux pastry.

3. Combine reserved pie dough with boiling water in saucepan and cook, stirring, until mixture is shiny and pulls away from pan.

4. Move cooked choux dough to food processor. Slowly pour in lightly beaten egg mixture as processor runs.

5. Cover each chilled dough rectangle with half of warm choux dough. Bake puffs for 1½ hours.

6. After puffs have baked and cooled, ice them with simple glaze and sprinkle them with sliced almonds.

1. FOR THE PASTRY: Adjust oven rack to middle position and heat oven to 400 degrees. Line rimmed baking sheet with parchment paper. Pulse flour, sugar, and salt together in food processor until combined, about 3 pulses. Add butter and pulse until mixture resembles coarse meal, about 10 pulses. Add ½ cup water and pulse until mixture forms dough, about 10 pulses.

2. Transfer half of dough (11 ounces) to lightly floured counter, knead briefly until dough comes together, and roll into two 12-inch ropes. Transfer ropes to prepared baking sheet. Press ropes with hand into 12 by 3-inch rectangles. Cover with plastic wrap and refrigerate until ready to use.

3. Meanwhile, lightly beat eggs and almond extract together in 2-cup liquid measuring cup. Bring remaining 1 cup water to boil in medium saucepan over high heat. Add remaining dough to boiling water and cook, stirring constantly, until ball forms, about 2 minutes. Reduce heat to low and cook, stirring constantly, until mixture is uniformly shiny and pulls away from sides of pan, 3 to 5 minutes.

4. Transfer hot dough to food processor and process for 10 seconds. With processor running, slowly add egg mixture until incorporated, scraping down sides of bowl as needed. Divide warm dough mixture between chilled dough rectangles and spread evenly.

5. Set baking sheet with pastry inside second rimmed baking sheet. Bake for 15 minutes, then reduce oven temperature to 350 degrees and bake until pastry is puffed and golden brown, about 75 minutes longer. Turn oven off and, using paring knife, make four ½-inch horizontal slits in each long side of both pastries. Prop open oven door with wooden spoon. Leave pastries in turned-off oven for 20 minutes. Remove from oven and let cool completely on baking sheet, about 1 hour.

6. FOR THE GLAZE: Whisk sugar, milk, salt, and almond extract together in bowl until smooth. Slowly whisk in melted butter until incorporated. Drizzle glaze over each pastry and top with toasted almonds. Serve.

DANISH PUFF PASTRY

CHOCOLATE ESPRESSO DACQUOISE

THERE COULD BE NO MORE STUNNING FINALE to a holiday celebration than a dacquoise: a decadent dessert featuring layers of crisp, nutty meringue and silky buttercream coated in sleek dark chocolate and studded with toasted nuts. But you rarely see dacquoise anywhere but fancy patisseries or high-end restaurants—and with good reason: Making one is a project to rival all projects. The good news? Not only can you make this impressive showpiece at home, but you can have it ready long before your guests arrive. In fact, this dessert improves when it's assembled a day or two before serving, as the flavors meld and the buttercream softens the meringue.

Here's how a pastry chef makes a dacquoise: She whips egg whites with sugar to make a meringue, into which she folds finely chopped nuts. Then she pipes the meringue into several flat layers, bakes them for up to three hours at a very low temperature, and then leaves them in the oven for an extended time to dry out completely. When the meringues are crisp, she layers them with buttercream (made from more egg whites, a screaming-hot sugar syrup, and a generous amount of butter). Finally, she coats the whole construction in a shiny ganache made with chocolate and warm cream.

To make this complex recipe manageable at home, I would have to eliminate some of its more bothersome features: namely, the fussy piping, the long baking and drying times, and that tricky sugar syrup. If possible, I also wanted to do something with all those orphaned egg yolks. And after all the time and effort I'd be putting in, I didn't want my dacquoise to just satisfy my guests; I wanted it to render them speechless.

Meringue is typically made by whipping egg whites (and perhaps an acid such as cream of tartar, which helps the egg white proteins bond for greater stability) until they begin to retain air and form soft mounds in the bowl. The sugar is then slowly added, while the whipping continues, until it dissolves and the mixture thickens, forming stiff, glossy peaks when the beaters are pulled from the surface. Finely ground nuts are folded in at this point, and then the meringue pieces are piped and baked. Meringue made this way, though, is a bit dense and crunchy, leading to a dacquoise that's hard to slice (and eat), even when left to sit for a while. I tried a technique I found for an "automatic meringue," in which the whites and sugar were combined at the start. The automatic meringue was indeed easy—I just dumped egg whites, cream of tartar, and sugar into the bowl of a stand mixer and let it rip—but it baked up as dense and firm as Styrofoam. Sugar, it turns out, interferes with the unfolding and bonding of egg white proteins, so adding it too early made for a slower process and denser meringue.

Obviously that was the wrong direction. But it gave me an idea: What if I went back to the traditional method of adding sugar once soft peaks formed but added less of it? Would that lighten up the texture? I gave it another go, this time adding just half the sugar between the soft- and stiff-peak stages and folding in the remainder at the end with the ground nuts. Now the egg white proteins were freer to expand, forming a light, airy foam in just four minutes. Once baked, this meringue had a crisp, delicate texture that was the perfect foil for buttercream—and was easier to slice and eat.

With the meringue's texture nailed down, I considered its shape. I wanted a rectangular dacquoise because it would be easier to slice neatly than a round one. Reluctant to use a pastry bag to pipe the meringue, I spooned it into four piles on two baking sheets and tried using an offset spatula to coax the piles into uniform rectangles. But despite my best efforts, they were all different sizes, with rounded blobs for corners.

Then I had a brainstorm: Why not bake the meringue in one big piece? That way, I could use just one sheet (eliminating the need to bake in batches) and trim the baked meringue into even pieces with squared-off edges. I drew a 13 by 10½-inch rectangle on a piece of parchment that I then placed on a rimless baking sheet. Using the lines as a guide, I spread meringue over it in an even layer.

Most dacquoise recipes call for baking the meringue at about 200 degrees for anywhere from one to three hours and then letting it dry in the oven for several hours more. I found that even two hours of baking, followed by a full three-hour rest, left my oversized meringue still chewy and impossible to cut neatly. With the temperature that low, I'd have to bake the meringue for a full three hours and rest it for at least as long in order to get it nice and crisp. While it was all hands-off waiting, I wanted to trim any time I could from the process.

What if I upped the heat? The meringue baked at 300 degrees was too brown and tasted slightly burnt. At 250 degrees I found my sweet spot: The meringue had a creamy taupe color, light caramelized taste, and a firm, crisp texture after only 90 minutes of baking and the same amount of time drying.

The higher temperature sped things up, but it also caused a new problem: The surface of the meringue was now drying out faster than the bottom, forming a brittle crust that ballooned out and crumbled as soon as I took a knife to it. Though meringue and moisture are normally bitter enemies, I wondered if lightly spritzing water on the top before baking would help. This counterintuitive solution worked: It delayed the setting of the surface until most of the moisture had evaporated from the bottom layer, forming a meringue that remained intact and cooked evenly.

At this point, I had what looked like a plank of acoustical tile. But it took some trial and error (and a small mountain of meringue shards) before I found the right tool and technique for dividing it into four strips. A long, serrated bread knife, a gentle and repeated scoring motion, and a ruler ensured that each piece was trimmed to a perfect 10 by 3-inch rectangle. I had the building blocks for my construction—now for the mortar to hold it together.

In its simplest form, buttercream is just powdered sugar and butter creamed together. I didn't want my dacquoise to be cloyingly sweet, so I ruled out that type from the start. The trouble is, most other buttercreams rely on egg whites, which would leave me with even more leftover yolks. I also wanted to avoid using a fussy hot sugar syrup (which requires a candy thermometer in order to bring the syrup to precisely 240 degrees), further narrowing the options. My salvation came in the form of a confection I'd never made before: a so-called German buttercream, which is whipped together from butter and pastry cream, a simple custard made with egg yolks that doesn't need a thermometer.

I whisked the yolks with cornstarch, milk, and sugar over medium heat for a few minutes until thickened. After cooling the pastry cream, I whipped it with an equal amount of softened butter until the mixture came together to form a velvety-smooth buttercream. It seemed a winner until I took a taste. Disappointingly, its flavor was flat and stodgy.

Dacquoise often includes a coffee-flavored element, and a few teaspoons of espresso powder mixed into the buttercream definitely improved matters. But something was still lacking. I found the missing element on the liquor shelf in the form of almond liqueur. Just an ounce gave the buttercream the sophistication it deserved and

complemented the nutty meringue. I stacked the strips of meringue, spreading buttercream between each layer; thinly coated the exterior with buttercream as well; and then let my dacquoise firm up in the fridge while I prepared its crowning glory—the shiny chocolate ganache.

To make the ganache, I poured warm cream over finely chopped bittersweet chocolate and stirred the mixture until it was smooth, adding a couple of teaspoons of corn syrup for enhanced shine. After it had cooled a bit, I poured the ganache over the chilled dacquoise and smoothed it over each side. For the final touch, I decorated the top of the dacquoise with toasted hazelnuts and patted some sliced almonds onto its sides.

It looked spectacular, but when I ate a slice, I knew that something was still missing. Only the outer edges of my dacquoise boasted chocolate flavor, and that just wasn't enough. Next time around, I made twice as much ganache and spread some on each layer of meringue, alternating with the buttercream. Now there was crisp, nutty meringue; rich buttercream; and silky ganache in every bite.

Tasters greeted this last dacquoise with a near-silence that made me nervous. Had I gotten it horribly wrong? Was it too sweet? Too crunchy? Had the meringue glued their jaws together? No. The dessert had merely rendered them speechless.

—ANDREA GEARY, *Cook's Illustrated*

Chocolate Espresso Dacquoise
SERVES 10 TO 12

The components of this recipe can easily be prepared in advance. Use a rimless baking sheet or an overturned rimmed baking sheet to bake the meringue. Instant coffee may be substituted for the espresso powder. To skin the hazelnuts, simply place the warm toasted nuts in a clean dish towel and rub gently. We recommend Ghirardelli Bittersweet Chocolate Baking Bar with 60% Cacao for this recipe.

MERINGUE
- ¾ **cup blanched sliced almonds, toasted**
- ⅓ **cup hazelnuts, toasted and skinned**
- 1 **tablespoon cornstarch**
- ⅛ **teaspoon salt**
- 1 **cup (7 ounces) sugar**
- 4 **large egg whites, room temperature**
- ¼ **teaspoon cream of tartar**

BUTTERCREAM

- ¾ cup whole milk
- 4 large egg yolks
- ⅓ cup (2⅓ ounces) sugar
- 1½ teaspoons cornstarch
- ¼ teaspoon salt
- 2 tablespoons amaretto or water
- 1½ tablespoons instant espresso powder
- 16 tablespoons unsalted butter, softened

GANACHE

- 6 ounces bittersweet chocolate, chopped fine
- ¾ cup heavy cream
- 2 teaspoons corn syrup

- 1 cup blanched sliced almonds, toasted
- 12 whole hazelnuts, toasted and skinned

1. FOR THE MERINGUE: Adjust oven rack to middle position and heat oven to 250 degrees. Using ruler and permanent marker, draw 13 by 10½-inch rectangle on piece of parchment paper. Grease baking sheet and place parchment on it, ink side down.

2. Process almonds, hazelnuts, cornstarch, and salt together in food processor until nuts are finely ground, 15 to 20 seconds. Add ½ cup sugar and pulse to combine, 1 to 2 pulses.

3. Using stand mixer fitted with whisk, whip egg whites and cream of tartar together on medium-low speed until foamy, about 1 minute. Increase speed to medium-high and whip whites to soft, billowy mounds, about 1 minute. With mixer running at medium-high speed, slowly add remaining ½ cup sugar and continue to whip until glossy, stiff peaks form, 2 to 3 minutes. Fold nut mixture into egg whites in 2 batches. With offset spatula, spread meringue evenly into 13 by 10½-inch rectangle on parchment, using lines on parchment as guide. Using spray bottle, evenly mist surface of meringue with water until glistening. Bake for 1½ hours. Turn off oven and allow meringue to cool in oven for 1½ hours. (Do not open oven during baking and cooling.) Remove from oven and let cool to room temperature, about 10 minutes. (Cooled meringue can be kept at room temperature, tightly wrapped, for up to 2 days.)

4. FOR THE BUTTERCREAM: Heat milk in small saucepan over medium heat until just simmering. Meanwhile, whisk egg yolks, sugar, cornstarch, and salt together in bowl until smooth. Remove milk from heat and, whisking constantly, add half of milk to yolk mixture to temper. Whisking constantly, return tempered yolk mixture to milk in saucepan. Return saucepan to medium heat and cook, whisking constantly, until mixture is bubbling and thickens to consistency of warm pudding, 3 to 5 minutes. Transfer pastry cream to bowl. Cover and refrigerate until set, at least 2 hours or up to 24 hours. Before using, warm gently to room temperature in microwave at 50 percent power, stirring every 10 seconds.

5. Stir together amaretto and espresso powder; set aside. Using stand mixer fitted with paddle, beat butter at medium speed until smooth and light, 3 to 4 minutes. Add pastry cream in 3 batches, beating for 30 seconds after each addition. Add amaretto mixture and continue to beat until light and fluffy, about 5 minutes longer, scraping down bowl thoroughly halfway though mixing.

6. FOR THE GANACHE: Place chocolate in heatproof bowl. Bring cream and corn syrup to simmer in small saucepan over medium heat. Pour cream mixture over chocolate and let stand for 1 minute. Stir mixture until smooth. Set aside to cool until chocolate mounds slightly when dripped from spoon.

7. TO ASSEMBLE: Carefully invert meringue and peel off parchment. Reinvert meringue and place on cutting board. Using serrated knife and gentle, repeated scoring motion, trim edges of meringue to form 12 by 10-inch rectangle. Discard trimmings. With long side of rectangle parallel to counter, use ruler to mark top and bottom edge of meringue at 3-inch intervals. Using serrated knife, score surface of meringue by drawing knife toward you from mark on top edge to corresponding mark on bottom edge. Repeat scoring until meringue is fully cut through. Repeat until you have four 10 by 3-inch rectangles. (If any meringues break during cutting, use them as middle layers.)

8. Place 3 rectangles on wire rack set in rimmed baking sheet. Using offset spatula, spread ¼ cup ganache evenly over surface of each meringue. Refrigerate until ganache is firm, about 15 minutes. Set aside remaining ganache.

9. Using offset spatula, spread top surface of remaining meringue rectangle with ½ cup buttercream; place on wire rack with ganache-coated meringues. Invert one ganache-coated meringue, place on top of buttercream, and press gently to level. Repeat 2 more times, spreading meringue with ½ cup buttercream and topping with inverted ganache-coated meringue. When last

ASSEMBLING THE DACQUOISE

Here's how to assemble the three different components of dacquoise—cooled, baked meringue; buttercream; and ganache—into a dessert that looks like it was made in a professional bakery.

1. Using serrated knife and gentle, repeated scoring motion, trim edges of cooled meringue to form 12 by 10-inch rectangle.

5. Invert one ganache-coated strip on top of buttercream-coated strip and press gently. Spread top with buttercream. Repeat twice to form 4 layers.

2. With long side of meringue parallel to counter, mark top and bottom edges at 3-inch intervals.

6. Lightly coat sides of cake with half of remaining buttercream; coat top with remaining buttercream. Smooth edges and surfaces; refrigerate until firm.

3. Repeatedly score surface by gently drawing knife from top mark to corresponding bottom mark until cut through. Repeat to make four 10 by 3-inch strips.

7. Pour ganache over top of cake and spread in thin, even layer, letting excess flow down sides. Spread thinly across sides.

4. Place 3 strips on wire rack and spread ¼ cup ganache evenly over each. Refrigerate for 15 minutes. Spread remaining strip with ½ cup buttercream.

8. Place toasted whole hazelnuts in line on top of cake and gently press sliced almonds onto sides.

---

ganache-coated meringue is in place, spread half of remaining buttercream to lightly coat sides of cake, then use remaining buttercream to coat top of cake. Smooth sides and top until cake resembles box. Refrigerate until buttercream is firm, about 2 hours. (Once buttercream is firm, assembled cake may be wrapped tightly in plastic wrap and refrigerated for up to 2 days.)

10. Warm remaining ganache in heatproof bowl set over barely simmering water, stirring occasionally, until mixture is very fluid but not hot. Keeping assembled cake on wire rack, pour ganache over top of cake.

Using offset spatula, spread ganache in thin, even layer over top of cake, letting excess flow down sides. Spread ganache over sides in thin layer (top must be completely covered, but some small gaps on sides are OK).

11. Garnish top of cake with toasted whole hazelnuts. Holding cake with 1 hand, gently press sliced almonds onto sides with other hand. Chill for at least 3 hours or up to 12 hours. Transfer to platter. Cut into slices and serve. For best results, slice with sharp knife that has been dipped in hot water and wiped dry before each slice.

VANILLA ICE CREAM

IN THE FIVE YEARS THAT I'VE OWNED MY CANISTER-style ice cream maker, I'd say that it has produced, optimistically, a mere couple of gallons of ice cream. It's not that I don't love the taste of homemade ice cream—believe me, I do. Rather, it's that the texture never measures up to the ultra-dense, impossibly smooth "super-premium" ice cream at the grocery store. Instead of thick, dense, and velvety, my results invariably turn out crumbly, fluffy, and icy. Before I decided to sell off my machine at my next yard sale, I wanted to try to come up with a recipe for ice cream with a texture rivaling that of the highest-quality commercial stuff.

I reviewed what I knew about custard-based ice cream: It typically calls for nothing more than milk, cream, sugar, eggs, and flavorings. Once the custard has frozen, the ice cream is composed of three basic elements: ice crystals of pure water; the proteins, sugars, and fats left behind as the water in the mix is crystallized; and air. The amount of air affects denseness, and both the makeup of the custard and how it is frozen contribute to smoothness. I decided to start with a standard custard base and focus first on finding the most effective way to freeze it.

Smooth ice cream isn't technically less icy than "icy" ice cream. Instead, its ice crystals are so small that our tongues can't detect them. One way to encourage the creation of small ice crystals is to freeze the ice cream base as quickly as possible. Fast freezing, along with agitation, causes the formation of thousands of tiny seed crystals, which in turn promote the formation of more tiny crystals. Super-efficient commercial "continuous batch" churners can turn a 40-degree custard base into soft-serve ice cream in as little as 24 seconds, or at most 10 minutes. To maintain this super-fine ice-crystal structure, the churned ice cream is then frozen in a matter of minutes at temperatures ranging from 20 to 50 degrees below zero. In contrast, my canister-style machine takes roughly 35 minutes to turn a chilled custard into soft-serve consistency. Then, depending on how often the freezer door is opened, the partially frozen custard can take up to eight hours to fully freeze. No wonder my results are always icy.

Since the speed of freezing is critical, I wondered if I could improve my results by starting with a colder base. After letting my hot custard cool for a few minutes, I transferred a cup of it to a small bowl, which I popped into the freezer. I cooled the rest of the custard in the fridge overnight. The next day, I stirred the frozen custard into the refrigerated stuff until the frozen custard dissolved, at which point the mixture registered around 30 degrees. Once in the canister, this base reached soft-serve consistency in just 18 minutes and exhibited less iciness than previous batches. Another bonus of this shortened churning time was that it allowed less air to be beaten into the mix; I needed some air, but too much only diluted the ice cream's flavor and lightened the texture. To my great disappointment, however, after four hours of hardening, this ice cream was almost as icy as before.

I couldn't make my freezer colder, but since the rate of cooling is a function of both temperature and surface area, there was still hope. For my next batch, instead of scraping my churned ice cream into a tall container before placing it in the freezer, I spread it into a thin layer in a chilled square metal baking pan (metal conducts heat faster than glass or plastic). In about an hour, my ice cream had firmed up significantly. Its hardening time had been cut significantly, and I could taste the difference—this was my smoothest batch yet.

However, as improved as the ice cream was, it still wasn't as smooth as store-bought. I turned my attention to the ingredients. Playing with the amounts of sugar and fat was out; my tasters felt that the ice cream had optimal sweetness and richness with ¾ cup of sugar, six egg yolks, and slightly more cream than milk. That left me with trying to manipulate the milk solids and water amounts. Milk solids interfere with the formation of crystals, so the more of them the better (up to a point—too much creates a sandy texture). And since crystals are created from water, the less of it the better (up to a point—too little water leads to gumminess). I tried replacing a portion of the milk or cream with condensed or evaporated milk, which contain less water than fresh dairy does. While both products proved effective at reducing iciness, they contributed a stale flavor. I also tried stirring in nonfat powdered milk to boost milk solids, but tasters deemed this ice cream "cheesy" and "funky."

Many commercial producers use powerful stabilizer mixes to immobilize free water in a gel, preventing it from freezing into large ice crystals. I wondered if I could approximate this effect with cornstarch, gelatin, or pectin, all of which thicken by trapping water in a weak gel. The ice crystals in all three batches were far less noticeable, but this easy success came at a price:

VANILLA ICE CREAM

Each ice cream had an artificial texture and strange melting properties. The sample with gelatin refused to melt, even after 10 minutes at room temperature.

I was getting nowhere with the milk solids and water, so I turned my attention to an ingredient that I had all but glossed over in my testing: sugar. I'd stuck with granulated white sugar, without looking further. But ice cream producers rely on a laundry list of different sweeteners to achieve particular textures and sweetness levels. One highly valued sweetener is invert sugar, a syrup made by cooking sugar water with an acid—a slow, finicky process that converts sucrose into glucose and fructose. With even more molecules than table sugar to interfere with ice formation, invert sugar dramatically lowers the freezing point of the ice cream mixture so that more of the water remains liquid in the freezer. While a boon to an ice cream shop that can hold its product at super-cold temperatures, a depressed freezing point spelled disaster in my home freezer. Even the smoothest ice cream eventually becomes coarse and icy in a home freezer due to inevitable shifts in temperature that cause thawing and refreezing. These temperature shifts have a more dramatic effect on ice creams with a depressed freezing point—they melt much more easily—than they have on ice creams that freeze harder at warmer temperatures. Furthermore, while professionals can buy ready-made invert syrup, I had to make my own—an activity that proved both time-consuming and unreliable. I crossed it off my list, along with two other unobtainable sweeteners: atomized glucose and dextrose powder. I rummaged through the pantry in search of neutral-tasting alternative sweeteners that I could use. The list was depressingly short: corn syrup. Containing about 25 percent water, corn syrup seemed like the last ingredient that might work in an effort to eliminate large ice crystals. But what did I have to lose?

I mixed up batches of my working recipe, replacing some of the sugar with increasing amounts of corn syrup. Right away, I could tell that something was different. The custard bases were more viscous than my all-sugar recipe straight out of the fridge, and they all churned to a thick, soft-serve consistency in record time. The real revelation, however, came when it was time to taste. The batch with ⅓ cup of corn syrup was the closest thing to super-premium perfection I had ever achieved. Not only was it dense, but it showed no trace of iciness. Though I was tempted to sit in the kitchen and finish off the rest of the quart, I was too eager to get back to my desk and figure out why this solution had worked so well.

After a few exchanges with our science editor, I had my answer. First, due to its viscosity, corn syrup prevents water molecules from grouping and freezing into large ice crystals. Second, corn syrup doesn't depress the

NOTES FROM THE TEST KITCHEN

WINNING ICE CREAM MACHINES

Home ice cream machines fall into two types: pricey self-refrigerating models that let you make batch after batch or cheaper models with a removable canister that must be refrozen each time. Our favorite self-refrigerating model, the **Whynter SNÖ Professional Ice Cream Maker** (left), $219.99, makes dense, creamy ice cream that's firm enough to eat right away. For the smoothest results, we recommend letting the machine run for five to 10 minutes to prechill it before adding the custard. Our favorite canister-style model and Best Buy, the **Cuisinart Automatic Frozen Yogurt-Ice Cream & Sorbet Maker** (right), $49.99, makes ice cream that rivals our top choice at a fraction of the price. It must be frozen for 24 hours before each use, but given its modest price, you can hardly go wrong.

TASTING VANILLA BEANS

For recipes in which vanilla is the star, we've always found that beans impart deeper flavor than extract. We tested five brands of vanilla beans, three mail-order and two from the supermarket, wondering if times had changed since we rated them more than a decade ago. At that time, we couldn't recommend any supermarket samples, finding them dried out and hardened, with few seeds and even less flavor. We used the beans first in an uncooked cream cheese frosting, then cooked in the base of our Vanilla Ice Cream and in a simple crème anglaise. Turns out times have changed: In a surprising reversal, we found the supermarket beans not only improved but better than the mail-order brands. Although all of the samples were acceptable—including cheaper Spice Islands, $8.49 for two—we recommend splurging on **McCormick Madagascar Vanilla Beans**, $15.99 for two, for their plump, seed-filled pods and "vivid," "robust" flavor.

freezing point as much as sugar does. My corn-syrup ice cream froze faster in the canister and remained harder at home-freezer temperatures than did the all-sugar recipe. This stuff was virtually free of large ice crystals, and it stayed that way for nearly a week in my freezer.

After months of churning countless batches of ice cream, I had tasted sweet victory. Another thing I could count on: My ice cream machine wouldn't be showing up at a yard sale anytime soon.

—DAN SOUZA, *Cook's Illustrated*

Vanilla Ice Cream

MAKES ABOUT 1 QUART

Two teaspoons of vanilla extract can be substituted for the vanilla bean; stir the extract into the cold custard in step 3. An instant-read thermometer is critical for the best results. Using a prechilled metal baking pan and working quickly in step 4 will help prevent melting and refreezing of the ice cream and will speed the hardening process. If using a canister-style ice cream machine, be sure to freeze the empty canister for at least 24 hours and preferably 48 hours before churning. For self-refrigerating ice cream machines, prechill the canister by running the machine for 5 to 10 minutes before pouring in the custard.

1   vanilla bean
1¾ cups heavy cream
1¼ cups whole milk
½   cup plus 2 tablespoons sugar
⅓   cup light corn syrup
¼   teaspoon salt
6   large egg yolks

1. Place 8- or 9-inch-square metal baking pan in freezer. Cut vanilla bean in half lengthwise. Using tip of paring knife, scrape out vanilla seeds. Combine vanilla bean, seeds, cream, milk, ¼ cup plus 2 tablespoons sugar, corn syrup, and salt in medium saucepan. Heat over medium-high heat, stirring occasionally, until mixture is steaming steadily and registers 175 degrees, 5 to 10 minutes. Remove saucepan from heat.

2. While cream mixture heats, whisk yolks and remaining ¼ cup sugar together in bowl until smooth, about 30 seconds. Slowly whisk 1 cup heated cream mixture into egg yolk mixture. Return mixture to saucepan and cook over medium-low heat, stirring constantly,

until mixture thickens and registers 180 degrees, 7 to 14 minutes. Immediately pour custard into large bowl and let cool until no longer steaming, 10 to 20 minutes. Transfer 1 cup custard to small bowl. Cover both bowls with plastic wrap. Place large bowl in refrigerator and small bowl in freezer and cool completely, for at least 4 hours or up to 24 hours. (Small bowl of custard will freeze solid.)

3. Remove custards from refrigerator and freezer. Scrape frozen custard from small bowl into large bowl of custard. Stir occasionally until frozen custard has fully dissolved. Strain custard through fine-mesh strainer and transfer to ice cream machine. Churn until mixture resembles thick soft-serve ice cream and registers about 21 degrees, 15 to 25 minutes. Transfer ice cream to frozen baking pan and press plastic on surface. Return to freezer until firm around edges, about 1 hour.

4. Transfer ice cream to airtight container, pressing firmly to remove any air pockets, and freeze until firm, at least 2 hours. Serve. (Ice cream can be stored for up to 5 days.)

CREAMY CHOCOLATE PUDDING

IN RECENT DECADES, HOMEMADE CHOCOLATE pudding has been pushed off the table by more glamorous, intensely flavored concoctions like truffle tarts and molten chocolate cakes. Today, diners clamor for increasingly darker, more bitter chocolate. Call me a wimp, but I don't always want my chocolate in lethal doses or in ever-higher cacao percentages. I miss the simplicity—and the restraint—of a good homemade chocolate pudding: that wonderfully smooth, dense, yet light marriage of chocolate and dairy thickened with cornstarch and maybe a few egg yolks. And making chocolate pudding from scratch couldn't be easier: Simmer dairy and sugar with cornstarch, whisk in chocolate and (sometimes) a few egg yolks, add vanilla extract, and chill.

That said, when I gathered some recipes and gave them a closer look, the variety among them was startling for a dish with so few steps and ingredients. Some called for unsweetened chocolate, others for bittersweet. Amounts ranged from a modest ounce to more than 10 times that amount. Still others ditched the solid chocolate for cocoa powder. As for the egg yolks, many recipes didn't include them, instead opting for a heftier dose of cornstarch to thicken things up. Then there was the dairy question: Should it be milk, cream, half-and-half—or some combination? And would adding butter be a good thing or overkill?

I decided to start conservatively, preparing a pudding from the 1975 edition of *The Joy of Cooking* that called for 1 ounce of unsweetened chocolate, milk, cornstarch, and no eggs. I wasn't surprised when tasters panned this pudding for its wan flavor and loose consistency. Fast-forwarding to 1990, I tried the version in Craig Claiborne's *The New York Times Cookbook*, which kicked everything up a notch, increasing the unsweetened chocolate to 3 ounces, swapping in some half-and-half for the milk, and adding a few tablespoons of butter. But it still garnered no fans.

Putting the old tomes aside, I went for a more drastic change and tried a blog-hyped bittersweet chocolate pudding recipe from the Scharffen Berger website. This formula—4 ounces of bittersweet chocolate, milk, and no eggs—produced a markedly richer, more complex chocolate pudding. Again, no surprise here—though 4 ounces of bittersweet chocolate is the rough equivalent of 3 ounces of unsweetened, we usually find the quality of good bittersweet far superior. But I hadn't hit the mark yet. Sure, this pudding's chocolate flavor had more oomph and dimension, but according to my tasters, I had yet to reach the chocolate ceiling.

I tried doubling the chocolate in my placeholder pudding base (made with milk, cornstarch, and no eggs) to 8 ounces. As I poured this latest batch into a bowl to chill, I sneaked a taste. The rich, dark, glossy pudding had a robust flavor that had been missing in the previous versions. But when the pudding set, my hopes were dashed; the once-smooth pudding was now marred by a distinctly grainy texture. I could only guess that the high proportion of chocolate solids was to blame. I began dialing back the chocolate to see how much I could incorporate while still keeping a velvety texture. To my disappointment, I found that 4 ounces was as high as I could go before the pudding turned gritty.

My only recourse was to highlight the modest chocolate flavor I had by cutting back on flavor-dulling ingredients like cornstarch and dairy. Replacing some of the cornstarch with low-sugar pectin produced pudding that was marginally more chocolaty but also considerably wetter. Trading some of the cornstarch for gelatin

worked no better, turning out pudding that was slick and springy. And when I swapped out 1 cup of milk for equal portions of water, coffee, or stout, these tests were also a bust.

With no other leads, I circled back to a recipe that I'd skipped because it sounded, well, uninspiring. The pudding from the "Big Red" *Betty Crocker's Cookbook* (1986 edition) calls for ⅓ cup of cocoa powder and no bar chocolate at all. My hesitation was twofold: First, gritty cocoa particles, in my mind, would equal gritty pudding; second, without richer-tasting solid chocolate, I didn't have high hopes for the chocolate flavor. Sure enough, my colleagues deemed this pudding's flavor simply "OK." But to my surprise, they raved about its silky texture—by far the smoothest pudding I'd turned out to date.

Why would cocoa powder—which typically consists of 80 to 90 percent cocoa solids and 10 to 20 percent fat, while a typical bar of 60 percent cacao bittersweet chocolate averages about 25 percent cocoa solids and 35 percent cocoa butter—make for a smoother pudding? Could it actually be that cocoa butter, not cocoa solids, caused grittiness in pudding when used in overly high amounts?

As a test, I took my working recipe with 4 ounces of solid chocolate and began adding cocoa powder to it, stopping when I got to 3 tablespoons. This pudding boasted not only deep chocolate flavor but also perfect smoothness. It seemed certain that cocoa butter—not cocoa solids—was the culprit.

Our science editor explained this curious phenomenon: Solid chocolate is manufactured so that its cocoa butter remains solid at room temperature but melts precisely at human body temperature. But when the same chocolate is melted, the crystalline structure of the cocoa butter is reorganized; it becomes more stable and melts at higher temperatures. If present in high enough amounts, this more stable form of cocoa butter creates a grainy texture. The upshot: For a pudding with both potent chocolate flavor and a supremely smooth texture, a combo of bittersweet chocolate and cocoa powder is the way to go.

With that mystery solved and the chocolate flavor exactly where I wanted it, I had just a few more tweaks to make. Thus far, I hadn't used egg yolks in my recipe, but the pudding was lacking a certain richness and body that yolks would surely provide. After a few tests, I determined that three yolks did the trick. Tasters also liked the added creaminess brought about by swapping

½ cup of the milk for heavy cream. Even better, with these adjustments, I was able to drop the cornstarch from 3 tablespoons to 2.

And yet something was still missing—some depth and roundness to the chocolate flavor. I thought back to my testing of nondairy liquids. While 8 ounces of coffee had competed with the chocolate, a smaller amount might perfectly enhance its roast-y undertones. I added just ½ teaspoon of espresso powder, and my pudding was finally complete.

With the help of two kinds of chocolate in a generous—but not lethal—amount, I daresay I had engineered a new classic.

—ANDREA GEARY, *Cook's Illustrated*

Creamy Chocolate Pudding

SERVES 6

We recommend using one of our favorite dark chocolates—Callebaut Intense Dark Chocolate L-60–40NV or Ghirardelli Bittersweet Chocolate Baking Bar. Garnish the pudding with whipped cream and chocolate shavings, if desired.

    2 teaspoons vanilla extract
    ½ teaspoon instant espresso powder
    ½ cup (3½ ounces) sugar
    3 tablespoons cocoa
    2 tablespoons cornstarch
    ¼ teaspoon salt
    3 large egg yolks
    ½ cup heavy cream
    2½ cups whole milk
    5 tablespoons unsalted butter, cut into 8 pieces
    4 ounces bittersweet chocolate, chopped fine

1. Stir together vanilla and espresso powder in bowl; set aside. Whisk sugar, cocoa, cornstarch, and salt together in large saucepan. Whisk in yolks and cream until fully incorporated, making sure to scrape corners of saucepan. Whisk in milk until incorporated.

2. Place saucepan over medium heat; cook, whisking constantly, until mixture is thickened and bubbling over entire surface, 5 to 8 minutes. Cook 30 seconds longer, remove from heat, add butter and chocolate, and whisk until melted and fully incorporated. Whisk in vanilla mixture.

3. Pour pudding through fine-mesh strainer into bowl. Press piece of lightly greased parchment paper against surface of pudding, and place in refrigerator to cool, at least 4 hours. Whisk pudding briefly and serve.

VARIATIONS

Creamy Mexican Chocolate Pudding
Add ½ teaspoon cinnamon, ¼ teaspoon chipotle chile powder, and pinch cayenne pepper to saucepan along with cocoa powder.

Creamy Mocha Pudding
Increase espresso powder to 1 teaspoon. Add 1 tablespoon Kahlua to vanilla mixture. Substitute ¼ cup brewed coffee for ¼ cup milk.

NOTES FROM THE TEST KITCHEN

PUDDING THROUGH THE AGES
Whether it's because our tastes have grown increasingly sophisticated or we just desire more taste sensation, the amount of chocolate in chocolate pudding recipes has inched steadily upward over the years. Here is the amount of chocolate per 3 cups of dairy in classic American recipes since the 1970s—along with our test kitchen's assessment of each pudding's flavor and our modern fix.

ERA	SOURCE	CHOCOLATE	RESULTS
1970s	*The Joy of Cooking*	1½ ounces unsweetened	No surprise: A minuscule amount of chocolate corresponded to minimal chocolate flavor.
1980s	The "Big Red" *Betty Crocker's Cookbook*	½ cup cocoa	All cocoa powder made for an extremely smooth texture but one-dimensional taste.
1990s	Craig Claiborne's *The New York Times Cookbook*	3 ounces unsweetened	A big increase in unsweetened chocolate wasn't enough. This pudding still lacked oomph.
2011	*Cook's Illustrated*	4 ounces bittersweet + 3 tablespoons cocoa	At last, the winning formula for a super-smooth pudding chock-full of chocolaty flavor.

TEST KITCHEN RESOURCES

Best Kitchen Quick Tips   278

Kitchen Basics Illustrated

25 Tips for Improving Flavor   280

Shrimp 101   282

Grilled Vegetables 101   284

Everyday Sweeteners 101   286

Holiday Cookies 101   288

Tastings & Testings*

Breakfast Sausage Patties   290

Low-Moisture Mozzarella   291

Supermarket Canned Tuna   292

Mayonnaise   293

Unsalted Butter   294

Hot Sauce   295

Ketchup   296

Tomato Soup   297

Spaghetti   298

Tastings & Testings (cont.)

Canned Whole Tomatoes   299

Premium Jarred Pasta Sauces   300

Cheese Tortellini   301

Cutting Boards   302

Innovative Cutting Boards   303

Knife Block Sets   304

Inexpensive Stockpots   305

Travel Mugs   306

All-Purpose Cleaners   307

Sauté Pans   308

Graters   309

Oven Mitts   310

Coolers   311

Measuring Spoons   312

Whisks   313

Conversions & Equivalencies   314

*Every product tested may not be listed in these pages. Please visit www.cooksillustrated.com to find complete listings and information on all products tested and reviewed.

BEST KITCHEN QUICK TIPS

Our readers are constantly showing us new ways to prep, cook, and problem-solve in the kitchen. Out of more than 1,000 tips we've published in our magazines and books, here are a handful we use every day.

CARING FOR BERRIES

Berries are prone to growing mold and rotting quickly. To keep mold at bay, rinse berries in a mild vinegar solution (1 part vinegar to 3 parts water) before drying them and storing them in a paper towel–lined airtight container.

TRACKING DOUGH RISE

Not every baker owns a dough-rising bucket with markings for tracking the rise of the dough, but any baker with a large, clear container can improvise one with this trick: After adding the dough to the container, mark its height by placing a rubber band around the container. This reference will make it easy to judge when the dough has doubled in volume.

MEASURING STICKY INGREDIENTS

Mist the inside of a measuring cup with vegetable oil spray before filling it with sticky ingredients such as honey and molasses. When emptied, the liquid will slip right out of the cup. Out of spray? Line the measuring cup with plastic wrap and discard after use.

KEEPING FRESH-BAKED BREAD FRESH

Without preservatives to keep it tasting fresh, artisanal loaves can quickly stale. We've found that storing the bread cut side down on a cutting board works better than wrapping the loaf in paper or plastic. The crust will stay dry, while contact with the board will keep moisture inside the crumb.

SPACE-SAVING VEGETABLE PREP

Many recipes call for adding ingredients at different points. Instead of a bowl for each prepped ingredient, layer them in a single large bowl, separated by sheets of waxed paper or plastic wrap. (The ingredients you'll need first should be on top.)

KEEPING COOKIE DOUGH ROUND

Using a cardboard paper towel roll to store refrigerator cookie dough helps the dough retain its shape. Once you've formed the dough into a log, roll it in plastic wrap and slide the dough inside the cardboard (slit lengthwise) to protect it in the fridge.

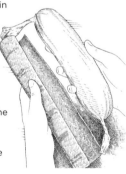

REMINDER TO RESERVE PASTA WATER

It's all too easy to forget to save a bit of pasta cooking water to thin a sauce when the recipe recommends it. Here's a surefire reminder: Before cooking the pasta, place a measuring cup inside the colander you'll use to drain it.

MAKESHIFT BOTTLE OPENER

Bottle opener gone missing during a backyard barbecue? Try your grill tongs, which have an opening inside the handles just large enough to catch the edge of a bottle cap so you can gently pop the cap off.

VINEGAR FLY TRAP

Since so-called fruit flies are actually vinegar flies attracted to the odor of fermenting fruits and vegetables, use this simple solution to rid your kitchen of these annoying pests: Place a few drops of dish soap in a small bowl of vinegar on the counter and stir to combine. The vinegar lures the flies into the liquid, and the soap breaks the surface tension, preventing them from escaping.

CITRUS REAMER SUBSTITUTE

Kitchen tongs are a great tool to use when juicing a lemon, lime, or orange. Holding the tongs closed, stick the pincers into the halved fruit and use a twisting motion to extract juice.

SALAD TO GO

Dressed salads prepared early and eaten later in the day are destined to turn limp. To transport a small amount of dressing, use one of the jars in which dry spices are packed. Their small size and tight seal are perfect for the job.

EASY PUREED GARLIC

In addition to grating nutmeg, citrus peel, and hard cheese, a rasp-style grater is an ideal tool for producing finely pureed garlic, shallot, or onion. For recipes such as Caesar salad or *aïoli*, peel a clove of garlic and grate it on the tool before adding it to the recipe.

EGG SLICER FOR FRUIT

Slicing individual pieces of fruit can be a tedious task. An egg slicer makes perfect slices of kiwi, strawberries (for shortcake), or banana in one quick motion.

PEELING GINGER WITH A SPOON

Knotty ginger skin is nearly impossible to peel with a knife or vegetable peeler. Instead, use the edge of a spoon to scrape it off quickly and efficiently.

FREEZING COOKIE DOUGH

Keeping some frozen dough on hand means you can bake just as many, or as few, cookies as you like without first having to whip up a batch of dough. Form the dough into balls and arrange them on a sheet pan or cookie sheet to freeze. Once the individual balls of dough are frozen, simply place them in a zipper-lock freezer bag and stow in the freezer for up to two months.

CHECKING A GAS GRILL'S FUEL TANK

There's nothing worse than running out of fuel halfway through grilling. If your grill doesn't have a gas gauge, use this technique to estimate how much gas is left in the tank. Boil a cup of water and pour it over the side of the tank. Feel the metal with your hand. Where the water has succeeded in warming the tank it is empty; where the tank remains cool to the touch there is still propane inside.

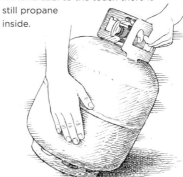

NO MORE "MYSTERY MEAT"

When freezing raw meat for later use, wrap the meat in plastic wrap, place it in a zipper-lock freezer bag, and then cut off the grocery label and put it inside, facing out. At a glance, you'll know the exact cut, weight, and—most important—date of purchase, allowing you to gauge how long the meat has been lingering in the freezer.

ORGANIZING POT LIDS

Many cooks store their pans and lids in a single drawer. To keep the lids from sliding around and under the pans, install a slender expansion curtain rod at the front. Stand the lids up straight against the rod, so they are within sight and reach.

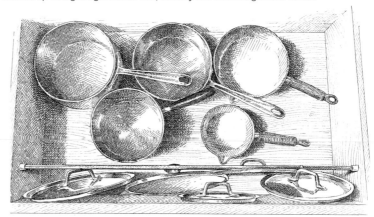

25 TIPS FOR IMPROVING FLAVOR

Reliable recipes and top-quality equipment will get you far, but sometimes it's the small touches that make the biggest difference. Here are the tricks we turn to most often in the test kitchen.

PREPPING

1. TRIM BEEF STEW MEAT THOROUGHLY; LEAVE A LITTLE FAT ON PORK

Remove all hard fat and connective tissue from the exterior of beef stew meat before cooking; its intramuscular marbling will keep it plenty moist and tender during cooking. But a thin layer (⅛ inch) of fat left on pork will baste and flavor the leaner meat.

2. KEEP THE TASTE IN TOMATOES

If excess moisture isn't an issue, ignore any instructions to remove the seeds and "jelly" from tomatoes. The guts are where the flavor is; in fact, they contain three times the amount of flavor-enhancing glutamic acid as the flesh.

3. AVOID ADVANCE PREP FOR GARLIC AND ONIONS

Chopping garlic and onions causes them to release sharp odors and flavors that intensify over time, so it's best to cut them at the last minute. Soaking sliced or chopped onions in a solution of baking soda and water (1 tablespoon per cup of water) tames their pungency for raw applications; just be sure to rinse them thoroughly before using.

4. SCORE MEAT BEFORE MARINATING

To help a marinade penetrate as quickly and deeply as possible (especially in thick cuts), prick the surface of the meat with a fork or make shallow scores with a knife.

7. KEEP FAT FRESH-TASTING

Fat equals flavor. But because the fatty acids in butter, oil, and oil-rich ingredients like nuts are particularly prone to rancidity—and because these ingredients easily absorb off-flavors—it's important to minimize their exposure to oxygen and heat.

FAT/NUT	BEST STORAGE METHOD
Butter	Slip the wrapped sticks into a zipper-lock bag and store them in the back of the fridge—not in the small door compartment—where it's coldest for up to 2½ weeks. For longer storage (up to four months), move the bag to the freezer.
Oil	Keep vegetable oils in a dark pantry or cupboard. Nut and seed oils should be stored in the fridge.
Nuts	The pantry is no place for nuts, unless you plan to use them within a couple of months. Placed in a zipper-lock bag (with the air pressed out) and stored in the freezer, they'll keep for at least a year.

5. FLIP OR STIR MEAT WHILE MARINATING

Place meat in a zipper-lock bag or use a large baking dish covered with plastic wrap. Flip the bag or stir the meat halfway through the soaking time to ensure that all of the meat gets equal exposure to the marinade.

6. OUT, DAMN SPROUT!

Remove any green shoots from garlic cloves before chopping. They contain bitter-tasting compounds that persist even after cooking.

COOKING

8. STRIKE—BUT NOT UNTIL THE PAN IS HOT

The temperature of the cooking surface will drop the minute food is added, slowing down flavorful browning, so don't rush the preheating step. If shallow- or deep-frying, check the temperature of the oil with an instant-read thermometer.

9. SPICE UP SPICES

To intensify the flavor of commercially ground spices and spice blends, cook them for a minute or two in butter or oil before adding liquid to the pan. If the recipe calls for sautéing aromatics, add the spices when the vegetables are nearly cooked.

10. ADD A RIND TO THE POT

Save your Parmesan rinds and do as the Italians do: Toss one into a soup or stew. It's an age-old trick for adding savory depth. Stored in a zipper-lock bag in the freezer, the rinds will keep indefinitely (no need to thaw them before using).

11. DON'T FORGET THE FOND

The caramelized brown bits that stick to the bottom of the pan after searing meat are packed with savory flavor. To incorporate them into a soup, stew, or pan sauce, deglaze the hot pan with liquid (wine, broth, etc.) and scrape them free with a wooden spoon.

12. SAVE THE MEAT'S JUICES

As cooked meat rests, it releases flavorful juices that can be added back to the skillet for pan sauces. If the juices thin the sauce, allow it to simmer an extra minute to restore the consistency.

13. MAKE NUTS NUTTIER

Toasting nuts brings out their aromatic oils for a deeper flavor. To toast more than 1 cup, oven-toast on a sheet pan, which offers more space than a skillet.

14. USE A LITTLE SUGAR

Lightly sprinkling lean proteins (and even vegetables) with sugar helps them brown better and faster, enhancing the flavor without the risk of overcooking.

BAKING

15. BROWN YOUR BREAD

Always bake bread until the crust is well browned—even if that means leaving the loaf in the oven beyond its recommended doneness temperature (most dough contains plenty of moisture and won't dry out). Flavor compounds in a browned crust are volatile and travel inward toward the crumb, enhancing the flavor of the loaf inside as well as out.

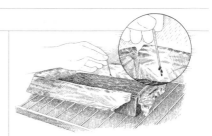

16. GO FOR DEEP GOLDEN PASTRY

Browning is also important in pastry: A well-browned crust will be more flavorful than a blond one. We bake all pies in glass pie plates so we can track color development. When working with puff pastry or other flaky dough on a baking sheet, we lift up the bottom of individual pieces and look for even browning.

17. DON'T OVERBAKE CHOCOLATE

Baking chocolate cakes and brownies past the point of doneness will not only dry them out but also dull the chocolate's flavor. To determine doneness, use a skewer and look for moist crumbs.

SEASONING

18. DROP (SALT FOR) ACID

Salt can boost the flavor of soups, stews, and sauces, but so can a drop of lemon juice or vinegar. Like salt, acid competes with bitter flavor compounds, reducing our perception of them as they "brighten" other flavors. Just a dash—⅛ teaspoon—can go a long way.

19. USE COARSE SALT WHEN SEASONING MEAT

Use kosher salt, not table salt, when seasoning meat. Its larger grains distribute more easily and cling well to the meat's surface. When a recipe calls for seasoning meat, use about ⅛ teaspoon of kosher salt per portion.

20. PEP UP, OR TONE DOWN, PEPPER

When you apply black pepper to meat will affect the strength of its bite. For assertive pepper flavor, season meat after searing; keeping the pepper away from heat preserves its volatile compounds. Seasoning before cooking tames pepper's punch.

21. SEASON COLD FOODS BOLDLY

Chilling foods dulls their flavors, so it's important to compensate by seasoning generously, but judiciously. To keep from overdoing it, season with a normal amount of salt before chilling, then taste and add more salt before serving.

22. INCORPORATE FRESH HERBS AT THE RIGHT TIME

Add hearty herbs like thyme, rosemary, oregano, sage, and marjoram to dishes early on in the cooking process; this way, they release maximum flavor while ensuring that their texture will be less intrusive. Save delicate herbs like parsley, cilantro, tarragon, chives, and basil for the last minute, lest they lose their fresh flavor and bright color.

23. ADD A LITTLE *UMAMI*

Common pantry staples like soy sauce, Worcestershire sauce, and anchovies contain high levels of glutamates that can give a savory umami boost to a dish. Try mixing a teaspoon or two of soy sauce into chili or adding a couple of finely minced anchovies to a chicken braise.

24. MAKE ADJUSTMENTS WHEN SEASONINGS GO AWRY

If you've added too much salt, sugar, or spice to a dish, the damage is usually done. In mild cases, however, the overpowering ingredient can sometimes be masked by the addition of another from the opposite end of the flavor spectrum. Consult this chart for ideas. And remember to account for the reduction of liquids when seasoning a dish—a perfectly seasoned stew will likely taste too salty after several hours of simmering. Your best bet is to season with a light hand during the cooking process and then adjust the seasoning just before serving.

IF YOUR FOOD IS	ADD	SUCH AS
Too salty	An acid or sweetener	Vinegar; lemon or lime juice; canned, unsalted tomatoes; sugar, honey, or maple syrup
Too sweet	An acid or seasonings	Vinegar or citrus juice; chopped fresh herb; dash of cayenne; or, for sweet dishes, a bit of liqueur or espresso powder
Too spicy or acidic	A fat or sweetener	Butter, cream, sour cream, cheese, or olive oil; sugar, honey, or maple syrup

25. ADD A FINISHING TOUCH

Even the most perfectly cooked soup, stew, or pasta dish can benefit from a last-minute burst of flavor. One of our favorite ways to liven up rich lasagnas or hearty braises is to sprinkle them with the classic Mediterranean garnish known as gremolata. This mixture features minced fresh garlic, citrus zest, and fresh herbs such as parsley or basil. We also turn to herb butter, made from blending finely minced herbs, garlic, and often shallot into softened butter, for a punch of flavor. Soups, pasta, fish, and just about any cut of meat will benefit from a dollop of herb butter.

SHRIMP 101

From shopping advice and prep tips to foolproof cooking methods, here's our guide to guaranteeing tender, juicy shrimp every time.

BUYING BASICS

Ensuring tender, briny-tasting shrimp starts at the seafood counter, where many of the rules that apply to buying fish don't hold true for shrimp.

GO FOR WHITE

Increasingly, seafood markets and gourmet shops sell a range of different shrimp species. We compared the three most commonly available types (pink, white, and black tiger) and found that white shrimp had the firmest flesh and the sweetest taste.

DON'T BE FOOLED BY "FRESH"

Just because shrimp is raw doesn't mean it's fresh. Since only 10 percent of the shrimp sold in this country comes from U.S. sources (more commonly, the sources include Thailand, Indonesia, and Ecuador), chances are the shrimp has been previously frozen. Unless you live near a coastal area, "fresh" shrimp likely means defrosted shrimp.

DON'T BUY DEFROSTED

Once shrimp are defrosted for the seafood case, the quality declines with each passing day. Unless you ask, there's no telling how long they have been on display—and in our tests, defrosted shrimp tasted noticeably less fresh even after a day of storage. But if you must buy defrosted, look for unblemished and firm shrimp that fill the shell and smell of the sea.

BUY INDIVIDUALLY QUICK-FROZEN

In general, IQF stands for "individually quick-frozen": Shrimp are spread on a conveyor belt and frozen at sea, locking in quality and freshness. All bagged frozen shrimp fall into this category; however, it's not always on the label. Shrimp are also sometimes frozen at sea with water in 5-pound blocks packed in boxes. We prefer bagged individually quick-frozen shrimp, as you can thaw exactly what you need.

CHECK THE INGREDIENT LIST

"Shrimp" should be the only ingredient listed on the bag or box. In effort to prevent darkening or water loss during thawing, some manufacturers add salt or STPP (sodium tripolyphosphate). Our tasters found an unpleasant texture in salt-treated and STPP-enhanced shrimp; the latter also had a chemical taste.

BUY WILD

We've found that wild shrimp have a sweeter flavor and firmer texture than farm-raised, making their higher price worth it. Unless you can purchase them right off the boat, only buy wild shrimp frozen. Fresh wild shrimp are minimally processed, so they are usually shipped with the heads on. The head contains enzymes that break down muscle proteins after death, resulting in mushy meat. Freezing halts this activity.

IT'S THE COUNT THAT COUNTS

There's no industry standard for labeling shrimp sizes, so one vendor's large may be another's extra-large. Instead of size, focus on count per pound, which always appears on the bag. The letter U stands for "under" (e.g., U/10 means under 10 shrimp per pound). Two numbers separated by a slash indicates a range. Most important: The smaller the number per pound, the larger the shrimp. Here are the most widely available sizes.

TEST KITCHEN NAME	COUNT PER POUND
Jumbo	16/20
Extra-Large	21/25
Large	26/30
Medium	41/50
Small	51/60

MAGIC NUMBER: 21/25
Extra-large shrimp (21/25) are our go-to when we want a browned exterior. This count is the most widely available in stores, and the shrimp's meaty size allows them to stay on the heat longer before turning rubbery.

PREP WORK

THE RIGHT WAY TO THAW

Frozen shrimp should be fully thawed before cooking—but how you defrost the shrimp affects its final flavor and texture. In tests, we got the firmest, juiciest results by defrosting the shrimp overnight in the refrigerator. For faster defrosting, place the bag under cold running water until the shrimp are fully thawed.

PEELING MADE EASY

Remove the telson, the small pointed section at the top of the tail. Holding the shrimp in one hand, move the thumb of your opposite hand up from the legs and around the shrimp, removing most of the shell. Pull gently on the tail to remove the remainder of the shell.

QUICK DEVEINING

For aesthetic reasons, we like to remove the thick, dark line that runs along the shrimp's back. Holding the shelled shrimp between your thumb and forefinger, use a sharp paring knife to make a shallow cut along the back, exposing the veinlike digestive tract. Lift it out with the knife's tip.

FOOLPROOF COOKING METHODS

GRILLING

When it comes to grilling, a modified two-level fire gives us a hot zone for cooking the shrimp and a cool side where we can keep a sauce at the ready. Here we add big flavor with a spicy lemon-garlic sauce.

1. Thread 1½ pounds extra-large (21/25) shrimp head to tail onto 3 metal skewers. Brush both sides with oil and season with salt and pepper; sprinkle one side with pinch sugar.

2. Pour 6 quarts lit coals over one-half of grill; leave other half empty. Cover grill and heat until hot.

3. Set disposable aluminum pie plate with 4 tablespoons unsalted butter, 4 tablespoons lemon juice, 3 minced garlic cloves, ½ teaspoon red pepper flakes, and ⅛ teaspoon salt on hot side of grill and heat 1½ minutes; move to cooler side when hot. Place skewers sugared sides down on hot side of grill; grill uncovered until lightly charred, 4 to 5 minutes. Flip and grill until second side is pink, 1 to 2 minutes.

4. Using tongs, slide shrimp off skewers into sauce and toss. Transfer to hot side of grill; cook, stirring, until shrimp are opaque, 30 seconds. Add ⅓ cup minced fresh parsley, toss to combine, and serve immediately.

PACK TIGHTLY
Threading shrimp front to back helps them cook more slowly so they don't dry out.

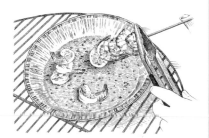

FINISH IN SAUCE
Sliding the almost-cooked shrimp into a flavorful sauce cooks them at a gentler pace.

PAN SEARING

A blazing-hot skillet produces nice browning but can quickly turn delicate shrimp tough. Our approach guarantees juicy shrimp—and a golden crust.

1. Heat 1 tablespoon oil in 12-inch skillet over high heat until just smoking. Meanwhile, toss 1½ pounds extra-large (21/25) shrimp, ¼ teaspoon salt, ¼ teaspoon pepper, and ⅛ teaspoon sugar in medium bowl.

2. Add half of shrimp to pan in single layer and cook until spotty brown and edges turn pink, about 1 minute.

3. Remove pan from heat; using tongs, flip each shrimp and let stand until all but very center is opaque, about 30 seconds. Transfer shrimp to large plate.

4. Repeat with 1 tablespoon oil and remaining shrimp; after second batch has stood off heat, return first batch to skillet and toss to combine. Cover skillet and let stand until shrimp are cooked through, 1 to 2 minutes. Serve immediately.

ADD SUGAR FOR BROWNING
Tossing the shrimp with a little sugar speeds up browning so they need less time over heat.

FLIP OFF HEAT
Removing the pan from the heat before flipping the shrimp prevents them from overcooking.

POACHING

We eschew the typical method for poaching shrimp—plunging them into hot water—for a far gentler approach.

1. Combine 1 pound extra-large (21/25) shrimp, ¼ cup lemon juice, spent lemon halves, 5 parsley sprigs, 3 tarragon sprigs, 1 tablespoon sugar, 1 teaspoon peppercorns, and 1 teaspoon salt with 2 cups cold water in medium saucepan.

2. Cook shrimp over medium heat, stirring frequently, until pink and centers are no longer translucent, 8 to 10 minutes (water should register 165 degrees and should just bubble around edges).

3. Off heat, cover and let shrimp sit in broth for 2 minutes. Meanwhile, fill bowl with ice water. Drain shrimp, discarding lemon halves, herbs, and spices, and place in ice water, about 3 minutes. Remove shrimp; pat dry with paper towels.

START COLD
Starting in cold water means the inside and outside of the shrimp cook more evenly.

FINISH OFF HEAT
Allowing the shrimp to finish cooking off the heat guarantees juicy results.

GRILLED VEGETABLES 101

Why heat up your kitchen to cook vegetables when you can get a crisp-tender texture and deep, smoky char from your grill? Here are our proven methods for getting the best results.

14 FAVORITE PICKS THAT DON'T REQUIRE PRECOOKING

ASPARAGUS

PREP: Snap off tough ends by holding asparagus halfway down stalk with one hand, then bend bottom half of stalk with other hand until it breaks.

COOK TIME: 5 to 7 minutes, turning once

TEST KITCHEN TIP: Pencil-thin asparagus will wither in the heat, while bulky specimens will burn before they cook through. If possible, purchase ½-inch-thick spears.

BABY BOK CHOY

PREP: Halve head through stem; rinse but don't dry.

COOK TIME: 6 to 7 minutes, turning once

TEST KITCHEN TIP: Water left clinging to the leaves will turn to steam on the grill, helping the bok choy cook evenly.

CORN

PREP: Remove all but innermost layer of husk; snip off silk.

COOK TIME: 8 to 10 minutes, turning every 1½ to 2 minutes

TEST KITCHEN TIP: Leaving the innermost layer of husk attached helps the corn take on grilled flavor without charring.

EGGPLANT

PREP: Slice crosswise into ¾-inch rounds.

COOK TIME: 8 to 10 minutes, turning once

TEST KITCHEN TIP: There's no need to salt eggplant destined for the grill. The intense heat will vaporize excess moisture.

ENDIVE

PREP: Halve lengthwise through core.

COOK TIME: 5 to 7 minutes, turning once

TEST KITCHEN TIP: Keeping the core intact keeps the leaves together for easy turning.

FENNEL

PREP: Trim fronds and cut thin slice from base. Cut bulb vertically through base into ¼-inch-thick slices, leaving core intact.

COOK TIME: 7 to 9 minutes, turning once

TEST KITCHEN TIP: Cover the fennel with an overturned aluminum pan while charcoal grilling to create an oven-like environment that cooks the interiors before the outside burns. (For gas grills, just use the lid.)

GREEN BEANS

PREP: Rinse but don't dry.

COOK TIME: 6 minutes, turning once

TEST KITCHEN TIP: Green beans (choose thick, mature specimens) are the one vegetable for which a grill pan is a must-have.

MUSHROOMS

PREP: For portobellos, wipe caps clean and snap off stems; for button and cremini, skewer through cap and stem so they are less likely to rotate when flipped.

COOK TIME: For portobellos, 8 to 10 minutes, turning once; for button and cremini, 8 to 12 minutes, turning every 3 minutes

TEST KITCHEN TIP: To keep mushrooms from becoming dry and leathery, brush liberally with oil before grilling.

ONIONS

PREP: Cut into ½-inch-thick slices parallel to equator; skewer parallel to counter.

COOK TIME: 10 to 12 minutes, turning once

TEST KITCHEN TIP: It's awkward to flip a skewer by the rounded "handle." Instead, grasp a centrally located onion slice with tongs and turn.

PEPPERS

PREP: Halve lengthwise; remove core, seeds, and ribs. Cut each half in thirds lengthwise.

COOK TIME: 7 to 9 minutes, turning once

TEST KITCHEN TIP: To grill-roast peppers, cook them whole until charred, transfer to a bowl, and cover with plastic wrap to loosen their skins. Then remove their skins, core, and seeds.

RADICCHIO

PREP: Cut head into 4 equal wedges.

COOK TIME: 4 to 5 minutes, turning every 1½ minutes

TEST KITCHEN TIP: For maximum grill flavor, turn each wedge twice so each side spends some time facing the fire.

SCALLIONS

PREP: Trim off root end and discard any loose or wilted outer leaves.

COOK TIME: 4 to 5 minutes, turning once

TEST KITCHEN TIP: For a well-charred exterior and a tender interior, use scallions that are at least ¼ inch in diameter.

TOMATOES

PREP: For round and plum, halve cored tomato along equator. Squeeze gently and shake out seeds. For cherry, thread onto skewers through stem end of fruit.

COOK TIME: For round and plum, 4 to 5 minutes, turning once; for cherry, 3 minutes, turning twice

TEST KITCHEN TIP: Start round and plum tomatoes skin side up to maximize charring.

ZUCCHINI/SUMMER SQUASH

PREP: Slice lengthwise into ½-inch-thick planks.

COOK TIME: 8 to 10 minutes, turning once

TEST KITCHEN TIP: Cutting the squash into planks keeps it from falling through the grates.

TOP 5 VEGETABLE GRILLING PRINCIPLES

1. BUILD A MEDIUM-HOT FIRE: Most vegetables respond better to moderate heat than to a blazing fire. To test the temperature of your grill, hold your hand 5 inches above the grill grate. You should be able to hold it there for three to four seconds.

2. MAKE THE (RIGHT) CUT: Preparing vegetables for the grill is all about maximizing their surface area to increase flavorful browning, and cutting them so they won't fall apart or slip through the grill grates.

3. BRUSH WITH OIL: Applying a thin layer of extra-virgin olive oil to vegetables (except corn) before grilling encourages even browning and helps prevent them from sticking to the grill grates. To contain the mess, lay the vegetables on a sheet pan and use a basting brush. Season with salt and pepper before cooking.

4. GO EASY ON THE CHAR: Browning vegetables is one thing; incinerating them is another. For the best results, keep the pieces moving to avoid hot spots and grill until they're just tender and streaked with grill marks.

5. GRILL MEAT FIRST ON A CHARCOAL GRILL: When grilling vegetables to accompany steak, chicken, or pork, we cook the meat first, while the fire is at its hottest. By the time the meat is done, the heat has subsided a bit and the vegetables can cook at more moderate temperatures while the meat rests. (Note: This plan works equally well on a gas grill, and waiting for the fire to die down is not an issue.)

GRILLED RATATOUILLE

Serves 6 to 8

Smoky char makes this classic dish even better. Depending on the size of your grill, you may have to cook the vegetables in batches. When grilling more than one vegetable at a time, be sure to take each one off the grill as it is done.

- 1 red onion
- 2 pounds eggplant
- 1½ pounds zucchini or summer squash
- 2 bell peppers
- 1 pound tomatoes
    Extra-virgin olive oil
    Salt and pepper
- 3 tablespoons sherry vinegar
- ¼ cup chopped fresh basil
- 1 tablespoon minced fresh thyme
- 1 garlic clove, peeled and grated to fine paste on rasp-style grater

1. Prepare vegetables according to instructions on page 284. Brush both sides of vegetables with oil; season with salt and pepper. Whisk ¼ cup oil, vinegar, basil, thyme, and garlic together in large bowl.

2. Grill vegetables over medium-hot fire, turning once, until tender and streaked with grill marks, 10 to 12 minutes for onion, 8 to 10 minutes for eggplant and squash, 7 to 9 minutes for peppers, and 4 to 5 minutes for tomatoes. Remove vegetables from grill; cool slightly.

3. When cool enough to handle, chop vegetables into ½-inch pieces, add to oil mixture, and toss to coat. Season with salt and pepper to taste; serve warm or at room temperature.

GET IN GEAR

Most grilling equipment you can do without, but these three well-designed tools make the job much easier.

NORPRO 12-INCH STAINLESS STEEL SKEWERS, $8.99 for 6 skewers
These thin, metal spears are reusable and won't burn. Plus, their flat (not round) surface prevents food from spinning around when turned.

OXO GOOD GRIPS 16-INCH LOCKING TONGS, $14.99
While keeping our hands far away from the fire, these long-handled tongs can firmly grip an ear of corn or multiple spears of asparagus.

WEBER PROFESSIONAL-GRADE GRILL PAN, $19.99
Narrow slits, rather than holes, prevent even thin-cut vegetables from slipping into the coals. The pan's raised sides keep food from sliding off and are easy to grip, even with heavy mitts.

EVERYDAY SWEETENERS 101

Not just for desserts, sweeteners play a crucial role in browning, tenderizing, adding structure to baked goods, and even enhancing savory dishes.

SWEETENERS

GRANULATED SUGAR

The relatively fine crystals and neutral flavor of granulated sugar, highly refined from sugarcane or sugar beets, make it the most versatile sweetener we know. Superfine sugar is simply granulated sugar processed into tinier crystals.

HOW WE USE IT: We almost always turn to granulated sugar in cakes, singling out the superfine kind when a delicate, grit-free texture is desired (e.g., in sponge cake, shortbread, and meringues). Superfine sugar is also ideal in drinks, where it dissolves almost instantly.

MAKE YOUR OWN SUPERFINE SUGAR: Process 1 cup plus 2 teaspoons of granulated sugar in a food processor for 15 to 30 seconds. Yield: 1 cup

TURBINADO AND DEMERARA SUGAR

Also referred to as "raw" sugar. The coarse amber grains of these products are the residue left after sugarcane has been partially processed to remove some of its molasses. They have a similar texture and delicate molasses taste, but turbinado sugar has been steam-washed and spun in a turbine.

HOW WE USE IT: The large crystals of these sugars do not readily dissolve—a reason to avoid them in dough. Instead, we like to sprinkle them on muffin tops to create crunch or to form the caramel crust on crème brûlée.

HONEY

Honey varies considerably depending on the type of nectar from which it's made. Color generally indicates depth of flavor: Lighter shades will be more mellow and darker shades richer and even slightly bitter.

HOW WE USE IT: In baking applications, we prefer milder honeys such as orange blossom and clover, which won't compete with other flavors.

BROWN SUGAR

Whether light or dark, brown sugar is refined cane sugar that has molasses added back in, contributing flavor and moisture. Dark brown sugar is 6.5 percent molasses; light brown is 3.5 percent.

HOW WE USE IT: We like how the caramel notes of brown sugar add dimension to sauces, glazes, and baked goods. These sugars can also add chewiness to cookies because they attract and absorb moisture from the surrounding air.

MAKE YOUR OWN: Mix 1 tablespoon of molasses into 1 cup of granulated sugar. (For dark brown sugar, use 2 tablespoons of molasses.) Yield: 1 cup

SWAPPING LIGHT FOR DARK: In taste tests, we found it hard to distinguish between light and dark brown sugars. In baked goods, if a recipe calls for less than ¼ cup, you're safe using the two interchangeably. Anything more than that and the difference in moisture levels between the sugars can begin to affect the texture.

PROPERLY PACKED: We're fans of weighing dry ingredients to eliminate any discrepancies in measuring. Whether light or dark, 1 cup of brown sugar that's densely packed should weigh the same as 1 cup of granulated sugar: 7 ounces.

CORN SYRUP

Unlike cloyingly sweet high-fructose corn syrup used in processed foods, ordinary corn syrup is only about 65 percent as sweet as sugar. It comes in two forms—light and dark—but we've found that flavor differences are very subtle.

HOW WE USE IT: Because corn syrup won't crystallize, it's particularly valuable in ice cream, candy, and frosting—even in sauces and glazes.

CONFECTIONERS' SUGAR

Confectioners' sugar is granulated sugar processed 10 times to an ultra-fine powder, with cornstarch added to prevent clumping.

HOW WE USE IT: Ideal for dusting finished desserts, this sugar's ability to dissolve easily also makes it a good choice for icings, glazes, and candy.

MAKE YOUR OWN: Process 1 cup of granulated sugar and 1 teaspoon of cornstarch in a blender or spice grinder for three minutes. Strain through a mesh strainer to remove any remaining large particles. Yield: 1 cup

MAPLE SYRUP

Maple syrup is the boiled-down sap of the sugar maple tree. It comes in four grades that reflect when the sap was harvested: grade A light, medium amber, and dark amber; and grade B. The lightest-colored, most delicate-flavored syrup is tapped at the beginning of the season, whereas darker, more robustly flavored syrup is tapped later.

HOW WE USE IT: For most cooking applications, we prefer the darker, more assertive flavor of grade B. Grade A dark amber is a close second for cooking and our preference for topping pancakes.

TEST KITCHEN FAVORITE: Maple Grove Farms Pure Maple Syrup

MOLASSES

A byproduct of the sugar-refining process, molasses boasts a naturally earthy, sweet, smoky flavor. With the exception of ultra-bitter blackstrap molasses, we find that all styles—mild, unsulfured, and robust—are equally acceptable in baking.

HOW WE USE IT: Molasses isn't just for gingerbread or baked beans. We like adding 2 teaspoons of molasses to chili to give it more dimension.

TEST KITCHEN FAVORITE: Brer Rabbit All Natural Unsulphured Molasses Mild Flavor

SUGAR: A MULTITASKER IN BAKING AND COOKING

BROWNING

During cooking and baking, some of the sucrose in sugar breaks down into glucose and fructose, which brown at lower temperatures, providing flavor and color in baked goods.

LEAVENING

Sugar is a prime contributor to the rise of cakes, cookies, and quick breads because it helps incorporate air bubbles into the batter during creaming.

TENDERIZING

Sugar is a major tenderizer. It inhibits gluten formation by preventing some of the water in the dough from hydrating flour proteins.

ON THE SAVORY SIDE

A dash of sugar in savory dishes has a complex, indirect impact on flavor, amping up tastes that might otherwise fade into the background. It can also bring balance to sour, salty, spicy, or bitter ingredients. What's more, sprinkling sugar over the surface of vegetables, fish, or raw meat or adding it to a brine can enhance browning.

STORAGE AND HANDLING

KEEPING BROWN SUGAR SOFT

Placing a soaked shard of terra cotta in a sealed container with brown sugar will keep it moist indefinitely.

QUICK FIX FOR HARD BROWN SUGAR

Microwaving hardened brown sugar can leave solid spots behind. We have a better way: Place the sugar in a pie plate and bake it in a preheated 250-degree oven for several minutes.

EASY SPOONING

Place metal measuring spoons under hot water or spray them with vegetable oil spray before dipping them in honey and maple syrup—the sticky stuff will slide right off.

MAKING HONEY CRYSTAL CLEAR

Honey never spoils, but it can crystallize and harden. To return honey to a clear, fluid state, microwave it in 10-second increments until the crystals dissolve or place the glass jar in a pan of hot water.

BUSTING UP CLUMPS

Even when stored in an airtight container, granulated sugar can form large, solid lumps. A few strokes with a potato masher will return it to a pourable state.

LOW-CALORIE SWEETENERS

There are plenty of sugar substitutes on the market. However, we tested seven types and have yet to find one that's a universal stand-in for the white stuff.

SWEETENER	PERFORMANCE
Agave Syrup: Natural sweetener made from the evaporated sap of the Mexican agave plant. **BRAND NAME:** Madhava Agave Nectar	About 1.5 times sweeter than sugar. Ideal for sweetening beverages, as it dissolves easily and has a relatively neutral taste. Not good for baking: Cookies were bready; cakes had a chewy layer of agave stuck in the pan.
Erythritol: Crystallized form of the sugar alcohol erythritol. **BRAND NAME:** Organic Zero	Terrific in beverages. Baking was another story: Sugar cookies turned out crumbly; cakes and muffins were chewy.
Granulated Sucralose: Sweetener derived from sucrose plus chlorine. **BRAND NAME:** Splenda	Perfectly acceptable in drinks, cobbler, and fruit-pie filling. But sugar cookies were overly soft and cakey and lacked sweetness.
Granulated Sucralose Blend: Mix of granulated sucralose and granulated sugar. **BRAND NAME:** Splenda	Drinks, cobbler, and fruit-pie filling all tasted fine. Sugar cookies had surprisingly decent texture but exhibited slight "artificial" aftertaste.
"Lite" Corn Syrup: Blend of glucose and sucralose. **BRAND NAME:** Karo	Sugar cookies and pecan bars had decent texture but unpleasant aftertaste. Frosting was downright rubbery.
Saccharin: Sweetener derived from petroleum. **BRAND NAME:** Sweet'N Low	Harsh, metallic aftertaste in drinks and baked goods. Sugar cookies were crumbly, and cakes and muffins were chewy. One upside: The metallic taste was less noticeable in fruit-pie fillings.
Stevia: Natural, calorie-free sweetener extracted from the leaves of the stevia plant (a sunflower cousin). **BRAND NAME:** Truvia	Mouth-puckering bitterness in beverages as well as in baked goods. Produced sugar cookies that were dry and crumbly rather than soft and chewy.

HOLIDAY COOKIES 101

Basic butter cookies are the perfect template for decorating—provided you start with a dough that's tailor-made for rolling, cutting, and embellishing. Follow these guidelines for cookies that look their holiday best.

START WITH THE RIGHT DOUGH

Rolling out the dough is usually sticky business, and the typical solution—adding more flour—makes for tough cookies.

WHY THIS DOUGH IS FOOLPROOF

- We use just enough butter for tenderness and rich flavor.

- Superfine sugar makes for a tight, compact crumb.

- Cream cheese adds subtle tang, and since it is softer than butter when chilled, it makes the dough easier to roll out.

- A "reverse" creaming method—in which the butter is beaten into the flour and sugar rather than creamed with the sugar—makes for flatter cookies that are easier to decorate.

USE THE RIGHT TOOLS

ATECO Plain Round Cutters (11-Piece Set), $15

No matter the shape, a good cookie cutter should be made of metal, with a thin, sharp cutting edge and a rounded top that won't cut into your hand as you press.

VOLLRATH Cookie Sheet, $24.95

Our favorite is roomy, with handles on the short sides, which makes it easy to slide cookies off.

ATECO Medium-Sized Offset Spatula (7.75-Inch), $8

Use a medium-size offset spatula for transferring cookies to and from the cookie sheet.

WILTON Angled 8-Inch Spatula, $4.79

A smaller offset spatula offers better control for spreading icing on a cookie.

JK ADAMS Plain Maple Rolling Dowel, $13.95

This 19-inch straight wooden barrel provides plenty of flat rolling surface, and the textured exterior holds onto flour to prevent dough from sticking.

ROLL WITH THE RIGHT TECHNIQUES

- **DO** roll dough between sheets of parchment paper. Handling the dough causes it to warm up and become tacky. To prevent it from sticking to the counter—and to the rolling pin—roll it between two large pieces of parchment paper.

- **DON'T** skip the chill after rolling. Cold, stiff dough will cut more cleanly than dough that's soft. Slide the bottom piece of parchment with the rolled dough onto a baking sheet to keep it flat, and refrigerate until firm, 10 minutes.

- **DO** minimize scraps. Cut shapes close together, starting from the outside and working your way to the middle. When making large and small cookies, we alternate cutters as we stamp to use as much dough as possible.

- **DO** peel away dough scraps—not the cookie. Use a small spatula to strip away the dough scraps from around the cookies. With excess dough out of the way, it is easier to cleanly lift the cookies and transfer them to a baking sheet.

- **DON'T** reroll more than once. Dough scraps may be packed into a ball and rerolled one time; working the dough any more will develop too much gluten and produce tough cookies. Make sure to chill the dough again before rolling and again before cutting.

FOOLPROOF HOLIDAY COOKIES

Makes 3 dozen cookies

The wrapped disks of dough can be refrigerated for up to three days or frozen for up to one month. If frozen, let the disks thaw in the refrigerator for 24 hours before using.

- 2½ cups (12½ ounces) all-purpose flour
- ¾ cup (5½ ounces) superfine sugar
- ¼ teaspoon salt
- 16 tablespoons unsalted butter, cut into 16 pieces and softened
- 2 teaspoons vanilla extract
- 2 tablespoons cream cheese, softened

1. Using stand mixer fitted with paddle, mix flour, sugar, and salt on low speed until combined, about 5 seconds. Add butter, one piece at a time; beat until mixture looks crumbly and slightly wet, about 1 minute. Add vanilla and cream cheese and beat until dough just begins to form large clumps, about 30 seconds.

2. Remove bowl from mixer; knead dough by hand in bowl for 2 to 3 turns to form large cohesive mass. Turn out dough onto counter. Divide in half, pat into two 4-inch disks, wrap each in plastic wrap, and refrigerate until dough is firm but malleable, about 30 minutes.

3. Adjust oven rack to middle position; heat oven to 375 degrees. Roll out 1 dough disk to even ⅛-inch thickness. Place rolled dough on baking sheet and refrigerate until firm, about 10 minutes. Meanwhile, repeat with second disk.

4. Working with first portion of rolled dough, cut into desired shapes using cookie cutter(s) and place shapes on parchment paper–lined baking sheet, spacing them about 1½ inches apart. Bake until light golden brown, about 10 minutes, rotating baking sheet halfway through baking. Repeat with second portion of rolled dough. Cool cookies on wire rack to room temperature.

DECORATE SIMPLY, BUT ELEGANTLY

ALL-PURPOSE GLAZE

Makes 1 cup; enough for 3 dozen cookies

To color, stir drops of food coloring into the glaze until it reaches the desired tint. For a citrus-flavored glaze, substitute orange, lemon, or lime juice for the milk. The glaze can also be flavored with ½ teaspoon of your favorite extract.

- **2 cups (8 ounces) confectioners' sugar**
- **3 tablespoons milk**
- **2 tablespoons cream cheese, softened**

Whisk all ingredients together until smooth. Spread glaze onto completely cooled cookies. Let glaze dry completely, about 30 minutes, before serving.

GUSSYING UP GLAZED COOKIES

DRAGGING
By applying dots of a contrasting colored glaze on top of another glaze and dragging a toothpick or thin skewer carefully through the center, you can create a variety of patterns and designs.

EMBELLISHING
Place decorations in the glaze while it is still soft; once the glaze dries, it will act like glue. In addition to the usual decorating options, consider cinnamon candies, jelly beans, crushed peppermint candies, gum drops, and chocolate morsels.

SUGARING
Once a glaze has been applied to a cookie, sprinkle it with colored sugar. For the most even distribution, hold your hand about 12 inches above the work surface. Excess sugar can be brushed or gently shaken off when the glaze is dry.

THREE WAYS TO GLAZE

SPREAD
For a simple, smooth coat, drizzle a little glaze in the center of the cookie and then spread it out in an even layer using the back of a spoon or a small offset spatula.

PIPE
To apply more intricate detail work, such as dots or lines, pipe the glaze directly onto the cookie. Fill a homemade parchment piping bag or a small pastry bag fitted with a small ¹⁄₁₆-inch round tip with glaze.

PAINT
Use a small paintbrush to apply different colored glazes to a cookie without overlapping or to fill in an outline.

MAKE A PARCHMENT PIPING BAG

1. Fold 12-inch square of parchment paper in half on diagonal. Using knife, cut it in half on fold into 2 triangles.

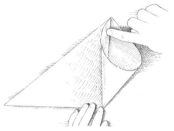

2. With long side of triangle facing you, fold bottom right-hand point up and under, giving it half twist until it meets triangle's top point.

3. Holding those points together, wrap left-hand point around outside of cone until all 3 points are perfectly aligned. Tape or staple points together.

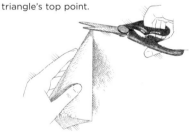

4. Use scissors to snip very small hole in point of cone.

DECORATORS' TIPS

MESS-FREE FILLING
To simplify the multi-handed job of filling a piping bag, place the bag upright in a tall drinking glass before filling. The glass also makes a good resting place for the bag while you are decorating.

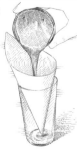

GLITTER STICKING POINTS
Unglazed cookies require a little surface preparation to ensure that embellishments will stick. We recommend lightly misting or brushing the surface of the dough with water before applying decorations.

TACKLE BOX FOR TRIMMINGS
To keep tiny trimmings close at hand and neatly organized for decorating, we corral each one in the individual cups of a muffin pan.

BREAKFAST SAUSAGE PATTIES

The mantra of modern cooking is that fresh is always better than frozen—but frozen is usually faster. We wanted to know if the trade-off was worth it when it came to breakfast sausage and pitted two fully cooked frozen patties against one brand of raw patties and four tube-style sausage rolls that we sliced into patties. Texture, which was dependent upon fat content, was the most important factor. Leaner brands were found to be chewy, while fattier brands were greasy; sausage with a moderate amount of fat was preferred, as it was tender but not greasy. Flavor was also important. Salt, black pepper, and sage are traditional seasonings for breakfast sausage, but many manufacturers add their own blend of spices as well. Tasters preferred higher amounts of sodium, a good amount of black pepper, and the inclusion of a sweetener. Style of sausage also played a role. Precooked patties have a definite advantage—after they are cooked to a specific level of browning and flavor development, antioxidants are added and the patties are frozen and vacuum-sealed to prevent flavor loss. Sausages are listed in order of preference; fat and sodium are per 2-ounce serving.

RECOMMENDED

JIMMY DEAN Fully Cooked Original Pork Sausage Patties
PRICE: $3.49 for 8 patties
STYLE: Precooked patties
FAT: 19 g SODIUM: 502 mg
COMMENTS: These fully cooked patties earned the top spot for being "meaty and well seasoned," with a "spicy, not too greasy taste." "Seasoning was perfect," according to one taster. Agreed another: "Coarser grain makes it more interesting and tender."

RECOMMENDED WITH RESERVATIONS

JONES DAIRY FARM Golden Brown All Natural Fully Cooked Sausage
PRICE: $2 for 6 patties
STYLE: Precooked patties
FAT: 20 g SODIUM: 373 mg
COMMENTS: These fully cooked patties struck tasters as "smoky" and "sweet," with a "peppery spice," but they lost points on texture with some tasters. "Thick and spongy, rubbery...like fast-food-restaurant style," wrote one. "Too bouncy!" agreed another.

JOHNSONVILLE Original Recipe Breakfast Sausage
PRICE: $3.99 for 8 patties
STYLE: Raw patties
FAT: 16 g SODIUM: 385 mg
COMMENTS: Tasters found these raw, preformed breakfast patties "way too chewy" and "chunky." They were compared to "fake vegan sausage" and "tofu." On the upside, they earned points for a "nice level of saltiness" and a "smoky," "mesquite-like flavor."

JIMMY DEAN All Natural Regular Pork Sausage
PRICE: $3.49 for 16-oz roll
STYLE: Roll-style, raw
FAT: 15 g SODIUM: 420 mg
COMMENTS: Tasters praised this sausage for a "well-seasoned" flavor that "tastes real, more like good sausage than fast food." However, its "grainy" and "coarse" texture proved its downfall.

RECOMMENDED WITH RESERVATIONS *(continued)*

FARMLAND All Natural Original Pork Sausage
PRICE: $2.49 for 16-oz roll
STYLE: Roll-style, raw
FAT: 16 g SODIUM: 310 mg
COMMENTS: Tasters found this sausage bland despite its "good meaty" taste and "tender" texture. It had the least amount of salt per serving, and tasters noticed. "Tasted like a tiny hamburger, not sausage," said one.

NOT RECOMMENDED

BOB EVANS Original Recipe Pork Sausage
PRICE: $4.29 for 16-oz roll
STYLE: Roll-style, raw
FAT: 15 g SODIUM: 460 mg
COMMENTS: While we liked this sample's "large black pepper grains" and "good herbal flavors," the texture was "rubbery," "chewy," and "dry, tough, and stringy," according to tasters. "Reminds me of beef jerky," one wrote.

FARMLAND Original Pork Sausage Roll
PRICE: $1.99 for 16-oz roll
STYLE: Roll-style, raw
FAT: 23 g SODIUM: 510 mg
COMMENTS: This product had the most fat and salt per serving among our samples, so it is no wonder we found it "salty," "extremely fatty," and "a grease bomb."

LOW-MOISTURE MOZZARELLA

Low-moisture mozzarella offers mellow flavor that blends seamlessly with bolder ingredients in baked pasta dishes and melts nicely in everything from lasagna to pizza. To find the best brand, we sampled nine different low-moisture mozzarellas, both block-style and preshredded, made with whole or part-skim milk, plain and on pizza. Preshredded cheeses quickly fell to the bottom of the heap; these are tossed with powdered cellulose (and sometimes potato starch) to absorb moisture, which prevents clumping and slows spoilage—but it also dulls the flavor of the cheese. As for the block-style cheeses, we preferred brands with more fat that were made from whole milk, not a cheaper alternative, such as condensed skim milk or nonfat dry milk, which can result in oddly sweet off-flavors and overbrowning when the cheese is melted. Also, tasters gave a thumbs-down to aged cheeses; they found the age-related tang and sharpness to be distracting. Mozzarellas are listed in order of preference; fat is per 28-gram serving.

RECOMMENDED

SORRENTO Whole-Milk Mozzarella (sold as Precious on the West Coast)
PRICE: $5.29 for 16 oz (33 cents per oz)
STYLE: Block FAT: 6.5 g
COMMENTS: Tasters raved that our favorite mozzarella's flavor was so "clean," "mellow," and "buttery" that it was "practically like drinking milk." Even better, its "smooth" texture boasted just a hint of "nice chew" that was great both eaten out of hand and melted on pizza.

KRAFT Low-Moisture Part-Skim Mozzarella
PRICE: $3.68 for 8 oz (46 cents per oz)
STYLE: Block FAT: 6 g
COMMENTS: The "creamy," "milky," "fresh-tasting" flavors that tasters praised when sampling this cheese plain turned up again when the cheese had been melted on pizza. There, it earned points for its "stretchy," "gooey" texture.

BOAR'S HEAD Whole-Milk Low-Moisture Mozzarella
PRICE: $7.49 for 16 oz (47 cents per oz)
STYLE: Block FAT: 7 g
COMMENTS: Though a few of us found this cheese's texture a bit too "chewy" on pizza, its flavor made up for it. Tasters noted that its balance of "creamy" and "milky" overtones, with "a touch of tang," made it ideal as a pizza topper.

RECOMMENDED WITH RESERVATIONS

KRAFT Low-Moisture Part-Skim Mozzarella
PRICE: $4.29 for 8 oz (54 cents per oz)
STYLE: Shredded FAT: 6 g
COMMENTS: Our favorite among the shredded cheeses, this sample's "creamy," "milky" flavor came through particularly well on pizza, where the dusty coating dissolved and gave way to a "smooth" texture with "good brown spots."

ORGANIC VALLEY Low-Moisture Part-Skim Organic Mozzarella
PRICE: $6.99 for 8 oz (87 cents per oz)
STYLE: Block FAT: 6 g
COMMENTS: Most tasters thought that this sample's "sharp," "cheddar"-like flavors, which stood out in the plain tasting, became "nice" and "milky" on pizza. As for texture some found it "rubbery", but others liked its "moderate chew."

RECOMMENDED WITH RESERVATIONS *(continued)*

SORRENTO Part-Skim Mozzarella
PRICE: $5.29 for 16 oz (33 cents per oz)
STYLE: Block FAT: 5.6 g
COMMENTS: Almost everyone noted that this cheese was comparatively "damp," "wet," and "a bit spongy," but that meant different things to different tasters. Many happily compared it to "fresh mozzarella"; others panned it as "limp," particularly when it was melted on pizza.

HORIZON Organic Low-Moisture Part-Skim Mozzarella
PRICE: $3.99 for 6 oz (67 cents per oz)
STYLE: Shredded FAT: 5 g
COMMENTS: One of the two leanest cheeses of the bunch, this sample—our least favorite in the plain tasting—was nothing you'd want to snack on. Many found it "dry" and "bland." Some picked up on sharp "pungent" flavors. On pizza, however, those harsh notes faded to a "creamy," "milky tang."

ORGANIC VALLEY Low-Moisture Part-Skim Mozzarella
PRICE: $4.29 for 6 oz (72 cents per oz)
STYLE: Shredded FAT: 6 g
COMMENTS: "Looks like cheap grated Parm—and kinda tastes like it, too," said one taster about these wispy shreds. Others agreed, citing "sharper, tangier" flavor than you'd expect from mozzarella. Its pizza performance redeemed it—but only slightly: Its higher fat content rendered it "stretchier" and "creamier" than other low-ranking samples.

NOT RECOMMENDED

SARGENTO Classic Mozzarella
PRICE: $3.49 for 8 oz (44 cents per oz)
STYLE: Shredded FAT: 5 g
COMMENTS: Though "void of flavor" to some, most found this cheese "overly sweet." The anti-caking residue made it "super-dry," "like there's a packet of mac and cheese powder dumped over it." On pizza, it was "dry and leathery," even "crunchy," with an odd "sweet" flavor.

SUPERMARKET CANNED TUNA

Canned tuna has never been high-class fare, but nowadays some manufacturers are upping the ante, offering premium versions of canned tuna with names like "select" grade and "prime fillet." Wondering if any of these were better, we trawled the tuna aisle and selected eight cans of solid white albacore tuna, most packed in water (our preferred style from an earlier tasting), and tasted them plain and in tuna salad. Though three large producers dominate the market, two smaller industry newcomers came in on top, with fresher, firmer fish that easily outshone the squishy, watery shreds of the lower-scoring brands. Instead of cooking their fish twice like the larger seafood producers do—once before it's canned, then again when it's heated inside the can to kill harmful bacteria—these smaller companies pack raw fish into the cans by hand and cook the meat only once, which preserves the fresh flavor and texture of the fish. They also don't use any packing liquid, which most producers include to enhance flavor and to cut costs—more liquid in the can means less room for fish. Tunas are listed in order of preference; sodium is per 2-ounce serving.

RECOMMENDED

WILD PLANET Wild Albacore Tuna
PRICE: $3.39 for 5 oz (85 cents per oz)
TUNA IN CAN: 3.99 oz (80% of total content)   SODIUM: 250 mg
INGREDIENTS: Albacore tuna and sea salt
COMMENTS: "Rich and flavorful, but not fishy," this hand-packed

tuna containing no extra liquid held its own in the mayonnaise-y salad and seemed "substantial" to tasters, who praised its "hearty" yet "tender" bite. In sum: "This one is aces."

AMERICAN TUNA Pole Caught Wild Albacore
PRICE: $4.99 for 6 oz ($1.00 per oz)
TUNA IN CAN: 5 oz (83% of total content)   SODIUM: 20 mg
INGREDIENTS: Albacore tuna
COMMENTS: The only other brand not packed in liquid, this prod-

uct stood out to tasters because it "actually tastes like tuna." The "distinct chunks" boasted fish flavor that was "pronounced" but not overpowering, and a texture that was "meaty," if "a little dry."

RECOMMENDED WITH RESERVATIONS

STARKIST SELECTS Solid White Albacore Tuna in Water
PRICE: $1.69 for 4.5 oz (47 cents per oz)
TUNA IN CAN: 3.6 oz (80% of total content)   SODIUM: 170 mg
INGREDIENTS: White meat tuna, water, salt, pyrophosphate
COMMENTS: Most tasters appreciated that this supposedly higher quality tuna's "solid chunks" stood out in the salad, but flavor-wise it was a mixed bag: To some the meat had "decent" tuna flavor, while others thought the fish fell flat in the presence of pickles, onions, and mayo. As we went to press,

StarKist slightly changed this product's formulation; tasters felt the new version was comparable in taste and texture.

BUMBLE BEE Prime Fillet Solid White Albacore Tuna in Water
PRICE: $1.99 for 5 oz (54 cents per oz)
TUNA IN CAN: 3.7 oz (74% of total content)   SODIUM: 140 mg
INGREDIENTS: White tuna, water, salt, pyrophosphate added
COMMENTS: The general consensus about this product whose manufacturer claims comes from a superior grade tuna? Ambivalence. Tasters described the meat's "very fine" texture as

"shredded without being squished," and though its flavor was "rather bland" and "mild," it was "moist and pretty tasty" and made a "good, basic tuna sandwich."

RECOMMENDED WITH RESERVATIONS (continued)

CHICKEN OF THE SEA Solid White Albacore Tuna in Water
PRICE: $1.99 for 5 oz (57 cents per oz)
TUNA IN CAN: 3.5 oz (70% of total content)   SODIUM: 180 mg
INGREDIENTS: Solid white tuna, water, vegetable broth (contains soy), salt, pyrophosphate
COMMENTS: The favorite non-gourmet offering of the "big three" brands, this tuna tasted familiar to many of us. Tasters found the

meat "decent" but "watery," and some admitted that this met their expectations. Others complained that it reminded them "why I never wanted this in my lunchbox."

CROWN PRINCE Natural Solid White Albacore Tuna in Water
PRICE: $2.99 for 6 oz (70 cents per oz)
TUNA IN CAN: 4.3 oz (72% of total content)   SODIUM: 105 mg
INGREDIENTS: Albacore tuna, spring water, sea salt
COMMENTS: Though this tuna consistently racked up points for its "distinct," "hearty" texture, tasters' votes were split when

it came to flavor. Depending on whom you asked, the fish tasted "meaty" and "pleasant," or was "very, very fishy" and "fermented tasting."

STARKIST Solid White Albacore Tuna in Water
PRICE: $1.67 for 5 oz (51 cents per oz)
TUNA IN CAN: 3.3 oz (66% of total content)   SODIUM: 190 mg
INGREDIENTS: White tuna, water, vegetable broth, salt, pyrophosphate; contains soy
COMMENTS: Without much tuna flavor to speak of, this conventional StarKist sample was more of a "family-friendly protein delivery system" than its premium sibling. That said, a few tasters

picked up on a big hit of salt—presumably a result of the meat soaking in vegetable broth, which seemed to affect this brand more than others.

BUMBLE BEE Solid White Albacore Tuna in Water
PRICE: $1.69 for 5 oz (46 cents per oz)
TUNA IN CAN: 3.7 oz (74% of total content)   SODIUM: 140 mg
INGREDIENTS: White tuna, water, vegetable broth, salt, pyrophosphate added; contains soy
COMMENTS: Though the tuna's "mild" flavor didn't offend anyone, it didn't impress either. Where this lesser Bumble Bee sample really lost points was in the texture department, where it elicited censure

for tasting "soupy" and "watery" and so "loose" that it seemed "more like a dip than a sandwich filling."

MAYONNAISE

Whether it's dressing potato salad, moistening a BLT, or holding crumbs in place on baked fish, mayonnaise is a kitchen staple. To find the best one, we gathered 15 top-selling jars, everything from classic mayo to olive oil– or canola-based versions to reduced-fat brands. After a preliminary tasting round, in which we sampled the mayos plain, we trimmed the list to seven and tried these brands in macaroni salad. In spite of a lineup of condiments with bells and whistles, we found that the best-tasting brands had the fewest ingredients and the simplest flavors. Tasters downgraded dressed-up variations that used cider vinegar instead of more neutral distilled vinegar, or honey instead of sugar for sweetness. They also didn't like add-ins such as dried garlic or onion, which turned plain mayonnaise into something closer to salad dressing. Our top-rated brand didn't even include lemon juice or mustard, though we use both in the test kitchen recipe for mayonnaise. Surprisingly, fat levels in the mayonnaises didn't affect the rankings; aside from the "light" version, all contained roughly the same amount. Not surprisingly, salt levels did make a difference, with tasters preferring brands with more salt rather than less. Mayonnaises are listed in order of preference; sodium, sugar, and fat are per 1-tablespoon serving.

RECOMMENDED

BLUE PLATE Real Mayonnaise
PRICE: $4.79 for 32 oz (15 cents per oz)
SODIUM: 80 mg
SUGAR: 0 g
FAT: 11 g
COMMENTS: Tasters praised Blue Plate's "great balance of taste and texture," calling it "solid, straight-up mayo" and "a close second to home-made." But while it's one of the top-selling brands in the country, you'll have to mail-order it unless you live in the South or Southeast.

HELLMANN'S Real Mayonnaise
PRICE: $4.79 for 30 oz (16 cents per oz)
SODIUM: 90 mg
SUGAR: 0 g
FAT: 10 g
COMMENTS: Our previous favorite, Hellmann's is the top-selling mayonnaise by a wide margin and is available nationwide (it's sold as Best Foods west of the Rockies). Tasters praised it as "creamy and tangy," with a "nice eggy flavor."

HELLMANN'S Light Mayonnaise
PRICE: $4.79 for 30 oz (16 cents per oz)
SODIUM: 125 mg
SUGAR: 1 g
FAT: 3.5 g
COMMENTS: With about one-third the fat of its full-fat sibling, this light mayonnaise won fans with its "eggy" flavor and "creamy" texture. "Tastes fatty, which you want in mayonnaise," one taster noted. A few people detected a "fake" aftertaste, but to most, this light product, with plenty of salt to boost flavor and starch for body, seemed like "the real deal."

SPECTRUM Organic Mayonnaise
PRICE: $5.79 for 16 oz (36 cents per oz)
SODIUM: 85 mg
SUGAR: 0 g
FAT: 11 g
COMMENTS: Tasted plain, this mayonnaise was "bright, sweet, eggy, creamy, and real," with a "pleasant and rich mayo texture" that was only slightly "oily." In macaroni salad, however, tasters found Spectrum a bit "greasy."

RECOMMENDED (continued)

DUKE'S Mayonnaise
PRICE: $3.50 for 32 oz (11 cents per oz)
SODIUM: 75 mg
SUGAR: 0 g
FAT: 12 g
COMMENTS: "Rich, smooth, and velvety," with a "strong, sharp vinegar taste" and "eggy" flavor—but "the balance is off." Despite its fanatical following in the South, Duke's Mayonnaise struck our tasters as merely fine.

RECOMMENDED WITH RESERVATIONS

SPECTRUM Organic Mayonnaise with Olive Oil
PRICE: $6.59 for 12 oz (55 cents per oz)
SODIUM: 75 mg
SUGAR: 1 g
FAT: 11 g
COMMENTS: Despite the "olive oil" in its name, this mayonnaise contains less olive oil than vegetable oil (listed as soy/canola on the label). Few tasters even noticed any olive oil flavor. While we liked Spectrum's "eggy, tangy, creamy, and sweet" qualities, we found it "oily," or worse ("way too greasy"). Plus, it's nearly triple the price of our winner and it tasted like salad dressing. Blame too much mustard, vinegar, and lemon.

KRAFT Mayo
PRICE: $5.59 for 30 oz (19 cents per oz)
SODIUM: 70 mg
SUGAR: 0 g
FAT: 10 g
COMMENTS: While this mayonnaise was "sweet and tangy," with "nice mild flavor," it lacked the "egginess" of our top-ranked brands, and tasters complained of off-flavors, from "sweet onion" to "Kraft mac and cheese powder."

UNSALTED BUTTER

Not too long ago, cultured butter, also known as European butter, was hard to come by. Nowadays, there are as many brands of this rich, pricey condiment in the dairy case as the standard sweet-cream variety. We wanted to know if we really had to spend more money for the best butter, so we sampled 10 brands, seven cultured and three sweet-cream, spread on crackers and baked into French butter cookies. While sweet-cream butters are quickly and cheaply mass-produced by churning cream that has undergone little or no storage, cultured butters are made more slowly, with cream that's allowed to ripen for a few days to develop flavor and then inoculated with bacterial cultures before churning. The higher-ranked brands nailed their mix of cultures, nicely balancing sweet, fresh-cream flavor with complex tang. They also included enough butterfat to make them decadent and glossy but not so rich that baked goods were dense or greasy. Only one sweet-cream variety made it into the top tier, coming in second, most likely because of its packaging; sticks of this butter are protected from refrigerator odors by a specially patented wrapper. Butters are listed in order of preference.

HIGHLY RECOMMENDED

PLUGRÁ European-Style Unsalted Butter
PRICE: $9.98 for 16 oz
STYLE: cultured cream   BUTTERFAT: 83%
COMMENTS: The cream of the crop, this "thick and luscious" cultured butter was "complex" and "just a bit tangy" and "grassy." Some deemed its flavor the most "robust" of all the samples.

RECOMMENDED

LAND O'LAKES Unsalted Sweet Butter BEST BUY
PRICE: $4.79 for 16 oz
STYLE: sweet cream   BUTTERFAT: 82%
COMMENTS: The most widely available supermarket butter—and the only sweet-cream sample to earn our recommendation—this product impressed tasters in spite of its plainer-tasting profile. We liked its "fresh-cream," "clean dairy flavor."

VERMONT CREAMERY European-Style Cultured Butter, Unsalted
PRICE: $11.98 for 16 oz
STYLE: cultured cream   BUTTERFAT: 86%
COMMENTS: This high-priced, high-fat cultured butter balanced "fresh-sweet dairy richness" with flavor that tasters described as "rich," "refreshing," and "barnyard-y" but also "mineral-y."

PRÉSIDENT Unsalted Butter
PRICE: $7.52 for 16 oz
STYLE: cultured cream   BUTTERFAT: 82%
COMMENTS: Though leaner than other cultured butters, this French import came across as "firm" and "silky," with "beautifully sweet and creamy" flavor that was also "buttermilk-y" and "slightly grassy."

ORGANIC VALLEY European-Style Cultured Butter, Unsalted
PRICE: $7.58 for 16 oz
STYLE: cultured cream   BUTTERFAT: 86%
COMMENTS: This sample was on the mellow side for a cultured butter, with some tasters deeming it "a bit timid." Others praised its "simple buttery flavor" and "floral undertones."

RECOMMENDED (continued)

ORGANIC VALLEY Cultured Butter, Unsalted
PRICE: $5.99 for 16 oz
STYLE: cultured cream   BUTTERFAT: 83%
COMMENTS: Though some tasters picked up on nothing but this butter's "rich" flavor and "welcome tartness," several detected an apparent storage problem. Seeping through this sample's waxed parchment wrapper were flavors that tasted "like the inside of a fridge."

LURPAK Imported Butter, Unsalted
PRICE: $11.98 for 16 oz
STYLE: cultured cream   BUTTERFAT: 83%
COMMENTS: Though enough tasters praised this butter for its "richness" and "complexity," it barely skated into the "Recommended" category, as others found it so "fake"-tasting that it drew comparisons to margarine.

RECOMMENDED WITH RESERVATIONS

CABOT Natural Creamery Unsalted Butter
PRICE: $5.29 for 16 oz
STYLE: sweet cream   BUTTERFAT: 81%
COMMENTS: At best, this butter was "mild"; but it was a little "boring," too. It was also another victim of poor wrapping: More than a few tasters detected "odd" flavors that reminded them of "the fridge."

KERRYGOLD Pure Irish Butter, Unsalted
PRICE: $5.98 for 16 oz
STYLE: cultured cream   BUTTERFAT: 83%
COMMENTS: It wasn't this Irish butter's texture that tasters objected to; in fact, several deemed it "luxurious" and "velvety." It was the "artificial," "movie-theater-popcorn flavor" that put many tasters off.

HORIZON Organic Unsalted Butter
PRICE: $5.49 for 16 oz
STYLE: sweet cream   BUTTERFAT: 81%
COMMENTS: Like the Cabot butter, this brand was "nothing special" and even struck some tasters as "watery" and "thin." Poor wrapping likely contributed to off-flavors that reminded one taster of "refrozen melted ice cream."

HOT SAUCE

Hot sauce isn't just for spicy dishes—we call for it in many other recipes to give dishes a little kick. We wanted to find the best all-purpose hot sauce, so we gathered eight brands in the traditional Cajun or Mexican style, plus one Sriracha, a thicker, sweeter Asian hot sauce that's grown in popularity in recent years, and sampled them on steamed white rice and in a Buffalo sauce on chicken tenders. Tasters preferred brands that had more salt (at least 100 milligrams per teaspoon), garlic, and a decent—but not overpowering—amount of vinegar. When it came to the variety of chile itself, tasters liked hot sauces made with mild, fruity-tasting cayenne and red jalapeño, both of which offer a moderate heat that allows other flavors to shine through. In the end, we had two winners that offered just the right combination of punchy heat, saltiness, sweetness, and garlic flavor. Hot sauces are listed in order of preference; sodium is per 1-teaspoon serving.

HIGHLY RECOMMENDED

HUY FONG Sriracha Hot Chili Sauce
PRICE: $4.29 for 17 oz (25 cents per oz)
SODIUM: 100 mg
INGREDIENTS: Chile (red jalapeño), sugar, salt, garlic, distilled vinegar, potassium sorbate, sodium bisulfite, xanthan gum
COMMENTS: Despite its unconventionally thick consistency and sweeter profile, this squeeze-bottle condiment (which we threw into the mix as a ringer) impressed tasters with its "full," "rich," "bright" heat. We even enjoyed its heavier body in Buffalo sauce; several tasters remarked that it coated the chicken "perfectly."

FRANK'S REDHOT Original Cayenne Pepper Sauce
PRICE: $2.29 for 12 oz (19 cents per oz)
SODIUM: 190 mg
INGREDIENTS: Aged cayenne red peppers, distilled vinegar, water, salt, garlic powder
COMMENTS: "Hello, Frank!" said one taster, who recognized this familiar-tasting condiment as the base for the original Buffalo sauce recipe. In both applications, it struck a perfect balance between tanginess and "tomatoey sweetness," with heat that "wasn't too hot" and "added to the food rather than overpowering it."

RECOMMENDED

ORIGINAL LOUISIANA Hot Sauce
PRICE: $0.99 for 6 oz (17 cents per oz)
SODIUM: 240 mg
INGREDIENTS: Peppers (cayenne), vinegar, salt
COMMENTS: Even with just three ingredients, this sauce had a "complex," "balanced" profile and "mild punch." A few tasters even picked up on "smoky," "roasted" notes with "a pleasant fruitiness." Its sodium content was at least double or even triple the amount found in most other brands.

TAPATÍO Salsa Picante
PRICE: $1.95 for 10 oz (20 cents per oz)
SODIUM: 110 mg
INGREDIENTS: Water, red peppers (undisclosed), salt, spices, garlic, acetic acid, xanthan gum, sodium benzoate
COMMENTS: Several tasters noted that this Mexican condiment delivered a "smoky" sweetness that reminded them of barbecue sauce or even Worcestershire sauce. Most of us agreed that the warm spice flavor is unusual for Buffalo sauce but not necessarily unwelcome.

RECOMMENDED *(continued)*

TEXAS PETE Hot Sauce
PRICE: $1.55 for 12 oz (13 cents per oz)
SODIUM: 100 mg
INGREDIENTS: Red peppers (3 undisclosed types), salt, xanthan gum, benzoate of soda
COMMENTS: When sampling it over rice, tasters found this bright red sauce "pleasingly hot and spicy," with a burn that "builds and lingers." A few tasters felt that the heat petered out a little once the condiment was mixed into Buffalo sauce, turning this hot sauce into a "milder," more "ketchup-y" version of Frank's.

EL YUCATECO Salsa Picante Roja de Chile Habanero
PRICE: $2.69 for 4 oz (67 cents per oz)
SODIUM: 90 mg
INGREDIENTS: Water, habanero pepper, tomato, salt, spices, acetic acid, xanthan gum, citric acid, sodium benzoate, FD&C red No. 40, calcium disodium EDTA
COMMENTS: This habanero-based sauce was "mouth-meltingly" hot but also "sweet," thanks to the addition of a little tomato. Those who liked it praised its "earthy, almost fruity" flavor, but others felt that it was out of place on Buffalo chicken.

RECOMMENDED WITH RESERVATIONS

CHOLULA Hot Sauce, Original
PRICE: $3.69 for 5 oz (74 cents per oz)
SODIUM: 85 mg
INGREDIENTS: Water, peppers (arbol and piquin), salt, vinegar, spices, xanthan gum
COMMENTS: Some tasters appreciated this Mexican sauce's "sweet" flavor and "mild smokiness," but others were unimpressed. Criticisms revolved around its low salt content, which a few tasters felt rendered the sauce "washed out."

NOT RECOMMENDED

TABASCO Pepper Sauce
PRICE: $3.49 for 5 oz (70 cents per oz)
SODIUM: 35 mg
INGREDIENTS: Distilled vinegar, red peppers (tabasco), salt
COMMENTS: Thanks to its high amount of vinegar and skimpy measure of salt, this top-selling hot sauce sank to the bottom of the chart. Tasters described it as "flavorless," "vinegary," "out of balance"—even "vile." Its consistency was off, too, saturating rather than saucing the chicken. (Tabasco also sells Buffalo Style Hot Sauce; we didn't test it since we were looking for an all-purpose product.)

KETCHUP

Since the 1980s, most ketchup has been made with high-fructose corn syrup (HFCS), which is cheap and easy to mix with other ingredients. But in recent years, HFCS has been blamed for rising obesity rates and other health problems, so many manufacturers now offer alternatives, such as ketchup made with white sugar. To find out if any of these reformulated ketchups tasted better, we gathered eight brands and sampled each one plain and with French fries. It was clear tasters wanted ketchup that tasted the way they remembered it from childhood: boldly seasoned, with all the flavor elements—salt, sweet, tang, and tomato—assertive yet harmonious. Sweetener did indeed play a role in our rankings: The top three ketchups were all sweetened with white sugar. Tasters also liked brands that had enough acid to balance the sugar and weren't stingy with the salt (our favorite brand had the highest percentage of salt). Ketchups are listed in order of preference; sweetener is per 1-tablespoon serving.

RECOMMENDED

HEINZ ORGANIC Tomato Ketchup
PRICE: $2.49 for 15 oz (17 cents per oz)
SWEETENER: Sugar, 4 g
SALT: 3.14 percent **pH:** 3.69
COMMENTS: Tasters praised the "bright and fresh," "well rounded ketchup-y flavor" of Heinz Organic. Its bold, harmonious punch of saltiness, sweetness, tang, and tomato flavor nudged it into first place. Altogether, "like ketchup should be."

HUNT'S Tomato Ketchup   `BEST BUY`
PRICE: $1.39 for 24 oz (6 cents per oz)
SWEETENER: Sugar, 4 g
SALT: 2.79 percent **pH:** 3.54
COMMENTS: The word "classic" popped up more than once to describe Hunt's ketchup. Tasters found it "perfectly aggressive" (meant in the nicest possible way) and "balanced." It won points for smoothness and color, too. "Love it. Classic. Tastes like ketchup should."

SIMPLY HEINZ Tomato Ketchup
PRICE: $2.59 for 32 oz (8 cents per oz)
SWEETENER: Sugar, 4 g
SALT: 2.92 percent **pH:** 3.64
COMMENTS: This sugar version of classic Heinz fooled several tasters into thinking it was their old (corn syrup) favorite: "Tastes the way I remember—nostalgia," wrote one. "Great balance, very classic-tasting. Heinz?" asked another.

HEINZ Tomato Ketchup
PRICE: $2.79 for 36 oz (8 cents per oz)
SWEETENER: High fructose corn syrup, corn syrup, 4 g
SALT: 2.53 percent **pH:** 3.6
COMMENTS: For the second time, America's number-one selling ketchup fell in the middle of the pack. Tasters praised its "tangy, sharp, a little zippy" flavor. They also liked the strong tomato presence. While it got respectable scores, it was edged out of the top because it "lack(ed) oomph and complexity."

DEL MONTE Ketchup
PRICE: $2.95 for 24 oz (12 cents per oz)
SWEETENER: High fructose corn syrup, corn syrup, 4 g
SALT: 2.61 percent **pH:** 3.74
COMMENTS: Our tasters found Del Monte acidic. Some liked that quality, praising the ketchup as "zippy" and "bright" with a "nice tangy flavor." A minority registered that latter quality as sour.

RECOMMENDED WITH RESERVATIONS

ANNIE'S NATURALS Organic Ketchup
PRICE: $3.99 for 24 oz (17 cents per oz)
SWEETENER: Cane sugar, 4 g
SALT: 2.09 percent **pH:** 3.59
COMMENTS: Annie's does not taste like classic ketchup. That appealed to a few tasters, who liked its "roasted" and "darker, richer" flavors and described it as "gourmet" ketchup. Others disagreed, finding the ketchup unbalanced: "Way too sweet. Okay tomato flavor but sugar overwhelms it all."

MUIR GLEN Organic Tomato Ketchup
PRICE: $3.49 for 24 oz (15 cents per oz)
SWEETENER: Naturally milled sugar, 3 g
SALT: 2.84 percent **pH:** 3.77
COMMENTS: Tasters split on this brand, which, again, didn't taste like "classic" ketchup; the critics found it closer to barbecue sauce, cocktail sauce, or marinara. Some praised it as "thick and flavorful." Others faulted both texture ("lumpy") and taste ("too much spice"). Summed up a taster, "Complex but weird."

NOT RECOMMENDED

ORGANICVILLE Organic Ketchup
PRICE: $3.50 for 24 oz (15 cents per oz)
SWEETENER: Agave nectar, 3 g
SALT: 2.11 percent **pH:** 3.83
COMMENTS: This brand hit rock bottom for its "gritty" texture and off-flavors. Tasters faulted the spiced flavor and "overwhelming sweetness." It uses agave nectar to sweeten. Although it had less sweetener per serving than our winning ketchups, it wasn't offset by salt and acidity. Tasters bellowed: "Impure ketchup! Impostor!"

TOMATO SOUP

In our quest to find a canned tomato soup with good tomato flavor that wasn't overpowered by too much salt, seasonings, or other additives, we rounded up eight brands (seven canned and one from a box), heated them up according to the instructions, and called tasters to the table. Some brands relied on tomato puree alone for tomato flavor, but tasters preferred those brands that included fresh, unprocessed tomatoes as well. Though we wanted the samples to have some sweetness, several of them went overboard with sweeteners. The four lowest-ranking soups have sugar or high-fructose corn syrup (HFCS) in the first three ingredients listed (by law, the order of the ingredient list must reflect the percentage of an ingredient within). Texture was also an important factor; our two favorite brands were closest to homemade, with medium body and a slightly chunky texture from real pieces of tomato. Tomato soups are listed in order of preference; sugars and sodium are per 1-cup serving.

RECOMMENDED

PROGRESSO Vegetable Classics Hearty Tomato
PRICE: $2.69 for 19 oz
SUGARS: 13 g SODIUM: 690 mg
TOMATO: Tomato puree, tomatoes
SWEETENER: Sugar and less than 2 percent corn syrup solids
COMMENTS: The "deep red" color and "tangy" flavor of this soup suggested actual tomatoes. Although it has the second highest amount of sodium among the brands we tasted, the flavors were balanced, and the "slightly herbaceous" seasoning "allowed the tomato to bloom."

IMAGINE Organic Vine Ripened Tomato Soup
PRICE: $3.29 for 14.5 oz
SUGARS: 12 g SODIUM: 610 mg
TOMATO: Tomato puree, tomatoes, tomato juice, tomato paste
SWEETENER: Evaporated cane juice
COMMENTS: This canned soup had the texture of homemade and nicely trod the line between sweetness and tang. "Tastes like real tomato, a balance between acidic and sweet flavors," one impressed taster noted. Although this soup contains no cheese, a few tasters thought they detected traces of Parmesan.

RECOMMENDED WITH RESERVATIONS

IMAGINE Organic Creamy Tomato Soup
PRICE: $3.99 for 32 oz
SUGARS: 7 g SODIUM: 620 mg
TOMATO: Tomatoes
SWEETENER: Rice syrup
COMMENTS: Unlike our top picks, this bright orange soup wasn't chunky. Instead, it was "comforting" and "thick." But many tasters objected to the strong vegetal flavors (primarily celery), which they felt "overpowered the tomato."

MUIR GLEN Organic Tomato Basil Soup
PRICE: $2.99 for 14.6 oz
SUGARS: 11 g SODIUM: 740 mg
TOMATO: Tomato puree, tomatoes
SWEETENER: Raw sugar
COMMENTS: Some tasters praised this "zesty" canned soup for its "good balance of spice and roast-y flavors" and "present tomato" taste. Others felt that the herbs sabotaged the tomato flavor. As one taster put it, "A little too herby—almost like a canned pizza sauce."

RECOMMENDED WITH RESERVATIONS *(continued)*

CAMPBELL'S Condensed Tomato Soup
PRICE: $0.99 for 10.75 oz
SUGARS: 12 g SODIUM: 480 mg
TOMATO: Tomato puree
SWEETENER: HFCS
COMMENTS: This soup incited no passion. "Not too thin, not too thick, just kind of dead center," one taster wrote. Other verdicts included "mild" and "bland but not off-putting." High-fructose corn syrup (which tastes sweeter than sugar) is the second ingredient listed; some tasters found this soup too sweet.

NOT RECOMMENDED

PROGRESSO Vegetable Classics Tomato Basil Soup
PRICE: $2 for 19 oz
SUGARS: 14 g SODIUM: 680 mg
TOMATO: Tomato puree
SWEETENER: Sugar and less than 2 percent corn syrup solids
COMMENTS: Although similar in some respects to our winning soup, this sample had no yeast extract (an ingredient that adds depth). Tasters found this variation "sickeningly sweet"; one likened it to SpaghettiOs. The third ingredient listed is sugar, and this soup had the most total sugars per serving of all the brands we sampled.

HEALTHY CHOICE Tomato Basil Soup
PRICE: $2.69 for 15 oz
SUGARS: 12 g SODIUM: 470 mg
TOMATO: Tomato puree
SWEETENER: Sugar
COMMENTS: A glut of herbs doomed this "heart healthy" soup. Tasters couldn't get past the "disgusting, powdery dried-herb dust." The "gelatinous" texture didn't help. As one taster wrote, the soup "seems thickened with duck sauce."

CAMPBELL'S Condensed Soup Healthy Request Tomato
PRICE: $1.49 for 10.75 oz
SUGARS: 10 g SODIUM: 410 mg
TOMATO: Tomato puree
SWEETENER: HFCS
COMMENTS: This "healthier" version of regular Campbell's uses a lot more water than the original. Our tasters found the soup "watery, thin, and bland." As one taster summed up, "Looks like tomato dishwater and tastes like it, too."

SPAGHETTI

Spaghetti is usually made of just semolina (coarsely milled durum wheat) and maybe added vitamins, yet when it comes to supermarket brands, its texture and flavor can vary tremendously. We sampled eight brands, dressed with olive oil and with tomato sauce, looking for one that delivered clean, wheaty flavor and a firm, nutty chew. The best brands stood out for their great texture, while the worst ones cooked up sticky or mushy; cloudier cooking water indicated which brands had a weak structure and broke down during boiling. Our top-rated spaghetti stuck to just semolina and vitamins and omitted durum flour, a finer, cheaper grind of durum wheat that was used in brands described as gummy. It is also likely extruded through well-maintained dies. Poorly maintained machines, no matter if the dies are traditional bronze or more modern Teflon-coated, cannot produce perfectly compact strands of spaghetti, and the texture of the pasta can suffer. Also, it is dried for a long period at a moderate temperature; ultra-high temperatures (190 degrees or higher) can speed up the process but may end up cooking out some of the flavor. Spaghettis are listed in order of preference.

RECOMMENDED

DE CECCO Spaghetti No. 12
PRICE: $1.39 for 16 oz   SOURCE: Italy
INGREDIENTS: Durum wheat semolina, niacin, ferrous lactate, thiamine mononitrate, riboflavin, folic acid
PROCESSING METHOD: Pressed through bronze dies; dried at 158°F
STARCH IN COOKING WATER: 4.88 percent
COMMENTS: This Italian import boasted "clean wheat flavor" and a "firm, ropy quality"; in fact, the lab confirmed these strands as the strongest of the samples. The texture was just as good with sauce—tasters found it "firm," with "good chew."

RUSTICHELLA D'ABRUZZO
Pasta Abruzzese di Semola di Grano Duro
PRICE: $4.56 for 17.5 oz ($4.17 for 16 oz)   SOURCE: Italy
INGREDIENTS: Durum wheat semolina
PROCESSING METHOD: Pressed through bronze dies; dried at 95°F
STARCH IN COOKING WATER: 5.78 percent
COMMENTS: Even though these noodles were dried at a fairly low 95 degrees, they retained a nice "firm" bite and chew. We also appreciated this pricey Italian brand's "nutty," "toasty" taste, which came through even under a coating of marinara.

GAROFALO Spaghetti
PRICE: $2.49 for 16 oz   SOURCE: Italy
INGREDIENTS: Durum wheat semolina, niacin, iron lactate, thiamine mononitrate, riboflavin, folic acid
PROCESSING METHOD: Pressed through bronze dies; dried at 176°F
STARCH IN COOKING WATER: 5.42 percent
COMMENTS: Tossed with olive oil, this Italian pasta ranked highest for flavor that was "buttery" and "rich-tasting" and had a "roughness" to the exterior. However, that pleasant coarseness was obscured by the sauce, which made the noodles slightly "gummy."

DELALLO Spaghetti No. 4
PRICE: $2.81 for 16 oz   SOURCE: Italy
INGREDIENTS: Semolina, ferrous lactate (iron), niacin, thiamine mononitrate, riboflavin, folic acid
PROCESSING METHOD: Pressed through bronze dies; dried at 167°F
STARCH IN COOKING WATER: 6.32 percent
COMMENTS: In general, tasters found this spaghetti to be "middle-of-the-road." It didn't stand out for having major flaws, and it didn't elicit rave compliments. Its taste was "light" but still "wheaty," while its texture was deemed "fine."

RECOMMENDED (continued)

RONZONI Spaghetti
PRICE: $1.39 for 16 oz   SOURCE: USA
INGREDIENTS: Semolina (wheat), durum flour, niacin, iron (ferrous sulfate), thiamine mononitrate, riboflavin, folic acid
PROCESSING METHOD: Pressed through Teflon-coated dies; dried at 190°F
STARCH IN COOKING WATER: 5.68 percent
COMMENTS: Overall, this brand passed muster. But perhaps due in part to ultra-high-temperature drying, which cooks out flavor, some tasters thought this mass-market American spaghetti "lacked nuttiness." The inclusion of fine-ground durum flour may have accounted for why some tasters found the texture "mealy."

BARILLA Spaghetti
PRICE: $1.67 for 16 oz   SOURCE: USA
INGREDIENTS: Semolina (wheat), durum flour, niacin, iron (ferrous sulfate), thiamine mononitrate, riboflavin, folic acid
PROCESSING METHOD: Pressed through Teflon-coated dies; dried at ultra-high temperature (company would not provide exact data)
STARCH IN COOKING WATER: 5.62 percent
COMMENTS: "There is something a little flat about the flavor of this," said one taster about this American bestseller, which we speculated must have been dried at a temperature high enough to make it taste less wheaty than some. Others agreed, some also noting the noodles' "gummy" consistency. Overall, though, tasters found the strands "OK" but "unremarkable."

RECOMMENDED WITH RESERVATIONS

MONTEBELLO Organic Spaghetti
PRICE: $2.99 for 16 oz   SOURCE: Italy
INGREDIENTS: Organic durum wheat semolina
PROCESSING METHOD: Pressed through bronze dies; dried at 130–150°F
STARCH IN COOKING WATER: 7.56 percent
COMMENTS: It wasn't flavor criticisms that sank this imported spaghetti to the lower rungs of the chart; most tasters praised the "clean," "bright," "almost nutty" taste. These strands lost the most starch during cooking, for a "mushy," "crumbly" texture.

CANNED WHOLE TOMATOES

If you believe the hype, San Marzano tomatoes, from southern Italy, are the best tomatoes in the world. We wanted to know if they were really the ultimate canned whole tomatoes, so we held a taste-off: San Marzanos versus everything else. We sampled 10 brands plain, in a quick cooked tomato sauce, and in a slow-simmered sauce. Disappointingly, none of the San Marzanos delivered the bold, deep taste we were expecting. Tasters liked tomatoes that had higher levels of sugar (judged according to the Brix scale, which measures amounts of sugar in liquid; a higher number indicates a greater level of sweetness) balanced by enough acidity; the San Marzanos were either not sweet enough, or too sweet but lacking ample acidity to counter the sweetness. When it came to texture, we liked tomatoes with a firm yet tender bite, even after a lengthy simmer. San Marzanos again scored poorly, as they are not treated with calcium chloride, which is added to domestic brands to help maintain firmness. As it turned out, the hype was all for naught—our favorite brand was domestic. Tomatoes are listed in order of preference.

RECOMMENDED

MUIR GLEN Organic Whole Peeled Tomatoes
PRICE: $2.99 for 28 oz   ORIGIN: USA
CALCIUM CHLORIDE: Yes   pH: 3.91   BRIX: 6
COMMENTS: "Reminds me of a real summer tomato," said one taster about our favorite sample. No wonder: Its strong acidity and high level of sweetness made for flavor that was "vibrant" and "sweet in a natural way." The addition of calcium chloride gave the tomatoes a "nice firm texture" that held up even after hours of simmering.

HUNT'S Whole Plum Tomatoes
PRICE: $1.95 for 28 oz   ORIGIN: USA
CALCIUM CHLORIDE: Yes   pH: 4.16   BRIX: 5.5
COMMENTS: Even after two hours of simmering, these calcium chloride–treated tomatoes were "meaty," with "distinct shape." A relatively high Brix value and low pH—an ideal combination for tomatoes—explained their "fruity," "bright" flavors.

RECOMMENDED WITH RESERVATIONS

RED GOLD Whole Peeled Tomatoes
PRICE: $1.36 for 14.5 oz   ORIGIN: USA
CALCIUM CHLORIDE: Yes   pH: 3.91   BRIX: 4.7
COMMENTS: These nicely "firm," globe-shaped tomatoes shared the same low pH (i.e., strong acidity) as our favorite brand, but they lacked its sweetness. As a result, several tasters found them "a bit sharp," even in long-cooked sauce. Others liked the big acid punch.

CENTO San Marzano Certified Peeled Tomatoes
PRICE: $3.79 for 28 oz   ORIGIN: Italy
CALCIUM CHLORIDE: No   pH: 4.25   BRIX: 7
COMMENTS: Although these non–DOP certified San Marzano tomatoes scored highest for sweetness, they lacked acidity, and tasters found their flavor merely "average"—even "untomatoey." That said, they fared best of all the Italian brands, particularly because their texture "held up" in sauce.

BIONATURAE Organic Whole Peeled Tomatoes
PRICE: $3.39 for 28.2 oz   ORIGIN: Italy
CALCIUM CHLORIDE: No   pH: 4.28   BRIX: 5.6
COMMENTS: Without calcium chloride, these Italian tomatoes were so "mushy" that they "tasted like sauce" before we cooked them, but their "sweet" flavor was praised by some tasters.

RECOMMENDED WITH RESERVATIONS (continued)

SAN MARZANO Whole Peeled Tomatoes
PRICE: $3.99 for 28 oz   ORIGIN: USA
CALCIUM CHLORIDE: Yes   pH: 4.26   BRIX: 6.4
COMMENTS: What's in a name? In this case, not much. These impostor "San Marzano" tomatoes were grown domestically with seeds from Italy's famous varietal. Some tasters picked up on their high level of sweetness, but without equally high acidity, the tomatoes' flavor was also "muted."

RIENZI Selected Italian Plum Tomatoes
PRICE: $1.95 for 28 oz   ORIGIN: Italy
CALCIUM CHLORIDE: No   pH: 4.22   BRIX: 5.4
COMMENTS: Tasters noticed this sample's lack of calcium chloride in all three applications, describing the tomatoes as "mushy" and "border-line soupy." Thanks to low acid and moderate sweetness, their flavor was middle-of-the-road.

EDEN Organic Whole Roma Tomatoes
PRICE: $3.79 for 28 oz   ORIGIN: Canada
CALCIUM CHLORIDE: No   pH: 4.31   BRIX: 4.2
COMMENTS: With the least amount of sweetness, not much acidity, and no added salt, these tomatoes didn't "pack much punch." Some tasters considered that effect pleasantly "clean" and "light," whereas others complained that they offered "no real tomato flavor at all," particularly in the long-simmered sauce.

PASTENE San Marzano Tomatoes of Sarnese Nocerino Area D.O.P.
PRICE: $4.53 for 28 oz   ORIGIN: Italy
CALCIUM CHLORIDE: No   pH: 4.32   BRIX: 4.6
COMMENTS: We had high expectations for these pricey DOP-certified San Marzano tomatoes but were disappointed. Because of low sweetness and acidity, their flavor translated as "weak" and "thin." Like the other calcium chloride–free samples, they broke down easily.

NOT RECOMMENDED

TUTTOROSSO Peeled Plum Shaped Tomatoes
PRICE: $1.79 for 28 oz   ORIGIN: USA
CALCIUM CHLORIDE: Yes   pH: 4.14   BRIX: 4.5
COMMENTS: We like a bit of firmness to our tomatoes, but thanks to their thick flesh, these samples were "tough," "chewy," and "fibrous." Worse, their low sweetness and acidity made them taste "muted" and "unbalanced."

PREMIUM JARRED PASTA SAUCES

Like a lot of other supermarket items, jarred pasta sauce has gone upscale. Nowadays, many manufacturers have branched out, jazzing up their sauces with red wine or special herb blends—and charging higher prices to match. But money and marketing aside, do any of them taste better? We sampled seven national brands of jarred sauce, plain and on pasta, to find out. Tasters preferred sauces with a chunky, homemade-style texture; brands that listed whole or diced tomatoes first in their ingredient list accomplished this better and scored higher than those that listed tomato puree first. Also, tasters liked sauces that weren't overly sweet. Many manufacturers include sugar when the tomatoes used aren't at the height of ripeness, but it must play a supporting role, adding a touch of sweetness, and not dominate the sauce or overshadow any bright tomato flavor. Sauces are listed in order of preference; sugar and fat are per ½-cup serving.

RECOMMENDED

VICTORIA Marinara Sauce
PRICE: $6.99 for 25 oz
SUGARS: 3 g
FAT: 4 g
COMMENTS: This "authentic"-tasting sauce earned praise for "robust, continuing flavor" comparable to "homemade." Medium-bodied, the sauce is made with imported Italian tomatoes and olive oil, as well as fresh onions, fresh garlic, and fresh basil. Its "nice, bright acidity" evoked fresh tomatoes, and the sauce was "restrained, rather than drowned in sugar."

CLASSICO Marinara with Plum Tomatoes and Olive Oil `BEST BUY`
PRICE: $2.79 for 24 oz
SUGARS: 6 g
FAT: 2 g
COMMENTS: Diced plum tomatoes are listed first on the ingredient list of this sauce, which tasters liked for a "great texture" that they described as "chunky" and "hearty." The second ingredient is tomato puree (a mixture of water and tomato paste). Tasters definitely noticed the two-layered tomato flavor, praising it as "stellar" and "very complete." A touch of heat lent a nice "slight kick."

RECOMMENDED WITH RESERVATIONS

RAO'S Homemade Marinara Sauce
PRICE: $8.69 for 24 oz
SUGARS: 3 g
FAT: 6 g
COMMENTS: This "rich and roasty" sauce won points from some for "long-simmered flavor" that tasters called "meaty" and "beefy." It had three times as much fat per serving as some brands, making it the fattiest sauce in our lineup (olive oil is the second ingredient). But while it secured points for flavor, it lost them for "watery" and "slightly thin" texture.

BARILLA Toscana Tuscan Herb
PRICE: $2.50 for 24 oz
SUGARS: 6 g
FAT: 2 g
COMMENTS: We liked the taste of this sauce, variously describing it as "tangy, nutty," and "roasted" and having "bright fresh-tomato flavor." We liked the "coarse consistency," too, finding that it "coated the pasta well." But many objected to "a punch in the face of oregano" that was "dusty-tasting" and "overly seasoned."

NOT RECOMMENDED

MEZZETTA Napa Valley Bistro Homemade Style Marinara
PRICE: $5.59 for 24.5 oz
SUGARS: 3 g
FAT: 5.5 g
COMMENTS: This brand's label boasted of imported Italian tomatoes from the San Marzano region. But the tomatoes were overshadowed by a "vegetal, dusty aftertaste" that was "musty," "drab," and "like a tin can." The sauce also had the second highest amount of fat per serving; some tasters found it greasy.

RAGÚ ROBUSTO! 7-Herb Tomato
PRICE: $1.67 for 24 oz
SUGARS: 9 g
FAT: 3 g
COMMENTS: This "thin and runny" tomato sauce was far from the chunky, homemade consistency that our tasters liked. But its sweetness is what really drove us away. "Way too much sugar; cloyingly sweet," one taster wrote. "Is this sugar sauce? Virtually no tomato flavor," said another. Sugar is listed third on the nutrition label.

BERTOLLI VINEYARD Premium Collection Marinara with Burgundy Wine
PRICE: $3.29 for 24 oz
SUGARS: 12 g
FAT: 2 g
COMMENTS: This "boozy" sauce topped the charts with the most sugar per serving, probably due to its third ingredient: Burgundy wine. The wine was also to blame for the sauce's last-place finish in our lineup. "Tastes like the wine hasn't been cooked down enough," one taster wrote. "Jarring," added another. The sauce wasn't helped by the fact that tomato puree is listed first on the label. (Tomatoes are listed second.) Plus, any tomato flavor was overwhelmed by the "raw wine" and "sour and off-tasting" flavor.

CHEESE TORTELLINI

Store-bought tortellini makes a good alternative to the homemade version, which can take hours to prepare. To find a suitable stand-in for homemade, we sampled seven supermarket brands of cheese tortellini, including two refrigerated, two dried, and three frozen. The ratio of pasta wrapper to filling was very important. Too much filling and the pouch will burst; too little, or too mild, and the tortellini tastes like unfilled pasta. The thickness of the pasta wrapper is also important—it must be sturdy enough to hold the filling and withstand boiling but not so thick that it becomes doughy. The filling's flavor was another factor we considered. Tasters preferred brands with both bold cheese flavor—our winner included a flavorful mix of ricotta, Emmentaler, and Grana Padano cheeses—and a higher sodium level. Tortellini brands are listed in order of preference; sodium is per 100 grams of tortellini.

RECOMMENDED

BARILLA Three Cheese Tortellini
PRICE: $4 for 8 oz (50 cents per oz)
STYLE: Dried
SODIUM: 310 mg
PASTA THICKNESS: 1.35 mm
COMMENTS: Although dainty, these tortellini packed a punch. Said one taster, "I like the small size, which makes the immodest taste (big, cheesy, robust, assertive) a pleasant surprise." The filling was a bold and generous combination of ricotta, Emmentaler, and Grana Padano cheeses. The wrapper was a hit, too: "Pasta is great—tender and delicate."

SEVIROLI Cheese Tortellini
PRICE: $7.49 for 14 oz (54 cents per oz)
STYLE: Frozen SODIUM: 230 mg
PASTA THICKNESS: 1.82 mm
COMMENTS: Tasters praised these frozen tortellini for their "good filling-to-pasta ratio." The wrapper was "firm but pliable" and "pleasant to chew." The filling, a combination of mild ricotta and sharper Parmesan and Romano cheeses, pleased us, too. "Filling is both creamy and full-flavored like aged cheese," said one taster. "Nutty, rich, pleasantly sharp," another wrote.

RECOMMENDED WITH RESERVATIONS

BUITONI Three Cheese Tortellini
PRICE: $5.65 for 9 oz (63 cents per oz)
STYLE: Fresh, refrigerated
SODIUM: 180 mg
PASTA THICKNESS: 1.2 mm
COMMENTS: Tasters liked the "delicate" and "tender" pasta in this brand of fresh tortellini. It was "fluffy and nice to chew." But we were disappointed with the filling: "Cheese is super mild—why bother?" one taster asked rhetorically.

ROSETTO Cheese Tortellini
PRICE: $4.53 for 19 oz (24 cents per oz)
STYLE: Frozen SODIUM: 200 mg
PASTA THICKNESS: 2.30 mm
COMMENTS: A few tasters liked the "firm, meaty bite" of this brand's thicker pasta; others compared its texture to Play-Doh. But the filling was criticized as "dry" and "powdery."

NOT RECOMMENDED

DAVINCI Tortellini Filled with Parmesan Cheese
PRICE: $2.12 for 7 oz (30 cents per oz)
STYLE: Dried SODIUM: 270 mg
PASTA THICKNESS: 1.36 mm
COMMENTS: Even the comparably high sodium level couldn't save these tiny tortellini. Their downfall was the filling—a mixture of Parmesan cheese, grated breadsticks, sunflower oil, and spices. The "crunchy" and "gritty" breadsticks made for "weird lumps of filling" that "resembled wood pulp."

ANGY'S Tortellini with Cheese
PRICE: $2.50 for 12 oz (21 cents per oz)
STYLE: Frozen SODIUM: 200 mg
PASTA THICKNESS: 2.25 mm
COMMENTS: Tasters struggled to eat this "too thick and chewy" pasta. "Hard to get your teeth through," complained one. Another compared its texture to "a leather handbag." The filling, made of ricotta and Parmesan, was no better. "The filling is like a blob of cotton," one taster commented. A second panned it as "a bland wad of nothingness."

NUOVO Tortellini Ricotta and Parmigiano
PRICE: $4.99 for 9 oz (55 cents per oz)
STYLE: Fresh, refrigerated
SODIUM: 120 mg
PASTA THICKNESS: 1.37 mm
COMMENTS: We were shocked to see this "chef-crafted" fresh brand at the bottom of our ratings, but tasters found themselves in "Bland City." "Barely detectable cheese. Scant, dry filling." The only praise (of sorts) for this "flavorless" pasta concerned its shape. After noting the "fancy ruffles," one taster added, "Reminds me of my bathing suit when I was five." That won't earn it a spot on our table.

CUTTING BOARDS

Last time we picked a winning cutting board, it warped after just a few years of use. To find a new winner, we put eight boards—wood, bamboo, plastic, and composite models priced from $22 to nearly $150—through three months of daily use with our test cooks. Wood and bamboo boards gripped the knives well; their soft, subtly textured surfaces offered just enough give for the knife's edge to stick lightly as we chopped. When it came to the wood and bamboo boards' performance, construction proved key; end-grain boards (in which blocks of wood are glued together with the exposed grain facing up) warped more easily than edge-grain boards (in which the grain runs parallel to the surface). For wood boards, we also considered maintenance; wood and bamboo need to be oiled regularly, but we found a teak winner that retained its soft, smooth, flat surface even after a few weeks of use with no oiling. Cutting boards are listed in order of preference.

HIGHLY RECOMMENDED	PERFORMANCE	TESTERS' COMMENTS
PROTEAK Edge Grain Teak Cutting Board MODEL: 107 PRICE: $84.99 MATERIAL: Mexican teak DIMENSIONS: 18 by 24 in WEIGHT: 15.05 lb DISHWASHER-SAFE: No	CUTTING: ★★★ DURABILITY: ★★★ USER-FRIENDLINESS: ★★★	Roomy, knife-friendly, and durable, this teak slab was worth every penny. It resisted warping and cracking, showed only minor scratches, and was easy to lift and clean, thanks to handholds on each end.

RECOMMENDED	PERFORMANCE	TESTERS' COMMENTS
OXO GOOD GRIPS Carving & Cutting Board BEST BUY MODEL: 1063789 PRICE: $21.99 MATERIAL: Polyproplene (plastic) DIMENSIONS: 14.5 by 21 in WEIGHT: 3.85 lb DISHWASHER-SAFE: Yes	CUTTING: ★★★ DURABILITY: ★★ USER-FRIENDLINESS: ★★★	Our favorite bargain board sports rubber strips on both sides that keep its lightweight frame anchored to the counter. It did suffer deep scratches and gouges but never split or warped, and it cleaned up stain-free.
JOHN BOOS Chop-N-Slice Reversible Cutting Board MODEL: 214 PRICE: $44.95 MATERIAL: Maple DIMENSIONS: 15 by 20 in WEIGHT: 9.4 lb DISHWASHER-SAFE: No	CUTTING: ★★★ DURABILITY: ★★ USER-FRIENDLINESS: ★★★	This reversible edge-grain board's slightly rough surface offered a secure hold on the counter and it gently gripped the knives. Though it absorbed stains and developed hairline cracks, it never warped.

NOT RECOMMENDED	PERFORMANCE	TESTERS' COMMENTS
SAGE Non-Skid Chop Board MODEL: SNS-14169S PRICE: $46.95 MATERIAL: Wood-laminate composite DIMENSIONS: 16 by 19 in WEIGHT: 3.15 lb DISHWASHER-SAFE: Yes	CUTTING: ★ DURABILITY: ★★ USER-FRIENDLINESS: ★★★	This model is thin and lightweight; dishwasher-safe; and stayed put thanks to its nonskid feet. Unfortunately, it warped after several commercial dishwasher runs and was the only model to commit the ultimate cutting board no-no: It dulled a knife.
THE CUTTING BOARD FACTORY Industrial Grade Polymer Cutting Board MODEL: CG-18024 PRICE: $27.93 MATERIAL: High-density polyethylene (plastic) DIMENSIONS: 18 by 25.25 in WEIGHT: 7.7 lb DISHWASHER-SAFE: Yes	CUTTING: ★★ DURABILITY: ★ USER-FRIENDLINESS: ★★	This plastic board is reversible and can be custom-cut to any size. It never warped, even in the commercial dishwasher. But chef's knives couldn't grip its slick surface, and the cleaver left cuts so deep that it pulled up strips of plastic.
CATSKILL CRAFTSMEN End Grain Chopping Block MODEL: 1822 PRICE: $79 MATERIAL: Yellow birch DIMENSIONS: 17 by 20.75 in WEIGHT: 17.6 lb DISHWASHER-SAFE: No	CUTTING: ★★½ DURABILITY: ★ USER-FRIENDLINESS: ★	What this hefty end-grain block offered in knife-friendliness (a cushiony, grippy surface for controlled cutting) it utterly lacked in durability. And this board cracked after a few rinses and eventually warped.
TOTALLY BAMBOO Congo Large Prep Board MODEL: 20-3476 PRICE: $140 MATERIAL: Butcher block–style bamboo DIMENSIONS: 16.5 by 21.75 in WEIGHT: 13.75 lb DISHWASHER-SAFE: No	CUTTING: ★★ DURABILITY: ★ USER-FRIENDLINESS: ★	Both copies of this end-grain board arrived slightly distorted, and the warping worsened somewhat over time. Though its feet kept it steady, the rubber pads peeled off.

INNOVATIVE CUTTING BOARDS

New styles of cutting boards promise to streamline food preparation, with built-in colanders and handles that allow you to easily scoop up and transport prepped ingredients. We wondered if any of these innovative boards would actually help cut down on prep time and compared eight to each other and to our favorite cutting board, the Proteak Edge Grain Teak Cutting Board (see page 302). Several boards failed at the basics, with cutting surfaces that were way too small or too slick, and the advertised innovations often solved one problem while creating another. Though we found one innovative board that actually worked, an over-the-sink bamboo model with a built-in colander, it doesn't replace our favorite board from Proteak. Cutting boards are listed in order of preference.

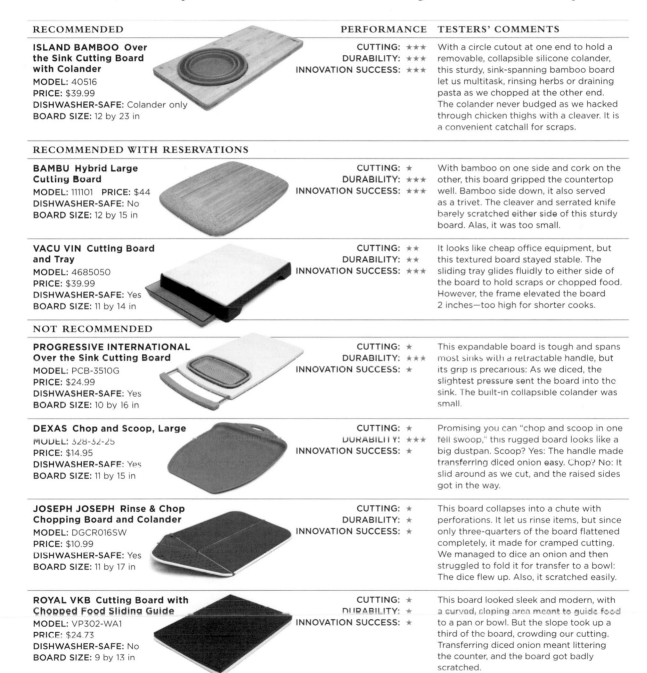

RECOMMENDED	PERFORMANCE	TESTERS' COMMENTS
ISLAND BAMBOO Over the Sink Cutting Board with Colander MODEL: 40516 PRICE: $39.99 DISHWASHER-SAFE: Colander only BOARD SIZE: 12 by 23 in	CUTTING: ★★★ DURABILITY: ★★★ INNOVATION SUCCESS: ★★★	With a circle cutout at one end to hold a removable, collapsible silicone colander, this sturdy, sink-spanning bamboo board let us multitask, rinsing herbs or draining pasta as we chopped at the other end. The colander never budged as we hacked through chicken thighs with a cleaver. It is a convenient catchall for scraps.

RECOMMENDED WITH RESERVATIONS		
BAMBU Hybrid Large Cutting Board MODEL: 111101 PRICE: $44 DISHWASHER-SAFE: No BOARD SIZE: 12 by 15 in	CUTTING: ★ DURABILITY: ★★★ INNOVATION SUCCESS: ★★★	With bamboo on one side and cork on the other, this board gripped the countertop well. Bamboo side down, it also served as a trivet. The cleaver and serrated knife barely scratched either side of this sturdy board. Alas, it was too small.
VACU VIN Cutting Board and Tray MODEL: 4685050 PRICE: $39.99 DISHWASHER-SAFE: Yes BOARD SIZE: 11 by 14 in	CUTTING: ★★ DURABILITY: ★★ INNOVATION SUCCESS: ★★★	It looks like cheap office equipment, but this textured board stayed stable. The sliding tray glides fluidly to either side of the board to hold scraps or chopped food. However, the frame elevated the board 2 inches—too high for shorter cooks.

NOT RECOMMENDED		
PROGRESSIVE INTERNATIONAL Over the Sink Cutting Board MODEL: PCB-3510G PRICE: $24.99 DISHWASHER-SAFE: Yes BOARD SIZE: 10 by 16 in	CUTTING: ★ DURABILITY: ★★★ INNOVATION SUCCESS: ★	This expandable board is tough and spans most sinks with a retractable handle, but its grip is precarious: As we diced, the slightest pressure sent the board into the sink. The built-in collapsible colander was small.
DEXAS Chop and Scoop, Large MODEL: 328-32-25 PRICE: $14.95 DISHWASHER-SAFE: Yes BOARD SIZE: 11 by 15 in	CUTTING: ★ DURABILITY: ★★★ INNOVATION SUCCESS: ★	Promising you can "chop and scoop in one fell swoop," this rugged board looks like a big dustpan. Scoop? Yes: The handle made transferring diced onion easy. Chop? No: It slid around as we cut, and the raised sides got in the way.
JOSEPH JOSEPH Rinse & Chop Chopping Board and Colander MODEL: DGCR016SW PRICE: $10.99 DISHWASHER-SAFE: Yes BOARD SIZE: 11 by 17 in	CUTTING: ★ DURABILITY: ★ INNOVATION SUCCESS: ★	This board collapses into a chute with perforations. It let us rinse items, but since only three-quarters of the board flattened completely, it made for cramped cutting. We managed to dice an onion and then struggled to fold it for transfer to a bowl: The dice flew up. Also, it scratched easily.
ROYAL VKB Cutting Board with Chopped Food Sliding Guide MODEL: VP302-WA1 PRICE: $24.73 DISHWASHER-SAFE: No BOARD SIZE: 9 by 13 in	CUTTING: ★ DURABILITY: ★ INNOVATION SUCCESS: ★	This board looked sleek and modern, with a curved, sloping area meant to guide food to a pan or bowl. But the slope took up a third of the board, crowding our cutting. Transferring diced onion meant littering the counter, and the board got badly scratched.

KNIFE BLOCK SETS

The biggest selling point when it comes to knife block sets seems to be the number of pieces the manufacturer can cram into one block, not the usefulness or quality of the blades. To find out if there was a knife block set on the market that would prove this assumption wrong, we tested eight sets containing six to nine pieces each and costing anywhere from $100 to nearly $700. After evaluating these sets against each other, comparing like components in a variety of tasks, we evaluated them against an à la carte selection of the test kitchen's favorite knives. In the end, our testing confirmed our suspicion that you are better off shopping for knives individually; that way, you get only what you really need—no weak links—and what you get is well constructed and of high quality. Knife block sets are listed in order of preference.

HIGHLY RECOMMENDED	PERFORMANCE	TESTERS' COMMENTS
TEST KITCHEN À LA CARTE KNIFE SET (7 pieces) TOTAL PRICE: $334.65 • Wüsthof Classic 3½-Inch Paring Knife (model 4066), $39.95 • Victorinox Fibrox 8-Inch Chef's Knife (model 40520), $29.95 • Wüsthof Classic 10-Inch Bread Knife (model 4151), $109.95 • Victorinox Fibrox 12-Inch Granton Edge Slicing/Carving Knife (model 47645), $49.95 • Victorinox Fibrox 6-inch Straight Boning Knife: Flexible (model 40513), $19.95 • Shun Classic Kitchen Shears (model 1120M), $39.95 • Bodum Bistro Universal Knife Block (model 11089), $44.95	WEAK LINKS: 0 of 7 	This "all-star" set of test kitchen favorites (all best-in-class winners in past tests) fits neatly into our favorite universal knife block by Bodum, designed to hold any variety of blades securely in its nest of plastic sticks. Best of all, at $334.65, this ideal collection costs less than many pre-packaged knife block sets.

RECOMMENDED WITH RESERVATIONS

	PERFORMANCE	TESTERS' COMMENTS
WÜSTHOF Classic 8-Piece Deluxe Knife Set MODEL: 8420 PRICE: $379.99 INCLUDES: 3½-inch paring, 5-inch boning, 8-inch chef's, 8-inch bread, 8-inch carving, sharpening steel, shears, 17-slot wood block 	PERFORMANCE: ★★½ EASE OF USE: ★★ USEFULNESS: ★★ WEAK LINKS: 3 OF 8	We were eager to try this set featuring our favorite paring knife and a shorter version of our favorite 10-inch bread knife. The results were mixed: The paring and boning blades fared admirably, but the 8-inch bread knife couldn't slice through a large loaf, the shears were wimpy, and the carving knife extraneous.
VICTORINOX 7-Piece Rosewood Knife Set MODEL: 46054 PRICE: $189.95 INCLUDES: 3¼-inch paring, 6-inch boning, 8-inch chef's, 8-inch bread, 10-inch slicing, sharpening steel, 6-slot wood block 	PERFORMANCE: ★★½ EASE OF USE: ★★ USEFULNESS: ★★ WEAK LINKS: 2 OF 7	While the knives in this set performed well and very few were filler, there was something that seemed cheap about it. The slots chipped as we slid the knives in and out, making the set look worn right away. The bread and slicing knives were sharp but a bit short.
SHUN Classic 9-Piece Knife Set MODEL: DMS0910 PRICE: $699.95 INCLUDES: 2½-inch bird's beak, 3½-inch paring, 6-inch utility, 8-inch chef's, 9-inch bread, 9-inch slicing, sharpening steel, shears, 11-slot bamboo block 	PERFORMANCE: ★★½ EASE OF USE: ★★ USEFULNESS: ★★ WEAK LINKS: 5 OF 9	These solidly constructed, razor-edged knives performed well overall. But the 9-inch bread knife couldn't handle large loaves, and the parer was like a mini chef's knife, making it hard to peel an apple. At this price, every piece should be essential.

NOT RECOMMENDED

	PERFORMANCE	TESTERS' COMMENTS
MESSERMEISTER Meridian Elite 9-Piece Knife Block Set MODEL: E/3000-9S PRICE: $351.94 INCLUDES: 3½-inch paring, 5-inch scalloped utility, 6-inch utility, 7-inch santoku, 8-inch chef's, 9-inch bread, sharpening steel, shears, 16-slot wood block	PERFORMANCE: ★★ EASE OF USE: ★ USEFULNESS: ★ WEAK LINKS: 5 OF 9	While some blades (particularly the nimble paring knife) shone in tests, this set's two utility knives and santoku were easily outperformed by the chef's blade on identical tasks. The bread knife was too short, and the block's finish chipped a little around the slots with repeated use.
GLOBAL 9-Piece Knife Set MODEL: G88/91ST PRICE: $661.95 INCLUDES: 3-inch paring, 4-inch paring, 5¼-inch utility, 5½-inch nakiri/vegetable, 6-inch serrated utility, 7-inch Asian chef's, 8¼-inch carving, 8¾-inch bread, 11-slot steel block 	PERFORMANCE: ★★ EASE OF USE: ★ USEFULNESS: ★ WEAK LINKS: 6 OF 9	Most of these sleek Japanese blades were agile, but many were also unnecessary: two utility knives, an extra paring knife, a carving knife, and a 5½-inch nakiri blade for vegetable prep.

INEXPENSIVE STOCKPOTS

While a 6- to 8-quart Dutch oven can handle day-to-day tasks of both boiling pasta and simmering chili and stews, there are occasions when a roomier pot—a stockpot—comes in handy, whether it's boiling corn or lobsters, or making a double batch of pasta. For this once-in-a-while pot, we didn't want to spend much. We selected seven 12-quart stockpots, priced under $40, and cooked big batches of spaghetti, corn, and chili in each. Short, wide pots were preferable, since they heated water faster, plus they let us see the contents of the pot and stir without burning our knuckles. Top-ranking pots were under 9 inches tall, with bottoms more than 8 inches wide. They also had big, protruding handles that were easy to grasp, even with oven mitts, and came with lids to trap steam and expedite boiling. Stockpots are listed in order of preference.

RECOMMENDED		PERFORMANCE	TESTERS' COMMENTS
ALPHA Heavy Gauge 12-Quart Stainless Steel Stock Pot with Glass Lid MODEL: S-5512 PRICE: $26 DIMENSIONS: 8¼ in tall, 10¼ in wide BOTTOM THICKNESS: 4.8 mm WEIGHT: 4.7 lb MATERIAL: Stainless steel with encapsulated aluminum disk bottom		HANDLING: ★★ BOILING: ★★★ SIMMERING: ★★ DURABILITY: ★★★	The wide bottom of this heavy pot accommodated corn easily, and water boiled rapidly. Large handles made it easy to carry, though its heft presented a challenge when pouring. Chili scorched a little around the edges of the pot, where the sides bulged over the encapsulated aluminum disk bottom.

RECOMMENDED WITH RESERVATIONS

		PERFORMANCE	TESTERS' COMMENTS
VASCONIA 12-Quart Aluminum Stock Pot with Lid MODEL: 5032030 PRICE: $14.99 DIMENSIONS: 8½ in tall, 10¼ in wide BOTTOM THICKNESS: 1.6 mm WEIGHT: 1.5 lb MATERIAL: Aluminum (with satin exterior finish)		HANDLING: ★★★ BOILING: ★★★ SIMMERING: ★★ DURABILITY: ★	This aluminum stockpot, the lightest and least expensive we tested, was easy to carry thanks to long handles with plastic grips that stayed cool. Chili barely scorched, because the aluminum was so responsive. But the pot discolored on the inside, and the bottom warped slightly.
ONEIDA 12-Quart Stock Pot MODEL: 62592 PRICE: $39.99 DIMENSIONS: 9¼ in tall, 9¾ in wide BOTTOM THICKNESS: 4.8 mm WEIGHT: 3.97 lb MATERIAL: Stainless steel with encapsulated aluminum disk bottom		HANDLING: ★★ BOILING: ★★★ SIMMERING: ★ DURABILITY: ★	This pan felt flimsy and bottom-heavy. It was a little too tall and skinny to maneuver easily, even though its handles were large and easy to grasp. Cooking chili, we found several hotspots where food stuck, plus it scorched around the edges of the pot.
PAULA DEEN 12-Quart Covered Stockpot MODEL: 51654 PRICE: $39.95 DIMENSIONS: 9 in tall, 10¼ in wide BOTTOM THICKNESS: 3.2 mm WEIGHT: 4.4 lb MATERIAL: Porcelain enameled steel		HANDLING: ★★ BOILING: ★★★ SIMMERING: ★ DURABILITY: ★	Water boiled quickly and the pot was easy to lift and pour—but beware of the searing hot lid and handles. It failed at making chili, cooking way too fast. Turning the heat down didn't help: A big scorch spot required a metal scrubber to clean. Enamel chipped inside the lid.

NOT RECOMMENDED

		PERFORMANCE	TESTERS' COMMENTS
NORDIC WARE 12-Quart Stock Pot without Cover MODEL: 22120 PRICE: $29.89 DIMENSIONS: 9¾ in tall, 10⅛ in wide BOTTOM THICKNESS: 1.6 mm WEIGHT: 3.7 lb MATERIAL: Aluminized steel with a nonstick interior		HANDLING: ★ BOILING: ★★ SIMMERING: ★ DURABILITY: ★★	The only pot sold without a lid—it costs an extra $8.50—is at a disadvantage, since covering pots of water makes them boil faster. Once the water was finally rolling, stubby handles close to the sides of the pot made it difficult to carry. The nonstick interior was helpful when cleaning a large spot of charred chili.
T-FAL Specialty 12-Quart Nonstick Stock Pot MODEL: A9228064 PRICE: $27.69 DIMENSIONS: 10¼ in tall, 9½ in wide BOTTOM THICKNESS: 3.2 mm WEIGHT: 3.8 lb MATERIAL: Aluminum with nonstick coating, inside and out		HANDLING: ★ BOILING: ★ SIMMERING: ★ DURABILITY: ★★	We had to stick our hands deep inside this tall skinny pot to stir; more than once we burned our knuckles. The bottom scorched the chili, and while the nonstick coating made it easy to clean, its presence on the exterior of the pot gave off awful fumes. (Eventually, the fumes abated.)

TRAVEL MUGS

A good travel mug makes it easy to enjoy your coffee or tea on the way to work—as long as it offers good heat retention and is easy to sip from. To find the best one, we selected seven travel mugs for testing, ruling out plastic and ceramic mugs for poor insulation, mega-mugs that contained 24 or more ounces of liquid, and mugs that required complete lid removal for drinking. We tested our mugs for heat retention by filling them with hot coffee and using thermometer probes to gauge heat loss over time. To find a rugged mug with a snug-fitting lid that didn't leak or drip, we turned full mugs over and shook them. We also took the mugs for a ride in the car, looking for models that were easy to open single-handedly and fit into car cup holders. Travel mugs are listed in order of preference.

HIGHLY RECOMMENDED	PERFORMANCE	TESTERS' COMMENTS
TIMOLINO Icon 16-Ounce Signature Vacuum Travel Mug MODEL: PCT-46K PRICE: $28.00 DISHWASHER-SAFE: Top rack only	SIPPING & HANDLING: ★★★ LEAKPROOF: ★★★ HEAT RETENTION: ★★	This sleek mug kept coffee drinkably hot for twice as long as it took for us to get to work (over an hour), but what really made this a top tumbler was its simple, leakproof lid design, which made it super easy to handle and a cinch to clean.
RECOMMENDED		
ZOJIRUSHI 17-Ounce Clear Stainless Mug MODEL: SM-DA50AX PRICE: $38.99 DISHWASHER-SAFE: No	SIPPING & HANDLING: ★★ LEAKPROOF: ★★★ HEAT RETENTION: ★★★	This slender, pretty carafe had the best heat retention of any mug in our lineup, and it opens easily with the press of a button. Too bad the open lid almost obstructed our view as we were driving (though train commuters won't mind). A colleague found her tea too hot to safely drink for the first half of her commute.
THERMOS Sipp 16-Ounce Vacuum Insulated Tumbler MODEL: NS105BK004 PRICE: $29.99 DISHWASHER-SAFE: Yes	SIPPING & HANDLING: ★ LEAKPROOF: ★★★ HEAT RETENTION: ★★★	A button in the center of the top opened this mug easily, but liquid poured out of opposite sides of the lid—we had to check alignment carefully. But it kept the contents hot, was impossible to overfill, and never leaked. The small hook inside the lid bottom designed to hold the string to a tea bag is a nice touch.
THERMOS Element 5 Travel Mug MODEL: E10500 PRICE: $34.99 DISHWASHER-SAFE: No	SIPPING & HANDLING: ★ LEAKPROOF: ★★★ HEAT RETENTION: ★★★	This rugged-looking mug retained heat superbly, staying well above 140 degrees for 2½ hours. But we needed two hands to twist open the lid unless the mug rested securely on a flat surface. The narrow neck made it hard to clean by hand, and the handle gets in the way of some car cup holders.
OXO LiquiSeal Travel Mug MODEL: 1055291 PRICE: $19.99 DISHWASHER-SAFE: No	SIPPING & HANDLING: ★★★ LEAKPROOF: ★★ HEAT RETENTION: ★★	With a soft rubber grip for comfortable handling and flawless, one-touch opening, our former test kitchen favorite was still a pleasure to take along. Coffee stayed above 140 for only an hour. It was easy to overfill this tumbler, which leaked if coffee got into the lid mechanism before we closed it.
BODUM Double Wall Travel Press with Bonus Lid MODEL: K11057-01 PRICE: $29.95 DISHWASHER-SAFE: Yes	SIPPING & HANDLING: ★★ LEAKPROOF: ★★★ HEAT RETENTION: ★★	A good mug but a flawed French press: Stray grinds seeped into the brew, and the lid prevented us from easily adding milk and sweetener. A non-French press lid (included) worked much better. Plus it retained heat reasonably well, sealed completely, and cleaned up in the dishwasher.
NOT RECOMMENDED		
TRUDEAU Board Room 16-Ounce Travel Mug MODEL: 087588 PRICE: $14.95 DISHWASHER-SAFE: No	SIPPING & HANDLING: ★ LEAKPROOF: ★★ HEAT RETENTION: ★	Dressed to impress, this faux-leather encased mug didn't. It lost heat like a sieve, letting coffee cool below a drinkable temperature in less than an hour. Liquid that got trapped inside the lid when we sipped dribbled out when the mug was turned upside down. And the handle got in the way of the car's cup holder.

ALL-PURPOSE CLEANERS

When it's time to clean grease, grime, and food splatters from your kitchen, a spray cleaner is a great solution. But store shelves teem with options, from all-purpose sprays to antibacterial products to "green" cleaning sprays, so how do you know which one to choose? We tested nine cleaning sprays, five labeled antibacterial and four billed as green or natural, on countertops and kitchen cabinets dirtied with vegetable oil. We also used them to tackle greasy stovetops, tomato sauce–splattered microwave interiors, and the grime on stainless steel range hoods. Finally, we rated the cleaners on their fragrances. All-purpose cleaners are listed in order of preference.

		PERFORMANCE	TESTERS' COMMENTS
HIGHLY RECOMMENDED			
METHOD All-Purpose Natural Surface Cleaner (French Lavender) **PRICE:** $3.79 for 28 oz (14 cents per oz)		SPRAYS TO CLEAN STOVETOP: 8 CLEANING: ★★★ STREAKING: ★★★ SCENT: ★★★	This spray embodies the winning combination of being pleasant to use and cleaning thoroughly and effectively with a minimum number of squirts. It cut grease, lifted stuck-on messes, and left surfaces shining.
RECOMMENDED			
LYSOL Antibacterial Kitchen Cleaner (Citrus Scent) **PRICE:** $2.99 for 22 oz (14 cents per oz) **ANTIBACTERIAL CLAIMS:** Kills 99.9% of *E. coli* and *Salmonella enterica* **WARNINGS:** Rinse food contact surfaces after use. Do not get in eyes, on skin, or on clothing. Wash thoroughly after handling.		SPRAYS TO CLEAN STOVETOP: 8 CLEANING: ★★★ STREAKING: ★★★ SCENT: ★★	Three stars for completely cleaning grease off the range hood in one swipe—and for leaving no streaks. It did fairly well with the splattered microwave, but we needed to rinse with water afterward. It cut grease on countertops and its smell was not bad, though it reminded some testers of Nair chemical hair remover.
RECOMMENDED WITH RESERVATIONS			
SEVENTH GENERATION Natural All Purpose Cleaner, Free & Clear **PRICE:** $5.49 for 32 oz (17 cents per oz)		SPRAYS TO CLEAN STOVETOP: 10 CLEANING: ★★ STREAKING: ★★ SCENT: ★★★	Some testers appreciated this product as the only unscented cleaner in the lineup; others preferred some scent, if only as an indicator that cleaning was going on. Its cleaning power was fair but left some streaks.
FANTASTIK Antibacterial All Purpose Cleaner Heavy Duty **PRICE:** $2.99 for 32 oz (9 cents per oz) **ANTIBACTERIAL CLAIMS:** Kills 99.9% of *E. coli* and *Salmonella choleraesuis* **WARNINGS:** Rinse all food-contact surfaces after use. Avoid contact with eyes, skin, or clothing.		SPRAYS TO CLEAN STOVETOP: 9 CLEANING: ★★ STREAKING: ★★ SCENT: ★	This product claims to kill household bacteria in as few as 10 seconds, and its spraying action has particularly good coverage. Unfortunately, it smells terrible, reminding one tester of Raid insect spray (both products are made by SC Johnson).
FORMULA 409 Antibacterial Kitchen All-Purpose Cleaner (Lemon Fresh) **PRICE:** $3.49 for 22 oz (16 cents per oz) **ANTIBACTERIAL CLAIMS:** Kills *Salmonella choleraesuis* **WARNINGS:** Rinse food-contact surfaces with water. Avoid contact with eyes, skin, or clothing.		SPRAYS TO CLEAN STOVETOP: 14 CLEANING: ★★ STREAKING: ★★ SCENT: ★★	Despite being antibacterial, this spray doesn't claim to kill *E. coli*, and it must stand for 10 minutes to kill any germs. It required extra sprays to clean the splattered microwave and greasy stovetop, and left streaks on stainless steel, although it did an adequate cleaning job.
CLOROX GREEN WORKS 97% Naturally Derived All-Purpose Cleaner **PRICE:** $3.29 for 32 oz (10 cents per oz)		SPRAYS TO CLEAN STOVETOP: 12 CLEANING: ★★ STREAKING: ★½ SCENT: ★★	A decent performer when it came to cleaning the countertops, greasy range hood, and stovetop, but it required extra sprays and wiping.
NOT RECOMMENDED			
MR. CLEAN with Febreze Freshness Antibacterial Spray (Citrus & Light) **PRICE:** $2.99 for 32 oz (9 cents per oz) **ANTIBACTERIAL CLAIMS:** Kills 99.9% of *E. coli* **WARNINGS:** Rinse all food-contact surfaces after use. Avoid contact with eyes or clothing.		SPRAYS TO CLEAN STOVETOP: 10 CLEANING: ★ STREAKING: ★ SCENT: ★	Its cleaning power was only so-so, it does not claim to kill salmonella, and it left plenty of streaks. In other words, this orange-tinted spray was a bust. Its scent was sickeningly sweet and chemical-y.

SAUTÉ PANS

Despite their name, sauté pans, which have a flat bottom and relatively high, straight sides, are not the best pans for sautéing or searing—for these tasks, we reach for a skillet, with its low, sloping walls that encourage evaporation and browning. But they are ideal for cooking down heaps of greens, for shallow-frying, and for certain braises. To find the best sauté pan on the market, we tested nine models, making fried chicken, braised cabbage, Mexican rice, Swedish meatballs, and crêpes (to gauge even browning) in each. Midsize (9½- to 10½-inch) pans performed best; larger pans tended to heat unevenly, and smaller pans didn't provide adequate surface area, so we had to fry our chicken in two batches. Pans that were moderately thick and moderately heavy were substantial enough to modulate heat but not so bulky that they retained too much of it and risked scorching our food. Also, pans that had a helper handle were much easier to move, especially when full. Sauté pans are listed in order of preference.

HIGHLY RECOMMENDED	PERFORMANCE	TESTERS' COMMENTS
VIKING Stainless 7-Ply 3-Quart Sauté Pan MODEL: VSC0303 PRICE: $219.95 WEIGHT (WITHOUT LID): 4.6 lb DIMENSIONS: 10½ in by 2¼ in; 3.88 mm thick MATERIAL: Stainless with aluminum core; metal lid OVENSAFE TEMPERATURE: 600°F	PERFORMANCE: ★★★ EASE OF USE:  ★★★ 	This midsize pan's heft was a boon to steady heating and even browning, and it's so well proportioned that the weight didn't bother us. The handle sported a ridge for a secure grip and stayed cool on the stove; the heavy, sturdy lid fit securely.
ALL-CLAD Stainless 3-Quart Tri-Ply Sauté Pan MODEL: 16711 PRICE: $224.95 WEIGHT (WITHOUT LID): 3.1 lb DIMENSIONS: 9¾ in by 2 in; 2.8 mm thick MATERIAL: Stainless with aluminum core; metal lid OVENSAFE TEMPERATURE: 500°F	PERFORMANCE: ★★★ EASE OF USE: ★★★ 	Our previous favorite is back in an updated induction-compatible version. The price hike is disappointing, but it cooks steadily, browns evenly, has a stay-cool handle, and is well balanced and relatively lightweight.

RECOMMENDED		
CUISINART MultiClad Pro Triple-Ply 3½-Quart Sauté Pan with Lid `BEST BUY` MODEL: MCP33-24H PRICE: $79.95 WEIGHT (WITHOUT LID): 3.4 lb DIMENSIONS: 9 in by 3 in; 3.7 mm thick MATERIAL: Stainless with aluminum core; metal lid OVENSAFE TEMPERATURE: 550°F	PERFORMANCE: ★★★ EASE OF USE: ★★½ 	Although its cooking surface is narrow, causing some crowding, this pan browned food evenly. Its well-balanced body made for easy lifting and pouring, and its handle stayed cool on the stove.
CALPHALON Tri-Ply Stainless 3-Quart Sauté Pan MODEL: 1767729 PRICE: $124.95 WEIGHT (WITHOUT LID): 3.2 lb DIMENSIONS: 9½ in by 2¼ in; 3.43 mm thick MATERIAL: Stainless with aluminum core; glass lid OVENSAFE TEMPERATURE: 450°F	PERFORMANCE: ★★½ EASE OF USE: ★★★ 	Even though this model fried chicken and braised meatballs just as well as our Best Buy—and offered slightly more surface area—it dropped a notch for costing roughly 50 percent more. It's light enough to lift easily, and the handle stayed cool.

RECOMMENDED WITH RESERVATIONS		
LE CREUSET Tri-Ply Stainless 3-Quart Sauté Pan MODEL: SSC5100-24 PRICE: $154.95 WEIGHT (WITHOUT LID): 2.9 lb DIMENSIONS: 9 in by 2¼ in; 2.32 mm thick MATERIAL: Stainless with aluminum core; metal lid OVENSAFE TEMPERATURE: 425°F	PERFORMANCE: ★★ EASE OF USE: ★★½ 	This was the lightest pan and also one of the thinnest; it ran hot, scorching braising cabbage. Its narrow surface accommodated only half a batch of chicken. The good news: Its light body and stay-cool handle made it comfortable to maneuver.
TRAMONTINA Tri-Ply Clad 12-Inch Stainless Steel Jumbo Cooker with Lid MODEL: 80116/510 PRICE: $64 WEIGHT (WITHOUT LID): 4.7 lb DIMENSIONS: 11¼ in by 2⅝ in; 3.71 mm thick MATERIAL: Stainless with aluminum core; metal lid OVENSAFE TEMPERATURE: 450°F	PERFORMANCE: ★★ EASE OF USE: ★★	A lot of bang for your buck when it comes to surface area. However, its extra-broad surface browned unevenly and required extra cooking oil. It was also one of the heaviest pans in the lineup, requiring two hands to lift. Fortunately, it features a helper handle.

GRATERS

A box grater has always been our go-to tool for shredding cheese and vegetables by hand. But given that most of us only ever use one side, leaving the other three grating surfaces unused, shouldn't there be a better option? To find out, we gathered nine graters, including everything from four-sided graters to flat paddles and two- or three-sided designs, and got to work grating. It was quickly evident that sharp teeth weren't as important as a generous-size grating plane and large holes, which let us effortlessly produce long, perfect strips of cheese. Also, the grater holes had to be stamped, rather than etched; stamped holes offered thicker, more rigid grating surfaces that didn't budge when we pressed firmly against them. Graters are listed in order of preference.

HIGHLY RECOMMENDED	PERFORMANCE	TESTERS' COMMENTS
RÖSLE Coarse Grater MODEL: 95022 PRICE: $35 STYLE: Stamped stainless steel GRATING SURFACE AREA: 7 in by 3.2 in DISHWASHER-SAFE: Yes	EASE OF USE: ★★★ PERFORMANCE: ★★★ DURABILITY: ★★★	This easy-to-store, flat grater made shredding a breeze, thanks to big, sharp holes; a large surface for better efficiency; and a solid, rigid frame that enabled continuous grating (rather than short bursts). It fit over medium and large bowls, and grippy rubber feet stuck securely to any work surface. Since most recipes call for coarse shreds—and we have a rasp-style grater for fine grating—we don't mind that it grates only in one size.

RECOMMENDED		
MICROPLANE Specialty Series 4-Sided Box Grater MODEL: 34006 PRICE: $34.95 STYLE: Chemically etched stainless steel GRATING SURFACE AREA: 4 in by 3.2 in DISHWASHER-SAFE: Yes	EASE OF USE: ★★★ PERFORMANCE: ★★ DURABILITY: ★★★	From the originators of chemical etching technology, this model frames four super-sharp grating planes with tough plastic, making it easier to handle than other etched graters. It quickly and flawlessly grated mozzarella on its large holes and rendered perfect shreds of ginger and Parmesan on its fine holes. But hard carrots and potatoes bounced off its thin metal surface.
CUISIPRO 4-Sided Box Grater with Bonus Ginger Base MODEL: 74-6850 PRICE: $29.95 STYLE: Chemically etched stainless steel GRATING SURFACE AREA: 5.25 in by 3.25 in DISHWASHER-SAFE: No	EASE OF USE: ★★ PERFORMANCE: ★★ DURABILITY: ★★★	With ultra-sharp etched teeth, a sturdy base, and a comfortable handle, this four-sided grater zipped through mozzarella, Parmesan, and ginger. But as with the etched Microplane grater, its thin surface bent under pressure, making it hard to create the thickest possible shreds of carrots and potatoes. Its razor-like teeth were tricky to clean—and it's not dishwasher-safe.

NOT RECOMMENDED		
OXO Good Grips Box Grater MODEL: 1057961 PRICE: $17.95 STYLE: Stamped stainless steel GRATING SURFACE AREA: 6 in by 3.25 in DISHWASHER-SAFE: Yes	EASE OF USE: ★ PERFORMANCE: ★★ DURABILITY: ★★★	The holes on this grater, a remake of our former favorite, open in two directions to enable upward and downward grating—an "improvement" that left mozzarella stuck to the surface and turned carrots and potatoes into mince. Grating downward alone produced decent shreds, but forget about cleaning: The dual openings trapped food.
ONEIDA Large Oval Shaped Grater MODEL: 50967 PRICE: $12.99 STYLE: Stamped stainless steel GRATING SURFACE AREA: 6.25 in by 4 in (at widest end) DISHWASHER-SAFE: Top rack	EASE OF USE: ★ PERFORMANCE: ★★ DURABILITY: ★★★	Shaped like a flattened box grater, this oval model was narrow and tippy and made grating feel like a dangerous operation. One side sports strips of both fine and medium holes, cutting grating space in half. This made channels in blocks of Parmesan, slowing down grating as testers stopped to reposition the cheese.
JOSEPH JOSEPH Fold Flat Grater MODEL: FFGG011HC PRICE: $20 STYLE: Stamped stainless steel GRATING SURFACE AREA: 5.5 in by 2.5 in (at widest end) DISHWASHER-SAFE: Yes	EASE OF USE: ★ PERFORMANCE: ★★ DURABILITY: ★★★	This dual-sided grater uses sharp stamped metal teeth that render medium and coarse shreds (but no fine grating) and folds completely flat for storage. But its grating surface was smaller than most other boxes, and the grater itself refused to stay unfolded for stable, comfortable use.
MICROPLANE Twist 'N' Grate Dual Sided Grater MODEL: 34304 PRICE: $19.95 STYLE: Chemically etched stainless steel GRATING SURFACE AREA: 4 in by 2.5 in (at widest end) DISHWASHER-SAFE: Yes	EASE OF USE: ★ PERFORMANCE: ★★★ DURABILITY: ★★★	The narrow planes of this round, collapsible grater made semicircular carvings in foods and slowed testers down. Worse, these curves were dangerous, enabling the teeth to snag testers' hands. The twist-close mechanism let us tuck the grater into tight kitchen drawers, but the mechanism loosened with use.

OVEN MITTS

The number-one purpose of an oven mitt is to prevent burns. But the best mitts should also be comfortable, dexterous, and durable. To find the best one, we gathered eight mitts and put them through their paces. Many mitts were oversize, thick, and awkwardly shaped, making it hard to get a grip on hot sheet trays. Thinner, more form-fitting styles were easier to maneuver. Moving scorching-hot oven racks revealed that some mitts couldn't take the heat and didn't adequately insulate our hands and fingers. In addition to being more form-fitting and withstanding heat, oven mitts should also be washable. After staining the mitts with ketchup, soy sauce, and vegetable oil, we headed for the laundry room. Only two mitts emerged from the washing machine as good as new. Oven mitts are listed in order of preference.

HIGHLY RECOMMENDED	PERFORMANCE	TESTERS' COMMENTS
KOOL-TEK 15-inch Oven Mitt by KatchAll MODEL: KT0215 PRICE: $44.95	DEXTERITY: ★★½ HEAT PROTECTION: ★★★ DURABILITY: ★★★	After 18 rounds of testing, Kool-Tek still came out on top. Made with layers of Nomex and Kevlar for heat protection, these mitts won fans for heat resistance and all-around dependability. What's more, this mitt emerged from the laundry as good as new. It never let us down.
ORKAPLUS Silicone Oven Mitt with Cotton Lining BEST BUY MODEL: A82305 PRICE: $14.95	DEXTERITY: ★★ HEAT PROTECTION: ★★★ DURABILITY: ★★★	Orka redesigned this mitt since our last testing. The old model had great heat resistance but was too stiff, plus it was unlined, so our hand got sweaty fast. This improved version features a removable cotton-terry lining that stays dry and comfortable and launders perfectly. This mitt is soft and extremely flexible.

RECOMMENDED		
CALPHALON 14-inch Oven Mitt MODEL: 52171 PRICE: $14.99	DEXTERITY: ★★ HEAT PROTECTION: ★★ DURABILITY: ★★½	The innovation for this otherwise standard cotton mitt was silicone striping over the hand portion. It performed solidly, though some testers found the mitt large and unwieldy. It shrank in the laundry, which actually improved the fit.

RECOMMENDED WITH RESERVATIONS		
OXO GOOD GRIPS Silicone Oven Mitt with Magnet MODEL: 1147503 PRICE: $14.99	DEXTERITY: ★½ HEAT PROTECTION: ★★★ DURABILITY: ★½	The silicone grip had excellent heat and stain resistance. Unfortunately, it was also stiff and oversize, which compromised dexterity. This mitt emerged unscathed from the flames. However, it didn't fare as well against soap and water, fading after just one wash.
LE CREUSET Oven Mitt MODEL: TH4911 PRICE: $14.95	DEXTERITY: ★★ HEAT PROTECTION: ★★½ DURABILITY: ★	This mitt was a tad oversize, which hindered dexterity, but it had decent heat resistance and performed well. But it failed on other counts: It shrank significantly in the wash; oil stains on the terry cloth grip remained after three cycles; and when it came in contact with flames, it caught fire within seconds.

NOT RECOMMENDED		
GLOVEN Oven Gloves MODEL: GRL01 PRICE: $19.99	DEXTERITY: ★★★ HEAT PROTECTION: ★½ DURABILITY: ★	We immediately took a liking to the tight fit and total finger control possible while wearing these gloves. However, these gloves lacked insulation between the fingers, hence ranked at the bottom in heat resistance. The glove discolored when it came in contact with flames and it emerged from the washer flecked with lint.
BUILT Sizzler Oven Mitt MODEL: OMXL-FVE PRICE: $17.99	DEXTERITY: ★★ HEAT PROTECTION: ★★ DURABILITY: ★	These Neoprene mitts were thin and form-fitting. The manufacturer claims these mitts resist temperatures up to 500 degrees, but the grip started melting when we pulled a casserole out of a 450-degree oven, began smoking during our heat-resistance test, and caught fire when exposed to flames. We'd say the "sizzler" in the name is about right.
PADERNO WORLD CUISINE Three-Finger Oven Mitts MODEL: 48517-03 PRICE: $35.55	DEXTERITY: ★ HEAT PROTECTION: ★★ DURABILITY: ★	Below average when it came to heat resistance, these leather mitts began scorching when they came in contact with flames. Their biggest drawback was a complete lack of dexterity: The three-finger design was a hindrance.

COOLERS

The first modern cooler, dating back to the 1950s, was a simple insulated box. Nowadays, coolers come in a variety of shapes, sizes, and materials. Bells and whistles range from wheels and telescoping handles to removable dividers and cup holders. Modern innovations aside, we wanted to know how effective the coolers were at keeping things cold and securely contained. We tested five models, ranging in price from $4 to $75. Every model kept prechilled sodas at the same temperature (45 degrees) for four hours; two models even dropped the sodas to a colder temperature. But beyond chilling capacity, the coolers had to be durable, which we tested by dropping them from a car tailgate. Models had to be sturdy but not heavy or awkward to move when full of food. We also liked brands that were easy to clean and didn't pick up food odors. Coolers are listed in order of preference.

RECOMMENDED		PERFORMANCE	TESTERS' COMMENTS
CALIFORNIA COOLER BAGS **T-Rex Large Collapsible** **Rolling Cooler** MODEL: 20109KYC PRICE: $75 INTERIOR DIMENSIONS: 15 in high, 16 in wide, 14.5 in deep		KEEPING IT COLD: ★★★ PORTABILITY: ★★★ COOLING ABILITY: ★★★ DURABILITY: ★★★ CLEANUP: ★★	Thanks to an ultra-insulating layer of plastic lining, this was the only nonelectric model to not only keep the sodas cool, but also chill them to 40 degrees. Wheels, a telescoping handle, a hatch in the lid to limit airflow, and a collapsible frame earned it plenty of convenience points, too. The only downside was cleaning its zip-in lining: Crumbs got caught in the teeth and a very slight fishy odor clung to the fabric.
CALIFORNIA COOLER BAGS **Large 48–52 Classic** **Collapsible Cooler** MODEL: 5-22010KYC PRICE: $36.40 INTERIOR DIMENSIONS: 12 in high, 16 in wide, 12 in deep		KEEPING IT COLD: ★★★ PORTABILITY: ★★★ COOLING ABILITY: ★★ DURABILITY: ★★★ CLEANUP: ★	This collapsible cooler isn't equipped with its larger sibling's insulating lining, but it still cooled sodas to 42 degrees. It also scored big for portability (a padded shoulder strap), space efficiency (stretchy fabric), and ruggedness. Odors clung to this cooler's interior.

RECOMMENDED WITH RESERVATIONS			
RUBBERMAID 5-Day **Wheeled Cooler** MODEL: 802697 PRICE: $48 INTERIOR DIMENSIONS: 14.5 in high, 20 in wide, 10.5 in deep		KEEPING IT COLD: ★★★ PORTABILITY: ★★★ COOLING ABILITY: ★★★ DURABILITY: ★ CLEANUP: ★★★	While this hard plastic tub sports bells and whistles like a split lid and cup holders, and cleanup-friendly features like a spout for emptying liquid, it isn't as durable as it looks. When we dropped it, one of the wheels came loose.
COLEMAN Collapsible **Chest Cooler** MODEL: 2000004139 PRICE: $39.99 INTERIOR DIMENSIONS: 12 in high, 22 in wide, 13 in deep		KEEPING IT COLD: ★★★ PORTABILITY: ★ COOLING ABILITY: ★ DURABILITY: ★★★ CLEANUP: ★★★	This cooler's spacious interior may seem like a perk, but once it's loaded up with food and drink, its wheel-free body is almost impossible to move by the short loop handle. That said, it can take a good bit of wear and tear and cleans up nicely, thanks to its smooth sides and antimicrobial fabric.
LIFOAM Styrofoam Cooler MODEL: 3542 PRICE: $4 INTERIOR DIMENSIONS: 12 in high, 17 in wide, 10 in deep	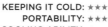	KEEPING IT COLD: ★★★ PORTABILITY: ★★★ COOLING ABILITY: ★ DURABILITY: ★ CLEANUP: ★½	You can't beat the price—but you don't get much for it. Though this Styrofoam cube kept drinks cool, it was too small to hold more than a few items. And given the crack that developed on the side during cleaning, it clearly wasn't meant for multiple uses.

MEASURING SPOONS

We recently tested eight sets of measuring spoons, both plastic and stainless steel, looking for an accurate set that was also comfortable and sturdy. In the test kitchen, we have found that the most accurate way to measure dry ingredients is to "dip and sweep," which means scooping up a heaping spoonful of the ingredient and then leveling the contents by sweeping across the spoon's rim with a flat blade. Some sets we tested had a bump or dip in the handle where it met the bowl, making it hard to get a clean sweep and resulting in inaccurate measurements. Also, dipping was difficult and uncomfortable with spoons that had thick handles and that were tightly attached to their mates, making us hold a fistful of spoons while we measured. Measuring spoon sets are listed in order of preference.

RECOMMENDED		PERFORMANCE	TESTERS' COMMENTS
CUISIPRO Stainless Steel **Measuring Spoons Set** MODEL: 74-7002 PRICE: $11.95 MATERIAL: Stainless Steel		FUNCTION: ★★½ ACCURACY: ★★★ COMFORT: ★★★	Comfortable and accurate with long handles, this set nests nicely. The rim of each spoon is flush with the handle so it is easy to sweep accurately. Our only gripe: The oval bowls made measuring liquids slightly tricky.
OXO GOOD GRIPS Measuring Spoons MODEL: 76081 PRICE: $5.99 MATERIAL: Plastic		FUNCTION: ★★★ ACCURACY: ★★★ COMFORT: ★★	The spoons were highly accurate with easy-to-read markings. They stayed on the ring securely but could be removed easily. But testers found these spoons bulky and slightly less sturdy than our top-rated metal set.
WILTON Scoop-It Measuring Spoons MODEL: 2103-325 PRICE: $4.84 MATERIAL: Plastic		FUNCTION: ★★½ ACCURACY: ★★★ COMFORT: ★★	These large plastic spoons were accurate with easy-to-read markings and soft-grip handles, but on the ring they were bulky. They were reasonably easy to pull off the ring, but pushing them back on took effort.
RECOMMENDED WITH RESERVATIONS			
JAMIE OLIVER Magnetic **Measuring Spoons** MODEL: JB3700 PRICE: $6.99 MATERIAL: Plastic		FUNCTION: ★★ ACCURACY: ★★ COMFORT: ★★	With a bowl on each end of a handle, three spoons offer six measures. But rounded handles got in the way of sweeping ingredients level, and one spoon in the set was consistently inaccurate (it was too large).
NORPRO Grip-EZ 6-Piece **Measuring Spoon Set** MODEL: 3017 PRICE: $4.89 MATERIAL: Plastic		FUNCTION: ★★ ACCURACY: ★★ COMFORT: ★½	These spoons have long, soft-grip handles, clear markings, and handles flush with the spoon bowls for easy leveling. But testers said the lightweight spoons felt cheap in the hand, and their triangular ring is clumsy.
NOT RECOMMENDED			
RSVP ENDURANCE 5-Piece **Measuring Spoon Set** MODEL: DSP-4 PRICE: $9.95 MATERIAL: Stainless Steel		FUNCTION: ★ ACCURACY: ★ COMFORT: ★½	These compact spoons have long handles and large markings. Unfortunately, they looked worn after a few washes. A bump where the handle met the bowl made sweeping difficult, leading to inaccuracy.
CIA MASTERS COLLECTION **Measuring Spoon Set** MODEL: 24419 PRICE: $21.99 MATERIAL: Stainless Steel		FUNCTION: ★ ACCURACY: ★ COMFORT: ★	This expensive, weighty set has large markings and long handles. But on the ring, its heft threw off the balance and made using a measuring spoon very uncomfortable. A dip near the bowl made sweeping difficult.
PROGRESSIVE INTERNATIONAL **5-Piece Stainless Steel** **Measuring Spoons** MODEL: GT3474 PRICE: $6.99 MATERIAL: Stainless Steel		FUNCTION: ★ ACCURACY: ★ COMFORT: ★	The spoons resemble safety pins, with a bowl attached to a short stainless steel loop. Their short handles couldn't reach into tall jars. Joints between bowls and handles trapped flour when sweeping. After dishwashing, we found rust in those joints.

WHISKS

We use whisks for numerous tasks in the test kitchen, from whipping cream and egg whites to making pan sauces. Looking for the best one, we tested ten French-style whisks and skinny balloon whisks on these tasks. When it came to whipping cream and egg whites, the best performers had at least 10 wires; whisks with more wires were faster, and better, at incorporating air than others. As for wire thickness, wire loops that were thin and flexible worked best at whipping cream and whites as they could be quickly pulled through the thickening mixture. But with pan sauces, thicker, stiffer wires were better; they were able to break up browned bits in the pan and incorporate them. Whisks with moderately thin wires were able to address both ends of the whisking spectrum. Whisks are listed in order of preference.

HIGHLY RECOMMENDED	PERFORMANCE	TESTERS' COMMENTS
OXO GOOD GRIPS 11-Inch Whisk MODEL: 74191 PRICE: $9.99 LENGTH: 11 in WEIGHT: 3.7 oz CONSTRUCTION: 10 wires, each 1.43 mm thick	SPEED/EFFICIENCY: ★★★ COMFORT/EASE OF USE: ★★★	With an ergonomic Santoprene rubber handle and a balanced, lightweight feel, this whisk was like an extension of a hand. It whipped cream and egg whites quickly, thanks to 10 wires that were thin enough to move through the liquid quickly but thick enough to push through heavy mixtures and blend pan sauces to smoothness.

RECOMMENDED	PERFORMANCE	TESTERS' COMMENTS
BEST MANUFACTURERS **Standard French Whip** MODEL: 1220 PRICE: $12.95 LENGTH: 12 in WEIGHT: 3.4 oz CONSTRUCTION: 10 wires, each 1.16 mm thick	SPEED/EFFICIENCY: ★★½ COMFORT/EASE OF USE: ★★½	This whisk weighs less than our winner and has thinner wires, making it a superb choice for whipping air into cream and egg whites. Its slender shape allowed it to easily reach pan corners. But for stirring heavy mixtures or scraping the fond in skillets for a smooth pan sauce, its wires proved a bit too thin.
RÖSLE Balloon Whisk/Beater MODEL: 95611 PRICE: $29 LENGTH: 12 in WEIGHT: 7.2 oz CONSTRUCTION: 12 wires, each 1.35 mm thick	SPEED/EFFICIENCY: ★★★ COMFORT/EASE OF USE: ★★	This slender model easily reached the corners of the saucepan. Although heavy in our hands, its 12 flexible, medium-thick wires easily whipped egg whites and cream. But those assets didn't justify the price: It costs at least twice as much as most other whisks in our lineup.
KUHN RIKON Balloon Whisk MODEL: 2303 PRICE: $16 LENGTH: 12 in WEIGHT: 7.2 oz CONSTRUCTION: 12 wires, each 1.35 mm thick	SPEED/EFFICIENCY: ★★½ COMFORT/EASE OF USE: ★★	This heavy whisk featured flexible wires that whipped cream and egg whites easily, but at 3 inches in diameter, it was a tad fat to reach into tight pan corners. A loop at the end of its steel handle, meant for hanging, made it uncomfortable when we were stirring something inside a deep saucepan.

RECOMMENDED WITH RESERVATIONS	PERFORMANCE	TESTERS' COMMENTS
NORPRO Krona Stainless **Steel Balloon Whisk** MODEL: 2320 PRICE: $12.49 LENGTH: 10 in WEIGHT: 5.5 oz CONSTRUCTION: 11 wires, each 1.35 mm thick	SPEED/EFFICIENCY: ★★ COMFORT/EASE OF USE: ★	With 12 medium-thick wires, this whisk whipped egg whites and cream with respectable speed. Shorter than all but one other whisk that we tested, its stature was a handicap, putting our hands dangerously near the hot skillet and getting lost in large mixing bowls. A loop at the base got in the way when we stirred in deep saucepans.
UPDATE INTERNATIONAL **12-Inch French Whip** MODEL: FW-12 PRICE: $2.49 LENGTH: 12 in WEIGHT: 7.2 oz CONSTRUCTION: 8 wires, each 2.25 mm thick	SPEED/EFFICIENCY: ★★ COMFORT/EASE OF USE: ★	With eight thick, stiff wires, this heavy stainless steel whisk meant business when scraping a skillet or stirring any thick mixture. But whipping air into egg whites and cream took too much time and effort. Plus, a pointed loop wire at the tip was a pain to clean by hand.

CONVERSIONS & EQUIVALENCIES

SOME SAY COOKING IS A SCIENCE AND AN ART. We would say that geography has a hand in it, too. Flour milled in the United Kingdom and elsewhere will feel and taste different from flour milled in the United States. So, while we cannot promise that the loaf of bread you bake in Canada or England will taste the same as a loaf baked in the States, we can offer guidelines for converting weights and measures. We also recommend that you rely on your instincts when making our recipes. Refer to the visual cues provided. If the bread dough hasn't "come together in a ball,"

as described, you may need to add more flour—even if the recipe doesn't tell you so. You be the judge.

The recipes in this book were developed using standard U.S. measures following U.S. government guidelines. The charts below offer equivalents for U.S., metric, and imperial (U.K.) measures. All conversions are approximate and have been rounded up or down to the nearest whole number. For example:

1 teaspoon   =   4.929 milliliters, rounded up to 5 milliliters
1 ounce   =   28.349 grams, rounded down to 28 grams

VOLUME CONVERSIONS

U.S.	METRIC
1 teaspoon	5 milliliters
2 teaspoons	10 milliliters
1 tablespoon	15 milliliters
2 tablespoons	30 milliliters
¼ cup	59 milliliters
⅓ cup	79 milliliters
½ cup	118 milliliters
¾ cup	177 milliliters
1 cup	237 milliliters
1¼ cups	296 milliliters
1½ cups	355 milliliters
2 cups	473 milliliters
2½ cups	591 milliliters
3 cups	710 milliliters
4 cups (1 quart)	0.946 liter
1.06 quarts	1 liter
4 quarts (1 gallon)	3.8 liters

WEIGHT CONVERSIONS

OUNCES	GRAMS
½	14
¾	21
1	28
1½	43
2	57
2½	71
3	85
3½	99
4	113
4½	128
5	142
6	170
7	198
8	227
9	255
10	283
12	340
16 (1 pound)	454

CONVERSIONS FOR INGREDIENTS COMMONLY USED IN BAKING

Baking is an exacting science. Because measuring by weight is far more accurate than measuring by volume, and thus more likely to achieve reliable results, in our recipes we provide ounce measures in addition to cup measures for many ingredients. Refer to the chart below to convert these measures into grams.

INGREDIENT	OUNCES	GRAMS
Flour		
1 cup all-purpose flour*	5	142
1 cup cake flour	4	113
1 cup whole wheat flour	5½	156
Sugar		
1 cup granulated (white) sugar	7	198
1 cup packed brown sugar (light or dark)	7	198
1 cup confectioners' sugar	4	113
Cocoa Powder		
1 cup cocoa powder	3	85
Butter†		
4 tablespoons (½ stick, or ¼ cup)	2	57
8 tablespoons (1 stick, or ½ cup)	4	113
16 tablespoons (2 sticks, or 1 cup)	8	227

* U.S. all-purpose flour, the most frequently used flour in this book, does not contain leaveners, as some European flours do. These leavened flours are called self-rising or self-raising. If you are using self-rising flour, take this into consideration before adding leavening to a recipe.
† In the United States, butter is sold both salted and unsalted. We generally recommend unsalted butter. If you are using salted butter, take this into consideration before adding salt to a recipe.

OVEN TEMPERATURES

FAHRENHEIT	CELSIUS	GAS MARK (imperial)
225	105	¼
250	120	½
275	135	1
300	150	2
325	165	3
350	180	4
375	190	5
400	200	6
425	220	7
450	230	8
475	245	9

CONVERTING TEMPERATURES FROM AN INSTANT-READ THERMOMETER

We include doneness temperatures in many of our recipes, such as those for poultry, meat, and bread. We recommend an instant-read thermometer for the job. Refer to the table above to convert Fahrenheit degrees to Celsius. Or, for temperatures not represented in the chart, use this simple formula:

Subtract 32 degrees from the Fahrenheit reading, then divide the result by 1.8 to find the Celsius reading.

EXAMPLE:
"Roast chicken until thighs register 175 degrees."
To convert:

175° F − 32 = 143°
143° ÷ 1.8 = 79.44°C, rounded down to 79°C

INDEX

A

Acidic ingredients, flavoring with, 281
Acidic or spicy foods, remedy for, 281
Agave syrup, about, 287
All-purpose cleaners, ratings of, 307
All-Purpose Glaze, 289
Almond(s)
    Chocolate Espresso Dacquoise, 266–69
    Danish Puff Pastry, 262–64, *265*
    Granola with Dried Fruit, 77–79
    Olives, and Oregano, Cucumber Salad with, 20–21
    Picada, 43
    Smoked, and Red Grapes, Chicken Salad with, 20
Anchovies
    Olive and Sun-Dried Tomato Stuffing, 150
    and Parsley, Olive Oil Sauce with, Fresh Pasta with,
        109, 112
Appetizers. *See* Starters
Apple(s)
    Crown Roast of Pork, 152–54
    and Crystallized Ginger, Cranberry Chutney with,
        67–69, *68*
    Dried, Spiced Walnut Granola with, 79–80
    French-Style Pot Roasted Pork Loin, 145–47
    Morning Glory Muffins, 80–82, *81*
    Waldorf Chicken Salad, 20
Artichoke(s)
    Crispy, and Sherry-Tomato Vinaigrette, Poached Fish
        Fillets with, 210–13, *211*
    and Porcini Stuffing, 151
Arugula
    –Goat Cheese Fresh Corn Salad, 23
    Roasted Garlic, and Chicken Sausage, Campanelle with,
        113–14
Asian-Style Sweet Potato Salad, 27
Asparagus
    grilling, 284
    Parmesan-Crusted, 53–54
Avocado(s)
    -Chickpea Fresh Corn Salad, 24
    preparing, 36
    and Tomato, Pan-Seared Shrimp with, *216*, 217–18

B

Babka, Cinnamon, 85–88, *86*
Back-to-Basics Bread Stuffing, 66–67
Bacon
    and Caramelized Onion, Potato Casserole with, 64–66
    Light Quiche Lorraine, 74–77, *75*
    and Pecans, Roasted Brussels Sprouts with, 53
    -Ranch Potato Tots, 61
Baked Chicken Imperial, 185–88, *186*
Baked Fish with Crispy Bread Crumbs, 207–8
Baked Mini Falafel with Yogurt-Tahini Sauce, 5–8, *7*
Baking tips, 281
Balsamic vinegar, taste tests on, 224
Barbecued Country-Style Ribs, 166–67
Barbecue Sauce, 170
Barley and Vegetable Soup, Farmhouse, 31–33
Basil pesto
    small-batch, preparing, 118
    Spaghetti with Turkey-Pesto Meatballs, 118–19
BBQ Grilled Chicken Wings, 182
Beans
    Baked Mini Falafel with Yogurt-Tahini Sauce, 5–8, *7*
    Black, and Rice, Lighter Cuban-Style (Moros y
        Cristianos), 234–36
    black, dried, taste tests on, 235
    Chickpea-Avocado Fresh Corn Salad, 24
    green, grilling, 284
    Tuscan Fresh Corn Salad, 24
    see also Lentil(s)
Beef
    Best Prime Rib, 143–45
    Green Bay Booyah, 43–46, *44*
    Grilled, Salad, Thai, 14–18, *17*
    Grilled Steak Burgers, 140–43, *141*
    Grilled Steak with Ancho Chile–Coffee Rub, 140
    Grilled Steak with New Mexican Chile Rub, 138–40
    Grilled Steak with Spicy Chipotle Chile Rub, 140
    Italian Wedding Soup, 37–40, *38*
    prime rib, preparing, 145
    Ragu alla Bolognese, 119–22
    Rigatoni with Genovese Ragu, 122–24
    Satay, Grilled, 11–14, *12*
    Stew, Catalan-Style, with Mushrooms, 41–43
    stew meat, trimming, 280

Berries
    frozen blueberries, buying, 257
    keeping mold from, 278
    Texas-Style Blueberry Cobbler, 256–57
    see also Cranberry(ies)
Best Crab Cakes, 202–4
Best Prime Rib, 143–45
Bisque, Shrimp, 48–49
Black and White Cookies, 240–41
Blueberries, frozen, buying, 257
Blueberry Cobbler, Texas-Style, 256–57
Blue Cheese
    Mushroom and Leek Galette with Gorgonzola,
        225–28, 227
Bluefish, Grilled Cumin-Crusted, with Corn Relish,
    209–10
Bok choy, grilling, 284
Bottle opener, makeshift, 278
Boursin and Prosciutto, Stuffed Mushrooms with, 4–5
Braised Turkey with Gravy, 196–99, 197
Bread(s)
    artisanal, storing, 278
    baking until well browned, 281
    Cinnamon Babka, 85–88, 86
    Cinnamon-Swirl, 88–91
    Cranberry-Pecan Muffins, 83–85
    Croissants, 92–97, 93
    Dilly Casserole, 102–3
    English Muffin, 98–99
    Herbed Croutons, 33–34
    Honey-Wheat Dinner Rolls, 99–102, 100
    Indian Flatbread, Quicker, 105
    Indian Flatbread (Naan), 103–5
    Morning Glory Muffins, 80–82, 81
    Stuffing, Back-to-Basics, 66–67
    tracking rise in dough, 278
Breakfast
    Granola
        Almond, with Dried Fruit, 77–79
        Hazelnut, with Dried Pear, 79
        Pecan-Orange, with Dried Cranberries, 79
        Spiced Walnut, with Dried Apple, 79–80
        Tropical, with Dried Mango, 80
    Light Quiche Lorraine, 74–77, 75
    Perfect Scrambled Eggs, 72–74
        for One, 74
        for Two, 74
Breakfast sausage patties, taste tests on, 290

Broccoli Rabe
    Chicken, and Roasted Garlic, Orecchiette with, 114
    preparing, 117
    and Sausage, Pasta with, 115–17, 116
Broiled Shrimp Cocktail with Creamy Tarragon Sauce,
    8–9
Broth, chicken, taste tests on, 66
Brownies, testing for doneness, 281
Brussels Sprouts, Roasted, 52–53
    with Bacon and Pecans, 53
    with Garlic, Red Pepper Flakes, and Parmesan, 53
    with Walnuts and Lemon, 53
Burgers, Grilled Steak, 140–43, 141
Butter
    herb, flavoring with, 281
    Lemon-Thyme, 34
    storing, 280
    unsalted, taste tests on, 95, 294
Butternut Squash Galette with Gruyère, 229

C

Cakes
    Carrot Layer, 252–55, 254
    chocolate, testing for doneness, 281
    Italian Cream, 250–52
    Pound, Chocolate, 248–50, 249
    Pound, Cream Cheese, 247–48
Campanelle with Roasted Garlic, Chicken Sausage,
    and Arugula, 113–14
Campanelle with Roasted Garlic, Shrimp, and Feta,
    115
Carrot(s)
    and Cilantro, Lentil Salad with, 26
    Layer Cake, 252–55, 254
    Morning Glory Muffins, 80–82, 81
Cashews, Curried Chicken Salad with, 19–20
Casserole Bread, Dilly, 102–3
Catalan-Style Beef Stew with Mushrooms, 41–43
Cheese
    Baked Chicken Imperial, 185–88, 186
    Butternut Squash Galette with Gruyère, 229
    Campanelle with Roasted Garlic, Chicken Sausage, and
        Arugula, 113–14
    Campanelle with Roasted Garlic, Shrimp, and Feta, 115
    Cheesy Polenta with Eggplant and Tomato Ragu, 230–31
    Dilly Casserole Bread, 102–3
    Easier Spinach Strudel, 231–34, 232

Cheese *(cont.)*

feta, taste tests on, 233

Goat, and Hazelnuts, Lentil Salad with, 26

Goat, and Olives, Spinach Strudel with, 234

Goat, –Arugula Fresh Corn Salad, 23

Goat, Potato and Shallot Galette with, 229

Grandma Pizza, 133–35, *134*

Lentil Salad with Olives, Mint, and Feta, 24–26

Light Quiche Lorraine, 74–77, *75*

mozzarella, taste tests on, 135, 291

Mushroom and Leek Galette with Gorgonzola, 225–28, *227*

Orecchiette with Roasted Garlic, Chicken, and Broccoli Rabe, 114

Parmesan, Spinach, and Walnuts, Lentil Salad with, 26

Parmesan-Crusted Asparagus, 53–54

Parmesan rinds, flavoring with, 280

Parmesan-Rosemary Potato Tots, 61

Piquillo Pepper and Manchego Stuffing, 150

Porcini and Artichoke Stuffing, 151

Roasted Brussels Sprouts with Garlic, Red Pepper Flakes, and Parmesan, 53

Southwestern Potato Tots, 61

Stuffed Mushrooms with Boursin and Prosciutto, 4–5

tortellini, taste tests on, 301

Vegetable Lasagna, 125–30, *127*

Walnut Cream Sauce, 112

Watermelon-Feta Fresh Corn Salad, *22,* 24

see also Cream Cheese

Chicken

Adobo, Filipino, 190–93, *191*

broth, taste tests on, 66

Chinese, Lettuce Wraps, 9–10

Citrus-and-Spice Grilled, 178–80, *179*

Green Bay Booyah, 43–46, *44*

Imperial, Baked, 185–88, *186*

inserting thermometer in, 177

Marbella, 188–90

Nuggets, Crispy, 182–85, *183*

Pie, Moravian, 194–96

Roast, Weeknight, 176–78

Roasted Garlic, and Broccoli Rabe, Orecchiette with, 114

Salad

Classic, 18–19

Curried, with Cashews, 19–20

with Red Grapes and Smoked Almonds, 20

Waldorf, 20

Sausage, Roasted Garlic, and Arugula, Campanelle with, 113–14

Chicken *(cont.)*

Tetrazzini, Reduced-Fat, 124–25

Wings, Grilled, 180–82

BBQ, 182

Creole, 182

Tandoori, 182

Chickpea(s)

-Avocado Fresh Corn Salad, 24

Baked Mini Falafel with Yogurt-Tahini Sauce, 5–8, *7*

Chile(s)

Ancho, –Coffee Rub, Grilled Steak with, 140

Chipotle, Rub, Spicy, Grilled Steak with, 140

Cucumber Salad with Jalapeño, Cilantro, and Pepitas, 21

Mint, and Basil, Cucumber Salad with, 21

New Mexican, Rub, Grilled Steak with, 138–40

Poached Fish Fillets with Crispy Jalapeños and Spicy Vinaigrette, 214

Spicy Cranberry Chutney, 69

Spicy Pork Tacos (al Pastor), 160–62

Chinese Chicken Lettuce Wraps, 9–10

Chocolate

Black and White Cookies, 240–41

cakes and brownies, testing for doneness, 281

cocoa powder, taste tests on, 240

Creamy Mocha Pudding, 275

Espresso Dacquoise, 266–69

Milk, Filling, Peanut Butter Sandwich Cookies with, 247

Pound Cake, 248–50, *249*

Pudding, Creamy, 273–75

Pudding, Creamy Mexican, 275

Chutney, Cranberry

with Apples and Crystallized Ginger, 67–69, *68*

with Fennel and Golden Raisins, 69

Orange, 69

with Pear, Lemon, and Rosemary, 69

Spicy, 69

Cilantro

and Carrots, Lentil Salad with, 26

Grilled Thai Beef Salad, 14–18, *17*

Jalapeño, and Pepitas, Cucumber Salad with, 21

Cinnamon

Babka, 85–88, *86*

-Swirl Bread, 88–91

Citrus-and-Spice Grilled Chicken, 178–80, *179*

Clam(s)

Chowder, Easy, 46–48, *47*

with Israeli Couscous, Chorizo, and Tomatoes, 221

with Israeli Couscous, Leeks, and Tomatoes, 220–21

Classic Chicken Salad, 18–19

Cleaners, all-purpose, ratings of, 307

Cobbler, Texas-Style Blueberry, 256–57

Cocoa powder, taste tests on, 240

Coconut

    Italian Cream Cake, 250–52

    Morning Glory Muffins, 80–82, *81*

    Tropical Granola with Dried Mango, 80

Coconut milk

    about, 236

    Filipino Chicken Adobo, 190–93, *191*

    Grilled Beef Satay, 11–14, *12*

    Peanut Sauce, *12,* 14

    Thai-Style Fish and Creamy Coconut Rice Packets, 214–15

    Thai Vegetable Green Curry with Jasmine Rice Cakes, 236–37

Coffee

    –Ancho Chile Rub, Grilled Steak with, 140

    Chocolate Espresso Dacquoise, 266–69

    Creamy Mocha Pudding, 275

Cookie dough

    freezing, 279

    keeping in round shape, 278

Cookies

    Black and White, 240–41

    decorating, 289

    equipment for, 288

    Gingersnaps, 241–45, *242*

    glazing, 289

    Holiday, 101, 288–89

    Peanut Butter Sandwich, 245–47

        with Honey-Cinnamon Filling, 247

        with Milk Chocolate Filling, 247

Coolers, ratings of, 311

Corn

    Chowder, 30–31

    cutting kernels from cob, 24

    grilling, 284

    Relish, Grilled Cumin-Crusted Bluefish with, 209–10

    Salad, Fresh, 23

        Arugula–Goat Cheese, 23

        Chickpea-Avocado, 24

        Tuscan, 24

        Watermelon-Feta, *22, 24*

    strippers, ratings of, 30

Cornmeal

    Fried Green Tomatoes, 54–56, *55*

Corn syrup, about, 286, 287

Cottage cheese

    Dilly Casserole Bread, 102–3

    Vegetable Lasagna, 125–30, *127*

Country-Fried Pork with Gravy, 154–56, *155*

Couscous, Israeli

    Chorizo, and Tomatoes, Clams with, 221

    Leeks, and Tomatoes, Clams with, 220–21

Crab

    Cakes, Best, 202–4

    taste tests on, 204

Cranberry(ies)

    Chutney

        with Apples and Crystallized Ginger, 67–69, *68*

        with Fennel and Golden Raisins, 69

        Orange, 69

        with Pear, Lemon, and Rosemary, 69

        Spicy, 69

    Dried, Pecan-Orange Granola with, 79

    -Pecan Muffins, 83–85

Cream Cheese

    Carrot Layer Cake, 252–55, *254*

    Italian Cream Cake, 250–52

    Pound Cake, 247–48

Creamy Chocolate Pudding, 273–75

Creamy Mexican Chocolate Pudding, 275

Creamy Mocha Pudding, 275

Creole Grilled Chicken Wings, 182

Crisp Roasted Fingerling Potatoes, 61–62

Crispy Chicken Nuggets, 182–85, *183*

Crispy Potato Tots, *58,* 59–60

Crispy Potato Tots for a Crowd, 60

Croissants, 92–97, *93*

Croutons, Herbed, 33–34

Crown Roast of Pork, 152–54

Cuban-Style Black Beans and Rice, Lighter (Moros y Cristianos), 234–36

Cucumber(s)

    Grilled Thai Beef Salad, 14–18, *17*

    Salad

        with Chile, Mint, and Basil, 21

        with Ginger, Sesame, and Scallions, 21

        with Jalapeño, Cilantro, and Pepitas, 21

        with Olives, Oregano, and Almonds, 20–21

    seeding, 21

    Watermelon-Feta Fresh Corn Salad, *22,* 24

Curry(ied)

    Chicken Salad with Cashews, 19–20

    paste, about, 236

Curry(ied) *(cont.)*

    Peanut Sauce, *12,* 14

    Thai Green, Vegetable, with Jasmine Rice Cakes, 236–37

Cutting boards, ratings of, 177, 302, 303

D

Dacquoise, Chocolate Espresso, 266–69

Danish Puff Pastry, 262–64, *265*

Deep-frying, keys to, 60

Desserts

    Chocolate Espresso Dacquoise, 266–69

    Creamy Pudding

        Chocolate, 273–75

        Mexican Chocolate, 275

        Mocha, 275

    Danish Puff Pastry, 262–64, *265*

    Paris-Brest, 257–62, *258*

    Texas-Style Blueberry Cobbler, 256–57

    Vanilla Ice Cream, 270–73, *271*

    see also Cakes; Cookies

Dilly Casserole Bread, 102–3

E

Easier Spinach Strudel, 231–34, *232*

Easy Clam Chowder, 46–48, *47*

Easy Salmon Cakes, 204–7, *205*

Easy Salmon Cakes with Smoked Salmon, Capers,
    and Dill, 207

Eggplant

    Grilled Ratatouille, 285

    grilling, 284

    and Tomato Ragu, Cheesy Polenta with, 230–31

    Vegetable Lasagna, 125–30, *127*

Eggs, Perfect Scrambled, 72–74

    for One, 74

    for Two, 74

Endive, grilling, 284

English Muffin Bread, 98–99

Equipment, ratings of

    all-purpose cleaners, 307

    coolers, 311

    corn strippers, 30

    cutting boards, 177, 302

    cutting boards, innovative, 303

    graters, 128, 309

    ice cream machines, 272

    knife block sets, 304

Equipment, ratings of *(cont.)*

    mandoline slicers, 65

    manual nut choppers, 252

    measuring spoons, 248, 312

    microwave rice cookers, 193

    muffin tins, 82

    oven mitts, 229, 310

    pineapple cutters, 162

    sauté pans, 308

    stockpots, inexpensive, 123, 305

    travel mugs, 306

    vegetable cleavers, 33

    whisks, 313

    whisks, all-purpose, 255

Erythritol, about, 287

F

Falafel, Baked Mini, with Yogurt-Tahini Sauce, 5–8, *7*

Farmhouse Vegetable and Barley Soup, 31–33

Farro, Wild Mushroom Ragu with, 224–25

Fennel

    and Golden Raisins, Cranberry Chutney with, 69

    grilling, 284

Feta

    Easier Spinach Strudel, 231–34, *232*

    Olives, and Mint, Lentil Salad with, 24–26

    Roasted Garlic, and Shrimp, Campanelle with, 115

    taste tests on, 233

    -Watermelon Fresh Corn Salad, *22,* 24

Figs and Port, French-Style Pot-Roasted Pork Loin
    with, 147

Filipino Chicken Adobo, 190–93, *191*

Finishing touches and garnishes, 281

Fish

    Baked, with Crispy Bread Crumbs, 207–8

    canned tuna, taste tests on, 292

    and Creamy Coconut Rice Packets, Thai-Style, 214–15

    Easy Salmon Cakes, 204–7, *205*

    Easy Salmon Cakes with Smoked Salmon, Capers,
        and Dill, 207

    Fillets, Poached, with Crispy Artichokes and Sherry-
        Tomato Vinaigrette, 210–13, *211*

    Fillets, Poached, with Crispy Jalapeños and Spicy
        Vinaigrette, 214

    Fillets, Poached, with Crispy Scallions and Miso-Ginger
        Vinaigrette, 213

    Grilled Cumin-Crusted Bluefish with Corn Relish,
        209–10

Fish *(cont.)*

removing fishy odor from, 204

see also Anchovies

Flavoring tricks, 280–81

Fly traps, 278

Foolproof Holiday Cookies, 288

French-Style Pot Roasted Pork Loin, 145–47

French-Style Pot-Roasted Pork Loin with Port and Figs, 147

Fresh Corn Salad, 23

Arugula–Goat Cheese, 23

Chickpea-Avocado, 24

Tuscan, 24

Watermelon-Feta, *22,* 24

Fresh Pasta with Olive Oil Sauce with Anchovies and Parsley, *109,* 112

Fresh Pasta without a Machine, 108–12

Fresh Pasta with Tomato and Browned Butter Sauce, 112

Fresh Pasta with Walnut Cream Sauce, 112

Fried Green Tomatoes, 54–56, *55*

Fruit

Dried, Almond Granola with, 77–79

slicing easily, 279

see also Berries; *specific fruits*

Fruit flies, trapping, 278

Frying, keys to, 60

G

Galettes

Butternut Squash, with Gruyère, 229

Mushroom and Leek, with Gorgonzola, 225–28, *227*

Potato and Shallot, with Goat Cheese, 229

Garlic

avoiding advance prep for, 280

Picada, 43

prepeeled versus fresh, 113

pureed, tip for, 279

removing green shoots from, 280

Roasted, and Rosemary Butter, Salt-Baked Potatoes with, 62–64, *63*

Roasted, Chicken, and Broccoli Rabe, Orecchiette with, 114

Roasted, Chicken Sausage, and Arugula, Campanelle with, 113–14

Roasted, Shrimp, and Feta, Campanelle with, 115

Sauce, Sichuan Stir-Fried Pork in, 170–73, *172*

Garnishes, 281

Ginger

Cranberry-Orange Chutney, 69

Crystallized, and Apples, Cranberry Chutney with, 67–69, *68*

Gingersnaps, 241–45, *242*

-Miso Vinaigrette and Crispy Scallions, Poached Fish Fillets with, 213

peeling, 279

Sesame, and Scallions, Cucumber Salad with, 21

Gingersnaps, 241–45, *242*

Glaze, All-Purpose, 289

Gnocchi, Potato, with Browned Butter and Sage, 130–32

Goat Cheese

–Arugula Fresh Corn Salad, 23

Campanelle with Roasted Garlic, Chicken Sausage, and Arugula, 113–14

and Hazelnuts, Lentil Salad with, 26

and Olives, Spinach Strudel with, 234

Potato and Shallot Galette with, 229

Gorgonzola, Mushroom and Leek Galette with, 225–28, *227*

Gouda cheese

Southwestern Potato Tots, 61

Grains

Cheesy Polenta with Eggplant and Tomato Ragu, 230–31

Farmhouse Vegetable and Barley Soup, 31–33

Fried Green Tomatoes, 54–56, *55*

instant polenta, shopping for, 230

Quinoa and Vegetable Stew, 34–36, *35*

rinsing, 36

Wild Mushroom Ragu with Farro, 224–25

see also Oats; Rice

Grandma Pizza, 133–35, *134*

Granola

Almond, with Dried Fruit, 77–79

Hazelnut, with Dried Pear, 79

Pecan-Orange, with Dried Cranberries, 79

Spiced Walnut, with Dried Apple, 79–80

Tropical, with Dried Mango, 80

Grapes, Red, and Smoked Almonds, Chicken Salad with, 20

Graters, ratings of, 128, 309

Gravy, Braised Turkey with, 196–99, *197*

Green Bay Booyah, 43–46, *44*

Green beans, grilling, 284

Greens
    Arugula–Goat Cheese Fresh Corn Salad, 23
    Campanelle with Roasted Garlic, Chicken Sausage, and Arugula, 113–14
    Chinese Chicken Lettuce Wraps, 9–10
    Italian Wedding Soup, 37–40, *38*
    see also Spinach
Green tea, taste tests on, 159
Gremolata, about, 281
Grilled dishes
    Barbecued Country-Style Ribs, 166–67
    Citrus-and-Spice Grilled Chicken, 178–80, *179*
    Grilled Beef Satay, 11–14, *12*
    Grilled Chicken Wings, 180–82
        BBQ, 182
        Creole, 182
        Tandoori, 182
    Grilled Cumin-Crusted Bluefish with Corn Relish, 209–10
    Grilled Ratatouille, 285
    Grilled Steak Burgers, 140–43, *141*
    Grilled Steak with Ancho Chile–Coffee Rub, 140
    Grilled Steak with New Mexican Chile Rub, 138–40
    Grilled Steak with Spicy Chipotle Chile Rub, 140
    Grilled Stuffed Pork Tenderloin, *148,* 149–51
    Grilled Thai Beef Salad, 14–18, *17*
    grilled vegetables 101, 284–85
    Hawaiian-Style Smoked Pork (Kalua Pork), 157–59, *158*
Grills
    equipment for, 285
    fuel tanks, checking level of, 279
    grill pans for, 285
Gruyère
    Butternut Squash Galette with, 229
    Light Quiche Lorraine, 74–77, *75*

H

Ham
    Slow-Cooker Holiday Glazed, 151–52
    Stuffed Mushrooms with Boursin and Prosciutto, 4–5
Hawaiian-Style Smoked Pork (Kalua Pork), 157–59, *158*
Hazelnut(s)
    Chocolate Espresso Dacquoise, 266–69
    and Goat Cheese, Lentil Salad with, 26
    Granola with Dried Pear, 79
    Paris-Brest, 257–62, *258*

Herb(s)
    butters, garnishing with, 281
    fresh, adding to recipes, 281
    Herbed Croutons, 33–34
    see also specific herbs
Holiday Cookies 101, 288–89
Honey
    about, 286
    crystallized, remedy for, 287
    measuring, 278, 287
    -Mustard Sauce, 185
    -Wheat Dinner Rolls, 99–102, *100*
Hot sauce, taste tests on, 295

I

Ice Cream, Vanilla, 270–73, *271*
Ice cream machines, ratings of, 272
Indian Flatbread (Naan), 103–5
Ingredients, tastings of
    balsamic vinegar, 224
    black beans, dried, 235
    breakfast sausage patties, 72, 290
    butter, unsalted, 95, 294
    cheese tortellini, 301
    chicken broth, 66
    cocoa powder, 240
    crabmeat, 204
    feta cheese, 233
    golden raisins, 82
    Greek yogurt, 6
    green tea, 159
    hot sauce, 295
    ketchup, 168, 296
    mayonnaise, 19, 293
    mozzarella, 135, 291
    pasta sauces, premium, 300
    spaghetti, 118, 298
    tahini, 6
    tomatoes, canned whole, 230, 299
    tomato soup, 297
    tuna, canned, 292
    vanilla beans, 272
Israeli Couscous, Chorizo, and Tomatoes, Clams with, 221
Israeli Couscous, Leeks, and Tomatoes, Clams with, 220–21
Italian Cream Cake, 250–52
Italian Wedding Soup, 37–40, *38*

K

Kalua Pork (Hawaiian-Style Smoked Pork), 157–59, *158*
Ketchup, taste tests on, 168, 296
Kitchen Quick Tips
    caring for berries, 278
    checking a gas grill's fuel tank, 279
    citrus reamer substitute, 279
    easy pureed garlic, 279
    freezing cookie dough, 279
    keeping cookie dough round, 278
    labeling frozen meat, 279
    makeshift bottle opener, 278
    measuring sticky ingredients, 278
    organizing pot lids, 279
    peeling ginger, 279
    saving pasta cooking water, 278
    slicing fruit quickly, 279
    space-saving vegetable prep, 278
    storing artisanal bread, 278
    tracking rise in bread dough, 278
    transporting salad dressing, 279
    vinegar fly trap, 278
Knife block sets, ratings of, 304

L

Lasagna, Vegetable, 125–30, *127*
Lemon grass, preparing, 14
Lemon(s)
    juice, boosting flavors with, 279
    juicing, 279
    -Tarragon Pan Sauce, 178
    -Thyme Butter, 34
Lentil(s)
    about, 25
    Salad
        with Carrots and Cilantro, 26
        with Hazelnuts and Goat Cheese, 26
        with Olives, Mint, and Feta, 24–26
        with Spinach, Walnuts, and Parmesan Cheese, 26
Lettuce Wraps, Chinese Chicken, 9–10
Lighter Cuban-Style Black Beans and Rice
    (Moros y Cristianos), 234–36
Light Quiche Lorraine, 74–77, *75*
Light Seafood Risotto, 218–20
Limes
    Citrus-and-Spice Grilled Chicken, 178–80, *179*
    juicing, 279

M

Macadamia nuts
    Tropical Granola with Dried Mango, 80
Main dishes
    Baked Chicken Imperial, 185–88, *186*
    Baked Fish with Crispy Bread Crumbs, 207–8
    Barbecued Country-Style Ribs, 166–67
    Best Crab Cakes, 202–4
    Best Prime Rib, 143–45
    Braised Turkey with Gravy, 196–99, *197*
    Butternut Squash Galette with Gruyère, 229
    Campanelle with Roasted Garlic, Chicken Sausage,
        and Arugula, 113–14
    Campanelle with Roasted Garlic, Shrimp, and Feta, 115
    Catalan-Style Beef Stew with Mushrooms, 41–43
    Cheesy Polenta with Eggplant and Tomato Ragu, 230–31
    Chicken Marbella, 188–90
    Chicken Salad
        Classic, 18–19
        Curried, with Cashews, 19–20
        with Red Grapes and Smoked Almonds, 20
        Waldorf, 20
    Citrus-and-Spice Grilled Chicken, 178–80, *179*
    Clams with Israeli Couscous, Chorizo, and Tomatoes, 221
    Clams with Israeli Couscous, Leeks, and Tomatoes, 220–21
    Country-Fried Pork with Gravy, 154–56, *155*
    Crispy Chicken Nuggets, 182–85, *183*
    Crown Roast of Pork, 152–54
    Easier Spinach Strudel, 231–34, *232*
    Easy Salmon Cakes, 204–7, *205*
    Easy Salmon Cakes with Smoked Salmon, Capers, and
        Dill, 207
    Filipino Chicken Adobo, 190–93, *191*
    French-Style Pot Roasted Pork Loin, 145–47
    French-Style Pot-Roasted Pork Loin with Port and Figs,
        147
    Fresh Pasta
        with Olive Oil Sauce with Anchovies and Parsley,
            109, 112
        with Tomato and Browned Butter Sauce, 112
        with Walnut Cream Sauce, 112
    Grandma Pizza, 133–35, *134*
    Grilled Chicken Wings, 180–82
        BBQ, 182
        Creole, 182
        Tandoori, 182
    Grilled Cumin-Crusted Bluefish with Corn Relish,
        209–10

INDEX   323

Main dishes *(cont.)*
  Grilled Steak
    with Ancho Chile–Coffee Rub, 140
    with New Mexican Chile Rub, 138–40
    with Spicy Chipotle Chile Rub, 140
  Grilled Steak Burgers, 140–43, *141*
  Grilled Stuffed Pork Tenderloin, *148,* 149–51
  Grilled Thai Beef Salad, 14–18, *17*
  Hawaiian-Style Smoked Pork (Kalua Pork), 157–59, *158*
  Lighter Cuban-Style Black Beans and Rice (Moros y
    Cristianos), 234–36
  Light Seafood Risotto, 218–20
  Moravian Chicken Pie, 194–96
  Mushroom and Leek Galette with Gorgonzola,
    225–28, *227*
  Orecchiette with Roasted Garlic, Chicken, and Broccoli
    Rabe, 114
  Pan-Seared Shrimp with Tomato and Avocado, *216,*
    217–18
  Pasta with Broccoli Rabe and Sausage, 115–17, *116*
  Poached Fish Fillets
    with Crispy Artichokes and Sherry-Tomato Vinaigrette,
      210–13, *211*
    with Crispy Jalapeños and Spicy Vinaigrette, 214
    with Crispy Scallions and Miso-Ginger Vinaigrette, 213
  Potato and Shallot Galette with Goat Cheese, 229
  Potato Gnocchi with Browned Butter and Sage, 130–32
  Quinoa and Vegetable Stew, 34–36, *35*
  Ragu alla Bolognese, 119–22
  Reduced-Fat Chicken Tetrazzini, 124–25
  Red Wine–Braised Pork Chops, 162–66, *165*
  Rigatoni with Genovese Ragu, 122–24
  Sichuan Stir-Fried Pork in Garlic Sauce, 170–73, *172*
  Slow-Cooker Holiday Glazed Ham, 151–52
  Smoky Indoor Ribs, 167–70
  Spaghetti with Turkey-Pesto Meatballs, 118–19
  Spicy Pork Tacos (al Pastor), 160–62
  Spinach Strudel with Olives and Goat Cheese, 234
  Thai-Style Fish and Creamy Coconut Rice Packets,
    214–15
  Thai Vegetable Green Curry with Jasmine Rice Cakes,
    236–37
  Vegetable Lasagna, 125–30, *127*
  Weeknight Roast Chicken, 176–78
  Wild Mushroom Ragu with Farro, 224–25
Manchego and Piquillo Pepper Stuffing, 150
Mandoline slicers, ratings of, 65
Mango, Dried, Tropical Granola with, 80

Manual nut choppers, ratings of, 252
Maple syrup
  about, 286
  measuring, 287
Mayonnaise, taste tests on, 19, 293
Measuring spoons, ratings of, 248, 312
Meat
  browned bits, preparing sauces with, 280
  cooking juices, preparing sauces with, 280
  marinating, tips for, 280
  raw, freezing and labeling, 279
  seasoning, 281
  see also Beef; Pork
Meatballs, Turkey-Pesto, Spaghetti with, 118–19
Microwave rice cookers, ratings of, 193
Mint
  Chile, and Basil, Cucumber Salad with, 21
  Grilled Thai Beef Salad, 14–18, *17*
  Olives, and Feta, Lentil Salad with, 24–26
Miso-Ginger Vinaigrette and Crispy Scallions,
    Poached Fish Fillets with, 213
Mocha Pudding, Creamy, 275
Molasses
  about, 286
  measuring, 278
Moravian Chicken Pie, 194–96
Morning Glory Muffins, 80–82, *81*
Mozzarella
  Grandma Pizza, 133–35, *134*
  taste tests on, 135, 291
  Vegetable Lasagna, 125–30, *127*
Muffins
  Cranberry-Pecan, 83–85
  Morning Glory, 80–82, *81*
Muffin tins, ratings of, 82
Mugs, travel, ratings of, 306
Mushroom(s)
  Catalan-Style Beef Stew with, 41–43
  Chinese Chicken Lettuce Wraps, 9–10
  grilling, 284
  and Leek Galette with Gorgonzola, 225–28, *227*
  Porcini and Artichoke Stuffing, 151
  Reduced-Fat Chicken Tetrazzini, 124–25
  Sichuan Stir-Fried Pork in Garlic Sauce, 170–73, *172*
  Stuffed, with Boursin and Prosciutto, 4–5
  Wild, Ragu with Farro, 224–25
Mustard-Honey Sauce, 185

N

Naan (Indian Flatbread), 103–5
Nut choppers, manual, ratings of, 252
Nuts
    Curried Chicken Salad with Cashews, 19–20
    storing, 280
    toasting, 280
    Tropical Granola with Dried Mango, 80
    see also Almond(s); Hazelnut(s); Peanut(s); Pecan(s);
        Walnut(s)

O

Oats
    Granola
        Almond, with Dried Fruit, 77–79
        Hazelnut, with Dried Pear, 79
        Pecan-Orange, with Dried Cranberries, 79
        Spiced Walnut, with Dried Apple, 79–80
        Tropical, with Dried Mango, 80
Oils, storing, 280
Olive Oil Sauce with Anchovies and Parsley,
    Fresh Pasta with, *109,* 112
Olive(s)
    Chicken Marbella, 188–90
    and Goat Cheese, Spinach Strudel with, 234
    Mint, and Feta, Lentil Salad with, 24–26
    Oregano, and Almonds, Cucumber Salad with, 20–21
    and Sun-Dried Tomato Stuffing, 150
Onion(s)
    avoiding advance prep for, 280
    Caramelized, and Bacon, Potato Casserole with,
        64–66
    grilling, 284
    Rigatoni with Genovese Ragu, 122–24
    Shoestring, 57–59
Orange(s)
    -Cranberry Chutney, 69
    juicing, 279
Orecchiette with Roasted Garlic, Chicken,
    and Broccoli Rabe, 114
Oven mitts, ratings of, 229, 310

P

Pan-Seared Shrimp with Tomato and Avocado, *216,*
    217–18
Paris-Brest, 257–62, *258*

Parmesan
    Baked Chicken Imperial, 185–88, *186*
    Cheese, Spinach, and Walnuts, Lentil Salad with, 26
    Cheesy Polenta with Eggplant and Tomato Ragu,
        230–31
    -Crusted Asparagus, 53–54
    Garlic, and Red Pepper Flakes, Roasted Brussels Sprouts
        with, 53
    Light Quiche Lorraine, 74–77, *75*
    Orecchiette with Roasted Garlic, Chicken, and Broccoli
        Rabe, 114
    Porcini and Artichoke Stuffing, 151
    rinds, flavoring with, 280
    -Rosemary Potato Tots, 61
    Vegetable Lasagna, 125–30, *127*
    Walnut Cream Sauce, 112
Pasta
    with Broccoli Rabe and Sausage, 115–17, *116*
    Campanelle with Roasted Garlic, Chicken Sausage,
        and Arugula, 113–14
    Campanelle with Roasted Garlic, Shrimp, and Feta, 115
    cheese tortellini, taste tests on, 301
    Clams with Israeli Couscous, Chorizo, and Tomatoes, 221
    Clams with Israeli Couscous, Leeks, and Tomatoes, 220–21
    cooking water, saving, 278
    Fresh
        with Olive Oil Sauce with Anchovies and Parsley,
            109, 112
        with Tomato and Browned Butter Sauce, 112
        with Walnut Cream Sauce, 112
        without a Machine, 108–12
    Italian Wedding Soup, 37–40, *38*
    long, breaking in half, 125
    Orecchiette with Roasted Garlic, Chicken, and Broccoli
        Rabe, 114
    Potato Gnocchi with Browned Butter and Sage, 130–32
    Ragu alla Bolognese, 119–22
    Reduced-Fat Chicken Tetrazzini, 124–25
    Rigatoni with Genovese Ragu, 122–24
    sauces, taste tests on, 300
    spaghetti, taste tests on, 118, 298
    Spaghetti with Turkey-Pesto Meatballs, 118–19
    Vegetable Lasagna, 125–30, *127*
Pastry, browning, 281
Peanut Butter
    Peanut Sauce, *12,* 14
    Sandwich Cookies, 245–47
        with Honey-Cinnamon Filling, 247
        with Milk Chocolate Filling, 247

Peanut(s)
  Asian-Style Sweet Potato Salad, 27
  Cucumber Salad with Chile, Mint, and Basil, 21
  Peanut Butter Sandwich Cookies, 245–47
    with Honey-Cinnamon Filling, 247
    with Milk Chocolate Filling, 247
  Sauce, *12, 14*
Pear
  Dried, Hazelnut Granola with, 79
  Lemon, and Rosemary, Cranberry Chutney with,
    69
Pea(s)
  Asian-Style Sweet Potato Salad, 27
  Reduced-Fat Chicken Tetrazzini, 124–25
  Thai Vegetable Green Curry with Jasmine Rice Cakes,
    236–37
Pecan(s)
  and Bacon, Roasted Brussels Sprouts with, 53
  Carrot Layer Cake, 252–55, *254*
  -Cranberry Muffins, 83–85
  Italian Cream Cake, 250–52
  -Orange Granola with Dried Cranberries, 79
**Pepitas, Jalapeño, and Cilantro, Cucumber Salad with,
  21**
Pepper, ground, seasoning with, 281
Pepper(s)
  bell, preparing, 27
  Grilled Ratatouille, 285
  grilling, 284
  Piquillo, and Manchego Stuffing, 150
  Sweet Potato Salad, 26–27
  Thai Vegetable Green Curry with Jasmine Rice Cakes,
    236–37
  see also Chile(s)
Perfect Scrambled Eggs, 72–74
  for One, 74
  for Two, 74
Pesto. *See* Basil pesto
Phyllo
  Easier Spinach Strudel, 231–34, *232*
  Spinach Strudel with Olives and Goat Cheese, 234
Picada, 43
Pies and galettes
  Butternut Squash Galette with Gruyère, 229
  Moravian Chicken Pie, 194–96
  Mushroom and Leek Galette with Gorgonzola, 225–28,
    227
  Potato and Shallot Galette with Goat Cheese, 229

Pineapple
  cutters, ratings of, 162
  Morning Glory Muffins, 80–82, *81*
  Spicy Pork Tacos (al Pastor), 160–62
Piquillo Pepper and Manchego Stuffing, 150
Pizza, Grandma, 133–35, *134*
**Poached Fish Fillets with Crispy Artichokes and
  Sherry-Tomato Vinaigrette, 210–13, *211***
**Poached Fish Fillets with Crispy Jalapeños and
  Spicy Vinaigrette, 214**
**Poached Fish Fillets with Crispy Scallions and
  Miso-Ginger Vinaigrette, 213**
Polenta
  Cheesy, with Eggplant and Tomato Ragu, 230–31
  instant, shopping for, 230
Porcini and Artichoke Stuffing, 151
Pork
  Barbecued Country-Style Ribs, 166–67
  breakfast sausage patties, taste tests on, 72, 290
  Chops, Red Wine–Braised, 162–66, *165*
  Clams with Israeli Couscous, Chorizo, and Tomatoes, 221
  Country-Fried, with Gravy, 154–56, *155*
  country-style ribs, buying, 167
  Crown Roast of, 152–54
  Hawaiian-Style Smoked (Kalua Pork), 157–59, *158*
  Italian Wedding Soup, 37–40, *38*
  Loin, French-Style Pot Roasted, 145–47
  Loin, French-Style Pot-Roasted, with Port and Figs, 147
  Pasta with Broccoli Rabe and Sausage, 115–17, *116*
  Ragu alla Bolognese, 119–22
  roast, double-butterflying, 146
  Sichuan Stir-Fried, in Garlic Sauce, 170–73, *172*
  Smoky Indoor Ribs, 167–70
  Tacos, Spicy (al Pastor), 160–62
  Tenderloin, Grilled Stuffed, *148,* 149–51
  tenderloin, stuffings for, 150–51
  trimming, 280
  see also Bacon; Ham
**Port and Figs, French-Style Pot-Roasted Pork Loin
  with, 147**
Potato(es)
  and Shallot Galette with Goat Cheese, 229
  Casserole with Bacon and Caramelized Onion, 64–66
  Corn Chowder, 30–31
  Crown Roast of Pork, 152–54
  Easy Clam Chowder, 46–48, *47*
  Fingerling, Crisp Roasted, 61–62
  Gnocchi with Browned Butter and Sage, 130–32

Potato(es) *(cont.)*
  Salt-Baked, with Roasted Garlic and Rosemary Butter,
      62–64, *63*
  Sweet, Salad, 26–27
  Sweet, Salad, Asian-Style, 27
  Tots
    Bacon-Ranch, 61
    Crispy, *58,* 59–60
    Crispy, for a Crowd, 60
    Parmesan-Rosemary, 61
    Southwestern, 61
Pot lids, organizing, 279
Poultry. *See* Chicken; Turkey
Prosciutto and Boursin, Stuffed Mushrooms with, 4–5
Puddings
  Creamy Chocolate, 273–75
  Creamy Mexican Chocolate, 275
  Creamy Mocha, 275

Q

Quiche Lorraine, Light, 74–77, *75*
Quicker Indian Flatbread, 105
Quinoa and Vegetable Stew, 34–36, *35*

R

Radicchio, grilling, 284
Ragu alla Bolognese, 119–22
Raisins
  Cinnamon-Swirl Bread, 88–91
  Golden, and Fennel, Cranberry Chutney with, 69
  golden, taste tests on, 82
  Morning Glory Muffins, 80–82, *81*
  Steak Sauce, 142
Ratatouille, Grilled, 285
Reduced-Fat Chicken Tetrazzini, 124–25
Red Wine–Braised Pork Chops, 162–66, *165*
Rice
  and Black Beans, Lighter Cuban-Style
      (Moros y Cristianos), 234–36
  Creamy Coconut, and Fish Packets, Thai-Style, 214–15
  Jasmine, Cakes, Thai Vegetable Green Curry with, 236–37
  Light Seafood Risotto, 218–20
  rinsing, 36
Rice cookers, microwave, ratings of, 193
Ricotta
  Easier Spinach Strudel, 231–34, *232*
  Spinach Strudel with Olives and Goat Cheese, 234

Rigatoni with Genovese Ragu, 122–24
Risotto, Light Seafood, 218–20
Roasted Brussels Sprouts, 52–53
  with Bacon and Pecans, 53
  with Garlic, Red Pepper Flakes, and Parmesan, 53
  with Walnuts and Lemon, 53
Rolling dowels, 288
Rosemary
  Butter and Roasted Garlic, Salt-Baked Potatoes with,
      62–64, *63*
  -Parmesan Potato Tots, 61
  Pear, and Lemon, Cranberry Chutney with, 69

S

Saccharine, about, 287
Sage and Browned Butter, Potato Gnocchi with,
    130–32
Salad dressings, transporting, 279
Salads
  Chicken
    Classic, 18–19
    Curried, with Cashews, 19–20
    with Red Grapes and Smoked Almonds, 20
    Waldorf, 20
  Corn, Fresh, 23
    Arugula–Goat Cheese, 23
    Chickpea-Avocado, 24
    Tuscan, 24
    Watermelon-Feta, *22,* 24
  Cucumber
    with Chile, Mint, and Basil, 21
    with Ginger, Sesame, and Scallions, 21
    with Jalapeño, Cilantro, and Pepitas, 21
    with Olives, Oregano, and Almonds, 20–21
  Grilled Thai Beef, 14–18, *17*
  Lentil
    with Carrots and Cilantro, 26
    with Hazelnuts and Goat Cheese, 26
    with Olives, Mint, and Feta, 24–26
    with Spinach, Walnuts, and Parmesan Cheese, 26
  Sweet Potato, 26–27
  Sweet Potato, Asian-Style, 27
Salmon
  Cakes, Easy, 204–7, *205*
  Cakes, Easy, with Smoked Salmon, Capers, and Dill, 207
Salt, seasoning with, 281
Salt-Baked Potatoes with Roasted Garlic and
    Rosemary Butter, 62–64, *63*

Salty foods, remedy for, 281

Sauces

    Barbecue, 170

    Honey-Mustard, 185

    hot, taste tests on, 295

    Olive Oil, with Anchovies and Parsley, *109,* 112

    Pan, Tarragon-Lemon, 178

    pasta, taste tests on, 300

    Peanut, *12,* 14

    Steak, 142

    Sweet and Sour, 185

    Tarragon, Creamy, Broiled Shrimp Cocktail with, 8–9

    Tomato and Browned Butter, 112

    Walnut Cream, 112

    Yogurt-Tahini, Baked Mini Falafel with, 5–8, *7*

Sausage(s)

    breakfast patties, taste tests on, 72, 290

    and Broccoli Rabe, Pasta with, 115–17, *116*

    Chicken, Roasted Garlic, and Arugula, Campanelle with, 113–14

    Clams with Israeli Couscous, Chorizo, and Tomatoes, 221

Sauté pans, ratings of, 308

Scallions

    Crispy, and Miso-Ginger Vinaigrette, Poached Fish Fillets with, 213

    grilling, 284

Scallops

    Light Seafood Risotto, 218–20

    preparing, 219

Seafood. *See* Fish; Shellfish

Seasoning tips, 281

Sesame, Ginger, and Scallions, Cucumber Salad with, 21

Shallot, Potato and, Galette with Goat Cheese, 229

Shellfish

    Best Crab Cakes, 202–4

    Clams with Israeli Couscous, Chorizo, and Tomatoes, 221

    Clams with Israeli Couscous, Leeks, and Tomatoes, 220–21

    crabmeat, taste tests on, 204

    Easy Clam Chowder, 46–48, *47*

    Light Seafood Risotto, 218–20

    removing fishy odor from, 204

    scallops, preparing, 219

    see also Shrimp

Shoestring Onions, 57–59

Shrimp

    Best Crab Cakes, 202–4

    Bisque, 48–49

Shrimp *(cont.)*

    buying, 282

    Cocktail, Broiled, with Creamy Tarragon Sauce, 8–9

    deveining, 9, 282

    grilling, 283

    Light Seafood Risotto, 218–20

    Pan-Seared, with Tomato and Avocado, *216,* 217–18

    pan-searing, 283

    peeling, 282

    poaching, 283

    Roasted Garlic, and Feta, Campanelle with, 115

    sizes and counts, 282

    thawing, 282

Sichuan Stir-Fried Pork in Garlic Sauce, 170–73, *172*

Sides

    Back-to-Basics Bread Stuffing, 66–67

    Cranberry Chutney

        with Apples and Crystallized Ginger, 67–69, *68*

        with Fennel and Golden Raisins, 69

        Orange, 69

        with Pear, Lemon, and Rosemary, 69

        Spicy, 69

    Crisp Roasted Fingerling Potatoes, 61–62

    Cucumber Salad

        with Chile, Mint, and Basil, 21

        with Ginger, Sesame, and Scallions, 21

        with Jalapeño, Cilantro, and Pepitas, 21

        with Olives, Oregano, and Almonds, 20–21

    Fresh Corn Salad, 23

        Arugula–Goat Cheese, 23

        Chickpea-Avocado, 24

        Tuscan, 24

        Watermelon-Feta, *22,* 24

    Fried Green Tomatoes, 54–56, *55*

    Grilled Ratatouille, 285

    Lentil Salad

        with Carrots and Cilantro, 26

        with Hazelnuts and Goat Cheese, 26

        with Olives, Mint, and Feta, 24–26

        with Spinach, Walnuts, and Parmesan Cheese, 26

    Parmesan-Crusted Asparagus, 53–54

    Potato Casserole with Bacon and Caramelized Onion, 64–66

    Potato Tots

        Bacon-Ranch, 61

        Crispy, *58,* 59–60

        Crispy, for a Crowd, 60

        Parmesan-Rosemary, 61

        Southwestern, 61

Sides *(cont.)*

Roasted Brussels Sprouts, 52–53

with Bacon and Pecans, 53

with Garlic, Red Pepper Flakes, and Parmesan, 53

with Walnuts and Lemon, 53

Salt-Baked Potatoes with Roasted Garlic and Rosemary Butter, 62–64, *63*

Shoestring Onions, 57–59

Sweet Potato Salad, 26–27

Sweet Potato Salad, Asian-Style, 27

Skewers, for grilling, 285

Slow-Cooker Holiday Glazed Ham, 151–52

Smoky Indoor Ribs, 167–70

Soups

Corn Chowder, 30–31

Easy Clam Chowder, 46–48, *47*

Green Bay Booyah, 43–46, *44*

Italian Wedding, 37–40, *38*

Shrimp Bisque, 48–49

tomato, canned, taste tests on, 297

Vegetable and Barley, Farmhouse, 31–33

see also Stews

Southwestern Potato Tots, 61

Spaghetti

taste tests on, 118, 298

with Turkey-Pesto Meatballs, 118–19

Spatulas, 288

Spiced Walnut Granola with Dried Apple, 79–80

Spices, intensifying flavor of, 280

Spicy Cranberry Chutney, 69

Spicy foods, remedy for, 281

Spicy Pork Tacos (al Pastor), 160–62

Spinach

Butternut Squash Galette with Gruyère, 229

Grilled Stuffed Pork Tenderloin, *148*, 149–51

Strudel, Easier, 231–34, *232*

Strudel with Olives and Goat Cheese, 234

Vegetable Lasagna, 125–30, *127*

Walnuts, and Parmesan Cheese, Lentil Salad with, 26

Squash

Butternut, Galette with Gruyère, 229

Grilled Ratatouille, 285

summer, grilling, 284

Vegetable Lasagna, 125–30, *127*

see also Zucchini

Starters

Baked Mini Falafel with Yogurt-Tahini Sauce, 5–8, 7

Broiled Shrimp Cocktail with Creamy Tarragon Sauce, 8–9

Chinese Chicken Lettuce Wraps, 9–10

Starters *(cont.)*

Grilled Beef Satay, 11–14, *12*

Stuffed Mushrooms with Boursin and Prosciutto, 4–5

Steak Sauce, 142

Stevia, about, 287

Stews

Beef, Catalan-Style, with Mushrooms, 41–43

Quinoa and Vegetable, 34–36, *35*

Sticky ingredients, measuring, 278

Stockpots, inexpensive, ratings of, 123, 305

Stuffed Mushrooms with Boursin and Prosciutto, 4–5

Stuffing, Bread, Back-to-Basics, 66–67

Stuffings (for pork)

Olive and Sun-Dried Tomato, 150

Piquillo Pepper and Manchego, 150

Porcini and Artichoke, 151

Sucralose, about, 287

Sugar

in baking and cooking, 287

brown, 286, 287

confectioners', 286

demerara, 286

enhancing browning with, 280, 287

granulated, 286, 287

storing and handling, 287

substitutes, 287

superfine, 286

turbinado, 286

Sweeteners 101, 286–87

Sweet foods, remedy for, 281

Sweet Potato

Salad, 26–27

Salad, Asian-Style, 27

T

Tacos, Spicy Pork (al Pastor), 160–62

Tahini

taste tests on, 6

-Yogurt Sauce, Baked Mini Falafel with, 5–8, 7

Tandoori Grilled Chicken Wings, 182

Tarragon

-Lemon Pan Sauce, 178

Sauce, Creamy, Broiled Shrimp Cocktail with, 8–9

Tea, green, taste tests on, 159

Texas-Style Blueberry Cobbler, 256–57

Thai-Style Fish and Creamy Coconut Rice Packets, 214–15

Thai Vegetable Green Curry with Jasmine Rice Cakes, 236–37
Thyme-Lemon Butter, 34
Tomato(es)
    and Avocado, Pan-Seared Shrimp with, *216,* 217–18
    and Browned Butter Sauce, 112
    canned whole, taste tests on, 230, 299
    coring, 24
    and Eggplant Ragu, Cheesy Polenta with, 230–31
    flavor in seeds and jelly, 280
    Grandma Pizza, 133–35, *134*
    Green, Fried, 54–56, *55*
    Grilled Ratatouille, 285
    grilling, 284
    Israeli Couscous, and Chorizo, Clams with, 221
    Israeli Couscous, and Leeks, Clams with, 220–21
    seeding, 218
    -Sherry Vinaigrette and Crispy Artichokes, Poached Fish Fillets with, 210–13, *211*
    soup, canned, taste tests on, 297
    Spaghetti with Turkey-Pesto Meatballs, 118–19
    Sun-Dried, and Olive Stuffing, 150
    Vegetable Lasagna, 125–30, *127*
Tongs, for grilling, 285
Tortellini, cheese, taste tests on, 301
Tortillas
    Spicy Pork Tacos (al Pastor), 160–62
Travel mugs, ratings of, 306
Tropical Granola with Dried Mango, 80
Tuna, canned, taste tests on, 292
Turkey
    Braised, with Gravy, 196–99, *197*
    -Pesto Meatballs, Spaghetti with, 118–19
Tuscan Fresh Corn Salad, 24

U

Umami flavors, 281

V

Vanilla beans, taste tests on, 272
Vanilla Ice Cream, 270–73, *271*
Veal
    Ragu alla Bolognese, 119–22

Vegetable cleavers, ratings of, 33
Vegetable(s)
    and Barley Soup, Farmhouse, 31–33
    Green Bay Booyah, 43–46, *44*
    grilling 101, 284–85
    Lasagna, 125–30, *127*
    and Quinoa Stew, 34–36, *35*
    space-saving prep work, 278
    Thai, Green Curry, with Jasmine Rice Cakes, 236–37
    see also specific vegetables
Vinegar
    balsamic, taste tests on, 224
    boosting flavors with, 279
    fly trap made with, 278

W

Waldorf Chicken Salad, 20
Walnut(s)
    Cream Sauce, 112
    Granola, Spiced, with Dried Apple, 79–80
    and Lemon, Roasted Brussels Sprouts with, 53
    Morning Glory Muffins, 80–82, *81*
    Spinach, and Parmesan Cheese, Lentil Salad with, 26
    Waldorf Chicken Salad, 20
Watermelon-Feta Fresh Corn Salad, *22,* 24
Weeknight Roast Chicken, 176–78
Whisks, all-purpose, ratings of, 255
Whisks, ratings of, 313
Wild Mushroom Ragu with Farro, 224–25

Y

Yogurt
    Greek, taste tests on, 6
    -Tahini Sauce, Baked Mini Falafel with, 5–8, *7*

Z

Zucchini
    Grilled Ratatouille, 285
    grilling, 284
    Thai Vegetable Green Curry with Jasmine Rice Cakes, 236–37
    Vegetable Lasagna, 125–30, *127*